International Business
Second Edition

International Business
Second Edition

▶ **Betty Jane Punnett**
University of Windsor

▶ **David A. Ricks**
Thunderbird—The American Graduate School
of International Management

Acquisitions Editor: Rolf Janke
Senior Development Editor: Mary Riso
Production Manager: Jan Phillips
Cover Designer: Calvin Nelson
Composition: AM Marketing
Cover Printer: Phoenix Color
Text Printer and Binder: Courier Westford

First edition published in 1992 by PWS-Kent Publishing Company, Boston, Massachusetts.

Second edition published in 1997 by Blackwell Publishers.
Reprinted 1998

Blackwell Publishers Inc.
350 Main Street
Malden, Massachusetts 02148
USA

Blackwell Publishers Ltd
108 Cowley Road
Oxford OX4 1JF
UK

Library of Congress Cataloging-in-Publication Data

Punnett, Betty Jane.
    International business / Betty Jane Punnett, David A. Ricks.
       p. cm.
    Includes bibliographical references and index.
    ISBN 1-55786-852-2 (hb), 1-55786-853-0 (pb)
    1. International business enterprises—Management. I. Ricks, David A. II. Title.
HD62.4.P865.199291-36662
658.1'8—dc20CIP

British Library of Congress Cataloguing-in-Publication Data

This book is printed on acid-free paper

For Don

For Traude, Susanne, Lorenz, Robert, and Anna-Sophie

Contents

The Changing World of International Business 442

Cases 458

Glossary 516

Name Index 525

Company Index 527

Subject Index 531

Preface

It seems clear that the business world of today is no longer limited by national boundaries and that organizations need a global perspective if they are to survive and prosper in this international environment. Many organizations will succeed or fail on the basis of their ability to deal with this dynamic environment. We wrote this book to help prepare students to function more effectively in a world made substantially more complex by the shrinking globe.

Global business appears to be a fact of life. Managing virtually any business in the 1990s and the 21st century will mean some international interactions. This is true for the small manufacturer that purchases foreign materials and employs immigrant workers; it is true for the large global organization that views the world as both its market and its source of supply; and it is true for all the various organizations between these two ends of the structural spectrum. We wrote this book to explore the issues faced by such organizations in this global environment.

Universities and colleges have been responding to the increasingly global business environment by internationalizing their curricula. Many courses are now offered that deal not only with international business in general, but also with more specialized areas, such as international marketing, international finance, or international accounting. We wrote this book to give students a thorough survey of the major issues associated with doing business in this international environment.

Several international business texts are available to students and instructors. We wrote this book because we believe we can provide a combination of content, format, and style that will stimulate learning and interest in the complex and dynamic field of international business.

Features

Many features of this book ensure that the material is lively and practical. Numerous illustrative examples ranging from mini-cases to international business "blunders" make studying international business interesting and enjoyable for students. For example,

1. The Japanese sogo shosha mini-case introduces these powerful and complex Japanese organizations, which are often unfamiliar to Western students.
2. An anecdote describes how Nigeria came to make a huge purchasing blunder that ultimately led to millions of tons of newly ordered cement being dumped into the sea because of problems unloading the delivery ships.

3. The Bata Shoe Organization mini-case discusses the policies, strategies, and corporate structure that have helped make the BSO the largest manufacturer and marketer of footwear in the world.
4. Two examples illustrate how an American shoe manufacturer and a telephone company both created ads that were offensive to their intended Eastern customers, through ignorance of the significance of human feet in different cultures.

Concepts presented in the text are linked to current issues facing international business in Chapter 16, "The Changing World of International Business."

Four full-length cases at the end of the book allow students to take a closer, more detailed look at specific multinational companies.

Supplementary Materials

A flexible and unique supplementary package is also available for the instructor and students.

Supplements for the instructor include

1. An instructor's manual complete with teaching notes, test questions, and suggestions regarding videos and additional readings.
2. A computerized test bank.

Supplements for the student include

3. A full-color removable map of the world.
4. *Blunders in International Business,* by David A. Ricks, which provides an anecdotal introduction to the perils and pitfalls awaiting the company that enters the international business arena.

If we have achieved all our aims, we expect that students and instructors will enjoy using this text. Because people learn best when they like what they are doing, enjoying this book will help make it a good learning tool. But, while we acknowledge the need to provide material in an enjoyable form, we have not sacrificed substance in the process. Our style is to simplify and enliven, while retaining sophisticated material and providing complete coverage of important topics. Although we have made every effort to ensure both enjoyment and learning, we are sure that the book can be improved. We would very much appreciate your comments and suggestions for future editions.

Acknowledgments

Many people contributed to this book directly or indirectly. Without the help of our colleagues, family, friends, and students, the book could never have been completed. These people have advised and encouraged us, and we owe them a great deal of gratitude.

There are too many people to thank everyone individually, but we do want to identify some individuals who have been especially helpful in the long, and sometimes painful and tedious, process of writing this book.

Several colleagues have contributed substantially to the final product. We thank particularly Maureen J. Fleming of the University of Montana, Richard H. Reeves-Ellington of Birmingham University, and Kathleen A. Rehbein of Marquette University. Their comments have improved the final version of this text.

In addition, many students have read early drafts of chapters and made helpful comments on these. Special thanks as well to Amanda Kelley of the University of Windsor for her extensive library research.

We owe our families a special debt of gratitude for putting up with us during the many hours that a project like this consumes. More important, we appreciate their encouragement in spite of these long hours. Don provided encouragement as well as many hours of extremely valuable editing and reediting of each draft of the manuscript.

We thank all of these people as well as the many others who have helped us write this book. We hope that they will feel that the final product is worthy of their interest and contribution.

About the Authors

Betty Jane Punnett

Betty Jane Punnett is Professor at the University of Windsor. A native of St. Vincent and the Grenadines, West Indies, she has lived and worked for extended periods in the Caribbean, the United States, and more recently Canada. Currently, she teaches international business and international management with Windsor's faculty of Business Administration. She holds a B.A. in English from McGill University and an MBA from Marist College, and received her Ph.D. in 1984 in international business from New York University.

Dr. Punnett's extensive international interests are illustrated by her research and teaching activities. Her past research has covered the Far East (China and Japan), the Caribbean, Europe, and North America; she has taught in Canada, China, Ireland, and the United States; and she has participated in management development programs involving South Asian countries. Dr. Punnett has guest edited issues of *International Studies of Management and Organizations*, examining research methods and a variety of management research sites around the world. She wrote *Experiencing International Management* (Boston: PWS-Kent Publishing Company, 1989) and *Global Management* (with Mark Mendenhall and David Ricks; Cambridge, Mass.: Blackwell Publishers, 1994) and edited *The Handbook for International Management Research* (with Oded Shenkar; Cambridge, Mass.: Blackwell Publishers, 1996). Her academic papers have been published in a wide variety of journals, including *Advances in International Comparative Management, International Studies of Management and Organizations, Caribbean Finance and Management, Canadian Journal of Latin American and Caribbean Studies, Canadian Journal of Behavioural Sciences Journal of Applied Psychology*, and the *Journal of International Management*. She has contributed book reviews to several journals, most recently to the *International Journal of Human Resource Management*, and she has a number of chapters in books, including *Advances in Chinese Industrial Studies* and *The Encyclopedia of Management*. Dr. Punnett has been division chair and program chair for the International Business Division of the Administrative Sciences Association of Canada and has served as a reviewer for the Academy of International Business and the Academy of Management, as well as several other international organizations. The Canadian government selected Dr. Punnett as a China scholar in 1990. She serves on the editorial board of the *Journal of International Management* and *Advances in International Comparative Management* and the advisory board of The Dushkin *Annual Editions: International Business*.

I

David A. Ricks

Dr. David Ricks is a Distinguished Professor of International Business at Thunderbird – The American Graduate School of International Management. He is also the editor-in-chief for the *Journal of International Management*. Previously, he taught at the Ohio State University (1970–1981) and at the University of South Carolina (1981–1992) where he served as the director of faculty development in international business, and as acting director of the Masters of International Business Studies Program.

Dr. Ricks has written 10 books. His most recent books are *Global Management,* and *Blunders in International Business.* He is also the author of scores of articles and papers, his most recent ones appearing in such publications as the *Strategic Management Journal,* the *Journal of Management,* the *Journal of International Business Studies, Organizational Dynamics,* and the *Columbia Journal of World Business.* He has appeared on the *Today Show,* testified before Congress, and has had his work favorably reviewed in *The Wall Street Journal, The New York Times, Business Week,* and *Forbes.*

Dr. Ricks is the consulting editor for the International Dimensions of Business Series, South-Western Publishing Company. In addition to having served as the editor-in-chief of the *Journal of International Business Studies* for eight years, Dr. Ricks is a member of the editorial board of 12 journals.

He has served both the Academy of Management and the Academy of International Business in many capacities, most notably as chair of the International Division of the Academy of Management and as the treasurer of the Academy of International Business. He is a fellow of the Academy of International Business.

P A R T

I

Introduction and Overview

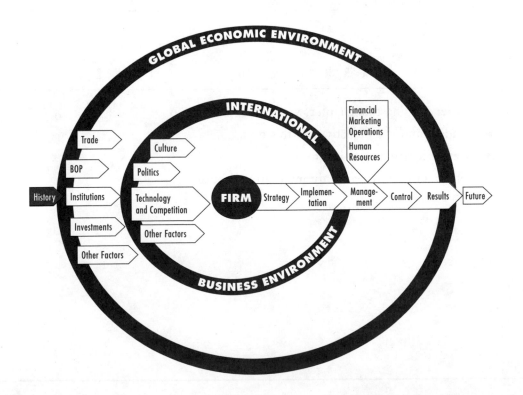

CHAPTER ▼ I

Studying International Business

LEARNING OBJECTIVES

After reading this chapter, you should be able to

▶ Understand the objectives of this text.

▶ Define international business.

▶ Understand why we study international business.

K E Y   T E R M S

▶ Ethnocentrism

▶ International business

▶ Domestic business

▶ Multidomestic

▶ Global

▶ Internationalization

▶ International company

▶ International firm

▶ Multinational company

▶ Transnational company

▶ Macrobusiness perspective

▶ Microfirm perspective

▶ Global economic environment

▶ International business blunder

T H O U G H T   S T A R T E R S

▶ It seems clear that the business world of today is no longer limited by national boundaries and that organizations need to have a global perspective if they are to survive and prosper in this international environment. Many will succeed or fail on the basis of their ability to deal with this dynamic environment.

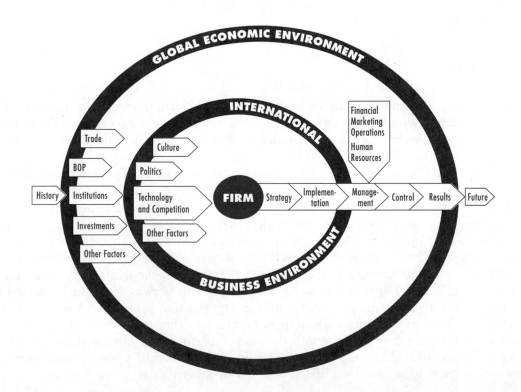

▶ Managing any business in the 1990s will mean some international contact. This is just as true of the small manufacturer that buys foreign materials and employs immigrant workers as it is of the global company, which views the world as both a market and a source of supply. The scope of these two examples is different, but both face an international environment, and neither can overlook its implications.

(Punnett 1994)

▶ International business is fraught with unexpected events. Fortunately, some of these surprising occurrences prove to be beneficial to the multinational corporations involved. For example, . . . a U.S. company which sold toothbrushes in the late 1960s experienced a major jump in sales, but it was not until years later that the company found out the Vietcong had bought the toothbrushes not to promote white teeth but to promote weapon cleaning.

  . . . These surprises, although sometimes controversial, are normally appreciated by the "lucky" corporations. However, not all companies experience such good fortune. Many surprises in international business are quite undesirable.

(Ricks 1993)

▶ A story is told of two companies that each sent representatives to Africa early in the 20th century to examine the market for shoes. One representative returned with the disheartening news that the people of Africa did not wear shoes so there was no market. The second returned with the good news that the people of Africa did not wear shoes so the market was untapped and enormous. The Bata Shoe Company is purported to be the second company. It now dominates the international shoe retail industry.

Introduction

There has been a growing recognition in the past decade that international business is the reality of the business world today. Entrepreneurs and bureaucrats, academics and practitioners, governments and ordinary people have acknowledged the significance of the international business environment. Most important for this text, you – students of business and management – have acknowledged this by creating an increased demand for courses dealing with international business topics.

  Although many people recognize the need to study international business because of its current significance, they nevertheless tend to view the world from an ethnocentric perspective. That is, their home country shapes their impression of the rest of the world. It is apparently a fact that, if asked to draw a map of the world, most people begin with their home country. The representation of the home country is generally in the center of the map, fairly accurate, and proportionally larger than it is in reality. As the drawing moves away from the home country, it becomes less accurate and more distorted in size. The fact that people know more about the shape of their home country and portray it more prominently than it should be is not surprising. The important lesson is that this is equally the case in all our ideas about foreign locations. A major goal of international business education, therefore, is to sensitize students to ethnocentrism and encourage them to see the world from different perspectives.

In response to the recognition of the international nature of business, many universities have developed courses focusing on international business topics, and academics have provided a variety of texts dealing with these topics. We wrote this text to add to the available resources for studying international business.

This introductory chapter of the text provides an overview of the field of international business and our approach to the topic. We begin with a brief statement of the learning objectives of the text. We next define terms relating to international business and then propose a general model, which serves to guide the text. Next is a brief overview of the topics to be covered throughout the text, with each topic related to the proposed model. The format of the chapters is presented, and the reasons for including various types of material are also explained. In addition, this chapter introduces a particular type of story, the business blunder, numerous examples of which will be illustrated throughout the text.

Objectives

We believe that students learn best when they enjoy what they are doing. We wrote the text with this in mind. Every attempt has been made to make the material easy to read and enjoyable. Theories and concepts are explained in simple terms without losing their sophisticated meanings. Examples, illustrations, stories, and interesting facts and figures are interspersed throughout the text to increase visual and intellectual stimulation.

We use both abstract and real-world approaches throughout the book. We discuss abstract theories and concepts and then illustrate and examine them from a realistic viewpoint. This combination of theories and concepts with real-world applications provides students with the background to approach and analyze new business situations and to determine practical action-oriented reactions to international opportunities and challenges.

This book is intended as an introductory text; therefore, it covers a wide range of topics. The material is presented with enough depth and practical guidance to give students a foundation on which to base actions in real-life situations in the international business environment. Each topic is discussed fully but not in the depth that would be more appropriate in a text for a specialized course. Rather, it gives students a broad but thorough survey of the field of international business. We hope that many students will find that the text increases their desire to study some of the topics in more depth and that they will seek additional courses and books on topics introduced here.

A particular aim of the text is to help students appreciate non-North American viewpoints. To this end, the cases, examples, illustrations, and situations include a substantial amount of non-North American information in addition to North American information. However, the theories and concepts presented should be applicable to any international organization; students outside North America should find this text as useful as those in Canada, Mexico, and the United States.

Students may expect clear-cut answers to issues, which often are not possible in studying international business. International business is naturally full of uncertainties, and this reality needs to be reflected in the material presented to students. To accomplish this, the text considers alternative views and examines varying approaches, without presenting one view or approach as more realistic than another.

Defining *International Business*

The study of international business begins with an understanding of what is meant by the term *international business* in the context of this text. The *American Heritage Dictionary* defines *international* as "of, relating to, or involving two or more nations" and *business* as "commercial, industrial, or professional dealings." Accordingly, the term **international business**, in this text, refers to any commercial, industrial, or professional endeavor involving two or more nations.

An alternative way to look at what is meant by international business is to distinguish it from domestic business. A **domestic business** operates in only one country, an international business in more than one. The fundamental characteristic that distinguishes international business from domestic business is that international business involves activities that take place across national borders. The implications of crossing these borders must be considered in all of the decisions and activities that international firms undertake.

The definition adopted here is intentionally broad and includes firms involved in limited exports and imports as well as those with operations around the world. The authors selected a broad definition because companies at all extremes of the definition face many common issues; thus, it seems appropriate to deal with these issues in a general framework.

This broad, general framework is appropriate for much of the discussion of international business activities, but it is also important to recognize specific differences in the way that business is conducted internationally. Many of the subsequent chapters identify the differences between firms described as multidomestic and those described as global. These are extremes and, in fact, most international companies combine attributes of both, but it is frequently helpful to distinguish between the two.

The **multidomestic** company does business in more than one country and thereby fits into the international business classification; the **global** company also operates in more than one country and is an international business. The distinction between them is as follows:

▶ A multidomestic firm conducts its foreign business through separate, local entities in foreign countries.
▶ A global firm views all of its foreign entities as interrelated and conducts business on a worldwide basis.

A good example of a multidomestic firm is the Bata Shoe Organization (the corporate literature describes the firm using this term). The firm generally establishes any subsidiary so that it operates for the local national market, using local suppliers and personnel. Bata sees this as one of its major strengths, and interestingly, Bata is believed to be a local firm in many locations. The word *bata* actually means "shoe" in some locations.

In contrast, the big oil companies may be considered global. These firms view the world as a single market, and their aim is to make the best product at a competitive price. These companies plan for integrated operations that promote efficiencies. In some larger firms, such as Nestlé, Procter & Gamble, or Sandoz, managers may even see themselves as linked more with the corporation than with a particular nationality.

These extremes are interesting to consider, but in reality, firms have to be concerned about both global integration and local adaptation. More critical, perhaps, for firms in today's competitive and rapidly changing environment is developing a "global philosophy." This means that a firm's managers consider all the world as a potential market, a potential source of supply, and a potential place for operations. Such a philosophy implies an openness to opportunities anywhere in the world. This can be important for all firms, because even small, domestic firms can be affected by international pressures and need to think globally.

These two types of firms are extremes of a continuum. This distinction is helpful in examining international business because the choices that international companies make are influenced by their overall multidomestic or global view. Throughout the text this distinction will be noted and its implications examined.

The definition adopted here implies a "business" perspective. Business in the North American context usually means private, for-profit enterprises. Certainly, these enterprises are the primary focus of the discussion in this text. At the same time, the general framework presented here is applicable to many organizations that would not be classified as businesses under this definition, such as government agencies, educational institutions, and charitable and other nonprofit organizations. The authors believe that most of the concepts developed in the chapters of this text can be applied to virtually any international organization with minor modifications.

The definition of international business proposed here is useful for general discussions. The authors believe that the broad, general definition in this text, which is intended for a varied group of students, is appropriate. It is important, nevertheless, to realize that, for more specific analyses, more precise definitions and finer distinctions may be appropriate. For certain decisions, degrees of **internationalization** might be a meaningful consideration. These degrees of internationalization can be measured in various ways; they are often determined by comparing a firm's domestic activities to its foreign ones. Some measures include foreign sales relative to domestic, foreign profits relative to domestic, foreign employment relative to domestic, and foreign investment relative to domestic. Other measures could be the number and type of foreign activities, the degree and form of foreign ownership, the form of overall corporate ownership, the makeup of top corporate management, and the mix of foreign and domestic management and technical personnel in various locations. These distinctions should be kept in mind when assessing particular international companies.

Thus far, the term *international business* has been used to refer to both a form of business and a type of organization. The term is used in both ways throughout the text. The terms **international company** and **international firm** are used interchangeably with the term *international business* to refer to a type of organization. A number of other terms also refer to international businesses and organizations. Some of the more common terms are **multinational company** (MNC), **transnational company** (TNC), and *global company*. Some authors distinguish among these as different forms of international organizations. Such distinctions are not stressed in this text, but if a distinction is believed to be needed in a specific instance, it will be specified at that time.

Importance of Studying International Business

There is little question that a large part of today's business is international in some form. This internationalization of the business world is not expected to decline in the foreseeable future. More likely, the reverse will take place, and internationalization will increase. In preparing for this, business students need to understand the factors that affect business activities that are international in scope.

International business is similar to any business in that the goals and objectives are often the same, and the management processes and functions are comparable. International business is more complex than purely domestic business, however, because the interactions and transactions take place across national boundaries. The introduction of different nations into the business process means introducing various ways to do business. These differences among countries result from the influence on business of a number of forces, such as laws and regulations, culture, language, currency, transportation systems, and distribution patterns, to mention a few. To be effective in an international environment, firms need to understand these influences and be able to use this understanding to their advantage.

Due to the internationalization of business and the complexity of the international business world, familiarity with international business practices is of growing importance to firms. Many universities and colleges have responded to this need for expertise in international business by internationalizing their curricula and offering a variety of international business and management courses. Students have responded by demanding more of these courses and more and better texts to accompany them. This text is a response to these developments, and it reflects the authors' conviction of the importance of studying international business. This text is intended both to inform students and to stimulate their interest in the exciting field of international business.

Organization of the Text

It is helpful for students to understand the reasons underlying the organization of a text so that they can follow the logical development of the topics covered. This section outlines the model that the authors used to organize the text.

The book is structured to move from a **macrobusiness perspective** to a **microfirm-management perspective.** This structure presents the overall environment in which international business takes place before focusing on management issues in international companies. The presentation gives students a thorough grounding in the theories and concepts that explain international business and its activities and allows them to understand how individual firms make decisions in this environment. A pictorial model of the elements of international business is presented in Exhibit 1.1. The model was used to guide the organization of the text and it appears at the opening of each part and chapter with the area that will be featured highlighted. Each section of the text is described and related to the model in the following discussion.

Sections of the Text

The following discussion of the content of the various sections and chapters in the text illustrates the flow of the material. The text is divided into four major parts: Introduction and Overview, The Global Economic Environment, The International Firm Environment, and Managing an International Business.

EXHIBIT 1.1   **Elements of International Business**

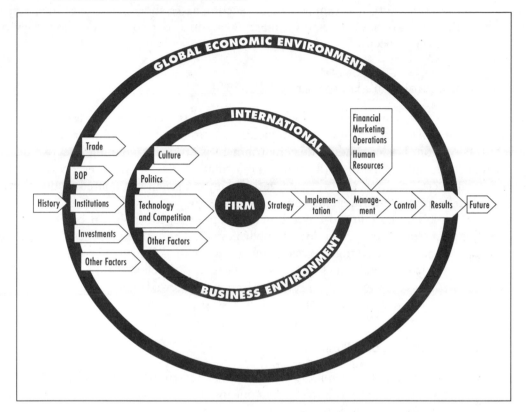

Part I: Introduction and Overview

This part gives students a general sense of the international business environment. Chapter 1 focuses on the need to study international business and the approach to this study found in this text; Chapter 2 examines the historical development of international business.

These two chapters put international business into context for the student; this context provides the framework for the balance of the text. The historical discussion and consideration of potential developments encourage students to incorporate current events into their thinking about issues throughout the text.

Part II: The Global Economy

This part examines the macrobusiness and global economic environment of international business, as represented by the outermost circle of the model. Chapter 3 considers trade, including reasons for it and the degree and direction of trade. Chapter 4 explains and discusses the balance of payments accounts and international institutions as they relate to international businesses. Chapter 5 examines world investment flows, including the reasons for investment and its level and direction.

These three chapters provide an overall assessment of why international business takes place; they also present the institutional framework that encompasses such business. Students need to have a thorough grasp of these issues on a macro scale in order to consider how they affect international firms on a specific level.

Part III: The International Firm's Environment

This part considers the environment in which international firms operate. The focus is on factors external to the organization that it cannot immediately control. The middle circle of the model represents this section. Understanding this environment is crucial to making effective decisions in a particular firm, and the use of environmental information for making international decisions is stressed in this section. Aspects of the international environment are related to decisions that international firms make and the management strategies they employ.

Chapter 6 looks at the cultural environment; Chapter 7, the political environment; and Chapter 8, the competitive and technological environment. These three business environmental facets are key external considerations to managing an international firm. These aspects incorporate most of the environmental issues of concern to organizations. The three chapters provide students with an appreciation of the need to assess the international business environment carefully, as well as models for accomplishing this assessment.

Part IV: Managing an International Business

This part turns to internal issues relating to managing international firms. The focus is on choosing appropriate international strategies and putting them into practice, as well as managing the various functions and processes of the international business. The specifics of international management are discussed in the context of the environment presented in the preceding chapters. This section is represented by the center section of the model.

There are eight chapters in this part. Chapters 9 and 10 discuss strategic decisions and their implementation. Chapters 11, 12, 13, and 14 focus on functional aspects of the international firm. The finance function, the marketing function, the operations function, and the human resource function are each discussed in separate chapters. Chapter 15 looks at the control process and its role in achieving international objectives. The final chapter, Chapter 16, reviews some events of the 1990s to illustrate the impact of such events on doing business internationally.

A Special Chapter

Chapter 16, the concluding chapter of the book, is to a large extent a summary as well as an opportunity to assess real-world events and their impact on international businesses. Students may find it helpful to refer to this chapter throughout; that is, after reading Chapter 2, it may be interesting to consider how Chapter 16 relates current events to issues discussed in Chapter 2.

A hallmark of the approach in this text is tying theories and concepts to real-world events. Students should constantly pay attention to news events and attempt to relate these to the discussions in the text. Consider these examples:

▶ In late 1995, the Province of Quebec held a referendum on separation from Canada. The results were very close, with a narrow margin voting against separation. The implications for international businesses are varied and complex. Among the implications, the vote indicates a relatively strong sense of frustration in Quebec for the "status quo." This in turn suggests a potentially unstable political situation. Businesses may see this as somewhat negative and select to invest outside of Quebec.

▶ In late 1995 and early 1996, budget deliberations by the federal government of the United States resulted in a shutdown of many government offices. This event has implications for international businesses. Among the implications, American businesspeople were not able to obtain or renew passports and travel documents and export permits were not processed. Some businesspeople were thus limited in their ability to travel internationally, and some international contracts were not fulfilled in a timely manner.

▶ In January 1996, elections were held for a new Palestinian Council, and the Palestinians took the first steps toward statehood. These elections have implications for international businesses. Elections should support the peace process and eventually lead to greater self-determination among the Palestinians. In turn, these factors may open new markets and provide the impetus for the development of new businesses in Palestine. Terrorist activities following the elections may be cause for delay in the peace process.

▶ Recently, the Islamic Republic of Iran opened government tourist offices in Brussels and Tokyo. This could have implications for a variety of international businesses. It offers new opportunities for tour operators in Europe promoting unusual destinations. It may also indicate a shift in anti-Western sentiment in Iran and thus the possibility that the Iranian market will eventually reopen to Western businesses.

▶ In 1996, the Central Bureau of Investigation in India charged 10 senior politicians of various parties with accepting kickbacks. This has implications for businesses considering India as a market or a place to locate. For a long time, India has been viewed warily by many international businesses because of its reputation for corruption. These charges may signal a serious attempt on the part of the Indian authorities to deal with corruption. In turn, this would encourage businesspeople to see business opportunities in India in a more positive light.

These events of late 1995 and early 1996 provide a sample of the impact that daily events have on doing business internationally. Businesspeople constantly monitor these events and factor them into their decisions. Students should begin to think globally by monitoring the news and asking, "What impact might that have on international business opportunities?"

Chapter Format

It is helpful for students to understand the authors' reasons for organizing chapters in a particular way and including certain types of material. Throughout the text the authors will relate theory, concepts, and practice to the real world and current events. The intent is, first, to provide students with a thorough grounding in the basic body of knowledge that relates to international business. The second intent is to ensure that students have a good grasp of the practical reasons for studying this body of knowledge. To accomplish these objectives, each chapter focuses on a particular aspect of doing business internationally; theories and concepts are illustrated with practical models and real examples.

The book contains a variety of materials that encourage students to think about each subject as it relates to international business. Each chapter begins with Thought Starters, relatively short quotes that provide an interesting starting point to the chapter. They are intended, as the name implies, to help students to start thinking about the topics that will be covered throughout the chapter. The chapters also include many examples and stories about real companies, which illustrate the conceptual points that are discussed. Most chapters end with a mini-case. The mini-case is a short description of a real company or situation that provides an opportunity to discuss some of the concepts in the chapter relative to a real situation.

In addition to the material outlined previously, most chapters contain additional sections that are helpful to students. At the beginning of each chapter is an outline of chapter topics, followed by a summary of the chapter's learning objectives, a list of key terms, and several Thought Starters. These sections prepare the student for the material that is discussed in the chapter. They are also helpful in reviewing the material.

Chapters conclude with a list of discussion questions, assignments, and selected references. Discussion questions and assignments stimulate further consideration of topics covered in the chapter. Selected references give students sources of additional information on the topics covered in the chapter. References in the body of the chapter have been kept to a minimum and are used only when specific mention is made of another author's work. The selected reference list encompasses major materials that support the chapter discussion.

Some chapters also have appendices that include material that is either of a specialized or an advanced nature. The material is included in this format because the authors believe it may be of special interest to some groups but of lesser interest to others. This format provides flexibility for the instructor. Students interested in the material may want to examine the appendices even if they are not assigned.

International Business Blunders

This book contains many examples, illustrations, and reports about firms' international experiences. Many of the reported experiences are about **international business blunders**. These factual stories about mistakes that companies have made in their international activities are used to provide valuable lessons about doing business internationally. Companies often relate business success stories, but they may be soon forgotten. Mistakes, on the other hand, although seldom admitted, are easy to remember and therefore are particularly helpful in illustrating the importance of doing things correctly. Blunders are an integral part of many chapters because students enjoy these stories and remember the theories and concepts associated with them. The boxed example illustrates these stories.

> Reuters News Agency — Singapore. Some owners of Italian-made Alfa Romeo 164s in Singapore are changing the car's model name to 168 because in the southern Chinese dialect [of] Cantonese, 164 sounds like "die all the way."   (*Globe and Mail* 1990)

Students will appreciate that there are lessons to be learned from mistakes. Many of these blunders are amusing in retrospect, but their impact on business at the time may have been very serious. Throughout the text there will be a number of similar international blunder stories illustrating how things can go wrong even in large and experienced firms. These blunders identify the need for international managers to develop international expertise to minimize their occurrence.

Summary

This text provides a broad coverage of issues that students need to understand so that they can become effective in the international business arena. This chapter defined *international business* and illustrated the need to study the topic. It also detailed the authors' approach to the topic and the organization of the text. The authors believe that students will enjoy the text and learn from it.

MINI-CASE
Barings Bank

In November 1994 an article in *The Economist* discussed the use of financial derivatives. This article concluded that many mutual funds bought and sold simple (*plain vanilla,* in the financial parlance) instruments to hedge their exposure to currency and other risks. At the same time, the article warned about the consequences of investing in increasingly complex instruments – in a very competitive environment, fund managers were encouraged to use more exotic derivatives to outperform rivals. All this seemed somewhat prophetic when the Barings Bank collapsed on February 26, 1995.

According to reports, Nicholas Leeson, a 28-year-old "whizzkid" derivatives trader in Barings' Singapore office lost close to US$1.5 billion on futures contracts on Japan's Nikkei stock market. This was substantially more than the bank's capital. Leeson's activities, which were described by many as gambling, apparently began in 1994 when he decided to sell put options and call options on Nikkei futures. These deals are profitable if the market proves less volatile than expected. By the end of 1994, Leeson had earned $150 million for Barings. There is substantial risk to such a strategy evidenced by the Barings story. The Kobe earthquake in January was said to have affected the stock market negatively, and Leeson's strategy began to fail. In an attempt to forestall failure he bought Nikkei futures on a huge scale, trying to reverse the downward trend. Given that the Tokyo stock market is the second largest in the world, one individual trying to influence its direction seems almost ludicrous. In fact, Leeson was unable to change the downward movement; and, even worse, the market plunged on January 23. To add to Leeson's desperation, bonuses were to be fixed on February 24; his desperation led to even wilder attempts to buy enough Nikkei futures to force the market to turn around. The result was almost inevitable.

The old-style bankers who form the majority of Barings' senior management appeared to be taken by surprise by the events in Singapore. The Barings' experience provides a reminder of how quickly disaster can strike – "how yesterday's rapid *expansion and ambitious investment can become tomorrow's sloppy management and fraudulent conspiracy*" ("The Collapse of Barings," *The Economist,* March 4, 1995, p. 19). Ironically, the Barings name and long-standing reputation probably contributed to its undoing. The bank was Britain's oldest bank, over 200 years old, steeped in tradition, with the reputation for caution and conservatism. Many people wondered how these events could have taken place. There was discussion of the need for new regulations and taxes to avoid similar events in the future. Some people went so far as to call for a ban on derivatives trading.

Discussion Issues

1. Discuss the pros and cons of banning trading in derivatives.
2. Discuss how Barings might have avoided the 1995 collapse.
3. Identify what subsequently happened to Leeson, Barings Bank, and trading in derivatives, following the collapse of the bank.

Selected References

Globe and Mail (December 4, 1990), section A2.

Jones, C. A., *International Business in the Nineteenth Century* (New York: New York University Press, 1987).

McCarthy, D. M. P., *International Business History* (Westport, Conn.: Praeger Publishers, 1994).

Punnett, B. J., *Experiencing International Management* (Boston: PWS-Kent, 1989), p. v.

Ricks, D. A., *Blunders in International Business* (Cambridge, Mass.: Blackwell Publishers, 1993), p. 1.

CHAPTER ▼ 2

International Business: Its History and Future

LEARNING OBJECTIVES

After reading this chapter, you should be able to

▶ Discuss the historical development and evolution of international business.

▶ Outline the characteristics of each stage of the four-stage model of development in the international business environment.

▶ Explain what impact several key issues will have on international business in the future.

K E Y   T E R M S

▶ Commercial era
▶ Explorative era
▶ Concessionary era
▶ National era

▶ Two-actor stage
▶ Three-actor stage
▶ Four-actor stage
▶ Multiactor stage

T H O U G H T   S T A R T E R S

▶ The harbor Herod built . . . Some 2,000 years ago, Caesarea Maritima welcomed ships. Caesarea was a major east–west trade route; Byzantium and Rome lay 20 to 60 days away by sail. The harbor handled local products – wine, flax, and grain – and silk and spices via caravan from Asia.

(Hohlfelder 1987)

▶ The city of Hotan lies 30 miles downriver and the fabled Kunlun Mountains about 70 miles upstream. Kunlun, the original "jade mountains," appear to have been Asia's sole source

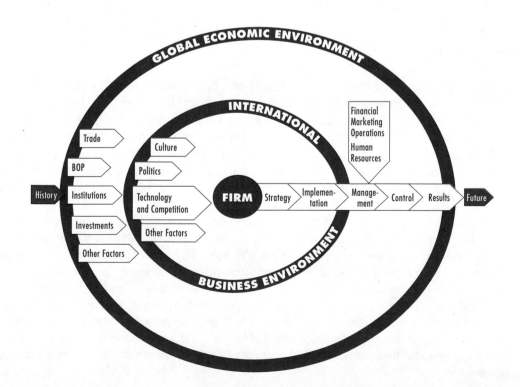

[of jade] from prehistoric times until the 1700s. For centuries jade pickers have roamed these shores collecting riches washed down in the spring floods. Camel caravans traveling west through this famed stop on the Silk Road carried Cathay's fabrics to the Middle East, and on their return trips packed the heavy jade boulders more than 2,000 miles for the emperors' workshops in Beijing. In this isolated desert, a European held Asian jade for the first time: Marco Polo, in 1272, observed "chalcedony and jasper, which are carried for sale to Cathay, and such is their abundance that they form a considerable . . . commerce."

(Ward 1987)

▶ Putting himself in the picture, an engineer at NASA's Ames Research Center uses a stereo-graphic viewer and DataGlove to manipulate a simulated fuel stream. With the glove, researchers can maneuver objects inside a computer image.

(Ward 1989)

▶ "Business in America has lost its way, adrift in a sea of managerial mediocrity, desperately needing leadership to face worldwide economic competition." So claims Mr. Abraham Zaleznik, a professor at Harvard Business School, in his book *The Managerial Mystique.*

(The Economist 1990)

▶ "One can discern . . . a move from technological optimism, whereby scientists thought they could offer certainty, towards an appreciation of the phenomena we experience as chaotic, 'chancy,' enigmatic, and paradoxical."

(Cummings and Haridimos 1995)

Introduction

This chapter explores the historical development and evolution of international business. The purpose of this discussion is to help the student better understand why we have international business and to place current events in the context of the international business field. This facilitates understanding the present international business environment. This chapter also suggests some directions toward which international business may be moving. Businesspeople cannot know what the future will bring, but they can analyze trends, developments, and other factors to make knowledgeable decisions in preparing for the future, whatever it is. This chapter therefore explores some future scenarios.

International business may seem to be a recent development; but in reality, business has taken place internationally for a long time. The ancient Egyptians, Greeks, and Phoenicians all traded with foreigners and encountered many of the same obstacles that present-day businesses encounter (e.g., different languages, different cultures, different customs and expectations, difficult transportation). In spite of these obstacles, there is evidence of extensive trade between nations as early as 3000 B.C. This international aspect to commerce developed when products available in one area were desired in other areas where they were not available and when people in one location had particular skills that were valued in other areas. Essentially, this is also true today, and international business continues for many of the same reasons that it began thousands of years ago.

Descriptions of the first Olympic Games held between 776 B.C. and A.D. 394 suggest a meeting that was part sport, part religion, and largely commerce. People traveled from all the Greek city-states (each the equivalent of a small independent nation), as well as from other countries, to attend the games every four years. Local entrepreneurs offered goods and services of all kinds at the games – some aimed at the very wealthy who would attend with a large contingent of servants and attendants, and some aimed at the poorer visitors camped in makeshift tents. Goods and services ranged from cheap trinkets to expensive jewelry, from prostitutes to prophecies of the future. Not unlike an international trade show today, this meeting provided merchants, entrepreneurs, and salespeople an opportunity to show off their wares while making valuable contacts with a variety of people with whom they might do business in the future.

More recently, the discovery and exploration of the New World in the late 1400s and 1500s were fueled by Europe's desire to facilitate trade with the Far East. During this period, the Dutch and the English, as well as other Europeans, began to build worldwide business empires, which were well established by the 1700s and 1800s. The British East India Company, for example, was chartered in 1600 and soon after had established foreign operations. In North America, the first English joint-stock company (the Company of Adventurers), which became the Hudson's Bay Company, was formed and its charter sealed on May 2, 1670. This company grew out of a conviction that the way to Cathay would be found by means of a Northwest passage via Canada's Hudson's Bay (Rich 1958).

When Sir George Simpson, the overseas governor of the Hudson's Bay Company, attended a state dinner in Oslo during a European tour in 1838, he was toasted as "head of the most extended Dominions in the known world – the Emperor of Russia, the Queen of England, and the President of the United States excepted." This was an appropriate tribute, given that the Hudson's Bay Company encompassed nearly 3 million square miles, and the company's trading posts once reached from the Arctic Ocean to Hawaii and its influence far beyond that. (Newman 1987)

Early forms of international business relied largely on trade, but in the 1700s American companies began to invest in foreign countries. These foreign activities were relatively short lived until 1868, when Singer Sewing Machine built a factory in Scotland.

During this period, there was "a widespread expectation, especially among those engaged in commerce, that free trade would bring to an end the era of despotism and war. Merchants trading internationally were inclined to see themselves, and to be seen by others, as agents of an individualistic and progressive liberal revolution" (Jones 1987, p. 1).

Historical Developments in International Business

International aspects of commerce have almost always been well known and accepted. While this is true, however, there has been an explosive growth in international companies in the second half of the 20th century. As we can see from Exhibits 2.1 and 2.2, world merchandise trade is increasing faster than world output.

EXHIBIT 2.1   Volume Growth of Merchandise Trade for Selected Regions, 1991–1993 (annual percentage change)

	Exports				Imports		
1991	1992	1993			1991	1992	1993
3	4.5	2.5	World		3.5	5	2.5
6	8	5.5	North America		0.5	8	11
2	7	9.5	Latin America		12.5	18	8
2.5	3	−0.5	Western Europe		3.5	2.5	−3.5
2.5	3	−1	European Union		5.5	3.5	−4
0	4.5	2	EFTA		−2.5	−1.5	−1.5
−19	−3.5	2.5	Central and Eastern Europe and the republics of the former USSR		−22	−7.5	10.5
8	5.5	6	Asia[a]		10	7.5	10.5
2.5	1.5	−1.5	Japan		4	−0.5	3
10.5	7.5	9.5	Six other Asian exporters of manufactures[a,b]		14	8	11.5

[a]Excluding Hong Kong re-exports and imports for re-export. Including Hong Kong's re-exports (and imports for re-export) the increase in world exports (and imports) would be 3 percent in 1993.
[b]Chinese Taipei, Hong Kong, Republic of Korea, Malaysia, Singapore, and Thailand.
Source: UN World Investment Report, 1994, *United Nations, 1994.*

EXHIBIT 2.2   Growth by Volume, of World Merchandise Trade and Output, 1980–1993 (annual percentage change)

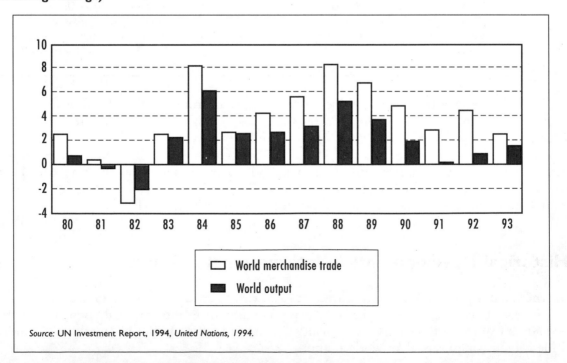

Source: UN Investment Report, 1994, *United Nations, 1994.*

The Commercial Era (1500–1850)

The **Commercial Era** began with the age of the great explorers, which followed Columbus's voyage to the New World. International trade during this era was very much a function of individual entrepreneurs seeking personal fortunes in distant lands. These men risked much, but the rewards were great. They purchased exotic goods (such as precious metals, spices, silk, and slaves), which could be sold at huge profits at home.

This era was also characterized by a close relationship between these entrepreneurs and European monarchs. After recognizing the profit potential of overseas ventures, European royalty wanted direct involvement in order to share in the returns. Further, members of the royalty used their influence to ensure maximization of profits. This resulted in the formation of the great chartered companies such as the Dutch East India Company, the Levant Company, the British Royal American Company, and the Hudson's Bay Company, which were granted exclusive trading rights and empowered to perform consular functions (e.g., make alliances, appoint governors, and deploy troops). Exhibit 2.3 shows the makeup of the top 100 multinationals, by home country, in the 1990s.

The Explorative Era (1850–1914)

The **Explorative Era** was characterized by the creation of industrial empires based on industrial products rather than exotic goods. The industrial revolution had changed the nature of the European enterprise, and businesses sought secure and cheap sources of raw materials in overseas investments.

EXHIBIT 2.3
Top 100 Multinationals by Home Country, 1992

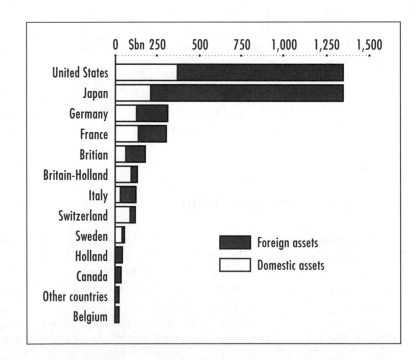

By the middle of the 19th century, many companies had large-scale investments in various countries. The increasing number of Europeans participating in foreign ventures as well as the importance of these investments to the home economies encouraged home governments to become involved in colonial rule. These colonies became more and more dependent on foreign investment and foreign rule, both industrially and politically.

At the same time, European investors found that the skills of local workers were often inadequate to operate the investor's enterprises. The European enterprises began to provide their own management, skilled workers, and technicians, thus further increasing the colonies' dependence on the foreign influences. In sum, this era represents a domination of host-country politics, economics, and culture by Western influences. Jardine Matheson in Hong Kong, MacKinnon MacKensic in India, and Fredrick Dalgety in New South Wales are good examples of the firms of this era.

The Concessionary Era (1914–1945)

The **Concessionary Era** was characterized by an increasing assumption of paternalistic responsibilities by Western enterprises in their host countries. The host countries reciprocated by granting major concessions to the Western companies, with the result that the companies became, to an extent, all-powerful and all-providing. Typical concessions were the early oil concessions in the Middle East and United Fruit's agreements in Central America. Such companies provided housing, health and sanitation services, finances, education, distribution of food and other goods, transportation, and protection for their workers – all services that governments often could not provide and therefore were happy to accept from foreigners.

For some time, the colonies seemed to accept this increasing dependence, but eventually, a sense of nationalism and economic development began to take place. The new sense of national identity combined with improved economic conditions eventually signaled the end of the Concessionary Era.

In addition, during the Great Depression of the 1930s, many companies began to replace high-priced home-country nationals with trained locals and cut back on the services the companies had previously provided in the host countries. These factors encouraged local governments and businesspeople to seek greater independence, both political and commercial, from their colonial masters.

The National Era (1945–1970)

The **National Era** is characterized by increasing hostility toward Western enterprises and antagonism toward foreigners' interference in local affairs. As noted previously, the emergence of a desire for sovereignty and self-government encouraged countries to seek economic independence from their former colonial masters. These countries often sought to exert their freedom by imposing restrictions on foreign enterprises.

The National Era was one of instability due to many changes occurring throughout the world in the political arena and because many of the newly independent countries were in fact ill-equipped to run their internal affairs effectively. This instability did not discourage international business, however. To the contrary, many companies found new opportunities around the world following World War II.

This was, in fact, a period of major global expansion for businesses, during which multinational companies, as we think of them today, were established. Businesses began seeking both markets and productive inputs around the world, and the idea of global rationalization (producing different components of an item in different parts of the world to achieve efficiency and cost effectiveness) first became popular. World War II had encouraged the development of worldwide communication and transportation systems, as well as the development of new technologies. These developments all contributed to the ability of businesses to take a global view of operations.

During the 1950s and 1960s, U.S. firms wholeheartedly embraced international business, and the multinational corporation became largely an American phenomenon. There were some multinational European firms, but U.S. firms dominated the international business scene. During this period, "going international" was the fashionable thing to do, and U.S. foreign direct investment rose from about $12 billion in 1950 to almost $80 billion by 1970.

Initially, these American companies entered the international arena for defensive reasons – largely to overcome trade barriers that were widespread in the 1950s. As these firms developed international expertise, however, they aggressively sought international opportunities, and by the 1960s many needed to develop a global strategy if they were to remain competitive.

In the 1960s, other countries in addition to the United States joined the move to international expansion. By 1965, large non-American companies were investing in foreign countries at about the same annual rate as U.S. companies, and foreign direct investment in the United States had increased. The Europeans were first to follow the U.S. lead, but the Japanese were not far behind. Between the mid-1950s and mid-1960s, Japan was the leader in international growth, followed by Continental Europe, with Canada, the United States, and the United Kingdom substantially behind.

More Recent Developments in International Business

By the 1970s, internationalization had lost some of its glamour. This situation, combined with increased host-government hostility toward foreign investment, led to a period of U.S. divestment in the early 1970s. This hostility was aimed particularly at U.S. companies probably because, in spite of their success, they often had been culturally insensitive to their hosts, believing that the "American way" was always the right way. U.S. companies adopted a more wary approach to foreign operations than they had previously. Between 1971 and 1975, American companies sold almost 10 percent of their subsidiaries. In addition, the number of new subsidiaries being formed declined substantially (Rose 1977).

Also during the early 1970s, Japanese companies became increasingly aggressive and successful in their internationalization and in selling their products in foreign markets. The mid-1970s through the mid-1980s was also a period of increased investment by other foreigners in the United States. For example, from 1975 to 1985, U.S. investment outside its borders doubled, while foreign investment in the United States increased by a factor of seven.

During this last period, a different shift in ownership was also occurring, which made identification and comparison of directions of investment more difficult. The difficulty resulted from a number of companies that were becoming truly global and, as such, had shares that were sold on stock markets around the world. Individuals and organizations investing in these markets were also increasingly global: Japanese were investing in U.S. markets, Americans in European markets, Australians in markets in the Association of South East Asian Nations (ASEAN). Consequently, ownership could no longer clearly be identified with the United States, Canada, or France, for instance.

The Actors in the International Business Play

An interesting way to look at developments in the international business environment is in terms of the actors involved at various stages (see Exhibit 2.4). Robinson (1981) described four stages of development, beginning with two main actors and progressing to a multiactor environment. These four stages are described as follows.

Two-Actor Stage

The **two-actor stage** encompasses the period from the end of World War II to 1955. During this decade, the two major players were the firm itself and its foreign commercial constituencies (customers, suppliers, partners, and so on). This was a period of relative simplicity for the company undertaking foreign transactions, and arrangements involved essentially the interests of only the two parties.

U.S. companies, such as the United Fruit Company, were dominant during this period. Europe and Japan were under reconstruction following the war, and U.S. technology, machines, and consumer goods were in great demand. Many of the less developed countries were not yet independent, national policies on foreign investment in most countries were in the process of formulation, and the regulations that did exist were poorly implemented. These factors combined to give the multinational company, particularly the U.S. multinational, a great deal of power.

Because of the success of the U.S. multinationals during this period, U.S. management was considered to be the embodiment of good management. U.S. firms were at the forefront of technological and managerial developments; around the world other companies sought to copy U.S. approaches. It is interesting to note that many Japanese management approaches were adapted from U.S. methods that were seen as particularly effective.

Three-Actor Stage

The **three-actor stage** lasted from 1955 to 1970. Three actors emerged as important in the international environment: the firm, its commercial constituencies, and the host government. Many countries were newly independent, nationalism among the newly independent countries was increasing, and during this period host governments were increasingly sensitive to the potential loss of power associated with foreign investment. These factors resulted in new regulations of foreign investment that were often stringently enforced.

EXHIBIT 2.4
The Actors in the International Business Environment

Two-Actor Stage
Time period — World War II to 1955
Key players — Firm and foreign constituencies
Characteristics — U.S. companies dominant

National foreign investment policies in process of formulation

United States viewed as forefront of management and technological developments

Three-Actor Stage
Time period — 1955 to 1970
Key players — Host governments increasingly important
Characteristics — Countries newly independent

Nationalism increasing

Host governments sensitive to potential loss of power associated with foreign investment

Japanese and European firms entering international arena

Four-Actor Stage
Time period — 1970 to 1980
Key players — Home governments increasingly important
Characteristics — Home governments seek to limit and prescribe appropriate company activities

U.S. companies retrench

Multiactor Stage
Time period — 1980 onward
Key players — Special interest groups, international agencies, economic alliances added
Characteristics — Greater complexity

Awareness of changing global perspectives and their assessment necessary

Japanese and European firms were then entering the international arena, and communist governments were offering assistance to many newly independent countries. The power base that had previously made U.S. companies virtually invincible was quickly eroding. No longer could multinationals expect to be successful by considering only the objectives of the firm and its commercial constituencies; the objectives of the host government had to be factored in as well.

Four-Actor Stage

The **four-actor stage**, from 1970 to 1980, reflects the growing importance of home governments. The interdependence of national economies was becoming clear to both host governments and home governments, and the home governments recognized that the activities of their multinationals could have a major impact at home. These home governments sought to limit and prescribe the appropriate activities for their companies abroad. Such regulation made the situation far more complex because home governments began to question and regulate the multinational's decisions in foreign locations although the home governments did not have any clear authority in the host countries.

The issue of extraterritorial enforcement of laws illustrates the four actors often involved at this stage. A U.S. firm (actor 1) could find a foreign partner and reach a mutually acceptable agreement with this partner (actor 2) that the host government (actor 3) found satisfactory, yet the U.S. government (actor 4) might object to the agreement. For example, imagine that the U.S. government prohibits U.S. companies from shipping certain chemicals to Iraq, but Jordan does not prohibit such shipments to Iraq. A U.S. joint venture registered as a Jordanian company is subject to Jordanian regulations, but the U.S. government will attempt to influence the company's business decisions by enforcing U.S. regulations outside of the U.S. through pressure on the U.S. partner.

During the four-actor stage, many U.S. companies chose to pull back rather than expand as the overall regulation of international business increased. Opportunities that would have been attractive to two actors only (the firm and its commercial constituencies) became less attractive when the objectives of both the host government and the home government were considered.

Multiactor Stage

The **multiactor stage** encompasses the period from 1980 to the present and involves many participants including a variety of different interest groups, all of which believe that the activities of multinational companies affect their members. Multinationals of this period must consider many groups whose membership transcends national boundaries: special-interest (racial, religious, ethnic) groups, international agencies, and economic alliances, among others. These groups have developed a certain degree of political power, and therefore the multinational cannot afford to ignore their demands. Environmental groups around the world, for example, have influenced businesses to incorporate "green," or ecological, issues into international strategic decisions.

The multiactor stage is one of great complexity, in which the balance of power is often not clear and may be shifting almost continuously in response to events around the world. To be successful in such an environment, companies need to be constantly aware of changing global perspectives and assess how such perspectives may affect their activities. The complexity of this environment presents an opportunity for those who study this exciting field of international business. Exhibit 2.4 summarizes the development of the actors participating in the international business environment.

The Future

Predicting the future is a risky business and generally the responsibility of fortune tellers and soothsayers. Major League Baseball manager Yogi Berra is reported to have said that predicting – especially the future – is tough. Exhibit 2.5 summarizes some forecasts of a century ago.

EXHIBIT 2.5
**Forecasts from a
Century Ago**

The Futurist reports the following forecasts from the 1890s:

No trees: Futurists saw the demand for wood totally consuming the supply, no reasonable alternative was foreseen.

Automobiles in war: General Greely predicted that eventually automobiles would play a role in war but that it would be a long time before they constituted a major means of transportation for an army – 15 years later, motorized warfare was a reality in Europe.

Quiet streets: A magazine writer thought that the automobile would produce quieter and less crowded streets.

Population, 60 million: Thomas Dixon, Jr., predicted that African-Americans would represent the major portion of American society by the end of the 20th century.

Technology: Storage batteries, nonrefillable bottles, and telephone advances were among the developments predicted.

Size of cities: Cities were expected to grow vertically, with different levels allocated to transportation, commerce, shopping, leisure, and living.

Freeways: In 1900, *Collier's Weekly* called for a "national highway."

Bullet trains: The passing of the steam locomotive was predicted by 1900, long before its final demise, and the development of a train able to travel at 300 miles per hour was suggested.

Source: Center 1990.

It is possible, however, to consider some of the major trends in the world and ask, "What do these mean for international businesses?" For instance, demographic information can be used to predict the makeup of certain populations in the future. These predictions serve as guides for businesses making decisions about their futures. The intent of this section is not to forecast the future but to identify some events and trends that may have major impacts on international business in the future.

An infinite number of issues in terms of the future of international business could be discussed. Space limits this discussion to only a few. Some events that appear likely to influence international business in coming years are briefly discussed in the following sections.

The Office of the Future

The increasing speed and efficiency of global communication make it possible to envision future office environments that are vastly different from current ones. No longer will it be necessary for employees to be physically located in the same place; instead, they will be able to work almost anywhere yet be instantly in touch with others. This has implications for both large and small companies.

The concept of a headquarters for a large organization could disappear if companies instead have networks of communication around the globe. Global participation for small companies could be possible without the previous overhead expense of coordinating such activities from a central location. For example, an article on the future of American business firms in *The Futurist* argued that middle-sized operations were vanishing as changing market conditions favored companies that were either very large or very small (Cetron, Rocha, and Lucken 1988).

One businessman lives in Vermont and runs a business in California. He says, "... [from] my farm in Vermont, about six months each year I run my $7m-a-year consulting business – in Palo Alto, California. That small business started selling overseas, via a joint venture, the year I set it up. It is now launching a new product. More than 20 subcontractors, from one-person shops to huge corporations, do everything from project management to design, packaging, and distribution. Simultaneous launch on three continents is a near-certainty." (*The Economist* 1989)

The State of the Environment

Environmentalists and conservationists have argued throughout the 20th century that humans would not survive long if they ignored their impact on the environment. In the late 20th century, people around the world have experienced on a personal level some of the effects of the continuing pollution and the dwindling of natural resources. These effects have included difficulties in disposing of toxic wastes, erratic weather conditions attributed to the Greenhouse Effect, a shortage of landfill sites for garbage disposal, and the evidence of cancers associated with chemicals in the air and food, among others. "Cheap gas or clean air – pick one. You can't have both. Not in a consumer economy like ours, anyway" (Iacocca 1989).

If the evidence continues to mount that humans will not survive unless greater attention is paid to damage to the environment, then it is likely that more and more people will consider this a serious issue and factor it into their purchasing and business decisions. Environmental damage is not contained by national boundaries; therefore, companies will increasingly assess their global operations relative to environmental issues. These issues provide opportunities and challenges for international companies – opportunities to develop new products and services in response to environmental problems and challenges associated with repairing damage created by current and past operations.

In 1990, Jim MacNeil, former secretary general of the World Commission on Environment and Development, said that public awareness and concern were at the highest level ever recorded throughout the world. Awareness and concern forced environmental issues to the top of political agendas "in all of the major capitals of the world, in the UN, in regional bodies like the OECD and ASEAN, in the World Bank and other multilateral banks, and in many of the companies listed in the Fortune 500" (MacNeil 1990, p. 48).

The issue of sustainable development is critical to the world's future. Current national accounting systems do not capture the value of natural resources or treat their degradation as a negative factor. There is substantial pressure for change in how we account for these resources and their degradation. Governments and the population at large are pushing for changes in accounting methods to encourage sustainable development.

Marilyn Waring, a former New Zealand member of Parliament (in a film entitled *Who's Counting?* produced by the National Film Board of Canada, 1995), commented that the Exxon *Valdez* environmental disaster was a very productive voyage, using traditional national accounting systems. The expenditures on clean-up, wildlife habitats, and so on, all contributed positively to the Gross Domestic Product. In contrast, there was no mechanism whereby deductions were made for the environmental degradation.

Concerns about the environment and sustainable development ("green" issues) consistently increased during the 1980s and into the 1990s. Firms have found that they cannot ignore these concerns, and an increasing number of firms are including "green" issues in their decisions. Interestingly, a number of firms have turned these concerns to their advantage. For example, concern with deforestation in the Brazilian rain forests has led to a realization among pharmaceutical firms that the rain forests are a likely source of new products.

It seems clear that "green" issues will continue to be important in international business through the 1990s and into the 21st century. Firms must be sure to factor these issues into their decisions. Further, firms need to be looking for opportunities to develop new products and services in the context of sustainable development.

Regulation of Global Social Responsibility

Many people believe that social responsibility cannot be left to individual companies because too many companies may ignore their responsibilities. Various attempts have been made within the United Nations to regulate multinational companies to ensure that they behave in ways considered socially responsible from a global point of view. The United Nations has given high priority to establishing an appropriate code of conduct for transnational corporations (TNCs) through the United Nations Commission on Transnational Corporations (UNCTC). The 1980s saw "attempts within the UN system to secure effective international arrangements for the operation of transnational corporations which are designed to promote the contribution of TNCs to national developmental goals and world economic growth while controlling and eliminating their negative effects" (Carasco and Singh, 1988).

More recently, the Caux Round Table Principles, for regulating social responsibility, have been developed by European, Japanese, and U.S. companies, indicating a trend toward self-regulation. Multinational companies generally prefer to regulate themselves than be regulated by outside bodies; therefore, they wish to keep such outside regulations to a minimum. To the extent that international business activities can be shown to be undertaken within the framework of global social responsibility, outside agencies are less likely to intervene. At the same time, some outside regulation appears to be inevitable, and international companies need to be involved in developing this regulatory framework as well as maintaining continual awareness of its likely impact on their operations. Exhibit 2.6 illustrates the benefits associated with a code of conduct for international companies, according to the UN viewpoint.

Changing Political Systems

The struggle between the ideologies of capitalism and communism was a major force in many of the developments of the 20th century. Some aspects of that struggle can be considered positive

EXHIBIT 2.6
**Benefits
Associated with a
Code of Conduct –
UN Viewpoint**

1. It would, most importantly, establish a balanced set of standards of good corporate conduct to be observed by transnational corporations in their operations and of standards to be observed by governments in their treatment of transnational corporations.
2. It would help ensure that the activities of transnational corporations are integrated in the development objectives of the developing countries.
3. It would establish the confidence, predictability, transparency, and stability required for expanded growth of foreign direct investment in a mutually beneficial manner.
4. It would, therefore, contribute to a reduction of friction, conflict, and painful disruption between transnational corporations and countries and permit the flow of foreign direct investment to realize its potential in the development process.
5. It would, as a consequence, encourage positive adjustment through the growth of productive capacities.

Source: United Nations 1987.

(such as space exploration) and others may be seen as negative (such as development and proliferation of nuclear weapons). Many communist countries had moved toward the more open capitalist ideology by 1990. At the same time, the United States and other Western countries were becoming more concerned over the plight of the homeless and the poor, and many people believed that there was evidence (e.g., statistics on infant mortality) that the United States had suffered socially in the previous decade and the government needed to be more socially conscious. Some people see in these movements a trend toward a common social, economic, and political ideology and a resulting reduction of world tensions. During the 1990s, the world has been in a state of change; the results of these changes will have a major impact on how future business is conducted worldwide.

There is little doubt regarding the globalization of today's business world and most people believe this will continue in the 21st century. International companies are particularly affected by the global political climate and need to monitor and analyze these changing relationships. One thing is certain in regard to politics and ideologies: Nothing is certain and everything changes.

Developments in the areas of global communication and travel, regional and global trade agreements, and the proliferation of multinational and global firms have all contributed to the new global reality. In spite of these developments and trends, some believe that the local context of business remains paramount. Events such as the balkanization of larger blocs, including the former Soviet Union, the separation of the Czech and Slovak Republics, and Quebec's desire for greater sovereignty suggest that local interests and needs have not been subordinated to the greater global good.

The end of the Cold War that came with the collapse of the Soviet Union was greeted by most people as the dawning of a brave new age, where many hoped the weapons of war would be put aside and the capital thus freed put into developing a better world for all. The reality so far has fallen short of expectations. The former communist states are in a state of flux, and no one can predict whether their experiments with capitalism will succeed or fail. Events around the world in the first half of the decade (1990–1995) suggested a time of chaos rather than the hoped for harmony. An article in the *Toronto Star* (Shawcross 1994) quotes Anthony Lake, President Clinton's national security advisor, as saying, "If order is created out of chaos, the post–Cold War era is giving us plenty of chaos to work from." To illustrate the chaos, Shawcross pointed to "brutal brushfires, savage skirmishes, hideous ethnic massacres and national implosions – Bosnia, Rwanda, Angola . . ." To add to the sense of chaos were the "uncertainties of Russia," and "the mutation of China into something quite unknown." Interestingly, these events were taking place in a world that was increasingly closely linked through trade and investment. Vaclav Havel summed up the world situation of this period by saying, "we live in the post-modern world where everything is possible and almost nothing is certain" (Shawcross 1994, p. E7).

Uncertainty

The Economist (1989, p. 19) described "tomorrow's companies" as operating in a world of unprecedented uncertainty. This is perhaps the one aspect of the future that we would be willing to forecast: All the evidence seems to indicate that the international environment is likely to become more complex and uncertain. The proper responses to this uncertainty, according to *The Economist,* are "flexibility, responsiveness, adaptiveness, born of new – especially information-based – technology" (1989, p. 19). Further, "mastering new technologies – and new forms of organization to go with them" (1989, p. 20) is vital. We concur.

The successful international company of the future will be one that can deal with a complex and uncertain environment. To do this, it must constantly monitor and assess its environment and be ready to change its strategy to fit the changing environment.

While this is certainly true of today's international venture, it was also largely true of the very early ventures. In 2000 B.C., international traders faced a host of dangers as they left home in their caravans or boats for a world outside that was largely unknown. These traders constantly had to "expect the unexpected." Similarly, the explorers and traders who followed Columbus to the New World had little idea of what to expect and were successful only if they were ready to adapt to new situations. In many ways, international business embodies both uncertainty and complexity. People throughout history have been willing to face this uncertain and complex environment because of the rewards it offered, in terms of both economic and personal success.

The field of business and management has changed in response to the globalizing of the business environment, and it reflects new realities. At the same time, a good argument can be made for learning from the past. In terms of Western thought, an article entitled "Awakenings: The Rediscovery of Ancient Greek Wisdom in Management Theory" (Cummings and Haridimos 1995) concluded that the current recognition of the importance of ambiguity, plurality, and idiosyncrasies reflects earlier Greek thought. It also discussed three surfacing themes in modern management thought and traced them to ancient Greek thought:

▶ The importance of practical reasoning and narrative sense making
▶ The reconnection of means and ends, facts and values
▶ The reacceptance of chaos, chance, and paradox

Similarly, in terms of Eastern thought, a greater understanding of modern management can be gained by focusing on philosophies and writing over the centuries. In China, for example, the influence of Confucian thought is often seen as resulting in a unique form of communism, which in turn influences business and management practices. In Japan, the Samurai pursuit of honorable objectives, the discipline founded on the philosophy of Zen, and the centuries-old tradition of rice farming have all been seen as contributing to Japan's management systems.

The world of business is full of change and yet it grows from its historical roots. Students of international business can benefit from thinking about the past, current events, and the future. We can learn much about current issues by drawing on the past. We can draw on knowledge of the past, combined with our understanding of current events, to be prepared for the future. At the same time, we need to recognize that unexpected shifts do occur and that the way we do business in the future will not be the same as the way we did business in the past.

Summary

This chapter introduced the world of international business and emphasized the importance of understanding the global economy, the international business environment, and operations in international businesses – topics to be dealt with in detail in Parts II, III, and IV of this text.

This brief discussion of the historical development of international business attempted to place the current state of the multinational company in perspective. Business across national and cultural boundaries has taken place for centuries; however, in the last half of the 20th century, the volume of international business has increased dramatically, and multinational companies now represent a major force in the world.

Tracing the development of international business indicates that the international environment is always complex and uncertain. As one looks to the future, this uncertainty can be expected to continue. To function effectively in an uncertain and complex environment, successful companies should monitor and assess information from the environment continually, and they should be flexible and adaptable.

MINI-CASE
Three Centuries of the Hudson's Bay Company

▶

May 17, 1670, Charles II granted to Prince Rupert and his 17 fellow investors a charter that led to the largest corporate landowner and oldest company in Western history. The trading posts of the Hudson's Bay Company once reached from the Arctic Ocean to Hawaii, and it is considered the oldest continuously operating Western commercial enterprise.

The Hudson's Bay Company (HBC) was formed by a group known as the Company of Adventurers; its original purpose was to exploit the riches of the Hudson Bay region through trade with Europe. The adventurers believed, like Sir Walter Raleigh, that "whosoever commands the seas, commands the trade; whosoever commands the trade of the world, commands the riches of the world – and consequently, the world itself."

In 1676, HBC reported profits of £19,000. The company remains a major economic force today. It is Canada's biggest department store chain and has a significant international role in real estate with projects in Canada, the United States, and the United Kingdom. The company is described as surviving the centuries by turning nearly every necessity into an opportunity and by not moving too fast.

In 1979, Kenneth Thomson purchased control of the company for $640 million cash. Through the early 1980s the company lost significant amounts; these losses were blamed on an economic recession and heavy debt resulting from reactive acquisitions. The advantages from low rents, large floor space, good locations, and large volumes were being dissipated by the company's inability to control key business components and a slow response to incursion by U.S. retailers. The new owners reacted by selling some of its "history-laden divisions," such as its fur auction houses. This upset some people, who commented that "a priceless heritage is gone forever." In contrast, Thomson defended these decisions as being in the interests of ensuring that the Hudson's Bay Company would be alive and well 300 years from now. These decisions were believed to be essential so that management and financial resources could be concentrated on what are now the company's core businesses of department store retailing and real estate.

George Kosich, president and chief executive officer of the company, recounted in 1990 the successful revitalization of the company as depending on understanding the market and the need to reinvest in people, assets, facilities, image, and innovation. He said in a speech that the future for the Hudson's Bay Company includes focusing on its core businesses, expansion in the United States, and exploration of its potential in Europe.

HBC has expanded its retail empire through the acquisition of Robinson's Department Stores in Ontario and Field's Outlets in Western Canada, a merger with Vancouver based Woodward's Ltd., and expansion of its Zeller's Discount Chain. It faces substantial competition, however, with the 1994 introduction of Wal-Mart Canada Inc. into the Canadian retail environment. Operating results in 1995 were mixed, with Zeller's operating profits falling, HBC's profits improving, and losses at Field's declining. Overall earnings were up but HBC failed to meet analysts' expectations.

Source: Kosich 1990; Newman 1985, 1987.

Discussion Issues

1. Discuss the advantages and drawbacks associated with a long corporate history and relate these to the Hudson's Bay Company.
2. Discuss the environmental factors that would influence a company like the Hudson's Bay Company to change the focus it has had during its long history.

> 3. Find recent information on the Hudson's Bay Company and iden-
>   tify its current business focus and level of success.

Discussion Questions

1. What current major issues might have an impact on international business in the future?
2. In your opinion, why have the following groups become actively involved in the operations of international business?
   a. host governments
   b. home governments
   c. special interest groups
   d. international agencies
   e. economic alliances
3. Why is it important to study the history of international business?

Assignments

1. Form groups of five or six students. As executives of a multinational corporation, you are asked to prepare a presentation for the company's CEO outlining the major world developments that the company should assess in the coming months.
2. As the executives in Assignment 1, select the most important development that you have identified and outline how it will affect each function in the company (finance, marketing, strategic planning, human resources, and public relations).
3. Consult recent publications and report the current growth patterns in the number and size of international companies.

Selected References

Averitt, R. T., "Time's Structure, Man's Strategy: The American Experience," in H. F. Williamson (ed.), *Evolution of International Management Structures* (Newark: University of Delaware Press, 1975).

Carasco, E. F., and J. B. Singh, "The United Nations Code of Conduct on Transnational Corporations: Some Unresolved Issues" (Windsor, Ont.: University of Windsor, working paper; reprint series no. R88-07). Reprinted from the *Proceedings of the Administrative Sciences Association of Canada*, vol. 9, part 8, International Division (June 1988), pp. 1–9.

Center, J., "Where America Was a Century Ago – History as a Guide to the Future," *The Futurist* (January–February 1990), pp. 22–28.

Cetron, M. J., W. Rocha, and R. Lucken, "Think Big or Think Small," *The Futurist* (September–October 1988), pp. 9–16.

Cummings, S., and T. Haridimos, "Awakenings: The Rediscovery of Ancient Greek Wisdom in Management Thought" (Coventry, UK: University of Warwick, Warwick Business School Research Paper No. 160, 1995).

The Economist (March 4–10, 1989), pp. 19, 20.

The Economist (June 2, 1990), p. 73.

Financial Post (May 5, 1992), p. 17.

Financial Post (August 26, 1994), p. 6.

Financial Post (March 10, 1995) p. 7.

Hohlfelder, R., "Herod the Great's City on the Sea – Caesarea Maritima," *National Geographic* (February 1987).

Iacocca, L., "The High Cost of Backsliding on Oil Conservation," reprinted in *Inside Guide* (Fall 1989).

Jones, C. A., *International Business in the Nineteenth Century* (New York: New York University Press, 1987).

Kidder, R. M., *Reinventing the Future: Global Goals for the 21st Century* (Cambridge, Mass.: MIT Press, 1989).

Kosich, G., speech to The Planning Forum (Toronto, November 1990).

Lorie, P., and S. Murray-Clark, *History of the Future: A Chronology* (Garden City, N.Y.: Doubleday, 1989).

Lutz, E., and M. Munasinghe, "Accounting for the Environment," *Finance and Development* (March 1991), pp. 19–21.

MacNeil, J., "A Threatened Future and Sustainable Development," *Inside Guide* (Winter 1990), pp. 47–48.

McCarthy, D. M. P., *International Business History* (Westport, Conn.: Praeger Publishers, 1994).

Naisbitt, J., "Technology Fuels Revolution in Marketing," reprinted in *Inside Guide* (Fall 1989).

Naisbitt, J., and P. Aburdene, *Megatrends 2000* (New York: Morrow, 1990).

National Film Board of Canada, *Who's Counting? Marilyn Waring on Sex, Lies and Global Economics* (Montreal: National Film Board of Canada, 1995).

Newman, P. C., *Company of Adventurers,* vol. 1 (Markham, Ont.: Penguin Books, 1985).

Newman, P. C., "Three Centuries of the Hudson's Bay Company: Canada's Fur-Trading Empire," *National Geographic* (August 1987).

Rich, E. E., *The Publications of the Hudson's Bay Record Society,* vol. 1 (London: The Hudson's Bay Record Society, 1958).

Robinson, R. D., *International Business Policy* (New York: Holt, Rinehart & Winston, 1964).

Robinson, R. D., "Background Concepts and Philosophy of International Business from World War II to the Present," *Journal of International Business Studies* (Spring–Summer 1981).

Ronen, S., *Comparative and Multinational Management* (New York: John Wiley, 1986).

Rose, S., "Why the Multinational Tide Is Ebbing," *Fortune* (August 1977), pp. 111–20.

Shawcross, W., "Present at a New Creation," *Toronto Star* (October 1994), p. E1.

United Nations, *General Reflections on the Code of Conduct* (New York: United Nations, 1987).

Uimonen, P., "Trade Policies and the Environment," *Finance and Development* (June 1992), pp. 26–27.

Ward, F., "Jade Stone of Heaven," *National Geographic* (September 1987).

Ward, F., "Images for the Computer Age," *National Geographic* (June 1989).

Wilkins, M., *The Emergence of Multinational Enterprise: American Business Abroad from the Colonial Era to 1914* (Cambridge, Mass.: Harvard University Press, 1970).

Williamson, H. F., ed., *Evolution of International Management Structures* (Newark: University of Delaware Press, 1975).

P A R T

II

The Global Economy

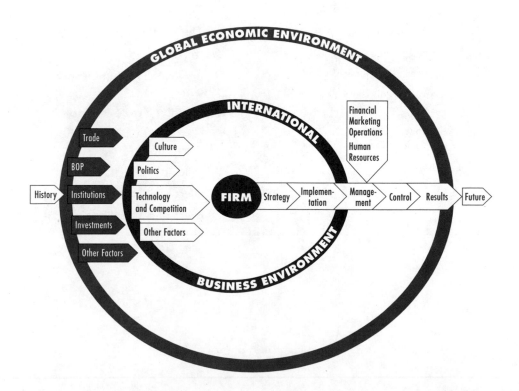

CHAPTER 3

International Trade Issues

L E A R N I N G   O B J E C T I V E S

After reading this chapter, you should be able to

▶ Outline the theories of trade.

▶ Explain why trade occurs between countries.

▶ Discuss the benefits and drawbacks to trade.

▶ Identify who benefits and loses, and why, from a move to freer trade.

▶ Identify barriers to trade.

▶ Explain why barriers to trade are used.

▶ Identify incentives for trade.

▶ Explain why trade incentives are used.

▶ Define countertrade and explain why it occurs.

▶ Explain the aim of trading agreements.

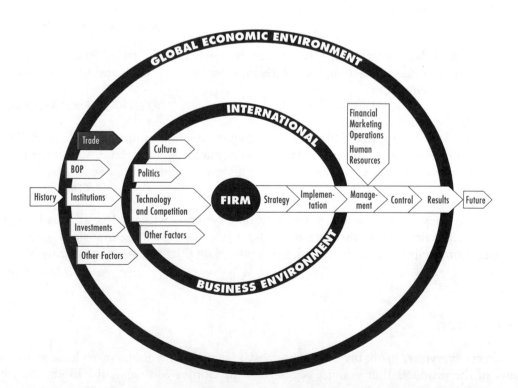

KEY TERMS

- Mercantilist theory
- Absolute advantage
- Closed economy
- Open economy
- Comparative advantage
- Factor endowments
- Infant industry
- Old industry
- Unfair trade
- Trade barriers

- Import tariff
- Countervailing tariff or duty
- General Agreement on Tariff and Trade (GATT)
- Export tariffs
- Nontariff barriers
- Subsidies
- Import quotas
- Voluntary export restraints
- Countertrade
- Trading agreements

THOUGHT STARTERS

▶ Why export? Export markets create more jobs for Americans. One billion dollars of trade activity creates close to 40,000 jobs directly and indirectly.

(U.S. Department of Agriculture 1989)

▶ No one knows how much trade is covered by countertrade arrangements. There is no information on some transactions, very little information on others, and suspect information on most of the remainder.

(U.S. Department of Agriculture 1989)

▶ An outward-looking approach to trade is the biggest single reason why some countries have done so much better than others. . . . classical economics [suggests] that trade allows countries to exploit their comparative advantage [and thus explain differential success].

(The Economist 1989)

▶ Over the past few years, the international trading system – which, after all, has brought the industrialized economies to their present prosperity – has shown the first signs of unraveling. In the economic climate that lies ahead, the pressures on this system will be greatly intensified.

(The Economist 1990)

Introduction

Trade affects everyone, probably on a daily basis. If you take a moment to look at the origin of many of the products that you use regularly – the clothes you wear, the foods you eat, the televisions you watch – you will quickly discover that they come from all around the world. These products get from their point of origin to their point of use through trade. Other less tangible items such as services and ideas are also traded regularly: Your fax directory probably contains data that were entered on a computer in another country, a software program that you use for word processing may include ideas imported from other countries, and management consultants may offer their services all around the globe.

Understanding existing trade patterns and the reasons for trade are important in international business because many business decisions involve the movement of goods (products and services) across borders. Decisions regarding imports and exports are clearly made in the context of trade, but decisions regarding foreign production are also, in effect, trade decisions. These second decisions, for example, may be made to access a particular market that is protected by trade barriers, or they may be made to take advantage of comparative advantages offered in a particular location. To make effective international decisions, businesspeople need to have a basic understanding of trade theory.

The purpose of this chapter is to provide students with a basic understanding of trade theory and global patterns of trade. The chapter begins with a discussion of trading patterns, an examination of the development of current theories of trade follows, focusing on why countries trade and the benefits of trade (the appendix demonstrates aspects of trade theory graphically). The chapter then explores the effects of moving from a closed economy with no trade to an open economy with free trade and considers the gains and losses associated with such a move. The chapter continues with a look at trade barriers and arguments for and against their use, as well as consideration of incentives for increased trade. The chapter concludes with a discussion of countertrade as a specific aspect of trade and a brief examination of some existing trade agreements and the European Union.

World Trade Data

Actual trading patterns depend on a variety of factors. Patterns are affected by factor endowments (that is, the relative availability of factors of production) and the comparative advantage (that is, the advantage derived from an abundance of a particular factor) of countries, but they are also affected by business decisions and government policies that restrict or encourage particular patterns of trade. It is important to recognize that these patterns are constantly changing due to changes in factor endowments, government policies, and business decisions. These patterns need to be analyzed by companies when they are making decisions about exports, imports, and foreign investment. Examining trade patterns leads one to ask why trade exists.

Trade statistics are included in a number of publications, such as the *Direction of Trade Statistics Yearbook*. In many cases, the information is in the form of lists of numbers pertaining to particular countries or groups of countries. These lists can be difficult to interpret. Often it is helpful to construct graphs and charts of various kinds to make the information more visually meaningful.

Exhibits 3.1 through 3.5 present world trade and output data in a variety of graphical forms, illustrating some of the ways in which such data can be portrayed. The specific data that are useful and their appropriate presentation depend upon the situation.

EXHIBIT 3.1   World Output 1980–1994 (Annual Average Percentage Change)

Country Groups	1980–1990	1991	1992	1993[a]	1994[b]
World	2.9	0.3	1.3	1.7	2.5
Developed market-economy countries	2.8	0.3	1.8	1.4	2.4
of which:					
United States	2.7	–1.1	2.6	3.0	3.4
Japan	4.1	4.0	1.3	0.1	0.5
European Union	2.4	0.7	1.1	–0.4	1.6
of which:					
Germany[c]	2.3	1.8	2.5	–1.3	1.0
France	2.3	0.7	1.4	–0.9	1.2
Italy	2.2	1.3	0.9	–0.7	1.2
United Kingdom	2.7	–2.3	–0.5	1.9	2.5
Central and Eastern Europe	2.1	–11.9	–15.5	–9.9	–6.8
Developing countries					
of which:					
America	1.3	3.5	2.7	2.9	2.5
Africa	1.9	1.6	0.8	1.2	1.8
Asia	4.6	4.7	4.8	5.0	5.2
Least developed countries	2.3	0.5	0.4	2.1	2.8
China	8.8	7.1	11.4	13.4	10.0
Memo item:					
World exports (volume)	3.7	2.0	5.4	2.5	5.0

[a]Estimate.
[b]Forecast.
[c]Including the eastern *Länder* after 1990.

Source: United Nations Conference on Trade and Development, New York, 1994.

Theories of Trade

International trade theory seeks to explain why trading occurs between the nationals of various countries. The reasons for trading are usually associated with the resulting gains that accrue to a country. Here we will examine the development of current theories about trade, beginning with mercantilism, the trade theory prevalent in the 17th and 18th centuries, and concluding with the theory of factor endowment, the basis for much of current thinking on trade.

Mercantilist Theory

The basic contention of the **mercantilist theory** was that to export was good and to be encouraged but to import was bad and to be discouraged. Mercantilists believed that a country would benefit from such a trade policy because it would increase its wealth and consequently its power

EXHIBIT 3.2
**World Output,
Percent of Shares,
1990**

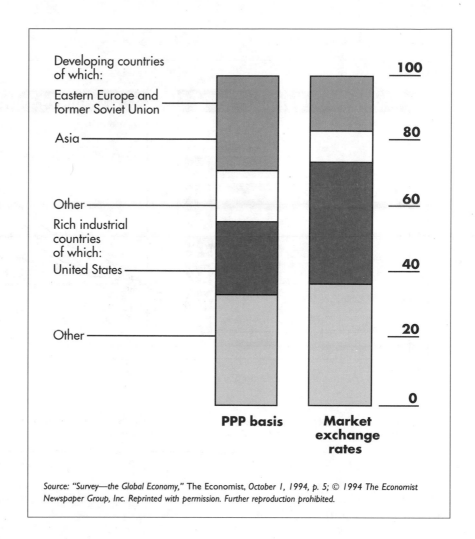

and strength. Proponents of this policy argued that a country's wealth and power were determined by its stock of precious metals, particularly gold. When countries exported goods, they received payments from other countries in gold, which increased the exporting country's wealth and power. The reverse happened when goods were imported: Payments in gold were made to other countries, and the importing country's wealth and power decreased.

The mercantilist argument has a certain appeal, and proponents of a similar viewpoint exist today. Many people take for granted that exports are good and should be encouraged but that imports are bad and should be discouraged. Today's proponents do not focus on gold and its ability to increase a country's power; rather, they focus on positive trade balances (i.e., exports greater than imports) as contributing to domestic jobs and domestic welfare. Their belief generally is that domestic industries should be protected.

The problem with the mercantilist theory is that it looks at only one side of the situation. At the extreme, suppose that a country (the exporter) were able to export much of its production

EXHIBIT 3.3   **A Seller's Market**

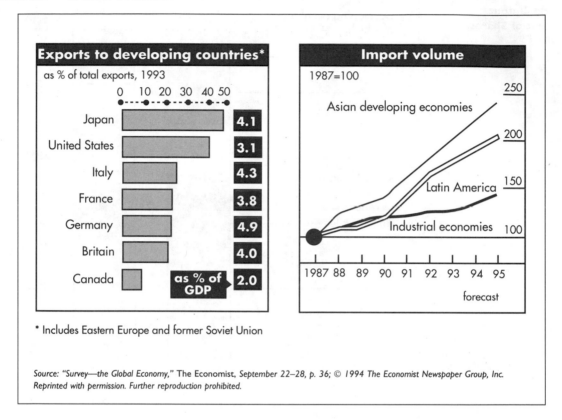

Exports to developing countries*

as % of total exports, 1993

0 10 20 30 40 50

Japan	4.1
United States	3.1
Italy	4.3
France	3.8
Germany	4.9
Britain	4.0
Canada	as % of GDP 2.0

Import volume

1987=100

250
200
150
100

Asian developing economies
Latin America
Industrial economies

1987 88 89 90 91 92 93 94 95

forecast

* Includes Eastern Europe and former Soviet Union

and avoid imports totally. What would be the consequences of this situation? A number of fairly obvious results would follow:

▶ Those countries buying the exporter's products would likely retaliate by refusing to continue because the exporter would not take their goods in return.
▶ If the importers did continue to buy, eventually they would use all of their reserves of foreign currency and gold and would no longer be able to afford to continue to purchase the exporter's products.
▶ The exporter's people would have to do without certain goods that they found desirable but that could not be produced locally.
▶ The exporter's consumers would pay more for domestically produced goods and services that could be produced more cheaply in other locations.
▶ To meet local demand for some products, producers would use resources inefficiently.

More recent theories of trade conclude that countries benefit only in the short run from a mercantilist policy, while two-way trade (i.e., encouragement of both exports and imports) serves to increase the long-term benefit. Two theories, those of absolute advantage and comparative advantage, illustrate the benefits of two-way trade.

EXHIBIT 3.4
U.S. International Sales and Purchases of Private Sectors, 1986–1993

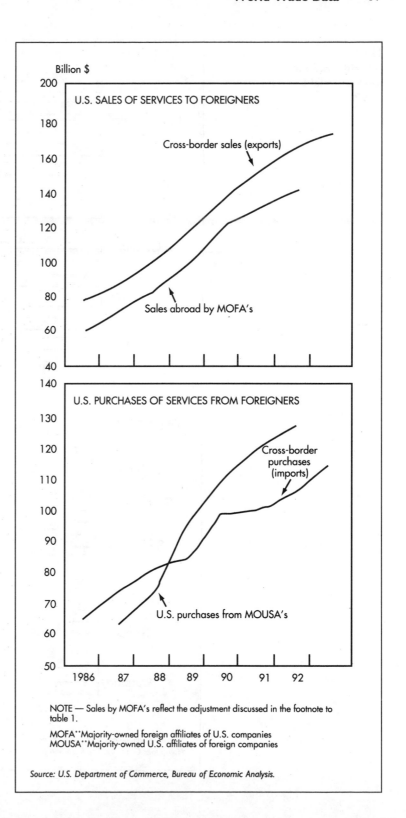

Billion $

U.S. SALES OF SERVICES TO FOREIGNERS

Cross-border sales (exports)

Sales abroad by MOFA's

U.S. PURCHASES OF SERVICES FROM FOREIGNERS

Cross-border purchases (imports)

U.S. purchases from MOUSA's

1986   87   88   89   90   91   92

NOTE — Sales by MOFA's reflect the adjustment discussed in the footnote to table 1.

MOFA"Majority-owned foreign affiliates of U.S. companies
MOUSA"Majority-owned U.S. affiliates of foreign companies

Source: U.S. Department of Commerce, Bureau of Economic Analysis.

EXHIBIT 3.5
World Trade in Commercial Services, 1992

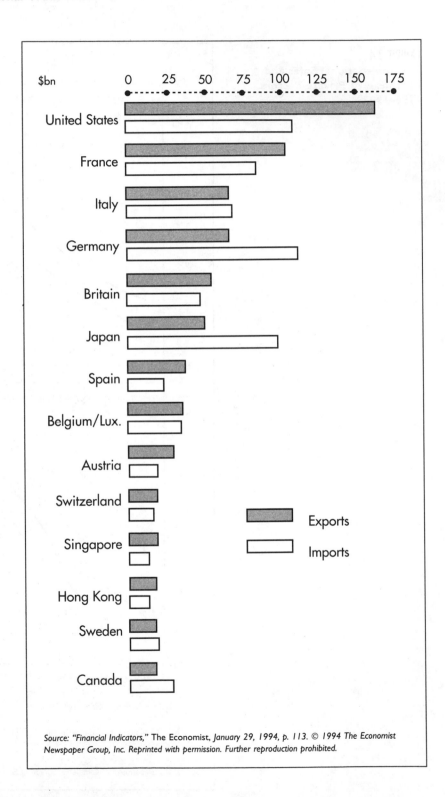

Absolute Advantage

The theory of **absolute advantage** postulates that a country can increase its welfare through international trade by specializing in the production of goods at which it is most efficient and using them to trade with other countries. This theory of absolute advantage is based on the assumption that the country is absolutely better (i.e., more efficient) at production of certain goods than its trading partners. From a cost point of view, absolute advantage deals with the situation in which one trading partner has the advantage in producing some goods at a lower cost, but the other partner has the cost advantage in producing other goods.

To illustrate the theory of absolute advantage in a very simple way, imagine two neighbors, Tom and Jean. Both Tom and Jean enjoy bread and peanut butter. Tom can make a loaf of bread in two hours with new fast-acting yeast while Jean takes five hours to make a similar loaf of bread. Jean, in contrast, has developed a new process that allows her to produce a pound of peanut butter in two hours while Tom uses an old method that requires five hours to make a pound of peanut butter. In essence, Tom is better and more efficient at making bread, and Jean is better and more efficient at making peanut butter. These relationships are summarized as follows:

	Bread	Peanut Butter
Jean	5 hours	2 hours
Tom	2 hours	5 hours

If Tom and Jean live in a neighborhood in which people avoid each other as much as possible (we might call these **closed economies** in trade terms), then, to have both bread and peanut butter, Tom and Jean each must work for seven hours. Tom must spend two hours making a loaf of bread plus five hours for his pound of peanut butter; Jean must spend two hours making a pound of peanut butter plus five hours for her loaf of bread. If these neighbors decide to become more friendly (in trade terms, to move to an **open economy**), they will find that they can benefit from specializing and trading with each other. Tom can spend four hours and make two loaves of bread while Jean spends four hours and makes two pounds of peanut butter. Then they can trade a loaf of bread for a pound of peanut butter. Each ends up with the desired bread and peanut butter, and each has worked for three fewer hours than before.

This example is extremely simplistic, but the basic idea can be expanded to the more general situation of two countries. For example, Canada produces electricity more efficiently than its neighbor the United States and therefore sells electricity to its neighbor to the south. The United States is more efficient at producing standardized bottles and therefore sells them to its neighbor to the north. Although there are situations in which countries have an absolute advantage in producing one good that they therefore specialize in and sell, the situation is usually much more complex. The theory of comparative advantage deals with a somewhat more complex trading situation.

Comparative Advantage

The theory of **comparative advantage** was first formulated by Ricardo in the early 1800s. According to this theory, even when one country is more efficient (i.e., has an absolute advantage) in all goods, it is still beneficial for it to trade with its less efficient neighbors. It may be helpful to think of this comparative advantage in terms of costs: In this case, one country has lower costs for all of its goods, but the relative costs of products within each country differ. For simplicity, consider only two countries and two products. Suppose that the countries Alpha and Beta both produce wine and cheese. Now suppose that Alphans take one day to produce two bottles of wine, but Betans produce only one bottle in one day (Alphans are more efficient at wine making than Betans). In addition, in one day Alphans can make four pounds of cheese while Betans can make only three pounds (Alphans are more efficient at cheese making as well). Would there be any advantage to trade between the Alphans and Betans? These relationships are summarized as follows:

	Wine	Cheese
Alpha	2 bottles/1 day	4 pounds/1 day
Beta	1 bottle/1 day	3 pounds/1 day

With no trade between countries, a bottle of wine would be exchanged in Alpha for two pounds of cheese; a bottle of wine would be exchanged in Beta for three pounds of cheese. An Alphan who can get more than two pounds of cheese for a bottle of wine would benefit from such a transaction (a Betan should be willing to pay up to three pounds). Similarly, a Betan who can get more than a bottle of wine for three pounds of cheese would have reason to trade (an Alphan should be willing to pay up to a bottle and a half of wine for three pounds of cheese). Even though the Alphans are absolutely better at producing both wine and cheese, Betans have a comparative, or relative, advantage in producing cheese. Hence, an incentive to trade exists because both countries can benefit from a trading arrangement. Any rate of exchange between the limits of one bottle of wine for two pounds of cheese and one bottle of wine for three pounds of cheese will benefit both sides. If the rate of exchange is close to the original rate of exchange in Alpha, then the Betans will benefit more, whereas if the rate is closer to the original rate in Beta, the Alphans will benefit more. Part of the appendix graphically illustrates changes in consumption and production that might occur as a country moves from no trade to trade; this shows that such a move benefits society as a whole.

> Comparative advantage can be thought of in terms of a skilled surgeon and her secretary. Imagine that the doctor is both a brilliant surgeon and an excellent typist, in fact a better typist than her secretary (that is, in economic trade terms, the surgeon has an absolute advantage both in surgery and typing). It would nevertheless make sense for the surgeon to concentrate on surgery and let her secretary concentrate on typing because of the comparative advantage she has in surgery.

The theory of comparative advantage illustrates that there are benefits to trade even when one trading partner is absolutely more efficient in production. This theory is simple relative to the real world. The theory of factor endowments looks at trade from an even more complex viewpoint.

Factor Endowments

The Heckscher-Ohlin theory of trade expands the comparative advantage approach by introducing the concept of the factors of production and their availability in a given country (how well endowed the country is with a particular factor). Production factors that are readily available within a country are said to be abundant, while those that are not readily available are said to be scarce. The **factor endowments** theory of trade concludes that a country should export products that use intensively its relatively abundant factors and import products that use intensively its relatively scarce factors.

This idea makes intuitive sense. Consider a country that has a relative abundance of capital (perhaps the United States) and a trading partner that has a relative abundance of labor (perhaps a developing country). It would seem to make sense that if capital is abundant it will be relatively inexpensive in the United States and that abundant labor in the developing country also should be relatively cheap. We would therefore expect the United States to export capital-intensive products to the developing country and import labor-intensive products from the same country. This would appear to be an efficient use of each country's resources.

This description of trade is much simpler than the real world, but is does provide a good beginning for understanding and examining global trade patterns and relationships. A variety of other factors need to be taken into account for a more complete understanding of trade patterns and relationships; for example,

▶ Political relationships – governments view some countries as more acceptable trading partners than others, and trade in some goods is encouraged while trade in other goods is discouraged or prohibited.
▶ Cultural preferences – trade between culturally similar countries may be easier than trade between culturally dissimilar countries.
▶ Geographic proximity – most countries consider neighboring countries as the more likely trade partners.
▶ Currencies and exchange rates – the availability, convertibility, and stability of currencies, as well as current and expected exchange rates, help determine the viability of particular exports or imports.
▶ Inflation – the price of domestic goods changes in response to inflation rates and, in turn, this affects the relative prices of domestic and imported goods and influences the level of imports.

It is clear that factors such as political relationships or inflation do not work in isolation; therefore, the interrelationships also need to be considered. For example, a political relationship may be based on cultural preferences and geographical proximity, and this relationship can create pressures that result in certain exchange and inflation rates. Exhibits 3.6a, b, and c provide information of imports into Canada, Mexico, and the United States. Students can use this information to discuss trading patterns. (It should be noted that Mexico's data are in thousands.)

This theory of factor endowments is closely related to that of comparative advantage because a country's comparative advantage is based on its factor endowment. In the previous comparative advantage example, if wine production is capital intensive and cheese production is labor intensive, we could conclude that Alpha had a relative abundance of capital, reflected in its

EXHIBIT 3.6a
**Top Ten Imports,
January–June
1994: Canada**

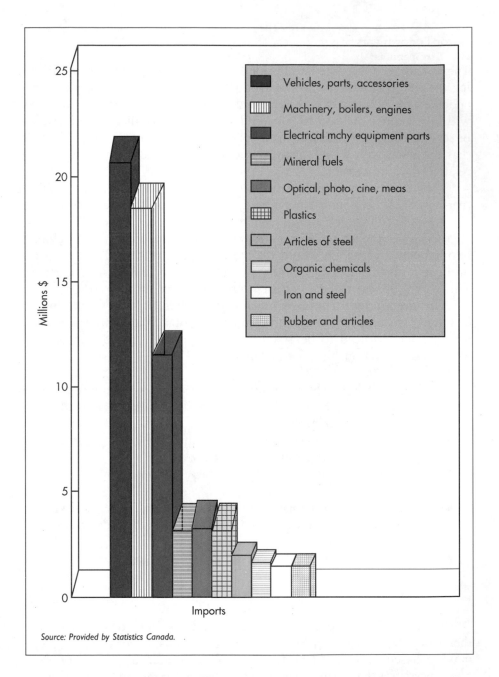

Source: Provided by Statistics Canada.

efficiency at wine making, whereas Beta had a relative abundance of labor, which was reflected in its comparative advantage in cheese making.

This theory of factor endowments is basic to current thinking regarding trade. It suggests that an efficient use of a country's resources relies on producing and exporting products that use its abundant resources while importing those that use scarcer factors. Capital, labor, and

EXHIBIT 3.6b
**Top Ten Imports,
January–June
1994: Mexico**

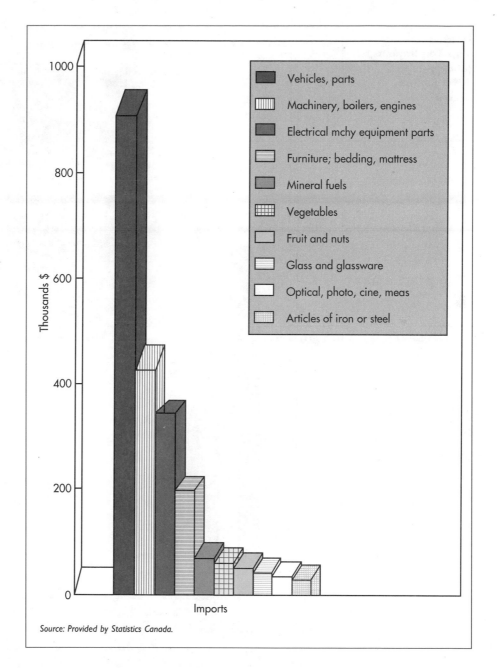

Source: Provided by Statistics Canada.

natural resources are among the major factors commonly examined in this framework, but the theory can encompass fine distinctions such as differences in labor (e.g., skilled versus nonskilled) and can include a wide variety of production factors (e.g., technology, management, experience).

The theories of trade discussed here are macroeconomic theories; that is, they deal with general movements of goods. Individual company decisions are affected by a variety of additional issues, but they nevertheless take place in this general macroeconomic framework. It is important

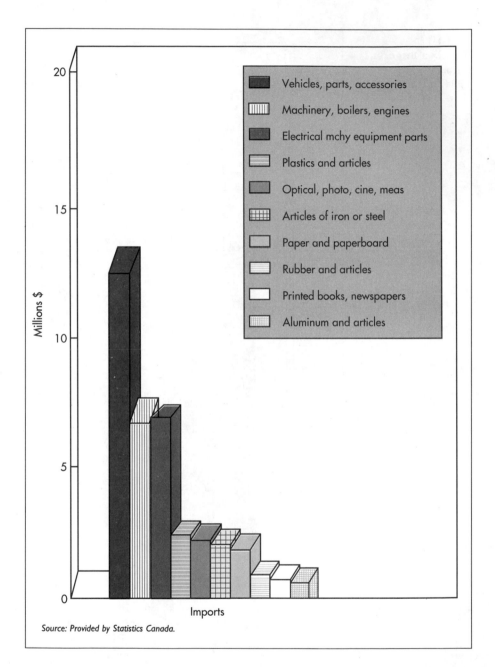

Source: Provided by Statistics Canada.

EXHIBIT 3.6c
Top Ten Imports, January–June 1994: United States

for international companies to understand the different theories of trade because their own individual patterns of trade are part of the overall global pattern. In addition, government advocates of different theories develop policies that affect individual companies. If companies are aware of the underlying arguments regarding different trade policies, they can argue in favor or against specific policies and anticipate the effects of particular policies that various governments might choose. Understanding the reasons for various trade policies gives companies an advantage in examining their environments and dealing effectively with them.

Gains and Losses from Trade

In general, Western economists agree that there are benefits to trade and that a movement from no trade to free trade results in a gain in welfare for the trading partners (see Exhibit 3.7 for evidence of this movement). The theories we have just presented explain why an open economy and reciprocal trade are recognized as more beneficial than the mercantilist approach. Nevertheless, as pointed out in the discussion of mercantilism, many people continue to adhere to protectionist beliefs, and some countries employ protectionist policies to limit imports. To understand why this is, one needs to look more specifically at those who gain and those who lose in a move from no trade (or limited trade) to free trade.

The following discussion makes some simple assumptions by examining transactions between two countries, using two products and two factors of production, when relative domestic prices are different from relative world prices of traded goods. The two countries are North and South; the two products are computers and shoes; and the factors of production are capital and labor. North has an abundance of capital and South has an abundance of labor; computers are capital intensive and shoes are labor intensive.

In a no-trade situation, both North and South would produce and consume both computers and shoes. According to our previous discussion, this would be inefficient; the two countries could benefit by specializing and trading with each other. If the countries decide to trade, North will increase its production of computers (which uses its abundant factor, capital, intensively) and export its surplus to South. At the same time, South will increase its production of shoes (which uses its abundant factor, labor, intensively) and export its surplus to North. The producers of the exported good in both countries will receive a higher price than they would at home (that is why they are willing to trade), and consumers of the imported good will benefit from a lower price (again, that is why they are willing to trade). There is a downside, however; producers of the imported good will receive less and consumers of the exported good will pay relatively more. The economy as a whole benefits but there are both winners and losers within each country (the appendix graphically depicts these trade relationships).

Economists argue that the overall benefit is the important factor. Winners can compensate losers and those in the losing industry will switch to the winning one, while consumers will change their consumption patterns to reflect the new price relationships. This is correct theoretically, but adjustments of this type take time. In the short run, they are painful and visible. The individual, personal, concrete dislocation can often be seen as more important than the more abstract societal good and therefore is reflected in political pressure to restrict trading. In the previous example, consider the individual who comes from a long line of shoemakers in North. There is pride associated with the family's selection of livelihood and with the current individual's choice to be trained and follow in the family's footsteps. Such an individual does not want to be retrained to make computers even if this would in some sense benefit the rest of society.

International companies that understand the gains and losses associated with freer trade use this understanding to make their international decisions more effective. An understanding of

EXHIBIT 3.7
Lower Tariffs, More Trade

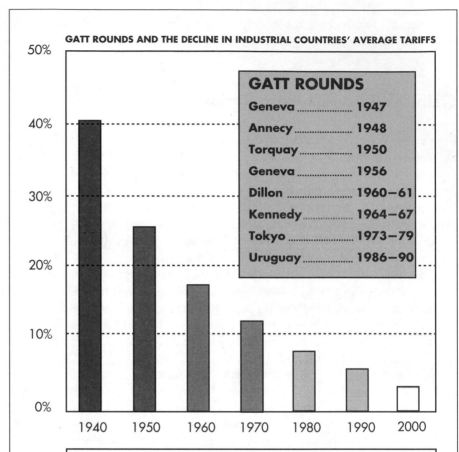

GATT ROUNDS AND THE DECLINE IN INDUSTRIAL COUNTRIES' AVERAGE TARIFFS

GATT ROUNDS

Geneva	1947
Annecy	1948
Torquay	1950
Geneva	1956
Dillon	1960–61
Kennedy	1964–67
Tokyo	1973–79
Uruguay	1986–90

	1913	**1950**	**1990**
France	21	18	5.9
Germany	20	26	5.9
Italy	18	25	5.9
Japan	30	—	5.3
Holland	4	11	5.9
Sweden	20	9	4.4
Britain	—	23	5.9
United States	44	14	4.8

Source: "Survey—World Trade GATT Rounds," The Economist, September 1990, p. 7; June 1990, p. 4; data from Paul Balroch and UNCTAD. © 1990 The Economist Newspaper Group, Inc. Reprinted with permission. Further reproduction prohibited.

these gains and losses allows a company to take advantage of the opportunities offered by freer trade as well as to deal with its potential problems.

Barriers to Trade

The previous discussion illustrated the theoretical benefits that accrue to society if a country is open to trade. In a move to freer trade, some groups always lose in the short run. Because of

International Trading Patterns

> Through Smith's eyes, it is possible to marvel afresh at this fabulously powerful mechanism and to relish, as he did, the paradox of private gain yielding social good. Only more so, for the transactions that deliver a modern manufactured good to its customer are infinitely more complicated than those described by Smith. In his day, remember, the factory was still a novel idea: Manufacturing meant pins and coats.
>
> A modern car is made of raw materials that have been gathered from all over the world, combined into thousands of intermediate products, sub-assembled by scores of separate enterprises. The consumer need know nothing of all this, any more than the worker who tapped the rubber for the tires knows or cares what its final use will be. Every transaction is voluntary. Self-interest and competition silently process staggering quantities of information and direct the flow of goods, services, capital and labor – just as in Smith's much simpler world. Far-sighted as he was, he would surely have been impressed. Mind you, modern man has also discovered something else. With great effort and ingenuity, and the systematic denial of personal liberty, governments can supplant self-interest and competition, and replace the invisible hand of market forces with collective endeavor and a visible input–output table. The result is a five-year waiting list for Trabants.
>
> Because Smith was convinced that the market would, literally, deliver the goods, he wanted it, by and large, left alone. He said that governments should confine themselves to three main tasks: defending the people from the "violence and invasion of other independent societies"; protecting every member of society from the "injustice or oppression of every other member of it"; and providing "certain public works and certain public institutions, which it can never be for the interest of any individual, or small number of individuals, to erect and maintain."
>
> *Source:* The Economist, July 14, 1990, p. 11. Used with permission.

these losses, many people advocate barriers to trade. A number of specific arguments are used to justify the imposition of trade barriers, and countries employ a number of different barriers to trade. The following discussion briefly examines the most common of these arguments and barriers.

Arguments for Trade Barriers

Arguments in favor of trade barriers recognize that there are economic costs associated with such barriers but believe that there are also benefits. If the benefits are deemed to outweigh the costs, trade barriers are seen as acceptable. The following discussion focuses on the most common arguments in favor of trade barriers.

Infant Industry

Many countries impose trade barriers to give new, or infant, domestic industries an opportunity to develop and become competitive. The argument in favor of such protection to the **infant industry** is that, in the short run, it is not competitive but, in the long run, it will have a competitive advantage. The country chooses to accept short-term welfare losses in expectation of long-term gains.

Established businesses may have a significant advantage in the short run because of economies of scale, established research and development, market know-how, and so forth. These advantages act as barriers to entry for new firms, and a country may choose to limit these advantages to allow domestic businesses to enter the industry and develop a competitive position. The country then limits imports through trade barriers so that its infant industry has greater access to the domestic market than it otherwise would have.

This approach has been used successfully in a number of instances. Many well-established industries developed because of protection at the infant stage. There are also problems with this approach, however. First, how does one decide which infant industries are worth protecting? To make this decision, one must compare the long-term gains with the short-term costs; this is not an easy task. Second, protection is often difficult to remove when it is no longer needed. Producers and workers in a protected industry often resist changes that increase competition. Third, and perhaps most important, protection tends to eliminate the need to become competitive. This can result in a protected industry that becomes a constant long-term drain on the society.

To gain the benefits of developing new competitive industries without risking the negative consequences, countries that wish to protect infant industries are usually advised to do so for a relatively short period of time that is determined in advance and to reduce protection gradually over a period of time. This approach encourages the infant industry to become increasingly self-sufficient and attempts to prevent its failure in the long run.

Old Industry

The **old industry** argument is similar to the infant industry argument except that in this case the industry is past its prime rather than at its beginning; a well-established industry is facing increasing competition and is losing. The concept is that a temporary period of protection from competitive forces will give this industry time to re-establish itself on a sound footing. Once again, the country limits imports through trade barriers to give the domestic industry the needed time to become competitive again. For example, the Canadian and U.S. governments have imposed trade barriers against imports of traditional home-country manufactured products (such as footwear, in Canada). These are usually labor-intensive industries in which Canada and the United States no longer have a comparative advantage.

Unlike the infant industry protection scenario, the old industry approach is more likely to fail than be successful. This is true because the industry has probably become uncompetitive due to shifts in comparative advantage. Protection of old industries often prolongs the process of dying by allowing an aging industry to continue operating inefficiently. The protected environment and consequent lack of competition may actually encourage inefficiency and an uncompetitive stance. Many people argue that if the industry has the potential to regain its former competitiveness, then the capital markets will respond appropriately and there is no need for government involvement. If the government is to become involved, a better role for it is to provide funding for retraining, feasibility studies, and so on to allow a smooth transition from the old industry to something more suitable for current conditions.

Retaliatory Actions

A country may impose its own barriers to trade because it believes its trading partners are engaging in practices that give their domestic companies an unfair advantage. Subsidies that trading partners pay to their domestic producers are often seen as **unfair trade** practices, and in such cases, the importing country can impose a countervailing tariff or duty to offset the effect of the subsidy.

In some situations, trading partners' practices can be clearly defined as being unfair, and the imposition of a countering trade barrier may be justified. In most cases, however, the situation is not at all clear. For example, suppose that the Canadian government provides health benefits for all of its citizens but that the United States does not. U.S. companies need to bear some responsibility to provide the health benefits to their employees and could argue that their Canadian counterparts have an unfair advantage because they do not have the same responsibility. If those U.S. companies affected by this practice convince the U.S. government that the Canadian companies are being unfairly subsidized, the United States might react by imposing a trade barrier to counter the practice that had been deemed unfair. As another example, some U.S. trading partners have argued that the high level of government spending on defense gives an unfair advantage to U.S. companies in the defense industry. The United States would certainly not consider this unfair just as Canada in the preceding example would not be likely to agree that its progressive health benefits could be interpreted as an unfair trade practice.

Noneconomic Arguments

A number of noneconomic arguments support trade barriers. These arguments recognize the economic losses associated with limiting trade but focus on other benefits that are believed to be more important than economic considerations. Proponents of trade barriers for noneconomic reasons are usually concerned about their country's ability to survive and develop along a path chosen by its own citizens. Some examples follow:

▶ Some people believe that it is important that their country be able to defend itself and that a domestic defense industry should be encouraged no matter what the economic cost.

▶ Some people believe that industries that support the country's cultural heritage (e.g., books, movies, entertainment) should be encouraged no matter what the economic cost.

▶ Some people believe that their country should not be dependent on others for food and that a domestic agricultural industry should be encouraged no matter what the economic cost.

These three examples illustrate the subjective nature of such arguments. What one person or group considers vital may well seem unimportant to others. Trade barriers imposed for these reasons cannot be assessed in an objective fashion; therefore, each country must make such choices for itself.

Domestic Economic Gains

Under certain conditions, a country or a group of countries can be in a position to influence the world price of certain products. This would be true, for example, when a country has a virtual monopoly on a product. In such a situation, the country may choose to limit the supply of the product in order to raise the price and maximize its own gains.

> The Organization of Petroleum Exporting Countries (OPEC) might be seen as a group of countries that controls a particular product and can therefore manage the supply of the product to benefit the producing countries. OPEC has achieved this control at times, but because a fairly large number of countries are in the group, agreement on supply policies has been difficult.

Such a policy is clearly not considered fair by outsiders and such actions tend to result in retaliations. Countries are unlikely, therefore, to admit to such policies but they may nevertheless engage in them under a more acceptable guise, such as conservation.

Types of Trade Barriers

The preceding discussion illustrates that, in spite of the advantages to trade, countries may choose to restrict it. A variety of **trade barriers** are commonly used for trade restriction. Trade restrictions are generally classified as tariff barriers or nontariff barriers.

Tariffs

Import Tariffs.   An **import tariff** or duty can be described simply as a tax on the import of a foreign-produced good. Most people are familiar with the tariffs or duties they must pay on foreign goods they have purchased while traveling abroad and brought back into their home country. Similar tariffs and duties apply when companies import products from foreign locations. Part of the appendix graphically illustrates the effect of a tariff on domestic prices, production, consumption, imports, and government revenues, as well as producer gains and losses due to a tariff.

If the world price of an imported good is $3 and domestic producers need to charge $4, clearly domestic producers will have difficulty competing with imports. If the country wishes to encourage domestic production, then it can raise the price of imports so that the difference is not so great. It can impose a tariff on imports to increase the price of these imports to, say, $3.75. The result will be that local producers can charge a higher price, and therefore consumers will pay a higher price than they would have without the tariff. The difference between local consumption and production will decrease; therefore, imports will decrease. Clearly, local producers benefit, but both local consumers and foreign suppliers are hurt. The government benefits because it collects the tariff and government revenues are increased.

An import tariff results in losses to consumers but gains to producers and the importing government; a comparison of these gains and losses indicates that the losses outweigh the gains. This builds on the earlier argument that a move to freer trade benefits society as a whole. In this case, the tariff moves to more restrictive trade and therefore hurts society as a whole.

The most common rationale for the imposition of a tariff is to encourage domestic production, but the revenue effect is also worth considering. Tariffs can be imposed to raise government revenues, to assist in redistributing income, or to discourage consumption. For example, if there is no domestic production of a particular item, a government might still choose to impose a tariff. The revenues raised would then be used for other projects that are believed to provide benefits that outweigh the costs associated with the tariff. If the tariff were imposed on a luxury item that only the wealthy would purchase and the revenues were used to assist the poor, then income would be redistributed. Finally, if imported products are considered undesirable (e.g., tobacco products), the country might impose a tariff to make them more expensive to local consumers and thus decrease consumption.

A special instance of a tariff is the **countervailing tariff or duty**. This tariff, imposed when a trading partner is seen to be engaging in an unfair trade practice, is intended specifically to counter the practice. Countervailing tariffs are usually levied on specific products or groups of products from particular countries.

Export Tariffs. **Export tariffs** are less familiar and used less frequently than other tariffs because the **General Agreement on Tariff and Trade (GATT)** generally does not sanction them, and the U.S. Constitution forbids them. These taxes are imposed by the exporting country to increase prices for their domestic products and increase the returns to the exporting country. They are feasible only if the country has control over supply and if demand is inelastic so that the increased price will not cause a substantial decrease in consumption. Export tariffs may also be used to raise government revenues.

Nontariff Barriers

Nontariff barriers (NTBs) to trade encompass a wide variety of payments and policies that intentionally or unintentionally limit trade. The most common of these are identified here.

Subsidies.   **Subsidies** are direct payments to domestic producers. The effect of a subsidy is to increase domestic production because the producer gets increased revenue; however, the price that consumers pay is not affected and therefore consumption does not decrease. Domestic producers supply a greater portion of the local market than would be the case without the subsidy; imports therefore decrease. Government revenues decrease, in contrast to the imposition of a tariff, because the government pays the subsidy. Although the price of the good does not necessarily change in response to a subsidy, consumers in general lose because the subsidy is paid out of general revenues, to which the consumer has contributed through taxes. The effect of a subsidy on production, consumption, imports, and government revenues is illustrated graphically in the appendix.

Import Quotas.   **Import quotas** are limits to the quantities or dollar values of a particular product that can be brought into the domestic market. The effect of a quota is similar to that of a tariff, although it is achieved differently. The limitation of supply increases the domestic price. This allows domestic producers to increase their production and causes domestic consumers to decrease consumption; of course, imports are limited by the quota. Government revenues are not necessarily increased, although fees may be associated with these quotas. The GATT agreements generally have prohibited import quotas; therefore, they are unusual. The same effect has been achieved by persuading trading partners to adopt voluntary export restraints. These restraints, in essence, are export quotas that the export country adopts, not because it wants to limit supply but because it is pressured to do so by a major trading partner.

Voluntary Export Restraints.   **Voluntary export restraints (VERs)** became an important tool of trade restriction in the 1970s and 1980s. They have been applied to industries and products, as varied as automobiles, electronic products, machine tools, textiles, clothing steel, and agriculture. These restraints are "voluntary" only in the sense that the exporting country prefers them to alternative barriers the importing country may implement. VERs were first used in 1935 when Japan was induced to limit its textile exports to the United States, but they became relatively widespread in the 1980s. The economic consequences of VERs are similar to those of limitations on imports and they contribute equally to limiting trade levels.

Buy National Policies and Programs.   These policies and programs are intended to give preference to local producers regardless of their competitiveness. This preference may be in the form of specific government policies that stipulate that government purchases of certain kinds must be from domestic producers. Other programs are more generally aimed at domestic consumers of a wide variety of products and services; these appeal to a sense of nationalism by encouraging the purchase of domestic products "for the good of the country." These policies and programs generally mean that local producers can charge a higher price than the world price and still be competitive. Domestic producers benefit from this, but consumers and the government pay a higher price, although they may do so willingly.

Customs Valuation Systems.   Classification systems for customs valuation are often imprecise in their language. Therefore, these systems can be manipulated to classify certain imports to protect local production. For example, a country might have an 8 percent tariff on toys and a 25 percent tariff on boats. Because the language of classification is imprecise, toy boats could be classified either as toys or boats. It would be to the benefit of local manufacturers of toy boats to have imported toy boats in the 25 percent category. Many companies find ways to take advantage of these valuation systems. For example, in many countries, finished goods have a higher tariff than goods that will be completed once inside the importing country. One U.S. company exporting running shoes to Canada found that without laces, the shoes could be classified as unfinished. Therefore, simply by removing laces before the shoes were sent across the Canadian border, the company paid a much lower tariff rate than if it had left the laces in the shoes.

Standards.   All countries have various standards that imported products must meet to be allowed into the domestic market. These standards are intended to protect consumers and ensure that imported products meet the same standards as domestic products. When used legitimately, such standards are not a barrier to trade; however, they can be designed to exclude certain foreign products (i.e., standards can be set in such a way that only local producers can meet them).

An example of this occurred when the Canadian government imposed standards regarding sterilization of imported cheeses, which the producers of French brie could not meet. The French producers argued that it was impossible to produce a high-quality brie if they met Canadian standards. The French producers argued their case successfully under the provisions of the GATT, and the standards were dropped. Interestingly, this event occurred when Canada wished to develop its domestic production of brie cheese. Exhibit 3.8 provides some examples of appeals under the GATT regarding restrictive trade practices.

In addition to the standards described previously, trade can be influenced in a variety of ways: for example, product definitions; regulations regarding health, safety, and labeling; import

EXHIBIT 3.8
Examples of Appeals under the GATT

In an argument under the provisions of the GATT, the United States noted that it had sought in two previous meetings to establish a dispute-settlement mechanism to examine Japan's restrictions on imports of beef, fresh oranges, and orange juice. The United States argued that these restrictions were inconsistent with Japan's obligations and were causing substantial harm to U.S. exports, with an estimated US$1 billion of trade at stake.

Japan, in turn, argued that beef and citrus products played a very important role in the development of its national agriculture and in the local economy of many regions. Its producers were trying to improve productivity under severe constraints. Japan believed that the United States had not shown sufficient understanding of Japan's efforts to improve the situation or of the difficulties in immediately liberalizing these products.

In another argument, the United States claimed that Norway maintained an import licensing system under which imports of apples and pears were restricted during certain seasons of the year. According to the United States, the prohibition on importation of the fruit was applied from the beginning of the harvest season for Norwegian apples and pears to the time the harvested crops had been sold.

Norway pointed out that the relatively free access of U.S. apples and pears to its market was shown by their significant import shares: two-thirds for apples and four-fifths for pears. Norway noted that the measures in question were adopted well in advance of GATT agreements and that its law was mandatory and could not be changed without legislative approval.

administrative procedures; and licensing systems can all be manipulated to serve as barriers to trade. Governments can also manipulate exchange rates to influence the degree and direction of trade.

Incentives to Trade

Just as there are barriers to trade, there are also incentives to trade. Many of these are offered by home governments to encourage exports, but host governments also offer preferential treatment to imports from preferred trading partners. Companies can and should take advantage of these incentives to improve their ability to do business internationally. The specific incentives that exist vary widely from location to location, but in general the following possibilities should be examined:

- ▶ Home-government assistance to attend trade shows in foreign locations
- ▶ Home-government assistance to explore potential export opportunities internationally
- ▶ Home-government sponsorship of foreigners to visit domestic producers and trade shows
- ▶ Home-government support in terms of advice and services (e.g., translators, transportation), facilities (e.g., offices, equipment), and so forth in foreign locations
- ▶ Special arrangements between selected foreign governments and the home country, either to give preferential treatment to imports from a particular location or to encourage exports to a particular location

Governments often maintain offices in foreign countries to provide information and help to companies seeking trade opportunities. Similarly, large banks maintain offices around the world to assist companies in developing trade opportunities.

Special Topics

The discussion to this point has focused on macroeconomic theories of trade, general gains and losses from trade, and barriers and incentives to trade. The chapter now turns to three special topics that students should understand to make business decisions regarding trade and investment. The topics to be discussed are countertrade, trading agreements, and the European Union.

Countertrade

Countertrade is a particular form of reciprocal trade that can be described as "a trading practice that conditions the completion of an import transaction on a separate purchase of goods from the importing country" (U.S. Department of Agriculture 1989).

Countertrade consists of three main types of transactions:

▶ Barter – two parties directly exchange products or services without any flow of money
▶ Counterpurchases – a seller agrees to purchase a given percentage of a contract's value in the form of products or services from the buyer's country
▶ Compensation arrangements – a selling company agrees to take full or partial payment in products as the result of a sale (e.g., a company selling machinery would take payment in products made from the machinery).

Countertrade arrangements can be either voluntary or mandatory. In the first case, two parties agree to a countertrade transaction because both parties agree that it is the best way to consummate a deal. In mandatory cases, countertrade is undertaken because a government mandates it. There are a variety of reasons for engaging in countertrade; some of the major reasons are briefly identified next.

Governments mandate countertrade to conserve foreign exchange reserves. Countries whose currencies are not readily convertible to hard currencies (such as the United States dollar) need to keep reserves of hard currencies to pay for their imports. These reserves are usually limited and efforts are made to conserve them. One approach is to require trading partners to accept goods, rather than currency, as payment for their products or services. The country that lacks a convertible currency generally sees itself as also lacking access to foreign markets and wishes to capitalize on its business partner's access to these markets. In addition, through countertrade arrangements, the country limits the marketing costs that it incurs.

Governments also mandate countertrade to implement industrial policies such as increasing exports. If a country wishes to increase its export sector, it may tie exports to imports through countertrade arrangements. In essence, this policy requires a country's trading partners to accept some of its products or services, and thus it increases its export sector. Again, the country relies on its business partner's foreign marketing expertise and avoids costs associated with marketing the products.

Private firms engage in countertrade to hold markets, expand them, or ensure stable flows of essential supplies. If a company wants to engage in trade with countries in which convertible currency is scarce, it may be necessary to accept countertrade as a means of doing business. In addition, countertrade arrangements can mean that the company gets a foreign product at a better price than it would on the open market. Most companies prefer to avoid countertrade but are willing to accept such an arrangement when it is the only way to conclude a trading agreement.

Countertrade provides both opportunities and problems for businesses. The opportunities arise because countertrade provides an alternative way to do business; thus, trade that might have been impossible without countertrade agreements can take place. The problems arise because such agreements are often more complex than buying or selling products and services for an agreed-on monetary compensation. Consider, for example, the experience of PepsiCo in the USSR. To establish its soft drink in the Soviet Union, PepsiCo agreed to a countertrade arrangement – its profits earned in the Soviet Union were paid in vodka rather than currency. The vodka was exported from the USSR to the United States and sold through distributors in the United States. Such an arrangement made it possible for PepsiCo to conclude an agreement that gave it access to an enormous market, but it also meant that the company found itself in a new and unfamiliar business, selling vodka. Companies may also find that they have agreed to accept goods in countertrade agreements that are not easily sold in the home market or other foreign markets; in such a case, the company may have to accept a lower price for these products, which means, in essence, a lower price for their own original goods.

Speaking at an interview at Moscow's Novosti Press Center, where the band had played its last concert, [the band's spokesperson] outlined some obstacles that had to be overcome. Most important was the tricky question of profits. Since the ruble is not convertible, musicians would be obliged to take their Soviet royalties in the form of a commodity. "I think Georgian cognac would be a great commodity, but it depends," [the band's spokesperson] said, adding that he would soon be meeting with the Ontario Liquor Control Board to discuss the possibility of marketing the product. He suggested that Russian lacquer boxes were another option. "There's a whole wealth of what could be brought back from this country into Canada," he said.

Indeed. In the past year, Soviet foreign trade negotiators have been known to offer, for example, racing camels, trained hunting hawks, and goat horns as barter for Rank Xerox photocopiers.

(Gransden 1990)

The U.S. government neither encourages nor discourages countertrade agreements that are freely negotiated. It does, however, oppose mandated countertrade. The government believes that freely negotiated countertrade probably reflects international market forces whereas mandated countertrade is likely to distort world trade. The U.S. government does offer advisory services and market information to prospective private countertraders. Canada, the European Community, and Japan have policies that are very similar to those of the United States. As might be expected, China, some Eastern European countries, and many developing countries have a different view of countertrade. This last group of countries lacks readily convertible currencies; therefore, it sees countertrade as a major opportunity to increase its overall trade.

Trading Agreements

A wide variety of **trading agreements** exists between and among countries. These are both bilateral (involving trade between two countries) and multilateral (involving trade among a group of countries). The aim of such agreements is to increase the trade that takes place between or among the signatory countries, generally by lowering or eliminating trade barriers between or among them. In most cases, the agreements are regional between countries that are linked geographically. These geographic links often mean that the countries are major trading partners in any case. The formation of regional trading blocs can increase trade within the bloc, but it can also deter trade with other countries outside it. This means that regional trading groups can both increase and decrease trade.

There is some evidence that trading blocs may be replacing the GATT in regulating trade (see the section on the GATT). This would represent a shift from a global view of trade to a regional focus. The situation is not clear, however, because the GATT and regional trading blocs are undergoing many changes. International firms will need to watch these events carefully.

European Union

The European Union (EU) represents an important trading agreement that affects international business. In fact, the EU is substantially more than a trading agreement, although it is based on such an agreement. It is to a large extent an economic integration that has been implemented over the last several decades.

The EU was initiated in 1957 when Belgium, France, West Germany, Italy, Luxembourg, and the Netherlands signed an agreement, the Treaty of Rome, which called for the progressive removal of all tariff and nontariff barriers among the member states. Subsequently, Denmark, Greece, Ireland, Portugal, Spain, and the United Kingdom have joined this community. In 1985, the EU heads of government committed themselves to completing this integration by 1993. The Single European Act, adopted in 1986, defined the *community* as a single market without internal frontiers, in which the free movement of goods, persons, services, and capital is ensured, and it outlined the legislative program needed to achieve these objectives by 1993.

The European Union was formerly known as the European Community (EC), and the change in terminology reflects the move toward a political union, often referred to as a *United States of Europe* rather than a trade agreement. The EU in 1995 provided essentially free movement of capital, labor, and goods among member countries; regulations were harmonized to support this movement; currency values were maintained; and as far as possible, within a relatively narrow band, economic and foreign policies were coordinated. The EU, however, had not achieved a political or monetary union, and serious questions remained as to whether, or when, these would be achieved. For example, the first target date of 1997 for monetary union seemed unlikely because of the varied economic conditions, and the member countries had disagreements ranging from fishing rights to UN peacekeeping roles.

The EU has faced numerous challenges over decades of moving toward integration, but it has made steady progress towards its goals. Whether a full political union evolves is less important to businesses than the current ease with which a large regional market can be accessed. Exhibit 3.9 provides GNP and population data for the EU.

The North American Free Trade Agreement

The North American Free Trade Agreement (NAFTA), which at the time of its inception created the world's largest trading bloc, was a major development in regional cooperation in the 1990s. The 1989 Canada–United States Free Trade Agreement (FTA), served as the basis for developing the extended trade agreement that initially included Canada, Mexico, and the United States. The NAFTA agreement was finalized in 1992 and came into force in January 1994. The agreement provided a set of rules to cover investment and trade.

In 1995, Chile was scheduled to join the agreement, and the vision of a free trade area that would eventually encompass all of the "Americas" – that is, South and Central America and the Caribbean as well as the countries of the North American continent – is coming closer to becoming a reality. The countries believed to be most likely for early admission were Argentina, Colombia, Costa Rica, Trinidad and Tobago, and Venezuela.

NAFTA opens opportunities for companies from all the signing countries. Firms can identify and capitalize on competitive advantages and needs in different locations. For example, Canadian

EXHIBIT 3.9   **Gross National Product and Population Data**

	1989 GNP (in billions of US$)	1989 Population (in millions)
European Community	4,232.2	325.1
Belgium–Luxembourg	136.9	10.2
Denmark	95.7	5.1
France	838.0	56.1
West Germany*	1,069.7	61.9
Greece	47.4	10.1
Ireland	28.3	3.5
Italy	741.2	57.3
Netherlands	195.7	14.8
Portugal	38.3	9.8
Spain	310.7	39.2
United Kingdom	670.8	57.1
*Unified Germany (estimate)	1,373.0	
United States	4,607.9	248.5

firms have extensive experience and expertise in telecommunications and banking, two areas of critical need in Mexico. Seventy percent of the Mexican population is under 30 while the populations in Canada and the United States are aging (see Exhibit 3.10 for a comparison of Canada and Mexico). United States retailing giants like Wal-Mart can capitalize on a Mexican preference for "American" products.

Despite clear benefits to the NAFTA, there are also concerns. The Mexican economy in 1995 was in a state of near collapse and this meant less disposable income to purchase goods and services from Canada and the United States. A severe devaluation of the Mexican peso had a negative impact on the other currencies, and a substantial amount of investment initially left Mexico. These events were seen as potentially exacerbating areas of concern – a collapsing economy and devaluing currency could mean efforts to reattract investment that would include less enforcement of environmental laws, lower wages, and poorer working conditions; it could also mean a resurgence of illegal immigration from Mexico into the United States. In contrast, the devaluation of the peso also meant that Canadian and U.S. investors saw Mexican investment opportunities as "cheap" and therefore attractive.

The NAFTA, like other trading agreements, changes trade and investment opportunities. Firms within a trading bloc, as well as those from outside, should carefully evaluate these agreements to identify the opportunities and challenges that are created.

General Agreement on Tariffs and Trade

The General Agreement on Tariffs and Trade, more commonly the GATT or simply GATT, is an agreement among member countries intended to promote trade. The GATT was adopted

EXHIBIT 3.10   **Age Distribution in Canada and Mexico**

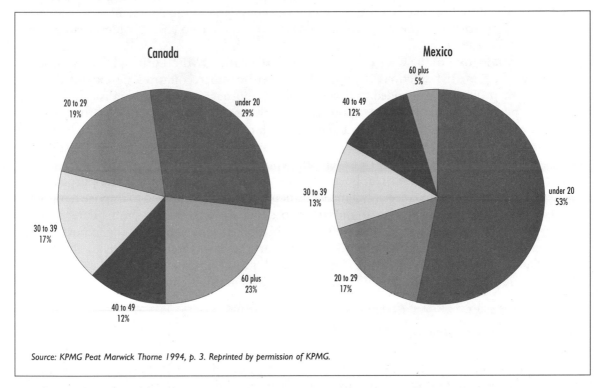

Canada

- under 20 29%
- 20 to 29 19%
- 30 to 39 17%
- 40 to 49 12%
- 60 plus 23%

Mexico

- 60 plus 5%
- 40 to 49 12%
- 30 to 39 13%
- 20 to 29 17%
- under 20 53%

Source: KPMG Peat Marwick Thorne 1994, p. 3. Reprinted by permission of KPMG.

following World War II in response to the protectionism that had preceded the war. This protectionism had resulted in decreased trade, which had had a negative effect on the economies of many countries. The adoption of GATT provided a means to liberalize trade among member nations. The GATT organization has since become recognized as the main forum for trade negotiations and agreements.

When it was ratified, the GATT had 23 signatory countries; this number has increased to nearly 100 members, including countries from all regions of the world, both industrialized and developing, and market economies as well as centrally planned economies. The GATT differs substantially from the regional trade groups previously discussed because its aim is to enhance trade on a worldwide scale.

The major activity undertaken under the auspices of GATT has been a series of "rounds" designed to bring signatory countries together to negotiate multilateral trade agreements. In these rounds of negotiations, signatory countries have agreed to a number of tariff reductions. Other steps have been taken to liberalize trade; for example, the Tokyo round in the 1970s focused on reducing nontariff barriers to trade as well as continuing tariff reductions.

The evolving terms of the GATT are administered by a permanent secretariat located in Geneva, Switzerland. This secretariat collects information on trade issues covered by the GATT. Signatory countries that believe a trade partner is not abiding by the agreements can make appeals under the GATT, and the cases will be investigated and a ruling rendered. Exhibit 3.8

illustrated some of these appeals. If it is determined that a country is violating the agreement, the country is required to take corrective action. The countries' mutual agreement to cooperate and their concern with avoiding protectionism have been enough to ensure widespread compliance with GATT rulings.

A dominant feature of the GATT is the most favored nation (MFN) principle. This principle requires that any tariff reductions negotiated between member countries be extended to all members. This provision is intended to ensure a global approach to trade liberalism rather than a bilateral approach. A number of exceptions to this provision, however, can lead to a bilateral approach. Most important, concessions associated with trade alliances (e.g., the Canada–United States Free Trade Agreement) do not have to be extended to other countries. In addition, preferential treatment can be given to developing countries.

Exceptions to the agreements can be granted to specific countries for specific purposes; for example, a country facing balance of payments difficulties could be allowed to impose temporary trade barriers. Countries have also found ways to avoid the agreements on a bilateral basis; voluntary export restraints are the most common method. In this situation, the exporter (e.g., Japan) agrees to limit exports of a product (e.g., cars) to another country (e.g., the United States). The result is the same as if the United States limited imports of Japanese cars; limiting imports would be contrary to the GATT agreements but limiting exports would not be.

The World Trade Organization

The Uruguay Round of GATT negotiations at times appeared destined for destruction, but after lengthy bargaining among GATT members, the World Trade Organization (WTO) was the result. The GATT Trade Negotiations Committee concluded the Uruguay round in Marrakesh, on April 15, 1994, by signing the "Final Act" and opening for signature the "Agreement Establishing the World Trade Organization." The WTO, which replaces the GATT, was officially launched on January 1, 1995. Peter Sutherland, its first director general, expects 155 states and territories to become members; however, a variety of negotiations continued during 1995 and 1996. A major issue was the question of membership for the People's Republic of China.

The WTO consists of a Secretariat headed by the director general, and a General Council that organizes meetings of the membership and coordinates the Dispute Settlement Body and Trade Policy Review Body. Ministerial meetings are scheduled for at least every two years. The main functions of the WTO are these:

- ▶ Facilitate the implementation, administration, and operation of the Uruguay round agreements
- ▶ Provide a forum for negotiations among members concerning their multilateral trade relations
- ▶ Act as a global trade referee by enforcing the standards that its members have agreed to accept
- ▶ Introduce a dispute resolution mechanism

The WTO is very new and its success is not yet established. Nevertheless, many believe its establishment provides a substantial strengthening of the multilateral trading system through

The WTO:
What It Is,
What It Does ▶

The World Trade Organization (WTO) was established on 1 January 1995. It will take charge of administering the new global trade rules, agreed in the Uruguay Round, which took effect on the same day. These rules – achieved after seven years of negotiations among more than 120 countries – establish the rule of law in international trade, which for goods and services together are estimated to have approached some $5 trillion this year. Through the WTO agreements and market access commitments, world income is expected to rise by over $500 billion annually by the year 2005 – and annual global trade growth will be as much as a quarter higher by the same year than it would otherwise have been.

How Different Is It From GATT?

▶ The WTO is more global in its membership than the GATT. Its prospective membership is already around 150 countries and territories, with many others considering accession.
▶ It has a far wider scope than its predecessor, bringing into the multilateral trading system, for the first time, trade in services, intellectual property protection, and investment.
▶ It is a full-fledged international organization in its own right while GATT was basically a provisional treaty serviced by an *ad hoc* Secretariat.
▶ It administers a unified package of agreements to which *all* members are committed. In contrast, the GATT framework includes many important side agreements (for example, anti-dumping measures and subsidies) whose membership is limited to a few countries.
▶ It contains a much improved version of the original GATT rules plus a lot more. The new version, called GATT 1994, clarifies and strengthens the original GATT rules for trade in goods.
▶ It reverses policies of protection in certain "sensitive" areas which were more or less tolerated in the old GATT. Under various agreements, export restraints on textiles and clothing will be dismantled, trade in agricultural reformed and "grey-area" trade measures – so-called voluntary export restraints – phased out.

What Does It Do?

The WTO administers, through various councils and committees, the many agreements contained in the Final Act of the Uruguay Round, plus a number of plurilateral agreements, notably on government procurement and civil aircraft. It also oversees the implementation of the significant tariff cuts (averaging 40 percent) and reduction of non-tariff measures agreed to in the negotiations.

It is a watchdog of international trade, regularly examining the trade regimes of individual members. In its various bodies, members flag proposed or draft measures by others that can cause trade conflicts. Members are also required to notify various trade measures and statistics, which are maintained by the WTO in a large data base.

As in any partnership, conflicts can arise among members. The WTO, from the very start of these conflicts, provides several conciliation mechanisms for finding an amicable solution. Trade disputes that cannot be solved through bilateral talks are adjudicated under the WTO dispute settlement "court." Panels of independent experts are established to examine disputes in the light of WTO rules and provide rulings. This tougher, streamlined procedure ensures equal treatment for all trading partners and encourages members to live up to their obligations.

The WTO is also a management consultant for world trade. Its economists keep a close watch on the pulse of the global economy, and provide studies on the main trade issues of the day.

Finally, the WTO will be a forum where countries continuously negotiate exchanges of trade concessions to further lower trade barriers all over the world.

Who Is In It?

All the 128 members of the old GATT automatically become WTO members upon acceptance of the Uruguay Round Agreements and submission of commitments on trade in goods and services. On the assumption that negotiations on the current membership applications of over 20 countries are ultimately concluded successfully, then the WTO will cover virtually the whole of world trade.

Participating and presiding over WTO meetings are representatives from members' diplomatic missions in Geneva and specialists from capitals.

The WTO Secretariat – numbering 420 of many nationalities – services all meetings of WTO bodies at its headquarters in Geneva. The Secretariat works with developing countries and countries undertaking economic reform to help them negotiate accession and draw maximum benefit from the WTO.

▶ More detailed rules to govern the application of a variety of trade policy measures, particularly those where weak or unclear wording had consistently been a source of trade tensions and the subject of trade disputes
▶ New multilateral trade rules to cover intellectual property and trade in services
▶ Tariff liberalization to maintain the movement toward freedom in multilateral trade

▶ Reductions in discriminatory aspects of regional trade agreements
▶ Increases in multilateral obligations of all countries to comparable levels, but with more favorable treatment for developing countries specified
▶ Linkage of various agreements within a formal, institutional framework, subject to an integrated dispute settlement mechanism

Summary

International business managers need to consider the trade patterns that exist in the world. Decisions about trade as well as investment are made within this context. Businesses need to understand why such patterns exist to make the best possible decisions about their products and services. This chapter has described world trade data, a number of trade theories, the benefits of trade, and barriers and incentives to trade, as well as countertrade and trading agreements. This discussion was intended to give students an overview of the global trade environment.

MINI-CASE
The Japanese Sogo Shosha

Sogo shoshas are well known in Japan, but North American business is not as familiar with them, although they are now more prevalent in the United States than they were formerly. The main role of the sogo shosha is to coordinate activities among a variety of organizations. This role has led to some sogo shoshas becoming some of the largest companies in the world; among them are Mitsubishi Corporation and Sumitomo Corporation.

Originally, the role of the sogo shosha was to match buyers with sellers of a variety of products. Japan's economic success has depended partially on its ability to import raw materials efficiently, process them, and export the finished products. This means that buyers and sellers often needed an intermediary to match their needs efficiently and effectively. The sogo shosha grew out of these needs. The sogo shosha began as a trading company and, subsequently, assumed a key role as intermediary between Japan's companies and the rest of the world. This has led, currently, to a more extensive role, including a focus on encouraging and promoting Japanese industrialization. The sogo shoshas became more and more powerful through the 1980s.

Sogo shoshas are involved in international business by facilitating trade, but they also participate through ownership in international companies (both Japanese and non-Japanese). They act as intermediaries, bringing corporations together and charging for this service. They are directly involved in a variety of other companies, purchased or founded as a result of trading activities, and profit from these activities as well.

> The Japanese sogo shoshas are complex organizations; they are involved in the flow of products from raw materials to finished products for companies and countries around the world. As a result, these organizations have immense power and responsibility.
>
> *Source: Yoshino and Lifson 1986.*
>
> **Discussion Issues**
>
> 1. Discuss the likely effect of Japanese sogo shoshas on trade between Japan and your home country, say, the United States, Canada, Australia, and so forth.
> 2. Would a similar type of organization be successful in your home country? Discuss why it would or would not be successful.
> 3. Identify several Japanese sogo shoshas by name and find information on their business activities.

Appendix: Trade Theories

The following descriptions and graphical diagrams illustrate the trade theories discussed earlier in this chapter.

Changes in Consumption and Production

Exhibit 3.11 reflects the changes in consumption and production that occur in one country as it moves from no trade to trade. Two products, wine and bread, are represented in the diagram. TT' represents the country's production possibilities: The country can produce any combination of wine and bread on this curve. I_o and I_i are social indifference curves: The society can consume any combination of wine and bread along one of these curves and be indifferent; I_i represents a higher level of social satisfaction than I_o.

PP' represents the domestic price ratios; $P_wP'_w$ represents the world price ratios. With no trade, the country will produce and consume the combination of wine and bread at E, where the domestic price line is tangent to the production possibility curve and the indifference curve I_o.

With trade, the country will produce where the world price line is tangent to its production possibility curve and its indifference curve I_i. The society is now able to consume at a level that represents a higher level of social satisfaction. Wine production now exceeds consumption; therefore, the surplus is exported. Bread production is less than bread consumption; therefore, the deficit must be imported.

The actual result of a change from no trade to trade depends on a variety of factors such as factor endowments (resource availability), social preferences, and domestic and world prices.

EXHIBIT 3.11
**No Trade
to Trade**

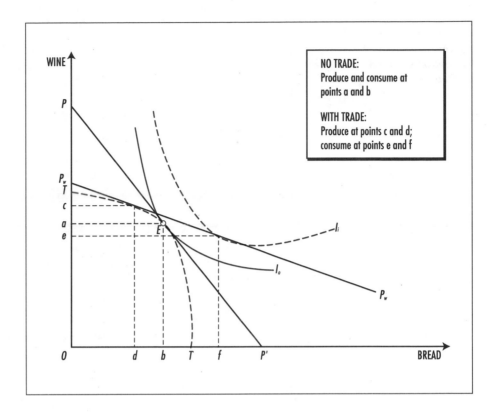

NO TRADE:
Produce and consume at
points a and b

WITH TRADE:
Produce at points c and d;
consume at points e and f

These factors are reflected in the production possibility curve, the social indifference curves, and the price lines but are not specifically addressed in this diagram.

Shifts in Production

Exhibit 3.12 shows how production shifts as two countries move from no trade to trade with each other. The two countries are North and South. North is abundant in capital and South is abundant in labor. The two countries produce two goods, Y and X. Y is capital intensive, and X is labor intensive. In the diagram, $P_n P'_n$ represents the production possibilities in North and $P_s P'_s$ represents the production possibilities in South; the shapes of these curves represent their respective factor abundancies. $P_n P'_n$ represents the price ratios in North and $P_s P'_s$ represents the price ratios in South; $P_w P'_w$ represents the price ratios in the world, or the price ratios if the two countries trade with each other.

The countries, without trade, will produce where their respective price lines are tangent to their production possibility curves: in North at Y_n and X_n, in South at Y_s and X_s. With trade, they will produce where the world price line is tangent to their respective production possibility curves: in North at Y'_n and X'_n and in South at Y'_s and X'_s.

This diagram illustrates that, with trade, North will produce more of Y and less of X than it would have without trade; South will produce more of X and less of Y than without **trade**.

EXHIBIT 3.12
**Factor
Endowment Effect
on Production**

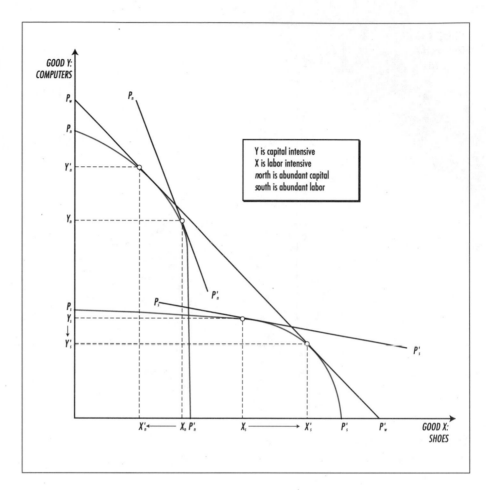

This shows that, with trade, each country will specialize in the product that uses more intensively its abundant resource.

Effect and Cost of a Tariff

Exhibit 3.13 illustrates the effect and cost of a tariff. In the diagram, D_x represents the demand for X, S_x represents the supply of X in a given country. P_w is the world price and $P_w + t$ is the world price plus the local tariff: This is the price that is paid for X in the country. At the higher price of $P_w + t$, production increases, consumption decreases, and imports (the difference between production and consumption) decrease.

   This diagram also illustrates the cost to society of a tariff, as follows. The triangle to the left of the demand curve and above the price line represents the consumer surplus given a particular price of a good. In effect, this represents the benefit to consumers who would have been willing to pay a higher price for this good and thus benefit from this lower price. A move

EXHIBIT 3.13
Cost of Tariff

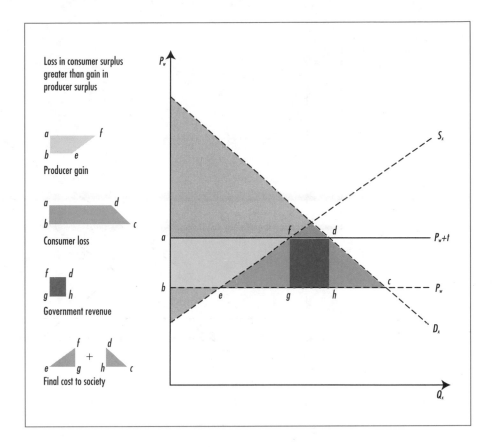

Loss in consumer surplus greater than gain in producer surplus

a   *f*
b   *e*
Producer gain

a   *d*
b   *c*
Consumer loss

f   *d*
g   *h*
Government revenue

f   *d*
+
e   *g*   *h*   *c*
Final cost to society

from the world price to the world price plus tariff decreases the size of the triangle. This decrease is represented by the area *abcd* in the diagram. This is the loss to consumers from the tariff.

The triangle to the left of the supply curve and below the price line represents the producer surplus given a particular price of a good. In effect, this represents the benefit to producers who would have been willing to produce the good at a lower price and thus benefit from this higher price. A move from the world price to the world price plus tariff increases the size of the triangle. This increase is represented by the area *abef* in the diagram. This is the gain to producers from the tariff.

A comparison of the loss to consumers and the gain to producers shows that the loss is greater than the gain. This entire difference is not lost to society, however, because the area *dfgh* is government revenue (imports × tariff). There is clearly a cost to society, nevertheless, and this is represented by the two triangles identified in the diagram.

Effect of a Subsidy

Exhibit 3.14 illustrates the effect of a subsidy on production, consumption, and imports. In the diagram, S_x represents the supply of X without the subsidy; S'_x represents the supply with the subsidy. In effect, producers receive a higher price at any level, due to the subsidy paid to them.

EXHIBIT 3.14
Direct Subsidy

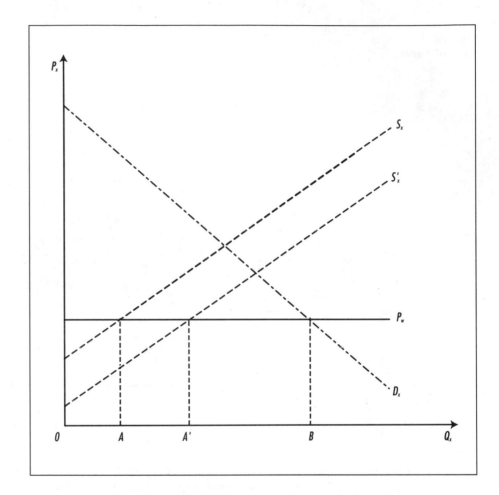

Thus, the supply curve is seen as having shifted to the right. D_x represents the demand for X and P_w the world price for X. Production increases from A to A′ because the price to consumers has not changed. Imports decrease from AB to A′B.

Discussion Questions

1. Define *absolute advantage* and *comparative advantage*.
2. Explain why it is beneficial to trade under conditions of absolute advantage and comparative advantage.
3. Discuss the gains and losses from trade.
4. Discuss the opportunities and risks associated with countertrade agreements.

Assignments

1. Select a country and examine its actual exports and imports. How do these fit with the theory of factor endowments?

2. Select a country and a product. Identify the tariff and nontariff barriers as well as incentives associated with the importation and exportation of the product.

3. Select a country and identify its comparative trade advantages. On the basis of these comparative advantages, identify the trade patterns you would expect for this country.

4. Identify developments relating to European Union (EU) integration that have occurred over the past 12 months.

5. Identify and discuss developments relating to the World Trade Organization (WTO) that have occurred over the past 12 months.

Selected References

Ball, D. A., and W. A. McCulloch, Jr., *International Business – Introduction and Essentials* (Plano, Tex.: Business Publications, 1988), chs. 2 and 3.

Boonecamp, C. F. J., "Voluntary Export Restraints," *Finance and Development* (December 1987), pp. 2–5.

Canadian Department of External Affairs and International Trade, *The NAFTA at a Glance* (EAITC, 1993).

Catoline, J., and J. Chopoorian, "The European Market in 1992: Strategies for U.S. Companies," *Advanced Management Journal* (Spring 1990), pp. 33–41.

Czinkota, M. R., P. Rivoli, and I. A. Ronkainen, *International Business* (Hinsdale, Ill.: The Dryden Press, 1989), ch. 2.

Daniels, J. D., and L. H. Radebaugh, *International Business – Environments and Operations* (Reading, Mass.: Addison-Wesley, 1986), chs. 4 and 5.

The Economist, "The Third World Survey" (September 23–29, 1989).

The Economist, "Modern Adam Smith" (July 14, 1990).

The Economist, "World Trade" (September 22, 1990), p. 5.

The Economist, "Lower Tariffs, More Trade" (September 22, 1990), p. 7.

The Economist, "The GATT Negotiations – Almost High Noon" (February 9, 1991), p. 70.

The Economist, "Off the Hook on Trade" (March 2, 1991), p. 18.

Garland, J., and R. N. Farmer, *International Dimensions of Business Policy and Strategy* (Boston: PWS-Kent, 1986).

Goette, E. E., "Europe 1992: Update for Business Planners," *Journal of Business Strategy* (March–April 1990), pp. 10–13.

Grandsen, G., "Singing for Supper Soviet Style," *Globe and Mail* (November 29, 1990), p. C7.

Greenspan, E., "Not Welcome," *Report on Business Magazine* (November 1990), pp. 25–26.

Grosse, R., and D. Kujawa, *International Business* (Homewood, Ill.: Irwin, 1988), chs. 3 and 8.

Heller, H. R., *International Trade* (Englewood Cliffs, N.J.: Prentice-Hall, 1973).

Kefalas, A. G., *Global Business Strategy* (Cincinnati: South-Western, 1990), chs. 4 and 5.

KPMG Peat Marwick Thorne, *NAFTA: A Canadian Perspective* (KPMG Peat Marwick Thorne, 1994).

Lawday, D., "Europe without Thatcher," *U.S. News & World Report* (December 31, 1990–January 7, 1991), p. 58.

Mosbacher, R. A., "U.S.-EC Cooperation Increases as the Single Market Takes Shape," *Business America* (January 1990), pp. 2–3.

Rugman, A., D. Lecraw, and L. D. Booth, *International Business Firm and Environment* (New York: McGraw-Hill, 1985), chs. 2 and 3.

Thurow, Lester C., "GATT Is Dead," *Journal of Accountancy in Inside Guide* (February 1991), pp. 27–30.

United Nations, *Direction of Trade Statistics Yearbook* (New York: United Nations, 199X).

United Nations Conference on Trade and Development, *Trade and Development Report* (New York: United Nations, 1994).

U.S. Department of Agriculture, World Trade Services Department, "Why Export?" (video workshop presented at the Global Trade Strategy Workshop, September 14, 1989).

Wittenberg-Cox, A., "Europe's Price for Free Trade," *Canadian Business* (June 1990), p. 27.

Yoshino and Lifson, *The Invisible Link* (Cambridge, Mass.: MIT Press, 1986).

CHAPTER ▼ 4

Balance of Payments Accounts and International Monetary Systems

LEARNING OBJECTIVES

After reading this chapter, you should be able to

▶ Define balance of payments (BOP) and identify each of the five types of balances and the various accounts.

▶ Differentiate among the various balances and accounts in the BOP statement.

▶ Discuss the practical implications of the BOP accounts.

▶ Discuss the international monetary system.

▶ Outline the differences between fixed and floating exchange rate systems.
▶ Discuss currency strength and weakness.
▶ Explain the practical implications of currency differences.
▶ Explain the role of the International Monetary Fund (IMF) and the World Bank in the international monetary system.

K E Y   T E R M S

▶ Balance of payments
▶ Current Account
▶ Capital Account
▶ Official Reserve Account
▶ Balance of trade
▶ Balance of goods and services
▶ Balance on Current Account
▶ Basic balance
▶ Official settlements balance
▶ Surplus account
▶ Deficit account

▶ Fixed exchange rate
▶ Floating exchange rate
▶ Clean float
▶ Dirty float
▶ Managed system
▶ Overvaluation
▶ Undervaluation
▶ Currency strength
▶ World Bank
▶ International Monetary Fund

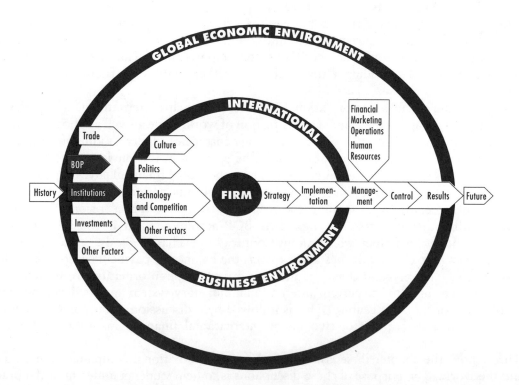

T H O U G H T   S T A R T E R S

▶ An international trading system in greenhouse gases would allow the countries which could reduce emissions most cheaply to earn money by selling gas-emitting allowances to those for which cuts were more expensive.

(The Economist July 7, 1990)

▶ The export-led growth of the Asian NICs [newly industrialized countries] is one of the biggest economic success stories of the past 30 years.

The main reason for the NICs' burgeoning trade surpluses in the second half of the 1980s was considerable undervaluation of their currencies.

(The Economist July 14, 1990)

Introduction

Different countries use different currencies; therefore, international arrangements across borders often involve currency exchanges. Doing business in an international framework can mean using assorted currencies for business transactions. To understand these transactions, it is necessary to understand the balance of payments (BOP) system currently used by countries around the world as well as the international monetary system.

The **balance of payments** system is used to report monetary transactions between countries. The international monetary system comprises the agreements, institutions, laws, and practices governing the movement of currency from one country to another. The international monetary system facilitates transactions, and the BOP system reports them. The international monetary system can be seen as providing a financial context that enables international companies to function across borders.

Understanding the meaning of national BOP accounts helps international companies make informed judgments about the volume and direction of world trade as well as about the potential economic performance of specific countries and their currencies. Understanding the international monetary system helps international companies be effective in this environment because such understanding gives them a better perception of how the global financial environment can affect their transactions. This chapter investigates the BOP and international monetary systems.

The chapter begins by examining the means by which countries record their financial exchanges with other countries through their BOP accounts. Then it considers the overall international monetary system, which allows countries to exchange goods, services, and capital with each other. The chapter defines and explains the balance of payments accounts, including various specific accounts, and considers the way firms use the information from the accounts. The chapter then turns to the current international monetary system and its development over the second half of the 20th century. This is followed by a discussion of currency strengths and weaknesses and a description of two major international financial institutions currently in operation.

Throughout the chapter these issues are related to international companies doing business around the world. The purpose of these discussions is to help students understand the practical business implications of payment balances and international monetary systems rather than to deal with these issues from a political or economic policy standpoint.

Balance of Payments

Balance of payments accounts provide a system for documenting economic transactions during a given period between and among the residents of one country and residents of the rest of the world, in a globally consistent manner and following generally accepted guidelines. Balance of payments information is published by governments and international institutions, such as the World Bank, and is readily available at most libraries.

A BOP statement documents a country's past economic transactions with other countries. As such, a country's BOP statement is like a company's annual cash flow, or sources and uses of funds, statement. A BOP statement provides a record of a how funds were generated from abroad (inflows from outside the home country) and used in foreign transactions (outflows to other countries) during a particular year. BOP statements are compiled on an annual basis, but interim data are often available on a monthly or quarterly basis.

BOP statements deal with only those transactions that take place across national borders. Therefore, any transaction on a BOP statement affects at least two countries. Thus, exports from the United States to Japan appear on the U.S. BOP as a source of funds and on the Japanese BOP as a use of funds.

Two basic concepts associated with BOP statements need to be understood. First, a BOP statement is made up of a series of balances, each of which can be in a surplus or deficit position. Second, a BOP statement must, by definition, balance; that is, economic inflows must equal outflows, or the sources of funds must equal the uses. The following sections define and describe the various accounts that make up a BOP statement and illustrates how these accounts are balanced.

Explanation of Accounts

BOP statements are divided into four major sections: the Current Account, the Capital Account, Errors and Omissions, and the Official Reserves Account. Each of these is described in terms of the various balances.

The Current Account

Included in the **Current Account** are imports and exports of goods and services, interest and dividend payments, and unilateral transfers of money such as gifts or inheritances. Exports are considered a source of funds because the exporting country receives payment for the goods and services. Imports are a use of funds because the importing country must pay for them.

The Capital Account

Included in the **Capital Account** are investments and loans. Investments in the home country by foreigners are considered a source of funds, and investments by locals in foreign countries are a use of funds. Money that is borrowed abroad is a source of funds and money that is lent to foreigners is a use. Interest payments on loans are recorded in the Current Account. The key in this account is the direction in which the cash moves, into or out of the country.

Errors and Omissions

The accounting system is not entirely accurate, and discrepancies can occur because of errors and omissions. The Errors and Omissions section compensates for these discrepancies.

The Official Reserve Account

The **Official Reserve Account** is a compensatory account that changes in response to surpluses or deficits in the Current and Capital Accounts. A surplus implies an inflow of funds greater than the outflow and consequently an increase in reserves. A deficit has the reverse effect and reduces a country's reserves.

BOP statements provide a useful guide for analyzing a country's economic position. The inaccuracies that may exist in these statistics need to be acknowledged, however, and considered in such an analysis. Later, we will consider briefly how international companies use the information in balance of payments statements.

Using the sources and uses of funds analogy with inflows of funds as sources and outflows as uses, it is possible to identify major inflows and outflows as follows.

Inflows, or sources, include

▶ Payments by foreigners for goods and services
▶ Dividends and interest payments from foreign investments
▶ Transfers (e.g., gifts) from foreigners
▶ Investments by foreigners
▶ Foreign government payments to local institutions or governments
▶ Borrowing from outside sources (including banks, governments, and institutions).

Outflows, or uses, include

▶ Payments to foreigners for goods and services
▶ Dividends and interest payments to foreigners
▶ Transfers to foreigners
▶ Investments in foreign locations
▶ Government payments to foreign institutions or governments (e.g., foreign aid)
▶ Loans to foreign debtors.

These sources and uses can be seen in more concrete terms in the following table:

Sources		Uses	
Exports of tires	100	Imports of shoes	80
Insurance exports	10	Service contract imports	15
Inheritances	1	Foreign charity	5
Sold foreign bonds	5	Foreigners sold equity	20
Totals	116		120

Change in reserves (calculated as sources less uses): $116 - 120 = -4$

Each of these can be examined separately as follows:

Net exchange of goods	+20	(surplus)
Net exchange of services	−5	(deficit)
Net exchange of short-term capital	−4	(deficit)
Net exchange of long-term capital	−15	(deficit)

Overall, the surplus on goods of +20 is less than the combined deficit in the other categories of −24, and therefore reserves decrease by −4.

Explanation of Balances

Five categories of balances are reported in a balance of payments statement.

1. The **balance of trade** reports a country's exports and imports of goods. The balance may be positive (a surplus) if exports are greater than imports (the country is selling more abroad than it is buying) or negative (a deficit) if exports are less than imports (the country is buying more abroad than it is selling).
2. The **balance of goods and services** reports exports and imports in both goods and services. This balance can likewise be either a surplus or a deficit.
3. The **balance on Current Account** reports short-term transfers of capital in addition to trade in goods and services. This balance can also be either a surplus or a deficit.
4. The **basic balance** reports movements of long-term capital as well as information in the previous three categories. Again, this balance may be either a surplus or a deficit.
5. The **official settlements balance** reports changes in a country's reserves needed to balance its surplus or deficit.

A simple example illustrates how these balances are derived and what they mean. These numbers can be reported in terms of the first four balances just defined, as follows:

Balance of trade	+20
Balance of goods and services	+15
Balance on Current Account	+11
Basic balance	−4

In this example, there is an overall deficit during the period in the country's exchanges with the rest of the world. The central government must now make up this deficit. For example, the central bank may sell four units of foreign treasury bills to cover the deficit; this means that the country's reserves have declined by four units.

This example illustrates the basis on which the various balances constituting a country's BOP are compiled and calculated as well as how surpluses or deficits are balanced. It is easy to imagine how complex this is in fact when multiple goods, services, and short- and long-term capital movements are involved among many different trading partners.

The complexity of estimating the various categories of the BOP statement means that room for error in these calculations exists. It is often difficult to obtain accurate and reliable information on these transactions, and governments may sometimes rely on estimates or even guesses. For this reason, a country's BOP figures are often revised over time, and one should expect some degree of inaccuracy in these statistics. In particular, the BOP figures for countries in which the needed information is not carefully and systematically collected may not be truly representative of the economic transactions occurring between that country and the rest of the world.

BOP figures can also misstate the real state of a country's economic interactions with other countries because the figures depict only legal transactions. Illegal and black market activities are not recorded in these statements, yet in some locations they are an important part of a country's international economic transactions. For example, in 1990, Colombia had substantial exports of illegal drugs, yet these are not recorded as part of its balance of payments statistics. Nor are the imports of illegal drugs into the United States recorded despite the widespread concern over such imports. Exhibit 4.1 illustrates a typical trade table, in this case for the United States.

Using Balance of Payments Information

A country's balance of payments statement is similar to a company's financial statements. Financial statements provide data that an informed user can interpret to assess the operations of a firm and identify important trends. Similarly, the BOP statement provides information that can be analyzed to understand better the economic conditions in a country. Careful analysis of BOP statements should, therefore, precede corporate decisions regarding doing business in a particular country.

The information provided in these statements also can be used to assess a country's economic relationships with the rest of the world. The information provides an initial point for estimating a country's strengths and weaknesses; that is, a country's comparative advantage is usually reflected in a **surplus account**, its disadvantages in a **deficit account**. These accounts therefore give a broad, general indication of a country's international economic performance.

In the trade terms presented in Chapter 3, a country that has abundant labor has a comparative advantage in products that use labor intensively and, in turn, its account in labor-intensive products should be in a surplus position. A country that has developed a comparative advantage in managerial expertise should be able to export this expertise; this advantage may be reflected in its balance of payments in the form of services or capital movements.

In analyzing a country's balance of payments, a company is usually interested in the general situation described by the five broad categories discussed earlier, as well as in the specifics that

EXHIBIT 4.1 U.S. International Transactions in Goods and Services (millions of dollars; monthly estimates seasonally adjusted)

			1993		1994 Jan.	Feb.	Mar.	Apr.	May	June	July	Aug.	Sept.	Oct.ʳ	Nov.ᵖ	Dec.
	1992	1993	Nov.	Dec.	Jan.	Feb.	Mar.	Apr.	May	June	July	Aug.	Sept.	Oct.ʳ	Nov.ᵖ	Dec.
Exports of goods and services	616,924	641,677	54,465	56,728	53,625	52,866	58,386	55,977	56,257	58,333	56,297	60,292	60,063	59,847	61,159	
Goods	440,361	456,866	39,364	40,953	38,533	37,425	42,065	40,378	40,276	42,028	40,128	44,121	43,596	43,380	44,535	
Foods, feeds, and beverages	40,270	40,628	3,476	3,665	3,346	3,163	3,405	3,087	3,268	3,088	3,052	3,676	3,698	3,925	3,998	
Industrial supplies and materials	109,140	111,814	9,615	9,630	8,974	8,721	10,604	9,625	9,914	9,820	10,254	10,739	10,320	10,604	10,720	
Capital goods, except automotive	175,915	181,696	15,491	16,894	16,022	15,318	17,309	16,747	16,555	17,727	16,284	17,656	17,830	16,893	18,030	
Automotive vehicles, engines, and parts	47,028	52,404	4,679	4,529	4,417	4,417	4,760	4,721	4,543	4,723	4,275	5,204	5,036	5,030	4,929	
Consumer goods (nonfood), except automotive	51,425	54,656	4,870	4,715	4,500	4,468	4,882	4,659	4,804	5,114	4,859	5,310	5,186	5,409	5,475	
Other goods	24,385	23,893	1,953	2,224	1,988	2,020	1,849	2,250	2,018	2,340	2,261	2,517	2,346	2,474	2,152	
Adjustments[1]	-7,805	-8,224	-719	-705	-714	-681	-743	-711	-828	-783	-857	-980	-820	-955	-770	
Services	176,563	184,811	15,100	15,774	15,092	15,440	16,322	15,599	15,982	16,305	16,169	16,171	16,467	16,467	16,625	
Travel	54,284	57,621	4,595	5,066	4,567	4,671	5,162	4,718	4,835	5,036	4,901	4,765	4,977	5,040	5,058	
Passenger fares	16,972	16,550	1,285	1,410	1,311	1,373	1,505	1,382	1,407	1,489	1,404	1,382	1,441	1,437	1,454	
Other transportation	22,704	23,151	1,924	1,996	1,901	1,864	2,107	2,001	2,017	2,030	1,996	2,125	2,084	2,100	2,159	
Royalties and license fees	19,922	20,398	1,698	1,697	1,763	1,780	1,790	1,795	1,816	1,847	1,930	1,954	1,960	1,960	1,955	
Other private services	50,992	54,870	4,740	4,762	4,678	4,867	4,851	4,745	4,919	4,890	4,895	4,886	4,937	4,871	4,922	
Transfers under U.S. military agency sales contracts[2]	10,828	11,413	801	784	802	816	841	908	940	964	980	992	998	1,000	1,016	
U.S. government miscellaneous services	861	808	57	60	70	70	67	50	48	49	63	67	69	59	61	
Imports of goods and services	657,308	717,402	61,997	61,253	61,455	62,460	65,285	64,559	65,477	67,178	67,250	69,352	69,417	69,944	71,690	
Goods	536,458	589,441	50,886	50,068	50,501	50,968	53,511	53,717	54,548	56,048	56,083	58,222	58,029	58,431	60,097	
Foods, feeds, and beverages	27,610	27,867	2,328	2,339	2,440	2,364	2,543	2,492	2,531	2,593	2,624	2,699	2,714	2,675	2,636	
Industrial supplies and materials	138,644	145,606	12,276	11,495	11,653	11,932	12,659	12,771	13,155	14,007	14,375	14,687	14,305	13,950	14,561	
Capital goods, except automotive	134,253	152,365	13,308	13,888	14,121	14,028	14,467	14,727	14,883	15,129	15,195	15,304	16,470	16,582	16,986	
Automotive vehicles, engines, and parts	91,788	102,420	8,856	8,728	8,683	8,787	9,549	9,491	9,481	10,153	9,911	11,057	9,870	10,230	10,755	
Consumer goods (nonfood), except automotive	122,657	134,015	11,526	11,281	11,603	11,502	11,335	11,845	12,136	12,138	12,023	12,479	12,630	12,787	12,953	
Other goods	17,713	18,386	1,686	1,710	1,598	1,566	1,837	1,808	1,801	1,820	1,701	1,632	1,815	1,926	1,935	
Adjustments[1]	3,795	8,783	905	629	404	789	1,120	582	560	209	254	364	225	281	271	
Services	120,850	127,961	11,112	11,185	10,953	11,492	11,774	10,842	10,929	11,130	11,167	11,130	11,388	11,513	11,594	
Travel	39,007	40,564	3,566	3,690	3,591	3,720	3,930	3,344	3,423	3,376	3,462	3,378	3,611	3,716	3,771	
Passenger fares	10,608	11,416	972	992	955	1,006	1,069	1,009	1,039	1,029	1,024	1,012	1,075	1,105	1,138	
Other transportation	23,460	24,502	2,091	2,039	1,952	1,980	2,159	2,080	2,096	2,175	2,190	2,271	2,211	2,248	2,246	
Royalties and license fees	4,987	4,840	446	448	450	713	444	434	436	481	516	491	499	507	513	
Other private services	26,625	32,119	2,905	2,889	2,861	2,926	3,025	2,866	2,840	2,980	2,886	2,891	2,906	2,873	2,870	
Direct defense expenditures[2]	13,862	12,176	954	946	938	932	926	890	877	868	867	864	863	853	845	
U.S. government miscellaneous services	2,301	2,344	178	181	207	216	221	219	220	221	222	222	223	209	210	
Memoranda:																
Balance on goods	-96,097	-132,575	-11,521	-9,115	-11,968	-13,542	-11,446	-13,339	-14,272	-14,020	-15,955	-14,101	-14,433	-15,051	-15,562	
Balance on services	55,713	56,850	3,988	4,589	4,138	3,948	4,548	4,757	5,052	5,175	5,002	5,041	5,079	4,954	5,031	
Balance on goods and services	-40,384	-75,725	-7,533	-4,526	-7,830	-9,594	-6,899	-8,582	-9,220	-8,845	-10,953	-9,060	-9,354	-10,097	-10,531	

ᵖPreliminary.

ʳRevised.

[1]Reflects adjustments necessary to bring the Census Bureau's component data in line with the concepts and definitions used to prepare BEA's international and national accounts.

[2]Contains goods that cannot be separately identified.

Source: U.S. Department of Commerce, Bureau of Economic Analysis and Bureau of the Census 1995.

make up these categories. The same approach is appropriate relative to specific trading partners. For example, a surplus or deficit in terms of goods gives a certain indication of a country's relative strength compared to that of the rest of the world. However, it may be important to know the specifics of this surplus or deficit as well. That is, within the general category of "goods" is a range of specific goods, some of which will have been exported and others imported. These specific goods give a more detailed picture of the transactions. Similarly, a surplus or deficit with the rest of the world provides some information, but it may be important to examine the relationship with specific countries. A country that has an overall trade surplus may nevertheless be in a deficit position relative to one or more of its trading partners. These specific trade relationships may be of more value than the general information for making business decisions.

In analyzing either the financial statements of a company or the BOP statements of a country, the potential investor or businessperson is interested in what occurred in the past, largely because this information can indicate what might occur in the future. The future is not usually a simple extrapolation of the past, however. To estimate future performance, one must understand what affected past performance as well as the changes in relevant factors likely to affect future performance.

Because the balance of payments statement is a historical description of transactions for a given period of time, a single statement is of limited use. Greater insight into future performance can be gained from assessing shifts in position in both the local and the global environments over time and analyzing changes and trends to understand why they occurred. The following examples illustrate such an analytical approach.

If a country has maintained a balance of trade surplus for an extended period but suddenly is in a deficit position, one might question the reason and wonder whether the deficit will continue. To determine why this occurred, one would examine specific aspects of the country's trade patterns; for example, perhaps a major trading partner imposed a new trade barrier or the home government eliminated export subsidies. To determine whether it will continue, one would identify other factors that could be important; for example, the formation of trading blocs might open new markets and increase exports or new developments in technology might decrease imports.

If a country's trade balance in services is increasing by a small but consistent amount over an extended period, one might wonder what caused it and how long it is likely to continue. To determine the cause, one would examine specific aspects of the country's trade patterns; for example, the cause may be a general increase in exports of services or an increase associated with one particular service for which there is a growing market. To determine whether this position will continue, one would identify other factors that may be important; for example, the worldwide market for services may be predicted to continue growing, or the specific service market currently being served may be expected to continue growing, or that market segment may be expecting increased competition.

If a country's inflows of capital normally exceed its outflows, one could question why it attracts capital and whether this situation is appropriate in the long-term. To determine why, one could look at the specific nature of the inflows; for example, they might be due to foreign investments or to foreign government aid or to World Bank loans. To determine the appropriateness of the situation, one could look at the foreign investment environment (including the nature of investments and the investment climate), the need for aid, or World Bank lending policies.

These examples illustrate that a balance of payments analysis involves more than simply looking at one statement and making a judgment that a country's situation is good or bad or that its currency is strong or weak. Surpluses are often equated with good and deficits with bad, but the situation is much more intricate than this. In effect, a good balance might be one that can be maintained over time. It is particularly misleading to examine one balance without considering the offsetting effect of others. For example, a deficit in trade in goods may be offset by a surplus in services; if this can be maintained, it may be considered good.

A country's BOP that is unstable and cannot be maintained represents a problem for which corrective action is needed. For example, a country consistently in a deficit position must constantly deplete its reserves. Such a situation can be sustained only to the extent that the country can continue to borrow externally. When the situation cannot be sustained, other changes must occur to bring the BOP situation back into a supportable position. Some likely changes to correct the situation follow.

1. Exchange rate changes – Exports, imports, investments, and loans are all affected by the relative value of a particular country's currency. A relatively undervalued currency means that exports are cheaper and imports more expensive; when currency is overvalued, the reverse is true. A BOP disequilibrium may, therefore, imply a currency value that is not at the equilibrium point. A currency revaluation would be expected to have a balancing effect on a country's BOP. Changes in currency values will take some time to be reflected in the BOP.

2. Domestic monetary and fiscal policy – Changes in domestic prices and income can have an impact on the BOP accounts. For example, decreased domestic prices will probably increase demand for domestic goods at the expense of imported goods and thus have an effect on the Current Account. Decreased domestic income might have a similar effect and might also decrease foreign investments, thus affecting the Capital Account. Implementing appropriate domestic policies can have a balancing effect on a country's BOP. These changes may be relatively minor and slow to be reflected in the BOP.

3. Trade and investment legislation – Offsetting legislation can be imposed in an attempt to correct BOP disequilibria. Such legislation might include trade and investment barriers and incentives. For example, if a deficit in trade in goods is seen to be a problem, the country may impose barriers to imports and offer incentives for exporters. If capital outflows are a problem, withholding taxes and other restrictions on these outflows could be imposed or incentives implemented to make the climate for inflows more attractive. These changes may have an immediate effect on the BOP, but they do not address the underlying problems causing the economic disequilibrium.

An international company can benefit from understanding and anticipating the reasons for surpluses or deficits in various accounts as well as government response to these balances. A thorough examination of a country's BOP statement gives the company a better understanding of the benefits and risks associated with doing business with that particular country. It is also important to recognize the relationships between investment and trade as illustrated in Exhibits 4.2 and 4.3. In the case of the People's Republic of China, for example, foreign direct investment as a percentage share in total exports rose from about 5 percent in 1988 to nearly 30 percent in 1993, going from US $20 billion to US $90 billion.

EXHIBIT 4.2 **Foreign Investment and Trade Linkages in Developing Countries**

A. Correlation Coefficients Between World FDI and Exports

	World Exports	Developed Countries' Exports	Developing Countries' Exports
World foreign direct investment	0.881	0.9118	0.786

B. Average Annual Rates of Change (Percentage)

	1970–1974	1975–1979	1980–1984	1985–1989
World foreign direct investment	26	13	4	34
World exports	30	15	3	11

Source: Foreign direct investment (FDI) data provided by the United Nations (Transportation Control and Movement Document, TCMD); export data provided by the statistical division of DESD.

International Monetary Systems

It is common today for countries to use currency as a means of economic exchange, in contrast to a barter system in which goods are exchanged for other goods of approximately equal value or to a system where goods are exchanged for gold or other precious objects that have an independently determined value. The use of currency facilitates buying and selling goods and services as the following examples illustrate.

In a barter system, the potential buyer may not have anything to trade for the desired goods; a farmer who raises chickens may want to purchase a dentist's service, but if the dentist is a vegetarian or does not like chicken, striking a bargain would be difficult. Establishing a trading agreement that seems fair to both parties is also often difficult; the dentist and the farmer might disagree on the number of chickens that should be exchanged for the extraction of a wisdom tooth even if the dentist wants chickens.

Payment with gold or other precious objects eliminates some of these difficulties because the precious objects have an objectively determined value. The farmer can sell chickens for a certain amount of gold and then use the gold to pay the dentist an agreed amount. The problem with this approach is that the means of exchange, such as gold, is often difficult to transport, and it may change its value so that buyers or sellers may feel cheated. The farmer may be able to carry the gold required for a wisdom tooth extraction but might find it impossible to carry around the gold needed for a child's orthodontic work. Or a dishonest farmer might shave small quantities from the gold bar and in effect cheat the dentist.

The complications and inconveniences associated with barter and gold resulted in today's common use of paper currency and coins. This facilitates domestic economic exchanges to a large extent. The international use of currency is more complicated, however, because each country usually requires its own currency to be used within its national borders (some countries do share a common currency; for example, several of the Caribbean island countries use a currency called the Eastern Caribbean currency).

Companies doing business across national borders often need to use different currencies and therefore must convert them from one denomination to another. The means by which this

EXHIBIT 4.3
**World Foreign Direct
Investment
and Exports**

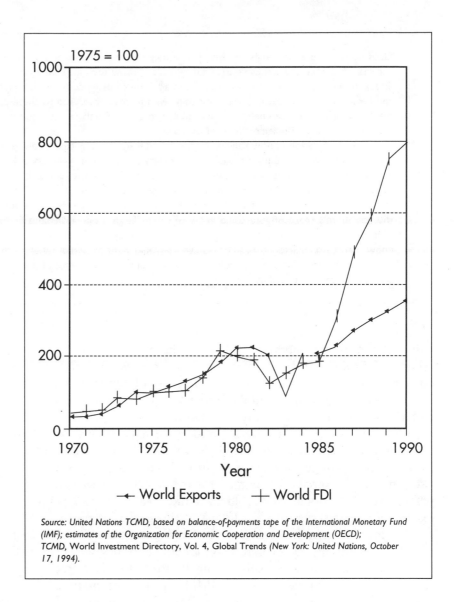

Source: United Nations TCMD, based on balance-of-payments tape of the International Monetary Fund
(IMF); estimates of the Organization for Economic Cooperation and Development (OECD);
TCMD, World Investment Directory, Vol. 4, Global Trends (New York: United Nations, October
17, 1994).

conversion is accomplished constitutes the international monetary system. In this section, we
will discuss only the overall characteristics of the international monetary system. Issues of
individual companies dealing with foreign exchange are considered in detail in Chapter 9.

Historical Overview of Foreign Exchange Rate Systems

In the first half of the 20th century, the international monetary system was based on a gold
standard (a practice used in various parts of the world for centuries). Countries kept a supply
of gold and printed currency, which represented its gold supply. Gold had a market-determined

Gold has been used throughout history as a medium of exchange because of several of its properties. It is relatively scarce and is thus considered valuable in many societies. Gold is also often considered beautiful and is in demand for decorative purposes. In addition to being considered beautiful, it can be worked and can be shaped into pieces of jewelry or coins with relative ease. Add to these properties its durability and the fact that it does not change when exposed to other metals and it is easy to see why it has been, and continues to be, a popular medium of exchange.

One explanation of how banking in the United Kingdom may have evolved concerns goldsmiths. When gold was used as a medium of exchange, ordinary people often kept a stock of gold; because this stock could be very valuable, it had to be kept in a safe place. Goldsmiths, because of their trade, also kept stocks of gold, which they kept in safes. The ordinary people would therefore have the goldsmith keep their gold and pay a small fee for the use of a safe. As more and more people took advantage of this opportunity the goldsmith's store of gold could grow to rather large proportions and people thought of him as very rich. Those who needed to borrow would therefore approach the goldsmith for a loan. The goldsmith knew that it was unlikely that all of his clients would want to withdraw all of their gold at the same time; therefore, he used the store of gold to provide loans to those whom he considered creditworthy. Thus, the banker came into being.

value; therefore, a country's currency value was determined from its currency in circulation relative to its stock of gold. In essence, currency was a useful substitute for gold and could be converted to gold at an agreed-upon price, or **a fixed exchange rate**.

This system became unstable during World War I, when many countries in need of money to pay for wartime expenditures printed money that was not backed by gold. The U.S. dollar at this stage was relatively stable and respected and was still based on the gold standard; therefore, countries began to keep U.S. dollars as reserves instead of gold. This system, known as the *gold exchange standard,* was formalized at a conference in 1944, which resulted in the Bretton Woods Agreement (named for the resort in New Hampshire where the meeting took place). The U.S. dollar held gold at a fixed value of $35 per ounce. Other countries could exchange their reserves of U.S. dollars at this exchange rate.

During this period, currencies had fixed stated values relative to the U.S. dollar. This value could fluctuate only by ±1 percent unless the currency was revalued to correct a fundamental disequilibrium. A major result of the Bretton Woods Agreement was the establishment of the International Monetary Fund (IMF) and the International Bank for Reconstruction and Development (World Bank). The roles of these institutions in the international monetary system are discussed separately in a subsequent section of this chapter. The system accepted at Bretton Woods worked for a period of time, but in the period 1967–1973 major dislocations occurred (for example, the British pound devalued by more than 14 percent) and concerns surfaced about the strength of the U.S. dollar. In response, a number of countries adopted essentially a floating exchange rate system.

The international community moved to a floating foreign exchange rate system formally during the 1976 Jamaica conference. A **floating exchange rate system** determines the value of a currency according to its supply and demand on the foreign exchange currency markets. Foreign currencies can be bought and sold at such markets. If governments do not intervene in the exchange of currencies, this system is called a **clean float**; when governments do intervene, it is said to be a **dirty float** or a **managed system**.

The Jamaica conference recognized the need for communication, cooperation, and consultation among countries regarding the international monetary system and foreign exchange rates. This meant that the foreign exchange system would be a managed system. The world has operated on this managed floating exchange rate system, to a large extent, since 1976. Market forces play an important role in determining exchange rates, but the current system is one of managed rates rather than freely floating exchange rates. The following statements summarize the monetary exchange situation as of 1995.

The larger market economies of the world have a managed floating exchange rate system. These countries allow their currencies to fluctuate relative to other currencies and be determined to a large extent by market forces of supply and demand. These countries attempt to manage their exchange rates, however. By buying and selling their own currencies on foreign exchange markets, by manipulating domestic interest rates, or by making agreements with other governments to buy and sell various currencies, for example, countries can influence the supply and demand for currencies.

Smaller market economies generally have adopted a system of tying their currencies to one of the major currencies. Each country has a fixed rate relative to the chosen currency that it maintains through its reserves of that currency. Its own currency fluctuates relative to others as the currency to which it is tied fluctuates.

Centrally controlled economies, such as the People's Republic of China, have fixed exchange rates determined by the government. Often these exchange rates have been unrealistically high, and the currencies have in effect, been unconvertible because foreigners are not willing to buy them at the fixed rate.

Closely linked economies (e.g., those with regional trade agreements) have adopted a version of a fixed-rate system whereby the currencies of the group of countries fluctuate relative to each other within only a narrow band, say ±1 percent. The formerly communist countries of Eastern Europe are in a state of change both politically and in terms of their monetary systems.

A floating exchange system seems normal to most Westerners today; and individuals, businesses, economies, and governments have generally evaluated the current international monetary system favorably. The floating exchange system is relatively new, however, and some people argue in favor of a return to the gold standard or some form of fixed exchange rate system.

These arguments gained strength in the mid-1990s, when a variety of currencies did not respond to government pressures. The Japanese yen, for example, was considered "too high" with negative consequences for Japanese exporters. In contrast, the U.S. dollar declined rapidly in spite of efforts to push up its value.

During this period it began to appear that the international monetary system had changed without major governments recognizing the changes. Increased speculation with currencies and technological developments that facilitate this speculation had forced changes in the international monetary system outside of the realm of government influence. This suggests that changes in the system may be forthcoming and that businesspeople need to remain current with changes and their likely impact on doing business.

Fixed versus Floating Exchange Rates

To understand the current international monetary system, one should consider the difference between a system in which the relative value of currencies is fixed and one in which these values fluctuate. To illustrate the difference between fixed and floating exchange rates, consider the U.S. dollar (US$) relative to other currencies, such as the Canadian dollar (C$) and the Japanese yen (¥). If exchange rates are fixed, then the US$ is worth a constant amount in C$ and ¥; this will not change in the short term unless one of the countries formally revalues its currency. Fixing US$1 at C$1.25 or ¥142.85 means that the various governments have agreed to these relative values. The value is often fixed to reflect the expected demand and supply for the currencies, but it does not change quickly in response to fluctuations in demand and supply. The value of these currencies changes only when it becomes evident that a disequilibrium has occurred and one of the countries formally increases or decreases the rate at which its currency is exchanged.

Both fixed and floating rate systems have advantages and disadvantages. The following summary identifies the major advantages and disadvantages from an international business perspective.

Floating exchange rates are constantly changing; therefore, companies that sign international agreements are at risk that the rates may move in an unfavorable direction. Fixed rates give a greater degree of certainty relative to future payments.

Fixed rates often change dramatically when a currency revalues up or down. Therefore, companies risk major losses if fixed rates are changed unexpectedly. Floating rates change constantly but by smaller amounts, thereby minimizing the degree of a potential loss.

Floating rates react to market pressures and encourage equilibrium of internal and external economies; therefore, a competitive company can benefit fully from the competitive advantages of these rates. Fixed rates introduce nonmarket forces, which may be more difficult to identify and anticipate.

Fixed rates provide a sense of security because they are known and controlled by government agreements. Floating rates are subject to unexpected shifts in demand and supply – for example, those created by speculators – and therefore can be difficult for companies to understand and anticipate.

The increased use of foreign currencies for investment, and buying and selling currencies to profit from changing rates, has had a major impact on the stability of currencies. When foreign currencies are used primarily for purchasing goods and services, changes in currency values tend to be small under a floating exchange rate system. In the mid-1990s, major shifts in investment in currencies resulted in fairly dramatic changes in currency values (this occurred in the case of the Mexican peso in 1995).

Currency Values

Currencies in a floating exchange rate system need to be converted from one denomination to another because they have different values. That is, one Japanese yen is not the same in value as one German deutsche mark or one Canadian dollar. The value of one currency relative to others depends on its supply and demand in the foreign exchange markets.

The foreign exchange market is distinguished from the domestic money market. One can think of the foreign exchange market as consisting of demand and supply for a currency outside of its home country. Exhibit 4.4 lists the major components of demand (uses) and supply (sources) for currencies outside their home countries.

EXHIBIT 4.4
External Supply and Demand for Currency (using the Australian currency as an example)

Supply	Demand
(A) payments for foreign goods and services	Payments by foreigners for (A) goods and services
(A) sent to foreigners (gifts, inheritances, etc.)	(A) sent by foreigners to U.S. residents
(A) invested outside of the United States	Money invested by foreigners in Australia
(A) transferred from Australia to foreign governments	Foreign government transactions in (A)

This demand and supply of a currency outside its home market can be thought of as similar to the demand and supply of any good. The demand and supply together usually determine the equilibrium price of the currency or, in this case, the rate at which that currency is exchanged for other currencies.

Although the exchange rate of various currencies can be determined partly by market forces, as explained, countries often do not allow the market to be the sole force determining exchange rates. A government's reaction results from exchange rates that affect its trade and payments balances. The strength or weakness of a currency encourages imports or exports and inflows or outflows of investment, as explained in the section on balance of payments.

If the fixed value of a particular currency differs substantially from its market value based on existing supply and demand, a black market in that currency is likely to develop. This is most likely to happen when a currency has a fixed value that is too high. Many communist countries in the past have had unrealistically high official values for their currencies. The result has been that other countries do not accept these currencies, thus making trade and investment more difficult for the communist countries. Further, their citizens have been willing to change local currency for foreign currencies at a much better rate than the official rate, thereby creating a black market for the overvalued currency.

The People's Republic of China has had two official currencies – the Foreign Exchange Currency (FEC), which foreigners use, and Renminbi (RMB), which locals use. When the official exchange rate was approximately FEC4 for US$1, and FEC1 was equal to RMB1. Foreigners found themselves constantly approached by locals of all ages, including old women and young children, asking to change money. The locals were generally willing to change foreign currencies at about six times the official rate; thus, a US$ could be exchanged for RMB24.

Exhibit 4.5 illustrates how a fixed exchange rate is affected by supply and demand. In part a of the diagram, there is a certain demand for the currency on foreign exchange markets (D_{fx}) and a certain supply (S_{fx}). P_e is the market-determined equilibrium price of fx, and P_f is the government-determined fixed price. If P_f is at the equilibrium rate of P_e, then demand and supply match each other. If, as the diagram illustrates, the exchange rate P_f is above P_e, then supply is greater than demand; but if P_f is below P_e, demand outstrips supply.

EXHIBIT 4.5   Fixed Exchange Rate: (a) Fixed Price (P_f) Does Not Equal Equilibrium Price (P_e); (b) Effects of Shifts in Demand and Supply

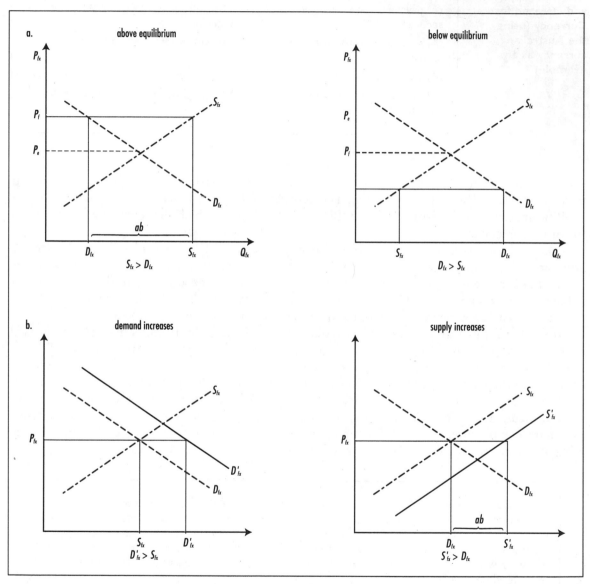

Similarly, as illustrated in part b, if demand increases (perhaps because other countries are importing more of the country's products and paying for them in that currency), the exchange rate will not respond because it is fixed by mutual agreement. The result is an imbalance, with demand for the currency greater than supply. Equally, an imbalance occurs if the supply changes. If the supply increases, say, because the country's citizens have increased the amount of currency that they have sent out of the country – perhaps seeking better yielding investments or to families abroad – the exchange rate still cannot change, and supply will be greater than demand.

In Exhibit 4.5, when supply exceeds demand by *ab,* the government will have to buy this excess on the international currency markets at the fixed rate to maintain that rate. Similarly when demand is greater than the supply, the government must intervene to sell its own currency to meet the excess demand; hence, it holds reserves for this purpose.

Minor short-term changes in demand and supply will not result in revaluations of a currency in a fixed system. If the changes are persistent and do not offset each other, the pressure on the currency over time will force a revaluation. The pressure the currency experiences may take the following forms.

Overvaluation means that the price of the currency is too high relative to other currencies and, therefore, supply is greater than demand. Suppose, for example, that the Canadian dollar is overvalued; this means that

► Exports from Canada to the rest of the world will fall because they will be relatively expensive.
► Imports to Canada will rise because they will be seen as inexpensive.
► Canada's trade balances will show a persistent deficit because imports will persistently exceed exports as long as the fixed high price continues (note that only the trade balance is in deficit; this does not refer to the overall balance of payments).
► Lower exports and increased external investment will decrease employment at home, thereby increasing political pressure from the unemployed and their representatives.
► Investment strategies can also put pressure on the currency: foreign investments in Canada may decrease because of expectations that the currency will be devalued; investments in Canada may also decrease because setting up a subsidiary there would be relatively costly. Canadian investments in foreign locations may increase because Canadians believe they can benefit from their dollar's high value before it is devalued.

Undervaluation means that the price of the currency is too low relative to other currencies, and therefore, supply is lower than demand. Suppose, for example, that the Japanese yen (¥) is undervalued; this means that

► Japanese exports will increase because foreigners see Japanese goods as good buys, and conversely, the high price of imported goods in ¥ will make them unavailable to many Japanese citizens, causing imports to decrease.
► Japan's trade balances will show a persistent surplus because exports will exceed imports; these persistent trade surpluses will anger trading partners.
► Higher prices for imports may be passed to customers by domestic producers and marketers and therefore lead to increased inflation.
► Foreigners will want to increase investment in Japan because they can get a lot for their money, while Japanese citizens may not invest as much abroad; increased foreign ownership of Japanese domestic industry, real estate, and so forth may be resented by locals.

Exhibit 4.6 summarizes the possible effects of overvaluation and undervaluation in a fixed exchange rate system. The pressures of a disequilibrium situation eventually mean that, if a currency is overvalued, it will be devalued and, if it is undervalued, it will be revalued upward.

EXHIBIT 4.6
Possible Effects of Overvaluation or Undervaluation in a Fixed Exchange Rate System

Overvaluation	Undervaluation
Decreased exports, increased imports	Increased exports, decreased imports
Deficit trade balance	Surplus trade balance
Decreased investment by foreigners, increased investment abroad	Decreased purchase of foreign-produced goods by locals
Increased unemployment	Trade surplus resented by trading partners
Increased likelihood of the development of a black market	Increased inflation
	Increased investment by foreigners, decreased investment abroad

In a fixed system, such changes usually do not occur often, but they can be dramatic and sudden. If changes do not take place, a black market is likely to develop.

Demand and supply can also be used to illustrate a floating exchange rate system. In this case, changes in exchange rates occur quickly in response to changes in supply and demand. These changes are likely to be relatively minor because they occur frequently. Exhibit 4.7 graphically depicts this situation.

In the graph, the supply of foreign exchange is represented by S_{fx}, and demand by D_{fx}. The original equilibrium point is at the price P_e; that is, the supply of and demand for this currency on the foreign exchange markets is such that this is the market-determined exchange rate. If the supply of this currency increases to S_{fx1}, perhaps because of investment in foreign locations,

EXHIBIT 4.7   **Floating Exchange Rate: Effects of Shifts in Supply and Demand**

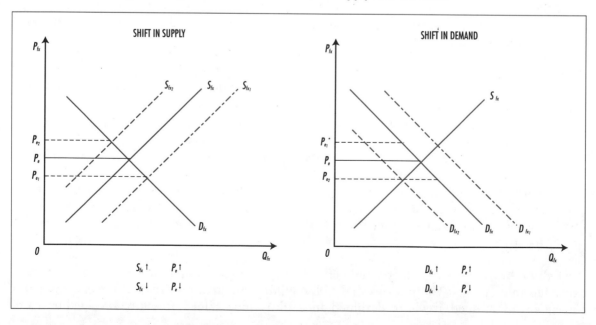

while the demand for the currency remains constant, then the price will fall to P_{e1}. If instead the supply decreases, the price will rise to P_{e2}. If demand for the currency increases to D_{fx1}, perhaps because foreigners want to buy more goods from the country in question while the supply of the currency remains constant, then the price will rise to P_{e1}. If instead demand decreases, the price will fall to P_{e2}.

Floating exchange rates also react and contribute to the domestic economic situation. These rates should lead to equilibrium externally and internally. For example, let us assume that all of the BOP accounts balance except for the trade account, then if imports are greater than exports (a trade deficit), the demand for the domestic currency outside the home country will be lower than the supply (demand related to paying for exports and supply related to paying for imports). This will lead to a fall in the price of the currency. As the price falls, exports will become relatively cheaper abroad and will increase; conversely, imports will become more expensive in domestic terms and will decline. This leads to a more balanced trade situation.

If exports are greater than imports (a trade surplus), the demand for the domestic currency outside the home country will be greater than the supply. This will lead to a rise in the price of the currency. As the price rises, exports will become relatively more costly abroad and will fall; conversely, imports will increase as they become cheaper. This leads to a more balanced trade situation.

If we assume that all BOP accounts balance except the investment account, then if foreign investments (say, Japanese investments in the United States) are greater than domestic investments in the foreign locations (e.g., U.S. investments in Japan), the supply of domestic currency (US$) in the foreign country (Japan) will be lower than the demand. That is, the Japanese will want US$ for their investments, but these dollars will not be readily available in Japan. This situation will lead to an increase in the price of the currency (US$ in Japan), which will make investments less attractive for foreigners (the Japanese) and foreign investments in the foreign country (Japan) more attractive for domestic investors (U.S. residents). This should result in a more balanced investment situation.

Currency Strength

Currencies are often referred to in terms of the **currency strength** or weakness, or in terms of increases or decreases in values. It is not always clear what this means and whether it is positive or negative. In fact, describing a currency as strong or weak is quite misleading; it should be described as strengthening or weakening as the following illustrates.

Exchange rates are quoted in terms of the relative relationship of two currencies. The US$ can be quoted relative to the Canadian dollar as US$1 = C$1.25 or C$1 = US$.80. Equally, US$ or C$ could be quoted relative to Hong Kong dollars as US$1 = HK$6 or HK$1 = US$.17, or C$1 = HK$4.8 or HK$1 = C$.21.

A currency may be described as worth more than one currency and less than another. Sometimes being worth more is equated with being stronger and being worth less with weaker. The Canadian dollar is worth less than the U.S. dollar and might be considered weaker, but it is worth more than the Hong Kong dollar and might be considered stronger in that respect. This statement may be quite misleading, however, because if the Canadian and Hong Kong currencies maintain their value consistently, then they could both be considered strong currencies.

If the Canadian dollar rises relative to the U.S. dollar, then it would be appropriate to say that it has become stronger but only in relation to the U.S. currency. At the same time, it could fall relative to the Hong Kong dollar and therefore be described as weaker in relation to the Hong Kong currency.

It is difficult to make blanket statements about the strength or weakness of a particular currency. When general statements of this type are made, they can mean one of several things:

▶ The currency has changed in the same direction relative to all of the major currencies in the world.
▶ The currency has changed in the same direction relative to the average of a group of currencies (a "basket" of currencies).
▶ The currency has changed relative to its major trading partner or a small group of major trading partners.
▶ The currency has changed relative to a major currency often used for comparative purposes, such as the US$.

From an international business perspective, it is important to distinguish among these meanings because a specific company may be concerned with one of them but not the others. Under some circumstances, specific currency movements will be of interest; while under other circumstances, more general information will be more useful. For example, a Nigerian company doing business with France and using French francs is concerned with the value of the Nigerian currency relative to the franc. If the company has agreed to use US$, then it will be concerned with movements of both the Nigerian and French currencies relative to the US$. A Taiwanese company evaluating alternative investment opportunities in Malaysia, Singapore, and Korea might be more interested in the general strengths or weaknesses of their currencies and might compare them all to one currency such as the US$ or some basket index of currencies.

There is a popular tendency to interpret strength in a currency as good and weakness as bad. This assessment is not necessarily appropriate. The international business activity affected by the currency in question determines whether strength and weakness are positive or negative. A firm seeking export markets will likely view strength of a foreign currency positively because a strong currency indicates that the market in the foreign country can afford the firm's products and that payment in the foreign currency will be acceptable. In contrast, a company seeking a source of supplies might believe that a supplying country's weaker currency is beneficial because the company's currency would be worth more in the supplying country.

> Canada's exports soared 21 percent last year to a historic $219.4 billion. Imports also rose sharply, but the trade surplus was in Canada's favor at more than $17 billion. Canada's major trading partner, the United States, bought 82 percent of the total 1994 Canadian exports. Of Canadian imports, 77 percent came from the United States. (A. C. MacPherson & Co., Inc. 1995, p. 1)
>
> Much of the reason for Canada's burgeoning exports is the relatively low level of the Canadian dollar, which makes its export very competitive on international markets.

A company that is assessing the currency situation should do so, as the previous examples illustrate, in terms of the particular decisions that will be affected by the currencies being assessed.

Usually, the currency's current strength as well as its performance over time should be considered. Companies are often concerned not only with the current exchange rates but also how they have changed over time. The stability or volatility of a currency – how often it changes and to what degree – and the trends it appears to follow often give a better picture of a country's foreign exchange situation than simply its current relationship to some other currency.

In addition to examining exchange rates to determine what impact they might have on a particular business decision, changes in exchange rates can help identify changes in the business environment in a particular country. A sudden strengthening of a currency, for example, could be attributed to a change in government, lowering corporate taxes, increasing central bank rates, new union regulations, incentives for exports, or any of a number of other changes in the business environment.

The previous sections have defined and explained the BOP accounts and the international monetary system in some detail because of their importance to international companies. The following section briefly considers two major international institutions and their relationship to the maintenance of the international monetary system. These are the International Monetary Fund and the International Bank for Reconstruction and Development (usually referred to as the World Bank).

The IMF and the World Bank

The International Monetary Fund (IMF) and the World Bank were established during the Bretton Woods meeting, and they continue to play an important role in the international monetary system. These institutions were established within the context of a fixed exchange rate monetary system, and their original roles reflect this. As the international monetary system has changed, the goals and activities of the two institutions have changed to reflect the new reality. The following discussion examines the original and changing roles of these two international institutions.

The IMF

The **International Monetary Fund** consists of member countries that elect to join together and follow a set of agreed-upon procedures. Each country pays a deposit to the IMF and receives voting rights and the entitlement to borrow from the fund. The deposit required depends on the country's economic size and, in turn, determines its voting rights. This system gives greater weight to the more economically developed member countries. Exhibit 4.8 details the IMF's original objectives.

A major concern originally was to maintain stable exchange rates by making IMF credit available to member countries to avoid changes in their fixed exchange rates. Only when a "fundamental disequilibrium," as reflected in a persistent balance of payments imbalance (either a persistent surplus or deficit), was evident were currency values to be changed by more than 1 percent.

EXHIBIT 4.8
**The IMF's Original
Objectives**

> ▶ To promote international monetary cooperation
> ▶ To expand world trade and investment
> ▶ To reduce government restrictions on international payments
> ▶ To make credit available to facilitate the maintenance of stable exchange rates
>   during temporary balance of payments imbalances
> ▶ To reduce the amplitude of balance of payments deficits and surpluses
>
> *Source: International Monetary Fund 1944.*

The major role of the IMF in the current international monetary system is as a lender to countries that experience persistent balance of payments deficits. The aim is not to avoid changes in exchange rates but rather to allow the countries the opportunity to make economic changes to redress imbalances. The IMF often imposes conditions of economic reform on countries receiving its loans. The long-term intent of these conditions is improved economic conditions, but the borrowing countries often see them as overly restrictive.

The World Bank

The **World Bank** was founded to help reconstruct European countries that had suffered economic hardships because of World War II. This reconstruction was accomplished by lending these countries funds provided by member countries.

The World Bank's current focus is quite different from its original purpose. Today the bank is involved mainly in the development of the poorer countries of the world. In addition to its public funding base, the bank raises money on the private capital markets and lends to developing countries for large-scale, long-term development projects. This approach allows high-risk borrowing countries to obtain money at better terms than they could on their own.

Changes in the IMF and the World Bank

The International Monetary Fund and the World Bank were created over 50 years ago in a very different economic climate than that of the 1990s. The IMF was intended to monitor a system of fixed exchange rates and help countries deal with short-term financial imbalances. The World Bank's major concern was financing reconstruction after World War II (note that the World Bank's formal name is the International Bank for Reconstruction and Development). Today, some people wonder whether these institutions any longer play an international role and, if so, what it should be. The answers to these questions are currently being debated by governments around the world, and changes in the mandates of both the IMF and the World Bank are likely before the turn of the century. The leaders of the Group of 7 (G7), the richest countries of the world, have promised to determine a framework for international organizations to prepare them for the 21st century. Leaders of non-G7 countries believe they should have more input into decisions about these institutions. New frameworks, and new mandates, seem likely, but what exactly these will be is not yet clear.

Summary

This chapter has examined the balance of payments and related accounts as well as the international monetary system, the IMF, and the World Bank. International transactions are all tied to these systems in some way; therefore, it is important for companies to understand how they work and what they mean. This chapter has explored these subjects to give students an appreciation of their impact on international business operations as well as an awareness of their value in assessing international business opportunities.

**MINI-CASE
Eureka
Management
Consultants**

Eureka is a small management consulting company located in southwestern Ontario, Canada, just across the Canadian–U.S. border. The company specializes in strategic planning workshops for international clients. The company consists of its founder, Donald Wood, and three associates. The company has clients in Canada, the Caribbean, China, and the United States.

Eureka has an expansion budget of approximately C$500,000 and has been considering establishing a small subsidiary in the United States. The company has analyzed the situation and believes that an office in the United States would be a profitable expansion; however, the company has a policy of allocating no more than 30 percent of its expansion budget to one country. This policy is based on the founder's conviction that expansion should not be tied to only one location.

The company has assessed the needed investment in a U.S. subsidiary to be approximately US$120,000. The exchange rate for the period 1993–1994 averaged around C$1 to US$.75. Eureka has been delaying its U.S. investment because it would represent more than 30 percent of its expansion budget.

If the Canadian dollar were to strengthen to C$1 to US$.80, Mr. Wood would reevaluate expansion to the United States.

Discussion Issues

1. Discuss how the decisions made by Eureka Management Consultants relate to the balance of payments accounts.
2. If the Canadian dollar and the U.S. dollar were fixed relative to each other, how would this affect Mr. Wood's decisions?
3. Identify the current value of the Canadian dollar relative to the U.S. dollar. At this exchange rate, should Mr. Wood invest in the United States?

Discussion Questions

1. Why should a firm doing business internationally be concerned with a country's balance of payments?
2. Would you describe the current exchange rate system as freely floating or managed?
3. What would you see as the major advantages of a fixed exchange rate system? A system based on a gold standard?

Assignments

1. Select a country and research its balance of payments statements over a five-year period.
   a. Report deficits and/or surpluses in the various balances.
   b. Based on the country's imports and exports, what do you see as its likely strengths and weaknesses?
   c. What trends can you identify over the five-year period?
2. Select a country and research its foreign exchange rates over a five-year period.
   a. Report changes in the currency's value relative to the U.S. dollar.
   b. Identify its major trading partner and examine changes in the currency's value relative to the partner's currency.
   c. What trends can you identify over the five-year period?
3. Select an international institution (e.g., the World Bank, the IMF, the OECD, United Nations Commission on Transnational Corporations) and research its recent activities. Discuss how these activities might be important to international firms.

Selected References

A. C. MacPherson & Co., Inc., *Stock Market Bulletin,* no. 106 (March 1995), p. 1.

Blair, D. C., "Canadian Cattle Drive into Soviet Market," *Canadian Business Review* (Summer 1990), p. 26.

Caves, R. E., and R. W. Jones, *World Trade and Payments* (Boston: Little, Brown, 1981).

The Economist, "Can Pay, Will Pay" (June 2, 1990), p. 83.

The Economist, "Trading Places" (July 7, 1990), p. 32.

The Economist, "Taming Little Dragons" (July 14, 1990), p. 67.

The Economist, "Business This Week" (August 4, 1990), p. 49.

Eiteman, D. K., and A. I. Stonehill, *Multinational Business Finance* (Reading, Mass.: Addison-Wesley, 1983).

Farmer, R. N., and J. F. Farmer, *Lust for Lucre: Explorations in International Finance* (Bloomington, Ind.: Cedarwood Press, 1986).

Gray, Peter H., *International Trade, Investment, and Payments* (Boston: Houghton Mifflin, 1979).

International Monetary Fund, *Articles of Agreement* (Washington, D.C.: IMF, 1944), Article I.

McKinnon, R. I., *Money in International Exchange: The Convertible Currency System* (New York: Oxford University Press, 1979).

Root, F. R., *International Trade and Investment* (Cincinnati: South-Western, 1984).

U.S. Department of Commerce, Bureau of Economic Analysis and Bureau of the Census, *Survey of Current Business* (January 1995).

Walter, I., and K. Areskog, *International Economics* (New York: John Wiley, 1981).

Willett, Thomas D., *Floating Exchange Rates and International Monetary Reform* (Washington, D.C.: American Enterprise Institute for Public Policy Research, 1977).

World Investment Flows

LEARNING OBJECTIVES

After reading this chapter, you should be able to

▶ Define foreign direct investment and outline the reasons why it occurs.

▶ Discuss the objectives of a firm and its host country relative to foreign direct investment.

▶ Explain the advantages and disadvantages of foreign direct investment from the point of view of both the firm and host country.

▶ Identify the main incentives and restrictions associated with foreign direct investment.

▶ Discuss the relationship between economic development and investment flows.

KEY TERMS

▶ Foreign portfolio investment

▶ Foreign direct investment (FDI)

▶ Factors of production

▶ International product life cycle

▶ Profit repatriation

▶ Economic development

▶ Gross domestic product (GDP)

▶ Less developed countries (LDCs)

▶ Newly industrializing countries (NICs)

▶ Centrally planned economies

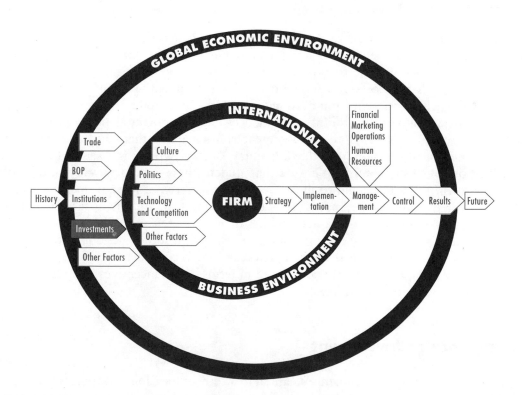

THOUGHT STARTERS

▶ A U.S. trade bill that included amendments that would have made it illegal for a U.S. subsidiary in Canada to do business with the communist government of Cuba was countered by a Canadian order forcing Canadian firms, including subsidiaries of U.S. firms operating in Canada, to ignore any U.S. prohibition on their trade with Cuba.

▶ It should be noted at the outset that foreign banks are enthusiastic and cooperative in promoting foreign investment in Canada, emphasizing businesses started by their national investors.

(Jarvis and Kirk 1986)

▶ The EC's competition law means that "the European Commission has exclusive rights to police big mergers and takeovers. The new regime offers businesses a 'one stop shop.' "

(The Economist 1990)

Introduction

This chapter examines foreign direct investment from a general perspective. It considers the reasons why foreign investment occurs and the determinants of the degree and direction of such investment. It discusses the objectives of a firm and its host country relative to investment and examines the benefits and costs of foreign investment as well as the incentives and regulations associated with such investment from both perspectives. The chapter also considers the impact of the level of development on the investment decision and potential new opportunities for investment. The chapter looks at foreign investment from a macro rather than a micro perspective. The foreign investment decision from the individual firm's viewpoint is discussed in Chapter 9.

The purpose of this chapter is to ensure that students have a broad understanding of why foreign investment takes place and to illustrate current patterns of foreign investment. Foreign investment involves many parties, particularly the investing firm and the host country in which such investment takes place. This chapter explores their distinct views of the investment process. Such distinct views of investment result from the differing, and sometimes conflicting, objectives of governments and investors. These distinct views can lead to conflict between host governments and international companies and are considered in terms of the incentives and restrictions that countries provide for foreign investors.

Defining *Foreign Investment*

Foreign investment is the commitment of capital in a foreign location in anticipation of returns. This investment can take several forms: public investment by governments, private investment by individuals or groups, or investment by firms. A distinction is usually made between portfolio investment and direct investment. We will focus here on direct investment, but the following sections distinguish between the two types.

Foreign Portfolio Investment

Foreign portfolio investment refers to the purchase of foreign stocks, bonds, or other securities in anticipation of returns. Companies, individuals, private groups, or public bodies can all invest in foreign locations through such purchases. For example, Rolls Royce (a British firm) might use its reserve funds to buy a few shares of American Express (a U.S. company), or a Japanese woman might purchase shares in Bell Canada on the Toronto Stock Exchange. A U.S. university pension fund could invest some funds in Japanese securities. The government in the United Arab Emirates might choose to buy long-term bonds in France with some of its oil revenues. The type of foreign investment in these examples is usually referred to as *portfolio investment*. This investment is made because of anticipated returns in the form of dividends, interest, or capital gains; the investors are not usually interested in establishing any control or management interest through the investment.

Foreign Direct Investment

Foreign direct investment (FDI), in contrast to portfolio investment, usually involves managerial commitment to foreign operations, which is the form of investment most firms prefer. This type of investment also anticipates returns, but specific returns may not be required from a particular investment. For example, a firm could choose to invest in locally unprofitable operations in a particular location in order to preempt the competition and thereby gain a global strategic advantage.

To be considered foreign direct investment, a movement of capital across borders usually takes place. This movement of capital for direct investment is often accompanied by transfers of management, technical, or other specialized personnel; technology or other expertise; or equipment. For example, if a Japanese company makes a direct investment in a Brazilian automotive plant, it will probably transfer much more than financial resources to ensure that the Brazilian operation is productive and profitable.

The foreign direct investment process is a complex one, and companies choose to engage in such investment for many reasons. The following section identifies and describes some of these reasons.

Explaining Foreign Direct Investment

Chapter 3 examined the reasons for trade between countries. An example in that chapter considered two countries, Alpha and Beta, which would trade wine and cheese. That example illustrated the benefits associated with Alphans specializing in wine production while Betans specialized in cheese production. In the trade example, one would conclude that cheese producers in Alpha, over time, would move to wine production, and similarly, in Beta, over time, wine producers would shift to producing cheese.

Rather than changing industries, the producers in Alpha and Beta could consider FDI. Alphan cheese producers might invest in cheese production in Beta, and Betan wine producers could establish wineries in Alpha. These producers would be likely to choose the foreign direct investment alternative if the returns associated with it were greater than those that were possible at home.

In the simple Alpha-Beta situation, for example, it is possible that the Alphan cheese producers could use their expertise at cheese making and take advantage of other resources available in Beta to realize returns on their investment. In contrast, they may find it costly to become wine producers at home because they would be competing with already established producers.

This example illustrates why companies might logically choose investment even when countries trade freely with each other. The following additional explanations of investment will help you understand why foreign direct investment takes place.

Factors of Production

Classical investment theory focuses on profit maximization and says that factors of production will move to the location where the highest returns are possible. If all **factors of production** (inputs into the production process) could move easily from one location to another, then labor would move to areas in which it was scarce, raw materials to areas in which they were scarce, and so on because each would get better returns in these new locations. This suggests that capital will move from countries where it is abundant to those where it is scarce. Foreign direct investment will flow from countries with an abundance of capital to those without it.

In addition, some factors of production are more mobile than others. Some inputs, such as land and natural resources, cannot be relocated. Some, like labor, may choose not to relocate for noneconomic reasons. Some governments restrict the movements of other inputs. Although many governments restrict the movement of capital, financial resources have generally been freer to move than other factors of production. This has encouraged foreign direct investors to take advantage of abundant nonmobile resources elsewhere.

This approach explains foreign direct investment, in brief, as the movement of capital from areas in which it is abundant to those in which it is scarce to take advantage of opportunities provided by the abundance of other factors of production. For example, savings rates in Japan during the 1980s were relatively high (averaging approximately 12 percent) and provided an abundance of capital for investment. Consequently, Japanese corporations engaged in a high degree of foreign direct investment in the United States, where savings rates were only about 5 percent and certain resources, such as land, were more readily available than in Japan.

International Product Life Cycle

In the mid-1960s, faculty members at Harvard University proposed another explanation of trade and investment patterns. This concept focused on the product life cycle and its relationship to production decisions. Based on observations of U.S. companies, the Harvard professors concluded that patterns of trade and investment were closely related to a product's stage in its life cycle. This concept is referred to as the **international product life cycle** concept and is described as follows.

Products are developed, initially, in response to domestic or home-market needs. During the early stages of product development, modifications in reaction to feedback from the domestic market are made and, therefore, production occurs near the domestic home market. As a product becomes well accepted at home and the firm's production experience grows, markets will develop in other countries similar to the home country, and domestic producers will export to these locations. Potential competitors will appear in these countries over time, and foreign direct investment may be the necessary reaction to competition. When the product matures and competition increases, efficiency and cost reduction concerns dictate production locations. Producers seek out low-cost locations and economies of scale during the maturity stage of the life cycle.

In summary, products in the birth and early growth stages of the product life cycle are produced at home; products in the later growth and early maturity stages of the cycle are produced in several locations to serve each of several foreign markets. Products in the late maturity and declining stages of the cycle are produced in a few locations where overall costs are minimized.

New and innovative products tend to originate in the more developed, wealthier countries. These countries have the resources to allocate to the development of such innovations and support the demand for new products. Other industrialized countries usually are the next users of new products, and direct investment often takes place initially among these more developed countries. When products mature or decline, production is likely to move to the less developed countries where costs are relatively low, according to the international product life cycle concept.

Chapter 8 covers the impact of the international product life cycle on competitive strategies and technological development.

Firm-Specific Strengths

Foreign direct investment can also be said to occur because firms are seeking to make the best possible use of the strengths that they have developed over time. This explanation of investment suggests that firms develop strengths based on the resources and markets at home but that over time these resources and markets become limiting. There is, therefore, an incentive to invest in foreign locations where these strengths can be used to better advantage.

Some Canadian companies, for example, have developed a strength in utilizing natural resources such as lumber, water, and minerals because of their relative abundance in Canada. This ability can be used to good advantage in many other locations around the world where similar natural resources exist; therefore, these companies will likely invest in some of these other locations.

Market and Location Differences

Foreign direct investment can also be explained by variations in markets and locations. These variations can be evident in a wide variety of circumstances, ranging from differential tariffs and trade barriers through varied government regulations and laws to different cultural and personal preferences. The existence of such differences from country to country provides opportunities for companies to benefit from direct investment in foreign locations.

For example, a firm whose product must be adapted substantially for different markets might choose to produce different versions in each of the locations in order to make appropriate modifications and react quickly to local needs. Another firm might invest in a particular foreign location to take advantage of incentives offered by that government or to avoid trade barriers that would limit its ability to serve the market through exports.

> The Japanese automakers substantially increased their foreign investment in U.S. plants during the latter half of the 1980s to avoid the trade barriers in the form of quotas previously imposed by the U.S. government.

Additional Observations

There are many reasons for foreign direct investment, as the previous explanations indicate. Hence, no one theory of foreign direct investment is fully supported by the empirical evidence of foreign direct investment. Patterns of investment reflect varied reasons for investment.

Even though the data in the tables in exhibits 5.7–5.12 appear to be precise and come from good sources, they may not be precise because estimating the magnitude of foreign direct investment is complex and often incorrect. One approach is to sum the yearly totals of all investments. This may not be completely accurate, however, because it does not consider current values (e.g., the value of an investment made in 1980 can be worth much more or less in 1990 than its original cost), divestment through high transfer payments is not included (e.g., companies may decrease the value of a foreign investment through payments made from the subsidiary to a headquarters), and investments may be double counted (e.g., if a U.S. company invests in Hong Kong, and the company in Hong Kong invests in the People's Republic of China, the investment will appear twice). There is general agreement, however, that the degree of foreign direct investment is large and increasing.

Globally, FDI inflows more than doubled in nominal terms in the period from 1975 to 1985, and they reached a record high in 1981 (see Exhibit 5.8, later in the chapter). In 1975, the United States was the source of more than half the total capital invested abroad, but by 1985 it was providing only 25 percent. In 1985, Western Europe had shifted from being the major host region for FDI to being the world's largest source; it was the dominant supplier with 50 percent. The main investing countries from Western Europe were the United Kingdom (15 percent of the total in 1985), the Federal Republic of Germany (9 percent), and the Netherlands (6 percent). Japan's share of FDI went from 6 percent in 1975 to 11 percent in 1985.

The following discussion briefly considers the roles of selected countries as investors and recipients of foreign investment.

> ▶ Australia (Royal Bank 1986a) – Traditionally, Australia has welcomed foreign investment, policies have been designed to encourage capital inflows, and the country has a strong net capital inflow. The United States, the United Kingdom, and Japan are the major sources of foreign investment, but inflows from the countries in the Association of South East Asian Nations (ASEAN) are increasing. The Foreign Investment Review Board (FIRB), established in 1976 as an advisory board, reviews certain types of proposals

by foreign interests. Generally, the government is flexible in administering its foreign investment guidelines.

▶ India (Royal Bank 1986b) – Foreign investment in India is tightly controlled. The Foreign Exchange Regulation Act sets the permissible levels of foreign equity ownership for various sectors of the economy. Companies that export their entire production or are located in a free trade zone can retain full ownership; otherwise, maximum foreign equity levels are stipulated and vary from sector to sector. All proposals for foreign investment require government approval. In addition, approval is needed to import machinery and equipment; issue new capital stock; and repatriate assets, service payments, and profit remittances. The largest group of foreign investors has been composed of nonresident Indians, and government policy has encouraged this group through relatively liberal policies.

▶ Japan (Royal Bank 1987; United Nations Centre on Transnational Corporations [UNCTC] 1988) – Following World War II, Japan limited foreign involvement in its economy, and until 1980, Japanese investments abroad grew faster than foreign investments in Japan. In 1973, Japan began to open itself to foreign firms, and, in 1980, a new law – the Foreign Exchange and Foreign Trade Control Law – freed many investments from government control, although they are still subject to review. The liberalization of the foreign investment climate has led to increased foreign investment in Japan, and prospects for further investment appear to be good. Japan's investments overseas are also growing, and the United States has absorbed significant volumes of Japanese investment.

▶ The United States (UNCTC 1988) – Since World War II, U.S. companies have been major foreign direct investors. Much of this investment has been in other developed countries, particularly the European countries and Canada. The United States remains a major source of foreign direct investment but also receives a substantial degree of investment from foreigners. Between 1975 and 1985, the inflows of FDI to the United States multiplied 7.5 times. In the 1970s, this FDI was largely from Western European firms, but more recently Japan's FDI has grown considerably. The United States is generally favorable toward FDI, but a number of sectors, such as nuclear energy, domestic air transportation, broadcasting, and shipping, are closed to it.

Objectives of Foreign Direct Investment

Many stakeholders are affected by a company's decision to make a foreign direct investment. The home country and parties in the home country are affected because the investment leaves the country and returns on it will come back. The host country is affected because it receives the investment with attendant benefits and drawbacks. Third countries (neither home nor host) and parties in those countries are also affected because the investment does not take place there, including its benefits and problems. The concerns of these countries and groups are important, and international companies should consider them, but the objectives of these third countries tend to be peripheral to the foreign investment decision. The objectives of the firm itself and the host country (the country receiving the investment) are clearly fundamental to the decision. The following discussion examines the objectives of the investing firm and the receiving country.

The Investing Firm's Objectives

The earlier discussion of the reasons for foreign direct investment indicated the possible objectives of the investing firm. In general terms, the firm wants an acceptable return on its investment, a relatively risk-free environment in which to operate, and host country operations that fit its overall strategy and structure.

The Host Country's Objectives

The host country accepts foreign direct investment because of its potential benefits. These benefits may accrue to particular individuals or to society as a whole, but the benefits must be seen to outweigh any costs associated with the investment. The foreign investment implies the presence of a foreign entity in the local economy and thus a degree of foreign influence on the local economy. This needs to be balanced against the degree to which foreign investment contributes to the host country's development and economic goals. Many average people think of foreign direct investment as negative. For example, a survey in the U.S. in 1988 asked a representative sample of adults how they felt about foreign investors – 74 percent agreed that FDI causes a loss of economic control because foreign investors can withdraw their money at any time; 77 percent favored a law to limit the extent of foreign investment; 89 percent believed that foreign investors should be required to register with the government (*Wall Street Journal*, 1988).

Potential Conflicts

Conflicts often occur because investing firms and their host countries have different objectives that each party needs to understand so they can be resolved. Extensive negotiations are often necessary to reach agreement on the specifics of a direct investment. Considering the investment from the two different viewpoints of the investing firm and the host government is helpful in understanding the reasons why conflicts arise.

Foreign Direct Investment Benefits and Costs to Host

To illustrate the possible conflicts between a foreign investor and its host country, we examine two extreme positions. At one extreme, the investment is considered from the viewpoint of the investor, which focuses on the benefits of investment to the host. At the other extreme, we consider the investment from the viewpoint of the host government, which examines the cost of the investment to its society.

If one asked a typical multinational company (foreign investor) about the impact of its foreign direct investment on host countries, the response would likely be in positive terms. If one asked a businessperson in the host country, the response might be more cautious. Exhibit 5.1 suggests the different perspectives that a foreign investor and a host-country businessperson might have to the same investment situation.

EXHIBIT 5.1
Different Viewpoints of Foreign Investor and Local Businessperson FDI

Foreign Investor

▶ We provide capital that the host economy needs. The host government has growth plans that cannot be achieved without this additional capital. The host's ability to generate funds internally is limited, and it needs to attract capital from abroad.

▶ We provide technology that the host needs to function in the modern world. The host society wants access to modern technology and modern conveniences, and we help it gain access to them. The host's ability to develop technology locally is limited because of limited finances and skills; therefore, access to technology through MNCs is the host's best option.

▶ We provide skills that the host needs to grow. The host economy has to grow to provide opportunities for a growing population. The host does not have the needed expertise and skills to allow the economy to grow at the desired rate. MNCs transfer managerial skills, business know-how, and technical expertise to the host, and train local people in all these areas.

Local Businessperson

▶ When outsiders provide resources and know-how, it increases our dependence on them. We need to develop our internal ability to produce capital, technology, and skills. We do not want to be dependent on outsiders for our survival and growth because they can withdraw and devastate our economy.

▶ MNCs are large and powerful relative to our economy and reduce our sovereignty. If we let them dominate our economy, they can exert pressure on our government by threatening to withdraw. Further, the business and management skills and approaches that they bring are foreign to us, and we believe that they are changing our cultural values and practices.

▶ Outsiders respond to different laws. Our laws and regulations are designed to support our interests and culture. Outsiders march to a different drummer and may disregard our laws when they conflict with their home government's wishes.

▶ Foreign companies are not concerned about the local environment and therefore they exploit us. They use up our nonrenewable resources and own our valuable assets. The capital that MNCs invest is much less than what they eventually take out as profits and dividends.

Foreign Investor

▶ We provide access to foreign markets. Some of these markets are largely controlled by MNCs, and the locals' size and inexperience means these markets are essentially closed to them without our help.

▶ We provide employment for locals. Host countries almost always want to increase employment, and we contribute to their ability to do so.

▶ We produce products locally that would otherwise have to be imported; therefore, we contribute positively to a host's trade balance. We may export our products and contribute even more to the trade balance.

▶ We provide foreign exchange through our investment and export earnings.

▶ We pay tariffs and taxes and contribute to government revenues.

Local Businessperson

▶ The technology that foreign investors provide is often not appropriate for us and not adapted for our use. Sometimes they send obsolete technology that does not help us domestically. Sometimes they send technology that is so advanced that our people cannot understand or use it and have to rely on foreign technicians.

▶ MNC investors usually choose our wealthy citizens as partners and local managers. This alignment with the elite encourages the concentration of wealth and disparity in income that already exists in our society. It hinders social change.

▶ Foreign production in our country increases local consumption because the products are less expensive than if they were imported. This decreases our savings and investment.

▶ Foreign investment discourages local investment even more because local industries do not believe they can compete with MNCs. Some local investors choose to invest abroad instead of investing locally.

▶ Foreign investment is often more capital intensive and less labor intensive than local investment would be; therefore, in the long run, it may actually cost us jobs.

▶ MNCs take out more foreign exchange in the long run than they bring in. MNCs' dividends and payments to their headquarters far outweigh the foreign exchange that they bring in.

The points presented in Exhibit 5.1 indicate how the same situation can seem quite different from two different positions. Both investors and host countries can improve the foreign direct investment process by understanding the objectives and attitudes of those with whom they will negotiate.

From the perspective of the international company, it is important that the investor realize that these different viewpoints can exist. It is far easier to reach an agreement if one understands the other side's perspective as well as one's own. The investing company can benefit from such an understanding of a host government's outlook so that the company can present the investment opportunity in the most positive way.

Most host countries recognize that foreign direct investment involves both benefits and costs. Many host countries have designed a set of incentives to encourage this investment to be able to derive the benefits. Coexisting with these incentives is a set of regulations designed to limit the activities of foreign investors and minimize the host's costs associated with the investment. The following sections examine and illustrate the most common of these incentives and regulations.

Foreign Direct Investment Incentives and Restrictions

Many countries supply and impose significant incentives and restrictions to foreign investment. These must be carefully examined by any potential investor before the decision is made to commit time, personnel, and funds into a project to ensure it will be a profitable endeavor.

Incentives for Foreign Investment

Incentives for foreign investment are intended to encourage foreign companies to invest, often in a particular location, a specific industry, or a definite type of investment. Some incentives are intended simply to increase investment in general because the country believes it can benefit from expanded investment in any sector. Other incentives target more specific investments that the host country has identified as particularly appropriate. The qualifying characteristics associated with the incentives offered by the host depend on the kind of investment it wants to attract. This desired investment is determined by the host's objectives. The following are some typical situations:

▶ Incentives tied to developing new industries – Many countries give preferential treatment for investment in any new (sometimes called *pioneer*) industry. Other countries identify specific new industries (e.g., food processing) for special treatment.

▶ Incentives to encourage a particular form of investment or type of company – Many countries favor companies that can demonstrate a transfer of technology associated with their investment. Others are more concerned with local employment, local content, or local ownership and assist foreign companies that will provide this local focus. Some countries may prefer foreign investments of a particular size and target their incentives toward these investments.

▶ Incentives to correct balance of payments imbalances – Countries may want to promote import substitution or exports, and they may want to build their foreign reserves. Incentives can be tied to any of these factors.

These incentives can take many varied forms, but the following are typical:

▶ Reduced tariffs – Many countries allow firms to import certain products without paying the normal duties. This can be a reduction of a certain percentage or the complete elimination of tariffs. This reduction typically applies to plant and equipment imports needed to establish a new operation and the inputs to a product to be exported. The tariff reduction is often linked to the development of a particular industry or location.

▶ Reduced taxes – Tax holidays are often offered to foreign investors. This can be a reduction in normal corporate taxes or their complete elimination. This reduction is typically for a specified period of time, which is estimated as the average time needed to establish efficient and competitive operations. The tax reduction is also frequently linked to the development of a particular industry or location. New industries often qualify for either reduced tariffs or reduced taxes or both.

▶ Provision of facilities – Host governments may construct factory shells or other facilities for foreign investors to use. A charge is usually associated with use of these facilities, but it is substantially lower than the investment needed to construct facilities.

▶ Provision of services – Services can range from accommodation during initial visits to translation services to labor negotiation advice and the use of government air services. These services might be difficult for foreigners to obtain on their own, and the assistance is intended to make the investment process easier.

▶ Subsidies – Host governments may provide subsidies in the form of low-interest loans, cash payments, preferred public utility rates, or other similar inducements to encourage investment in desired sectors.

▶ Monopoly rights – Host governments sometimes grant foreign companies the exclusive right to produce and sell certain products within the country for a certain period of time.

Restrictions on Foreign Investment

As noted previously, countries also try to control foreign investment and avoid the potential drawbacks associated with it. Restrictions, like incentives, may be tied to certain forms of investments. Typical restrictions include the following:

▶ Host employment – Foreign investments may have to qualify for approval or incentives by guaranteeing to employ a certain number, or percentage, of host-country nationals in their operations. This is often further specified in terms of management, technical staff, research personnel, and so forth. The purpose of this restriction is to ensure that the investment does in reality result in the desired creation of jobs in the host country. Further restrictions relative to management, technical staff, and research personnel are intended to ensure that these skills are transferred to the host country, not simply provided by foreigners.

▶ Foreign management – In addition to general employee specifications, many countries focus particularly on management personnel and restrict the number of foreign managers who can be appointed in a given time period. This occurs because management skills are seen as particularly important to the host economy; therefore, this restriction is designed to ensure that host-country nationals are trained and develop expertise in management.

▶ Host ownership – Many countries do not allow wholly owned foreign subsidiaries and specify the degree of host ownership necessary to obtain permission to invest. In some locations, foreign firms are limited to a minority share. This provision is intended to ensure that host interests are central to decision making and that host country nationals benefit from the profits generated in their country. In Japan, "certain enterprises, mostly in energy and high technology, are designated as sensitive to foreign investment, and foreign ownership is generally restricted to a maximum of 50 percent" (Royal Bank 1987).

▶ Local content – Countries often specify the degree of local content that must go into items that are produced by foreign investors. Local content refers to the inputs to the product and where these inputs originate. This restriction is intended to ensure that the investment contributes to the economy as a whole through the spin-off benefits of purchases of inputs from other host-country suppliers. The restriction also avoids increasing imports to serve the foreign investment.

▶ Trade balance focus – Countries may specify that foreign investments are permitted only if they can demonstrate that they will contribute to exports or provide a substitute for current imports. Countries faced with chronic trade deficits that they hope to correct will often adopt these measures. Similarly, countries with limited foreign reserves will use these approaches to conserve their available resources.

▶ Training – Countries quite often demand that investors provide training for host-country nationals to improve their skills. This is usually intended to relate to those employed by the organization that is the focus of the foreign investment, but countries sometimes require training programs for others as well. This restriction has the effect of upgrading the skills of host-country nationals and ensuring that the country does not increase its dependence on others.

▶ Location – Many countries limit the locations where foreign investment is permitted. This can be designed to avoid further investment in areas that are already overcrowded. It is often used to ensure development of regions that are currently poor and underdeveloped. Investors may be required to provide their own infrastructure (e.g., roads, electricity, water) in these regions and thus further contribute to the host country's development objectives.

▶ Research and development – Many countries want to ensure that research and development occur locally to develop their research expertise. Countries therefore may require that investors guarantee to perform certain research functions locally or to spend specified amounts locally on research.

▶ Profit repatriation and reinvestment – Many countries try to ensure that foreign companies do not take all of their profits out of the local economy and that the foreigners continue to invest locally. These countries may have limits on the level of profits that can be repatriated (**profit repatriation** refers to profits returned to the home country) in a specific time frame and may stipulate specific levels of reinvestment.

▶ National concerns – Many countries review investment proposals to determine how they will affect the host country in terms of national security, public safety, and so on. Investments are either allowed, modified, or disallowed, depending on this review. In Japan, for example, "transactions may still be suspended or modified if the minister concerned sees them as a threat to national security, public order, public safety, the economy in general or the maintenance of equality of treatment for investors from other countries" (Royal Bank 1987, p. 18).

Trade-offs between Incentives and Restrictions

The degree and direction of foreign investment is to some extent influenced by these host government incentives and restrictions. In making a foreign direct investment decision, the international firm should attempt to weigh all of the arguments for and against a particular location and to compare each location with others. The existence of particular incentives or restrictions in a particular location, therefore, sometimes can be the deciding factor as to whether to invest in that location.

These considerations are, however, likely to be secondary. In many cases, incentives and restrictions balance each other. In other cases, the firm's plans are already consistent with the host's requirements and so restrictions are not viewed as negatives. Most countries have similar incentives and restrictions; therefore, they may not be a major factor on the volume and direction of foreign direct investment.

Application of Investment Incentives and Restrictions

The incentives and regulations that host governments impose on foreign investors usually are stated as applying equally to all investors. In fact, they are not always equally applied. Some countries may be moving toward differentiated sets of regulations and incentives tailored to suit particular situations. Host countries are often willing to negotiate arrangements that differ from their stated policies if a particular foreign investor can indicate that its investment proposition is especially worthwhile. In addition, some host governments have found that it is appropriate to negotiate specific restrictions and incentives in terms of the host's requirements and each investor's needs and potential contribution to the host's goals. The common incentives and restrictions described earlier are generally applied evenhandedly, but managers and negotiators in international companies need to be alert to potential departures from them.

Levels of Economic Development

The level of economic development of a country or region can have a substantial influence on investment flows. To examine this influence and the reasons for it, let us first consider what *economic development* means.

Defining *Economic Development*

Economic development is usually measured in terms of **gross domestic product (GDP)** per capita, a measure of a country's productivity and income. This is only a crude measure because it ignores illegal and underground economic activities, nor does it consider the quality of life achieved at different levels of per capita GDP. Other measures that are interesting to consider are wealth distribution, daily calorie consumption, leisure time, energy consumption, and various demographic (e.g., literacy, life expectancy) and health (e.g., infant mortality, doctors per capita) statistics. Consideration of an array of measures is more likely to give an accurate picture of the level of development in a given country or set of countries. GDP per capita seems to be the most convenient to use, however, and often serves as a proxy for other measures.

Categories of Levels of Economic Development

Countries have been classified in terms of development in a variety of ways, and these classifications are continually shifting. The following categories therefore should be viewed as only suggestive of the distinctions that can be found:

▶ Third World – The poorer countries of the world are often referred to in this way. This term is in contrast to the developed market economies (the rich countries), which constitute the first world, and the centrally planned economies, which make up the second world. The terms *first world* and *second world* are not commonly used, but Third World has become a common epithet for the poor countries.

▶ Less developed countries (LDCs) – The poorer countries are also often referred to as less developed countries. This is relative to the more developed (sometimes called just *developed*), richer countries. The LDCs were once called *backward* or *underdeveloped,* but these terms are seldom used currently because they offend many people.

▶ Developing countries – Some Third World countries recently have been called *developing countries.* This is in contrast to the developed, rich countries. The term *developing,* as opposed to *Third World* or *LDC,* has a sense of moving forward, and therefore some people prefer it.

▶ Newly industrializing countries – Newly industrializing countries (NICs) are in the process of moving from the poor category to the rich; they are developing countries of the Third World that have experienced rapid industrial growth in the last quarter of the 20th century. Countries such as South Korea, Taiwan, Hong Kong, Singapore, and Thailand currently fall into this category.

▶ Centrally planned economies – The centrally planned economies are the centrally planned, communist countries. The changes of the early 1990s suggest that it is possible that only a few countries will continue to follow this economic model in coming years.

▶ Developed or industrialized countries – These are the wealthier countries of the world. Their economies have generally been based on industrialization and free markets. Many of these countries are also referred to as *Western.*

The Effect of Level of Development on Investment Flows

Developing countries generally have a scarcity of their own capital for investment, and capital theoretically flows to them. In addition, for the most part, these countries have incentives in place to encourage foreign investment. The reality is somewhat different from what theory might expect. Traditionally, relatively little investment occurred in the developing countries.

The following points provide some reasons for this lack of investment.

▶ The international product life cycle explanation of investment suggests that investment initially will be made in similar, more developed countries and only later in low-cost developing countries. Combine this with a competitive and rapidly changing technological environment that leads to short product life cycles, and the result is little investment in developing countries.

▶ Companies seeking to utilize their established strengths want to do so in relatively safe environments. The developing countries have generally been seen as riskier than the developed ones. The result is a preference for investment in the developed countries.

▶ Companies do not see the developing countries as representing important markets. Even though these countries constitute approximately 80 percent of the world's population, their poverty makes them relatively unattractive markets. The result is that countries choose to exploit markets in the developed countries and to invest near these markets before considering those in the developing countries.

▶ The developed countries tend to be more similar culturally to each other than they are to the developing countries. Companies are more comfortable dealing with others that are reasonably like them. The result is that, other things being equal, companies choose to invest in developed countries rather than developing ones. Exhibits 5.2 through 5.4 illustrate a variety of investment flows.

Prior to 1990, the developed countries had invested little in the centrally planned economies. This can be attributed to stringent investment restrictions in these countries, a lack of hard currency for profit repatriation, government intervention in company operations, and a concern on the part of investors about understanding how to do business in these countries. The opening of Eastern Europe that occurred in 1990 has encouraged many companies to consider the potential of investment in these countries.

It is important to recognize that the world is changing and look ahead to what the world economy may be like in the future. *The Economist,* for example, expects the developing countries of today to account for a substantially greater proportion of world output in the future, as illustrated in Exhibits 5.5 and 5.6.

New Opportunities for Investment

Investment opportunities change over time; consequently, investment patterns also shift. International companies are constantly looking for new opportunities to expand and grow. This section

EXHIBIT 5.2   **Foreign Direct Investment Flows, All Industrial Countries and Asia ($ billions)**

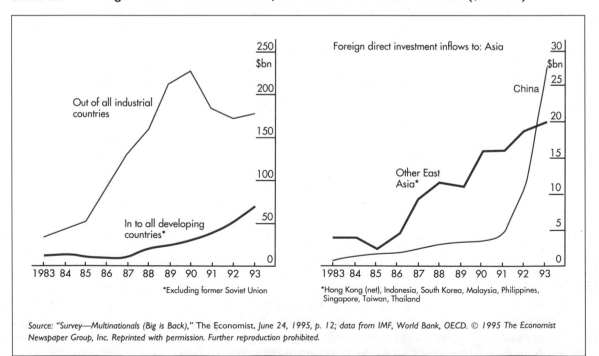

Source: "Survey—Multinationals (Big is Back)," The Economist, June 24, 1995, p. 12; data from IMF, World Bank, OECD. © 1995 The Economist Newspaper Group, Inc. Reprinted with permission. Further reproduction prohibited.

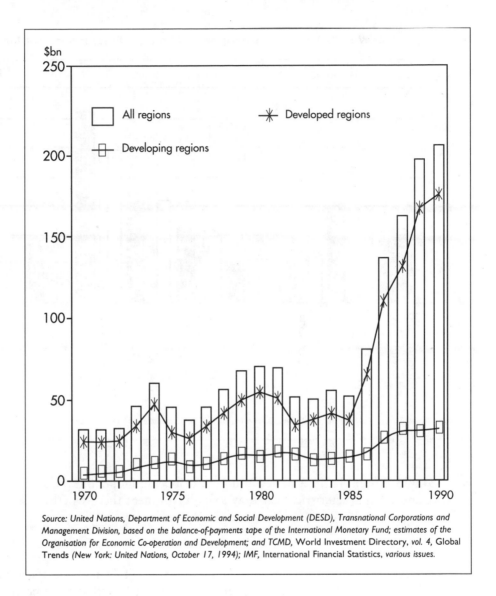

EXHIBIT 5.3
**Real Foreign
Direct Investment
Inflows**

Source: United Nations, Department of Economic and Social Development (DESD), Transnational Corporations and Management Division, based on the balance-of-payments tape of the International Monetary Fund; estimates of the Organisation for Economic Co-operation and Development; and TCMD, World Investment Directory, vol. 4, Global Trends (New York: United Nations, October 17, 1994); IMF, International Financial Statistics, various issues.

takes a brief look at some of the opportunities for investment that seem most interesting in the 1990s.

Developing Countries and Centrally Planned Economies

In spite of the reasons for little investment in developing and centrally planned economies, these countries offer vast potential. International companies willing to undertake such investment may be able to gain a competitive advantage over their less adventuresome counterparts. It may be that some international companies avoid these countries simply because they seem too foreign. This foreignness in itself might signal opportunities in terms of both production and markets.

EXHIBIT 5.4   **The World's Ten Largest Recipients of Foreign Direct Investment Inflows in the 1990s**

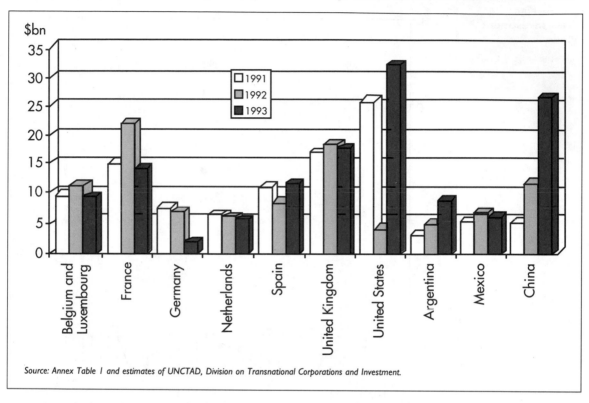

Source: Annex Table 1 and estimates of UNCTAD, Division on Transnational Corporations and Investment.

For example, Africa, Latin America and the Caribbean, India, and the smaller countries of Asia all have special characteristics that may make investment there worthwhile.

Eastern Europe

Changes that began in 1990 in the communist countries of Eastern Europe are having an impact on global investments. These countries provide new markets that have been undersupplied for a lengthy period. Many Japanese, North American, and Western European firms are considering the potential advantages to investing in these countries. Nevertheless, investment has been relatively slow as changes continue to make this region somewhat unstable.

The Pacific Rim

The Asian countries of the Pacific Rim continue to present interesting, new, and exciting investment opportunities. Some of these countries, such as Taiwan, have fast-growing economies and are becoming investors themselves. Others, such as the People's Republic of China, offer an enormous (over a billion people) untapped market. These countries have been particularly attractive to investors in the 1990s.

EXHIBIT 5.5   **Economy versus World Output**

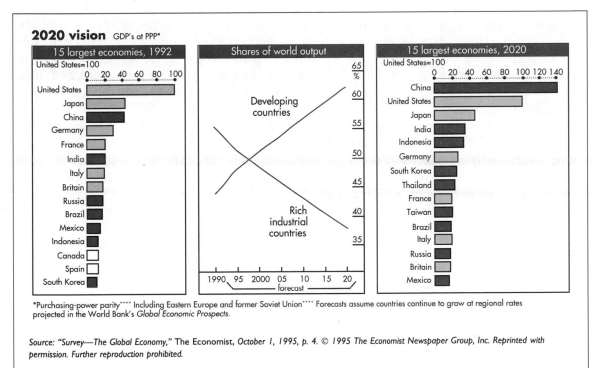

*Purchasing-power parity**** Including Eastern Europe and former Soviet Union**** Forecasts assume countries continue to grow at regional rates projected in the World Bank's *Global Economic Prospects*.

Source: "Survey—The Global Economy," The Economist, October 1, 1995, p. 4. © 1995 The Economist Newspaper Group, Inc. Reprinted with permission. Further reproduction prohibited.

EXHIBIT 5.6   **Percentage Growth in Industrial and Developing Countries**

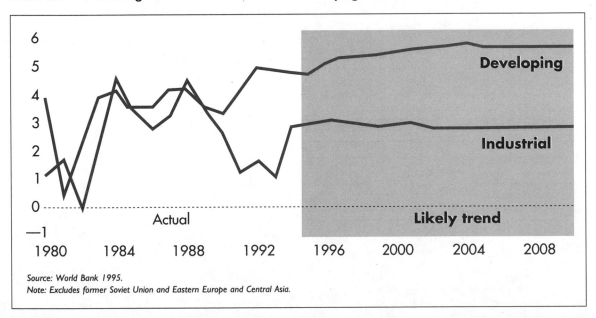

Source: World Bank 1995.
Note: Excludes former Soviet Union and Eastern Europe and Central Asia.

Regional Groupings

Several closely linked regional groups of countries provide attractive investment options. Canada, Mexico, and the United States signed a free-trade agreement. The European Community became the European Union, and countries not previously part of this group seemed likely to join it. Countries of the Pacific Rim moved toward closer economic linkages with each other, and other regionally grouped countries (e.g., Africa, South Asia, and Latin America) considered expanding their regional linkages.

These regional agreements encourage trade and investment movements among member countries but may discourage movement into and out of the region. Investment flows therefore can be substantially influenced by the formation of such groups. Exhibits 5.7 through 5.12 on the next several pages provide information on the direction of investment. Earlier investments flows are depicted in Exhibits 5.13 and 5.14.

EXHIBIT 5.7 Regional Direction of Foreign Direct Investment Inflows (percentages)

To:	United States 1985	1988	Japan 1985	1988	Europe 1985	1988	France 1985	1988	Germany 1985	1988	Spain 1985	1988	United Kingdom 1985	1988	Developing countries 1985	1988	Total
From:																	
United States	—	—	3.7	7.8	57.7	52.2	7.4	11.5	2.5	-12.4	1.1	4.3	22.2	29.0	33.7	21.8	100
Japan	44.2	46.1	—	—	15.8	19.4	0.5	1.0	1.4	0.9	0.7	0.3	3.0	8.4	35.2	27.8	100
France	42.6	23.0	0.8	—	25.7	63.4	—	—	4.3	4.5	2.6	4.8	4.6	16.6	28.4	4.1	100
Germany	53.3	47.0	0.9	1.3	36.9	45.6	5.7	4.6	—	—	3.1	4.4	5.9	8.0	6.9	2.2	100

Source: United Nations, DESD, TCMD 1993.

EXHIBIT 5.8 **Regional Direction of Foreign Direct Investment Stocks (percentages)**

To:	United States		Japan		Europe		France		Germany		Spain		United Kingdom		Developing countries[b]		Other		Total
From:	1985	1988	1985	1988	1985	1988	1985	1988	1985	1988	1985	1988	1985	1988	1985	1988	1985	1988	
United States	—	—	4.0	5.4	45.7	47.1	3.3	3.9	7.3	6.5	1.0	1.5	14.3	14.8	22.9	23.3	27.4	24.3	100
Japan	32.2[a]	40.3[a]	—	—	13.1	16.2	—	—	—	—	—	—	—	—	42.0[b]	34.3[b]	12.6	9.3	100
France	—	33.6	—	0.4	—	51.3	—	7.9	—	4.3	—	5.4	—	10.0	—	13.1	—	1.6	100
Germany	30.1	27.0	1.5	2.2	43.7	49.3	8.0	—	—	—	3.4	5.0	4.7	5.8	12.7	11.2	12.0	10.3	100

[a]Includes Canada.
[b]Represents Asia and Latin America.

Source: *United Nations, DESD, TCMD 1993.*

EXHIBIT 5.9   Inflows and Outflows of Foreign Direct Investment, 1981–1993

Country	(Billions of Dollars)								Share in Total (Percentage)					Growth Rate (Percentage)[b]				
	1981 to 1985 Annual Average	1986 to 1990 Annual Average	1988	1989	1990	1991	1992	1993[a]	1981 to 1985 Annual Average	1986 to 1990 Annual Average	1991	1992	1993	1981 to 1985 Annual Growth Rate	1986 to 1990	1991	1992	1993
Developed countries																		
Inflows	37	130	131	168	176	121	102	109	74	84	74	65	56	1	24	-32	-5	7
Outflows	47	163	162	212	222	185	162	181	98	96	96	95	—	3	24	-17	-12	12
Developing countries																		
Inflows	13	25	28	27	31	39	51	80	26	16	24	32	41	-4	17	25	32	54
Outflows	1	6	6	10	10	7	9	14	2	4	4	5	—	33	49	-28	33	55
Central and Eastern Europe[c]																		
Inflows	0.02	0.1	0.015	0.3	0.3	2	4	5	0.04	0.1	1	3	3	1	90	716	85	25
Outflows	0.004	0.02	0.02	0.02	0.04	0.01	0.03	—	0.01	0.01	0.005	0.02	—	-11	20	-74	172	—
All countries																		
Inflows	50	155	159	196	208	162	158	194	100	100	100	100	100	-0.1	23	-22	-2	23
Outflows	48	168	168	222	232	192	171	195	100	100	100	100	—	3	24	-17	-17	14

[a]Based on preliminary estimates.

[b]Compounded growth rate estimates, based on a semi-logarithmic regression equation.

[c]Former Yugoslavia is included in developing countries.

Note: The levels of worldwide inward and outward FDI flows and stocks should balance; however, in practice, they do not. The causes of the discrepancy include differences between countries in the definition and valuation of FDI; the treatment of unremitted branch profits in inward and outward direct investment; treatment of unrealized capital gains and losses; the recording of transactions of "offshore" enterprises; the recording of reinvested earnings in inward and outward direct investment; the treatment of real estate and construction investment; and the share-in-equity threshold in inward and outward direct investment.

Source: UNCTAD, Division on Transnational Corporations and Investment, based on UNCTC, 1992a; UN-TCMD, 1993a, UNCTAD-DTCI, 1994a, 1994b, 1994c; International Monetary Fund, balance-of-payments tape, retrieved in April 1994, and estimates of the Organisation for Economic Co-operation and Development; and annex tables 1 and 2.

EXHIBIT 5.10   Outflows of Foreign Direct Investment from the Five Major Home Countries, 1981–1993

Country	(Billions of Dollars)								Share in World Total (Percentage)					Annual Growth Rate (Percentage)				
	1981 to 1985[a]	1986 to 1990[a]	1988	1989	1990	1991	1992	1993[b]	1981 to 1985[a]	1986 to 1990[a]	1991	1992	1993[b]	1981 to 1985[a]	1986 to 1990[a]	1991	1992	1993[b]
France[c]	3	17	14	19	35	24	31	21	6	10	12	18	11	-17	45	-31	29	-32
Germany[c]	4	16	13	18	29	22	16	17	9	9	12	9	9	13	27	-22	-29	5
Japan[c]	5	32	34	44	48	31	17	12	11	19	16	10	6	8	32	-36	-46	-29
United Kingdom	9	28	37	35	19	16	16	26	19	17	8	9	13	-2	4	-18	1	61
United States[d]	11	22	14	34	24	33	33	50	23	13	17	19	25	-5	15	38	-0.03	52
Total[e]	32	115	113	151	155	126	113	126	67	68	66	66	64	-.03	23	-19	-10	11

[a]Compounded growth rate estimates, based on a semi-logarithmic regression equation.

[b]Based on preliminary estimates.

[c]Not including reinvested earnings. In the case of France, reinvested earnings are not reported after 1982.

[d]Excluding outflows to the finance (except banking), insurance, and real estate industries of the Netherlands Antilles. Also excludes currency-translation adjustments.

[e]Totals may not add up, due to rounding.

Source: UNCTAD, Division on Transnational Corporation and Investment, based on UN-TCMD, 1993b; International Monetary Fund, balance-of-payments tape, retrieved in April 1994; annex Table 2.

EXHIBIT 5.11   **Japanese Outflow of Foreign Direct Investment by Region (Percent)**

Host Region	1980	1985	1989	1990	1991	Average 1951–1991
North America	34.0	45.0	50.2	47.8	45.3	44.0
Latin America	12.5	21.4	7.8	6.4	8.0	12.4
Asia	25.2	11.8	12.2	12.4	14.3	15.2
East Asia	24.8	10.7	11.9	12.2	14.2	15.1
Other	0.4	1.1	0.3	0.2	0.1	0.1
Middle East	3.4	0.4	0.1	0.0	0.2	1.0
Europe	12.3	15.8	21.9	25.1	22.5	19.5
Africa	3.0	1.4	1.0	1.0	1.8	1.9
Pacific Islands	9.6	4.3	6.8	7.3	7.9	6.1
Total	100	100	100	100	100	100

Source: Transnational Corporations 3, no. 1 (February 1994).

EXHIBIT 5.12   **Share of the Ten Largest Host Countries in Foreign Direct Investment Inflows to Developing Countries, 1981–1992**

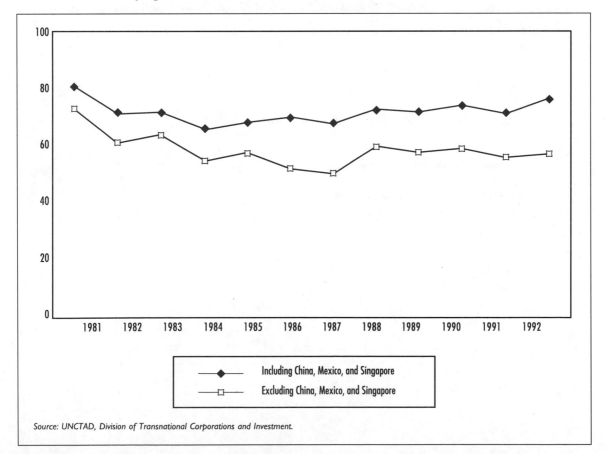

Source: UNCTAD, Division of Transnational Corporations and Investment.

EXHIBIT 5.13   **Foreign Direct Investment Inflows, by Major Regions, 1970–1985 (in $ billions)**

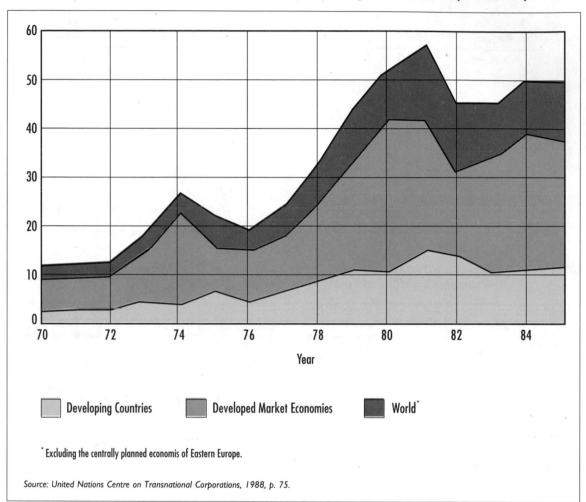

* Excluding the centrally planned economis of Eastern Europe.

Source: United Nations Centre on Transnational Corporations, 1988, p. 75.

EXHIBIT 5.14
**Inward Foreign Direct
Investment Stocks, by
Country or Region of Origin,
1975–1986
(in $ billions)**

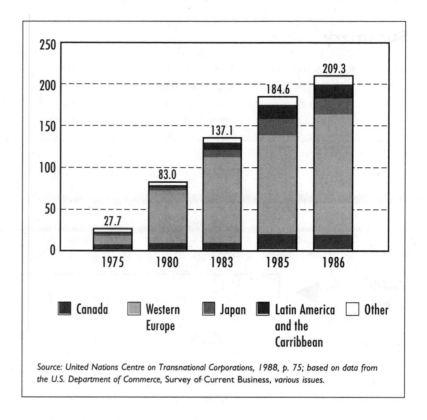

Source: United Nations Centre on Transnational Corporations, 1988, p. 75; based on data from
the U.S. Department of Commerce, Survey of Current Business, various issues.

Summary

This chapter focused on the direction and degree of foreign direct investment. It did not consider how individual companies make investment decisions; rather, it explored the factors influencing investment in general. *Foreign direct investment* was first defined, and then the reasons why such investment takes place were identified. The views of the two major players in the investment decision, the investing company and the host country, were explored. The differing views of these two players is a function of their various objectives relative to the foreign investment process and can result in conflicts and, sometimes, seemingly incongruent government policies and regulations. The role of economic development was identified as another factor that shapes the direction and degree of foreign direct investment. *Economic development* was defined and various categories of level of development were identified so that the influence of this factor on foreign direct investment could be examined. The chapter concluded with a short discussion of some current developments that could influence foreign direct investment in the future.

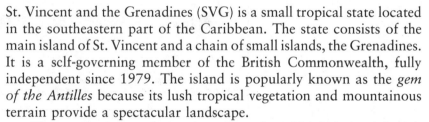

MINI-CASE

Investment in St. Vincent and the Grenadines

St. Vincent and the Grenadines (SVG) is a small tropical state located in the southeastern part of the Caribbean. The state consists of the main island of St. Vincent and a chain of small islands, the Grenadines. It is a self-governing member of the British Commonwealth, fully independent since 1979. The island is popularly known as the *gem of the Antilles* because its lush tropical vegetation and mountainous terrain provide a spectacular landscape.

The country's population is estimated at 134,000; its colonial, slave-based plantation history remains evident in present society. About 95 percent of the population is descended from African slaves. A white elite, only 2 percent of the population, dominates upper-class occupations.

SVG is socioeconomically a rather typical less developed, or developing country, as the following characteristics demonstrate:

▶ It is dependent on a small number of agricultural commodities that are subject to wide price fluctuation.
▶ Ownership is concentrated in the hands of a small minority.
▶ It is predominantly poor, with a low GNP per capita.
▶ It suffers from high unemployment and underemployment.
▶ Trade deficits with other nations are chronic.
▶ It is rural and isolated, with limited access by air and poor transportation outside the capital city.
▶ Educational levels are low – qualified teachers are in short supply and functional literacy is low.
▶ It lacks local economic opportunity.

The following profile of SVG's foreign direct investment strategy can be identified. The SVG government wants to encourage sound and balanced economic and social development while providing opportunities for citizens to create wealth and improve their living standards. Foreign direct investment is sought to create domestic income, contribute positively to the external trade account and diversify investment, strengthen the agricultural and tourist sectors, and encourage labor-intensive industry.

SVG identifies its endowments as

▶ Natural resources – rich soil, springlike, year-round temperatures, unspoiled varied terrain, good snorkeling and scuba diving, good swimming and beaches, outstanding sailing
▶ Infrastructure – good transportation and communication; abundant water supply and electricity; high standards of telecommunications, banking, insurance, and financial services, good educational system
▶ People – healthy and literate, young and willing to be trained, calm and friendly, low wage rates and good labor relations
▶ Government – stable and democratic, dedicated to providing basic fundamental rights and freedoms for all people
▶ Location – easy access to a variety of markets

Specific opportunities for investment are identified as

▶ Industry related – manufacture of garments; accessories; sporting goods; costume jewelry; cosmetics; leather products; toys; plastic products; high-quality furniture; fiberglass boats; components for solar, wind, and geothermal energy facilities; electrical fixtures and accessories; assembly of electronic components, medical equipment, automotive components, and accessories; pharmaceutical packaging; data processing facilities
▶ Tourism related – construction and management of hotels, resorts, restaurants, marinas, convention centers, yacht charters, water sports facilities
▶ Agriculture related – production and exportation of a variety of products including cigars, cigarettes, coir (from coconuts), snack foods, sauces, canned tropical fruits and vegetables, fresh fruits and vegetables, flowers, plants, live tropical fish, poultry, pork, and fish

Investment incentives include

▶ Development corporation – stimulates and facilitates investment by providing advice to investors and factory shells
▶ Tax holidays – offers approved enterprises 15-year holidays if local value added is 50 percent or more of total sales value; 12-

year holidays if value added is between 25 percent and 50 percent; 10-year holidays between 10 percent and 25 percent; 15-year holidays if 100 percent of production exported outside regional area; 15-year holidays for capital intensive investment (over $25 million EC, with US$1 = EC2.7); 10-year holidays for new hotels

▶ Duty-free access – exporting companies exempt from duties, and imports for hotels are exempt from duties

▶ Other incentives – no limitation on dividend payments; dividends to local residents exempt from income taxes; liberal depreciation, capital expenditure, and loss carryforward provisions.

In spite of the identified endowments and liberal incentives, SVG has had little success in attracting foreign investment.

Discussion Issues

1. Why do you think SVG had not been more successful, at the time of the case, in attracting more foreign investment?
2. How do you think SVG (and other similar countries) could improve their ability to attract foreign investment?
3. Find recent information on SVG and identify the current level of foreign investment there. If possible, identify the sources and types of recent investments.

Discussion Questions

1. Explain why governments use reduced tariffs, taxes, and other incentives to encourage foreign companies to invest in their countries.

2. What incentives for foreign direct investment do you believe are most likely to attract investment? Why do you believe these are particularly important?

3. Discuss the international product life cycle concept in the 1990s. What factors might affect its validity in today's world?

4. Are American Express shares purchased by Rolls Royce on the London Stock Exchange or Bell Canada shares purchased by a Japanese woman on the Tokyo exchange foreign investments?

Assignments

1. Choose a country and research its current incentives and restrictions that relate to foreign direct investment.

2. Choose two neighboring countries and identify the sectors in which each has invested in the other. How do these investments relate to the countries' comparative advantages?

3. Select a country to investigate and identify changes in its foreign direct investment policies over the last 20 years.

Selected References

Aggarwal, R., "Investment Performance of U.S.-Based Multinational Companies: Comments and a Perspective on International Diversification of Real Assets," *Journal of International Business Studies* (Spring–Summer 1980), pp. 98–104.

Calvett, A. L., "A Synthesis of Foreign Direct Investment Theories and Theories of the Multinational Firm," *Journal of International Business Studies* (Spring–Summer 1980), pp. 43–59.

Caves, R. E., *Multinational Enterprise and Economic Analysis* (Cambridge, Mass.: Harvard University Press, 1980).

Corcoran, T., "St. Joe Averts 30-Second Cuban Crisis," *Globe and Mail* (November 7, 1990), p. B8.

Dunning, J. H., *International Production and the International Enterprise* (London: Allen and Unwin, 1981).

The Economist (September 22, 1990), p. 81.

The Economist, "Multinationals – Survey" (June 24, 1995).

The Economist (October 1, 1995), p. 4.

The Futurist, "Looking at the Future of American Business – An Interview with Marvin Cetron" (March–April 1986), pp. 25–27.

Goldar, J. D., and M. Jelinek, "Plan for Economies of Scope," *Harvard Business Review* (November–December 1983), pp. 141–148.

Jarvis, M., and F. Kirk, Jr., eds., *Foreign Direct Investment in Canada: The Foreign Investors Perspective* (Ottawa: Carleton University Press, 1986), p. 4.

McGregor, J., "Rescuing China's Economy," *Globe and Mail* (November 7, 1990), p. B8.

Royal Bank, *Market Guide Australia* (Toronto: The Royal Bank of Canada, 1986a).

Royal Bank, *Market Guide India* (Toronto: The Royal Bank of Canada, 1986b).

Royal Bank, *Market Guide Japan* (Toronto: The Royal Bank of Canada, 1987).

Rugman, A., "A New Theory of the Multinational Enterprise: Internalization versus Internalization," *Columbia Journal of World Business* (Spring 1980), pp. 23–29.

Rugman, A., *Inside the Multinationals: The Economics of Internal Markets* (New York: Columbia University Press, 1981).

United Nations, DESD, TCMD, *World Investment Directory 1992,* vol. 3, *Developed Countries* (New York: United Nations, 1993).

United Nations Centre on Transnational Corporations, *Transnational Corporations in World Development – Trends and Prospects* (New York: UNCTC, 1988).

Vernon, R., "International Investment and International Trade in the Product Cycle," *Quarterly Journal of Economics* (May 1966).

Vernon, R., "The Product Cycle Hypothesis in a New International Environment," *Oxford Bulletin of Economics and Statistics* (November 1979).

Wall Street Journal, "Public Opinion on FDI in the U.S." (March 8, 1988).

Wells, L. T., Jr., "A Product Life Cycle for International Trade?" *Journal of Marketing* (July 1968), pp. 1–6.

World Bank, *Global Economic Prospects and the Developing Countries 1995* (Washington, D.C.: World Bank, 1995).

PART

III

The International Firm's Environment

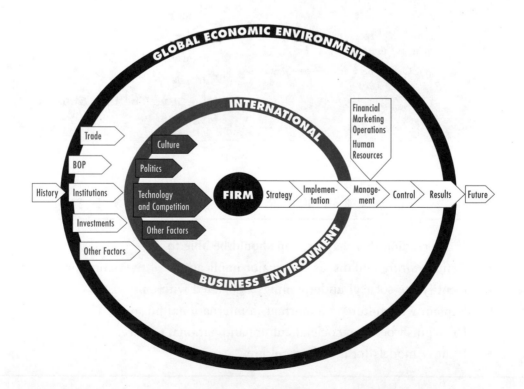

CHAPTER 6

The Cultural Environment of International Business

LEARNING OBJECTIVES

After reading this chapter, you should be able to

▶ Define *culture* and discuss the major implications of the definition.

▶ Identify the societal underpinnings associated with culture.

▶ Explain why culture is important in international business.

▶ Distinguish between societal culture and national culture.

▶ Identify models for assessing culture.

▶ Explain Hofstede's cultural model.

▶ Explain Kluckhohn and Strodtbeck's cultural model.

▶ Explain how culture affects management.

▶ Discuss ways to deal with cultural differences.

K E Y   T E R M S

▶ Culture

▶ National variables

▶ Societal variables

▶ National culture

▶ Societal culture

▶ Corporate culture

▶ Professional culture

▶ Individual values

▶ Country clusters

▶ Cultural antecedents

▶ Cultural values

▶ Hofstede's Value Survey model

▶ Individualism

▶ Uncertainty avoidance

▶ Power distance

▶ Masculinity

▶ Kluckhohn and Strodtbeck's value orientations

▶ Relationship to nature

▶ Time orientation

▶ Basic human nature

▶ Activity orientation

▶ Human relationships

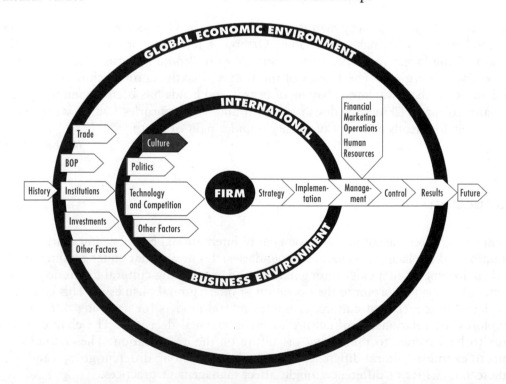

T H O U G H T   S T A R T E R S

▶ A Chinese story tells of a raging flood. A monkey, caught in the flood, was able to scramble up a tree and save himself. He looked down and saw a poor fish swimming against the current. Feeling sorry for the fish, the monkey decided to save it; he reached into the water and lifted the fish out.

▶ Herodotus, in the fourth century B.C., reported the following. Darius, when he was king, summoned those Greeks who were with him and asked them what sum of money would induce them to make a meal of their dead fathers; and they said nothing would induce them to do this. Darius then summoned the Callatian Indians, who do eat their parents, and asked them how much money they would take to burn their dead fathers in a fire (as the Greeks did); and they raised a great uproar, telling him not to speak of such a thing.

▶ I leave to your imagination how Chinese businessmen felt taking off from Hong Kong during the inauguration of our concierge services for first-class passengers. To mark the occasion, each concierge was proudly wearing a white carnation . . . a well-known oriental symbol of death. . . . Perhaps the most embarrassing mistake was our in-flight magazine cover that showed Australian actor Paul Hogan wandering through the Outback. The caption read, "Paul Hogan Camps It Up." Hogan's lawyer was kind enough to phone us long distance from Sydney to let us know that "camps it up" is Australian slang for "flaunts his homosexuality."

(Zeeman 1988)

▶ The ancients believed a hairy man is a strong man. The Greeks and Romans shaved or tore out their hair as offerings to the Gods. Orthodox Jews are forbidden to shave "the four corners of the face." In battle, ancient Britons wore drooping moustaches dyed green blue to irk Caesar's legions. The Franks of the fifth and sixth centuries chose their kings from the hairiest of their warriors. Shaving of beards and heads has been a common punishment in many cultures. Chinese males in the 16th and 17th centuries had to wear pigtails and shave their foreheads as a sign of loyalty – under pain of death.

(Globe and Mail 1990)

Introduction

This chapter explores the cultural environment of international business. International business, by definition, takes place across national boundaries; this means that understanding the different cultural environments that exist among nations and considering cultural differences in all facets of business are very important to the operation of international businesses. This chapter defines and explains the concept of culture, examines several models for assessing different cultures, and explores the relationship of culture to organizational decisions. The chapter encourages students to be sensitive to the impact of culture on the organization. The chapter also helps students to examine cultural differences and similarities among different groups and determine how these similarities or differences might affect management practices.

Defining *Culture*

Culture is a concept that pervades our thinking; books, magazines, periodicals, and newspapers are filled with articles that include the word *culture*. It is difficult, however, to define specifically what the concept means. This is illustrated by the fact that in the mid-1900s, two anthropologists (Kroeber and Kluckhohn 1952) catalogued 164 separate and distinct definitions of the word *culture*. This issue is further complicated because the word has several quite different meanings. At one level, *culture* refers to a shared, commonly held body of general beliefs and values that define what is right for one group (Kluckhohn and Strodtbeck 1961; Lane and DiStefano 1988). At a very different level, culture refers to socially elitist concepts, including refinement of mind, tastes, and manners based on superior education or upbringing (Heller 1988). Equally, culture often refers to artistic output that is characteristic of a particular ethnic or regional group. Culture is further used to describe a medium for growing biological specimens and a germ for growing a product (yogurt culture).

The word *culture* apparently originates with the Latin *cultura,* which is related to *cultus,* which can be translated as "cult" or "worship." This meaning is helpful in understanding the use of the term in this chapter. Members of a cult believe in specific ways of doing things and hence develop a culture that enshrines those beliefs. *Culture* in this chapter will be used in this general sense. Specifically, a definition proposed by Terpstra and David (1985) delineates what is meant by the word *culture* in this context: "Culture is a learned, shared, compelling, interrelated set of symbols whose meaning provides a set of orientations for members of a society. These orientations, taken together, provide solutions to problems that all societies must solve if they are to remain viable" (p. 5).

This definition contains several elements that are important to understanding the relationship of cultural issues and organizational decisions.

- ▶ Culture is learned – It is not innate; as such it is possible for a person who goes to another culture to learn the new culture.
- ▶ Culture is shared – The focus is on those things that members of a particular group share rather than on individual differences; therefore, it is possible to study and identify group patterns.
- ▶ Culture is compelling – Behavior is determined by culture without individuals being aware of the influence of their culture; understanding culture is important in order to understand behavior.
- ▶ Culture is interrelated – Although various facets of culture can be examined in isolation, they should be understood in the context of the whole; a culture needs to be studied as a complete entity.
- ▶ Culture provides orientation – A particular group reacts in general in the same way to a given stimulus; understanding a culture can help to determine how group members might react in various situations.

This definition suggests that one can learn other cultures and that culture is basic to how people behave. One's own culture is basic to how one behaves. To understand how other cultures are similar to, or different from, one's own, it is necessary first to examine and understand one's own culture. This is difficult to do because people generally are unaware of the cultural influences that affect their values and behaviors. The exercise suggested at the end of this chapter provides an opportunity for students to discuss and examine their own culture.

Much cross-cultural organizational literature focuses on national boundaries rather than specific cultural boundaries; that is, "culture has often served simply as a synonym for nation without any further conceptual grounding" (Bhagat and McQuaid 1982). This means, in effect, that the focus is on what might be called a *national culture.* This can be somewhat misleading because there are clear cases in which cultures transcend national boundaries (e.g., aspects of British culture can be found in many Commonwealth countries) and other cases in which several cultures are evident in one nation (e.g., French and English cultures in Canada). On the whole, however, from an organization's viewpoint, a focus on national cultures appears appropriate.

Nations appear to be formed generally as a political expression of cultural similarity. Nations composed of several different cultures with no superordinate and uniting values are unlikely to survive in the long run. In such cases, the original nation may break into smaller units or one group may forcefully impose its values on the others, or an external threat may result in a united front. All of this suggests that, over time, it is appropriate to expect the emergence of a national culture.

Further, MNCs' activities are legally constrained by national requirements rather than cultural ones. For example, companies must comply with national constraints regarding ownership, reporting practices, taxes, and so on. The MNC is subservient to these aspects of national sovereignty and therefore naturally focuses on national issues, not purely cultural ones.

The human resource considerations that encourage an MNC to take a national perspective are even more important from a cultural analysis point of view. The organization's work force is usually predominantly a national work force. Labor mobility within a country is usually greater than between countries; consequently, the majority of employees are generally from the country where the organization is located, but they may come from many different parts of that country. This means that management systems need to be designed with this national character of the work force as a major consideration. Governments encourage this through legislation. In most cases, laws and regulations regarding interactions with employees encompass all citizens of a country and do not apply differentially. Laws and regulations regarding employees differ quite dramatically from country to country, but within a particular country they are usually consistent and apply to everyone. The MNC has to function in this system and therefore should begin its cultural analysis at the national cultural level. Once overall management systems have taken the national culture into account, the company can then consider subcultures within the national culture and make modifications for those groups as appropriate.

Assessing the Influence of Culture on Individual Values and Behavior in Organizations

It is important to examine the relationship between culture and organizations. The abstract and complex nature of culture, however, makes it difficult to identify and analyze. This examination of culture is therefore simplistic and must be understood in that context. The model depicted in Exhibit 6.1 shows the factors influencing the development of individual values and the relationship of these values to behavior. The model consists of seven factors, which will be described briefly.

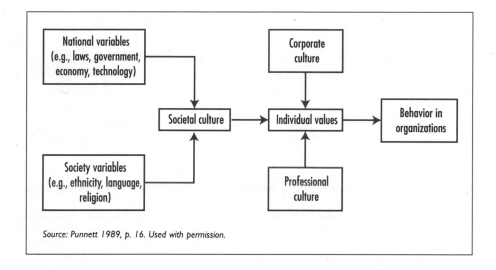

EXHIBIT 6.1
Model of the Influence of Cultural and National Factors on Individual Values and Behavior in Organizations

Source: Punnett 1989, p. 16. Used with permission.

▶ National Variables – Although in reality there is no clear distinction between national and societal characteristics, **national variables** are depicted here as the more concrete and observable factors that distinguish one nation from another. National characteristics include such factors as laws and regulations, economic conditions, and political ideology. They are generally used to describe an entire nation.

▶ Societal Variables – **Societal variables** may be shared with people of several nations. Conversely, a variety of social groups may exist within one nation who do not share all societal variables. Societal characteristics include ethnicity, language, and religion, among others.

▶ Societal and National Cultures – **National and societal cultures**, taken together, serve to develop a particular shared set of values typical of the people of one nation.

▶ Corporate Culture – The organization, through its leadership, work design, reward systems, and so on provides a culture of its own, a **corporate culture**; thus a shared set of values is typical of the people within one organization.

▶ Professional Culture – The group (for example, accountants, managers, manual workers) with which a person associates professionally also often provides a certain culture of its own, a **professional culture**; thus a shared set of values may be typical of people within one professional grouping.

▶ Individual Values – The individual in an organization expresses specific values that are formed partially by societal and national cultural values and partially by the corporate culture and the individual's professional culture. These constitute the person's **individual values**.

▶ Behavior – The actual behaviors that individuals engage in depend on their particular values; these values, as depicted in Exhibit 6.1, are the result of a wide variety of forces.

A complete understanding of individual behavior in organizations is very complex and, in fact, probably impossible. Clearly, the organization cannot hope to assess all of the variables included in the model. One alternative is for an organization to assess the relative similarity or dissimilarity of national cultures and then to deal with the major differences.

One means of analyzing similarities and differences has been through the identification of countries that appear to share similar values. Exhibit 6.2 uses information presented by Ronen and Shenkar to cluster countries based on the similarities of their cultural values.

These **country clusters** are based on the results of a variety of studies that examined employee attitudes, beliefs, values, and so on. The countries included in the list, therefore, are only those countries for which such research has been performed. Many countries and certain groups (e.g., Eastern Europe and Africa) are not represented. It may be possible, however, to make informed judgments regarding the likely position of countries that are not represented based on information about their cultural antecedents.

Using information from Punnett and Ronen, Exhibit 6.3 shows similarities and differences in cultural factors that shape cultural values (these are labeled **cultural antecedents**). These cultural antecedents are presented for each cluster of countries. According to data in Exhibit 6.3, countries in the Anglo cluster share, to a large extent, their language, religion, race, and level of economic development; note that other clusters share some of the Anglo characteristics but that other clusters have no overlapping with the Anglo group. It would seem that countries that share these characteristics have a degree of cultural similarity; where none are shared, there is relative cultural dissimilarity. An Arabic cluster would be different from the Anglo cluster in terms of language, religion, race, and level of economic development; therefore, the national culture of countries in such a cluster would be very different from the culture of countries in the Anglo cluster.

EXHIBIT 6.2
Country Clusters

Cluster 1 – Anglo
    Canada, Australia, New Zealand, United Kingdom, United States
Cluster 2 – Germanic
    Austria, Germany, Switzerland
Cluster 3 – Latin European
    Belgium, France, Italy, Portugal, Spain
Cluster 4 – Nordic
    Denmark, Finland, Norway, Sweden
Cluster 5 – Latin American
    Argentina, Chile, Colombia, Mexico, Peru, Venezuela
Cluster 6 – Near Eastern
    Greece, Iran, Turkey
Cluster 7 – Far Eastern
    Hong Kong, Indonesia, Malaysia, Philippines, Singapore, South Vietnam, Taiwan
Cluster 8 – Arab
    Bahrain, Kuwait, Saudi Arabia, United Arab Emirates
Independent (not closely related to other countries)
    Japan, India, Israel

Note: Countries within a cluster are considered similar with regard to their cultural values. Clusters are arranged in an approximate order of cluster similarity; that is, the Anglo cluster is more similar to the European clusters (Germanic, Latin European, and Nordic) than it is to the Latin American, Near Eastern, Far Eastern, and Arab clusters.

Source: Punnett 1989, p. 17. Used with permission. Based on information presented by Ronen 1984.

EXHIBIT 6.3 Cultural Antecedents Among Country Clusters Relative to Anglo Values

Anglo	Germanic	Latin European	Nordic	Latin American	Near Eastern	Far Eastern	Arab	Independent
Language (English)	*	X	X	X	X	X	X	India ?[a]
Religion (Judeo-Christian)	*	*	*	*	X	X	X	X
Race (Caucasian)	*	*	*	?	X	X	X	X
Economy (Industrial)	*	*	*	X	X	X	X	Japan

Similarities are indicated by an *, differences by an x, and some overlap by a ?.

[a]English is a commonly spoken language in India.

Source: Betty Jane Punnett, Experiencing International Management (Boston: PWS-KENT, 1989), p. 18. Based on information presented by Punnett and Ronen, 1984.

Framework for Cultural Analysis

To assess cultural similarities and differences, a framework with which to work is necessary. A variety of models for cultural analysis have been proposed that examine groupings of cultural values, and these are helpful. The two such models presented here are not mutually exclusive nor are they all-encompassing; rather, they provide different ways to examine cultural similarities and differences. Each approach provides somewhat different insights; therefore, each can be useful on its own or in combination with other models. In essence, however, cultural models provide only a simplified way to examine cultures. All cultures are far more complex than these models suggest, and it is important that this complexity be recognized.

Hofstede's Value Survey Model

The **Hofstede Value Survey Model** (VSM) (1980) proposed four dimensions, or indices, of culture. They were developed on the basis of a worldwide survey of employees in a large U.S. multinational company. As such, it is the most comprehensive study that incorporates culture as a factor in explaining variations in management. The indices measure four characteristics: individualism, uncertainty avoidance, power distance, and masculinity. Scores on each index range from 0 to 100; these scores should be interpreted as indicating a general sense of the values likely to be found in a particular country. The index characteristics and their impact on management policies are defined and described as follows.

Individualism (IDV) refers to the degree to which individual decision making and action are accepted and encouraged by the society. A society with a high IDV index emphasizes the role of the individual; a low IDV index (often referred to as *collectivism*) indicates that the society emphasizes the role of the group. Some societies view individualism positively and see it as the basis for creativity and achievement; others view it with disapproval and see it as disruptive. Effective management in high IDV countries incorporates policies, practices, and procedures that allow for individuals to take initiative, make decisions, and work on their own. In low IDV countries, the reverse is appropriate; group decisions, group action, and group work are preferred.

Uncertainty avoidance (UAI) refers to the degree to which the society is willing to accept and deal with uncertainty. The society with a high UAI index seeks certainty and security and wishes to avoid uncertainty; a low UAI index indicates a society that is comfortable with a high degree of uncertainty and is open to the unknown. Some societies view certainty as necessary, so that people can function without worrying about the consequences of uncertainty; others view uncertainty as providing excitement and opportunities for innovation and change. Effective management in countries with high UAI indexes provides job security, a well-defined work role, and opportunities to decrease uncertainty through consensus building. In countries with low UAI indexes, the reverse is true; job security is not stressed, risk taking is encouraged, and decisions are often made quickly and with relatively little information.

Power distance (PDI) refers to the degree to which power differences are accepted and sanctioned by society. Where the PDI index is high, the society believes that there should be a well-defined order in which everyone has a rightful place; where the PDI index is low, the prevalent belief is that all people should have equal rights and the opportunity to change their position in the society. Some societies view a well-ordered distribution of power as contributing to a well-managed society because each person knows what his or her position is, and people, in fact, are protected by this order. Others view power as corrupting and believe that those with less power inevitably suffer at the hands of those with more. Effective management in countries with high PDI indexes incorporates a well-defined hierarchy, centralized decision making, and authoritarian leadership. In countries with low PDI indexes, the reverse is true; flatter organizations with fewer levels of management, fewer supervisors, and democratic leadership are more successful.

Masculinity (MAS) refers to the degree to which traditional male values (assertiveness, performance, ambition, achievement, and material possessions) are important to a society. Societies with high MAS indexes have clearly differentiated sex roles, and men are dominant. Societies with low MAS indexes have sex roles that are more fluid and have predominately feminine values (focus on quality of life and the environment as well as nurture and concern for the less fortunate). Some societies see the traditional male values as being necessary for survival (i.e., men must be aggressive and women must be protected). Others view both sexes as equal contributors to society and believe that a dominance by traditional male values is destructive. Effective management in a society with a high MAS index differentiates work roles, stresses achievement, and rewards high performers with money. A low MAS index indicates accepted gender equity, emphasis on quality of work life, and less tangible rewards that are based on factors other than performance alone.

Each of these indices has been described in its extremes. Most countries are somewhere along the continuum in the moderately high or moderately low areas; thus, effective management practices seldom reflect an extreme. It is helpful in assessing cultural values to group countries into four quartiles: high, moderately high, moderately low, and low. Exhibit 6.4 presents the countries examined by Hofstede using the quartile format. The countries are further grouped according to the country clusters identified in Exhibit 6.2.

The index scores for members of the Anglo cluster are high on individualism, moderately low on uncertainty avoidance and power distance, and moderately high on masculinity. This seems to fit an intuitive profile of Anglo culture (especially in Australia and the United States) that values the individual, is ready to accept change, believes in equality (within the parameters of sex distinctions indicated by a relatively high MAS score), and stresses achievement and tangible rewards. The Germanic cluster is similar to this except that its index is higher in terms of uncertainty avoidance. The Latin European cluster also has a relatively high index on individualism but its index scores on uncertainty avoidance and power distance are higher, and its score on masculinity is mixed (among countries in that cluster). The Nordic cluster is similar to the Anglo cluster except for quite a dramatically low score on the masculinity index (the Nordic countries are the only ones that score in this quartile on masculinity). Latin American index scores are generally low on individualism, moderately high on uncertainty avoidance, and mixed on the other two indices. The Far Eastern group score is also low on individualism, but is rather high on power distance and mixed on the others; the Near Eastern group is similar. Finally, the independent group, as one would expect, has varied scores and does not clearly fit with any other group.

This analysis suggests that, within certain clusters, some but not necessarily all cultural values may be held in common. The Anglo cluster, for example, is clearly individualistic (this

EXHIBIT 6.4   **Countries Examined by Hofstede**

Cluster	IDV	UAI	PDI	MAS
Anglo				
Australia	H	ML	ML	MH
Canada	H	ML	ML	MH
Ireland	MH	L	L	MH
New Zealand	H	ML	L	MH
South Africa	MH	ML	ML	MH
United Kingdom	H	L	ML	MH
United States	H	ML	ML	MH
Germanic				
Austria	MH	MH	L	H
Germany (East and West)	MH	MH	ML	MH
Switzerland	MH	ML	ML	H
Latin European				
Belgium	MH	H	MH	MH
France	MH	MH	MH	ML
Italy	H	MH	ML	H
Portugal	ML	H	MH	ML
Spain	MH	MH	MH	ML
Nordic				
Denmark	MH	L	L	L
Finland	MH	ML	ML	L
Norway	MH	ML	L	L
Sweden	MH	L	L	L
Latin American				
Argentina	ML	MH	ML	MH
Chile	L	MH	MH	L
Colombia	L	MH	MH	MH
Peru	L	MH	MH	ML
Venezuela	MH	MH	L	H
Far Eastern				
Hong Kong	L	L	MH	MH
Philippines	ML	ML	H	MH
Singapore	L	L	H	ML
Taiwan	L	MH	MH	ML
Thailand	L	MH	MH	ML
Near Eastern				
Greece	ML	H	MH	MH
Iran	ML	ML	MH	ML
Pakistan	L	MH	MH	MH
Turkey	ML	MH	MH	ML
Independent				
Brazil	ML	MH	MH	ML
India	ML	ML	H	MH
Israel	MH	MH	L	ML
Japan	ML	H	MH	H

Note: H = high (1st quartile); MH = moderately high (2nd quartile); ML = moderately low (3rd quartile); L = low (4th quartile)

Source: Betty Jane Punnett, Experiencing International Management *(Boston: PWS-KENT, 1989), p. 19. Used with permission.*

is consistent with the English language capitalization of the word *I*). The Nordic cluster is clearly feminine, consistent with an emphasis on social welfare and attempts to attain equality of the sexes.

Examination of profiles of different countries shows the variety that is possible considering these four dimensions. Some examples illustrate how these profiles might influence management practices in particular countries.

▶ New Zealand as a society is individualistic, does not avoid uncertainty, and believes in equality and traditional male values. This suggests that organizational structures will be relatively flat with individuals making decisions on their own and competing for scarce resources.

▶ Italy as a society is individualistic, avoids uncertainty, and believes in equality (within the confines of sex distinctions) and traditional male values. This suggests a similar structure but also a reliance on gathering information for decisions and an emphasis on job security and seniority as important components of the management system.

▶ Singapore as a society is collectivist, does not avoid uncertainty, believes in power distinctions, and has a low MAS score. This suggests a paternalistic leadership system, with the leader expressing concern for subordinates and the quality of life but without a stress on job security.

▶ Japan is a collectivist society but also high on the uncertainty avoidance as well as the masculinity indexes, and relatively high on power distance. These characteristics suggest a system that seeks consensus among group members but is competitive and has clear distinctions in terms of power; job security is stressed, and jobs are allocated on the basis of sex.

It is important to stress that the indexes identified by Hofstede were developed from data obtained from employees within one organization, a large U.S. multinational company. The fact that certain types of individuals are attracted to such an organization is reflected in these scores. These scores should not, therefore, be interpreted as an accurate description of a national culture as a whole but as an indication of the similarities and differences that one might expect to find among employees in this type of organization in different countries.

These index scores represent a central tendency in a particular population, but there is likely a wide array of values in any country; organizations and industries attract and retain individuals with value systems that fit into the organizational culture. For example, a study of fast-food restaurant managers in Canada and the United States revealed a very low level of individualism combined with no uncertainty avoidance and high power distance and masculinity (Punnett and Withane 1990). These characteristics are quite dissimilar from the Canadian and U.S. value profile presented in Exhibit 6.4, but they appear appropriate in an industry in which people must work in close coordination, have little job security, and experience clear distinctions of power and a great deal of competition.

The process of management is often described as consisting of four essential stages: planning, organizing, directing, and controlling. This framework can be used to examine the potential influence of cultural differences on the process of management. These four stages of management can be discussed relative to the four cultural dimensions developed by Hofstede. The two extremes of each of the cultural dimensions are considered relative to selected aspects of these four processes; for example, planning and decision making can be looked at in terms of individualism and collectivism, structuring and organizing in terms of high or low uncertainty avoidance, staffing and directing in terms of masculinity and femininity, and communicating and controlling in terms of power distance.

Kluckhohn and Strodtbeck's Value Orientations

Another way to view cultural similarities and differences is in terms of basic problems that all human societies face. Anthropologists Kluckhohn and Strodtbeck (1961) identified five such problems:

1. Relationship of humans to nature
2. Humans' time orientation
3. Beliefs about basic human nature
4. Humans' activity orientation
5. Relationship of humans to other humans

The concept underlying this approach to cultural similarities and differences is that there are different ways to cope with these problems, and different societies have adopted different solutions. Like the Hofstede framework, these ways of coping represent the central tendency in a society, but individuals deviate from this general preference. The following sections discuss these five problems, **Kluckhohn and Strodtbeck's value orientations**.

Relationship to Nature: *Subjugation, Harmony, and Mastery*

Societies that view themselves as subjugated to nature view life as essentially preordained: People are not masters of their own destinies, and trying to change the inevitable is futile. Societies that view themselves as living in harmony with nature believe that people must alter their behavior to accommodate nature. Societies that view themselves as able to master nature think in terms of the supremacy of the human race and harnessing the forces of nature.

The Muslim view of events occurring as God wills exemplifies the first view; the Native American wish to preserve nature as it is is a good example of the second; the third is seen, for example, in the English-speaking world's desire to conquer natural phenomena.

Time Orientation: *Past, Present, and Future*

Societies that are oriented toward the past look for solutions in the past; they wonder what their forebears would have done. Societies that are present oriented consider the immediate effects of their actions; they wonder what will happen if they do something. Societies that are future oriented look to the long-term results of today's events; they question what will happen to future generations if certain things are done today.

The Chinese veneration for older people suggests an orientation to the past; the reported American desire for instant gratification suggests an orientation toward the present; the Japanese emphasis on long-term planning might be considered an orientation toward the future.

Basic Human Nature: *Evil, Good, and Mixed*

Societies that believe that people are primarily evil focus on controlling the behavior of people with specified codes of conduct and sanctions for wrongdoing. Societies that believe that people are essentially good are more likely to exhibit trust and to rely on verbal agreements. Societies that see people as mixed probably see people as changeable and focus on ways to modify behavior – to encourage desired behavior and discourage undesirable behaviors.

The view of people by North Americans as both good and bad is reflected in their treatment of employees with a general emphasis on rewarding "good" behavior and punishing "bad" (the same might be said of the penal system). The Japanese suggest an attitude of people being good; an employee is not singled out for good performance because this is simply living up to expectations. The 17th century Puritan concept that people are born with a burden of original sin exemplifies the view that humans are inherently evil but they still hold hope for erasing the evil.

Activity Orientation: *Being, Containing and Controlling, and Doing*

Societies that are primarily being oriented are emotional; people react spontaneously based on what they feel at the time. Those concerned with containing and controlling focus on moderation; people seek to achieve a balance in life and in society. Those who are doing oriented are constantly striving to achieve; people are driven by a need to accomplish difficult tasks.

The Latin temperament might be considered essentially being because it is emotional. The British, on the other hand, could be seen as controlling or stressing moderation. The view that work is good and that "idle hands make mischief" represents the doing orientation.

Human Relationships: *Individual, Lineal, and Colineal*

Societies that are primarily individual believe that individuals should be independent and take responsibility for their own actions. Those that are lineal are concerned with the family line and the power structure that underlies a hierarchy. Those that are colineal are group oriented and emphasize group interactions and actions.

English-speaking societies tend to be individualistic, stressing the role of the individual in society. The Indian society is probably largely lineal, placing emphasis on the individual's lineage. The Japanese may be considered predominantly colineal.

These value orientations affect the management practices that are effective in different locations. The following examples illustrate how these orientations can be related to management:

▶ In a society that believes humans are subjugated by nature, the very act of planning is futile because the future is preordained.

▶ In a society that is present oriented, rewards for performance should be closely tied to the actual performance.

▶ In a society that believes in the basic goodness of humans, participative management is likely to be the normal approach.

▶ In a society that is primarily being oriented, decisions are likely to be intuitive with less concern for logic.

Examples of cultural misunderstandings show clearly the role of cultural differences in cross-cultural encounters. A few such examples are highlighted in the box on cultural misunderstandings.

In the United States, the invitation "Come any time" may simply be a polite expression, but in India it represents a serious invitation. The Indian is requesting a visit but is politely allowing the guest to arrange the time. If no time is set, the Indian assumes the invitation has been refused.

A true anecdote about an American couple touring Asia might best illustrate the risks involved when relying on nonverbal forms of expression while in a foreign environment. A wealthy couple, accompanied by their pet poodle, was enjoying a lengthy cruise around the world. At one of the ship's Asian stops, the couple, with their inseparable pet, decided to sightsee in the town. After a lengthy walk, they chose to dine at a pleasant-looking restaurant. Since the restaurant employees could not speak English and the tourists could speak no other language, they ordered their meals by pointing to various items on the menu. Knowing the poodle was also hungry, the couple tried to order food for it. For a long time the waiter had a difficult time understanding, but after several attempts he seemed to have figured it all out. He pointed to the dog and then pointed to the kitchen. The couple interpreted this to mean that their pet could not eat in the dining area but must eat in the kitchen where the waiter had some food for it. They therefore agreed to let the waiter take the dog to the kitchen. After waiting a particularly long time, the waiter and the full staff proudly entered with the couple's order. One can imagine the tourists' horror when the chef lifted one of the lids to display how well he had cooked the poodle!

Cultural Underpinnings

The focus of both the Hofstede value indexes and the Kluckhohn and Strodtbeck value orientations is on expressed cultural values. It is important in international business to understand the role that other cultural factors play in intercultural interactions. Although a wide variety of factors could be examined in this context, the approach here is to focus on a limited number of factors that seem to be of particular importance to organizational effectiveness. The following discussion will examine the influences of language, religion, education, and social systems in the business environment.

Language

Language seems to be important in people's socialization, and Whorf (1967) described language as defining and perpetuating a particular worldview. The important nature of language is illustrated by the belief that one cannot really speak a foreign language until one learns to think in that language. The reason is that the thought patterns that go with one language are different from those that accompany another; thus, language influences even the way people think. Further, the vocabulary of each language reflects the primary concerns of that society. This is seen in the more than 6,000 words in Arabic for describing the camel and its equipment; similarly, the Inuit (Eskimo) have an extensive list of words for describing snow. While English is certainly limited relative to these two languages in terms of camels and snow, it has become accepted as the language of commerce because of its extensive vocabulary dealing with business-related issues. Although it is helpful for English-speaking peoples to know that English is the most commonly spoken second language, they should not adopt the attitude that other languages, therefore, are unimportant.

Language provides people with an important means of communication, and because communication is integral to all aspects of business, how to communicate when different languages are spoken is an issue that international companies must settle. An example of the operations of a hypothetical company serves to illustrate the language needs that one company might have.

Imagine Company A, headquartered in Toronto, Canada, with a French-speaking CEO from Quebec. The company has the following international activities:

▶ A wholly owned manufacturing subsidiary in Trinidad that supplies other Caribbean islands
▶ A licensee in France that supplies the European market, including the United Kingdom, Germany, Sweden, and Finland from facilities in France
▶ A joint venture with a Brazilian company that manufactures in Brazil and exports to the rest of South America and Central America
▶ A joint venture with the Indian government that consists of small manufacturing facilities throughout India
▶ Negotiations currently under way with a Japanese company to establish a joint venture to develop and exploit new technologies
▶ Exports from Canada to the People's Republic of China
▶ Consideration of a merger with a U.S.-based competitor.

A variety of levels of communication would take place in such an organization. These include communication between the headquarters and managers in foreign locations, the headquarters and foreign partners, the headquarters and foreign governments, the headquarters and foreign customers, suppliers, creditors, and so on. Managers in foreign locations also communicate with employees, unions, their governments, suppliers, customers, local partners, and so on, and with other managers and staff at different locations. Each of these communications may involve more than one language.

Company A's activities might involve the following languages: English (quite a variety – American, British, Canadian, Trinidadian), French (Canadian, Parisienne, Caribbean), Spanish, Portuguese, German, Swedish, Finnish, Japanese, Chinese (Mandarin), and probably several different languages in India. The international company facing such a situation has a number of options available; each has its benefits and disadvantages as will be discussed.

Translations and Translators

A company may hire outside translators or have on staff employees whose job it is to translate from one language to another. Most companies that have interactions in different languages will, at some time, use translators and translations. Many translation services provide an adequate means to go from one language to another, but there is a great deal of room for error in translations. Very often, translations are literal translations of words rather than meanings, and they may be quite misleading in the foreign language. Most of us have come across instructions for use of foreign-made products that have been translated into English in such a way that it is almost impossible to follow them. The box on language and cultural interactions illustrates some of these.

One U.S. banker in Australia began on the wrong foot when he indicated that he was "full." The subsequent nervous laughter suggested that something was wrong, so he tried to clarify the situation by saying that he was "stuffed." One can imagine his astonishment when he was informed that "full" implied drunk and that "stuffed" indicated being involved in sexual intercourse.

Otis Engineering Corporation's representatives could not discern why its display won Soviet snickers as well as praise. Much to their disappointment and embarrassment, they discovered that a careless translator had rendered a sign that identified "completion equipment" as "equipment for orgasms."

Quebec has been the site of a number of corporate blunders. One promotion was supposed to say "Don't be half-sure, be Ponko-sure." Instead, it declared "Ne Soyez pas DEMI-SUR, soyez PONKO-SUR." At the root of this translation mishap was the word *sur*. *Sûr* means sure, but if the accent over the *û* is left off, the word *sur* takes on the meaning "sour." The company, therefore, was saying "Don't be half-sour, be PONKO-sour."

Sumitomo used a Tokyo-based, Japanese agency to help develop its advertisements. The company named a specific steel **Sumitomo High Toughness,** and the name was promoted by the acronym SHT in bold letters. So bold, in fact, that the full-page ads run in U.S. trade journals were three fourths filled with SHT. Located at the bottom of the page was a short message that ended with the claim that the product "was made to match its name."

General Motors was troubled by the lack of enthusiasm among the Puerto Rican auto dealers for its Chevrolet Nova. The name Nova meant "star" when literally translated. However, when spoken, it sounded like "no va," which in Spanish means "it doesn't go."

Ford encountered translation problems with some of its cars. It introduced a low-cost truck, the Fiera, into some of the less developed countries. Unfortunately, the name meant "ugly old woman" in Spanish. Ford also experienced slow sales when it introduced a top-of-the-line automobile, the Comet, in Mexico under the name Caliente. The puzzlingly low sales levels were finally understood when Ford discovered that *caliente* is slang for streetwalker.

A U.S. airline that proudly advertised swank "rendezvous lounges" available on its Boeing 747 jets may have wished that its promotion had never reached Brazil. The company belatedly learned that *rendezvous* in Portuguese represents a room rented out for prostitution.

When the Coca-Cola Company was planning its strategy for marketing in China in the 1920s, it wanted to introduce its product with the English pronunciation of Coca-Cola. A translator developed a group of Chinese characters that, when pronounced, sounded like the product name. The characters were placed on the cola bottles and marketed. Was it any wonder that sales levels were low? The characters translated to mean "a wax-flattened mare" or "bite the wax tadpole."

The difficulty in translation is illustrated by one researcher's experience when having a questionnaire translated from English into Korean. A student who spoke both Korean and English prepared the translation. Fortunately, the questionnaire in Korean was translated back into English; this translation revealed a major problem with one question. This question, attempting to discuss the amount of conflict in an organization, meant in Korean, "Is there a lot of hitting and fighting among employees?"

The accuracy of translations can be improved through the back-translation approach. The communication is translated from one language (e.g., English) into a second language (e.g., German) by one individual, then translated from the second language (German) back into the first (English) by a second translator. The two versions in the first language are then compared for discrepancies; where differences are found, a further translation is undertaken. It is generally best to have each translator translate into her or his native tongue. These approaches increase accuracy, but they also increase cost and take additional time. The increased benefits and costs must be weighed. Generally, if the communication is vital to the company, accuracy is important; if time is available, then these complex approaches are generally adopted. If the communication is less important, the added accuracy may not be seen as worth the added cost.

Language Training

Employees from the home country can be trained in the foreign languages that they will encounter, and foreign employees can be trained in the home-country language. Most companies engage in some degree of language training, and certainly it is desirable that employees have some knowledge of the different languages that they may encounter. Language training can be expensive and time consuming, however; and some people find it difficult to learn a new language. Again, the company should weigh the costs against the benefits. If interactions among people of different languages will be frequent, it is probably important for them to be able to communicate directly. If interactions are infrequent, then language training can be reduced.

One of the most critical aspects of communication in international companies is between subsidiary and parent. To allow for regular, frequent, and accurate communication between parent and subsidiary, having at least a certain number of bilingual or multilingual managers is usually desirable. These may be foreign managers who speak the home language or expatriate managers who speak the foreign language. It may sometimes be possible to hire individuals who are already able to speak the required languages, but in many cases, managers with the required technical and interpersonal skills may not speak the desired language. In such cases, language training is needed.

Outside Consultants

A number of communication tasks can sometimes be best accomplished by outside consultants, and it may be appropriate for a company to use these services rather than translations or language training. Negotiations with governments and media development are two areas in which companies may choose to delegate the task to an outsider. Companies or individuals specializing in government negotiations or media development offer an intimate knowledge not only of the language but also of the culture and the activity being delegated. At the same time, the dollar cost of using outsiders is often high and, in addition, the company is entrusting a critical function to someone outside the organization.

In facing the communication difficulties that arise because of language differences, a company should weigh carefully the benefits to be gained from improved communication against the costs associated with the improvement. For example, English is generally accepted as the common language of business and in some cases it may be appropriate to rely on this rather than attempt to learn a foreign language. Equally, there are situations in which understanding at least some of a foreign language may provide a manager with a real advantage. The final choice for a particular situation may involve a combination of approaches.

Religion

Religion has been identified as a "socially shared set of beliefs, ideas, and actions that relate to a reality that cannot be verified empirically yet is believed to affect the course of natural and human events. Because such belief conditions people's motivations and actions, it affects their actions" (Terpstra and David 1985, p. 79). Clearly, religion is closely associated with the development of cultural values, and it has an impact on many day-to-day activities in a society. International companies, therefore, need to understand the role of religion in the societies in which they operate.

The international company is usually interested in several dimensions of a country's religious profile. These dimensions are, first, the dominant religion or state religion; second, the importance of religion generally in the society; third, the degree of religious heterogencity or homogencity; and fourth, the tolerance or intolerance of religious diversity.

The dominant religion influences many day-to-day activities, such as opening and closing times, days off, holidays, ceremonies, and foods. A company's operations and activities should be organized relative to those specific religious practices that affect management. Religious beliefs and events can affect both production and consumption, and the effective organization makes its plans to accommodate these beliefs and events. In the United States, Sunday is customarily a day off from work, Christmas day is a holiday for most employees, and production over the entire Christmas period is often slow while consumption is at a peak. These customs clearly reflect the dominance of Christian religion in the United States and the fact that U.S. businesses clearly plan their operations around these events. Although it may seem self-evident that different religious events must be accommodated in countries that are not Christian, people all too often forget to consider this.

The importance of religion in a particular society is also a major consideration for a business. Where religion plays a relatively minor role, people, for the most part, are relatively flexible in terms of religious adherence and tolerant of religious mistakes that foreigners make. Where religious beliefs are fundamental to the society and represent deeply held convictions of the people, however, there is little flexibility or tolerance. This affects a company's activities; for example, scheduling extra work on a religious holiday might be possible in the former country but not the latter. Advertising using religiously unacceptable themes might simply be corrected in the first but can cause lasting damage in the second.

Religious diversity is also an important factor. Although most countries have a dominant religion, many also have groups who adhere to different religions. This can be particularly difficult for a foreign company to accommodate because it can mean different working hours, different holidays, different ceremonies, and so on for different groups of employees. Although this diversity may be difficult to accommodate, a company that is aware of the necessity to treat each group according to its religious dictates can devise ways to do so. If the company is not aware of the need, it may alienate some groups of employees and suffer the consequences of low motivation, turnover, absenteeism, and so on without understanding the cause.

Religious tolerance, or lack thereof, is another serious concern for companies operating in foreign environments. In many cases, lack of tolerance for other religions is associated with religious beliefs that are held very deeply. It is not surprising that, if religion is very important in a society, people in that society will believe that their particular religion is right and others are wrong. Such a situation clearly has the elements for conflict if employees within the same organization come from different faiths. It may not be possible to avoid some conflict in such situations, but the company that is aware of the potential for conflict can make efforts to minimize the likelihood and develop approaches to manage it if it should surface.

Fortunately for international companies, it is relatively easy to obtain information about the religious profiles of particular countries, and literature on the beliefs and practices of most of the world's religions is readily available. Companies, therefore, should investigate the religious makeup of any country in which they expect to have activities. The *World Christian Encyclopedia* (Barrett 1982) contains a census of the world's religions and can be a starting point for religious investigation. A lack of religious understanding has been the demise of many an international business endeavor, as illustrated in the box on religion and cultural interaction.

England's East India Company may have lost control of India in 1857 because it failed to modify a product it provided. In those days, bullets were often encased in pig wax, and tops had to be bitten off before the bullets could be fired. The Asian Indian soldiers were furious when they discovered the pig wax since it was against their religion to eat pork. The soldiers revolted, and hundreds of people on both sides were killed before peace was restored.

One soft-drink company inadvertently offended some of its customers in the Arab world because its labels incorporated six-pointed stars. The stars were considered to be only a decoration by the firm, but they were interpreted by the Arabs as reflecting pro-Israeli sentiment.

A refrigerator manufacturer used for its advertisement a picture of a refrigerator containing a centrally placed chunk of ham. The typical refrigerator advertisement often features a refrigerator full of delicious food, and because these photos are difficult to take, the photos are generally used in as many places as possible. This company used its stock photo one place too many, though, when it was used in the Middle East where Moslems do not eat ham. Locals considered the ad to be insensitive and unappealing.

Saudi Arabia nearly restricted an airline from initiating flights when the company authorized "normal" newspaper advertisements. The ads featured attractive hostesses serving champagne to the happy airline passengers. Because alcohol is illegal in Saudi Arabia and unveiled women are not permitted to mix with men, the photo was viewed as an attempt to alter religious customs.

Education

Education is a process of learning, through which members of society gain specific information and share social expectations. Education, like language and religion, is an integral part of the development of a societal culture. Education implies teaching and the passing of information and knowledge from older people to younger. Adults teach children from infancy what they know about the world. This serves as a method of passing on cultural knowledge and developing patterns of thinking that result in acceptance of cultural values. The educational system is the formal approach that a society uses to provide information and knowledge to its children. The educational system provides information related to the society's cultural system, and it also influences and molds values by providing the information in a particular format, at a particular time, by particular people, and so on. For example, in societies that believe knowledge comes with age, education of children may be the task of the elders in the society; in contrast, where knowledge is associated with expertise, education is the task of anyone who has studied and mastered a particular body of knowledge.

Companies need to consider all aspects of education in a foreign location but they will often focus on the educational system and its impact on their activities. It is virtually impossible for a company to function effectively in a society without understanding its educational system, as shown in the box on education and cultural interaction.

> One laundry detergent company wishes it had contacted a few locals before it initiated its promotional campaign in the Middle East. All of the company's advertisements pictured soiled clothes on the left, its box of soap in the middle, and clean clothes on the right. But, because in that area of the world people tend to read from right to left, many potential customers interpreted the message to indicate the soap actually soiled the clothes.

The interaction of education and the organization is seen most clearly in a company's relationships with employees. The levels and types of education in a country determine the skill level of the work force, the amount of additional training the company must provide, and the communication skills of the workers. The quality of the educational system affects the degree and type of training of staff that must be undertaken; it also influences the degree of decentralization possible and the communication systems that are employed.

A focus for most Western companies is the educational level that exists in a particular country. The higher the level of education, the more likely it is that all jobs can be staffed locally, that many decisions can be made at the local level, that training methods can be transferred, and that standard written communication will be adequate. A lower level of education decreases the likelihood of these factors. In this case, the company must consider staffing with foreigners, particularly at higher and more technical levels; extensive training programs that may have to be adapted according to the abilities and customs of the workers may be necessary; less delegation will be possible; and the company may find that written communication is not adequate.

The more economically developed countries of the world generally have relatively high levels of education, which makes these staffing issues somewhat easier. Even in such cases, it may be important to adjust to the traditional system. Rohlen (1973) tells of a training program for a Japanese bank that incorporated Zen meditation, military training, working for strangers for no pay, time spent in an agricultural community, and a 25-mile endurance walk. This training might be met with resistance if implemented in North America. Training programs that are effective in North America can be ineffective elsewhere if they depart dramatically from the type of educational system operating in that country.

The role of educational systems is particularly important in a company's employee relations and in its interaction with other groups. It can affect a company's policies regarding customers and consumers. If consumers cannot read, for example, written descriptions of products or directions are not useful; customers respond to pictures and interpret products in this situation. An enlightening example of how this can backfire is described in the box on interpreting pictures.

In areas in which many of the people are illiterate, product labels usually depict a picture of what the package contains. This very logical practice proved to be quite perplexing to one big company. It tried to sell baby food in an African nation by using its regular label showing a baby and stating the type of baby food in the jar. Unfortunately, the local population took one look at the labels and interpreted them to mean the jars contained ground-up babies.

Illiteracy can be particularly important with products or processes that are potentially dangerous. Employees or customers who cannot read warning labels are subject to dangers because they cannot understand written warnings. Companies in such situations must devise means other than written statements to warn and direct users.

Social Systems

All societies rely on systems for organizing behavior, and these form an important part of the society's culture. Social systems provide a context for appropriate interactions among individuals and groups – they encompass a wide variety of structures that delineate what is acceptable in different circumstances. Social systems include such diverse activities as courting and marriage rituals, entertaining practices, interaction among people of higher and lower classes, kinship units, and business ownership, to name only a few.

Global companies have to function within the confines of the established social systems in a particular location. This means accommodating these systems or attracting local employees who are willing to accept alternative systems. The manager needs to gather information on the social systems in foreign locations, assess the impact on operations, and then decide if and how much to adapt the organization's traditional practices to accommodate the new social system.

We cannot fully discuss the variety of social systems that influence how business is conducted, but consider some examples:

- ▶ In Japan it is acceptable for a male supervisor to introduce female subordinates to prospective husbands.
- ▶ In the United States it is normal to invite a colleague of the opposite gender for a meal to discuss business.
- ▶ In the West Indies it is usual to discuss business over a few alcoholic drinks.
- ▶ In Saudi Arabia it is traditional to segregate working women from working men.

▶ In Moslem countries it is expected that work will stop for prayers throughout the day.

▶ In Canada it is likely that business will close for extended periods over the December 25 Christmas festival.

Clearly, any of these practices which form part of a well-established social system seems standard to members of the society, but to nonmembers they may appear unusual or even bizarre. It is important that managers in foreign locations recognize the importance of social systems to the effective functioning of a business, and that they take the time and make the effort to understand these systems.

Summary

This chapter explored the concept of culture and identified the implications it has for effective management. Two models for assessing cultural differences were presented, and various specific aspects of culture were discussed. This chapter should provide students with a general appreciation of the importance of culture in managing international companies, as well as some guidance for assessing and managing cross-cultural encounters.

MINI-CASE
The Bata Shoe Organization

A story is told that, following World War II, two footwear companies sent representatives to assess the African market. One returned and said that there was no market because the people did not wear shoes. The second returned and said that the market was huge because the people did not wear shoes. The second representative is said to have been from the Bata Shoe Organization (BSO), which now has subsidiaries throughout Africa.

BSO is the world's largest manufacturer and marketer of footwear, with operations in more than 100 countries worldwide. The company was started as a family business in the late 1800s in Czechoslovakia. In 1988, it was still a family business, with Thomas G. Bata, grandson of the founder, as chief executive officer.

BSO is headquartered in Toronto, Canada, but most of its business (95 percent) is outside Canada. BSO has the enviable reputation of being considered a local company almost everywhere it operates. This may be partly because the name *Bata* is not easily associated with any particular nationality. It is certainly also due to the corporate culture that BSO cultivates. BSO describes itself as a multidomestic organization; its subsidiaries are virtually self-governing and autonomous. The company's corporate brochure describes it as "an international organization of companies rooted in their communities and essentially 'national' in spirit." The company says that its first allegiance is to the communities and countries in which it does business. Subsidiaries operate as local companies and rely largely on local markets, local suppliers, and local staff.

In contrast, a policy of standardization appears to be one of the company's competitive strengths. Factories and stores are built and maintained to the same specifications wherever they are located; employees worldwide have access to the same management and technical training opportunities; universal policies govern all subsidiaries. BSO maintains this global control by establishing wholly owned subsidiaries wherever possible (85 percent of subsidiaries are wholly owned).

This mix of decentralization and global standardization is achieved partly through a training program that affects all Bata employees throughout their careers. Bata's philosophy is that a successful company relies on its people and that these people need to be properly trained.

Training at BSO takes place at all levels of the organization. There are programs for top management, middle management, supervisors, and operators; there are also training programs for trainers. Training is stressed, and there seems to be a genuine belief that proper training results in tangible benefits for both the organization and its people. The documented benefits of training programs include higher productivity, lower absenteeism, improved industrial relations, and increased employee satisfaction.

The Cultural Challenge

BSO operates in more than 100 countries worldwide. A major challenge has been to develop training programs that are culturally sensitive and can travel throughout the world. To paraphrase one executive, it is difficult to talk about face-to-face communication in a country where women employees are expected to sit on the floor facing the wall, with their backs to their male superiors.

To achieve its desired mix of standardization and cultural sensitivity in its training programs, the company has instituted an interesting approach to training. The program for first-line supervisors illustrates that approach.

First, executives at the company developed an agenda of issues that they believed affected all supervisors, no matter where they were located. This agenda included general issues such as motivation, discipline, assigning work, and communication. A general overview of these issues was developed for use worldwide, describing in simple language what was meant by each concept.

Next, individuals in different countries and regions met to discuss the issues that had been identified. Small groups were used to develop policies for dealing with a variety of issues. These groups considered various situations and identified culture-specific solutions to different situations.

In this way, the company achieved a standardized training program for use worldwide; it was also sensitive to the cultural differences that could be expected in different locations.

Conclusions

Companies such as BSO that operate in a large number of countries worldwide face a major challenge in terms of developing effective practices and procedures that can be transferred around the world. BSO has instituted a particular worldwide training program that seems to be effective in ensuring that similar issues are considered at all locations and, at the same time, different approaches are accepted in culturally different locations.

Source: Bata Shoe Organization, corporate literature and interviews.

Discussion Issues

1. Considering the product that Bata manufactures and sells, discuss the advantages and disadvantages of cultivating a local image as Bata does.
2. Do you agree with the Bata executives that managers in all countries face universal management issues? Develop a list of such issues and discuss them.
3. Examine recent reports on the Bata Shoe Organization and identify the countries and regions of the world in which it currently operates.

Discussion Questions

1. Define *culture* in your own words and list some of the characteristics of culture that you believe to be particularly important when traveling in foreign locations.
2. Select one characteristic of culture that you believe affects international business and management and explain its impact on doing business in foreign locations.
3. Share different cultural experiences that you have had and discuss how these would affect your management style in a particular foreign country.
4. Try to define your own culture and some of its key characteristics.

Assignments

1. Choose a country and research its cultural profile.

2. Choose two countries that you expect to have different cultures and contrast those cultures.

3. Select a particular aspect of management (leadership, motivation, planning, etc.) and discuss how it could be influenced by cultural differences.

Selected References

Barrett, D. B., ed., *World Christian Encyclopedia* (New York: Oxford University Press, 1982).

Bhagat, R. S., and S. J. McQuaid, "Role of Subjective Culture in Organizations: A Review and Directions for Future Research," *Journal of Applied Psychology Monograph* 67, no. 5 (1982), pp. 635–685.

Globe and Mail, "Hair: The Long and Short" (November 19,1990).

Globe and Mail, "Social Studies" (November 19, 1990), p. A10.

Heller, F. A., "Cost Benefits of Multinational Research on Organizations," *International Studies of Management and Organization* 18, no. 3 (1988), pp. 5–18.

Hofstede G., *Culture's Consequences: International Differences in Work Related Values* (Beverly Hills, Calif.: Sage Publications, 1980).

Kluckhohn, C., and F. Strodtbeck, *Variations in Value Orientations* (Westport, Conn.: Greenwood Press, 1961).

Kroeber, A., and C. Kluckhohn, "Culture: A Critical Review of Concepts and Definitions," *Papers of the Peabody Museum of American Archaeology and Ethnology,* Harvard University (1952), pp. 1–223.

Lane, H. W., and J. J. DiStefano, *International Management Behavior* (Scarborough, Ont.: Nelson Canada, 1988).

Punnett, B. J., *Experiencing International Management* (Boston: PWS-Kent, 1989).

Punnett, B. J., and S. Ronen, "Operationalizing Cross-Cultural Variables," paper delivered at the 44th Annual Meeting of the Academy of Management, Boston, 1984.

Punnett, B. J., and S. Withane, "Hofstede's Value Survey Module: To Embrace or Abandon?" in *Advances in International Comparative Management* (Greenwich, Conn.: JAI Press, 1990).

Ricks, D., *Big Business Blunders* (Homewood, Ill.: Dow Jones-Irwin, 1983).

Ricks, D., *Blunders in International Business* (Cambridge, Mass.: Blackwell Publishers, 1993).

Rohlen, T. P., "Spiritual Education in a Japanese Bank," *American Anthropologist* 75, no. 5 (1973), pp. 1542–1562.

Ronen, S., *Comparative and Multinational Management* (New York: John Wiley & Sons, 1984).

Terpstra, V., and K. David, *The Cultural Environment of International Business* (Cincinnati: South-Western, 1985).

Whorf, B. L., *Language, Thought, and Reality* (Cambridge, Mass.: MIT Press, 1967).

Zeeman, J., Academy of International Business Annual Meeting, 1988.

CHAPTER 7

The Political Environment of International Business

L E A R N I N G   O B J E C T I V E S

After reading this chapter, you should be able to

▶ Define *political risk* and discuss the concept and its assessment and management in an international context.

▶ Outline the political risk process that enables a company to estimate the degree of risk that exists in a given situation and then decide how to deal with that risk.

▶ Identify and discuss factors associated with countries and companies that contribute to their riskiness.

▶ Differentiate between defensive and integrative political risk management strategies.

▶ Understand how the political system and the objectives of the home and host governments are critical to the political environment facing international firms.

▶ Discuss negotiations between international firms and governments.

▶ Describe the major political systems in the world today.

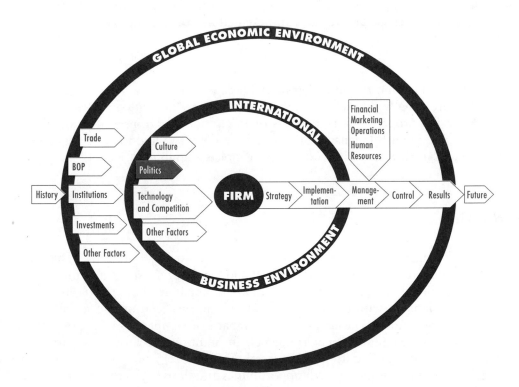

KEY TERMS

- Political risk
- Forced divestment
- Confiscation
- Expropriation
- Nationalization
- Unwelcome regulation
- Political risk analysis

- Political risk management
- Defensive political risk management
- Integrative political risk management
- Capitalism
- Socialism
- Communism

THOUGHT STARTERS

▶ Kuwait found an unexpected benefit in Iraq's invasion of the tiny kingdom; the subsequent tumble in stock prices around the world presented a great buying opportunity for its huge investment portfolios.

(Globe and Mail August 23, 1990)

▶ Even the name of a country can cause trouble because the names given to Eastern countries by the West are usually different than those used by the Eastern countries themselves. The failure to use the proper country name is often considered an insensitive or offensive act. For instance, the English-language catalog of a Swedish firm had to be changed because the catalog cited "North Korea" instead of the "People's Republic of Korea."

Introduction

International companies, by definition, operate across national boundaries. This means that these companies interact within different political and regulatory systems and must consider the impact of these political systems on their operations. Companies that are largely domestic will consider their relationship with the local political system; this relationship usually is relatively familiar and well understood. The international company often operates in one or more unfamiliar and little understood political environments. In addition, because of its foreignness, an international company may find itself the brunt of discriminatory practices in certain locations. The political environment provides both opportunities and drawbacks for international companies, and therefore, understanding and managing this environment is an important component of international management. This chapter focuses on the concept of political risk to explore the political environment and the opportunities and threats provided by this environment.

The chapter explores the concept of political risk and its assessment and management in an international context. Various types of risks are identified and specific models of political risk management presented. The chapter discusses the relationships between international companies and host governments as well as their differing objectives and how these can be reconciled. Also considered are negotiations with governments and how these can be conducted effectively, as well as the impact of the home government in the activities of the MNC. Finally, general forms of government-business relationships are examined.

Defining *Political Risk*

Political risk includes a variety of factors ranging from government confiscation of a firm's assets to government encouragement of negative attitudes toward foreign businesses. To encompass this wide range of factors, **political risk** can be defined as the possibility of unwanted consequences of political activity (i.e., political risk occurs because of the uncertainty associated with political activities and events). Companies face three major categories of political risk: forced divestment, unwelcome regulation, and interference with operations.

Forced Divestment

Forced divestment occurs when a government wishes to acquire the assets of a company against the company's will. At worst, the host government may **confiscate** company assets; that is, take them over with no compensation. Alternatively, the host may force the company to sell its assets to local interests, usually the government itself. Forced divestment can take the form of **expropriation** (usually the takeover of one firm) or **nationalization** (generally the takeover of an entire industry). When Cuba took over companies in 1960, for example, it refused to pay for them. This confiscation is considered the largest in modern times. Chile, on the other hand, took over the copper industry within its borders by paying for the local companies. The payments, however, were below what the nationalized firms wanted to receive.

Such actions on the part of a government may occur for a variety of reasons: The government may believe it can make better use of the assets; it may believe that acquisition of the assets is beneficial to the government's image; or the government may wish to control specific assets for defense or developmental reasons. Exhibit 7.1 identifies major forced divestments in the oil producing countries over a 60 year period. Oil exploration and production around the world have gone from being largely foreign owned at the beginning of the 20th century to being virtually entirely nationally owned at the end of the century.

Forced divestment is legal under international law as long as it is accompanied by prompt and equitable compensation. Such a takeover does not usually involve the risk of a total loss of assets (sometimes assets are confiscated by a host government and, in this case, there is a total loss); the greater risk is that the payment will be less than what the company considers equitable, that the payment will be in nonconvertible currency or nonnegotiable government bonds, or that the loss of a particular subsidiary will affect the rest of the organization's operations.

These are serious risks, but, in fact, the number of unwanted takeovers is relatively low in comparison to total foreign investment. Companies should be aware of the possibility of forced

EXHIBIT 7.1   **Forced Divestment of Petroleum Production**

Year	Country	Action
1918	USSR	Nationalized entire oil industry.
1937	Bolivia	Confiscated operations of Standard Oil of New Jersey and National Oil Company (NOC) took over operations.
1938	Mexico	Nationalized 100% of Shell, Esso, Sinclair, and others (in total, 17 companies) and NOC took control of all petroleum operations.[a]
1951	Iran	Nationalization act passed following Mossadeq's election as Prime Minister. Nationalized 100% of Anglo-Iranian Oil Co. (subsidiary of British Petroleum [BP]).[b]
		1954 Agreement reached with Iranian Consortium, which gave it effective control over production.
		1973 Agreement reached with consortium to abolish existing arrangement and give NOC 100% control of operations.
1961	Iraq	Passed Public Law 80, which withdrew IPC's (BP, 23.75%; Shell, 23.75%; Compagnie Francaise du Petrol [CFP], 23.75%; Exxon, 11.85%; Mobil, 11.85%; Gulbenkian, 5%) rights to areas where they were not producing — approximately 99% of original concession.
		1967 Barred the return of any known reserves to International Petroleum Company (IPC) and gave NOC the right to exploit these reserves by itself or with others as partners.
1962	Burma	Government decree increased government ownership from 51% to 100% in Burmah Oil Co., Indo-Burma Petroleum Co., British Burmal Oil.
	Egypt	Forced sale of shares of BP and Shell in Anglo-Egyptian oilfields. Nationalized 100% of Société Egyptienne pour le Raffinage et le Commerce du Petrol (Egyptian government, 62.7%; Société Cooperative Egyptienne des Petroles, 13.3%; Industrie Petroliere, 10%; individuals, 7%).
		1964 Nationalized 50% of Ente Nazionale Idrocarburri (ENI).
1963	Argentina	Nationalized 100% of all production operations (Union Oil Co., Esso Argentine, Inc., Tennessee Argentina, S.A., Transworld Drilling Co., Continental Oil Co., Argentina, Argentine Cities Service Development Co., Shell Production Co., Pan American International Oil Co.).
	Indonesia	Legislation limited future foreign activity to contractual; 50-50 profit-sharing agreements changed to 60-40 production sharing. Stanvac, Shell, and Caltex became contractors to NOCs.
		1967 Concluded production-sharing agreements with Mobil, Gulf, Atlantic Richfield, Conoco, Independent Indonesian American Petroleum Co., and others.
1964	Dubai	NOC bought into Duma (NOC, 30%; CFP, Hispanoil, 25% each; Deutsche Texaco, A.G., 10%; Dubai Sun Oil, Delfzee Dubai Petroleum, 5% each).
		1975 Agreement modified to provide "financial equivalency" instead of participation.
1968	Peru	Nationalized 100% of IPC.
1969	Bolivia	Nationalized 100% of Gulf.[c]
	Nigeria	Petroleum decree established the state's right to acquire part ownership in oil companies.[d]
		1972 Began negotiations for participation in oil companies.
		1973 Announced intention to take over petroleum industry.
		1974 Increased government participation to 55% in Japan Petroleum Co., Occidental Petroleum Co. of Nigeria, Société Anonyme Française de Recherches et d'Exploitation de Petrol, Nigerian-Petroleum Co., AGIP-Phillips Oil, Texaco-Chevron, Mobil Oil, Gulf Oil.
		1979 Increased government participation to 60%. Nationalized 100% of BP and BP's 20% of Shell-BP Concession giving government 80% of Shell.
1971	Algeria	Nationalized 100% of all non-French operations (including Mobil, Shell, Phillips)[e] and 51% of French operations (including Total Algerie, Enterprise de Recherches et d'Activities Petrolieres).
	Libya	Announced negotiations on participation. ENI told to send representative to begin talks, concluded with 50-50 participation agreement. Nationalized 100% of BP.

EXHIBIT 7.1   **Forced Divestment of Petroleum Production (*continued*)**

Year	Country	Action
		1972 Nationalized 51% of Bunker Hunt and announced intention to nationalize 51% of all oil companies. Occidental gave up 51%[f]; Oasis gave up 51%; Socal and Texaco refused and 100% nationalized.
		1974 Nationalized 81% of Occidental, 50% of Exxon and Mobil, Shell's share of Oasis.[g]
	Abu Dhabi	NOC acquired 25% of Abu Dhabi Petroleum Company (ADPC) (subsidiary of IPC) and ADMA (BP 2/3, CFP 1/3).
		1974 Equity ownership increased to 60% after becoming a member of OPEC.
1972	Abu Dhabi, Qatar, Iraq, Kuwait,[h] Saudi Arabia[i]	General participation agreement provided for 25% government participation beginning January 1, 1973, rising to 51% by 1983. Iraq nationalized 100% of IPC.
		1973 Kuwait national assembly opposed the idea of limited participation. Iraq nationalized Near East Development Corp. (Exxon, Mobil).
		1974 Qatar raised share in Qatar Petroleum Company (BP, Shell, CFP, 23.75% each; Exxon, Mobil, 11.876% each; Partex, 5%) and SCQ (Shell) to 60%. Kuwait raised share in Gulf, BP, and Japanese Arabian Oil to 60%. Abu Dhabi raised share in ADPC and ADMA to 60%. Saudi Arabia agreed with Arabian-American Company (ARAMCO) (Exxon, Texaco, Socal, 30% each; Mobil, 10%) to raise equity share to 60% retroactive to the beginning of the year.
		1975 Iraq nationalized 100% of all foreign holdings in the oil industry. Saudi Arabia and ARAMCO agreed in principle on a complete takeover. Kuwait announced all assets of Kuwait Oil Co. nationalized.[j]
		1976 Qatar purchased remaining 40% of SCQ onshore operations.
		1977 Qatar purchased remaining 40% of SCQ concession. Kuwait nationalized 100% of Reynolds.[k] Saudi Arabia scheduled negotiations for complete takeover of ARAMCO.
		1980 Saudi Arabia completed takeover of 100% of ARAMCO.
	Ecuador	Contracts with foreign oil companies negotiated and transfer of producing interest to NOC begun.
		1973 New contract gave NOC right to buy into Texaco/Gulf consortium.
		1974 Purchased 25% of Texaco/Gulf operations.
		1976 Purchased Gulf's 35.5% share of operations, increasing NOC's total share to 62.5%.[l]
		1979 Exercised option to take Texaco's 18.5% royalty in oil instead of cash.
	Gabon	Acquired financial equity in foreign oil operations (10% Shell; 12% ELF; 30% Société Gabonaise de Raffinage; 51% National Petroleum Production Distribution Corp.).
		1973 Renegotiated all agreements to include government participation of 12.5% of any oil discovered.
		1976 Increased financial equity in ELF and Shell to 25%.
		1979 NOC created.
	Oman	Forced sale of 60% of Petroleum Development Co. (Shell, 85%; CFP, 10%; Gulbenkian, 5%).
1974	Malaysia[m]	Established NOC and set a six-month period for negotiating conversion of existing contracts to production-sharing agreements.
		1976 Production-sharing agreement reached with Exxon and Shell.[n]
	Bahrain	Forced sale of 60% of Bahrain Petroleum Co. (Caltex, Standard Oil of California).
		1977 Completed 100% takeover of production operations.
	Trinidad & Tobago	Bought 25% of Deminex; 15% of Occidental; 20% of Texaco; 50% of BP.
		1979 Minimum government participation increased to 60%.[o]
		1981 Parliament announced intention of acceleration participation and ownership in petroleum operations. Nationalized 100% of oil industry.

EXHIBIT 7.1   **Forced Divestment of Petroleum Production (continued)**

Year	Country	Action
1975	Venezuela[p]	Law passed reserving operation of petroleum industry to the state; nationalization of 100% to become effective on January 1, 1976. Total of forty companies including Occidental, Amoco, Atlantic Richfield, Chevron/Socal, Continental, Creole Petroleum/Exxon, Mene Grande/Gulf, Mobil, Phillips, Sinclair, Sun, Superior, Texaco, Texas Petroleum Corp.[q]
1976	Angola	Law of Petroleum granted NOC exclusive right to hydrocarbon exploration and production. **1977** Nationalized 100% of Angol (Portuguese) and NOC replaced Angol in concessions where Angol had been a participant; nationalized 51% of Gulf Oil. **1978** Abrogated all previously existing foreign-held petroleum rights to NOC and set a minimum NOC participation level of 51%.[r]
1981	India	Plans to Nationalize Assam Oil (100% owned by Burmah Oil Co.) and Burmah Oil's 50% ownership in Oil India Ltd., retroactive to January 1980.[s]

[a]Shortly after nationalization, the government paid $130 million in compensation.

[b]This was followed by a collective boycott of Iranian Oil resulting in a decrease in exports from $400 million in 1950 to less than $2 million in 1951–1953.

[c]NOC reached agreement in 1970 with a Spanish company, Camba, to market oil with Gulf to be compensated out of sales ($78,622,171 over 20 years).

[d]In 1970, new concessions included 50% state ownership; in 1971, offshore concessions included 51% state ownership, and the state assumed its optional 33% of AGIP and AGIP's joint venture with Phillips; in 1973, the state agreed to a production-sharing contract with Ashland Oil Co.

[e]British and American companies agreed to minor compensation.

[f]Occidental accepted immediate cash settlement of $135 million "on account."

[g]Companies were compensated for net book value of assets. BP agreed to a cash settlement of $42 million based on net book value of $150 million less $108 million for back taxes, royalties, etc.

[h]In 1960, Kuwait's concession with Shell included the privilege of taking a 20% interest in operations.

[i]In 1965, Saudi Arabia's agreement with Regie Antonomes des Petroles included government participation.

[j]Kuwait began negotiations with Gulf and BP regarding compensation.

[k]Reynolds was compensated $179.7 million in 1982.

[l]Gulf accepted an initial cash payment of $82.5 million, eventually receiving a total of $115.5 million.

[m]In 1968, the Petroleum Rules Act called for surrender of the orginal concession area after five years and 75% after ten years.

[n]The government sets the base price on which profits are split 70-30 with an additional payment of 70% of difference between market price and base price.

[o]Participation was to increase based on achievement of specified production levels.

[p]In 1970, a hydrocarbons reversion law required that all concessions revert to the state at expiration of existing contracts; in 1974, the government called for early revision of all contracts.

[q]The compensation totaled $1.02 billion with approximately 1/2 reserved as a guarantee of physical assets; 1/3 of this was eventually deducted to replace and restore equipment.

[r]Part of this may be assigned to others.

[s]Actual nationalization was not confirmed.

References: Ajami, R. A., *Arab Response to the Multinationals* (New York: Praeger, 1979); Akinsanya, A. A., *The Expropriation of Multinational Property in the Third World* (New York: Praeger, 1980); Allen, L., *OPEC Oil* (Cambridge, Mass.: Qelgeschlager, Gunn, & Hain, 1979); Blair, J. M., *The Control of Oil* (New York: Pantheon Books, 1976); Ghadar, F., *The Evolution of OPEC Strategy* (Lexington, Mass.: Lexington Books, 1977); Ingram, G. M., *Expropriation of U.S. Property in South America* (New York: Praeger Publishers, 1975); *International Petroleum Annual* (Washington, D.C.: U.S. Department of the Interior, 1975, 1977); Johnson, W. A., and R. E. Messick, *Vertical Divestiture of U.S. Oil Firms; The Impact on the World Oil Market, Law, and Policy in International Business*, vol. 8 (1976), pp. 963–989; Levy, B., "World Oil Marketing in Transition," *International Organization* (Winter 1982), pp. 113–33; *Oil and Gas Journal* (October 19, 1970), p. 52, (December 7, 1970), p. 34, (November 1, 1971), p. 40, (December 20, 1971), p. 36, (October 23, 1972), p. 40, (March 5, 1973), p. 119, (July 9, 1973), pp. 3 and 64, (August 13, 1973), p. 54, (August 20, 1973), p. 24, (December 2, 1974), p. 39; Rustow, D. A., and J. F. Mugno, *OPEC: Success and Prospects* (New York: New York University Press, 1976); Sampson, A., *The Seven Sisters* (New York: Bantam, 1976); Shwadran, B., *The Middle East, Oil, and the Great Powers* (New York: John Wiley & Sons, 1973); U.S. Department of Energy, *Energy Industries Abroad* (Washington, D.C., 1981); *Wall Street Journal* (August 13, 1981), p. 22.

Source: S. J. Kobrin and B. J. Punnett "The Nationalization of Oil Production, 1918–1980," in D. W. Pearce, H. Siebert, and I. Walter, eds., Risk in the Political Economy of Resource Development *(London: Macmillan Press, 1984). Reprinted by permission of The Macmillan Press Ltd.*

divestment and its possible consequences, but they should also recognize that the likelihood of such divestment is relatively low. Exhibit 7.2 illustrates expropriation acts by sector from 1960 to 1985. As this exhibit indicates, expropriations rose during the 1970s and peaked in 1975–1976. They have declined through the 1980s and 1990s. In fact, privatization – the reverse of nationalization – has become more common in the 1990s.

Unwelcome Regulation

Unwelcome regulation refers to any government-imposed requirements that make it less profitable for a company to operate in a particular location. These provisions include corporate or income taxes, local ownership or management requirements, restrictions on reinvestment and repatriation of profits, and limitations on employment and location. Companies expect to have to operate in the context of government regulations, and where these are known and expected, they do not constitute risk. The unexpected imposition of such regulations, however, should be considered.

Many European and American firms, for example, found that some African nations suddenly changed the rules on them during the 1970s. Firms were ordered to become partners with the

EXHIBIT 7.2   **Frequency of Expropriation Acts by Sector (Total Area), 1960–1985**

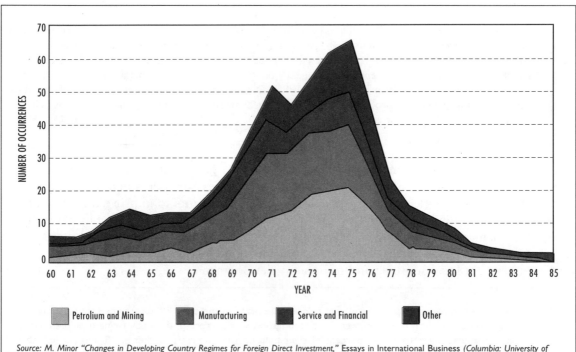

Source: M. Minor "Changes in Developing Country Regimes for Foreign Direct Investment," Essays in International Business (Columbia: University of South Carolina, September). Reprinted by permission of The University of South Carolina.

government or with local citizens, were forced to hire more local people, or were taxed at much higher rates. The political climate in many of these countries became so bad that firms chose to leave if they were not forced out.

Privatization is essentially the reverse of nationalization. It refers to the process of turning government-owned and -operated assets into privately owned and operated assets. In contrast to the use of expropriation in the late 1960s and early 1970s (as illustrated in Exhibit 7.2), privatization has increased dramatically in the 1990s. This is partially due to the breakup of the former USSR and the shift in Eastern Europe from centrally controlled economies to market-oriented ones. The same trend is apparent, however, in a variety of other countries, both in the developing and the industrialized world. To a large extent these privatization efforts are aimed at reducing government debt, but they are also encouraged by a prevailing view that the private sector is more efficient and productive than the public sector.

Privatization should provide opportunities for international firms, and this new political philosophy is generally viewed favorably by those looking for international opportunities. Privatization has not always been successful, however; for example, it has proceeded rather slowly in Eastern Europe, sometimes with questionable results; in some developing countries, privatization has resulted in layoffs; and there is concern in countries like Canada that privatization of airports and railways may lead to safety concerns.

The current global acceptance of private enterprise does not guarantee that businesses are safe from government intervention in their activities. In spite of the increase in privatization in the 1990s, international businesses need to continually monitor government attitudes toward business in general and foreign firms in particular.

The complexities of foreign investment laws have also been frequent sources of problems. The 3M Company, for example, submitted an application to the Japanese government to establish a joint venture with 15 firms of the Sumitomo industrial group. The company's failure to consider all of the applicable Japanese investment laws delayed the governmental approval required. By the time the approval was obtained – four years later – domestic manufacturers such as Sony and Tokyo Denki Kagaka had succeeded in streamlining the production of magnetic tape products and, unfortunately, Sumitomo-3M's share of the market was held to a very small percentage of the total Japanese market.   (Ricks 1993)

Governments generally impose regulations to increase government revenue and encourage particular aspects of development. If a government's priorities are understood, then the purpose of regulation is usually clear. For example, if a government wants to improve local managerial skills, it will likely impose regulations regarding the employment and training of local managers; if a government is concerned with unemployment, it will likely establish local employment requirements; if a government wishes to establish a broadly based industrial complex, it may require maximum local sourcing and technology development.

A foreign-owned paper pulp producer that operated in Brazil in the early 1980s assumed that it could sell all of its product on the world market. That assumption was correct until Brazil, facing a pulp shortage, required manufacturers to sell 20 percent of their pulp on the domestic market at 20 percent less than world market prices.   (Bertrand 1990)

Unlike the threat of forced divestment, incidents of unwelcome regulation occur regularly. Therefore, companies should be particularly alert to these possibilities. In contrast to forced divestment, governments do not usually reimburse companies for losses in profitability resulting from the imposition of regulations.

Interference with Operations

Interference with operations refers to any government activity that makes it difficult for a business to operate effectively. This type of risk includes such things as government encouragement of unionization, government expression of negative comments about foreigners, and discriminatory government support of locally owned and operated businesses. Governments generally engage in these kinds of activities when they believe that a foreign company's operations could be detrimental to local development or because they expect that these activities will result in increased support from important local constituents. Such activities may be seen as improving a government's popularity and thus enabling it to remain in power. The box on the impact of labor and political instability on investment success discusses the effects of such interference.

> One investor had the unfortunate experience of basing a decision to locate a business in a foreign country on what appeared to have been a thorough feasibility study, only to discover later that the study dealt with just one of a number of factors that should have been considered in going overseas.
>
> An unusual opportunity had developed to erect an iron and steel mill, one that this foreign investor zealously pursued. The feasibility study confirmed the market and profitability potential. The mill was built but closed within a year; the building was stripped and the equipment removed. The problem was one of labor and political instability. Although the feasibility study had properly concluded that jobs were scarce and thus ample labor could be attracted, it failed to consider and recognize the nature of the social and political environment. The area was notoriously known as a politically turbulent place; history showed that private investment rarely flourished despite the strong private sector that characterized the country. Almost all manufacturing was publicly owned and operated, consistent with the scheme of social reform that permeated government policy. Labor had long been encouraged to believe in the threat of "capitalistic" exploitation. This belief was even more pronounced because the labor force came largely from farms where exploitation was common and owners were detested and distrusted.

Governmental interference can even occur because of prejudices or the international political situation. Japanese companies need to keep a low profile and can expect some problems in Korea because of the Japanese occupation of Korea before and during World War II. American firms, on the other hand, often find a more friendly environment in Korea.

This type of political risk is particularly difficult to assess and manage because it can occur in many different and subtle forms. Forced divestment and unwelcome regulations have an immediate and identifiable impact on operations; the activities described as interference with operations may be less obvious and the effects unclear. These effects, while not immediately obvious, can nevertheless have a great impact over time (through lost sales, increased costs, difficult labor relations, and so forth); therefore, companies should consider this aspect of political risk as important as the other two.

Understanding the reasons for political activity enables a company to assess the likelihood of a particular activity occurring, as well as devising ways to deal with such occurrences. Effective assessment and management of political risk begins, therefore, with an understanding of the risks that companies face and why they occur.

> More than a few firms have experienced unexpected problems with joint ventures. One U.S. firm that entered into a joint venture with some South American capitalists did not fully comprehend its initial errors until some five years later. At the time of the company's commitment, its South American partners were in favor with those in the local government. However, the joint venture began to gradually experience various forms of host government harassment and, consequently, profits slowly declined. Investment money, effort, and time were lost by the U.S. partner. What had happened? The U.S. company had failed to analyze the situation thoroughly. Early research should have revealed both the existence of a volatile political scene and high degree of political involvement in local business practices. (Ricks 1993)

Development of a Political Risk Strategy

Formal systems of political risk management are relatively new to international businesses. Kobrin (1979) found that assessment of political risk in most companies was an informal, subjective activity. Events in Iran in the 1970s resulted in substantial losses for many U.S. companies; these events helped to establish the need for a greater awareness of the political risks associated with foreign investments. Events in China in 1989 and in the Middle East during the early 1990s again underscored the need for political risk analysis and management. According to Bertrand (Donath 1990), corporate cost cutting in the 1980s "put political risk analysts on the endangered species list" (p. 4), but in the late 1980s and early 1990s, management again welcomed the risk assessment function.

The initial focus for most companies is the assessment of political risk associated with potential investment opportunities. An equally important focus can be the ongoing management of risk; this involves assessing potential risks and then taking steps to minimize the effect of such risks on the company's operations.

Sources of Information

Political risk strategies continue to rely largely on subjective judgment, although risk assessment is increasingly being formalized by international companies. Nevertheless, a number of methods can help ensure that such judgment is based on the best information available. **Political risk analysis** usually involves rating a particular location (using a scale from very risky to not risky) on a number of dimensions considered to represent risk. Information for such ratings comes from a variety of sources.

External Sources

Many sources external to a firm can provide country risk information; these include banks, consultants, periodicals, and country risk services. Each of these may also provide different viewpoints, and companies may want to utilize several of them. Companies need to recognize how rapidly the world can change and how quickly information can become outdated.

Internal Sources

Sources of information within a company include "old hands" (people with substantial international experience), subsidiary and regional managers (people with firsthand experience of a particular location), and staff personnel (people specializing in political risk analysis). Each of these provides a somewhat different viewpoint, and companies can benefit from combining input from all of them.

Some sophisticated political risk systems are computer based and incorporate a wide variety of country and company information. This information is provided from internal and external sources.

The Xerox political risk management system was described as having included the following steps:

1. Each managing director of a major foreign affiliate prepared a quarterly report listing the 10 most salient political issues in the local environment. These issues were analyzed, in terms of their implications for Xerox, and alternative action plans for dealing with them were suggested.
2. These reports went to the operating vice-president and the director of international relations at the company headquarters, who considered the combined implications of all the reports.
3. Decisions about responses to political events were made by the operating vice-president and the director of international relations, incorporating the managing directors' recommendations. These decisions were incorporated into the company's annual plans.

Chemical Bank was reported to have used a different process. It incorporated political spreadsheets that were completed for each given location. Significant political issues and actors were identified for each location; the actors were evaluated in terms of their stands on issues, their power to enforce a stand, and their degree of concern about it. Overall, this provides both a rating for a given location and details regarding political issues of concern. The spreadsheet was completed by local managers and reviewed by headquarters.

The Royal Bank of Canada used a ranking method to gauge the relative risk it faced in each nation (Bertrand 1990). This ranking covered the country's economic, business, and political environments. To rank a country's economy, the bank's analysts examined the country's economic structure and resources (including natural resources), its recent economic trends and policies, its foreign debt and liquidity, and its short- and long-term economic outlook. Assessing the business environment included determining the quality and skills of the labor pool and business leaders, the legislative environment including rules for ownership and taxation, and the financial strengths and competitiveness of the country's top companies. The political environment was examined as to the quality and stability of the government as well as social factors such as the impact of special interest groups or civil unrest and relationships with its neighbors, superpowers, and Canada. Once the bank had all the data, it ranked countries on a scale of 0 (worst) to 100 (best). The bank's Country Review Committee reviewed all 80 countries in which the bank did business at least once each year.

Developing a Process for Dealing with Political Risk

The political risk process can be thought of as comprising both assessment of risk and management of risk. The process enables a company to estimate the degree of risk that exists in any situation and then decide how to deal with that risk.

- ▶ If the risk in a particular location is judged to be very high, then the company will expect commensurably higher returns (these returns should be viewed in terms of the total organization, not simply the specific subsidiary).
- ▶ If higher returns are not available to offset higher risks, the company will likely forgo that opportunity or find ways to reduce its exposure to risk.
- ▶ If the returns are expected to justify the risks, the company will select methods to deal with the identified risks to limit the likelihood of their occurrence and their impact.

False assumptions regarding the level of host government support have led to many problems. Massey-Ferguson, for example, believed it had won Turkish support to establish a tractor producing plant. The company relied heavily on that support to help with sales. Unfortunately, the support never materialized and the venture eventually died.

> Sometimes companies win government support when perhaps they should not. For example, it is possible at times to gain legal approval to do (or not to do) things that should not (or should) be done. This legal support offers a business protection, but it can prove to be temporary or controversial. Several firms have found all too suddenly that, as times change, the definition of what is acceptable can change.
>
> Consider a company in Spain that obtained permission from the Spanish government to use badly outdated technology that polluted the atmosphere. A sudden change in weather created a dangerous health situation. Several people died, the local population rioted, the government withdrew its approval, and the company paid the price for hiding behind the legal protection of the government.   (Ricks 1993, p. 129)

The process of **political risk management** can be thought of as consisting of five separate steps (Gregory 1989) as shown in Exhibit 7.3.

Step 1. Identify Risks

The purpose of this step is to identify government policies and activities that could affect company operations. An important aspect of this step is to recognize that different policies and activities

EXHIBIT 7.3   Risk Management

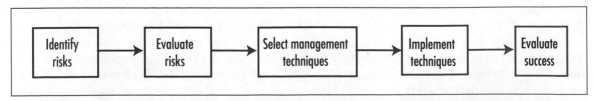

can affect different companies in different ways. Companies want to concentrate their attention on government actions that are most likely to affect their operations.

Step 2. Evaluate Risks

This step evaluates the likelihood of pertinent government policies and activities actually occurring as well as determines their specific impact on company operations. Various political risk services provide information on different countries, and these services can provide basic information for estimating political events. However, because of their specific operations, some companies are more or less likely to be affected by specific events than others. Organizations should concentrate on the events most likely to occur and expected to have the most impact on their operations.

Step 3. Select Management Techniques

The purpose of this step is to decide how to deal with the risks that have been identified. Risks can be reduced, transferred, or avoided altogether with a variety of techniques. Different approaches are appropriate, depending on the circumstances. Specific approaches are addressed later in this chapter in our discussion of defensive and integrative political risk management. Companies should choose those approaches that best protect their most important interests. There are many opportunities in risky situations, but the risk needs to be recognized and managed. It is sometimes more risky to avoid such situations than to pursue them while paying attention to the identified risks.

Many countries provide insurance to protect their own companies from losses incurred in foreign locations due to political events. The Overseas Private Insurance Corporation (OPIC), a U.S. government agency, insures against risks of expropriation, war, or currency nonconvertibility. Similar insurance is offered in the United Kingdom by the Export Credit Guarantee Department and in Canada by the Export Development Council. These agencies provide insurance in exchange for the payment of insurance premiums.

Step 4. Implement Techniques

The purpose of this step is to put into action those techniques that have been identified as most appropriate for a particular company. This turns risk management from analysis to action. It may not be possible to adopt all the preferred techniques, and it may be necessary to make trade-offs at this stage. Companies should insist on those approaches that protect their competitive strengths and be willing to forego others.

Step 5. Evaluate Success

The purpose of this step is to evaluate the effectiveness of the company's political risk management. This step provides the opportunity to reassess the likelihood of various risks and appraise the effectiveness of the risk management techniques that have been adopted. Political risk management should be an ongoing process because the political situation embodies change. Companies that are aware of their political environment are less likely to encounter negative effects from unwanted political activity.

Vulnerability to Risk

Studies (Kobrin *et al.* 1980; Poynter 1982) suggest that the degree of risk a company faces is a function of both the particular country and the particular company's operations. Country characteristics such as type of government, level of economic development, stability of social and political systems, and so on make a country more or less risky. Company characteristics such as the industry, technology, ownership, management, and so forth increase or decrease vulnerability to risk. Exhibit 7.4 identifies country characteristics that are generally associated with increased risk.

In general, instability is associated with increased risk: Instability implies uncertainty, which implies risk. Clearly, for most companies, frequent government changes, an unstable economy, and social upheavals increase the business risk associated with a particular location. Wars and revolution or the prevalence of terrorism imply personal and property risks as well as business risks. When a gap exists (as is the case in many less developed countries) between what the people expect (particularly in terms of material goods) and what they have access to, the population may be hostile toward foreigners who seem to be better off than locals.

Acts of terrorism, although relatively rare, are especially worrisome to international firms. They may occur anywhere and any time, usually unexpectedly. For example, in the summer of 1990, the Irish Republican Army struck at the heart of the British financial establishment by setting off a bomb inside the London Stock Exchange. Fortunately, no one was hurt because warning calls were received and the building was evacuated. In the bombing of PanAm flight 103 over Scotland, the passengers and crew were not so fortunate.

Although instability, war, and terrorism imply increased risk for many companies, it is also true that some companies benefit from them, and a fair number are not affected. At the extreme,

EXHIBIT 7.4
Country Characteristics Associated with Risk

Government Instability

Economic Instability

Social Instability

War and Revolution

Terrorism

a company whose business is selling guns or training executives to counter terrorism benefits from situations that most companies would seek to avoid. Equally, a company that specializes in providing certain material goods at a low cost might be attracted to a location in which the expectations/reality gap is high. Other companies are involved in businesses that are not particularly affected by changes in government, the economy, or society (for example, a company manufacturing cardboard boxes might fall into this category), and therefore, they can to some extent ignore these instabilities.

Dealing with terrorism is problematic for international firms. The United States and other Western countries do not allow companies to make payments, such as ransom, to terrorists for ethical reasons. At the same time, many companies believe that, also for ethical reasons, they must protect their employees and consequently do make such payments.

Certain industries appear to be more subject to government activity than others. This is frequently because these industries are seen as being important to development, and therefore, the government wishes to maintain control over them. In addition, these industries are often highly visible to the local population and so the government can use them as a means to maintain political control. Extractive businesses and those that use natural resources, banking and insurance companies, and companies involved in infrastructure projects (e.g., railroads, airlines, communications) have been historically most likely to be affected by direct government intervention.

Companies with complex, globally integrated operations appear to be relatively safe from government intervention. These operations would be difficult to take over or regulate successfully. Operations of this type often mean that the parent company controls sources of supply or markets, or both; this control makes it difficult for a host government to manage such operations and makes it possible for the parent to avoid some of the regulations imposed against it.

High technology companies and those that have high research and development expenditures are also relatively safe from government intervention. The explanation is much the same here – local governments would be unable to manage such companies themselves, and effective regulations are difficult to impose.

Companies with little competition are often in a similar situation. The host government cannot turn to other sources to replace the products or services offered by this foreign firm. The government and country therefore may be quite dependent on this particular firm and unwilling to impose undesirable restrictions for fear that the firm might choose to withdraw.

A company's ownership is also an important component of its vulnerability to risk. Local ownership is usually viewed favorably by governments; hence, wholly owned subsidiaries are at greater risk, while joint ventures with local private partners are less risky. Such joint ventures are seen positively; local partners provide valuable local information. In contrast, joint ventures with governments have often been riskier, presumably because the government develops the expertise to intervene in operations effectively.

Management makeup is another important consideration. An entirely foreign management has a risk similar to 100 percent foreign ownership, but total local management is also risky, because this implies that there is no need for foreign involvement, and this arrangement reduces corporate control over subsidiary activities.

The size of a company appears to have no real effect on political risk. On the one hand, a large company attracts attention and may be the target of government intervention, but the large company is likely to be relatively powerful. On the other hand, a small company may be the target because of the ease of takeover or regulation, but it may not provide a politically noticeable event. Exhibit 7.5 summarizes the company characteristics that influence level of political risk.

This discussion notes that the degree of risk in any situation is a function of both the country and the company. In assessing and managing political risk, companies need to consider both sets of factors.

There are basically two approaches to managing political risk. These have been classified as defensive and integrative (Gregory 1989). **Defensive political risk management** is intended to protect a firm's strengths by reducing its dependence on any single subsidiary. **Integrative political risk management** is designed to make a firm an integral part of the host society and thus to protect its strengths. The two approaches are quite different, but most companies use a combination of them in their political risk management. The following sections define and discuss these two approaches to political risk management.

Defensive Approaches to Political Risk Management

Defensive approaches generally rely on locating a crucial aspect of the company's operations beyond the reach of the host. This is intended to minimize the firm's dependence on the host or to make it costly for the host to intervene in operations. A summary of the major defensive techniques that companies employ follows.

Financial

▶ Borrow locally. Negative host government actions can affect local creditors more than the company itself.
▶ Raise capital from a variety of sources (including host government, local banks, international institutions, local customers and suppliers, third-country institutions). This tech-

**EXHIBIT 7.5
Company Characteristics Influencing Level of Political Risk**

Type of Industry

Type of Operations

Level of Technology and Research and Development

Degree of Competition

Form of Ownership

Nationality of Management

nique involves a variety of parties that would be affected by any unwanted government actions, and the government may be unwilling to antagonize some of these groups.

▶ Enter into joint ventures with firms from the host country and third countries. This technique spreads the risk among several firms, each of which may have a different influence on the host government.

▶ Obtain host-government guarantees for investment. Although the host may not always live up to these guarantees, they give a company a good bargaining position.

▶ Minimize local retained earnings. Both headquarters' costs on behalf of subsidiaries and dividend payments serve to reduce retained earnings. Companies legitimately charge their subsidiaries for a variety of services that the headquarters provides, and it is particularly important that these costs be identified in locations where companies want to minimize retained earnings.

Management

▶ Minimize the use of host nationals in strategic positions and limit locals to junior and symbolic positions. This technique ensures that parent-country nationals are in control.

▶ Train and educate necessary host nationals at the headquarters. This may serve to ensure an understanding of headquarters' objectives and approaches.

Logistics

▶ Locate a crucial segment of the company's process outside the host country. This makes the local enterprise depend on the parent.

▶ Balance the production of the same components among several countries. This reduces the company's dependence on a single subsidiary.

▶ Concentrate research and development in the home country. This increases subsidiaries' dependence on headquarters.

Marketing

▶ Control markets where possible (e.g., have parent or subsidiaries purchase products from other subsidiaries). This makes it difficult for the host government to take over local operations because it would have no ready-made market.

▶ Maintain control over transportation. The host would have to develop an independent transportation system if it were to take over the subsidiary.

▶ Maintain a strong, single global trademark, corporate image, and so on. This makes it difficult for anyone else to attempt to use these corporate symbols.

Integrative Approaches to Political Risk Management

The aim of integrative political risk management approaches is to make the foreign company an integral part of the host society, in effect, to make the company appear local. If the company is seen as a good local citizen, local government intervention is less likely. A summary of the major integrative techniques that companies use follows.

Management

▶ Employ a high percentage of locals throughout the organization, including top positions. This gives the subsidiary a local image and provides evidence that the company trusts its local personnel.

▶ Ensure that expatriates understand the host environment. This avoids situations in which personnel from the parent company misinterpret the local situation.

▶ Establish commitment among local employees. This provides a loyal work force that will react negatively to unwanted government actions.

Government Relations

▶ Develop and maintain channels of communication with members of the political elite. This keeps the company in contact with political events and allows it to take appropriate action to avoid unwanted actions.

▶ Be willing to negotiate agreements that seem fair to the host and renegotiate those no longer perceived as fair. A company that is seen as acting in an equitable manner is likely to be treated favorably.

▶ Provide expert advice when asked. Foreign companies are often in a position to provide expertise to local governments and they should be willing to do so if asked.

▶ Provide public services. Foreign companies may also be able to provide services such as education, health care, or transportation and should be ready to do so when it seems appropriate.

Operations

▶ Maximize localization in terms of sourcing, employment, and research and development. This enhances the subsidiary's local image and is beneficial to the local economy.

▶ Use local subcontractors, distributors, and professionals wherever possible. This increases dependence on locals and thus any negative impact from government is felt throughout the local economy.

Financial

▶ Raise equity in the host country. This involves local creditors who consequently would be affected by any negative government action. (Note that this approach is also defensive in that it shifts the risk from the company to local creditors.)

▶ Establish joint ventures with local participation. This ensures that local interests will be concerned with the subsidiary's success.

▶ Ensure that internal pricing among subsidiaries and between headquarters and subsidiaries is fair. Host governments are particularly concerned with an MNC's ability to use internal prices to move profits between subsidiaries. Companies can establish and use objective prices for goods and services to guarantee that these transfer prices are appropriate.

▶ Establish open reporting systems. Providing access to financial statements and bookkeeping information can help portray the foreign company and its subsidiary in a positive light to local interests.

Choosing the Right Combination

Both defensive and integrative approaches to political risk management have their advantages and disadvantages. In general, a global firm emphasizes defensive approaches because they fit into its overall strategy; a multidomestic firm (as defined in Chapter 1) emphasizes integrative approaches. Using largely defensive techniques tends to encourage a global or geocentric view of the firm; using largely integrative techniques tends to encourage a fragmented and localized or polycentric view. Although certain companies may favor one approach or the other, many firms combine the two.

The specific mix of risk management approaches that is appropriate depends on the situation – the particular company and the particular country of operations. The model presented in Exhibit 7.6 suggests an analysis of a company's competitive strengths and weaknesses combined with an analysis of the political environment, leading to decisions regarding a desired mix of defensive and integrative approaches. This is followed by bargaining with the host country government and, finally, structuring corporate activities to reflect agreements reached with it.

EXHIBIT 7.6
Designing the Political Risk Management System

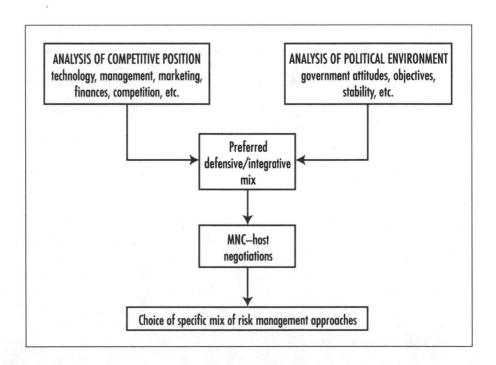

A major company concern is ensuring protection of firm-specific advantages. These are the strengths that allow it to operate successfully. These strengths vary from company to company and can include a wide variety of attributes. For example, control of a particular technology; use of a well-known brand name, well-developed distribution systems, and well-trained international managers; access to low-cost financing; and familiarity with a particular country or region could be firm-specific advantages. Once a company has identified those aspects of its activities that are most critical to its success, it should decide how it can best protect them.

> Coca-Cola considers its "secret formula" for producing the special taste of Coke a key component to its success and protects this secret. The company has been willing to forgo foreign investments in countries such as India because the investment would put the secret formula at risk. The potential of profitable operations was not enough of a benefit to offset the risk associated with loss of such an important firm-specific advantage.

The best way to protect a company's firm-specific advantages depends on the particular country that is being considered. The decision as to which risk management approaches are preferred should be made in terms of both the company's competitive position and the political environment in a specific country. Generally, the more positive the political environment, the more integrative approaches a company is willing to employ; the more negative the environment, the more likely defensive approaches will be appropriate.

> European companies investing in the United States are often thoroughly integrated into the U.S. environment – employing U.S. managers at the highest levels, relying on U.S. sources of supply where possible, carrying out research and development in the United States, and leaving day-to-day decisions to U.S. managers. These same companies investing in the Far East often employ quite different practices: top managers are European, supplies are coordinated from Europe, local research and development is limited, and day-to-day decisions are carefully monitored.
>
> To some extent these decisions are based on the availability of local expertise and resources, but they are also a function of the degree of risk perceived in the particular location.

A company can decide on its preferred means of political risk management, but this does not necessarily mean that it will be able to implement all of its preferred approaches. Negotiation with the host government is often necessary before final decisions can be made about how a company's activities will be structured. In such negotiations, the company must be willing to make concessions but not to jeopardize its competitive position. As noted in the example of the Coca-Cola Company in India, companies sometimes must forgo attractive opportunities to safeguard their firm-specific advantages. Following negotiations, the firm implements its mix of risk management approaches.

Negotiating with Host Governments

The model discussed in the previous pages identifies negotiation between the MNC and the host government as an important component of the political risk management process. Such negotiation generally takes place in most locations and can be time consuming and frustrating because the two sides often see the same situation very differently. This section discusses some of the different viewpoints and makes suggestions for improving the negotiation process.

It is important to recognize that foreign direct investment (FDI) is an important component of economic development in any country (particularly a less developed country) and that FDI usually implies the presence and influence of MNCs. MNC activities, therefore, are of serious concern to host countries, and governments consider it necessary to regulate, at least partially, these activities.

In general terms, the MNC's objective in any investment is to establish operations that fit its overall strategy and provide a reasonable return in a relatively risk-free environment. The host's general objective is a positive contribution to its development objectives. These general objectives need not be in conflict, and the aim of negotiations should be to establish the means by which each party can accomplish its objectives and find ways in which operations can be mutually beneficial.

Although it is true that the MNC's objectives need not conflict with those of the host, the different views of the same situation by the host and the MNC often make it seem that their objectives are in conflict. To reach agreement with the host and to achieve its own objectives, the MNC needs to understand how the host views a particular situation. The following discussion illustrates, in general terms, how the two sides may view a typical investment by an MNC.

MNC View

Typical investment by an MNC may be seen in a positive light as essentially beneficial to the host country, particularly a developing host country. The following are some of the benefits that the MNC may identify.

- ▶ Capital for growth and development – Ambitious growth plans require capital. Often this capital cannot be generated internally and must be attracted from abroad. The MNC sees itself providing needed capital, through investment, which contributes to its host's development objectives.
- ▶ Technology for modernization – Most countries want access to advanced technology. Often this technology cannot be developed locally and needs to be acquired from abroad. MNCs often see themselves as providing access to needed technology.
- ▶ Skills for local industry – Many countries lack sufficient numbers of people with business know-how, managerial expertise, and technical skills. It may be easier to import these skills and learn from foreign experts rather than develop them internally. MNCs often provide needed expertise and skills, as well as training for locals in various needed areas.
- ▶ Access to foreign markets – MNCs often exert a fair amount of control over markets to which small developing nations find entrance on their own to be very difficult or

impossible. Even sizable countries can find it difficult to access markets that are controlled by large companies. MNCs see themselves as providing the means of entrance into such markets.

▶ Positive contribution to balance of trade – The products or services of many MNCs are substitutes for imports, or are exported, thus contributing either to decreased imports or increased exports. The MNC sees itself as having a positive effect on the host's trade balance.

▶ Provision of employment – The MNC's local operations provide employment for host country nationals at various levels and may provide opportunities for employment in other locations and at headquarters. Many developing countries have chronic high unemployment and any creation of employment is beneficial.

▶ Provision of foreign exchange – Many developing countries have limited amounts of foreign currencies (e.g., US$), which they need to pay for their imports. Through investment and export earnings, MNCs provide increased foreign exchange.

▶ Tax revenues – MNCs are subject to local corporate taxes and tariffs, and their employees (both local and foreign) pay income taxes. These payments contribute to government revenues.

▶ Development of entrepreneurs – Developing countries often lack skilled local entrepreneurs. MNCs believe that they provide an example to, as well as a starting place for, host-country nationals who are potential entrepreneurs.

Viewed in this way, MNC investment appears extremely positive, and many MNC executives are surprised that they are not always welcomed and treated as benefactors, particularly by LDC host governments. A look at how the host government may view the situation illustrates why this occurs.

Host View

The host government may see foreign investment as potentially providing the benefits outlined previously but may also see a negative side to the investment as explained in the following (these negative aspects are often magnified if the host is a developing country).

▶ Increased dependence – The provision of needed resources (capital, technology, and expertise) appears positive but may be seen as increasing local dependence on the outside world. For example, many developing countries believe that they need to develop their internal abilities rather than rely on others. Further, MNCs are seen as usually aligned with the host country's elite, and thus they can retard social change by supporting the status quo.

▶ Decreased sovereignty – The provision of needed resources and consequent dependence on MNCs translate into a loss of control by the host government. Many countries, particularly small ones, believe that large MNCs can have a major, possibly harmful, impact on their economic, social, and political systems (for example, through encouragement of local consumption, imposition of Western values in place of traditional ones, or support of a particular political party).

Canada has always depended on outside interests for much of its economic development. During the period of rapid economic growth that followed World War II, this outside contribution was particularly extensive. In manufacturing and other key sectors such as energy, foreign controlled companies expanded their roles, sometimes controlling as much as 75 percent of a particular industrial sector. The Canadian public's concern over the consequences of this situation resulted in federal government foreign investment guidelines, followed by the establishment of the Foreign Investment Review Agency (FIRA) in 1974, and restrictions in the energy sector through the National Energy Program (NEP) in 1980. These controls were highly publicized by the government and media and were met by hostile foreign reactions and a drop in investment. A change in public attitudes in Canada, as well as a change in government, resulted in FIRA's replacement by Investment Canada in 1986 and an extensive campaign to persuade investors that Canada was "open for business."

(Jarvis and Kirk 1986)

Equity capital comes mainly through transnational corporations, whose size and economic power pose difficulties for small states in their relations with them. In terms of bargaining power, negotiating skills, and access to relevant information, small states are usually seriously disadvantaged in dealing with these firms. Their economic strength tends to give the corporations considerable political influence, which in some instances they have used in order to wrest special concessions: for example, favorable adjustment in tax regulations. Small states have endeavored to alleviate some of the constraints of size through regional cooperation. In the Caribbean, Southern Africa, and the South Pacific, a number of these states participate in regional arrangements that extend beyond economic cooperation. (Commonwealth Secretariat 1985)

Another threat is from unscrupulous foreign business firms and "adventurers" that are attracted to the tourist industry and off-shore financial activities on which small states increasingly rely to secure economic progress. The heart of the problem is the weak power and administration of small states and the encouragement these economic activities give to corruption, fraud, commercial crime, drug trafficking, prostitution, and political interference. (Commonwealth Secretariat 1985)

▶ Increased exploitation – MNCs are often seen as using up nonrenewable resources, repatriating profits rather than reinvesting them, excluding locals from valuable local resources, and generally profiting at the expense of the local community. In addition, MNCs may make new products or services available locally. This can increase consumption and decrease local savings and investment.

▶ Inappropriate technology – In many cases, the technology provided by MNCs is seen as being either outdated or too advanced. Sometimes it seems that an MNC is getting rid of its old technology by sending it to the host; in other cases, the newest technology is transferred even though the host does not have the expertise to utilize it properly. LDC hosts believe that many MNCs pay little attention to the real needs of the country from a technological point of view and that technology is seldom adapted to local needs.

▶ Displacement of local firms – Local firms may believe that they cannot compete with the MNC and may forgo local investment. At the extreme, this can mean a flight of local capital to foreign investments. Moreover, some governments might argue that local investments would be labor intensive, while foreign investments are capital intensive; thus, the net impact of FDI on employment is actually negative.

▶ Outflow of foreign exchange – The apparent foreign exchange benefits from investment and exports can be more than offset, over time, by payments for imported machinery and parts and repatriation of profits through dividend payments and other intrafirm transfers.

Looked at in this light, one can better understand why host governments are cautious about foreign investment. Not all host countries, of course, put much weight on these negative thoughts. If anything, the trend seems to be away from a negative view. More and more companies are welcoming foreign investment and its benefits. However, if the MNC understands the potential concerns of the host, then it is in a better position to negotiate successfully because it can deal with these concerns.

Different viewpoints are particularly obvious in interactions between MNCs and LDC hosts, probably because development objectives are of special importance to LDC governments. This means that negotiations with these governments may be particularly time consuming. It also means that identifying how the firm will contribute to LDC objectives can be a critical aspect of negotiations.

Love-Hate Relationship

A host country wants the potential contributions of FDI (e.g., economic benefits of improved trade balances, increased employment, more foreign exchange, and increased power and prestige) but fears the potential negative consequences such as loss of sovereignty, technological dependence, and control of key economic sectors. This can lead to conflicting emotions, or sometimes to what can be described as a love-hate relationship between an MNC and its host government. That is, the host country wants and "loves" the benefits associated with foreign investment and MNCs but, at the same time, seeks to avoid or "hates" the negative implications of the presence of MNCs.

This relationship results in a variety of host government policies designed both to attract and restrict MNCs. Exhibit 7.7 identifies the major incentives and restrictions in place in many

EXHIBIT 7.7
Typical Government Investment Incentives and Restrictions

Incentives	Restrictions
Tax holidays	Local ownership
Exemption from duties	Local content
Tax incentives	Local personnel
Monopoly rights	Local training
Provision of buildings	Location
Low-interest loans	Profit repatriation
	Foreign exchange use

countries. To negotiate successfully with host governments, it is necessary for MNC personnel to understand what these incentives and restrictions are intended to accomplish.

Relations with host governments are more likely to go well when the company can demonstrate that it gives more to the country than it takes out. It is generally recommended that this hold true for every year the firm expects to do business in the country. This is usually easy in the early years, when money and technology often flow into the host country and jobs are created. The local population tends to forget this over time and takes the benefits for granted. In later years, the host may notice only the money leaving the country. When firms can no longer demonstrate that they are giving more than they are receiving, they face a greater likelihood of political risks.

The potential for facing larger political risks later can be reduced by the timing of benefits and costs. Rather than bring in all the investment early, a firm can begin by borrowing locally and then repaying later from the parent company. Expansions in plant operations can be done later and with parent funds. Profits can be invested locally. Many options exist. The important point for firms to remember is that they must always be able to justify their presence in the host country.

The Balance of Power

The outcome of any negotiation is partially a result of the strength of each side. This strength depends on how much each party needs the other and how much control each side can exert on the other.

At one extreme, if a company believes a particular location is very important to its overall operations and the host has many companies interested in coming, then the host is strong, and the company in a relatively weak position. In this situation, the company must be willing to accept most of the terms demanded by the host. At the other extreme, if the host is anxious to attract the firm and the company has many other countries interested in it, then the company is strong, and the host is in the relatively weak position. In this situation, the company can largely dictate the terms of its investment. Most situations are not this clear-cut. Rather, each side has certain strengths and weaknesses. In these situations, the negotiating skill of each side becomes very important.

The bargaining position that a particular company or country adopts can be considered in terms of the model in Exhibit 7.8.

The Role of the Home Government

The strength and bargaining position of a firm is also influenced by its home government and the relationship between the home government and the host government. A positive relationship between the two governments is likely to make negotiations smoother, whereas a negative relationship often complicates issues. The likelihood of the home government supporting the firm in case of unwanted political activities and the influence that the home government can have on the host are additional factors to consider.

EXHIBIT 7.8
Bargaining Posture: MNC and Host Country

Both Sides Weak	Quiet, unobtrusive posture; aim for little interaction
One Side Relatively Strong	Assertive, competitive posture; aim to dominate
One Side Relatively Weak	Cooperative, accommodative posture; aim to satisfy
Relative Strength Unclear	Compromising, bargaining posture; aim for trade-offs
Both Sides Strong	Collaborative, informative posture; aim for integration of concerns

Source: Adapted from T. N. Gladwin and I. Walter, Mulitnationals Under Fire: Lessons in the Management of Conflict (New York: John Wiley & Sons, 1980).

The interests of the home government often coincide with those of its MNCs. This is because the profit that a firm earns overseas is returned to its home-country shareholders in the form of dividends and capital appreciation. Employees in the home country can also benefit from foreign operations because a profitable firm can pay higher wages. In turn, the home country benefits generally through increased taxation. Insofar as their interests are seen as compatible, the MNC can expect support from the home government.

Concern has been expressed in the Bahamas that the neighboring superpower has attempted to exercise extraterritorial jurisdiction by compelling Bahamas-based corporate financial entities with branches in the United States to disclose information on their commercial operations, contrary to the banking laws of the Bahamas and in open breach of accepted concepts of national sovereignty. Banking is such a central segment of the Bahamas' economy that such actions could constitute a threat to the continued survival of its role as an off-shore banker.   (Commonwealth Secretariat 1985)

Although from an overall economic view, the interests of the home country and the MNC seem to coincide, there is an opposing view as well. The decision to invest in foreign locations may be seen as not investing at home, and some groups will be negatively affected by this decision. For example, jobs will be created in the host country rather than at home, foreign suppliers may be used rather than those at home, and prices of certain goods may change as a result of the decision. Those groups that are adversely affected by the foreign investment decision will push for restrictions on MNC activities.

The government and people of the home country also often expect the firm to act in the best interests of the home nation rather than in the best interests of the firm. This can lead to demands by the home government that conflict with the MNC's preferences. This may be particularly true when, for political reasons, the home government tries to control the activities of MNC subsidiaries. The situation can become very complex for the subsidiary caught between conflicting laws and politics as the following incident illustrates.

When the U.S. government wanted to impose restrictions on exports of technology-intensive products to the Soviet Union in retaliation for its activities in Afghanistan, this was relatively easy to accomplish with exports from the United States but more difficult when it was expanded to include subsidiaries of U.S. firms operating in Europe. The European hosts insisted that the subsidiaries, located in their nations, comply with their regulations and policies, not those of the United States. This left the subsidiaries in a no-win situation, in which any action would antagonize one or the other government. In 1995 a similar situation arose when the United States decided to blacklist non-U.S. companies with ties to Cuba. Companies on the blacklist were to be barred from dealing with U.S. firms.

Cuba offers an interesting case in point, because economic opportunities have been strongly influenced by politics. Not only did the Cuban government change from a form of capitalism to a form of communism, but it did so in a dramatic manner that included confiscating many firms and their assets. Reaction was especially negative in the United States, and American firms were ordered not to do business with Cuba. Other countries gradually adjusted to the changes in Cuba, and many firms renewed business ties that were profitable to all parties involved. Canada, a country many people consider fairly similar to the United States, has a difference in its foreign trade policy with Cuba, and Canadian firms have been doing business in Cuba while American firms have had to turn down opportunities. Clearly, both the foreign government and the home government can create major problems for a firm wanting to do business overseas.

Government-Business Relations

Much of what has been discussed so far in this chapter, and throughout the text, has assumed that countries permit private ownership and free enterprise. In fact, this is not always the case; sometimes governments prohibit some or all private ownership and free enterprise. It is important to examine the major types of national governments that currently exist and understand how the types of government influences government-business relationships.

Governments are often divided into three groups: capitalist, socialist, and communist. These distinctions are used for our brief discussion of the types of relationships that firms can expect under different governments. The discussion is meant to provide a very basic review of the major differences between these systems.

Capitalism is most familiar to Americans because the American system is based on capitalist beliefs. This system believes in free enterprise, a market-based economy, and the private ownership of the factors of production. The government provides necessary services that are not provided by the private sector.

The basic element of this philosophy is the primacy of individual rights and freedoms. This primacy implies the right of individuals to enter into agreements with other individuals concerning the production and consumption of goods and services; it also means that each individual has a right to her or his own preferences if these do not impinge on the rights of others. This sounds appealing, but there are limits to these rights; the government may enact certain restrictions for the good of the public (e.g., require that cigarette packages carry warnings regarding the effects of smoking on health), and sometimes controls are placed over individual preferences (e.g., a preference for heroin is not considered acceptable).

Socialism is prevalent in a number of developing countries. This system believes in government ownership of the basic means of production, combined with private ownership of other factors.

The basic element of this philosophy is the need for government control of those industries that directly affect the well-being of the people. The belief rests on evidence that a free market often does not provide for the unfortunate. This is appealing because it provides for the less fortunate in society, but government interference with market forces often tends to distort supply and demand and may cause problems in the availability of goods and services.

Communism is the system followed in the People's Republic of China, Cuba, and some other developing countries. This system believes in government ownership of most factors of production. Prior to its breakup, the USSR was the world's major communist power, and communism was practiced throughout most of Eastern Europe. That situation changed in the early 1990s and most Eastern European countries are moving toward more open, capitalistic economies.

A basic element of the communist philosophy is the need for a centrally planned economy to ensure that all citizens benefit equally from the country's output. The government is supplier as well as market in such a system and makes the decisions regarding the country's needs. This is appealing to those concerned with ensuring equality for all, but the inefficiencies created by such a system are apparent in the disparities between supply and demand.

Individual governments may be seen as falling somewhere along a continuum, with pure communism at one extreme and pure capitalism at the other, and degrees of socialism in between, although all countries have some elements of socialism in their government-business relationships. The closer a system is to communism, the more limited the role of private business; the closer to capitalism, the greater the role of private business. In countries at the communist extreme, foreign companies have relatively limited access to markets, and trade and investment are tightly controlled. In countries at the capitalist extreme, foreign companies have relatively free access to markets, and trade and investment are relatively open.

These systems change over time; therefore, one cannot expect countries to continue to maintain the same government-business relationships over long periods of time. Particularly in the early 1990s, there were signs of major shifts in these relationships. Many communist countries underwent economic and political changes. Countries (e.g., Poland) that had previously embraced communist ideals were moving to a capitalist approach to private ownership and free enterprise. Even countries that maintained their adherence to the principles of communism (e.g., the People's Republic of China) were liberalizing their control of private business. These events suggest an expansion in international business opportunities in the coming decades. Exhibit 7.9 discusses changes taking place in the Czech and Slovak Republics in the mid-1990s.

The three systems identified are helpful to understanding the types of government interactions that companies can expect based on the ideology of the country. The government always plays some role in business, but the largest role is in communist countries; doing business in such countries consistently requires interactions with the government.

All political systems, of course, have the potential for helping or hurting the international firm. Each system creates various opportunities and threats. Capitalist systems usually allow more direct contact with local businesses, but these do not necessarily result in profitable or risk-free contracts. Communist governments usually require that international business be negotiated with government officials, but they can sometimes be very profitable for the outside firm. For example, government contracts with the Soviet Union were very reliably paid, with few surprises or risks (once the contract was agreed on). In contrast, Russia is now seen as less politically stable and having higher levels of risk for many Western firms.

It is important to keep in mind also that these generalizations are not always as clear-cut in reality as they are conceptually. In any country, the stated ideology may differ from actual

EXHIBIT 7.9
Vouchers and Governance: The Czech and Slovak Experiment

Skeptics had reservations when Czechoslovakia launched its massive program in 1992 to privatize state-owned enterprises. The state's voucher scheme gave almost every citizen a chance to own shares in one or more companies. But critics complained that having so many owners would mean that nobody would be in control. There would be no effective way for shareholders to manage the managers. However, hundreds of new investment funds emerged that traded their own equity for vouchers. That gave the funds the heft to bid for large blocks of stock in newly private companies and led to a greater concentration of ownership than expected. Whether it also leads to improved corporate governance is another matter.

The program gave all citizens over 18 a chance to buy a package of vouchers for about $35, then equal to about the average weekly wage. Vouchers represented points that the owner could use to bid for shares in any of 1,491 enterprises. Most people turned their points over to one or more of the 430 investment funds formed by banks and other sponsors. The funds ended up owning 70 percent of the bidding points. But the concentration of ownership was even greater than that suggests. The 10 largest bank-sponsored funds, including several managed by the same institution, picked up 43 percent of the points.

Despite the strength of the funds, they did not obtain dominating equity positions. Although some funds, notably in Slovakia, have exceeded the limit, all are technically prohibited from holding more than 20 percent of the shares of an individual firm. Moreover, the funds tended to bid for the shares of larger firms and then, because of the bidding, paid more points per share. As a result, only two funds have a position in a firm exceeding 30 percent of the stock. With dispersed ownership, of course, an investor can have effective control with only a small fraction of shares. And in many cases, two or three funds could have combined control of an enterprise. There is no company in which two funds have a combined majority stake, but in almost half the companies in the program, the two funds with the largest number of shares jointly have a controlling position. (Individual domestic or foreign direct investors have effective control of about 100 companies.)

There has been too little time and too many shocks – including the country's split – to judge the effect of new ownership arrangements on the performance of the privatized firms. But share prices in the final round of bidding and in the secondary market theoretically should anticipate the benefits of concentrated ownership. Other things being equal, the shares of a company with a controlling ownership and, presumably, better corporate governance should trade at higher prices than the stock of a firm with more diffuse ownership. But that has been so only when ownership is highly concentrated, with a single owner or group holding an absolute majority. Relative control, especially when it is held by one or two funds, has had a negative effect on share prices.

One explanation for the way share prices have reflected the concentration of ownership could be the potential conflict of interest for investment funds controlled by banks. In many cases, these banks are major creditors of the firms in which the funds have a large equity interest. Other investors might be less willing to bid up share prices without more separation between fund management and commercial lending. A possibly stronger factor is that the investment regulations of both republics require absolute majorities for important decisions such as removing directors and supermajorities for fundamental corporate changes. As a result, only a very large shareholder is legally able to restructure a firm and carry out the radical changes needed to ensure profitable growth.

> One lesson to be taken from the program is the importance of small shareholders. In some markets a well-developed proxy system allows a stakeholder with less than majority ownership – for example, a bank in Germany – to solicit the support of small shareholders and thus exercise control even in the presence of high majority requirements. So far, small Czech and Slovak shareholders have not taken an active interest and their votes are essentially lost. The result is weaker shareholder control and – the ultimate penalty for the investor – lower share prices.
>
> *Source: World Bank Policy Research Bulletin, vol. 6, no. 2, March-April 1995.*

practice. Companies doing business in foreign environments should consider both aspects of the political environment.

Summary

Developing an effective strategy to deal with political risk is an important aspect of successful international operations. The political environment that an international company faces is complex, and therefore the assessment and management of political risk are not easy tasks. This chapter focused on the factors that make a particular situation risky, suggesting ways to assess the degree of risk that a company faces in any location as well as various means to manage exposure to risk.

Bargaining between firm and host is an integral part of managing political risk, and effective bargaining depends to some extent on understanding the objectives of the other side. Therefore, this chapter examined the contrast between a firm's view and a host's view of FDI. Overall, understanding the political system and the objectives of the host is critical to a successful political risk strategy. An additional complication in the relationship between MNC and host is the role of the home-country government. In some ways the interests of the MNC coincide with those of the home government, but this is not always the case; therefore, the home country can sometimes be supportive of MNC activities and sometimes critical.

MINI-CASE
The Big Gun

The story of Iraq's attempt to build a big gun is truly international in scope. It involves governments and individuals around the world, in countries as small as Barbados and as large as China, from the North American continent to the Middle East. It embodies political risk in a variety of forms.

The big gun story begins in the 1960s when a Canadian scientist, Gerald Bull, was working on a joint Canadian-U.S. government research project, the High Altitude Research Project (HARP). HARP was intended to determine the feasibility of using super artillery to send small satellites into space orbit. A number of strategies for orbital and suborbital ranges up to 6,200 miles (10,000 kilometers) from a variety of barrel diameters were developed, and a 600-pound projectile was reportedly shot 1,150 miles. Research on the project was carried on both in Canada and in the Caribbean island of Barbados.

Bull is described by those who knew him as a brilliant scientist. When the Canadian government canceled the HARP project, he raised the capital to open an 8,000-acre establishment in Highwater, Quebec, where he designed and refined high-tech weapons systems that he sold to a number of governments, including China, South Africa, and Israel. He became widely known as the world's foremost authority on heavy artillery.

> "HARP (High Altitude Research Project) was dedicated to the idea that satellites could be launched from large caliber guns. One gun had been installed on the Caribbean island of Barbados, and a trip to participate in the launches was a carrot in front of every student working for the project."
>
> "Dr. Bull was in the offices infrequently and did not condescend to speak to engineering students."
>
> "Dr. Bull was rarely around but it was always evident that he was running the show. He provided the theoretical base for the operations in Highwater and he was able to obtain the contracts to keep the place running."
>
> "The foundation for the big gun was done on a tight schedule and the pouring of the concrete would not be delayed for something as inconsequential as a blizzard." (Anstead 1990)

In the 1970s, Bull became an American citizen. In 1980 he was convicted of exporting arms technology to South Africa in defiance of an embargo and went to prison for six months. When he was released in February 1981, Bull moved to Belgium where he reestablished his business. He is known to have traveled widely, visiting clients around the world.

In early 1990, the British monthly *Defense* reported that Iraq was probably proceeding with its own version of HARP under Bull's direction. British authorities were concerned that one of Bull's subsidiaries could be developing technology in Belfast to be used in Iraq's attempts to perfect a medium-range missile to deliver nuclear warheads.

The severity of the situation was realized in April 1990 when customs officials seized pipe sections supposedly for delivery to an Iraqi petrochemical plant. The British government confirmed that the giant cylinders were actually parts for the barrel of a super gun capable of leveling a city block with every shot from ranges previously thought impossible.

Michael O'Brien, a leading defense specialist, warned, "the next time we hear about the Iraqi super gun may be the sound of its first firing." No one knows how many additional companies around the world, knowingly or unknowingly, may have been supplying parts for the big gun.

Bull's son denied his father's involvement in the Iraqi gun but Gerald Bull could not shed any light on the situation. He was murdered outside of his Brussels apartment on March 22, 1990. The Belgian police believe that his engagement in selling weapons was the reason for his death. He had just returned from the Middle East when an unknown assailant killed him with a silenced handgun as he unlocked his front door. The precision with which he was killed and the fact that about $25,000 in cash was left untouched in his wallet led the Belgian police to conclude that he was killed by a professional assassin for political reasons. The most likely suspects were Iraq's enemies, Israel and Iran, both of whom had also been clients of Bull.

Sources: Anstead 1990 Anstead, as a student, worked for Gerald Bull; Grant 1990, pp. D1, D5; MacLean's 1990, pp. 22–24.

Discussion Issues

1. Given the risks that Dr. Bull faced in doing business with Iraq, why do you believe he was willing to undertake this project?
2. Evaluate the risk-benefit trade-offs from the point of view of the Iraqi government.
3. Find current information on the political situation in Iraq and discuss the risks associated with doing business there. How do the risks differ for companies from different countries (e.g., Canada, China, Korea, or the United States)?

Discussion Questions

1. What characteristics of a company do you think make it more vulnerable to political risk?
2. Given the characteristics identified in Question 1, how should companies prepare to manage their exposure to political risk?
3. Why do companies fear sudden changes in government?
4. Would you expect political risk assessment to be more common and more formalized in companies today than in the past? Why or why not?

Assignments

1. Select a country to investigate and evaluate its level of political risk.

2. Select a country and trace the political developments that have occurred there over the past five years. Do these events make it more or less attractive for international business?

3. In groups of four students each, identify recent (in the past 12 months) political events and discuss what impact they would have on doing business internationally.

Selected References

Anstead, C. J., interview conducted by B. J. Punnett (November 28, 1990).

Bertrand, K., "Politics Pushes to the Marketing Foreground," *Business Marketing* (March 1990), pp. 51–55.

Brander, J. A., *Government Policy Towards Business* (Toronto: Butterworths Canada, 1988).

Commonwealth Secretariat, *Vulnerability: Small States in the Global Society* (London: Commonwealth Secretariat Publications, 1985), pp. 21, 29, 35.

Coplin, W. D., and M. K. O'Leary, "1990 World Political Risk Forecast," *Planning Review* (April 1990), pp. 41–47.

Donath, B., "Coping with Trade's Dark Side," *Business Marketing* (March 1990), p. 4.

Gladwin, T. N., "Conflict Management in International Business," in I. Walter, ed., *Handbook of International Business* (New York: John Wiley & Sons, 1982).

Gladwin, T. N., and I. Walter, *Multinationals Under Fire: Lessons in the Management of Conflict* (New York: John Wiley & Sons, 1980).

Globe and Mail (August 23, 1990), p. B18.

Grant, D., "The Doomsday Gun," *Toronto Star* (April 21, 1990), pp. D1, D5.

Gregory, A., "Integrative and Protective Techniques in Reducing Political Risk: A Comparison of American and Canadian Firms in Indonesia," in J. Rogers, ed., *Global Risk Assessments,* vol. 3 (Riverside, Calif.: Global Risk Assessments, 1988).

Gregory, A., "Political Risk Management," in A. Rugman, ed., *International Business in Canada* (Scarborough, Ont.: Prentice-Hall Canada, 1989), pp. 310–329.

Grosse, R., and J. Stack, "Noneconomic Risk Evaluation in Multinational Banks," *Management International Review* 1 (1984).

Harrigan, K. R., "Joint Ventures and Competitive Strategy," *Strategic Management Journal* 9, no. 2 (1988), pp. 141–158.

Jarvis, M., and F. Kirk, Jr., eds., "Foreign Direct Investment in Canada: The Foreign Investors Perspective," International Business Study Group, School of Business, Carleton University (1986).

Kobrin, S. J., "Political Risk: A Review and Reconsideration," *Journal of International Business Studies* (Spring–Summer 1979), pp. 67–80.

Kobrin, S. J., J. Basek, S. Blank, and J. LaPalombra, "The Assessment and Evaluation of Noneconomic Environment by American Firms: A Preliminary Report," *Journal of International Business Studies* (Spring–Summer 1980), pp. 32–47.

Korbin, S. J., and B. J. Punnett, "The Nationalization of Oil Production, 1918–1980," in D. W. Pearce, H. Siebert, and I. Walter, eds., *Risk in the Political Economy of Resource Development* (London: Macmillan Press, 1984).

MacLean's, "A Doomsday Gun Mystery" (April 23, 1990), pp. 22–24.

Mahini, A., *Making Decisions in Multinational Corporations – Managing Relations with Sovereign Governments* (New York: John Wiley & Sons, 1988).

Minor, M., "Changes in Developing Country Regimes for Foreign Direct Investment," in *Essays in International Business* (Columbia: University of South Carolina Press, 1990).

Poynter, T. A., "Government Intervention in Less Developed Countries: The Experience of Multinational Companies," *Journal of International Business Studies* (Spring–Summer 1982), pp. 9–25.

Ricks, D. A., *Big Business Blunders – Mistakes in Multinational Marketing* (Homewood, Ill.: Dow Jones-Irwin, 1983).

Ricks, D. A., *Blunders in International Business* (Cambridge, Mass.: Blackwell Publishers, 1993).

Rogers, J., ed., *Global Risk Assessments: Issues, Concepts, and Applications* (Riverside, Calif.: Global Risk Assessments, 1986).

Shaw, A., "Guyana's Mineral Potential," *Mining Journal* (May 1989), pp. 358–360.

Simon, J. D., "Political Risk Assessment: Past Trends and Future Prospects," *Columbia Journal of World Business* (Fall 1982), pp. 62–71.

Weiss, S. E., "Creating the GM-Toyota Joint Venture: A Case in Complex Negotiation," *Columbia Journal of World Business* (Summer 1987), pp. 23–37.

Weiss-Wik, S., "Enhancing Negotiators' Successfulness," *Journal of Conflict Resolution* 27, no. 4 (1983), pp. 706–739.

Wells, L. T., "Negotiating with Third World Governments," *Harvard Business Review* (January–February 1977), pp. 72–80.

World Bank, *World Bank Policy Research Bulletin* 6, no. 2 (March–April 1995).

Yaprak, A., and K. T. Sheldon, "Political Risk Management in Multinational Firms: An Integrative Approach," *Management Decisions* (1984), pp. 53–67.

CHAPTER ▼ 8

The Competitive and Technological Environment

LEARNING OBJECTIVES

After reading this chapter, you should be able to

▶ Discuss the types of competition found in the global environment.

▶ Outline the forces that encourage or limit competition.

▶ Discuss the relationship between competition and technology in international business.

▶ Explain how companies can succeed internationally in terms of competition and technology.

▶ Discuss the role of technology and technology transfer in the international environment.

- ▶ Competitive environment
- ▶ Barriers to entry
- ▶ Barriers to exit
- ▶ International product life cycle
- ▶ Competitive advantage
- ▶ Technological environment

- ▶ Technological advantage
- ▶ Creative chaos
- ▶ Transfer of technology
- ▶ Intrafirm bonds
- ▶ Interfirm bonds

T H O U G H T   S T A R T E R S

▶ The multinationals have for years been the only human agencies on earth to take a long term, 20-year look into the future. . . . It won't be some cottage industry that makes the alternative safe refrigerants, it will be the multinational chemical industry.

(Lovelock 1990)

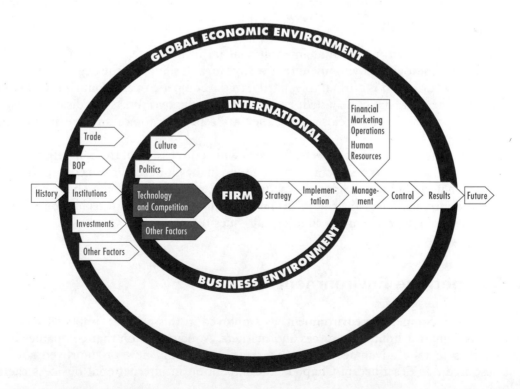

▶ Nippon Telegraph and Telephone, Japan's biggest company, chose voice technology from Motorola, an American telecoms equipment manufacturer, as the standard for Japan's cellular phone network, beating off domestic competition. Motorola shares soared to a one-year high.

(The Economist 1990)

▶ The 20th century wasn't a competitive century. Especially after World War II, it was an era of niche competition.

The 21st century became the century of head-to-head competition, as opposed to niche competition, concludes a historian of the future.

(Randall 1990)

Introduction

A quote from an article in the *Academy of Management Executive* illustrates the close connection of competition and technology for today's international businesses.

> With the increasing globalization of international business, the high-technology sector has become a major segment of foreign trade. Such industries as the semiconductor computer chips, commercial aircraft and engines, and industrial robots have become the battleground where firms fight to increase their market share to survive and prosper in international competition. (Keller and Chinta 1990, p. 33)

The competitive environment that international businesses face, to a certain extent, is a function of the technological environment that we live in, and similarly, the degree of technological innovation in our world is attributable, partly, to the competitive environment. Competition and technology therefore are closely tied. For this reason, the two topics are discussed together in this chapter. In spite of their close links, they are separable topics and are first discussed separately.

This chapter has three distinct aspects. It begins with a discussion of the competitive environment. In this discussion, the types of competition found in the global environment are considered, as are factors that encourage or limit competition. The second part of the chapter focuses on technological issues, including the role of technology and the transfer of technology. The final section relates the competitive and technological issues to each other.

The Competitive Environment

The concept of a **competitive environment,** as employed in this chapter, implies two or more organizations vying for limited resources and markets. A major reason that companies become international is to take advantage of new markets and to find new or improved sources of various resources, as described in Chapter 9. Competition in international business therefore often is intense, and the number of competitors in a given situation can be large and varied as to nationality, strategic objectives, and competitive strategy.

The claim that one distinguishing feature of doing business internationally, compared to domestically, is increased competition should not surprise most readers. The sources and nature of competition are likely to increase as a company crosses international boundaries. Very simply, there are more sources of competition, and the various competitors may play by different rules. In the sections of this chapter dealing with the international competitive environment, the sources of competition and the nature of competition are examined first and then the degree of international competitiveness. The product life cycle and its influence on competitive approaches is considered. The discussion concludes with a consideration of international companies' competitive strategies and the impact of government regulations on the competitive environment.

Sources of Competition

Competition in the global environment comes from a wide variety of sources. It may originate with the public or private sector, come from large or small organizations, be domestic or international, be established in developed or developing nations, and stem from traditional or new competitors. Perhaps the most distinguishable characteristic of international competition is its variety. First, it is evident that there may simply be more competitors in the international arena because there are potentially more players. A number of additional components to the competitive environment can be identified.

Organizations in both the public and private sectors often compete internationally. This is generally less likely to be the case in any single national location. The reason for this is that individual countries may distinguish between those industries or businesses that it chooses to operate within the public sector and those to be run by the private sector. Within a given country, there may be little competition between public sector organizations and private sector ones. Different countries may identify these distinctions differently; what is considered an appropriate public sector business in one location may be private in another and vice versa. This means that a U.S. company accustomed to competing in the private sector at home can find itself competing with organizations that are in the public sector elsewhere. In particular, countries with centrally planned and controlled economies make greater use of public organizations controlled by the government than do countries with free market systems.

Organizations of differing sizes may compete internationally. This is less likely to be the case in any single national location. Industries within a given country tend to develop so that larger organizations compete mainly with other larger organizations, and smaller ones with other relatively small ones. This pattern develops because of the availability of resources and the structure of the markets served within a particular country. Resources and markets may differ from location to location, and therefore industries tend to follow varied patterns in different locations. An Italian company that is accustomed to competing with relatively small companies in Italy can find itself competing with large companies in Germany in the same business.

Exhibit 8.1 illustrates the interrelationships among the Mitsui Group in Japan. Japanese companies usually have extensive corporate and financial linkages that are unusual (or impossible because of regulations) in the United States. The linkages in the Mitsui Group include

EXHIBIT 8.1 The Mitsui Group

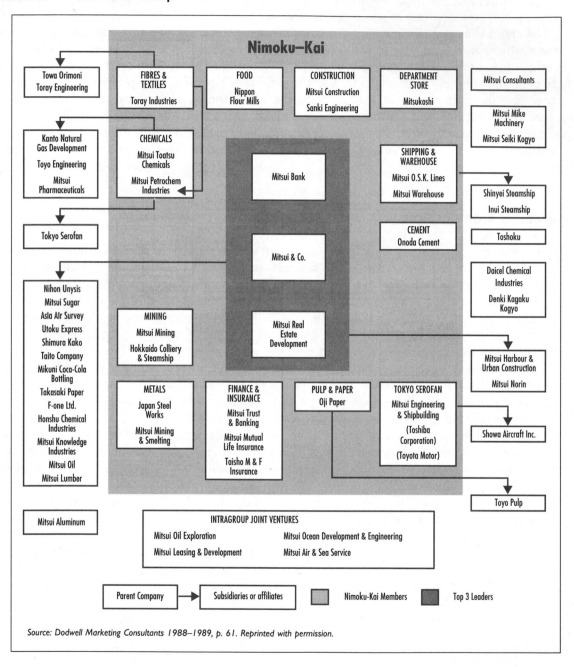

Source: Dodwell Marketing Consultants 1988–1989, p. 61. Reprinted with permission.

▶ Three leading companies – Mitsui Bank, Mitsui & Co., and Mitsui Real Estate Development
▶ Second-tier companies – among others, Toray Industries (fibers and textiles), Nippon Flour Mills, Mitsui Construction, Sanki Engineering, Mitsukoshi (department store), Mitsui Toatsu Chemicals, Mitsui Petrochem Industries, Mitsui Mining, Hokkaido Colliery & Steamship, Oji Paper, Japan Steel Works, Mitsui Mining & Smelting, Mitsui Warehouse, Onoda Cement
▶ Subsidiaries and affiliates – among others, Toray Engineering, Mitsui Pharmaceuticals, Mitsui Sugar, Mikuni Coca-Cola Bottling, Mitsui Knowledge Industries, Mitsui Oil, Mitsui Lumber, Mitsui Aluminum, Mitsui Consultants, Shinyei Steamship, Mitsui Harbour & Urban Construction, Showa Aircraft, Inc., Toyo Pulp.

Competition with Mitsui in one industry (for example, in the chemical industry with Honshu Chemical Industries) can be affected by its relationships with other companies in the group and other subsidiaries (for example, Shinyei Steamship, Showa Aircraft, Inc., or Mitsui Oil). The competitive nature of business can be different internationally from that found at home because relationships such as those pictured for Mitsui may exist in foreign locations but not at home.

> Japanese corporations are carefully positioning themselves on an all but invisible combat ground. This war will go beyond any previous Japanese corporate campaigns directed at individual markets, industries or technologies. The new contest will be over the basic culture of capitalism – and the Japanese aim to win it.
>
> "An age of competition between variant systems of capitalism has begun," says Professor Ken-ichi Imai of Tokyo's Hitotsubashi University. "Ultimately, it will involve a struggle for leadership in shaping the economic systems of the century to come."
>
> This struggle, argues Prof. Imai, will centre on the huge business alliances called keiretsu (pronounced CAY-re-tsu), which stitch together a spectrum of Japanese industry and banks through networks of cross shareholdings, financing arrangements, and exclusive trading and business relationships.
>
> As the keiretsu increasingly become the main channel for Japanese business and investment abroad, the clash with Western business may leave them the ascendant form of global business organization.
>
> (*Globe and Mail* 1990)

In any given location, the competitors may be both domestic and international. International companies may find that they compete with other international companies as well as local companies that are essentially domestic. In some locations, domestic companies are given preferential treatment and protected to a certain extent. These local companies are able to compete more effectively because of such preferential treatment and protection. This means, for example, that a multinational company headquartered in Canada can find itself competing with local companies, say in Latin America, who would not normally be competitive, except for their government's support. Local companies may have real advantages as well. Experience and established presence often put local companies in a superior position relative to foreign firms.

Organizations from both the developed and developing nations may compete in any location. The number of organizations originating in developing countries has been steadily increasing in the last decade. International business is no longer the sole domain of organizations from

> To illustrate the complexities of international competition in Japan: Japanese financial institutions have emerged as world-class players. But the pension fund business in Japan is also slowly but steadily being invaded by non-Japanese institutions – American, British, Swiss. Most of the large hospitals in Japan are maintained by the Japanese affiliate of a Chicago-based maintenance company. In Southern California, a Japanese-owned and run advanced management school is being founded. (Drucker 1990)

the developed countries. The different economic conditions faced at home by these organizations can mean that they compete differently in their international operations. This means, for example, that a British company may find itself trying to sell the same products in Canada as a Taiwanese company.

> The biggest question marks in the competitive strategy of the developed business world are the role and position of the developing world.
> There are experts today who advocate a business strategy that confines itself to the "Triad"; that is, to the three increasingly interrelated large developed regions of North America, Western Europe, and the Far East....
> And yet can you exclude two-thirds of humanity – soon to be three-fourths? And, if possible, is it prudent? (Drucker 1990)

Established companies may find that unexpected new entrants appear internationally. Unexpected new entrants appear domestically as well, but it is more difficult to estimate their likelihood in the international arena. Barriers to entry into a particular industry are reasonably well known in the home situation, and the probability of new entrants can be estimated on this basis. These barriers are less well known in the international sphere; therefore, unforeseen new entrants are more likely. An established Japanese firm, accustomed to competing with American and European companies, may find unexpected competition from a company headquartered in South Korea.

The type and source of international competitive advantage can be based on organizational advantages as well as national advantages. Country-specific advantages associated with a particular nation provide the basic resources that translate into competitive advantage for various organizations. In addition, nations themselves compete for resources and markets. In assessing global competition, companies need to consider both sources of competition.

> Alexander Graham Bell developed the telephone in Canada and the United States, and North American companies are still at the forefront of new technologies in the telecommunications industry today – but they are exploring new horizons in terms of both technology and locations. Hong Kong is a particularly important maker of telecommunication products and is used as a showplace for the entire region. The Hong Kong market is unique because there is little government regulation of this industry and people are willing to accept new concepts, and try new products. One executive warned, however, that it is a risky market because products become obsolete very quickly and competition can be cutthroat.

Nature of Competition

The preceding discussion suggests that global competition may be distinct from competition at home. Different participants around the world often compete in different places and varied ways. Companies develop their initial, domestic competitive approaches based on their home environments. Factors such as government regulations, economic scale and conditions, availability of resources, and culturally accepted practices all combine to create an array of effective international competitive approaches. The combination of these factors frequently varies from location to location, and consequently, competitive approaches also vary.

The following examples illustrate the array of factors that can influence a company's competitive posture. This is not an exhaustive list, but it includes important considerations for most situations.

Government regulations affect how companies compete because firms must comply with regulations in the countries in which they operate. For example, regulations affecting competition vary from those that encourage competition through the prohibition of organizations working together to those that prohibit direct competition by regulating virtually all of the activities of organizations operating within the country's boundaries. Governments often seek to impose these regulations extraterritorially on home companies as well. Clearly, companies learn to compete quite differently in these varied environments. Companies must understand government regulations, both at home and in foreign environments, that shape the way they can compete.

Economic conditions influence how companies compete because firms focus on those areas in which they can expect to gain a competitive advantage, given economic conditions. For example, in a poor country, products designed to appeal to the masses should be relatively inexpensive; hence, cost and price may be important competitive factors. In a relatively wealthy country, factors such as quality and service may be more important. To choose a competitive approach in a particular location, a firm should examine the economic conditions that are likely to affect its business in that location.

The availability of resources also has an impact on competitive factors because availability, or lack thereof, encourages companies to focus on certain issues. If resources are scarce, companies must put time and energy into obtaining needed resources. Where resources are scarce and in demand, one can expect that competition for these limited resources will be intense.

Cultural practices are another important contributor to the form that competitive approaches take in various locations. For example, in some locations, specific relationships are expected between buyers and sellers. In other locations, social interactions between management and government officials are required to facilitate transactions. In some locations, open and aggressive competition is encouraged but this is frowned upon in others. Numerous cultural conventions have an impact on the form of competition that exists and is effective in any given location. Successful international companies are sensitive to these often subtle cultural conventions and use them to their advantage.

Competitive forces in the home environment are usually relatively well known to a successful domestic company. One could argue that companies that survive and prosper do so because they compete effectively. These companies assess the local competition competently and take strategic and operational actions that enable them to continue successfully. In the international arena, the rules of the game may be quite different than at home, and companies often find that

One can still lose by low labor productivity. But one can no longer establish and maintain competitive leadership through blue-collar productivity or low blue-collar labor costs. The productivities that will determine competitive position are new and different ones. Very few businesses pay much attention to them. First, there is the cost and productivity of capital. The biggest advantage the Japanese have today in worldwide competition is their low capital costs. But even the Japanese, by and large, do not do a good job of managing the productivity of money in business. Increasingly, this will be a key factor.

But then we will also have to work on the productivity of the new people in the work force and above all the productivity of the knowledge worker. Knowledge workers already outnumber blue-collar workers in all advanced countries. Yet very little attention so far has been focused on their productivity. But knowledge work is one area in which North America, both Canada and the United States, should have a distinct advantage, in part because of the abundant supply of people prepared for knowledge work and because knowledge work is hedged in North America by far fewer political and social restrictions than in either Europe or the Far East.   (Drucker 1990)

the international competitive environment is full of surprises. Some examples will serve to illustrate these potential surprises.

▶ Competing for market share – Companies in one location may be accustomed to competing largely in terms of price to gain market share for a particular product or service. In such a situation, companies concentrate on lowering costs and offering attractive deals to be able to offer the product at a competitive price. In another location, competition in terms of the same product or service could revolve around quality, distribution, or after-sales service, among other factors. The company that uses the competitive strategies and tactics appropriate for the first situation in the second may find that it is unsuccessful. Alternatively, these approaches by a newcomer, because they are unusual, may prove to be very successful and cause problems for established local competitors.

▶ Competing for resources – Companies may gain access to needed resources in one location through a network of relationships. In such a situation, companies put substantial effort into establishing and cultivating the appropriate relationships. Competition for the same resources in another location may be based solely on price. For a company accustomed to the first situation that uses the relationship approach, where price is all-important, it may find that it wastes valuable time and effort. Again, of course, an unusual approach can prove to be an advantage and cause problems for established competitors.

▶ Competing in terms of demand and supply – Companies accustomed to a free enterprise economic system are used to prices being determined, at least to some extent, by the demand for and supply of a particular product. In such a system, companies make certain decisions depending on estimates of future demand and supply. In centrally planned economies, decisions are made by central planners regarding the desired level of supply, and prices are set by the planners as a means to shift resources. Companies accustomed to the free-market approach will find it disconcerting to compete in a situation in which demand and supply are predetermined and prices are not allowed to respond to expected forces.

The Degree of Competitiveness

The degree of competition in an industry depends to some extent on the number of competitors in the industry. The number of competitors depends in turn on the barriers to entry and exit in the industry. **Barriers to entry** are those things that make it difficult for new companies to get into an industry and **barriers to exit** are those things that make it difficult to get out.

Barriers to entry include factors such as high initial capital investment and the need for continuing investment, protected technology, and controlled resources, distribution, or markets. A company considering entry should evaluate these factors as deterrents to entry and should choose to become a new entrant in the industry only if the company can establish an effective means to overcome the barrier(s). The higher are the barriers to entry for a particular industry, the fewer new entrants there are likely to be.

Barriers to exit include factors such as highly specialized assets that are difficult to dispose of, existing contracts and commitments that cannot be transferred, and investment in research and development. A company considering exit should evaluate these factors as deterrents to exit and should decide to leave the industry only if these barriers can be overcome. If there are many barriers to exit for a particular industry, only a small number of companies will leave it. If barriers to exit are substantial and known, they may also serve as barriers to entry for potential new entrants.

In general terms, if the barriers to entry are high and the barriers to exit are low, the number of competitors in that industry is likely to be small. In such an industry, companies can leave easily, thus decreasing the number of competitors, but companies cannot enter as readily to make up the decrease. When the barriers to both entry and exit are high, the number of competitors will also likely be small. When the barriers to both entry and exit are low, a large number of competitors will likely be entering and exiting frequently. Where the barriers to entry are low and those to exit are high, the situation is less clear. This might suggest many competitors because of many entrants and few leaving. If the exit barriers are well known, however, there will be fewer entrants in spite of the low barriers to entry.

Barriers to entry and exit are assessed in the international environment just as they are in the domestic situation. The challenge faced by international companies, however, is to understand what constitutes a barrier in different national environments. In particular, political forces and government policies can reverse the barriers to entry and exit from one location to another. For example, in one location foreign investment in a particular industry may be encouraged and incentives for investment promoted by the government; the same industry in another country could be seen as a strategic industry in which foreigners are unwelcome. Similarly, barriers to

> When Drexel Burnham Lambert Group Inc. collapsed, the U.S. government was willing to stand aside and allow its dissolution. The Japanese reaction illustrates how differently the same situation may be viewed. In Tokyo, management called the Japanese Ministry of Finance to say that they had been told by headquarters to liquidate the office immediately. They were told they could not close. The Japanese could not understand how something like that could be allowed to happen and said Drexel had responsibilities to take care of. The Japanese approach was essentially, "We license you. Therefore, you cannot simply close; we have to give you permission."   (Sterngold 1990)

exit can be a function of government policies. In one country, it may be possible to declare bankruptcy relatively easily and shut down operations, but in another, the firm that goes out of business may still have numerous legal obligations that it must meet.

Product Life Cycle and Competitive Approach

The stage of the product life cycle of a firm's products or services also influences the type and form of competition it is likely to encounter. Four stages of the product life cycle are examined here in terms of competitive forces. These four stages are infancy, growth, maturity, and decline. These are considered in general terms first; then implications of the **international product life cycle** issue are examined.

Infancy

Infant products, or new products in infant markets, are characterized by their differentiation from current products. These products are essentially unique in an unknown market. Potential customers are initially unaware of the product or service; therefore, a major focus is on gaining visibility and awareness, thus creating demand. Promotion is important, and effective managers for such products often have an entrepreneurial, risk-taking mentality. An individual or small group with personal commitment and high energy may be needed to launch and develop infant products. Often such people operate best with minimal corporate control or accountability.

The initial market for an infant product is necessarily small, but if it is successful, the market will grow rapidly. These products will be a net cash drain for the company because of the need to spend large amounts on facilities, promotion, and sales efforts before sales are made. The firm must be prepared to provide funds for facilities and distribution as demand grows as well.

Because they are unique, infant products or services initially have no established competitors. Competition, however, can be expected to develop as soon as other firms see opportunities in the new market. This creates a sense of urgency to be the first company to establish a dominant position before others enter. Once competitors enter the market, competition for customers' attention is the main concern of all the firms vying for the market. This results in a focus on price and added features, as competitors work vigorously for market share and dominance.

Growth

Growth markets are defined as markets growing faster than the economy as a whole. Products in growth markets are characterized by increasing demand and competition for sales. The needed mentality at this stage is that of a salesperson. Financial controls remain relatively loose at this stage, with high advertising and promotional expenditure. The firm's focus is on market share with an attempt to achieve market dominance. Again, advance spending can be substantial, and growth products or services are usually a drain on a firm's financial resources.

Competition tends to be intense during the growth phase. Because of the growth, the market attracts a large number of competitors, both large and small. The competition is frequently well organized and professional, often with an emphasis on client assistance, quality, timing, after-sales service – anything that will entice customers to a particular brand. Customers have many options from which to choose as competitors develop new and imaginative offerings. Many companies enter and exit such a growth market.

Maturity

A mature market grows at about the same rate as the economy. Mature products are well accepted and somewhat standardized. A professional management approach is important at this stage. This includes market research, testing new approaches, and refinements in the product or service. Processes are well established, and cost controls and efficiencies are important to success. Financial management becomes important, and tight controls are necessary. Expenditures are evaluated relative to options and target returns.

Market size is well established, and firms are trying for minor improvements in market share. There is probably a fairly stable complement of competitors because many firms will have dropped out of the market as it matured. (As the product matured, the less efficient producers dropped out and the more efficient ones remained.) Growth is at the expense of competition, and companies compete in terms of product innovations, packaging, service, and so forth to increase profits. Customers are familiar with the products and choose among alternatives, so that the competitive approach is to advertise the merits of the product or company or to use comparative advertising and competitive pricing. Competitors may consider mergers to consolidate market shares. Vertical integration may also be attractive as competitors seek to gain advantages in sources of supply and key distribution points.

Decline

A declining market is usually made up of a small number of large established participants in a market in which growth is less than the overall growth of the economy. Customers have established loyalties; little change in market share can be expected. Products in declining markets should be generating cash because the production and distribution processes are well established and there is little need for extensive promotion. The mentality of a financial controller is most important at this stage, with tight cash management a priority and expenditures carefully weighed against options.

Each participant has a particular reason to remain in a declining market (e.g., location, patent, customer relations), and little real product differentiation is possible. Competition through price cutting, usually in terms of discounting, is often used to keep current customers. Companies are considering strategic alternatives at this stage.

International Implications

International variations in economies, customer tastes, technology, governments, and so on offer opportunities to prolong a product life cycle and find new uses for established products. This means that a firm may have a product facing a mature market in one location and an infant market somewhere else, which leads to the need for different management priorities, systems, and procedures in different locations. For example, a professional manager successfully managing a mature product in Germany may suddenly be faced with an entrepreneurial colleague insisting that there is a new market for the product in a small African country if the firm moves quickly. The professional manager is accustomed to achieving success through careful research and planning, while the entrepreneurial manager needs to take immediate risks and cannot research and plan carefully in an unknown market.

Once again, our story of the Bata Shoe Organization illustrates the two approaches to an unknown market. Recall that two people were investigating the African market in the 1920s. One (the professional) did some research and concluded that people did not wear shoes and therefore there was no market. The other (the entrepreneur) looked around and saw that no one wore shoes and concluded that there was an enormous untapped market. In this situation, the entrepreneurial mentality was needed.

To take advantage of opportunities for finding new uses for products and prolonging the product life cycle internationally, companies need to recognize the different approaches that may be needed in different locations. Companies need to be flexible enough to accept these different styles within the same organization.

> Coleman kerosene lanterns are seldom used in developed countries; the major consumers in these countries for these lanterns are cottagers and campers. In contrast, there are many developing locations where electricity is uncommon and Coleman lanterns are found in most households.

Although there can be international opportunities to prolong product life cycles, forces are also at work to shorten the life cycle. New products may be developed in foreign locations that have an impact on a product's life cycle domestically. To compete effectively on a global scale, companies are constantly seeking to develop new products and technologies. This emphasis on innovation has tended to shorten many product life cycles. Companies need to be constantly aware of this international competitive environment and its impact on the life cycle of their products. Monitoring the international environment is complex but necessary if the firm is not to be taken by surprise.

> Large mainframe computers were still in the growth phase of the product life cycle in many developing countries when they had already moved to the mature stage in the developed countries. The emergence of personal computers with expansive memory capability at a relatively low price cut short the cycle for mainframes in these developing countries.

Companies make different decisions depending on their relative dominance in a particular market. *Dominance* is often defined as selling at least twice that of the nearest competitor. Companies in dominant positions may be in a position to dictate the nature of competition because they are the leaders; they are usually the most profitable. These companies stress their leadership position and focus on protecting this position. Companies in minor positions seek smaller niches in which they can specialize. These firms issue challenges to the leader and focus on their own special strengths. A firm's dominance in one market can be used to establish a new position elsewhere. Equally, however, companies can find themselves in different positions of dominance in several international markets and must respond to these differently. A company that dominates in one market may find that it is a minor player in another. Furthermore, the nature of the international competitive environment, as well as varied levels of dominance, can lead to unexpected collaborations. Companies may compete intensely in one location and form an alliance in another location with the same competitor. For example, automobile manufacturers (e.g., GM, Ford, Toyota, Nissan) are fierce competitors in some locations, but they have formed joint ventures in other locations.

Companies' trademarks, copyrights, brand names, and so on that are well recognized in one location can provide a competitive advantage if they can be transferred effectively to new international locations. Equally, a well-recognized trademark in one location can cause difficulties in another. For example, British Petroleum's BP trademark, which was well recognized in the United Kingdom and internationally, ran into problems when it entered the Canadian market. Imperial Oil of Canada also used BP as the logo for its Building Products division; this was a well-established and recognized logo in Canada. Both firms offered some similar petroleum-based products. Clearly, there was a conflict; both companies could not continue using almost identical corporate symbols in the same marketplace.

Competitive Strategy

Companies seldom succeed internationally by chance alone. Rather, they actively seek to create **competitive advantages** for themselves. Successful international companies are "caught up in a never-ending process of seeking out new advantages and struggling with rivals to protect them" (Porter 1990, p. 577). Porter identified five principles that are particularly important in global competition:

1. Competitive advantage grows fundamentally out of improvement, innovation, and change. An essential challenge for any company is the ability to improve and innovate. In the international arena, firms gain a competitive advantage over their rivals because they find new ways to compete that anticipate foreign as well as domestic needs.
2. Competitive advantage involves the entire value system. The value system is described as the array of activities involved in a product's creation and use. Competitive advantage often comes from identifying new ways to configure and manage the value system. The availability of different elements of the value system around the globe can provide opportunities for companies to identify new approaches that give them global advantages.
3. Competitive advantage is sustained only through relentless improvement. The factors that give a company a competitive advantage can always be imitated by other companies, so firms that remain stationary are eventually overtaken by rivals. Advantages are sustained through ongoing modifications to value systems and challenges to established wisdom. Traditional ways of doing things are particularly vulnerable in the international context when others are likely to look at things in innovative ways. To continue to compete successfully

at the international level, firms may need to actively seek outsiders with new and innovative ideas.

4. Sustaining advantage demands that its sources be upgraded. A company's competitive advantage may grow from any activity in the value chain, and these sources of advantage differ in their sustainability. Some can be replicated easily by international competitors (e.g., factor cost advantages), but others are more difficult to duplicate (e.g., internal technical capability). Companies cannot rely on initial sources of competitive advantage to continue to give the same advantage over time. Successful international companies seek to expand their sources of advantage and move from those that are easily replicated to those that are difficult to duplicate.

5. Sustaining advantage ultimately requires a global approach to strategy. The international environment provides both threats and opportunities for companies seeking innovation and change as described in the first four points. A global approach to strategy allows a firm to supplement its home-based advantages and overcome its home-based disadvantages. Using a global perspective and strategy enables firms to identify and seek advantages in the global environment.

These essentials of successful international competitive advantage, according to Porter, constitute a mindset that is not present in many companies, a mindset that accepts and seeks change and challenge. Most companies tend to value stability and protect ideas and techniques that have proven successful in the past. Contrary to this, successful international competition often relies on creating an impetus for innovation that changes the established ways to do things. Porter suggests a number of approaches as specific steps that can be taken to overcome the natural tendency of firms to prefer stability. These steps are identified in Exhibit 8.2.

There are clear reasons for many companies to innovate to be successful in the global environment. There are also opportunities for companies that are not innovative to find market niches for specialized products or services. For many of these companies, the innovation comes in recognizing the need for established products in new market niches and locations.

Government Regulations

Government regulations are an important component of the competitive environment. Corporate laws and regulations in different countries are often designed to deal specifically with the competitive environment. These regulations may apply nationally as well as extraterritorially and are often designed both to limit and to encourage competition.

EXHIBIT 8.2
Proactive Approaches to Creating Innovation

- ▶ Sell to the most sophisticated and demanding buyers and channels.
- ▶ Seek out buyers with the most difficult needs.
- ▶ Establish norms of exceeding the toughest hurdles or product standards.
- ▶ Source from the most advanced and international suppliers.
- ▶ Treat employees as permanent.
- ▶ Use outstanding competitors as motivators.

Extraterritorial jurisdiction of the U.S. antitrust laws was applied to the creation of Canadian Industries Limited (CIL) in 1954. This was a joint venture between U.K.-based International Chemical Industries (ICI) and U.S.-based DuPont. DuPont was forced to divest because of the threat of unfair competition with U.S. companies, even though CIL was incorporated outside the United States. Regulations that affect competition can follow a variety of patterns, as can be seen by the following examples.

▶ Traditionally, the United States has encouraged competition through legislation that is more stringent than regulations found in most other countries. The U.S. antitrust regulations are designed to limit monopolistic practices by restricting corporate combinations that might substantially decrease competition.

▶ In general, European countries encourage company mergers that they expect to result in larger companies that are better able to compete internationally (i.e., they are willing to accept decreased competition at home if this improves their companies' international competitive advantage).

▶ Countries such as Japan and South Korea encourage a close link between the government and large firms in planning and financing major investment initiatives.

▶ Some centrally planned economies, such as the People's Republic of China, allow free enterprise for small enterprises but maintain tight government control of all other enterprises.

▶ Other communist countries, such as North Korea and Cambodia, maintain a virtually complete antimarket approach, with all enterprise controlled by the central government.

These are only general descriptions of government policies toward business. The specific regulations in each location differ and must be carefully assessed. Equally, government policies toward private sector business change over time, and the regulations in force as well as the degree to which they are enforced also change.

In its early years, the Reagan administration pushed up the value of the dollar to the point where American exports became noncompetitive on the world market. U.S. manufacturers decided, in the great majority, to try to maintain profit margins rather than market standing. They increased their foreign prices to yield the same dollar income. As a result, within two years, they lost sales, market standing, and profits. A few years later, when the Reagan administration decided to push down the value of the dollar so as to make it difficult for the Japanese to flood the American market, the Japanese decided to sacrifice profit margins to maintain their market standings. As a result, Japanese sales in the United States did not go down. They continued to go up and within 18 months the Japanese had recouped their profit margins, and were, in fact, making larger yen profits in the United States than they had made before when the dollar-yen exchange rate was much more favorable to them. And the Germans, who followed the Japanese example in the U.S. market, have obtained the same results. (Drucker 1990)

The Technological Environment

A characteristic of the 20th century has been the speed with which technological advances have been made. There is little reason to believe that the pace of technological development will slow in the 21st century. International companies are, therefore, destined to function in this environment of rapidly changing technology. *Technological development* in this context refers to the development of new and improved products or services as well as new and improved processes for producing, marketing, and delivering products or services. The following sections, focusing on the **technological environment**, discuss innovative strategies and the transfer of technology. This discussion is followed by an examination of the relationship between competitive advantage and technology – specifically, developing, protecting, and using technological advantage.

The *Encyclopedia Britannica* from 1898 provides a good lesson in how the world has changed in this century. Everyday words such as *airplane, computer, telephone,* and *robot* simply are not there. Science fiction stories from the 1940s and 1950s also highlight how our world has changed. Many of these stories seem laughable today because the technological innovations that are portrayed as far in the future have actually occurred. *Star Trek* fans may not be able to "beam up" or travel at "warp" speed yet, but technologies now exist to enable them to do most of the other things that the crew of the original Enterprise could do.

Technology Defined

Technology can generally be thought of as falling into three categories: product technology, process technology, and management technology. *Product technology* relates to the specifics of a product or service: its features and uses. *Process technology* relates to the process by which a product or service is produced: the inputs, procedures, machinery, and so on. *Management technology* refers to the human skills involved in managing an organization. All firms have these three types of technology and can develop a competitive **technological advantage** in any or all.

Developing new and improved products, processes, and management implies the need for innovative thinking and for understanding how locations differ in terms of abilities and requirements. To function well in this environment, firms need to have innovative strategies and the ability to transfer technology effectively from one location to another.

> In the 1960s, America went to the moon because it was there and because it was good geopolitical PR. In the 90s, the United States is joining with Canada, the Europeans, and the Japanese to place a $41 billion space station in orbit 500 km above the earth because it's an ideal place to manufacture everything from pharmaceuticals to industrial ceramics as well as being a logical assembly and launch point for new generations of satellites. It will also be the jumping off point for a broader space exploration effort in the early decades of the 21st century, an effort that will often be aimed at commercial objectives such as lunar mining. The space station, in other words, is going to be good for business.   (Davies 1990)

Innovative Strategies

Companies that foster innovation make the conscious decision to live in a dynamic environment. These companies create an organizational culture that welcomes change. This is not easy to do because many people prefer to deal with a stable environment and to continue doing things as they were done in the past. It is particularly challenging for a successful company to make the decision to change its way of doing things. After all, this worked in the past, so, why change?

An organizational culture that fosters innovation and welcomes change must reward both. The development of such a culture must be created and encouraged by top management. Leadership in such organizations is extremely important in providing a vision and moving the firm toward achieving this vision. The concept of creative chaos described by Nonaka (1988) may be a particularly appropriate model for international companies in a rapidly changing globalized technological environment.

The concept of **creative chaos** is based on the physicists' proposition that nonequilibrium is the source of new order. This concept of order out of chaos suggests that organizations that compete through innovation should foster nonequilibrium. These organizations see equilibrium as a state of stagnation whereas managed disequilibrium provides the desired creative environment.

Creative chaos is described as requiring permissive management that leaves room for decentralized creativity and strategic ambiguity (Hughes 1990). Such chaos is achieved by moving into an uncertain environment, where markets fluctuate constantly and technology is always changing. An open system encourages countercultures, unpredictable ideas, subordinate challenges to existing ways, and a lack of common values, all of which contribute to creative chaos.

Transfer of Technology

A critical aspect of succeeding in an international environment of rapid technological change is the **transfer of technology** from one location to another. That is, companies that operate across national boundaries often need to transfer know-how from one location to others. This can be complex internationally because factors such as culture, laws, markets, social circumstances, and physical conditions all influence the transfer.

One of the first considerations for these firms is the appropriateness of a particular technology to a specific location. The concept of appropriate technology is that the technology can be used efficiently and effectively in the local environment. Technology may be unacceptable because of culture, laws, and social or physical conditions. Some examples illustrate the difficulties.

Heavy machinery designed for use by people of a certain strength could result in only male operators being able to use the machinery, but it might be culturally unacceptable for men to undertake the kind of work involved. For example, in some countries agricultural work is the responsibility of women, but they may have physical constraints relative to certain types of agricultural machinery due to its construction.

Laws might prohibit the importation of certain products that are needed to make use of advanced technological processes. For example, some computer systems rely on particular types of paper for printouts, but the importation of such paper may be precluded because it competes with locally produced paper.

Cultural conditions can make it difficult for local people to understand and use certain types of equipment properly. For example, detailed written instructions may be required for proper use of some machinery, but the people likely to use the equipment may have limited literacy skills.

Physical conditions can render advanced technologies less than useful. For example, processes designed for use in a dust-free environment will not operate effectively in places where it is impossible to maintain the needed physical environment.

China was recently forced to cancel a $5 billion contract it had negotiated with several Western companies because it miscalculated its needs and abilities. The plan for building the giant Baoshan Iron and Steel Works near Shanghai was doomed from the start. Negotiations on both sides failed to recognize that there were inadequate port, transportation, and power facilities in the area and an additional $9 billion would have been required to develop these needed facilities. Furthermore, the oil revenues that the planners had projected to generate the original $5 billion needed fell far short of expectations. China lost face, and its jilted Western partners lost confidence in China.   (Ricks 1993, pp. 15–16)

A French firm set up a timber mill in East Africa and was all set to open when the French realized that usually there was not enough electrical power in the area to run the mill. Unfortunately, there may never be adequate power and the firm had to dismantle the mill.

Sometimes it is not the plant location that is the problem but the plant layout. For example, an English pulp and paper company entered into a joint venture arrangement with another British firm hoping to utilize the timber resources of British Columbia. They obtained a concession of enormous timberland acreage. The sawmill, however, was designed and set up by British engineers who were unfamiliar with the characteristics of British Columbian lumber. As a result, the mill was constructed with a setup that was not flexible enough to adjust to the numerous varieties and sizes of Canadian trees. Within three years the firms sold the mill at a substantial loss.   (Ricks 1993, p. 17)

These examples illustrate the need for careful assessment of the host environment relative to a particular technology transfer prior to transfer. If a transferred technology proves inappropriate, then the transfer has wasted valuable resources. If it is assessed as inappropriate prior to the transfer, then substitutes can be sought or adaptations made. These can be in terms of the technology, or they can be in terms of the environment. That is, the technology can be changed or the environment within which it is to perform can be changed.

To assess the transferability of technology, one can look generally at factors that hinder transfers and those that facilitate transfers. Keller and Chinta (1990) identify home- and host-country barriers as follows:

▶ Home country – Many countries preclude the transfer of certain technologies to other countries. This may be to limit the likelihood of foreign competition, or it may be for political and ideological reasons.

▶ Host country – Many countries prohibit the importation of certain technologies. This may be to limit the competition at home, or it may be to protect jobs in a home industry. Standards also vary from country to country, and host-country standards can be incompatible with certain technologies.

Facilitating Technology Transfer

Keller and Chinta (1990) identify intrafirm and interfirm bonds as facilitating transfers as follows:

▶ **Intrafirm bonds** – The relationships within a firm that go across national boundaries and encourage the transfer of technology. The more that various parts of a company work together, the more likely they are to share technology and transfer it successfully from one part of the organization to another.

▶ **Interfirm bonds** – Relationships among firms across national boundaries also encourage the transfer of technology. Many alliances are formed specifically to encourage technology transfer, and many countries require local participation in foreign investments because this is believed to foster localization of the technology.

Copeland and Griggs (1985) identified the following obstacles to transferring technology from the United States, particularly to the developing countries:

▶ The small pool of potential managers and skilled employees – Inadequate preparation of local employees in developing countries may mean that they are ill equipped to learn the technical or administrative skills needed to implement new technology.

▶ More than a technology gap – Local employees who are unfamiliar with Western approaches cannot simply be trained to use new technology because the cultural and social differences affect the learning process.

▶ Hostile attitudes – Local employees may believe that a company's primary purpose is to provide jobs and welfare; therefore, the Western focus on profits is interpreted as ruthless profiteering, and locals resist efforts to introduce new technology, particularly if it is seen as labor saving.

▶ Lack of trainers and training materials – The job of training often falls to the company manager who may not be adequately prepared to carry out this function and thus locals, in fact, are not properly trained.

▶ Resistance to American teaching techniques and style – Americans are comfortable with a combination of coaching and feedback as a teaching approach, but this style may be uncomfortable for other cultures and locals will resist learning.

▶ Americans overlook what foreigners do know – Some of the previous issues lead Americans to discount local information and skill that may in fact be very relevant to the technology being transferred.

The experience of an American and German company in South America illustrates the costs associated with failure. The foreign companies were building a nuclear power plant in a location that their Indian laborers disapproved of. The foreign engineers paid no attention to their warnings until it became apparent that the Indian name "weak rock" meant that the rock was really weak and the ground shifted with the tide. Altogether, about $3 million in cost overruns was spent to shore up the buildings, but with little success.   (Copeland and Griggs 1985, p. 144)

Recognizing these issues means that companies can plan technology transfers so as to minimize the problems they are likely to encounter. Prior to undertaking a transfer of technology, companies need to assess the receiving organization and country relative to the proposed technology. If this assessment is positive, the sending company then needs to plan the actual transfer.

This includes selecting and training people to accomplish it. All of this may be time consuming, but it is usually worth the investment to avoid a failed attempt.

Competitive Advantage and Technology

According to Porter (1990, p. 45), "Firms create competitive advantage by perceiving and discovering new and better ways to compete in an industry and bringing them to market, which is ultimately an act of innovation." He continues to define *innovation* as "improvements in technology and better methods or ways of doing things." These comments, like the quote at the beginning of the chapter, indicate that competition in today's global environment is typically driven by technology.

Companies are constantly under pressure to discover and implement technological changes that will make them better than other firms. This is true in any location, but it is particularly true of companies competing internationally.

The international environment is characterized by technological competition. There are opportunities for distinct technological developments to occur in a variety of locations and be disseminated on a global basis. In Chapter 3, we discussed a country's factor endowments as the basis for its comparative advantage in the production of certain goods and services. A similar argument applies in terms of technology.

A country's resources – including human capital, financial capital, current technology, physical environment, and so forth – provide the ability to develop certain technologies. In addition, a country's needs tend to provide the motivation to develop technologies that meet those needs. Resources and needs vary from country to country because of national and cultural differences. These differences provide the impetus for distinct technological developments.

In addition to the likelihood of distinct technological developments occurring in different locations, today's world is characterized by fast and effective communication. This means that technological developments in one location can quickly be available in other locations. The combination of rapid innovation and communication can lead to unexpected shifts in competitive advantage among companies. Therefore, to be effective in such an environment, companies need to monitor developments globally and foster internal innovations that can give them a global advantage.

Developing a Competitive Technological Advantage

Companies seeking to develop a competitive technological advantage essentially have two choices: They can develop the superior technology themselves or they can seek to acquire it. This is basically a make-versus-buy decision. There are pros and cons to each of the possibilities.

Developing superior technology internally takes a substantial investment of time and resources with no certainty of the outcome. Some companies may find the investment impossible or decide that the costs outweigh the potential benefits. It is often worthwhile, however, because of the learning process involved. The need to develop new technology is continually important and should probably be developed internally, particularly for companies that depend on technology as a key competitive advantage.

Acquiring superior technology that has been developed by another company means that the investment is known, as is the technology being acquired. This is appropriate where the desired technology is available and for sale or license. On the negative side, the acquiring company is limited to what is already available, it may not be capable of using the technology to its best advantage, and it does not develop its own technological capability. The buy decision is most likely when a company needs a specific technology that it does not have the time or resources to develop and that may not be the main focus of the company's business.

Protecting the Competitive Technological Advantage

Once a competitive technological advantage has been established, firms face the challenge of protecting the advantage and using it as effectively as possible. There are both legal and managerial approaches to protecting technology. Firms should consider both. Legal approaches include copyrights, patents, trademarks, and contracts (see Exhibit 8.3 for a definition of these terms). Managerial approaches involve efforts to maintain control over vital aspects of the technology through proprietary knowledge and techniques. Coca-Cola, for example, keeps its formula secret so that imitators cannot produce the "real thing."

A particular issue faced internationally is the variation in protection available from country to country. Legal protection is effective where it is enforced but meaningless in countries where it is not. Counterfeit production has become a major concern for companies in a wide variety of industries. A number of Asian countries are known to produce fake brand name products. Rolex watches bought on the streets of New York City for $20 look like Rolexes but certainly were not produced by Rolex. Initially, counterfeiting was largely a problem for name brand consumer items – Rolex watches, Calvin Klein jeans, Apple computers, and the like – but more recently counterfeiters have moved to everything from automotive parts, to agricultural products, to prescription drugs.

Counterfeiting is a serious problem. It costs companies billions of dollars in lost sales and royalties, and counterfeit automotive parts, agricultural products, or prescription drugs that do not conform to required standards can cause serious damage to consumers. The serious nature

EXHIBIT 8.3
Definitions of the Legal Means of Technology Protection

Copyright – gives the owner of a literary, audio, or visual work the exclusive right to display or reproduce the work for a limited time. The copyright covers the actual form of the work rather than the more general ideas on which the work is based.
Patent – gives the developer of a new or substantially improved product or process monopoly rights for a limited period of time.
Trademark – a distinctive design unique to a particular organization that cannot be used by another organization without formal permission.
Contract – a legal document that can be prepared to bind partners, employees, and so on to maintain the developer's proprietary rights in a certain technology, often confining its use geographically.

of the problem has led governments, industries, and individual companies to take steps to fight the problem, and efforts are being made to establish a worldwide approach to dealing with counterfeiters. In 1996, however, counterfeit products were still readily available in Southeast Asian countries and on the streets of New York, Toronto, London, Paris, and around the world.

Using the Technological Advantage

Making the best use of one's technological competitive advantage often involves a strategy of gaining a dominant market share in major markets as quickly as possible. This makes it more difficult for potential competitors to enter the market successfully. An international company needs to identify the major markets as well as the best sequence for introducing new technology to these markets. Three strategies for introduction are suggested by Keller and Chinta (1990):

▶ Simultaneous introduction in the home and host countries
▶ Introduction in the home country followed by introduction into the host countries
▶ Introduction in the host countries after the life cycle has reached maturity in the home country

The first option is generally appropriate where life cycles are short and companies want to make the most of this cycle globally. This also creates a global presence that can create a barrier to entry for other companies. This approach generally requires centralized management and a multiplant strategy. The disadvantages include the different regulations in various countries that make it inappropriate to introduce the same product, the need for similar markets, extensive premarket costs, and little opportunity to apply learning from one market to others. In addition, failure in the host markets can affect success at home.

The advantages of the second option are the ability to adapt to new markets, learn from the home market, and accommodate local requirements. This may be appropriate with longer life cycles, when time is available to take advantage of the learning effects. The disadvantages include the delay that allows competitors to enter the host country, the development of newer technology in the host country, and the host country's desire to have the most advanced technologies available as soon as possible.

The third option can prolong the profitable life of a technology and allows adequate opportunity for adaptations. This option may provide a better match between technology and developing country needs. Disadvantages include resistance from the host country, which believes it is receiving outdated technology; decreased competitiveness, because others have introduced newer technologies; and a need for a decentralized organization to deal with dissimilar environments.

The advantages and disadvantages of these approaches are summarized in Exhibit 8.4. Companies should consider their particular technological competitive advantage relative to the strategies described and choose the one that provides them the most benefits and the fewest drawbacks.

EXHIBIT 8.4
**Technology
Introduction
Strategies**

Simultaneous Introduction in Home and Host Countries
Advantages

▶ Good for products or processes with short life cycles
▶ Global presence a barrier to entry for competition
▶ Good with centralized management and multiplant strategy

Disadvantages

▶ Different regulations may cause problems
▶ Large premarket development costs
▶ Markets need to be similar in different countries
▶ Failure in host may affect sales at home
▶ Little learning curve effect

Introduction in Home then Host Countries
Advantages

▶ Good for longer life cycles
▶ Significant learning curve effects
▶ Allows for product modification and improvement
▶ Can adapt to different regulations

Disadvantages

▶ May lag technology in host countries
▶ Delay may attract competitors
▶ Host wants state-of-the-art technology

Introduction to Host Countries after Life Cycle at Home Country Complete
Advantages

▶ Prolongs profitable life
▶ May match needs of developing countries
▶ Allows adaptation to dissimilar host-country environments

Disadvantages

▶ Uncompetitive with newer technologies
▶ Host-country resistance to outdated technology
▶ Needs decentralized organizations to deal with dissimilar environments

Summary

This chapter dealt with two interconnected subjects: competition and technology. These topics are closely connected because technological abilities give companies their competitive advantage, and competition stimulates technological developments. It is important to understand the connections between competition and technology as well as the unique considerations of each of these aspects of doing business internationally. To accomplish this, the chapter examined each topic separately and then looked at the interplay between them.

The discussion in this chapter highlighted the degree of competitiveness and the rate of technological change that characterize the world of the late 20th century and are expected early in the 21st century. These are two facets of the global environment that successful international companies must constantly monitor and assess. This chapter is intended to give the reader a basic understanding of the issues involved in such monitoring and assessment.

**MINI-CASE
Frost, Inc., in
Great Britain** ▶

Frost, Inc., is a small manufacturing company with a single location near Grand Rapids, Michigan. During the 1980s, Chad Frost, the grandson of the founder and current CEO, moved the company from an old-line manufacturing facility to a highly progressive, technologically sophisticated company. It employs the latest in CAD-CAM technology. It is now one of the lowest cost producers of the highest quality door moldings and trim serving the manufacturing enterprises of the Midwest. The automobile companies are its biggest and most demanding customers. They want and get cost, quality, and timeliness of delivery from any company that wants to continue to be a supplier.

Frost, Inc., has been able to survive and even prosper in the highly competitive and demanding industry by combining high technology with high involvement human resource management practices. Frost is famous in the Midwest for offering employment security to its employees if they commit themselves to flexible job assignments and retraining. Frost operates in a very open environment with few secretaries and few secrets. Being in the western part of Michigan has enabled Frost to attract a work force dedicated to hard work and without the need to be represented by a union.

Over the past two years, Frost has been supplying Nissan USA with door moldings and trim for its facilities in Tennessee. Nissan has been so impressed that it is now asking Frost to become a sole supplier for its new plant in Sunderland, England. Although Chad Frost knows that the automobile business is a worldwide industry, he has no particular experience in operating internationally. He does acknowledge, however, that this is an opportunity that comes around only once. He further acknowledges that with his consulting arm, Amprotech, which specializes in advising firms seeking to automate their operations, he has the technological know-how to set up a plant anywhere.

Source: Written by Randall S. Schuler, research professor, Stern School of Business, New York University, used with the author's permission.

Discussion Issues

1. Discuss the impact of accepting Nissan's offer on Frost's competitive posture. What are the advantages to accepting this offer? What are the potential disadvantages?
2. Discuss the role of Frost's human resource practices relative to the type of Frost's business. Are these practices transferable internationally?
3. Get information on the automotive parts manufacturing industry and discuss the competitive nature of the industry from an international perspective.

Discussion Questions

1. Why has the competitive environment in international business intensified?

2. What do you believe to be the "mindset" needed to succeed in international competition, and why is this important?

3. How does international competition differ from domestic competition?

4. Why can the technological and competitive environments be discussed together in an international context?

Assignments

1. Choose an international industry of interest and do the following:
   a. Identify the barriers to entry and exit in this industry.
   b. Identify the main competitors in this industry and their home countries.
   c. Relate the characteristics of this industry to the competitive advantages of the home countries identified.

2. Choose a country of interest and do the following:
   a. Identify characteristics of this country that would influence the level of technology that would be appropriate.
   b. Evaluate these characteristics for the country selected.
   c. Identify the country's competitive advantages.

Selected References

Baranson, J., *Technology and the Multinational: Corporate Strategies in a Changing World Economy* (Lexington, Mass.: Lexington Books, 1978).

Brada, J., "Technology Transfer Between the United States and Communist Countries," in R. Hawkins and J. Prasad, eds., *Research in International Business and Finance: Technology and Economic Development* (Greenwich, Conn.: JAI Press, 1981).

Caves, R. E., "Multinational Enterprises and Technology Transfer," in A. Rugman, ed., *New Theories of the Multinational Enterprise* (New York: St. Martin's Press, 1982).

Caves, R. E., M. E. Porter, and A. M. Spence, *Competition in the Open Economy: A Model Applied to Canada* (Cambridge, Mass.: Harvard University Press, 1980).

Contractor, F., and T. Sagafi-Nejad, "International Technology Transfer: Major Issues and Policy Responses," *Journal of International Business Studies* 12, no. 2 (1981), pp. 113–135.

Copeland, L., and L. Griggs, *Going International* (New York: Random House, 1985).

Davidson, W., and J. de la Torre, "Key Characteristics in the Choice of International Technology Transfer Mode," *Journal of International Business Studies* 16, no. 2 (1985), pp. 5–21.

Davies, C., "Getting High-Tech off the Ground," *Challenges, Ontario's Business: Issues and Opportunities* (Winter 1990), p. 21.

Dodwell Marketing Consultants, *Industrial Groupings in Japan,* 8th ed. (Tokyo: Dodwell Marketing Consultants, 1988–1989).

Drucker, P. F., "Global Competition: The New Realities," *Challenges* (Winter 1990).

Dunning, J., *Multinational Enterprises' Technology and Competitiveness* (Winchester, Mass.: Unwin Hyman, 1988).

The Economist (June 2, 1990), p. 69.

Globe and Mail, "Report on Business" (September 22, 1990), p. B1; (November 15, 1990), p. B22.

Grant, D., "The Doomsday Gun," *Toronto Star* (April 21, 1990), pp. D1, D5.

Hughes, G. D., "Managing High-Tech Product Cycles," *Academy of Management Executive* 4, no. 2 (1990).

Kedia, B., and R. Bhagat, "Cultural Constraints on the Transfer of Technology Across Nations: Implications for Research in International and Comparative Management," *Academy of Management Review* (October 1988), pp. 559–571.

Keller, R. T., and R. R. Chinta, "International Technology Transfer: Strategies for Success," *Academy of Management Executive* 4, no. 2 (1990).

Lovelock, J., *The Economist* (September 8, 1990), p. 26.

Nonaka, I., "Creating Organizational Order out of Chaos: Self-Renewal in Japanese Firms," *California Management Review* (Spring 1988).

Osborn, R. N., A. Strickstein, and J. Olson, "Cooperative Multinational R&D Ventures: Interpretation and Negotiation in Emerging Systems," in U. E. Gattiker and L. Larwood, eds., *Managing Technological Development* (New York: Walter de Gruyter, 1988), pp. 33–54.

Porter, M. E., *Competitive Strategy* (New York: The Free Press, 1980).

Porter, M. E., *The Competitive Advantage of Nations* (New York: The Free Press, 1990).

Randall, R. M., "Dean Thurow's 'Historian of the Future' Solves an Economic Mystery," *Planning Review* (July–August 1990), pp. 40–47.

Ricks, D. A., M. Y. C. Fu, and J. Arpan, *International Business Blunders* (Columbus, Ohio: Grid, 1974).

Ricks, D.A., *Blunders in International Business* (Cambridge, Mass.: Blackwell Publishers, 1993).

Rosenberg, N., and C. Frischtak, eds., *International Technology Transfer: Concepts, Measures, and Comparisons* (New York: Praeger, 1985).

Sterngold, J., "Contrasts in How Japan, U.S. Handle Business Failures," *Globe and Mail* (May 1, 1990), p. 52.

PART

IV

Managing an International Business

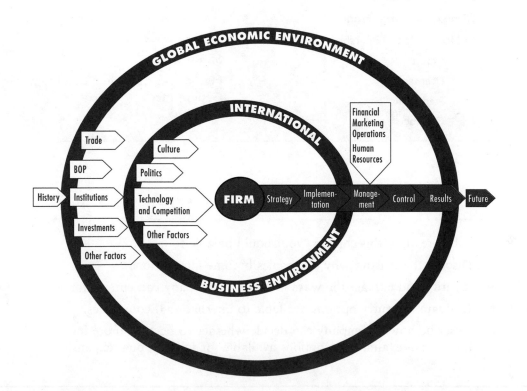

CHAPTER ▼ 9

Going International: Strategic Decisions

LEARNING OBJECTIVES

After reading this chapter, you should be able to

▶ Discuss the reasons why companies become international.

▶ Identify and explain the ways in which a company can enter a foreign location.

▶ Evaluate the entry options available to international companies.

▶ Describe how a company can decide whether to become more international and how it can evaluate the options available for international expansion.

KEY TERMS

- ▶ Multidomestic company
- ▶ Global company
- ▶ Economies of scale
- ▶ Reactive reasons for going international
- ▶ Proactive reasons for going international
- ▶ Firm-specific advantages
- ▶ Synergy
- ▶ International decision process
- ▶ Exports

- ▶ Licensing agreement
- ▶ Franchising
- ▶ Contracts
- ▶ Turnkey operations
- ▶ Joint ventures
- ▶ Sole ownership
- ▶ Company capability
- ▶ Location attractiveness
- ▶ Perceived risk

THOUGHT STARTERS

▶ The Japanese consumer electronics giant Sony Corporation which bought Columbia Pictures for $5 billion announced a $2.7 billion write-off on the acquisition of the studio. This was

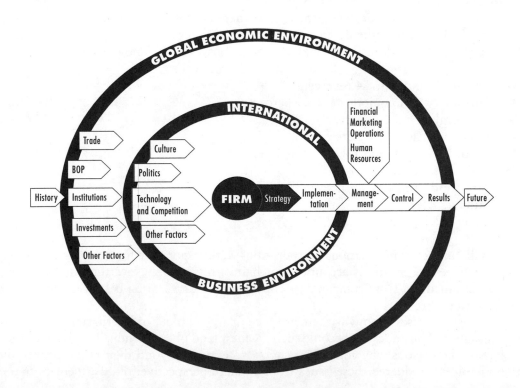

one of the largest losses in Japanese corporation history. It was attributed to factors such as management problems which had not been addressed or even acknowledged.

(Globe and Mail November 21, 1994, p. B1)

▶ Unilever, an Anglo-Dutch conglomerate, is negotiating to buy Faberge, the perfumes company owned by Meshulam Riklis and thought to be worth about $2 billion. Don't those suds smell simply divine?

(The Economist 1989)

Introduction

International business has been growing constantly and dramatically since World War II, and the number of enterprises that are classified in some sense as international is now very large. Foreign direct investment (i.e., investment outside the home country) is a major force in today's world. A listing of the top 100 multinationals by home country in the June 24, 1995, issue of *The Economist* shows the following order: United States, Japan, Germany, France, Britain, Britain-Holland, Italy, Switzerland, Sweden, Holland, Canada. According to the United Nations Center on Transnational Corporations (UNCTC 1988, pp. 33–34), in 1985 the 600 largest transnational corporations engaged in industrial or agricultural production (i.e., not including banking and financial institutions, construction, tourism, shipping, and other services) had total sales of about US$3 trillion. These 600 companies, very large multinationals with affiliates scattered throughout the world, generated more than one-fifth of the total industrial and agricultural value added in both the developed market economies and the developing countries.

The primary lines of business for these companies were as follows:

▶ Petroleum and gas, 24.6 percent
▶ Machinery and equipment, 24.5 percent
▶ Chemicals, 13.5 percent
▶ Motor vehicles, 12.6 percent
▶ Food, beverages, and tobacco, 10.4 percent
▶ Basic metals, 6.6 percent
▶ Paper and printing, 3.8 percent
▶ Mining, 1.6 percent
▶ Others, 2.5 percent

A small number of international corporations were responsible for a large share of economic activity; only 69 corporations accounted for half of total sales. Nevertheless, the contribution of small- and medium-sized companies is considerable, representing half of the total number of firms investing abroad.

The question arises as to why there are such a large number of international enterprises and why international business has become such a widespread phenomenon. To address these issues, we examine the reasons why companies choose to expand beyond their home-country borders. Earlier chapters considered these issues from a macro perspective; that is, theories that explain the overall worldwide flows of goods and services and foreign investment have been examined. The intent of this chapter is to examine issues from a micro, or individual company, perspective; that is, consideration is given to specific reasons companies choose to become international or expand internationally, as well as the options they have to accomplish such expansion.

This chapter is intended to provide a concise overview of reasons for foreign expansion and means to accomplish this expansion. It first identifies reasons for international expansion and then proposes a model for assessing whether international expansion is appropriate. A discussion of various forms of entry follows; this discussion concludes with a model for assessing the degree of foreign involvement desirable for a particular company in a particular location. Managers of international businesses must have a clear idea of what options are available to them and what the benefits and drawbacks are for various options. These decisions form the basis for international activity. The student, on completion of this chapter, should be able to identify and explain reasons for international expansion and various forms of entry into foreign locations. In addition, the student should be able to assess the desirability of expansion and specific forms of entry from the point of view of a specific company.

Why Companies Are International

A distinction has been made between companies whose international subsidiaries are largely autonomous and self-governing, often called **multidomestic companies,** and those companies whose international operations are global in nature. The subsidiaries of multidomestics operate, to a large extent, as though they were a series of separate domestic companies, hence the label. **Global companies,** in contrast, operate as one entity worldwide with globally integrated strategies and operations. This distinction is useful for discussion purposes, but in reality, many companies combine aspects of the two approaches. There are benefits to each approach; neither is inherently more advantageous than the other. The advantages for a particular company depend largely on its activities.

On the one hand, some businesses are multidomestic by nature (i.e., products or services need to be tailored to local requirements and conditions, and the nature of their operations lacks sufficient **economies of scale*** to provide a competitive edge from global operations); many accounting firms operate on this basis because accounting requirements differ from country to country.

On the other hand, many businesses can benefit from global operations and seek to establish a worldwide system of products and markets to establish a competitive position. According to Hout, Porter, and Rudden (1982), these companies seek to control leverage points, ranging from cross-national production scale economies to the foreign competitor's sources of cash flow; the potential for global competition is greatest when significant benefits are gained from worldwide volume.

The following discussion illustrates some of the differences between global and multidomestic firms in 1995.

---

*With economies of scale, increased production in one large facility lowers the per-unit cost and creates economies based on the large volume of production.

Business Week's Global 1000 (July 10, 1995) and *Fortune*'s Global 500 (August 7, 1995) provide a picture of the makeup of the world's largest firms. Depending on how one looks at size, slightly different pictures emerge:

▶ In terms of revenues, Japanese firms dominate. Of the top ten, six are headquartered in Japan (Mitsubishi, Mitsui, Itochu, Sumitomo, Marubeni, Nissho, three in the United States (General Motors, Ford, Exxon), and one in Britain/Netherlands (Royal Dutch Shell).

▶ In terms of profits, U.S. firms dominate. Of the top ten, eight are headquartered in the United States (Ford, Exxon, General Motors, General Electric, Philip Morris, AT&T, Chrysler, Citicorp). The United Kingdom follows with Royal Dutch Shell (Britain/Netherlands) ranked number one and Standard Life Assurance listed number eight.

▶ In terms of employees, U.S. firms also dominate. Of the top ten, seven are headquartered in the United States (U.S. Postal Service, General Motors, Wal-Mart, Pepsico, Sears Roebuck, Ford, K-Mart) and three are headquartered in Germany (Siemens, Deutsche Bank, Deutsche Post).

While firms from Japan and the United States, with the United Kingdom and Germany following, clearly dominate the list of global giants, firms come from many countries. Included in the lists are firms from Australia, Austria, Belgium, Canada, Demark, Finland, France, Hong Kong, Ireland, Italy, the Netherlands, New Zealand, Norway, Singapore, Spain, Sweden, and Switzerland. A striking aspect of this list is the complete absence of firms from most of the developing world, even from among the Asian Tigers (Hong Kong and Singapore being the exceptions).

A wide variety of industries are represented by these multinational firms. *Business Week*'s list includes the following:

▶ Energy (energy sources, electric and gas utilities)
▶ Materials (building materials and components, chemicals, forest products, paper, nonferrous metals, steel, miscellaneous materials and commodities)
▶ Capital Equipment (aerospace and military technology, construction and housing, data processing and reproduction, electrical and electronics, electronic components and instruments, energy equipment and services, industrial components, machinery and engineering)
▶ Consumer Goods (appliances and household durables, automobiles, beverages and tobacco, food and household products, health and personal care, recreation and consumer goods, textiles and apparel)
▶ Services (book editing and publishing, business and public services, leisure and tourism, merchandising, telecommunications, airlines, road and rail, shipping, wholesale and international trade)
▶ Finance (banking, financial services, insurance, real estate)
▶ Other (multi-industry, gold mining)

While these data provide a picture of the multinational firm makeup in 1995, it is important to recognize that this picture changes as economies change. It was not long ago that U.S. firms were losing to Japanese firms, and in the coming decades, firms from other countries may well increase in importance. These data also focus on the giants only. There are a myriad of small firms located around the world doing some international business. Many students will be as interested in the management of these small firms as in the management of the giants. The information provided in this book is intended for managers in both.

Global Firms

Caterpillar, Inc., has been described as a global company. Caterpillar has chosen the advantages offered by a global approach to its international operations. The global approach can increase profits by achieving economies of scale, and a global viewpoint allows companies to take advantage of opportunities that their multidomestic counterparts might overlook. The company's main advantages stem from its ability to establish major barriers to entry into the industry through a globally independent distribution system and worldwide production scale. The company first established independent dealerships to service fleets of Caterpillar equipment left overseas after World War II. These dealerships formed the basis of the current dealership network, which is larger and better financed than its competitors' distribution systems. Economies of scale have been achieved because product lines are limited and use identical components, allowing a few large-scale manufacturing facilities to fill worldwide demand. These facilities are augmented by assembly and production of local adaptations, in its major markets. The very strength of this approach can be its weakness, however. In a globally integrated company, the entire organization can suffer because of events that affect only one part.

In the case of Caterpillar, Inc., the company went from 48 years of continuous profits in 1982 to 3 years of losses totaling almost US$1 billion. Some of the company's main customers were in Third World nations, and when they experienced extremely bad economic conditions combined with their enormous international debt payments, their purchases declined. At the same time, the U.S. dollar's value was rising and Caterpillar's large-scale facilities in the United States were manufacturing products that were increasingly expensive, forcing its overseas customers to consider other suppliers.

Multidomestic Firms

The Bata Shoe Organization (BSO) describes itself, in its corporate literature, as a multidomestic organization. BSO is clearly an international company with subsidiaries around the world, in more than 90 countries, and approximately 95 percent of its business is outside its home country of Canada. It is not, however, a global company, because its subsidiaries operate as local companies wherever they are located, relying largely on local markets, local suppliers, and local staff. BSO states that it believes that "an international organization of companies rooted in their communities and essentially national in spirit would be stronger than one responding only to central direction and policies made by people in places far away." BSO has chosen advantages it believes are offered by a multidomestic approach to international operations.

BSO avoids the risks associated with integrated operations. A negative impact in one subsidiary does not necessarily have any impact on the rest of the organization; in fact, BSO can open or close a subsidiary without substantial impact on the organization as a whole. The drawback to this approach is that BSO does not take advantage of potential opportunities for economies of scale or production in low-cost locations. It is likely that BSO could increase its profits and competitive position through a more globally integrated approach; but, in so doing, it would incur the additional risks associated with globally integrated operations.

Although there are certainly companies whose operations are fairly clearly multidomestic and others whose operations are clearly global, most international companies exhibit some aspects of each type. Many companies globally integrate certain aspects of their operations and act like multidomestics in others; for example, Caterpillar Tractor uses independent local dealerships, and BSO has a worldwide corporate culture.

Reasons for Going International

Companies in the international arena experience many benefits; however, the complexity of the international business environment means that international ventures are inherently more risky than purely domestic ones. For rational business decisions to justify international activities, therefore, the perceived benefits must outweigh the expected risks.

Companies that choose to go international or expand their international presence do so to gain from the perceived benefits. They also want to minimize the risks to which they are exposed. The decision is made in the context of their particular internal and external environments. Very simply, internally, they consider strengths and weaknesses; externally, they consider opportunities and threats.

The following discussion examines the most likely reasons for becoming more international; these reasons have been grouped as reactive and proactive (Exhibits 9.1 and 9.2 summarize these). **The reactive reasons for going international** assume that the company is responding to something happening in its environment, generally something beyond its control and in its external environment. **The proactive reasons for going international** assume that the company is seeking advantages and benefits available internationally; thus, the focus is both internal and external. Although it is helpful to consider these as two distinct categories, in many cases companies are both reactive and proactive at the same time.

EXHIBIT 9.1
Summary of Reactive Reasons for International Business

Outside Occurrence	Explanation of Reaction
Trade barriers	Tariffs, quotas, buy-local policies, and other restrictive trade practices can make exports to foreign markets less attractive; local operations in foreign locations therefore become attractive.
International customers	If a company's customer base becomes international and the company wants to continue to serve it, then local operations in foreign locations may be necessary.
International competition	If a company's competitors become international and the company wants to remain competitive, foreign operations may be necessary.
Regulations	Regulations and restrictions imposed by the home government may increase the cost of operating at home; it may be possible to avoid these costs by establishing foreign operations.
Chance	Chance occurrence results in a company deciding to enter foreign locations.

EXHIBIT 9.2
**Summary of
Proactive Reasons
for International
Business**

Advantage or Opportunity	Explanation of Action
Additional resources	Various inputs – including natural resources, technologies, skilled personnel, and materials – may be obtained more readily outside the home country.
Lowered costs	Various costs – including labor, materials, transportation, and financing – may be lower outside the home country.
Incentives	Various incentives may be available from the host government or the home government to encourage foreign investment in specific locations.
New, expanded markets	New and different markets may be available outside the home country; excess resources – including management, skills, machinery, and money – can be utilized in foreign locations.
Exploitation of firm-specific advantages	Technologies, brands, and recognized names can all provide opportunities in foreign locations.
Taxes	Differing corporate tax rates and tax systems in different locations provide opportunities for companies to maximize their after-tax worldwide profits.
Economies of scale	National markets may be too small to support efficient production, while sales from several combined allow for larger-scale production.
Synergy	Operations in more than one national environment provide opportunities to combine benefits from one location with another, impossible without both.
Power and prestige	The image of being international may increase a company's power and prestige and improve its domestic sales and relations with various stakeholder groups.
Protect home market through offense in competitor's home	A strong offense in a competitor's market can put pressure on the competitor that results in a pull-back from foreign activities to protect itself at home.

Reactive Reasons Illustrated

Many companies do not actively seek international involvement; this can be because the risks and costs are seen as too high, the payoffs are seen as relatively low, or the company does not have adequate resources to pursue international opportunities actively. These companies, nevertheless, often find that internationalization is forced on them because of events outside of their control. The following issues illustrate reactive internationalization.

Trade barriers imposed by trading partners who are customers for a company's product or services often encourage a company to initiate international operations. These trade barriers can make a product or service too expensive (tariffs), unavailable (quotas), or unattractive (buy-local policies). If the product or service is produced locally, it is not subject to the same trade barriers and can benefit from the status as a local product.

For example, Japan's auto makers established operations in the United States to avoid protectionist barriers and moved into the European market for a similar reason. European quotas in the mid-1980s kept the Japanese share of the European market to only 10 percent, served largely by exports. To increase this share, Japanese auto makers set up local production and joint ventures in Europe.

If a company's customers choose to become international, the company may have to follow their lead to retain them as customers. Many international companies prefer to deal with a small number of suppliers worldwide; therefore, a supplier that cannot meet their needs in foreign locations may lose the business as a domestic supplier as well.

A good example involves accounting firms. When their customers set up operations in foreign locations, they want to deal with branches of their current firms. A firm that has no branch in a particular location may find it worthwhile to set one up to avoid the risk of its customer going to a competitor for all its accounting needs.

If the competition becomes international, a company may have to follow this lead to remain competitive. If international competitors become well established in foreign environments, this may put them in a position to attack the domestic market with lower costs of operation. In addition, if competitors become well established in international markets, a domestic company may find it difficult to compete in these markets at a later date. Many companies, therefore, follow the international lead of their competitors.

For example, until the early 1970s, manufacturers of wiper blades for vehicles were apparently quite happy with the level of profits generated in domestic markets. Then one company (Tridon Limited) developed a major innovation in wiper blades and found it could sell them readily in foreign markets as well as at home. These new blades soon became the standard for the industry, and other wiper blade companies were forced to either go out of business or expand and compete internationally as well.

Home governments can impose regulations and restrictions that increase the costs of operating. These include environmental, health and safety, and insurance regulations, among others. If less rigorous regulations and restrictions exist elsewhere, other factors being equal, companies may decide to operate in the less restrictive environment.

As an example, in the late 1980s, many Hong Kong capitalists decided to invest in business ventures and real estate outside Hong Kong. This outflow of capital was believed to be in anticipation of changing and more restrictive regulations resulting from the transfer of control of Hong Kong from Great Britain to the People's Republic of China. Finally, many companies seem to become international purely by chance. A chance meeting between a company's CEO and a potential foreign associate on a plane trip can result in the decision to set up foreign operations of some kind.

For example, the president of Wagner Woodlands in Vermont was on a vacation in Ireland when he met a young woman whose father was a businessman in the Caribbean. Later the U.S. executive visited the family in the Caribbean. This chance occurrence resulted in the formation of a joint venture between Wagner Woodlands and a local group of businesspeople to establish two tourist developments, Windward Islands Plantations and Parklands on the island of Bequai.

Proactive Reasons Illustrated

International differences in customs and cultures, as well as differing factor endowments, often provide many opportunities for companies outside their home borders. The following issues illustrate proactive foreign investment.

Resources are available in some locations but not in others; they are easier to access in certain locations, or they may be cheaper or subject to fewer restrictions. This is true of natural, human, technological, and financial resources. If a company needs a resource that is scarce at home, it will seek that resource elsewhere, and if the resource cannot be readily transported, the company will move operations to that location.

For example, a U.S. company needed workers who could do smocking (similar to hand embroidering) on children's clothes. Smockers were readily available in the Caribbean island of St. Vincent, but these women could not be brought to the United States. Therefore, the company set up a manufacturing subsidiary in St. Vincent.

Costs are lower in some locations than in others. Natural resources are less expensive where they are plentiful, and labor costs are lower where labor is abundant. Costs such as energy and transportation also may differ, depending on the location of production facilities relative to markets. In addition, the costs of doing business, including interest rates and taxes, vary from country to country. Companies can take advantage of these cost differentials by locating facilities in countries in which particular costs are low. If a natural resource (e.g., lumber) is an important component of a product, then it is logical for the company to seek locations, whether at home or abroad, where this resource is least costly. Similarly, if a product or service is labor intensive, it is logical to seek locations where wages are low. The same is true of any input that is a major part of the cost of a product or service. As costs of labor have increased in North America, many North American companies have moved operations offshore to take advantage of low labor costs in the Caribbean, the Far East, Latin America, and so on.

As an example, the number of U.S. companies taking advantage of the opportunities offered by the Mexican *maquiladora* (see Exhibit 9.3) clearly illustrates this. In 1987, more than 1,152 U.S. manufacturers operated assembly facilities on the northern border of Mexico.

Many countries believe that they benefit from foreign investment (this investment may be seen as providing needed foreign exchange, employment, technology, skills, training, and so on). Therefore, the governments of these countries offer incentives to encourage foreigners to invest there rather than elsewhere. Incentives offered by host governments include such things as providing industrial buildings, insurance, tax exemptions, tax holidays, and low-interest or interest-free loans. The home government may also want to encourage domestic companies to choose certain foreign locations over others and may offer its own incentives, including trade assistance, subsidies, low-interest loans, and risk insurance. These incentives can increase profits and decrease risks, making foreign operations more attractive than they would be otherwise. Companies can seek these opportunities around the world to maximize their net returns.

For example, Polysar was a global company with operations in more than 90 countries around the world. During an interview, its director of corporate strategy said that, other things

EXHIBIT 9.3
**A Brief
Description
of the Mexican
*Maquiladora***

The in-bond, or *maquiladora,* industry in Mexico increased substantially in the 1980s. The in-bond regulation allows imports into Mexico duty-free if the finished products are to be exported – the imports remain in-bond while being further processed. Estimates of exports from the *maquiladora* industry suggest an average annual increase of 37 percent from 1967 to 1987, and between 11 and 16 percent through the early 1990s. The *maquiladora* industry is expected to continue in Mexico, but the implementation of the North American Free Trade Agreement (NAFTA) provisions will likely have an impact on its growth.

The *maquiladora* industry is based on U.S. and other foreign firms engaging in processing and assembly operations in Mexican facilities without paying duties on the materials and components brought into Mexico. This allows companies to take advantage of the lower production costs available in Mexico while providing needed materials and technology from outside.

The in-bond provision is available in many locations, but there are special advantages to Mexican operations for many U.S. companies; notably, the proximity to U.S. and Canadian markets and that U.S. managers can live in the United States and manage operations in Mexico. Many border towns have capitalized on this proximity, and the *maquiladora* industry has grown, particularly along the Mexico-U.S. border. NAFTA is likely to diminish the importance of the *maquiladora* industry, as Canadian and U.S. products will be able to enter Mexico with little or no duty and vice versa.

being equal, government incentives can be the deciding factor in an investment decision. He stressed that many other factors are considered first (costs, availability of supplies, infrastructure, labor, and so forth) but given two locations with fairly comparable situations, government incentives become important.

Different levels of economic development and different lifestyles, customs, and conditions throughout the world provide reasons to consider foreign investment. A mature product in a declining market at home may be an innovative product in a growth market somewhere else. Outdated technology at home may be welcomed elsewhere. New products not suited to the home market may be appropriate for foreign locations. Conditions elsewhere may be more suitable for certain processes. The opportunities are almost endless.

A British manufacturer of heaters, for example, was somewhat surprised to find that Venezuela, Brazil, and Jordan imported large quantities of heaters. It turned out that in Jordan they were used at night when the temperature dropped rapidly, and in Venezuela and Brazil they were used for drying coffee.

Company strengths that originate at home can be easily advantageous in the global environment. A well-known brand name, a technological lead, and a recognized company image are potential global strengths. Many companies have found that they are able to take their domestic **firm-specific advantages** (FSAs) and turn them into global advantages.

As previously discussed, the Coca-Cola company has been able to use its well-known trademark *Coke* in many parts of the world. Coke is distributed in at least 155 countries around the world and is consumed more than 303 million times each day. The Coca-Cola company makes its profits from the sale of its concentrate to bottlers; it is important therefore to retain control of its secret formula. The importance of this formula is illustrated by the company's willingness to forgo the very substantial Indian market rather than put production of the formula in the hands of a subsidiary with less than 100 percent ownership.

Tax differentials among countries are important to companies that operate internationally. A company can minimize the corporate taxes it pays globally by locating its various operations in appropriate countries. In essence, an international company wants to maximize its profits in countries with low corporate tax and minimize profits in countries with high corporate tax. This can be accomplished by establishing operations in countries that offer these tax advantages.

Take the following example. In a speech delivered to the Canadian Tax Foundation, Alexander McKie proposed a hypothetical Barbados company, owned by a Canadian corporation, which purchased whiskey from Scotland for sale in Venezuela, qualified for a tax exemption in Barbados, and distributed its profits tax-free to its Canadian parent corporation. He ended with the comment "tax-free profit from whiskey – an intoxicating idea!" Tax deferral is possible, but profits are taxed in the home country when repatriated. So, the final benefits may be limited.

Economies of scale that are not available in a single market may be possible on a larger international scale. The sheer size of the potential global markets means that, for those products or services that can benefit from economies of scale, there is great potential.

As an example, car manufacturers generally have found that their markets are essentially global. Rather than produce locally for local markets, they can achieve substantial cost savings and efficiencies by producing for this worldwide market.

A certain degree of **synergy** can be created through international operations. Operations in more than one national environment provide opportunities to transfer learning from one location to another; this is impossible without both locations.

In the early 1960s, for example, IBM was pressured by Japan to offer its basic patents to Japanese companies, and it did. In 1985, when Japan had developed its own leading technologies, IBM was able to win access to Japan's government patents.

A search for increased power and prestige also may provide a reason for seeking international activities. Being international can give a company the image of being powerful and prestigious; this image can improve its domestic sales, as well as relations with various stakeholder groups. Customers at home may believe that if a company is international, its products or services must be world class; suppliers may believe that relations with an international company are more important than those with a purely domestic company; shareholders may believe that share value is enhanced by international recognition. Many companies, in their domestic literature (advertising, corporate reports, public relations announcements, and so on) stress their international nature to enhance their image.

For example, the Bridgestone Tire Company of Japan described its investment in the United States as, at least partly, a function of prestige; the president of Bridgestone explained that if the company could be successful in the very competitive U.S. market, it would create a desirable image in the world tire market.

Some firms have found that the best defense of the home market is a strong offense in the foreign competitor's home market. If a firm can put enough pressure on the competitor in the competitor's own home market, then that competitor may need to pull back from its foreign activities to protect itself at home.

As an example of this, during the 1980s, Kodak found itself under increasing pressure in the United States from Fuji. To combat this pressure, Kodak significantly expanded its marketing activities in Japan in the late 1980s. Fuji was forced to scale back its budget and marketing plans in the United States to protect itself better in Japan.

A Model of the International Decision Process

The following model summarizes the **international decision process** for a company considering new or increased international operations. It considers factors that may force the company to expand internationally and opportunities from internationalization, as well as the company's capability in the international context. The model is developed in terms of a series of questions that a company can ask itself.

1. The company begins by asking the following: Must we be more international? To answer this question, the company assesses factors in its home market to which it may need to react: the competition, trade policies, and the regulatory environment. If its home market is limited or its customers are becoming international and want to use the same supplier worldwide, the answer is yes. If the domestic competition is becoming international or foreign competition is increasing, the answer is probably yes. If there is a high probability of increased trade barriers that will affect the company's export markets, the answer is yes. If the regulatory environment is making current operations less attractive, the answer is probably yes. If none of these is occurring, the answer is probably no.

2. If the answer is no, the company asks this: Should we be more international? To answer this question, the company assesses factors that offer it potential advantages; all of the factors that are listed as proactive reasons for internationalization would be examined. If specific international opportunities are identified, the answer is yes. If none is compelling, the answer is probably no. If the answer is no, the company should concentrate on domestic opportunities.

3. If the answer to question 1 or 2 is yes, the company asks this question: Are we capable of becoming more international? To answer this question, the company assesses its strengths and weaknesses. This assessment is essentially an internal inventory and should include consideration of factors such as management, finances, products, equipment, expertise, technology, distribution, and so on. An important point is that this assessment is internationally oriented. This means that it will be different from an assessment for domestic strategy decisions. A strength at home may prove to be a weakness internationally or a weakness a strength, as the following examples indicate:

▶ An employee's facility with foreign languages might not be considered important in domestic operations but might be of critical importance in certain foreign operations.
▶ Participative management approaches that work well are a strength at home but may be totally ineffective in some foreign locations.
▶ Outdated machinery might be considered a liability in domestic operations but could prove the best kind in technologically less advanced situations.

If the company is generally strong in terms of assets that will be useful internationally and if no critical weaknesses are uncovered in this assessment, then the answer is yes. If there are critical weaknesses or a general lack of strength, then the answer is no.

4. If the answer is no, the company asks this question: How can we improve our capability? The company has previously determined that it must or should expand internationally; now it wants to be sure that it can do so successfully. The previous assessment will have identified specific weak areas or a general lack of strength. The company must now design programs to strengthen those areas before undertaking international expansion.

5. If the answer to 3 is yes, the company asks the following: What specific opportunities should we pursue? The answer to this question depends very much on the previously identified reasons for international expansion. Only a limited number of options can be explored in detail, because this analysis is time consuming and costly. Those options to be examined, therefore, should be chosen with care. If, for example, the company is reacting to government regulations and also seeking locations where specific raw materials are available, then regions or countries where different regulations are in effect and the particular raw materials are available should be identified. If, in contrast, the company is seeking new markets for products that are mature at home, then regions or countries where the products are likely to be in the growth stage will be identified. If the company is reacting to competitors' moves, the specific actions taken by the competition are examined to help determine regions or countries to be assessed.

6. The company now asks this question: How should we enter a specific location? To answer this question, the company must assess the costs and benefits of various possible modes of entry into a particular location. In general, the choices can be seen as a continuum ranging from no ownership in foreign locations through joint ventures to sole ownership of a foreign subsidiary.

Each of these options has specific benefits as well as drawbacks (which are described in more detail in the following section); these benefits and drawbacks must be weighed by the company to make an appropriate choice. Once a choice is made, an action plan is designed to achieve the desired foreign activity. This model should be thought of as incorporating an iterative process (i.e., having been through the model once, a company will periodically return to the first question and repeat the process). This has the effect of converting a reactive strategy to a proactive one. The model is summarized in Exhibit 9.4, and Exhibit 9.5 provides a flowchart of the decision process.

Choice of Entry Mode

A major aspect of global strategy for many companies is the appropriate form of entry into a given foreign location. Companies can enter foreign locations in a variety of forms ranging from exports, through licenses and contracts, to ownership of foreign operations. Entry decisions are not necessarily either/or decisions; rather, each may involve a variety of forms in combination. For example, the Fiat Group's operations in the 1970s included the following:

▶ Wholly owned stamping, body assembly, and mechanical engineering concentrated around Turin, Italy
▶ 80 percent equity in a manufacturing and marketing division that coordinated activities in Italy, France, and the Federal Republic of Germany
▶ Engine production in Brazil for shipment to Fiat plants around the world
▶ A licensing agreement with the SEAT company in Spain

EXHIBIT 9.4
**The Decision
Model
Summarized**

1.	Ask:	Must we become more international?
	Assess:	Limits to home markets, competitors, customers, etc.
	Answer:	No, then go to step 2. Yes, then go to step 3.
2.	Ask:	Should we become more international?
	Assess:	Potential advantages in terms of markets, costs, etc.
	Answer:	No, then concentrate on domestic opportunities. Yes, then go to step 3.
3.	Ask:	Are we capable of becoming more international?
	Assess:	Company's international strengths and weaknesses.
	Answer:	No, then go to step 4. Yes, then go to step 5.
4.	Ask:	How can we improve our capability?
	Assess:	Specific weaknesses.
	Answer:	Design programs to strengthen, then go to step 5.
5.	Ask:	What specific opportunities should we pursue?
	Assess:	Reasons for expansion relative to opportunities.
	Answer:	Recommend specific regions and/or countries, then go to step 6.
6.	Ask:	How should we enter a particular location?
	Assess:	Benefits and drawbacks of various options.
	Answer:	Recommend form of entry and action plan.

▶ 41 percent equity in a Turkish production group
▶ Assembly of cars in Egypt
▶ Cooperative agreements in Poland and Yugoslavia
▶ Provision of equipment and technical expertise to the Soviet Union.

The nature of business activities that a particular company undertakes in a particular location is a function of that company's specific situation. The following sample of companies doing business internationally illustrates a variety of entry mode choices.

Avis, Inc., through its subsidiary Avis Rent a Car System, Inc., and the latter's subsidiaries, rents and leases vehicles worldwide through a group of largely independent franchises. About 70 percent of its international operations are independently owned, about 20 percent are wholly owned by Avis, and the remainder are joint ventures.

Overseas Keyboarding Services in Philadelphia provides a computer data entry service and sells contracts for data entry work, done in India, all over North America.

Moore Corporation, a forms supplier, prefers to retain 100 percent ownership in subsidiaries in about 50 countries around the world but has set up joint ventures in Japan, Venezuela, Barbados, Jamaica, and Central America, partly due to perceived political risks and partly in response to restrictions on foreign investment.

The most common forms of entry (entry modes) are described next. The general benefits and drawbacks of each option are discussed briefly. These are grouped as involving no foreign ownership, joint ventures, or sole ownership (ownership is discussed in more detail in Chapter 10).

EXHIBIT 9.5
**Flowchart of
Decision Process
for Going
International**

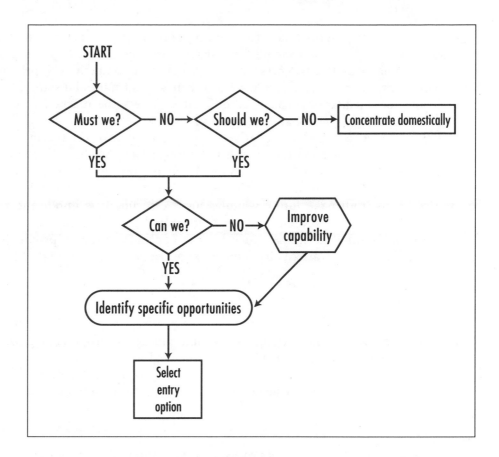

No Foreign Ownership

Companies can be involved in foreign locations in many ways and can even generate most of their revenue and profits from foreign markets without ownership or direct investment. The following paragraphs outline the major opportunities of this type.

Exports

A firm supplies foreign demand from home production. This approach is appropriate when excess capacity exists at home and the product reaches the foreign markets in a timely manner and at a competitive price. **Exports** are relatively easy to undertake and are often the first international step for a company. The company essentially continues operations as when purely domestic but now exports some output to foreign markets.

The company benefits from increased sales and can test its products or services in foreign markets with relatively little risk. The operational risks are low because there is little change in operations. There are financial risks because of potential changes in exchange rates; however, these can be minimized through currency markets or contracts (as will be explained in Chapter 11).

Exports are very appropriate for certain products; however, certain factors may make exporting undesirable. For example, if transportation costs are high or tariffs apply to the product, the final price to customers may be too high to be competitive. If products are perishable or delicate, it may not be possible to transport them any substantial distance. If nontariff barriers exist in the foreign market, it may be difficult to access the market. If after-sales service is important, a local presence may be necessary.

Although exports provide a relatively risk-free means to test the international waters, a company may not realize the full market in a foreign location through exports. In most cases, companies rely on a foreign importer to distribute and promote their product(s), but this may not be done adequately; even worse, if the foreign importer fails, the failure can reflect badly on the company and make future ventures more difficult. It is important, therefore, that an exporter consider its corporate trading partner carefully. In addition, an exporter should assess various export options to decide which is most appropriate for its product(s) and market(s). Exhibit 9.6 illustrates a variety of potential export options.

Licenses

A firm (the licensor) grants the rights on some intangible property (e.g., patents, processes, copyrights, trademarks) to a foreign firm (the licensee) for an agreed-on compensation (a royalty). This approach is appropriate when foreign production is preferable to production at home, but the licensor does not wish to engage in foreign production itself. A **licensing agreement** gives

EXHIBIT 9.6
Potential Export Options

The exporting company can go directly to the customer or through home-country agents, such as

► export houses
► resident foreign buyers
► export commission houses
► export associations
► export brokers

The exporting company, the home-country agent, or both can go directly to the customer or through foreign agents, such as

► individuals
► import brokers
► import houses
► distributors
► sales branches
► sales subsidiaries

Some combination of these is often used (e.g., export company to export house to export broker to import broker to import house to distributor).

the company access to foreign markets and foreign production without the necessity of investing in the foreign location.

Licensing agreements vary from agreement to agreement, depending on the bargaining power of the two parties and the assistance and so on provided by the licensor. Often the licensee pays a sum when signing the agreement and then a periodic percentage of sales for the period of the contract. The licensing company benefits from sales in the foreign location and increased revenues through royalties without having to provide capital or management. This is particularly attractive for a company that wants to access foreign markets through local production but does not have the financial or managerial capacity to do so on its own.

The drawbacks to licensing arrangements are as follows:

▶ If the product or service is successful, the company's revenue is less than it would have been had the company set up operations itself.
▶ The company depends on the foreign licensee for quality, efficiency, and promotion of the product or service; if the licensee is not effective, this reflects on the licensor.
▶ The company may be creating a potential competitor.
▶ A certain amount of technology sharing is necessary, and the licensor may risk losing its technological edge.

These disadvantages mean that the licensor should choose its licensee carefully to be sure that the licensee will perform at an acceptable level and is trustworthy. The agreement is very important to both parties; it should ensure that the licensee is encouraged to be efficient, that the licensor benefits from increased profits, and that the licensor's technology is adequately protected.

The stories in the box on licensing pitfalls illustrate some of the problems associated with the licensing decision. As they show, the decision not to license can be as traumatic as the decision to license.

Franchising

A **franchising** firm (the franchiser) grants, for a fee, an independent foreign firm (the franchisee) the use of a trademark or other asset that is essential to the operation of the franchised business. This approach is appropriate for firms that have developed such an asset (e.g., McDonald's, Kentucky Fried Chicken) and can locate appropriate foreign franchises.

The benefit for the franchising firm is the ability to expand rapidly without investing its own resources. In addition, the franchiser does not need local knowledge; that is left to the franchisee. The drawbacks are the need for appropriate franchisees and the difficulty of maintaining control over a specific asset. Franchisees must be able to put up the capital necessary to set up operations and be capable of running the franchised business; such individuals may be difficult to find, particularly in unfamiliar environments. A franchise is workable only when the franchiser can maintain control of the needed asset; otherwise, the company simply creates a competitor in the franchisee.

Fast-food operations that started as franchises in the domestic market have successfully expanded the concept to international markets. McDonald's is a prime example of successful franchising outside its home country. The franchising approach has worked well for McDonald's

Licensing decisions are as difficult as those around creation of a joint venture. Failure to make the correct decision at the right time can result in the loss of substantially long-range business prospects and potential profits. In one case, a U.S. manufacturer not only licensed the manufacture and sale of its product to an English firm, but also granted the firm the exclusive right to sublicense the U.S. expertise to other countries. At the time the decision was made, the company was not interested in expanding overseas. The firm believed that it was best to simply collect the royalties and thus eliminate the need to provide additional investment money. Within a few years, however, worldwide markets for the firm's products developed. Naturally, the company greatly regretted its earlier decision to permit exclusive licensing.

A similar case involved a U.S. pharmaceutical firm that licensed its manufacturing techniques to an Asian company. The Asian company, heavily promoting the products, enjoyed great success. As a result of the licensing terms, however, the Asian partner reaped almost all of the tremendous profits. Having never realized the product's potential, the U.S. company had permitted the licensing. If the U.S. firm had committed to a more direct form of involvement, such as equity participation, it could have earned a greater profit. In this instance, the company's failure to study the market carefully and product opportunities eventually resulted in a lost opportunity.

Sometimes the licensee, although pleased to have been granted the license, is not as enthusiastic about the product as the licensor. One U.S. firm discovered this when it granted an exclusive license to a Japanese company. The Japanese company was given the right to manufacture and sell the U.S. firm's specialty products for a period of 20 years. Market studies had indicated that the product, which had been extremely successful in the United States, was destined to replace some of the more conventional materials currently in use in Japan. The U.S. firm had carefully studied its potential licensees and had chosen the Japanese company because of its strength of distribution, size, and record of profit performance. However, the Japanese firm, continuing to push the more conventional materials, failed to promote the new products actively. Since the contract included no agreement concerning minimum royalties, the U.S. company earned no income for the first 10 years. Having failed to recognize the Japanese company's lack of marketing initiatives and interest, the U.S. firm was forced to accept the fact that it could not enter the market itself until the expiration of the 20-year license.   (Ricks 1993, pp. 104–105)

because it has a name and an overall look (the golden arches) that are so well marketed and publicized that it is known worldwide. In addition, McDonald's procedures and marketing strategy are well developed and controlled by the franchiser. This means that McDonald's franchises are in demand around the world, and franchisees cannot simply learn from McDonald's and then set up in competition because they cannot hope to be successful without the support of the franchiser.

Companies considering franchising internationally should probably have experience franchising at home. Success at home does not guarantee success in other environments, however. The Canadian Tire company found that its Canadian franchising formula was not successful when it tried to expand to the United States. To franchise successfully around the world, a company must have a formula that can be transferred successfully across national and cultural boundaries. Even successful global franchisers can run into difficulties in certain locations.

Contracts

A firm provides general and specialized services (including management, technical expertise, operational know-how) in a foreign location for a specified time period for a fee. This is appropriate for firms that have talents not being fully utilized at home and in demand in foreign locations.

Contracts are attractive because they allow a company to use its resources effectively, they are relatively short term, and revenues are specified in the contract. The major drawback is their short-term nature; this means that the company must constantly be developing new business and negotiating new contracts. This negotiation is time consuming, costly, and requires skill at cross-cultural negotiation. The company's revenues from international contracts are likely to be uneven and the company must be in a position to weather periods when new contracts do not materialize. Further, the company's revenues can be affected if the customer faces an economic downturn; it may be difficult to collect fees, restrictions on the movement of foreign exchange may be imposed, and currency values may change. The specific form of each contract, therefore, is very important to protect the company's economic interests.

Turnkey Operations

A firm constructs a facility, starts operations, and trains local personnel; this facility is transferred (the keys are turned over) to the foreign owner when it is ready to commence operations or when it is running smoothly. Projects of this kind are undertaken, almost entirely, in the less developed countries and by companies from the developed countries. In many cases, these operations are financed by international organizations such as the World Bank, and they tend to be megaprojects with specialized requirements; therefore, they are suitable for only a few large companies. These companies often have control over assets or resources that make it difficult for other companies to compete against them in bidding for projects.

Turnkey operations, because of their size, can mean very substantial revenues for the company providing the service; equally, if cost overruns occur, there can be substantial losses. Cost overruns can be the result of inadequate understanding of and preparation for working in the host-country environment.

Joint Ventures

Looked at very broadly, a **joint venture** (JV) consists of two or more partners sharing in a project. Using this broad definition, joint ventures can take many forms depending on what is shared, the degree of sharing that occurs, the number of partners involved, the type of project, and the time frame. As such, it is impossible to identify discrete opportunities; rather, options in terms of each of these variables are discussed.

What to Share

Most commonly, joint ventures are thought of as involving shared ownership. Two or more parties contribute capital or other resources with a specified value to create a separate entity that the partners jointly own. Sharing ownership with locals is required by law in many countries; it is equally appropriate wherever one company wishes to establish a viable foreign operation on its own but is unable to do so.

In conjunction with sharing ownership, companies may share technology, or other specialized inputs. Two or more companies can each provide specialized technology for one project. This is appropriate when each of the different technologies is required for the project and no one company has access to all the different technologies. Similarly, companies can each provide specialized inputs (including raw materials, access to markets, distribution systems, management, and so on) to one project. This is appropriate when each of the different inputs is essential to the project but no one company controls all of them.

Sharing ownership, technology, or other inputs is often the only way to make a project viable; thus, it offers the benefit of establishing a foreign operation that could not otherwise be established. In addition, the risk is shared with partners. Companies involved in a joint venture can gain from each other and develop a certain synergy. Sharing inevitably involves conflict, however, and companies have a number of concerns about entering joint ventures.

The two major concerns regarding shared ownership are lower profits and less control than one company could expect without the other owner. First, profits must be shared among the partners; thus, the profit potential may be lower than if the company were sole owner of the subsidiary. Second, if ownership is shared, decision making may be shared as well, and there is likely to be disagreement among partners stemming from different objectives and values. The major concern regarding sharing technology or other inputs is that another party, possibly a rival, has access to proprietary information. Given these concerns, companies need to weigh carefully the potential benefits that may accrue from a joint venture against potential losses in order to decide what they are willing to share.

How Much to Share

Each joint venture project involves decisions as to how much each partner contributes and what each partner gets in return for that contribution. In the case of ownership, there is a range from very low ownership (e.g., 10 percent of equity), through equal shares (50–50), to high ownership (e.g., 90 percent of equity). In many cases, the degree of ownership implies a certain degree of control and decision making and a certain share in profits, but this is not necessarily the case.

With Whom to Share

The choice of partners is extremely important to the success of a joint venture. Joint ventures have often been compared to marriages, and like a marriage, they are most successful when the partners work well together. There are many potential partners for a joint venture; they can be from the home country, the host country, third countries, or some combination of these. Partners may be individuals, local companies, multinational companies, governments, international organizations, or some combination. Finally, there may be a few partners or many, and partners can take many roles (from silent to active). The choice of appropriate partners depends on the specific project and the specific location as well as the availability of potential partners.

How Long to Share

Joint ventures have been found to be unstable in general, perhaps because most joint venture partnerships are formed for a specific undertaking; thus, implicitly they are intended to last for only a limited period of time. It is appropriate for JV partners to give explicit attention to this point when forming a JV. Further, the partners should deal specifically with the question of what to do if the JV fails: how to dissolve the partnership and who gets what in the divorce settlement.

Sole Ownership

A company sometimes establishes a subsidiary that the parent company owns entirely. This approach is appropriate when control of decisions and policies is important to the parent, and the parent can provide the needed resources to operate the subsidiary effectively. The company choosing this mode of entry has access to all of the subsidiary's profits and, subject to government regulations, retains control of decision making; equally, the company assumes all of the risk associated with the subsidiary's operation.

Sole ownership was the preferred entry mode of U.S. companies because of the desire for parent control. This appears to be changing, with a variety of strategic alliances, and combined approaches, becoming relatively more popular than in the past. This shift seems to have occurred primarily for three reasons: (1) the necessity of local involvement imposed by host governments, (2) greater recognition of the potential benefits of other forms of entry, and (3) the competitive advantages offered by strategic alliances.

Strategic Alliances

Strategic alliances are arrangements among firms to cooperate for strategic purposes. In this very broad sense, a firm could be said to have formed a strategic alliance when it works with a supplier to improve quality. More specifically, strategic alliances are thought of as involving firms working together on major strategic initiatives, for example, developing new technology of benefit to all the cooperating firms. While firms of any size can enter a strategic alliance, the alliances that one hears of most often are among some of the major international firms, for example, IBM and Apple Computers, and General Motors and Toyota.

Strategic alliances have become more prevalent in the 1990s. This seems to have occurred because many projects are seen as too large for any one firm (even one of the "giants") to undertake in isolation. Drawing on the strengths of two or more firms is often seen as the only means to undertake really large ventures. At the same time, strategic alliances have not always been successful, financially and otherwise. A feature of many of these alliances is that the firms involved in an alliance, which incorporates cooperation in one location, may compete fiercely in other locations. This means that a particular concern for firms is loss of their competitive advantage to rivals in a strategic alliance.

While large firms make the news when they form strategic alliances, small- and medium-sized firms can also benefit from alliances. A strategic alliance may allow a smaller firm to take part in international ventures that it could not consider on its own. Alliance should be entered cautiously, however, and the advantages and risks weighed carefully.

Making the Right Entry Choice

The view that sole ownership is generally the best entry mode and that the other options should be examined only when sole ownership is not possible simplified the entry mode decision for many companies. The changing emphasis in terms of preferred forms of entry makes the decision more complex. At the same time, it is clear that assessment of the various possible options is extremely important to identify the optimal approach in each situation. The following approach is proposed to assist in the choice of entry for a particular location.

The approach identifies three dimensions, each of which must be assessed to reach an entry decision: (1) company capability, (2) location attractiveness, and (3) perceived risk. The entry choice is discussed in terms of degree of involvement desired for a particular location. A company's desired level of involvement in a particular foreign location is a function of the company's capability, the location's attractiveness, and the perceived risk, as depicted in Exhibit 9.7. Specifically, desired level of involvement increases as capability and attractiveness increase and risk decreases. Assessment of these dimensions is discussed next.

Company Capability

Assessment of **company capability** was described previously in question 3, "Are we capable of becoming more international?" This analysis leads to a judgment of the company's overall capability to undertake an international venture.

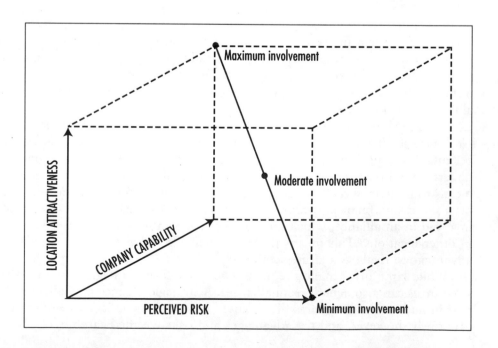

EXHIBIT 9.7

Involvement as a Function of Capability, Risk, and Location Attractiveness

Attractiveness of Location

Assessment of **location attractiveness** involves consideration of the net benefit to the company of operations in a particular location. This includes consideration of competition, entry barriers, exit barriers, incentives, potential markets, regulations, supplies, taxes, and so on. The analysis of this dimension should focus on both opportunities and challenges that operations in this location would engender. Assessment of a particular location could be based on its potential as a market or a source of supply, or both, and should consider this location as part of the company's overall operations. Although profit potential is an important part of this assessment, the focus is not necessarily on profits in this location but on the impact that operations in this location will have on overall corporate profits.

The attractiveness of a particular location depends on the company doing the analysis; that is, what is attractive to one company may be meaningless to another. The following examples illustrate this:

▶ A company seeking increased markets for a low-cost product (e.g., toilet paper) considers a country with a large population and low income attractive, whereas one with a relatively expensive product considers this location less attractive.

▶ A company seeking low-cost labor considers a country in which unskilled labor is abundant and wage rates are low attractive, but one that needs skilled labor might consider it less attractive.

▶ A company seeking rare raw materials considers any location where they are available attractive, in spite of conditions such as extreme cold (e.g., Siberia) that might make it unattractive to most other companies.

Perceived Risk

Assessment of **perceived risk** involves consideration of how safe operations are likely to be in a particular location. This assessment should consider the social environment, the economic environment, and the political environment. Risk in this analysis is equated with the likelihood of unwelcome events occurring.

This analysis should examine the stability and compatibility of a particular location. Stability can be thought of in terms of the degree and frequency of unplanned change; the greater the likelihood of such change, the greater is the risk. Compatibility can be thought of as the degree of divergence between the company and country in terms of objectives, culture, systems, and so on. The more compatible (similar) the company and country are, the more likely that operations will be relatively safe; the more incompatible (different), the more likely that disagreement and consequent unwelcome events will occur.

The degree of risk that exists in any situation depends on the particular company. A risky situation for one company may be quite safe for another. Some examples will illustrate this.

▶ Frequent changes in government suggest a risky environment for a company that relies on government support but are relatively safe for a company whose operations are of little interest to the host government.

▶ Anti-American feelings are a risky environment for an American-owned and operated company but could be quite safe for an Australian or Canadian company.

This assessment of company capability, location attractiveness, and perceived risk should lead a company to identify external opportunities and threats and internal strengths and weaknesses. These factors can then be related to the entry options available to the company. The company should choose a form of entry in a particular location to maximize the benefits and minimize the drawbacks that the previous assessment identified.

The entry choice can be thought of in terms of the degree of involvement that a company would like in a particular location. If the situation is very favorable, the company would like to maximize its involvement; if it is unfavorable, it would want to minimize involvement; if it is mixed, it would prefer moderate involvement. It is important to note that degree of involvement and ownership is not necessarily the same (although increased ownership often implies increased involvement): Joint ventures and other forms of foreign participation can also be undertaken at varying levels. The entry modes considered for a particular location are limited to those permitted within the regulations of a given location.

The classifications in Exhibit 9.8 rate company capability (CC), location attractiveness (LA), and perceived risk (PR) as either high or low, resulting in eight cells. Each of the cells, with possible entry choices, will be discussed briefly. Not all of the appropriate choices for each cell

EXHIBIT 9.8
Rating Foreign Market Entry Choices

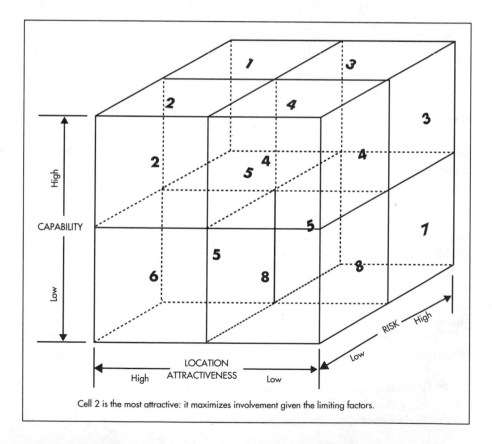

Cell 2 is the most attractive: it maximizes involvement given the limiting factors.

are considered; rather, the emphasis is on the logic of identifying various options as appropriate for a particular company in a particular location. Of course, in a real-world assessment, the choices would be limited by the regulations that exist in any location, and the company would consider only those options permitted.

1. Cell 1: High CC, High LA, High PR – In this cell, the investing company must be concerned with reducing and managing the perceived risk. The exact option depends on the type of risk foreseen. If the company is concerned about foreign exchange risk, it structures its investments to minimize assets that are exposed to changes in exchange rates. If the company is concerned about social risks, such as lack of acceptance by locals, it may wish to engage in a joint venture with locals. If the concern is political risk such as feared nationalization of assets, the company may prefer to limit ownership or locate key aspects of its business externally.

2. Cell 2: High CC, High LA, Low PR – This is the ideal cell from the company's viewpoint. The company maximizes its presence in this location, given the regulations that exist. If wholly owned subsidiaries are permitted, it chooses this option; if not, it maximizes ownership within the regulations that do exist.

3. Cell 3: High CC, Low LA, High PR – Relatively low location attractiveness and high perceived risk are the issues for this cell; this suggests that the company can use its capabilities more effectively and safely elsewhere. If the company chooses to maintain a presence in this location because it believes the situation may change, it should do so through exports or licensing.

4. Cell 4: High CC, Low LA, Low PR – The concern here is the limited attractiveness of this location; however, it is a safe environment and the company may want to maintain a presence to be ready if the location becomes more attractive. A company in this situation opts for limited involvement: probably exports or a licensing arrangement, possibly a sales branch.

5. Cell 5: Low CC, High LA, High PR – In this situation, the company's capability and the perceived risks are both concerns. The attractiveness of the location means, however, that the company would like to maintain some presence here. This company might consider a joint venture that would offset its weaknesses and limit its exposure. The company's choice of partner is very important relative to the degree of risk to which the company is exposed. In all low capability cells, the company should also pursue programs to improve its capability.

6. Cell 6: Low CC, High LA, Low PR – This is an attractive situation, but the company's capability is questionable. In this situation, the company wants to maximize its ownership and looks for a joint venture partner that can provide specific complementary strengths.

7. Cell 7: Low CC, Low LA, High PR – This cell is the least interesting from the company's point of view and no presence is probably the appropriate choice.

8. Cell 8: Low CC, Low LA, Low PR – This cell is unattractive, but the safe environment might suggest maintaining a minimal presence. Such presence might be maintained through exports or a licensing agreement that does not place undue strain on the company's capabilities.

In more general terms, a company might react to these three dimensions as follows:

1. If the company believes that it is capable of international investment and operations, it should aggressively seek opportunities; if, in contrast, it has identified important deficiencies in its abilities, it should seek to rectify them by seeking partners or by building up its own resources.

2. If a company believes that a location is attractive, it should maintain as high a presence as possible, given the constraints that it faces, and seek to expand its involvement over time; if, in contrast, it has identified a location as unattractive, it should maintain only enough presence to allow it to increase its involvement if the situation changes positively.

3. If a company believes that a situation is relatively safe, it should maintain a presence appropriate to the attractiveness of the location and its capability; if a situation is seen as risky, the reduction and management of risk become primary concerns in that location.

This approach, as presented, is relatively simplistic. Each dimension could be assessed on a scale, from 1 to 10, to give a greater precision to the analysis. Even in this simple form, however, this approach delineates the foreign entry decision process and thus assists companies in making appropriate choices.

Summary

This chapter examined the foreign entry decision from the point of view of the individual firm. Reasons for becoming international or expanding international operations were explained and different options for entry assessed. The emphasis was on decision making as it might be applied to a specific company in a specific situation. A model was presented to illustrate the decision-making process. This model can serve as a guide for making real decisions about real companies. An approach that can be used for further assessment of specific entry choices was also presented. This approach can also serve as a guide for decision making.

MINI-CASE
**Capsule
Technology
Group, Inc.**

Capsule is a Canadian-based medical supply company. The company manufactures gelatin capsules and develops and sells technology around the world. In 1989, the company had capsule manufacturing operations in Canada, at a wholly owned subsidiary in Puerto Rico, and through joint ventures in Venezuela, Colombia, and France. In 1989, it embarked on its first pharmaceutical product, a fish oil concentrate. The company believed that this and other pharmaceutical products would be a major source of revenue in the future. The company's major revenues up to this time had been from the development and installation of turnkey capsule plants.

The company's early approach to the worldwide market was unusual in the medical supply industry. Capsule focused initially on the design and installation of turnkey gelatin capsule production plants. At the end of 1988, Capsule had completed 18 turnkey plants in 16 countries in less than six years.

This early market approach is perhaps best understood by considering the events leading to the establishment of Capsule. Stephen Lucas, the president and chief executive officer, established the company at a time when he had to abide by a five-year noncompetitive agreement with his previous employer (Parke-Davis). He spent much of this time researching the turnkey opportunity. He found that there were private pharmaceutical companies and foreign governments around the world that wanted to establish capsule manufacturing capabilities of their own rather than depend on others for their supply of capsules.

At the end of the 1980s, management at Capsule Technology was changing its focus for the 1990s. It believed that the company could capitalize on its capsule-producing technology and its long-standing relationships in the pharmaceutical industry to form joint venture projects. A joint venture agreement with the French pharmaceutical company, Laboratoire Genneau, illustrates this strategy. The joint venture company, Genneau Caps, was established to manufacture gelatin capsules and market Laboratoire Genneau's pharmaceutical products, thus combining the manufacturing expertise of one parent with the marketing expertise of the other.

The founder of Capsule Technologies began with a specific plan for entering the international environment. His stated intent was to establish an international presence through the sale of turnkey plants with the intention of becoming a pharmaceutical company within 15 years. In 1989, after 12 years of operation, the plan was largely on track.

Discussion Issues

1. Evaluate the costs and benefits associated with turnkey operations and compare them to the costs and benefits associated with joint ventures for Capsule Technology.
2. Identify other international expansion strategies that Capsule Technology could consider and evaluate these options.
3. Find information on the capsule production industry and identify the main companies involved in this industry. How have these companies expanded internationally?

Discussion Questions

1. What are the relative advantages and drawbacks to a global strategy versus a multidomestic strategy?
2. Given the current international business environment, which type of company would you expect to be most prevalent, global or multidomestic? Explain why you believe this.
3. Identify a recent international event that may influence international company strategy. What impact do you believe it will have?

Assignments

1. Select two contrasting cells in the model presented in Exhibit 9.8 and identify in detail the considerations implied by each of these cells. How would a company's strategy differ depending on which cell it fell into?

2. Select an international company to research. Based on the literature available, describe the company's strategy in terms of the global-multidomestic contrast.

3. Select an international company to research. Identify different entry modes that this company employed in different situations and explain why it probably chose these options.

Selected References

Bata Shoe Organization, company reports (1988).

Boddewyn, J. J., "Foreign Direct Divestment Theory: Is It the Reverse of FDI Theory?" *Weltwirtschfliches Archiv.* (1983), pp. 345–355.

Contractor, F. J., "In Defence of Licensing: Its Increased Role in International Operations," *Columbia Journal of World Business* (1981).

Czinkota, M. R., and W. J. Johnston, "Exporting: Does Sales Volume Make a Difference?" *Journal of International Business Studies* (Spring–Summer 1983), pp. 147–153.

The Economist, Business This Week section (January 14–20, 1989), p. 59.

The Economist, "Multinationals – Survey" (January 24, 1995), p. 15.

Globe and Mail (November 21, 1994), p. B1.

Grosse, R., *Foreign Investment Codes and Location of Direct Investment* (New York: Praeger, 1980).

Hout, T., M. E. Porter, and E. Rudden, "How Global Companies Win Out," *Harvard Business Review* (September–October 1982), pp. 98–103.

Meyers, G. C., with J. Holusha, *When It Hits the Fan – Managing the Nine Crises of Business* (New York: Mentor Books, 1986).

Polysar, company interviews (1988).

Porter, M. E., and M. B. Fuller, "Coalitions in Global Strategy," in M. E. Porter, ed., *Competition in Global Industries* (Boston: Harvard Business School Press, 1986).

Punnett, B. J., "International Human Resource Management," in A. Rugman, ed., *International Business in Canada: Strategic Approaches to Management* (Toronto: Prentice-Hall Canada, 1989).

Ricks, D. A., *Blunders in International Business* (Cambridge, Mass.: Blackwell Publishers, 1993).

Stopford, J. M., "Changing Perspectives on Investment by British Manufacturing Multinationals," *Journal of International Business Studies* (Winter 1976).

United Nations Centre on Transnational Corporations, *Transnational Corporations in World Development* (New York: United Nations, 1988).

CHAPTER 10

Implementing International Strategic Decisions

LEARNING OBJECTIVES

After reading this chapter, you should be able to

▶ Discuss the major considerations associated with the various forms of entry into foreign locations.

▶ Explain the advantages and disadvantages of major export routes.

▶ Discuss the use of licensing and contracting from an international perspective.

▶ Evaluate the cost/benefit trade-offs of various ownership options.

▶ Differentiate between joint ventures and strategic alliances and explain why they both have become popular choices for international companies.

▶ Understand the importance of the joint venture partner and aspects of a successful joint venture or strategic alliance.

▶ Identify the main factors that affect international negotiations.

K E Y   T E R M S

▶ Export routes

▶ Export intermediary

▶ Import intermediary

▶ Export documentation

▶ Product preparation

▶ Licensing agreement

▶ Licensor

▶ Licensee

▶ Contracting

▶ Ownership

▶ Joint ventures

▶ Strategic alliances

▶ Negotiations

▶ Stages of the negotiation process

▶ Variables in the negotiation process

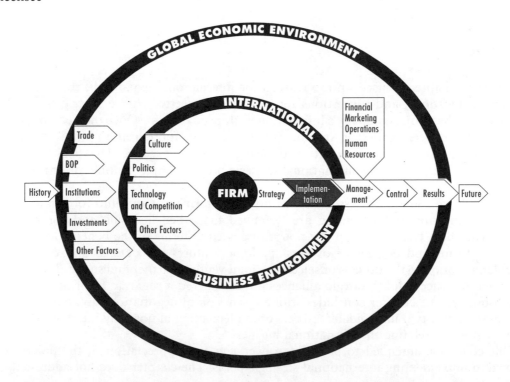

▶ A U.S. pineapple firm was unable to transport its fruit down the river to its processing plant because the prevailing river conditions were unsuitable.

(Ricks 1993, p. 16)

▶

The Soviet Union built a large, expensive steel mill for India only to discover that the mill had been located in an area without adequate transportation facilities.

(Ricks 1993, p. 111)

▶

International business is a rough game and no place for the naive idealist or the faint-hearted. Your competitors use bribes and, unless you are willing to meet this standard, competitive practice, you will lose business and, ultimately, jobs for workers at home. Besides, it is an accepted practice in those countries, and when you are in Rome you have to do as the Romans do. "Moralists," on the other hand, believe that cultural relativity is no excuse for unethical behavior.

(Lane and Simpson 1990)

▶

It might seem that the creation of a joint venture, for example, would eliminate all of the problems encountered by a company "going overseas." With the combined expertise and efforts of both local and foreign firms, potential problems or possible blunders would surely be eliminated. However, although certain types of errors are definitely less likely, a multitude of other problems can arise and pose serious threats to the venture's success.

(Ricks 1993, p. 101)

Introduction

The previous chapter focused on the reasons for international expansion, the forms of entry into foreign locations, and suggestions for making an effective choice among options. These factors are the basis of a company's international strategic process. Once the decision to become international has been made and specific avenues of internationalization have been identified, the company turns its attention to putting these decisions into practice. The focus of this chapter is on the second aspect of the international strategic process: implementing the strategic choices made.

The major considerations associated with various forms of entry into foreign locations are discussed. Exporting and importing are examined first, then licensing and contracting, and finally ownership. The ownership decision is discussed in terms of the benefits and drawbacks of various forms and degrees of ownership. Joint ventures are defined and discussed, with particular attention to the process of selecting a joint venture partner and suggestions for making a joint venture successful. Strategic alliances are considered a separate form of doing business internationally. The chapter concludes with a discussion of negotiations and company-government interactions, two unavoidable aspects of implementing almost any international strategy, and ethical issues relating to international business.

This chapter is intended to provide an overview and appreciation of the practical issues involved in implementing international strategic plans. The chapter does not address the legal, accounting, or tax issues associated with such implementation. These questions are specialized in nature and differ from one decision to another; therefore, companies often use specialists to assess these aspects of strategic decisions.

Exporting and Importing

Companies typically begin their international involvement by exporting or importing goods or services. These aspects of doing business internationally often remain important to companies even when they become involved in other forms of international business. To some degree, exporting and importing are relatively simple forms of international business; however, the following discussion illustrates that they are more complex than many people realize. Robinson (1978, p. 69) illustrates this complexity.

> It should be clearly understood that exporting requires a set of highly specialized skills having to do with packaging; marking; documentation; selection of carriers; insurance; foreign import regulations; foreign export finance; and the selection of overseas commission houses, representatives, and/or agencies; as well as the sensitivity to know when direct entry into a foreign sales branch or subsidiary is advantageous.

A company generally chooses to export its products or services when it has the capacity to do so and it can make profits. A company chooses to import products or services because it can secure a better source of supply outside domestic sources. This sounds simple, and because exports and imports involve relatively limited interaction with other countries, some of the risks of international interactions are minimized, but many decisions still have to be made to approach exports and imports effectively. The major concerns regarding export routes, transportation issues, payment methods, export documentation, and product preparation are discussed briefly in the following sections. They are discussed from the exporter's point of view for simplicity, but they are equally important considerations for importers.

Most companies try to save money by purchasing supplies in large quantities. There are, however, logical limits governing this strategy. One example of excessive supply purchasing occurred in Chile. Until recently, the Chilean government levied high tariffs on automobile imports. Over time, this policy created a large, pent-up demand for cars. In the late 1970s, the government began to radically reduce tariffs and, consequently, demand quickly outstripped supply. By 1981, these tariffs had dropped so low that large numbers of Chileans could afford new autos. Because dealers were unable to fill the vast number of orders, a five-month waiting period for most automobile models was not unusual. Believing that this demand might be unlimited, dealers ordered up to 10 times their normal number of cars for 1982 even though the economy began experiencing a recession and the new models were higher-priced. A flooded market resulted. Most of the demand for autos had already been satisfied, and few of the fairly new cars needed to be replaced. Economic uncertainty and higher prices also kept customers away. The result was that inventories are so high that dealers had no room to store cars. Many loads (more than a year's supply) were left on-board ships lying offshore, incurring high storage costs. The lesson: Optimistic, straight-line projections on sales figures are obviously dangerous. Temporary cause of demand should be analyzed and estimates made to determine the amount of pent-up demand still remaining.   (Ricks 1993, p. 108)

Export Routes

The previous chapter identified a number of alternative **export routes** that companies can utilize. Here we examine the advantages and disadvantages of four major export options. Broadly, these options are (1) direct from the exporter to the foreign buyer, (2) from the exporter through a domestic **export intermediary** to the foreign buyer, (3) from the exporter through a foreign **import intermediary** to the foreign buyer, and (4) from the exporter through a domestic export intermediary and a foreign import intermediary to the buyer.

The first option can be the simplest because it involves essentially only two parties, the exporter and the foreign buyer. This approach minimizes certain costs and provides certain benefits but increases other risks as summarized in the following points.

Benefits include

▶ Costs associated with intermediaries are minimized.
▶ The parties communicate directly.
▶ The firm develops exporting skills internally.
▶ The firm becomes familiar with its export markets.
▶ The exporter's interests can be the dominant focus.

Drawbacks include

▶ Internal specialists are needed.
▶ Internal specialists may be costly to find or develop.
▶ The foreign buyer may not be a competent importer.
▶ The exporter assumes much of the financial risk.

The second option involves a third party in the export transaction. This adds certain costs but provides other benefits and decreases some risks, as summarized in the following points.

Benefits include

▶ Specialized outside expertise is utilized.
▶ The intermediary may have established access to certain locations and have developed good working relationships with relevant local people.
▶ The firm's internal resources are not tied up with exporting details.
▶ Some financial risk may be transferred to the outside specialists.

Drawbacks include

▶ There are added costs of the intermediary.
▶ The intermediary deals with many exporters and markets, and this can lead to difficulty in attaining or retaining high-priority status if there are conflicting interests.
▶ No development of internal expertise takes place.
▶ The intermediary may not have in-depth knowledge of a specific foreign buyer or location.

The third option also involves a third party, but, in this case, the third party is located in the foreign buyer's country. This again adds certain costs but provides benefits and decreases risks, as summarized in the following points.

Benefits include

▶ Specialized knowledge of a particular foreign environment is provided.
▶ The intermediary is likely to have desired contacts with a variety of parties (government officials, potential customers, transportation companies, and so on) in the foreign location.

Drawbacks include

▶ Interactions may be difficult due to language and other communication barriers.
▶ The firm must still provide export expertise.
▶ The added costs of the intermediary become part of the transaction.

The fourth option combines the second and third options. This is the most complex of the options in that it involves several players. This option removes the exporting firm from the export process and relies on the expertise of outsiders. As might be expected, the benefits and drawbacks are a combination of those listed for the second and third options. In general terms, specialized know-how regarding exporting and the foreign location and a transfer of some of the risk from the exporting firm to the intermediaries are the major benefits. However, the costs may be high, and the firm's removal from the process can mean that its best interests are not always served.

The exporting firm should weigh the costs and benefits of the available exporting options relative to its own position in a particular location to make the most effective choice. Factors such as the need for adaptation, the degree of standardization, the firm's familiarity with the local market, the complexity of the foreign environment, and the maturity of the market may need to be factored in to the decision, but these factors will affect different firms in varied ways. For example, if a product needs to be adapted substantially for a particular market, one firm might decide that its lack of knowledge of the local market suggests the need for an intermediary who is more familiar with this location; another firm might believe that it needs to develop this local expertise itself to make appropriate adaptations.

Transportation Issues

A major consideration in exporting goods is the physical movement of products from the point of production to the foreign buyer. Transportation choices involve trade-offs in terms of cost, speed, safety, reliability, and convenience. The major forms of transportation that firms normally consider are sea, air, rail, truck, and electronic. Each of these involves different benefits and drawbacks that need to be related to the particular product and location being considered. Some illustrations of the trade-offs follow.

Sea transportation is relatively inexpensive and appropriate for products of varying sizes and weights; it may be particularly appropriate for large items. Sea routes are often slow and indirect because ships stop at many ports, shipping lines differ in terms of the degree of safety and reliability that they offer, scheduled arrival times may not be precise, and ground transportation has to be arranged to and from the docks. The convenience of sea routes often depends on the location of the exporting firm and the foreign buyer.

Air transportation is quick and direct, but it is relatively expensive and may be appropriate only for smaller or high-value items. Air transportation is usually relatively safe, reliable, and convenient to major locations but less so to remote locations. Ground link transportation also must be arranged, often separately.

Rail transportation is relatively inexpensive, safe, and reliable. It is slower than air transportation and depends on the availability of rail lines and spurs to serve specific customers. If spurs are not available, then transportation to and from rail lines must be arranged.

Truck transportation is versatile and can provide door-to-door pickup and delivery; trucks can often service locations that cannot be served by other means. Although off-road vehicles and helicopters are available for areas that cannot be reached by road, most truck transportation relies on an adequate system of roads and receiving facilities.

Electronic transportation is quick and direct, but it is expensive and limited to rather specific items. Some items that can be transmitted electronically are contracts, plans, reports, computer programs, and data lists. If the product is appropriate and the technology available, electronic transfers can be reliable and convenient; however, a lack of privacy may be associated with such transfers.

Large department stores often purchase stock from many sources, including foreign countries. It is especially important for the buyers of these goods to be familiar with local foreign customs. They should also be fluent in the required language or procure translation assistance. One overconfident buyer created quite a problem for her Italian firm. Believing that she knew English fairly well, she was sent to Britain to purchase clothing. When she found some appropriate sweaters . . . , she attempted to request "four to five thousand pounds' worth." It became quite obvious, however, that there had been a "misunderstanding" when she returned to Italy and the delivery trucks began arriving. They were carrying the "forty-five" thousand pounds worth (US$90,000) that she had actually ordered. (Ricks 1993, p. 110)

A similar event occurred on a small island in the Caribbean (population 90,000) when a small shop ordered a variety of sizes of men's trousers from a company in Britain. The shop's owners wanted about two dozen pairs of trousers in total, but their order was interpreted to mean two dozen in each size available. When the order of several thousand trousers arrived, the owners were totally overwhelmed. Not only could they not hope to sell this number of rather expensive trousers, they could not afford to pay for them. To make matters worse, the costs of shipping them back to Britain meant that the option of returning them was not practical. Needless to say, the relationship between the Caribbean shop and its British supplier was not good after this event.

Payment Methods

The means by which the exporting firm receives payment for its products is an important consideration in the export process. This question includes the timing, form, and currency of payments. These issues are dealt with in Chapter 11 and are discussed here only briefly.

Payments can be taken in a variety of forms and at different times. These choices depend on the relationship between the buyer and seller. A seller that wishes to eliminate the risks associated with payments can ask for payment in advance, but this may discourage the buyer. A firm that wants to encourage sales can extend credit to its customers but takes the risk of not receiving the expected payment. As in all of these decisions, the firm needs to consider the trade-offs to make an appropriate choice. Generally, a seller that is in a strong position relative to a buyer can arrange terms that are in its own favor, and a seller that is in a relatively weak position may accept terms that are more in the buyer's favor.

Consider a multinational firm that had carefully test marketed its specially modified washing machines and concluded that they would sell well in Latin America. Sales were slow even though a large shipment had been made available. Eventually the firm discovered the trouble: Local competitors were making their sales on credit. Apparently, people participating in the market test had assumed that credit would be made available since it was the local business practice. So, when asked during the test if they would buy, they replied "yes." Only after they discovered that no credit would be provided did they change their minds and decide not to purchase the product.

Export arrangements also involve specification of the currency in which payment is to be made because of fluctuations in currency values. If payment is made in the seller's currency, the seller knows exactly how much will be received and does not face the uncertainty associated with receiving a foreign currency. If payment is made in the buyer's currency and the seller plans to convert it, there is uncertainty about the exact amount of the seller's currency that will be received. If payment is in a third currency and each party is converting this currency, then both are unsure of the exact payment in their currency.

Export Documentation

Export documentation is a necessary part of the export process. A variety of documentation forms have to be completed, and the exporting firm must comply with certain procedures before it can actually move its goods from the domestic location to the foreign location. These forms and procedures relate to products leaving the home country, arriving in the foreign country, and passing through other countries. Each country has its own regulations regarding the movement of products in and out of its borders, and all of these regulations must be met if an export transaction is to be completed satisfactorily. Prior to undertaking an export obligation, a firm should ascertain the documentation that will be necessary to complete its obligation and ensure that it can comply with the necessary procedures. There are specialists who can provide information on export documentation. Firms that plan not to use intermediaries may need to seek advice from such specialists.

Among the many documents that may have to be prepared are bills of lading, commercial invoices, export licenses, insurance certificates, certificates of product origin, inspection certificates, and payment documents. Overlooking even one necessary form will delay the entire export transaction; therefore, companies should be sure that they have accurately prepared all of the documents required at both ends of the export process as well as during transit. Not all documents are required for all shipments; therefore, the exporter must identify which documents are needed for a particular shipment. The requirements depend on factors such as the types of goods being shipped, the method of shipment, the origin of the shipment, and the destination of the shipment. The main documents likely to be required will be briefly described.

Bills of lading are issued by the shipping company or its agent as evidence of a contract to ship the goods. The bill of lading shows that the exporter delivered the goods to the shipping company. Shipments by air use air waybills, and shipments involving several types of transportation (e.g., rail to air to truck) may use a combined transport document.

Commercial invoices are itemizations written by the exporter that describe the details of the merchandise and the terms of payment.

Export licenses are issued by the regulatory agency in the country of origin and give the exporter the legal right to export the goods being shipped.

Insurance certificates are issued by the insuring company and specify the goods that are insured and the terms of the insurance contract.

Certificates of product origin are issued by regulatory agencies in the country of origin and provide evidence that the goods were made in a particular country. These certificates are needed to assess various tariffs and regulations imposed by the importing country.

Inspection certificates can be issued by regulatory agencies either in the exporting country or the importing country and provide evidence that the goods have been inspected and meet the prescribed standards for goods of their type.

Payment documents ensure that the exporter receives payment for the goods. The most common form of payment is a letter of credit. An export letter of credit is issued by a buyer/importer's bank and promises to pay the seller/exporter a specified amount when the bank has received certain documents specified in the letter of credit by a specified time. Most letters of credit are designated as *confirmed and irrevocable,* which means that once accepted, they cannot be changed. Exhibit 10.1 is an example of a letter of credit.

Export documentation is discussed further in Chapter 11 as it relates to short-term financing.

Product Preparation

The issue of product adaptation for foreign markets is discussed in detail in Chapter 13. The focus here is on the **product preparation** to make it ready for the exporting process and foreign markets. The major issues that must be considered are foreign requirements, language, and packaging for shipment. Dealing with each of these issues can involve some modifications to the product or packaging or both and thus costs. These costs need to be examined as part of the overall decision to export.

Foreign requirements regarding product standards, labeling, and so on should be determined before exporting. These requirements often differ from those at home, and so, the product or the label may need to be modified to comply with these foreign requirements. Definition of the product for customs purposes may be critical to ensure expeditious clearance through customs and correct classification for duty purposes.

Language is also an important consideration for exporters. If a firm exports to a country in which a different language is spoken, the firm needs to translate its labels and product

EXHIBIT 10.1
**Sample Letter
of Credit**

Letter of Credit – Confirmed and Irrevocable

Date of issue: January 15, 1996

Issuing bank: The International Bank of Business, London, England, U.K.

In favor of: The International Exporting Company, New York, New York, U.S.A.

For account of: The International Importing Company, Birmingham, England, U.K.

Amount: US$45,000 (forty-five thousand U.S. dollars)

Covering merchandise described as dill pickles

Available by sight draft when accompanied by:

Commercial invoice: 1 original and 2 copies

Certificate of origin: 1 original and 2 copies

Certificate of inspection: 1 original and 2 copies

Original insurance certificate

Air waybill consigned to The International Importing Company

This agreement will be in force until May 15, 1996.

Authorized signatures _____

Authorized signatures _____

---

information. This can be an expensive and time-consuming process, particularly where product information is extensive or complex.

The appropriate packaging for shipment must also be resolved before the exporting process can be undertaken. Packaging can be extremely important to a product's arrival at its destination in an acceptable condition. The appropriate packaging depends on the product, the method of shipment, and the country to which the product is being shipped. It may be necessary to develop a new form of packaging or to modify the existing packing; again, this can be costly and time consuming.

A firm in Taiwan shipped some drinking glasses to the Middle East. The company used wooden crates, and padded the glasses with hay. Most of the glasses, however, were broken by the time they reached their destination. As the crates had traveled into the drier Middle East, the moisture content of the hay had dropped. By the time the crates were delivered, the thin straw offered the glasses almost no protection. What works well in one part of the world doesn't necessarily work well everywhere.

A similar problem was encountered by another Taiwanese firm. The Iranians refused payment on a shipment of wool because they claimed the shipper lied about the weight of the shipment. After expensive delays, it was discovered that wool in humid countries (such as Taiwan) loses moisture when shipped to dry countries (like Iran) and therefore, weighs less after being shipped.   (Ricks 1993, p. 27)

Licensing, Contracting, and Franchising

Licensing, contracting, and franchising represent intermediate levels of foreign involvement relative to exports, imports, and foreign ownership. Although there are many forms of licensing, contracting, and franchising, the focus here is on licensing technology, contracting services, and franchising, particularly in the restaurant industry. The goal of the discussion is to convey a flavor of the practical considerations related to decisions regarding these intermediate levels of foreign ownership.

Licenses

Generally a **licensing agreement** involves granting rights to intangible property such as patents, copyrights, trademarks, or procedures. An agreement that specifies the terms of use and the payment for use is made between the owner (**licensor**) of the property and a user (**licensee**). A firm, as owner or licensor, should consider several issues prior to entering into a licensing agreement. Major considerations are choice of the licensee, payment terms and time frames, and protection of assets. These are complex issues, and firms generally obtain legal advice, either internal or external, prior to finalizing a licensing agreement. The following points should be considered.

The licensee should be trustworthy and capable of using the licensed asset effectively; license agreements should be finalized only after the licensee has been checked thoroughly. It may be advisable to consider several licensees before reaching a choice.

Payment terms should provide an adequate return to both the licensor and licensee; it may be appropriate to provide for renegotiation of payment terms once both parties have had an opportunity to evaluate the potential of the licensing agreement. Time frames are closely tied to payment terms and should be of reasonable duration for both parties. Again, it may be appropriate to renegotiate the agreement at specified times.

Protection of licensed assets can be vital from the licensor's viewpoint. These assets can cost millions of dollars to develop, and the licensor must ensure that they cannot be lost through the granting of a license. Firms may limit the extent to which they give licensees access to key aspects of their technology, and they may try to ensure through legal means that their assets remain safe.

Not all countries are signatories to international agreements regarding patents, copyrights, and so on. The firm's legal rights should be carefully established to ensure protection of its vulnerable assets.

An unfortunate decision made by Gillette nearly cost the company the razor blade market. The firm had developed a superior stainless steel blade, but because the new blade was so outstanding and would require fewer replacements, the company preferred not to market it. So Gillette sold the technology to a British garden tool manufacturer, Wilkinson. Because Gillette had assumed that Wilkinson would use the new technology in the production of its garden tools, it failed to restrict Wilkinson from competing in the razor blade market. However, Wilkinson Sword Blades were promptly introduced and sold as fast as they could be produced. Gillette's superior marketing skills and experience in the razor blade market enabled it to eventually recover, but the challenge was unwelcome and expensive.   (Ricks 1993, p. 122)

Contracts

Many companies provide services to foreign buyers based on their particular expertise and skills (e.g., computer, economic, engineering, management, marketing). These skills are generally provided on a contract basis (i.e., deliverables and time frames are specified in a contract and associated with specific payments).

Companies considering **contracting** their services face a number of complex decisions, as do their licensing counterparts. These firms need to invest substantially in business development activities if they are to be selected as contractors; they need to assess the client organization and its ability to fulfill its end of a contract, and they need to be particularly culturally sensitive because the nature of their business necessitates cross-cultural interactions.

Many firms invest hundreds of thousands of dollars in business development activities in their efforts to land a particular contract. Business development can involve extensive worldwide travel and substantial preliminary project design. Prior to incurring these costs, the firm should understand the contracting organization and the project in question. It is important to estimate the likelihood that the contract is actually open to all firms and has not been promised to another firm because of its relationship with the contracting organization. It is also important to determine the contracting organization's objectives and whether the firm can meet these objectives in an efficient and effective manner. The contracting organization's ability to live up to its part of the contract – in terms of provision of services, materials, and prompt payments – should also be assessed. If the assessment of the contracting organization is positive, then the time and money necessary to bid for the contract can be compared to the expected returns. In addition, consideration needs to be given to obtaining work permits, income tax responsibilities, and other issues related to working in a foreign location.

Contracting firms rely on their communicating and negotiating ability throughout the process of bidding for, signing, and completing a contract. Many firms are very successful international contractors, but many more find that the costs often outweigh the benefits. Contracting provides unique opportunities for firms with specialized skills that are in demand internationally, but firms should not make the mistake of thinking that it is easy to obtain international contracts.

Franchises

Many firms have been able to develop a company image and name that is identified with desirable characteristics such as quality, service, cleanliness, good value, and so on. Once this image is established, the company is in a good position to consider franchising.

The first issue to be addressed is whether the established image can be transferred to other locations around the world. Success at home is based on providing a particular product or service that appeals to consumers in the home culture (e.g., speed and quality at McDonald's). The company considering franchising in foreign locations should determine whether this product or service will be desirable in those locations.

The second issue to be addressed is whether the factors contributing to success at home can be transferred. Franchising success is often attributable to standardization, high identification because of aggressive promotion, and cost control. The company considering franchising in foreign locations must consider whether these will be equally possible in other locations or whether local conditions and regulations will make it difficult to achieve the needed degree of standardization, identification, and cost control.

If a company believes that it has the potential for successful franchising in foreign locations, it must evaluate the benefits and costs carefully. Franchising offers many benefits, particularly providing the opportunity to expand internationally with relatively little investment, sharing the risk of international operations with the foreign franchisees, and drawing on the local knowledge and input of the franchisees. There are also costs, particularly associated with identifying and assessing potential franchisees and with legally establishing and enforcing franchise agreements. The risks of establishing foreign franchises that prove to be unsuccessful and may have repercussions at home also must be considered. The specific benefits and costs vary from company to company and location to location; therefore, this cost/benefit analysis should be undertaken for each new location.

Franchising is more common in the United States than elsewhere in the world, and U.S. companies currently represent the major international franchisers. However, many other countries have generated franchise operations, and growth in international franchising appears likely. Among U.S. restaurant chains that have expanded internationally through franchises are Burger King, Dairy Queen, Dunkin' Donuts, Kentucky Fried Chicken, McDonald's, and Pizza Hut. The fastest growth areas for U.S. companies have been Canada, Japan, and the United Kingdom, but there are franchises in most parts of the world.

> Cynics said the Chinese wouldn't touch a Big Mac with a 10-foot chopstick. But they certainly proved to be wrong. When McDonald's opened its first restaurant in the People's Republic of China in 1990, thousands of people rushed to have their first taste of the famous American fast food, just as they did when McDonald's opened its first restaurant in the Soviet Union.

Foreign franchising opportunities may be tempered by the fact that franchising is not common in some locations and local financing may be difficult for franchisees to secure. Firms that decide to pursue the franchise approach internationally may have to develop promotional packages to explain the concept and opportunities both to potential franchisees and financing organizations. In addition, firms must often modify their traditional operations to deal with local customs, regulations, and constraints. Overall, franchising internationally provides benefits for the right companies, but specific costs and benefits should be carefully evaluated to determine whether this approach can work for a particular company.

Ownership

Many international businesses opt for ownership in some or all of their international ventures. In many ways, the decision to adopt ownership arrangements is seen as a natural progression that occurs as companies become more familiar with the international environment. Once a company establishes subsidiaries or associated organizations in which it participates through

Fast-food corporations offer an example of how ownership-specific advantages and internalization advantages interact in foreign markets. McDonald's, the industry's leader, is such an example.

In 1985, McDonald's opened on average one restaurant a day in the United States. In addition, McDonald's has increasingly looked to foreign markets for investment (and, consequently, profits). Of the total establishments opened in 1986, 23 percent were located outside the United States, compared to 17 percent in 1980. Of the firm's 9,410 units in 1986, 2,138 were located in more than 40 countries and accounted for 27 percent of its $11 billion in revenues, but only 21 percent of its operating income and a smaller share of its profits. Most restaurants are franchised, that is, franchisees (carefully selected for their entrepreneurial acumen) have to invest their own capital and, therefore, acquire a direct interest in the success of the enterprise. (In the United States, it costs at least $250,000 to open a new unit.) McDonald's does, however, also enter into joint ventures or establish its own subsidiaries if need arises.

What McDonald's sells abroad is more than just fast food – it sells, above all, a firm-specific package of management, marketing, and technology which is characterized by strict standards of quality, service, cleanliness, and value.

At a general level, the parent corporation tries its best to infuse each store with a common company culture and an overarching company loyalty. It is not uncommon that restaurant owners from one country meet with those from another. But most important are stringent requirements to observe a detailed set of procedures for operations. Each franchisee obtains an operating manual which deals with everything – from the temperature of the shortening used to prepare french fried potatoes, to the way in which the bag containing the hamburger has to be given to the customer, to the number of times the bathrooms have to be cleaned daily. Each job is broken down into its smallest steps; the cooking and bagging of fries, for instance, consists of 19 separate steps. To ensure that these procedures are understood properly, each foreign operator has to attend one of McDonald's four Hamburger Universities in the Federal Republic of Germany, Japan, the United Kingdom, and the United States (complete with exchange programs), and consultants regularly visit franchisees to offer advice on such issues as promotional campaigns and employee training.

There is, however, room for some creativity within this management approach. In some countries, a few modifications from the menu are permitted. In Brazil, for example, guarana softdrinks are sold. In fact McDonald's most important new product developments (for example, the Big Mac and Egg McMuffin) were both developed by franchisees.

McDonald's insists on the strict observation of procedures to assure consistency and, above all, product and service quality. High standards are not only imposed on its own outlets, but also on suppliers. In fact, in many countries one of the greatest difficulties the company faces is to ensure a supply system that meets its standards, be it for meat, potatoes, buns, coffee, or straws. In one Western European country, for example, McDonald's had to build its own plant after repeated efforts to obtain buns corresponding to its specifications from local bakeries were unsuccessful. Sometimes, in other words, ownership-specific advantages can only be realized if certain transactions are internalized.

(United Nations Centre on Transnational Corporations 1988)

ownership, its commitment to international operations increases. By contrast, operations based solely on exports and imports can be eliminated relatively easily if a decision is made to focus more on domestic markets and supplies, and agreements such as licenses and contracts are usually of limited duration and do not need to be renewed if the firm's international strategy changes. **Ownership** implies a longer-term commitment; and it is more difficult, costly, and time consuming for a firm to divest itself of ownership than of other forms of involvement. This implied commitment means that ownership options must be considered carefully and ownership decisions made deliberately and strategically after weighing the relative advantages and disadvantages. The discussion in this section begins by examining different forms of ownership possible and their benefits and drawbacks.

Ownership can vary from 100 percent (wholly owned) to as little as 5 or 10 percent. The major ownership possibilities discussed here are

- ▶ 100 percent ownership
- ▶ Public sale of shares
- ▶ Ownership fadeout
- ▶ Low ownership
- ▶ Joint ventures

100 Percent Ownership

Many companies prefer to have a 100 percent interest in their foreign operations because they believe that the parent company can more closely retain control of operations with this arrangement. However, there are both benefits and drawbacks to this choice. These are summarized as follows.

The wholly owned option does give the parent company more decision-making control relative to foreign operations; 100 percent control can be a major consideration when centralized control is necessary or desirable (e.g., in globally integrated operations). This option eliminates the need to bargain with local or other shareholders, who can have different views or objectives than those of the parent. The parent can rationalize its operations on a global basis even when this involves making decisions that do not favor the particular subsidiary. In addition, there is no sharing of profits; and the parent may not want to accept lower profits, particularly when profit potential is substantial.

No sharing of profits implies no sharing of losses; therefore, the wholly owned option involves assuming all of the risks associated with a foreign venture. It also means that the parent undertakes the entire initial investment, which may be high. A larger potential drawback is that wholly owned foreign subsidiaries may be viewed negatively and resented by locals. This situation can result in a multiplicity of difficult relationships with local managers, employees, suppliers, and creditors, as well as the host government. In the worst case, these negative views and difficult relationships can single out the company for government intervention and thus increase the political risk associated with a particular location.

Having encouraging results from a preliminary market study, a major U.S. manufacturer of mixed feed for poultry decided to establish a market in Spain. Although local business people advised the firm against forming a subsidiary that was foreign-owned, the company went ahead with its plans. A factory was built, a technical staff was brought in, and operations were set up. However, once production began, the firm discovered that it could not sell its products. Why? The Spanish poultry growers and feed producers comprised a closely knit family, and newcomers were not welcome. To overcome this obstacle, the firm bought a series of chicken farms to support its feed population. To its dismay, the company discovered that no one would buy its chickens either. Had the company heeded the local advice and understood the local business practices, these difficulties could have been avoided.   (Ricks 1993, p. 119)

Public Sale of Shares

Companies may choose to sell shares in foreign operations on the open market. Where stock markets exist, such sales would be made through the stock market; however, public offerings can be made using other local arrangements if there is no formal stock market. Companies may choose this option if they want to raise outside capital and spread the risks but maintain a fair degree of control. Stock offerings may be limited to local participation or may be global in nature. The benefits and drawbacks of this approach are summarized as follows.

This option allows the company to raise capital and share the risks of the foreign operation while maintaining a relatively high degree of decision-making control. Decision-making control is maintained because the ownership is usually spread over a fairly large number of small minority stockholders. This means that the parent usually can exert control even with a relatively small percentage of the shares because the minority stockholders are not likely to act in concert against the major stockholder as long as satisfactory results are being achieved. A sale of shares to local individuals and groups means that the company may be viewed in a favorable light by the local community because it is seen as essentially a local company. This, in turn, can enhance local relationships and reduce political risk. This option retains some of the benefits of 100 percent ownership while overcoming some of the disadvantages. A major disadvantage to this option is the lack of stock markets in many countries, especially developing countries.

Although other means for making a public offering of sales do exist, these methods may be cumbersome and inefficient and can result in unwanted concentration of ownership in the hands of a few powerful locals. This approach also involves specific costs associated with a stock offering; therefore, the size of the offering must be large enough to warrant such action, which could be difficult in a small or relatively poor foreign country, where buyers for large offerings may be scarce. In addition, it is possible that even a diverse group of stockholders will decide to act together and wrest control from the parent or, alternatively, that one stockholder will buy out others and establish majority ownership this way. Finally, most countries have laws that deal with the rights of minority shareholders. Therefore, a company choosing this option cannot make decisions that would negatively affect these stockholders even though such decisions might be in the parent's best interests.

Ownership Fadeout

The concept of a fadeout is that the company begins with 100 percent of the equity, or at least a majority share, and, over time, sells shares in the company until its ownership is reduced to a minority position or even no ownership. Although not very common, this approach may be attractive in some situations. This ownership option allows the company to retain decision-making control in the early stages of foreign operations and gives the parent access to all profits initially, and it appeals to local interests because it is clear that over time the subsidiary will be localized. In a situation in which control is particularly important in the start-up phase and less so later on or in one for which a continuing infusion of capital is needed after start-up and the company does not wish to commit itself to additional investment, this arrangement is appropriate. In such an arrangement, the company makes its profits early and does not incur a long-term risk.

The obvious disadvantage to this approach is that the company gives up control over time and participates less and less in the profits. If the company can accurately forecast the need for control and expected profits, it can structure the fadeout to its advantage. Unfortunately, if its forecasts are incorrect, it may find that it has selected an undesirable ownership option. There is a natural tendency in such an arrangement, because of the short-term commitment, to focus on short-term profits, which is often detrimental to the foreign entity itself.

Low Ownership

A company is likely to choose this option if it wants to participate in a foreign venture that it believes is attractive but it is not in a position financially or managerially to take a greater share of ownership. The company in a minority position benefits from the successes of the foreign venture but may not need to make a substantial investment or tie up its own management in day-to-day operations. Such a position might be particularly attractive if the foreign operation were likely to become a customer or supplier. Of course, to a large extent, the company choosing to accept a minority share limits its ability to influence the direction of the foreign entity. The minority position also means that the company participates in profits only to a limited degree while it still suffers the negative consequence of losses. This can be a very difficult situation if the losses appear to be attributable to its inability to influence the direction of the foreign entity.

The degree of ownership sought by particular companies in foreign locations is influenced by legal and tax issues as well. Different choices have different tax implications and affect shareholders in the parent company and other subsidiaries. These questions should be examined by experts in the relevant fields before a final ownership decision is made.

Joint Ventures

Joint ventures, as discussed here, involve shared ownership. They are differentiated from sharing ownership through a public sale of shares or taking a minority position in a foreign entity, however, because they are discussed in terms of partnerships (although they may not necessarily take the technically legal form of a partnership). This implies an agreement between the partners regarding their respective rights and responsibilities.

Joint ventures or partnerships have become reasonably common in international business because a number of factors encourage their use; specifically, economic, social, and political factors encourage such ventures. In broad terms, joint ventures provide needed capital and expertise and allow companies to blend their respective strengths while sharing the risk in foreign undertakings. Joint ventures often improve the local image when they involve local partners and satisfy government regulations and incentives that mandate or encourage the involvement of local partners. According to the United Nations Centre on Transnational Corporations (1988), a major proportion of expansion is through joint ventures. Exhibits 10.2 and 10.3 provide some information on cooperative joint ventures among international companies, specifically in the automobile industry and at Siemens AG.

Joint ventures, like other forms of ownership, have both benefits and drawbacks. Joint ventures provide a means to spread large capital needs over a number of parties; major projects

EXHIBIT 10.2
Cooperation among International Companies in the Automobile Industry

Joint ventures, mergers, and minority equity investments have become more prominent in automobile production. General Motors and Toyota are assembling automobiles in the United States in a joint venture, New United Motors, Inc., in which each partner owns 50 percent. Toyota is managing the factory. General Motors seeks experience with Japanese production technology, while Toyota wants to learn from the marketing practices of General Motors. Toyota is building its own assembly plant in the United States, while General Motors has established a new division to build small cars. Thus, the two firms will continue to compete with each other, while cooperating in this joint venture. At the same time, General Motors has minority equity interests in two other Japanese producers, Subaru and Isuzu.

Various other cross-national relationships exist in the automobile industry. For some time, Chrysler has held a minority interest in Mitsubishi and has sold its cars under Chrysler brand names in the United States. Now, Chrysler and Mitsubishi are jointly constructing an assembly plant in the United States. Meanwhile, Mitsubishi owns 15 percent of Hyundai (Republic of Korea) and has supplied the latter with components and technology for the cars that Hyundai exports to the United States and Canada.

The acquisition of technology is a motive behind recent mergers and acquisitions by automobile producers. For example, Chrysler (United States) purchased American Motors (United States), in which Renault (France) had previously held a majority interest, in order to obtain American Motors' four-wheel drive technology. Both General Motors and Daimler-Benz have purchased large, military-oriented electronics corporations with the objective of more rapid integration of electronics technology into the production and design of motor vehicles.

are often feasible only if a partnership is possible. This spreading of the initial investment also spreads the risks among the partners. Different parties can bring specific skills and know-how to the partnership, making the foreign operation more effective than it would be if one party alone undertook it. Overall, a successful joint venture provides synergy; that is, it is a better undertaking because of the partnership than it would have been without it.

Host-government approval is another extremely important variable in the determination of a company's overseas success. Massey-Ferguson learned this when it reportedly experienced some difficulties after it entered into a 51 percent ownership venture in Turkey to produce tractors. A large-scale plan was developed that permitted an initial annual production capacity of 50,000 engines and called for the later addition of a second facility that would produce another 30,000 tractors a year. The company's high hopes were never realized. Massey-Ferguson reportedly failed to investigate thoroughly the implications of the economic and political scene in Turkey and the stability of the government. To assure its market success, the company needed strong governmental backing. This support never fully materialized (a result that some claim could have been predicted), and the venture was formally terminated in 1970.   (Ricks 1993, p. 121)

The benefits of joint ventures can easily be negated, though. Such partnerships have the potential for conflicting objectives, which lead to disputes between the interested parties. Once disputes arise, decision making slows down and foreign operations can become unresponsive

EXHIBIT 10.3
**Siemens AG and
Its Main
International
Cooperative
Agreements,
1984–1987**

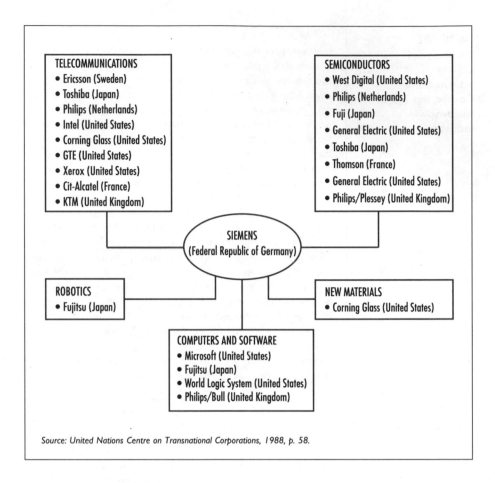

TELECOMMUNICATIONS
- Ericsson (Sweden)
- Toshiba (Japan)
- Philips (Netherlands)
- Intel (United States)
- Corning Glass (United States)
- GTE (United States)
- Xerox (United States)
- Cit-Alcatel (France)
- KTM (United Kingdom)

SEMICONDUCTORS
- West Digital (United States)
- Philips (Netherlands)
- Fuji (Japan)
- General Electric (United States)
- Toshiba (Japan)
- Thomson (France)
- General Electric (United States)
- Philips/Plessey (United Kingdom)

SIEMENS
(Federal Republic of Germany)

ROBOTICS
- Fujitsu (Japan)

NEW MATERIALS
- Corning Glass (United States)

COMPUTERS AND SOFTWARE
- Microsoft (United States)
- Fujitsu (Japan)
- World Logic System (United States)
- Philips/Bull (United Kingdom)

Source: United Nations Centre on Transnational Corporations, 1988, p. 58.

and inefficient. Even without disputes, decision making can be slow because all parties must agree on major issues, and differing viewpoints can make this process complex.

Joint Venture Partners

The more general benefits and drawbacks of a joint venture can vary depending on the makeup of a particular joint venture. There are a variety of partners from which to choose, and each can be helpful or cause problems in different ways. The ability of partners to work well with each other is a key aspect of joint venture success; therefore, choosing the right partner is an extremely important step. The partner or partners may be selected from a number of groups. The main groups considered here are host governments, private host parties, and other foreign companies.

Host governments quite often act as the local partner in a joint venture. This is likely to be the case if the host government controls resources that the joint venture needs to function or if no suitable private partners are available and the country does not allow wholly owned foreign operations. Joint ventures with host governments are inevitable where most commerce is centrally controlled, and they are common in resource-based industries in which the government controls the natural resources that the venture will be using.

In some respects, a joint venture with the host government is appealing because this clearly puts the foreign partner in touch with the people currently in control. The government could be expected to smooth the way for the joint venture because it is as interested in its success as is the foreign partner.

These benefits occur in some cases, but there are many situations where they do not materialize. First, when changes in government occur, the joint venture can be associated with the previous regime and it may be singled out for negative treatment. Second, the government, as a partner, has access to the joint venture's policies, procedures, techniques, technology, and so on. Once it is familiar with them, the government may conclude that there is no need for foreign involvement and choose to nationalize the venture. Third, the objectives of the government and the foreign parent will probably clash at some point because the fundamental nature of their strategies is different; for example, the government might want to expand domestic employment to support its development priorities, but the foreign parent might believe that automation will cut costs over time and result in better quality and higher profits. Fourth, governments are not structured for the same kind of decision making as private firms, and bureaucratic complexities may become problems in these partnerships.

On balance, it appears that host governments are not particularly good joint venture partners; so, companies may prefer to avoid these partnerships if possible. Nevertheless, companies sometimes find such alliances desirable. Companies entering into such joint ventures need to be particularly aware of the potential problems inherent in such alliances so that they can be prepared to deal with them.

Many companies seek private partners in the host environment. These partners can be described, broadly, as silent or active. A silent partner holds shares in the local company but does not become actively involved in the operations of the company. An active partner participates in terms of ownership as well as management. Some investing companies wish to select silent partners; others see greater benefits from active partners.

A local private partner usually provides local know-how relative to creditors, employees, government, markets, suppliers, unions, and so forth. At the same time, the involvement of a local partner means the likelihood of differing objectives and dilution of profits. An enterprise that incorporates local ownership is likely to be viewed positively by the host government and people, but it also means that decisions, expertise, technology, and so on must be shared.

Silent partners are advantageous because they provide local acceptance, local knowledge, and local capital while agreeing to remain outside the day-to-day decision-making process. For some foreign enterprises, a silent partner allows the parent company to take advantage of the benefits of localization without the expected loss of control over decisions associated with having a local partner. This may be especially important when the foreign parent needs to protect some firm-specific advantage (e.g., proprietary technology) that would be exposed in the joint enterprise. Silent partnerships can backfire if the partner that was expected to be silent demands an active role in the enterprise or if the host government decides that the enterprise is not truly localized because the silent partner is merely a front to mask real control by the foreign firm.

Active local partners provide more in-depth local knowledge because of active involvement in operations, and this local know-how is vital to many enterprises. Many multinational companies seek this local knowledge from local partners so that the subsidiary can be more responsive to local markets. The price paid is a decrease in decision-making control and often slower decisions. Slower decision making, however, does have some benefits. A high degree of involvement of locals in the decision-making process often means that the reasons for decisions are clearly understood and the decisions are supported by locals. In turn, cooperation is enhanced and implementation of decisions is quick and smooth, compensating for the slower decision making.

Joint ventures between multinational companies are also fairly common. These arrangements are generally entered into when the skills of each of the multinational companies are needed to ensure the success of a particular venture. This choice is often appropriate when the project is large and it is not likely that any one company can undertake the entire project effectively.

A joint venture among a group of multinational companies provides some security for each member because all pool their resources and there is strength in numbers relative to the local community. This approach can, however, result in disputes over respective roles and increased visibility, which can result in increased local resentment.

Making a Joint Venture Successful

Once a company has made a decision regarding the kind of partner it prefers, it should then move to a more detailed examination in choosing a particular partner.

> *The Economist* (1991) has reported that cross-border alliances were reaching fad proportions. Among the biggest joint venture agreements reported were IBM with Siemens, Texas Instruments with Kobe Steel and Hitachi, Motorola with Toshiba, AT&T with Mitsubishi Electric and NEC, Volvo with Renault, Pilkington with Nippon Sheet Glass, and Daimler-Benz with Whitney. *The Economist* argues that although there are good reasons for alliances, even small companies, and many big ones, can compete on their own in global markets.

Joint ventures have often been compared to marriages. The analogy is particularly apt in terms of choosing the right partner. Marriages between people who have conflicting objectives are not as likely to succeed as those in which basic objectives are complementary; the same is true of a joint-venture partnership. People considering marriage are often advised to consider more than one partner before making a final selection and to get to know the anticipated partner well before taking the marriage vows. The advice to companies entering joint ventures is similar: Check out a variety of possible partners and do not rush into an agreement. The first advice to companies contemplating a joint venture arrangement is to choose its partner(s) carefully.

> Weiss (1987) described negotiations between Toyota and Ford and Toyota and General Motors. Toyota negotiated with Ford for 13 months unsuccessfully, and negotiations with General Motors were described as "long," "hard," and "frustrating." The negotiations with GM were successful, however, and led to the formation of New United Motor Manufacturing, Inc. (NUMMI), which became a symbol for international cooperation within the auto industry.

The choice of partner is complicated in international joint ventures because the people negotiating the agreement may not be the people responsible for carrying it through. It is possible for negotiators to develop a close, trusting relationship, suggesting that a joint undertaking will be a success, only to have the deal fall apart because the managers selected by each side did not relate well. Clearly, it is important to establish good relationships at both levels before proceeding.

> A company should create a joint venture only after giving the idea careful consideration. Although another firm may be prepared to become a partner, its eagerness does not necessarily assure success. One U.S. manager found this to be especially true. During an inspection of his company's European operations, he met with a number of Belgian pump-manufacturing executives. Because one particular company exhibited a great deal of interest in forming a partnership, a joint enterprise was quickly formed. A Belgian was installed as the president of the new company, and the U.S. firm's manager in Belgium became the vice-president for manufacturing and engineering. However, the combination of friction between these two men and company losses precipitated a crisis. The partnership was dissolved, and the U.S. company bought up all of the Belgian shares at book value. The result: It was many years before the operation became profitable. Undoubtedly the U.S. firm's unfortunate choice of partner hindered this venture's success. Partners must be selected with caution, and employee personalities should be considered.   (Ricks 1993, pp. 102–103)

A substantial number of joint ventures end unhappily, and such endings, like divorces, can be messy and costly. Companies entering into joint ventures want to do everything possible to avoid an unhappy ending. The potential problems in joint venture enterprises need to be addressed prior to undertaking the agreement if the venture is to be successful. Harrigan (1984) advises the following:

- ▶ Do not accept a joint-venture agreement too quickly; weigh the pros and cons.
- ▶ Get to know a partner by initially doing a limited project together; if a small project is successful, then bigger projects are more feasible.
- ▶ Small companies are vulnerable to having their expertise lost to larger joint venture partners; small companies need to structure such deals with great care and guard against potential losses.
- ▶ Companies with similar cultures and relatively equal financial resources work best together; keep this in mind when looking for an appropriate partner.
- ▶ Protect the company's core business through legal means such as unassailable patents; if this is not possible, then do not let the partner learn your methods.
- ▶ The joint enterprise should fit the corporate strategy of both parents; if this is not the case, conflicts are inevitable.
- ▶ Keep the mission of the joint enterprise small and well defined; ensure that it does not compete with the parents.
- ▶ Give the joint enterprise autonomy to function on its own and set up mechanisms to monitor its results; it should be a separate entity from either parent.
- ▶ Learn from the joint enterprise and use what has been learned in the parent organization.
- ▶ Limit the time frame of the joint enterprise and review its progress often (as often as every three months).

To be successful, a joint venture should probably have clearly defined goals as well as established measures of performance to which the parents have agreed. The exact nature of each parent's contribution in terms of finances, management, technology, know-how, and so on should be established to both parties' satisfaction. Conflicts are almost inevitable in a joint venture; therefore, a conflict resolution mechanism should be in place. In addition, a "prenuptial" agreement that specifies the conditions for dissolution of the venture and division of assets in case of a divorce is a very good idea. Establishing agreement on these issues prior to undertaking a joint venture eliminates many of the potential causes of conflict.

> Joint venture success cannot always be judged on the basis of longevity. A joint venture in the Caribbean illustrates this point. A local businessman wished to purchase a parcel of land locally as a tourist development. He was unable to raise the capital on his own and believed that outside expertise would be extremely helpful in planning and implementing the development project. A joint venture was formed with a U.S. firm to undertake the project, and the joint venture continued for more than 15 years. On the surface, it was a success because a divorce did not take place. Unfortunately, during this period, very little profitable development took place, and the project did not live up to local expectations. It seemed that the U.S. partner viewed the property as a vacation spot that would be spoiled if others were attracted to it. The final outcome was that the local government acquired the property because it believed the property was not being adequately utilized.

Even when initially successful, partnerships can end in divorce. A number of U.S. companies have found that their apparently successful partnerships with foreign companies have ended in messy divorces. The *Wall Street Journal* (1991) reported that Borden (U.S.) and Meiji Milk (Japan), considered the epitome of joint venture success between a Japanese company and a U.S. company, were undergoing "divorce" after 20 years of partnership. The *Wall Street Journal* also reported additional divorces among international companies, including Ralston Purina, Microwave Systems, Bayer, and Monsanto.

Strategic Alliances

Joint ventures, as discussed here, imply shared equity by two or more partners in a separate enterprise. **Strategic alliances** are differentiated from joint ventures because they involve non-equity arrangements as well. Strategic alliances can be thought of simply as cooperative ventures with two or more organizations choosing to cooperate with each other for specific purposes and a defined period of time. Clearly, this concept of a strategic alliance incorporates a wide variety of possible cooperative ventures. For example, two companies might choose to pool their R&D expertise to develop a particular technology that would benefit both companies. A company with a good product might cooperate with another company with a well-developed distribution or marketing network. One company with expertise in a particular location might work with a supplier company to establish operations in that location. In none of these cases is a separate entity established with joint ownership. Rather, the companies choose to cooperate because each believes that it can benefit from the cooperation.

Strategic alliances or cooperative ventures differ from traditional joint ventures, but they involve many of the same problems and should be handled as carefully, if not more so. Certainly, the risk of loss of firm-specific advantages is as present in these alliances as in joint ventures, and the likelihood of conflict also exists. The joint venture may actually be less risky than the strategic alliance because the parents are establishing a separate entity that can be dissolved or taken over by one partner if that is desirable. The option of dissolution or takeover does not exist for a strategic alliance when no separate entity is created. Dissolving a strategic alliance agreement prematurely can fundamentally affect one or another partner's ability to operate effectively.

Choosing the right partner with whom to ally or cooperate is a key element of success in strategic alliances. Each party to a strategic alliance or cooperative agreement must trust the others because, without trust, it will be unlikely to cooperate fully. To develop the needed trust, getting to know potential partners is of parmount importance. The risks are too great to enter into such arrangements without first establishing a relationship with which all partners are comfortable.

Strategic alliances of all kinds appear to be increasing. The rates of technological change and global competition in the last decade of the 20th century have increased to a level at which such alliances have become necessary for certain successful global operations. These trends show no signs of abating; hence, companies can expect that the need to form these alliances will increase in the future. It is important, therefore, that international companies have a sound understanding of the implications of such alliances.

Strategic alliances may be beneficial from a firm's point of view but not from that of governments. In the United States, for example, antitrust legislation may prevent the formation of such alliances. In other countries, legislation may either prohibit or encourage alliances of various kinds. The legal dimensions of these decisions, both at home and in foreign locations, should be carefully examined prior to entering into a binding agreement.

Negotiations

Negotiations can be described in broad terms as discussions between two or more parties aimed at reaching a mutually acceptable agreement. Negotiations are an implicit aspect of implementing any international strategy. A company involved in exports negotiates prices, quantities, payment terms, delivery times, and so on with its trading partner. A company that licenses or contracts its technology or services negotiates the terms of various licenses and contracts with the licensee or contractor. A company seeking a joint venture negotiates the makeup of the joint enterprise in terms of capital, ownership, management, and so on with potential partners. A company that establishes a wholly owned subsidiary in a foreign location negotiates the terms and conditions of its investment with the host government. Understanding the process of cross-cultural negotiation is therefore very important for international companies.

The cultural orientation of the parties in a negotiating process often influences their views of the process. Each party may have different expectations of what negotiations entail, and this can lead to unwanted friction and stress and less than optimal agreement. Understanding one's own negotiating style as well as that of others in the negotiating process can enhance negotiations

A typical situation involves an American negotiating with Japanese managers in order to buy or sell some product or service. The American, often anxious to complete the deal, tends (in the eyes of the Japanese) to rush the negotiation. All too often, when the time for price discussion arrives, the American will quickly suggest a price. Being used to the give-and-take of negotiating, the American usually does not make the best possible offer at the start nor necessarily expect it to be accepted. Here is where the troubles arise. When people hesitate, an American tends to assume that the price mentioned is an unacceptable one. Therefore, an American will sometimes hastily improve the offer even before it is rejected or the process is unsuccessfully terminated. But the American negotiating with Japanese managers may commit a blunder by quickly altering the price.

This has happened on numerous occasions but in at least one reported case, an American raised the price he was willing to pay three times after the Japanese were prepared to accept. Unaware of Japanese customs, he did not realize that the hesitation and discussion between the Japanese (in Japanese, of course) were not a result of unhappiness over the price quoted. With each higher offer, the Japanese negotiators expressed amazement (in Japanese) but then proceeded to check out their colleagues' opinion. This delay only unwittingly encouraged the American to offer even more.   (Ricks 1993, p. 68)

and result in better agreements. To understand how the negotiation process can differ among cultural groups, two models of the process are discussed.

Graham's Four-Stage Model

A four-stage model of the negotiation process presented by Graham (1981) is helpful in understanding negotiations. This model suggests four **stages of the negotiation process**: nontask sounding, task-related exchange of information, persuasion, and concessions and agreements. Although all negotiations include these four aspects, the content, duration, and sequence can differ from culture to culture.

The following describes these four stages in more detail followed by a contrast of American and Japanese negotiating styles.

Nontask Sounding

This stage of negotiations focuses on establishing a relationship among the negotiating parties. During this stage, information specific to the issue under negotiation is not considered; rather, the parties seek to get to know each other.

Westerners see Japanese negotiators as stressing this aspect of negotiations and spending substantial time on building a relationship. This stage may include entertainment and gift giving. The Japanese believe that if a harmonious relationship can be established at the beginning of the negotiating process, conflicts can be avoided later on.

American negotiators, in contrast, see this stage of negotiations as rather a waste of time and prefer to get down to business matters as quickly as possible. Americans expect that once an agreement has been reached, relationships will develop between the parties as they work together.

Task-Related Exchange of Information

This stage of negotiations focuses on providing information directly connected to the issue under negotiation. During this stage, each party explains its needs and preferences.

Japanese negotiators are concerned with understanding the other side's point of view. The Japanese tend to provide relatively little information; they are polite and seek to avoid offending other negotiating parties. They present their needs and preferences in ways that to them are tactful. They find that their American counterparts are embarrassingly frank.

American negotiators, in contrast, stress openness and honesty in information exchange. They are direct and frank, providing information clearly and to the point. Japanese tact often appears hypocritical to Americans, who would be more comfortable if the Japanese would "tell it like it is."

Persuasion

This stage of negotiations focuses on efforts to modify the views of other parties and sway them to one's way of thinking. This stage of negotiations is often intertwined with other stages (i.e., persuasion goes on while exchanging information and making concessions).

Japanese negotiators believe that little persuasion should be necessary if the parties have taken the time to understand each other thoroughly. The time allocated to the first two stages of the negotiation process means that Japanese negotiators do not feel the need to allocate much time to persuasion. The Japanese tend to listen to persuasive arguments and respond with silence, which means simply that they are considering the arguments presented. They react negatively to open disagreement and aggression.

American negotiators, in contrast, spend a lot of time and effort on persuasion. They are often aggressive in their attempts to persuade and use tactics such as threats to break off negotiations. Americans are uncomfortable with silence and interpret it to mean that their arguments have not been understood or, alternatively, that the other party is not willing to agree. There is a tendency for Americans to fill silence with additional explanations or concessions.

Concessions and Agreement

Essentially, this stage is the culmination of the negotiating process at which an agreement is reached. To reach an agreement that is mutually acceptable, each side frequently must give up some things; therefore, concessions by both sides are usually necessary to reach an agreement.

Japanese negotiators tend to make all concessions at the end of the negotiation process and expect that these will lead immediately to the conclusion of the agreement. The Japanese believe at this stage that they should understand the other side's position and how it relates to their own so that they are in a position to decide what concessions are needed to reach a final agreement.

American negotiators, in contrast, tend to make concessions throughout the negotiation process and to evaluate their progress toward agreement continuously. They are put off when other parties do not seem to be willing to offer concessions early in negotiations and may interpret this to mean that their side needs to offer even more concessions. Americans believe that the earlier stages of the negotiations should culminate in both sides recognizing that they have reached a mutually agreeable position.

As this brief contrast of negotiating styles indicates, negotiations can easily break down because of a lack of understanding of the cultural component of the negotiating process. Negotiators who take the time to understand the approach likely to be used by the other parties and adapt their own styles to match are likely to be more effective negotiators. The American and Japanese styles have been contrasted here; the American negotiating style contrasts with that of many other groups as well, and it is well worth the time that it takes to investigate these differences prior to entering into a negotiation situation.

Weiss's Twelve Variables

Weiss (1987 and Weiss-Wik 1983) identified 12 variables in the negotiation process that should be examined to understand negotiating styles better. These variables are explained briefly; again, a contrast between Americans and Japanese is used to illustrate the points.

1. Basic Concept – Different groups view the purpose and process of negotiation differently. Negotiation may be seen as a conflict in which one side wins and another loses, as a competition to identify who is best, or as a collaborative process to formulate some undertaking. Americans tend to see negotiations as a competitive process; the Japanese see it as collaborative.
2. Criteria for Selecting Negotiators – Different groups choose negotiators on the basis of a variety of factors. Negotiators may be selected on the basis of their previous experience, their status, knowledge of a particular subject, or personal attributes, such as trustworthiness. Americans tend to select negotiators on the basis of ability and experience; the Japanese look for high-status negotiators.
3. Issues Stressed – Different groups stress different aspects of the negotiation. In broad terms, some groups stress substantive issues directly related to the agreement while others stress relationships. Americans tend to stress substantive issues (e.g., price, quantities, quality); the Japanese are more concerned with building relationships.
4. Protocol – Different groups have their own particular etiquette associated with the negotiation process, and their adherence to protocol varies according to its perceived importance. Protocol factors that should be considered are gift giving, entertainment, dress codes, seating arrangements, numbers of negotiators, timing of breaks, and planned duration of the process of negotiations. In general, the degree of formality or informality is an important component of protocol that should be assessed. Americans tend to be informal; the Japanese, on the other hand, are conservative and formal.
5. Communications – Different groups communicate in different ways and are more comfortable with one or another form of communication. Some groups rely on verbal communications; others on nonverbal communications including gestures, space, and silence. Some groups rely to a great extent on one method; others use a mixture. The more varied the methods of communications, the more complex is the communication context and the more care must be given to understanding this context. Americans tend to be verbal, but the Japanese often use periods of silence.

6. Nature of Persuasive Arguments – Different groups attempt to persuade others, and are in turn persuaded, by the use of a variety of different types of arguments. Some rely on facts and logical arguments, others on tradition and the way things were done in the past, still others on intuition or emotion, and others on the beliefs associated with a particular religion or philosophy. Americans emphasize empirical information and rational arguments; the Japanese rely more on sensitivity and intuition.

7. The Role of the Individual – Individuals play different roles in different societies. In some groups, the individual is seen as very important, and a particular individual's success or failure can depend on the outcome of the negotiation process. In other groups, individuals are subordinate to the home negotiating party, and personal ambitions are contained. Still others may view the entire group as consisting of all negotiating parties, both home and host, as the most meaningful unit and be most concerned with achieving overall success. Americans are individualistic, giving negotiating responsibility and authority to individuals; the Japanese are collectivist and rely on the group as a whole in negotiations.

8. Basis for Trust – Trust is a necessity if groups are going to work together to their mutual benefit, and all groups seek to establish trust with the other parties in the negotiation process. Each group, however, may establish trust on a different basis. Some groups look to past experience and past records, others rely on intuition and emotion, and still others are most comfortable when sanctions exist to guarantee performance. Americans look to the past record of those with whom they are negotiating and trust in sanctions. The Japanese are more concerned with the relationships that have been built with their counterparts.

9. Risk-Taking Propensity – Negotiations involve a degree of risk because the final outcome is unknown when the negotiations begin. Different groups view uncertainty and risk as relatively desirable or undesirable. Some groups therefore are open to new ideas and unexpected suggestions whereas others prefer to remain within the expected boundaries and accustomed agreements. Americans tend to take risks and accept uncertainty, while the Japanese are more averse to risk and uncertainty.

10. View of Time – The value of time differs from one group to another. Some people view time as limited and something to be used wisely; therefore, punctuality, agendas, and specified time frames are important to them. Others view time as plentiful and always available; therefore, they are more likely to expect negotiations to progress slowly and be flexible about schedules. Americans have a relatively short time horizon and believe that time must be used efficiently. The Japanese, however, are likely to take a longer-term view of activities.

11. Decision-Making Systems – Decisions are made differently in different groups. They may be made by individuals or by the group as a whole. Further, within a group, participants may defer to the person of highest status or to the most senior group member; alternatively, some groups accept the decision of the majority of group members; other groups seek consensus among group members and will not make a decision until all members have agreed. Americans expect individuals to make decisions, and if there is disagreement among individuals, they accept the decision supported by the majority of group members; the Japanese expect decisions to be made by the group as a whole and continue discussion until they reach consensus among group members.

12. Form of Agreement – The final form of the agreement can also vary from culture to culture. In some cultures, written agreements are expected; in others, verbal agreements or

a handshake is accepted. In some cultures, agreements are detailed and set out as many points as possible, discussing contingencies and potential events; in others, broad general agreements are preferred with details to be worked out as they arise. In some cultures, agreements are expected to be legally binding; in others, there is little faith in legal contracts and much more emphasis is placed on a person's obligation to keep his or her word. Americans tend to prefer written, explicit, relatively detailed contracts. The Japanese favor written agreements that are brief and identify basic principles.

This second model provides a detailed framework that can be used to analyze the negotiation process in different countries. Each of the variables discussed in the model can be examined both for the home country and for foreign countries to identify similarities and differences in approaches.

As an example, here is the profile of an Arab negotiator:

▶ Basic concept – Social, nondirective
▶ Selection criteria – Family and personal ties, personal loyalty
▶ Issues – Social and personal
▶ Protocol – Adherence to social norms of hospitality
▶ Communication – Mixture of verbal and nonverbal, nonverbal actions important (e.g., showing the sole of one's foot, which is considered insulting), verbal exaggerations common
▶ Persuasion – Based on emotion, tradition, and ideology; empirical reasoning infrequent
▶ Role of individual – Individualism stressed
▶ Trust – Based on personal friendship, family relationships
▶ Risk taking – Fatalistic, things happen "if Allah wills"
▶ Time – Casual approach, "There's always tomorrow"
▶ Decision making – Centralized but consultative
▶ Agreements – Words are binding; duty to fulfill obligations

Company–Host-Government Interactions

Company interactions with the host government are almost inevitable, no matter which form of entry into a foreign location a company chooses. These interactions may be minor if the company is exporting through intermediaries, but even in this case the company should understand the host government's requirements relative to its exports. Interactions are likely to be significant if a subsidiary is being established in the foreign location. Foreign direct investment of any kind is likely to be subject to host-government review and various approvals.

Companies often find themselves negotiating the terms of their investment with the host government, including the degree of investment, ownership and management structure, employment levels, location, level of exports and imports, and so forth. They may also have to negotiate incentives with the host government, including tax and tariff exemptions, favorable loan terms, subsidies, government services, and provision of land or buildings.

The host-government literature, and even legislation, may serve as only a starting point for possible arrangements. In many cases, unique conditions can be negotiated for specific companies.

Further, many of the questions that a company may have or the issues that it needs clarified prior to investment may not be covered in official government communications but must be addressed in personal interactions. Companies can, therefore, expect to be involved in substantial interactions with host governments in the initial stages of foreign expansion.

The U.S. lock manufacturer, Yale and Towne, can attest to the desirability of gaining not only local government support but also the acceptance of local competitors. In the 1960s, in order to gain entry into the Japanese market, Yale and Towne planned to form a joint venture with Copal Co., Ltd., a local Japanese camera shutter manufacturer. The plans were quite ambitious and included a projected annual production target of 600,000 units, or 20 percent of the Japanese market. Local manufacturers, threatened by these plans, petitioned the Japanese Ministry of International Trade and Industry requesting the prevention of this investment. Not surprisingly, Yale and Towne experienced a delay in the processing of its application. By April 1965, the lock industry had been included in a list of industries that fell under the law for Acceleration of Modernization of Small Enterprise (a section of the 1950 Foreign Investment Law). The industry therefore gained special protection and development incentives from the government. Eventually, the Yale and Towne application was rejected. Had the company initially shown more discretion, the local manufacturers may have accepted the new competition without pursuing governmental protection. (Ricks 1993, pp. 121–122)

Interactions with host governments are likely to be ongoing throughout the life of the company's involvement in a foreign location. This is because the company and the government's situation are likely to change over time, and these changes lead to the need to negotiate new agreements or renegotiate existing ones.

To have productive interactions with host governments, companies need to consider two important points. First, a successful relationship is more likely if both parties believe that the deal is fair. Second, the company and the host government probably have different cultures; a relationship is most effective when this fact is considered.

The first point means that the company must seek to understand the host government's objectives and strategies so that the firm can structure its project to contribute to these while achieving its own objectives. The second means that the company must seek to understand the host culture and establish its negotiating style in light of this. Successful companies have a clear sense of what they want from a foreign venture and ensure that they attain these goals through the establishment of good relations with the host government.

Ethical Issues

The actions of international firms have been the subject of much criticism in light of varying standards of ethical conduct. The result of being accused of acting unethically is usually negative and can have wide-ranging repercussions, including bad publicity, consumer boycotts, lawsuits, and government intervention.

A number of examples of alleged behavior, considered unethical by some and reported by the media, follow. These examples present only one side of the ethical situation, the side that views the behavior as unethical. There may be valid arguments for the "violator's" position, however. The intent here is simply to report situations in which ethical issues have been involved; it is not to evaluate the moral positions of various parties.

▶ The Nestlé Company markets infant formula to mothers in the Third World. Some people view this as unethical. The argument is that these are uneducated, poor women and their infants have been hurt by the use of formula. Opponents believe that these women discontinued breast-feeding and substituted formula in response to "aggressive marketing techniques." Formula cost them more than breast-feeding (which the poor can ill afford), it may not have been as healthy for the infants, and mothers seeking to stretch it or unable to read the directions may have mixed it incorrectly.

▶ Union Carbide suffered a major chemical accident in Bhopal, India. The argument is that the facilities did not meet safety standards required in more developed countries, and the workers were not supervised adequately. The accident has been reported as the result of unethical behavior and a lack of concern for Indian workers.

▶ The Vanguard Corporation was reported to have continued manufacturing and exporting pesticides to Third World countries after their use was prohibited in the United States. This has been considered unethical because it endangers the environment and the health of the people in the Third World.

▶ Lockheed executives were accused of engaging in payments to officials in foreign countries. This was considered to be bribery and to have encouraged corrupt practices and therefore was unethical.

▶ Firestone Tire & Rubber Company dominated the rubber economies of Malaysia and Liberia. Such reliance on a foreign company has been considered potentially damaging to these countries and therefore unethical on the part of the company.

In addition to the companies in these examples, other firms have been accused of unethical behavior for continuing operations in countries that violate human rights, for influencing the outcome of elections, for transferring jobs to foreign countries where wage rates are lower, for operating in countries with few environmental regulations, and for a variety of other activities.

International firms need to act in ways that are socially and morally acceptable, or ethical, because this is both the right way to behave and it avoids the negative consequences of unethical behavior. There are difficulties, however, because what is considered ethical in one location may be seen as unethical elsewhere. Two examples illustrate this dilemma.

Continued manufacture and sales of a banned pesticide seem unethical from the U.S. viewpoint, but a poor country might knowingly choose to continue to use the pesticide if it increases agricultural yields. The poor country might argue that feeding its people now is more important than longer-term concerns with their health or the environment.

Unrecorded payments to facilitate projects are considered unacceptable in North America and considered to be bribes, but they are the norm in some other countries. Some foreigners argue that activities considered normal in North America, such as taking business colleagues out to restaurants, are in fact "payments" to facilitate projects. *The Economist* (May 27, 1995) describes corruption in Asia as "endemic." The interesting aspect is that an expensive bribe for a construction contract is not unusual and more subtle "bribes" also are common – such as inviting a potential partner's son to study at a U.S. university. The big risk in any such dealings is that the government will crack down on "corruption," and a firm associated with anyone accused of corruption will be suspect.

To determine what is ethically appropriate, companies must consider the impact of their decisions on a variety of stakeholders, both at home and in foreign locations. These stakeholders are the groups affected by a particular decision. There is no practical way to find decisions that will be acceptable to all stakeholders (as illustrated in the previous examples, there may be conflicting issues and views); however, by considering the impact on the major stakeholders, companies can make informed judgments. Many companies have developed guidelines to help international managers evaluate the ethical aspects of various decisions.

In the area of questionable payments, U.S. firms have guidance in the Foreign Corrupt Practices Act (FCPA) of 1977. The objective of the FCPA is to stop U.S. multinational companies from initiating or perpetuating what are believed in the United States to be corrupt practices in foreign locations. The FCPA requires companies to report all payments made in foreign locations. The Justice Department prosecutes firms for contravening the FCPA; therefore, international firms need to be familiar with the details of the act. The United Nations Centre on Transnational Corporations (UNCTC) has developed a code of conduct for international companies, which can also be helpful to firms in defining what is ethical and what is not.

The Economist (June 24, 1995, p. 15) notes that "businesses do not have a natural propensity to do good" and there is no guarantee that business will not "rape the environment, indulge in slavery or rip off their customers." This is supported by an article in *California Management Review* (Badarocca and Webb 1995) that concludes that the ethical climate of organizations is very fragile. On a more positive note, the White House is developing a code of ethics for American businesses intended to bring about a "worldwide standard" of conduct (*The Economist,* April 8, 1995, p. 57), and consumers have succeeded in pressuring big businesses to behave in ethically responsible ways. A recent example of the impact of consumers occurred in 1995 when a consumer boycott forced Royal Dutch/Shell to drop plans to dispose of an offshore storage buoy by sending it to the bottom of the Atlantic. The development of international principles on the part of firms themselves is also a current trend.

Arguments continue over the appropriateness of legislating morality based on a particular cultural viewpoint. Some people believe that ethics should be governed by local customs, and others believe that the developed countries and their companies should take the lead in establishing ethical standards on a worldwide basis.

Summary

This chapter explored some of the issues associated with implementing international expansion decisions. Specifically, concerns relative to exports and imports, licensing, contracting, franchising, and ownership were addressed. Joint ventures and strategic alliances were also considered. The final focus was on interactions with host governments and ethical issues. International companies continually face these issues. The international expansion decision is an ongoing one that must be addressed again and again. Each of the concerns discussed in this chapter will probably affect every international company at one time or another. Companies often face many of these issues simultaneously and need to be prepared to deal with the implications of all of them together. The chapter presented the major considerations that companies will likely face in implementing various international decisions. These considerations were examined in a general sense only; each company has specific concerns and faces unique situations. Legal advice, therefore, often is necessary before proceeding with the implementation of a chosen course of action. Similarly, each decision has implications from an accounting and tax perspective that need to be considered prior to executing strategic decisions.

MINI-CASE
The
Foundation
Company

The Foundation Company is a member of the Banister-Foundation Construction Group headquartered in Scarborough, Ontario, in Canada. The Foundation's mission is to be the industry leader in civil and building construction in North America, and it describes itself as a company with a global vision. The company's activities are primarily in

▶ Power generation projects
▶ Dams and irrigation systems
▶ Underground structures
▶ Transportation infrastructures
▶ Defense-related installations
▶ Residential, industrial, commercial, and institutional buildings.

This activity profile makes the Foundation a prime candidate for major international infrastructure projects. An ongoing hydroelectric project in India illustrates the complexity of such projects. The total cost of the project is US$1,465 million, the contract value is C$430 million, and the project is financed by the World Bank, supplier's credits, and the Indian government.

The following exhibits outline some details of the project. Exhibit 10.4 provides a timeline and Exhibit 10.5 briefly describes the project. Exhibits 10.6–10.8 are the firm's evaluation of how it succeeded, the elements leading to success for projects of this kind, and lessons learned from the process.

Source: Information provided by Harry Chan, VP marketing, the Banister-Foundation Inc.

Discussion Issues

1. Evaluate the Foundation Company's success factors for the type of business in which it is involved.
2. Evaluate other forms of entry for the Foundation Company.
3. Suppose the Foundation Company were seeking a joint venture partner. Prepare a list of partner characteristics.

EXHIBIT 10.4
Project Milestone Dates

1980 – Liaison between Foundation & Continental began

1985 – First joint bid for Nathpa Jhakri Dam Project

1986 – Foundation started tracking the Nathpa Jhakri project

1988 – Submitted pre-qualification

Oct. 1991 – Bidding document issued by owner

Jun. 1992 – Original closing date of bid

Jul. 1992 – Actual closing date of bid

May 1993 – Letter of Intent issued by owner

Aug. 1993 – Signing of Contract #1

Sep. 1993 – Signing of Contract #2.1

EXHIBIT 10.5
Project Description

The 1500 MW Nathpa Jhakri Hydroelectric Project, located in Kinnaur and Shimla Districts of Himachal Pradesh, is a run-of-the river type development, proposed to harness hydroelectric potential of the upper reaches of the river Satluj. A design discharge of 405 cumecs is proposed to be diverted through a 60.5m high concrete gravity dam, four intakes and four underground desilting chambers, a 10.15m diameter head race tunnel (HRT) terminating into 21m diameter and 225m deep surge shaft. Along its route, the 27,295m long HRT encounters Manglad creek which is proposed to be crossed by lowering the tunnel to cross it at its bed level. Three pressure shafts, each of 4.9m diameter taking off from the surge shaft, will feed the discharge to six generating units of 250 MW each housed in an underground power house to utilize a design head of 425m.

EXHIBIT 10.6
How We Did It

Concentrated effort in Bid Preparation	– Over 5,000 man hours in 4 months; $500,000 salary and expenses.
Working closely with Local JV Partner	– Over 20% of the project cost required input from local JV Partner.
Bid Reconciliation	– Each JV partner prepared its own estimate, based on its methodology and schedule. Reconciliation of each cost item was made before bid submission.
Pre-determined Bidding Strategy	– Recognizing the geographical linkage between Contract 1 and Contract 2.1, a special price consideration was offered if these two contracts were awarded together.
Neutralized Competitors' Advantage	– JV was organized to take advantage of the 7.5% price preference for domestic bidders.

EXHIBIT 10.7
Elements of
Success

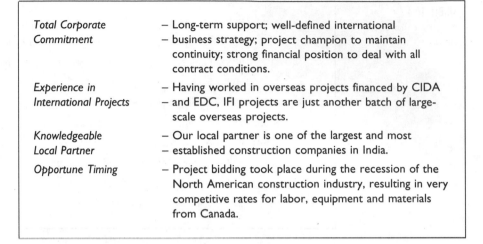

Total Corporate Commitment	– Long-term support; well-defined international
	– business strategy; project champion to maintain
	   continuity; strong financial position to deal with all
	   contract conditions.

Experience in International Projects	– Having worked in overseas projects financed by CIDA – and EDC, IFI projects are just another batch of large- scale overseas projects.
Knowledgeable Local Partner	– Our local partner is one of the largest and most – established construction companies in India.

Opportune Timing	– Project bidding took place during the recession of the
	   North American construction industry, resulting in very
	   competitive rates for labor, equipment and materials
	   from Canada.

EXHIBIT 10.8
Lessons Learned

IFI project cycle takes a long, long time to complete. The key factors must be re-evaluated at the beginning of each stage.

Protect your low bid. Despite the relatively open and transparent bidding process, it is essential to have local representation all the time to protect your interest, especially during the bid evaluation phase.

Canadian government supports were not adequate, at least not for this project.

Very serious weakness in the Canadian construction industry in developing the pool of hands-on construction people with overseas experience. Need a long-term solution.

Cofinancing is going to be one of the important elements of success in IFI projects. Canada must be prepared.

Discussion Questions

1. Why might a company decide to bypass exporting intermediaries and sell directly to foreign customers?

2. How is a joint venture different from a strategic alliance? Discuss the relative benefits and costs of each.

3. How does culture influence negotiations? Explain and use examples.

4. If you were visiting a subsidiary in a foreign location and were asked to make a payment that you considered questionable, how would you react?

Assignments

1. Contact a local customs broker or import/export agency and get samples of import/export forms; contact a local bank and get samples of actual letters of credit.

2. Research the recent literature on joint ventures and prepare a checklist for establishing and managing a successful joint venture.

3. Research a variety of actual joint ventures and find examples of some that have succeeded and some that have failed. To what are success or failure attributed?

4. Select a country to research. Identify characteristics of the country that would influence a company's decisions regarding ownership (e.g., culture, regulations, politics, economics) and discuss how these would be likely to affect ownership decisions.

Selected References

Adler, N., and J. L. Graham, "Business Negotiations: Canadians Are Not Just Like Americans," *Canadian Journal of Administrative Sciences* 4, no. 3 (1987), pp. 211–238.

Badarocca, J., and A. Webb "Business Ethics: The View from the Trenches," *California Management Review* 37, no. 2 (1995).

Bilkey, W. J., "An Attempted Integration of the Literature on Export Behavior of Firms," *Journal of International Business Studies* (Summer 1978), pp. 33–46.

Bowie, N., "The Moral Obligations of Multinational Corporations," Hilton Business Ethics Day, Loyola Marymount University (Fall 1986).

Contractor, F. J., "Strategies for Structuring Joint Ventures: A Negotiations Planning Paradigm," *Columbia Journal of World Business* (Summer 1984), pp. 30–39.

The Economist (May 5, 1991), p. 16.

The Economist (April 8, 1995), p. 57.

The Economist (May 27, 1995), p. 61.

The Economist (June 24, 1995), p. 15.

Ferrel, O. C., and J. Fraedrich, "International Business Ethics," in *Business Ethics – Ethical Decision Making and Cases* (Boston: Houghton Mifflin, 1991).

Franko, L. G., *Joint Venture Survival in Multinational Corporations* (New York: Praeger, 1971).

Graham, J. L., "The Influence of Culture on the Process of Business Negotiations: An Exploratory Study," *Journal of International Business Studies* 16, no. 1 (1985), pp. 81–96.

Graham, J. L., "A Hidden Cause of America's Trade Deficit with Japan," *Columbia Journal of World Business* (Fall 1981), pp. 5–15.

Harrigan, K. R., "Joint Ventures and Global Strategies," *Columbia Journal of World Business* (Summer 1984), pp. 7–16.

Killing, J. P., "How to Make a Joint Venture Work," *Harvard Business Review* (1982), pp. 120–127.

Lane, H., and D. Simpson, "Bribery in International Business: Whose Problem Is It?" *International Management Behavior* (1990), p. 236.

Lyles, M. A., "Common Mistakes of Joint Venture Experienced Firms," *Columbia Journal of World Business* (Summer 1987), pp. 79–85.

Poynter, T. A., "Government Intervention in the Less Developed Countries: The Experience of Multinational Companies," *Journal of International Business Studies* (Spring–Summer 1982), pp. 19–26.

Ricks, D. A., *Blunders in International Business* (Cambridge, Mass.: Blackwell Publishers, 1993).

Robinson, R. D., *International Business Management – A Guide to Decision Making* (Hinsdale, Ill.: Dryden Press, 1978).

Shenkar, O., and S. Ronen, "The Cultural Context of Negotiations: The Implications of Chinese Interpersonal Norms," *Journal of Applied Behavioral Science* 23, no. 20 (1987), pp. 263–275.

Shenkar, O., and Y. Zeira, "Human Resource Management in International Joint Ventures: Directions for Research," *Academy of Management Review* 12, no. 3 (1988), pp. 546–557.

United Nations Centre on Transnational Corporations, *Transnational Corporations in World Development – Trends and Prospects* (New York: UNCTC, 1988).

Wall Street Journal (February 21, 1991), p. B1.

Weigand, R., "International Investments: Weighing the Incentives," *Harvard Business Review* (July–August 1983), pp. 146–152.

Weiss, S., "Creating the GM-Toyota Joint Venture: A Case in Complex Negotiation," *Columbia Journal of World Business* (Summer 1987), pp. 23–37.

Weiss-Wik, S., "Enhancing Negotiators Successfulness," *Journal of Conflict Resolution* 27, no. 4 (1983), pp. 706–739.

Wells, L. T., "Negotiating with Third World Governments," *Harvard Business Review* (January–February 1977), pp. 72–80.

CHAPTER ▼ 11

International Financial Management

LEARNING OBJECTIVES

After reading this chapter, you should be able to

▶ Discuss the impact international risks have on international financial management.

▶ Identify and explain foreign exchange rate risks and markets.

▶ Recognize that managers have many ways to reduce their exposure to foreign exchange rates.

▶ Discuss how MNCs finance overseas operations for both the short term and the long term.

▶ Explain the roles of various types of bankers.

▶ Discuss capital budgeting in MNCs.

K E Y   T E R M S

- ▶ Foreign exchange rate risk
- ▶ Foreign exchange
- ▶ Foreign exchange rate
- ▶ Spot market
- ▶ Forward market
- ▶ Net exposure
- ▶ Open account basis

- ▶ Foreign collections basis
- ▶ Eurocurrency
- ▶ Eurodollars
- ▶ Bearer shares
- ▶ Eurobonds
- ▶ Development banks
- ▶ Investment bankers

T H O U G H T   S T A R T E R S

▶ Several firms have started foreign operations only to discover that they are not permitted to take profits out of the country.

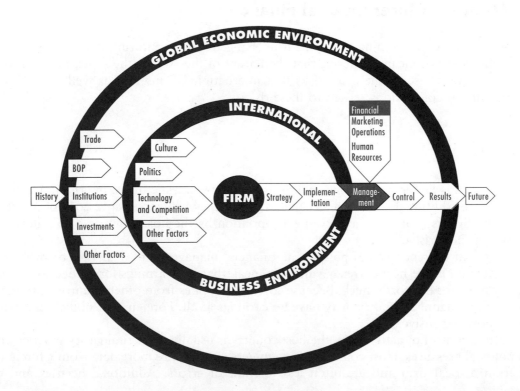

▶ Many companies have been promised payment in a foreign currency on delivery of goods sold. However, by the time the goods arrive, the foreign currency has lost value and results in an unprofitable sale.

▶ It is relatively easy for a subsidiary of a large multinational corporation to borrow foreign money, even though the subsidiary, not the large parent company, promises to repay. Sometimes the temptation to borrow is too great and the subsidiary borrows more than it can repay. Lenders then complain that they thought they were lending to the parent firm and would have demanded a higher interest payment from the more risky subsidiary. Foreign competitors also complain that the subsidiary is taking advantage of this "halo effect" and borrowing at an unfairly low interest rate.

Introduction

This chapter explores issues associated with financial management in international companies. The chapter also considers the risks of doing business internationally from a financial perspective and discusses ways to deal with them. One of the reasons international business managers make blunders is that they sometimes forget they are facing more risks than their domestic counterparts.

The Nature of International Finance

The basic concepts concerning risk remain unchanged when venturing into the international arena. This does not mean, however, that the nature of the risks is the same, far from it. The following sections discuss the extra risks that international firms face as well as a variety of concepts and misconceptions related to these risks.

Extra Risks

The set of risks is larger for international firms than for domestic firms. International financial managers face additional risks such as changes in currency values, selective control of activities because the firm is "foreign," and even expropriation by the host country. The following are examples of these risks.

Changes in currency values present the financial manager with a myriad of problems. A major reduction in the host currency value can mean that any earnings forwarded to the parent company may not be worth much. Because costs for supplies from other countries can increase far more than planned, the firm may have no earnings at all. Foreign debt obligations can also become more expensive.

Selective control of activities by the host country is usually a discriminatory practice arising from political pressures. Host-country tax examiners may require more data from a foreign firm than from a local firm and are often less tolerant of errors. Additional licenses and other documents are often required, and the local laws may be more strictly enforced. Not all multinational corporations (MNCs) face such discrimination, of course, but the risks always exist and must be considered.

The risk of expropriation is also present. There are ways to reduce this risk, but it cannot be completely eliminated or ignored. The general public holds the false impression that the expropriation of a firm by a foreign government is an act of confiscation. Except in times of war, such outright seizures are extremely rare; governments almost always pay for the company being expropriated. The real question is how much the firm is worth. The risk of being forced to sell at a price below the firm's estimated value is an important consideration. (Chapter 7 contains a more complete discussion of these international business risks.)

Concepts and Misconceptions

As previously stated, the basic concepts of financial risk remain the same for both domestic and international financial managers; however, because international financial management involves extra risks, some additional concepts must be considered. One of the most basic concepts concerning risk and return is the principle that higher risks should not be accepted without higher expected returns. This risk-return concept remains unchanged in international business.

In fact, this concept is often used to argue that foreign opportunities may need to promise higher returns than domestic ones. These demands for higher returns have led some critics of MNCs to charge "profiteering" when, in fact, the firm is simply following apparently sound financial practices by examining both risks and returns. Managers might well ask, "If our firm is not permitted to earn a higher return on foreign operations, then why should it take on the added risks?"

A company should examine the total risk picture, not just the risk of a single project or the risks in a single country. By investing in many different economies, a firm may be able to hold an internationally diversified "portfolio" that would provide better results and be less risky than a portfolio consisting of an individual opportunity. Of course, to be successful, diversification requires economies without high degrees of correlation, but it could mean that the MNC need not always require higher rates of return to invest in risky projects.

A common belief is that MNCs must be more profitable overseas than the local competition because they face more risks, but risk returns need not be higher than those made by other companies. MNCs that invest only in countries where they can outperform all others are much more vulnerable to outside criticism and will lose those good investment opportunities when the returns would justify the risks, even the unique international risks of expropriation, discrimination, and currency fluctuations.

The impact of these additional risks will become more apparent later in this chapter. Because of these extra risks, additional financial management techniques have been developed that are unique to international financial management.

Foreign Exchange

Of all the unique risks that international financial managers encounter, the **foreign exchange rate risk** generally proves to be the most troublesome. Most surveys of international businesspeople show that exchange rate risk is the top concern, causes the most problems, and demands the most attention. To understand foreign exchange rate risk, one must first understand foreign exchange, foreign exchange rates, and foreign exchange markets.

Foreign exchange is the currency of other countries. This money can be of one foreign currency or many. American firms owning French francs, therefore, have foreign exchange. French firms holding U.S. dollars count these dollars as at least part of their foreign exchange holdings.

The **foreign exchange rate** is the price at which one currency can be bought with or sold for another currency. In other words, it is the rate at which a firm might exchange one currency for another. Since at least one of these currencies is foreign, it is called the *foreign exchange rate.* Let us say, for example, that a U.S. businessperson wants to buy 200 stereos in Japan costing 1,500 Japanese yen (¥) each. This person needs ¥300,000. If the foreign exchange rate between the Japanese yen and the U.S. dollar is ¥100 equals $1, then the American needs US$3,000.

Foreign exchange and foreign exchange rates are usually unavoidable aspects of international business. Since one party has either to pay or receive a foreign currency, people must be able to convert currencies. This conversion takes place in what is known as the *foreign exchange market.*

The foreign exchange market usually involves the use of such intermediaries as bankers, currency traders, and brokers. A great deal of currency trading occurs in New York City, but money is also converted in most major cities of the world. Some of this money is even exchanged, legally or illegally, on street corners. This is all part of the foreign exchange market.

Multinational corporations, of course, deal primarily with large transactions and, therefore, normally use the assistance of banks or financial institutions. Many of these transactions, however, are so large that even the banks require specialists. In New York City alone, more than a dozen firms do nothing but handle foreign exchange arrangements for banks.

Most foreign exchange transactions are made over the telephone or with electronic equipment, and written contracts are rare. The honor system, although unusual in most other forms of international business, is necessary because the foreign exchange market is so dynamic.

Most foreign exchange transactions involve the U.S. dollar, the Japanese yen, the British pound, the Swiss franc, the French franc, or the German mark. A few other currencies are becoming more important, but fewer than 10 currencies dominate market activity.

There are actually two major types of foreign exchange transactions. One type of transaction involves the immediate exchange of currencies in the **spot market**. The other involves promises to make an exchange of currencies in the future in the **forward market**

The Spot Market

The spot market is used when a company wants to change one currency for another "on the spot." The procedure is extremely simple. A banker can either handle the transaction for the firm or have it handled by another bank. Within minutes the firm knows exactly how many units of one currency are to be received or paid for a certain number of units of another currency.

For example, a U.S. firm may want to buy 1,000 books from a British publisher. The publisher wants two thousand British pounds (£2,000) for the books, so the American firm needs to change some of its dollars into pounds to pay for the books. If the British pound is currently being exchanged for US$1.65, then £2,000 equals US$3,300. The U.S. firm simply pays $3,300 to its bank and the bank exchanges the dollars for £2,000 to pay the British publisher.

Looking at this another way, let us say that you are thinking of buying a BMW in Germany. The price there is 70,000 German marks (DM70,000). You are wondering if you should buy it there or buy it in the United States for US$55,000. If the foreign exchange rate is US$1 equals DM1.40, then DM70,000 equals US$50,000. If the car would cost less than US$5,000 to bring into the United States, then you should buy it in Germany.

Risks are involved with any currency. No matter what currency a company holds or expects to hold, the exchange rate may change so that the firm is hurt if it is unlucky or careless. There are also risks that what the company owes or will owe is stated in a currency that becomes more valuable and, therefore, possibly harder to obtain and use to pay the obligation.

Let us suppose, for example, that you work for a U.S. firm that promised to sell some computers to a British company for £500,000. If the sale were to occur today and the payment were to be made today, then the transaction probably would not involve much more. You would simply deposit the money in a bank and ask that the pounds be converted (at the spot price) to U.S. dollars.

In this scenario you have no choice regarding the conversion price – it is quoted on a "take-it-or-leave-it" basis. In the United States, you usually find the conversion price quoted in two different ways. One is an expression of how many foreign units (in this case, British pounds) are needed to buy one U.S. dollar. The other quotation states how many U.S. dollars are required to buy one foreign unit (e.g., British pound). In recent years, the spot price of £1 has been about US$1.5000 or about £0.6667 British pounds to the dollar. Most quotations are four digits past the decimal point. In this example, if these were the prevailing rates, then the £500,000 could be exchanged for about US$750,000.

Business deals are seldom so simple. There is usually a delay between the time an agreement is made and when the payment is due. This delay accounts for some of the most common exchange rate risks. Refer to the example once again. If the £500,000 were to be paid in 90 days, the firm runs the risk that the value of the pound might decline (depreciate) during that period. If the firm took no action to protect itself and the pound depreciated during the 90 days by 10 percent, then the £500,000 would convert to only about $675,000. The risk, therefore, is that exchange rate fluctuations might cause the firm to receive less money than expected. Of course, just the opposite could happen, and the firm could end up with more money.

It is also possible that the company might be the one buying a product and that it may have to pay for it in the future. Depending on the currency in which the purchase price is stated and the changes in exchange rates, the firm could be forced to pay more or less than anticipated.

For example, assume that a Canadian firm promises to buy 1,000 bottles of Austrian wine in six months. The agreed total price is 150,000 Austrian schillings (S150,000). If the spot price is C$1 equals S7.5000, then the Canadian firm has agreed to pay C$20,000, if the bill were due now. Since the bill is not due for six months, however, there is the risk that the exchange rate will change. If, for instance, the rate becomes C$1 equals S10, then S150,000 would be worth only C$15,000 and the Canadian firm would actually pay less than it would have six months earlier. On the other hand, if the exchange rate becomes C$1 equals S5, then the Canadian firm would have to pay C$30,000.

The Forward Market

Businesspeople generally dislike uncertainty. This is a major reason for the existence of the forward market. A forward contract guarantees which currencies are to be traded, when the exchange is to occur, how much of each currency is involved, and which side of the contract each party is on (each party's beginning and ending currencies). A German firm, for example, could promise to pay a bank 40,000 German marks in 90 days for 20,000 British pounds. By entering into a forward contract, a firm eliminates one uncertainty, the exchange rate risk of not knowing what it will receive or pay in the future; however, note that any possible gains in exchange rate changes are also eliminated and the contract may cost more than it turns out to be worth.

For example, suppose that the 90-day forward price of the British pound is US$2.0000 (US$2.00 per £1) and that the current spot price is US$1.6500. If a company enters into a forward contract at the forward exchange rate, it indicates a preference for this forward rate to the unknown rate that will be quoted 90 days from now in the spot market. However, what if the spot price of the pound increases (appreciates) by 100 percent during the next 90 days? Then the pound would be worth US$3.3000. The firm having a forward contract promising to sell pounds at $2 each would have been better off with no forward contract. The forward market, therefore, can remove one uncertainty, that of not knowing how much the firm will receive or pay; however, it creates another uncertainty, whether the firm might have been better off by waiting.

Daily spot and forward exchange rates for most major currencies are reported in such financial publications as the *Wall Street Journal*. For example, Exhibit 11.1 contains the foreign exchange rates quoted in the *Wall Street Journal* on January 10, 1996. Minor exchange rate fluctuations occur frequently, but daily changes of more than 5 percent are rare and create a great deal of attention. Students might want to look up the most recent rates and compare them to those quoted in 1996 to see how much the exchange rates have changed.

Managing Foreign Exchange Risk

It has been demonstrated that businesspeople who operate in the international arena face a number of problems that domestic businesspeople are able to avoid or ignore. Problems generated by exchange rate risks are the most frequently encountered; therefore, firms must thoroughly understand the risks involved and be prepared for them.

The threat of a devaluation can disrupt the normal operating procedures of subsidiaries in the threatened country. In an effort to reduce exposure to devaluation, capital expenditures are often postponed or local currency borrowing increased. Capital remittances to the parent company may be speeded through dividends, royalties, or a variety of fees as well as repayment of debt or interest payments. The local subsidiary must be able to finance these outflows and operate on the remaining funds. Under these conditions, the subsidiary should not hold excess cash and should reallocate funds to other areas of the system. These techniques are effective and feasible, however, only to the extent that government regulations permit them, local financing is available, and the added costs of transfers are less than the expected losses from devaluation.

EXHIBIT 11.1   **Currency Trading**

EXCHANGE RATES

Tuesday, January 9, 1996

The New York foreign exchange selling rates below apply to trading among banks in amounts of $1 million and more, as quoted at 3 p.m. Eastern time by Bankers Trust Co., Dow Jones Telerate Inc. and other sources. Retail transactions provide fewer units of foreign currency per dollar.

Country	U.S. $ equiv. Tues.	U.S. $ equiv. Mon.	Currency per U.S. $ Tues.	Currency per U.S. $ Mon.
Argentina (Peso)	1.0007	1.0001	.9993	.9999
Australia (Dollar)	.7433	.7462	1.3454	1.3402
Austria (Schilling)	.09850	.09872	10.152	10.130
Bahrain (Dinar)	2.6532	2.6525	.3769	.3770
Belgium (Franc)	.03368	.03379	29.690	29.591
Brazil (Real)	1.0288	1.0288	.9720	.9720
Britain (Pound)	1.5495	1.5505	.6454	.6450
30-Day Forward	1.5475	1.5492	.6462	.6455
90-Day Forward	1.5458	1.5473	.6469	.6463
180-Day Forward	1.5424	1.5437	.6483	.6478
Canada (Dollar)	.7345	.7348	1.3615	1.3610
30-Day Forward	.7312	.7346	1.3676	1.3613
90-Day Forward	.7338	.7345	1.3628	1.3615
180-Day Forward	.7338	.7338	1.3627	1.3627
Chile (Peso)	.002454	.002454	407.55	407.55
China (Renminbi)	.1202	.1202	8.3215	8.3215
Colombia (Peso)	.001010	.0009990	990.10	1001.00
Czech. Rep. (Koruna)...	....	....	....	....
Commercial rate	.03733	.03743	26.788	26.718
Denmark (Krone)	.1791	.1795	5.5840	5.5695
Ecuador (Sucre)...	....	....	....	....
Floating rate	.0003415	.0003415	2928.50	2928.50
Finland (Markka)	.2291	.2291	4.3645	4.3645
France (Franc)	.2028	.2026	4.9315	4.9365
30-Day Forward	.2029	.2026	4.9282	4.9367
90-Day Forward	.2031	.2027	4.9235	4.9331
180-Day Forward	.2033	.2028	4.9200	4.9308
Germany (Mark)	.6949	.6947	1.4390	1.4395
30-Day Forward	.6941	.6955	1.4407	1.4378
90-Day Forward	.6962	.6975	1.4364	1.4336
180-Day Forward	.7013	.7006	1.4259	1.4273
Greece (Drachma)	.004241	.004240	235.81	235.84
Hong Kong (Dollar)	.1293	.1293	7.7330	7.7335
Hungary (Forint)	.007164	.007179	139.59	139.30
India (Rupee)	.02793	.02793	35.800	35.800
Indonesia (Rupiah)	.0004361	.0004361	2293.00	2293.00
Ireland (Punt)	1.5997	1.5997	.6251	.6251
Israel (Shekel)	.3187	.3187	3.1377	3.1380
Italy (Lira)	.0006358	.0006345	1572.72	1576.00
Japan (Yen)	.009567	.009508	104.53	105.18
30-Day Forward	.009560	.009537	104.60	104.85
90-Day Forward	.009634	.009615	103.80	104.00
180-Day Forward	.009810	.009731	101.94	102.76
Jordan (Dinar)	1.4104	1.4104	.7090	.7090
Kuwait (Dinar)	3.3395	3.3411	.2994	.2993
Lebanon (Pound)	.0006270	.0006270	1595.00	1595.00
Malaysia (Ringgit)	.3910	.3910	2.5577	2.5577
Malta (Lira)	2.9851	2.8297	.3350	.3534
Mexico (Peso)	....	....	....	....
Floating rate	.1336	.1331	7.4850	7.5150
Netherlands (Guilder)	.6200	.6200	1.6128	1.6130
New Zealand (Dollar)	.6588	.6588	1.5180	1.5180
Norway (Krone)	.1573	.1575	6.3573	6.3476
Pakistan (Rupee)	.02920	.02923	34.247	34.216
Peru (new Sol)	.4292	.4267	2.3299	2.3435
Philippines (Peso)	.03810	.03810	26.247	26.250
Poland (Zloty)	.4032	.4027	2.4802	2.4833
Portugal (Escudo)	.006681	.006681	149.68	149.67
Russia (Ruble) (a)	.0002142	.0002144	4668.00	4665.00
Saudi Arabia (Riyal)	.2667	.2666	3.7495	3.7504
Singapore (Dollar)	.7015	.7015	1.4255	1.4255
Slovak Rep. (Koruna)	.03367	.03372	29.697	29.660
South Africa (Rand)	.2756	.2753	3.6282	3.6325
South Korea (Won)	.001269	.001269	788.02	788.20
Spain (Peseta)	.008261	.008260	121.05	121.06
Sweden (Krona)	.1511	.1511	6.6181	6.6183
Switzerland (Franc)	.8602	.8606	1.1625	1.1620
30-Day Forward	.8590	.8627	1.1641	1.1592
90-Day Forward	.8642	.8678	1.1571	1.1523
180-Day Forward	.8762	.8754	1.1413	1.1423
Taiwan (Dollar)	.03650	.03653	27.397	27.371
Thailand (Baht)	.03959	.03959	25.259	25.260
Turkey (Lira)	.00001687	.00001691	59284.50	59130.00
United Arab (Dirham)	.2724	.2722	3.6711	3.6731
Uruguay (New Peso)...	....	....	....	....
Financial	.1393	.1393	7.1788	7.1800
Venezuela (Bolivar)	.003448	.003448	290.00	290.00
SDR	n.a.	n.a.	n.a.	n.a.
ECU	1.2862	1.2862	....	....

Special Drawing Rights (SDR) are based on exchange rates for the U.S., German, British, French and Japanese currencies. Source: International Monetary Fund.

European Currency Unit (ECU) is based on a basket of community currencies. n.a.-Not available. c-Corrected.

a-fixing, Moscow Interbank Currency Exchange

Source: Wall Street Journal, *January 10, 1996, p. C6.*

Managers, therefore, must be able to obtain accurate forecasts of the probability of devaluations and of their probable amounts. To make such estimates, the forecaster must understand the causes of currency value fluctuations.

Factors Affecting Foreign Exchange Rates

Foreign exchange rates can be affected by many variables. Some of the most common include the following:

1. Rates of inflation
2. Political stability
3. Labor conditions
4. Balance of payments
5. Monetary and fiscal policy
6. Ties to other currencies
7. Speculation

If the local rate of inflation increases, then the exchange rates usually change so that the local currency declines in value. If the political stability improves in a country, the value of its currency increases. If labor conditions (e.g., strikes) worsen, the value of its currency decreases. If a country's balance of payments improves, the value of its currency increases. If a country spends more than it takes in or prints more money than it used to, then its currency is likely to decline in value. If a country's currency value is fixed relative to be worth that of another country's, then its currency changes with the other's currency (e.g., if the dollar in Panama is worth a dollar in the United States, then Panama's dollar declines when the U.S. dollar declines). If currency speculators buy a currency in anticipation of an increase of its value, then their speculation tends at least temporarily to drive up the value of that currency. These relationships are summarized in Exhibit 11.2.

Many of these factors are subjective and, thus, difficult to quantify. Even if the firm has accurately analyzed the economic pressures against a currency, the influence of government policy makes it difficult to be sure what will happen, when it will happen, and therefore, how best to protect the firm.

Exposure-Reduction Strategies

A company's susceptibility to exchange losses is usually measured in terms of net exposure. **Net exposure** represents the net monetary value of assets and liabilities that would be affected by a currency devaluation. For example, if a company has $500,000 worth of assets and liabilities that would be hurt by a devaluation and if only $100,000 worth of its assets and liabilities would be helped by the devaluation, then its net exposure is $400,000. A 25 percent devaluation, therefore, would hurt the company by about $100,000.

There are ways to reduce a company's net exposure. In general, a firm likes to maintain its asset accounts in strong currencies and denominate its liability accounts in weak currencies. Procedures available to reduce exposed items include the following:

1. Increasing local liabilities of weak currency subsidiaries
2. Speeding payments denominated in strong currencies
3. Delaying investments in weak currency subsidiaries
4. Self-insuring through reserves (putting some earnings into a special account to cover exchange losses)

EXHIBIT 11.2
Factors Affecting Exchange Rates

Variable	Effect
Inflation up	Currency drops
Political stability up	Currency strengthens
Labor conditions improve	Currency strengthens
Balance of payments up	Currency strengthens
Government spending up	Currency drops
Currency tied up	Currency strengthens
Speculation that currency value will increase	Currency strengthens

5. Arranging protection in the foreign exchange markets (obtaining guarantees to sell or buy a currency at a predetermined price and time)

Exposure reduction strategies largely depend on management's attitude toward risk. Since American firms generally favor steady increases in U.S. dollar earnings per share (EPS), they tend to avoid large losses in a single period. They want the short-term costs to be a small percentage of overall potential losses. Some companies therefore are willing to accept the small extra expenses of using the preceding procedures all the time to avoid a large loss every so often.

Unfortunately, the optimal timing for the purchase of a forward contract or the use of any other method of exposure reduction is difficult to determine. All economic factors may be correctly identified and analyzed, but unpredictable political factors can profoundly influence currency rate changes. As a result, the timing and use of exposure reduction measures are tricky. The reduction of exposed accounts must be sought before major currency declines. However, as devaluation grows more likely, the costs of exposure reduction also increase (if the options even remain). The manager's challenge is to reduce the exposure only when it is worthwhile.

To reduce exposure effectively, an estimate of devaluation probabilities is necessary. Accurate estimates are hard to derive and require good information from the subsidiary. However, the routine working capital decisions of multinational firms are often decentralized: Cash needs are forecast locally and banking is handled locally. To increase the efficiency of foreign exchange risk management, centralized cash-mobilization centers are becoming increasingly common. Companies have found that a centralized depository permits many economies of scale, specialization, and broader perspectives on risks and investment opportunities for excess cash.

When a centralized depository is used, subsidiaries are encouraged to hold minimum balances and no precautionary reserves to reduce risks. Excess cash is transferred by wire or telex to the central fund. These centers are usually established in countries with well-developed capital and foreign exchange markets, stable governments and currencies, liberal tax regulations, and minimal restrictions on the flow of funds. The use of a centralized depository permits better control, profitability, and efficiency in the management and evaluation of the variables that influence the firm's exchange rate risk. Naturally, even though this helps minimize global risks for the multinational corporation, it means that some subsidiaries have to bear higher risks or costs than they otherwise would have chosen.

Foreign Exchange Models

The following list specifies some of the many factors that must be examined when determining optimal cash levels in different countries:

1. Liquidity and risk factors
2. Transfer costs
3. Rates of return earned on excess funds
4. Government restrictions on funds transfers
5. Short-term investment opportunities
6. Advantages of cash funds in bank accounts for future loan requests

With so many variables, more and more managers are looking for computer models that can keep track of the situation, make forecasts, and then make recommendations. Various models have been developed, but unfortunately, these models usually require probability estimates of the size and time of devaluations. The limitations of computer models have tended to discourage their widespread use in the business world.

No known model that can fully predict all aspects of exchange rate risks has yet been developed, but models have allowed managers to gain important insights into the problems, interrelationships, and techniques necessary for risk reduction and protection. Extremely accurate reporting systems and forecasting techniques for the quantification of subjective factors are critical when using the majority of models. The most effective and operational models seem to be programming models that allow sensitivity analyses to determine probable changes in costs and returns as a result of changes in input variables.

Financing Foreign Operations

A firm needs neither to be considered a multinational corporation nor to be engaged in international business to take advantage of the many ways available to raise money and capital in foreign locations. Unfortunately, domestic firms seldom consider foreign funding sources. For MNCs, however, access to foreign money and capital markets is an integral part of doing business, as can be seen in the box detailing a financial management mistake.

> Misinterpretation can sometimes cause major financial losses. One company, for example, decided to spend $2 million for a Brazilian plant it seems was not needed. The company's decisions to invest the money was based upon an incorrect interpretation of data. The reported sales figures (stated in Brazilian cruzeiros) appeared very promising, but they had not been adjusted to account for high inflation. Only the number of cruzeiros had grown, not the number of products sold. It is often more prudent to evaluate sales levels employing physical measures (such as weight, volume, number of units, etc.) rather than financial ones. Then inflation and currency value fluctuations are less likely to cause such errors. (Ricks 1993, p. 132–133)

Short-Term Financing

Both domestic and international firms require short-term financing to meet working capital needs, for seasonal or temporary fluctuations in capital, and for times when longer-term capital is not yet available. However, there are major differences between domestic and international money market operations.

One major difference is that the variety of sources available internationally is far greater than that at home. This larger variety requires a firm to acquire a broader range of knowledge of and a more sophisticated approach to decision making. The foreign exchange risks, for example, increase for international money markets, but many multinational firms believe that the risks are worthwhile and often use international money markets. The most important and widely used sources of short-term funds and methods of available financing might be better understood if three interrelated topics – trade documents, commercial banks, and the Eurocurrency market – are considered.

Trade Documents

Most governments pay a great deal of attention to all aspects of international trade, so the documents required to do business domestically are much less numerous and complex than those required by two or more governments for international trade. Different currencies also add complexity. Furthermore, in international trade, the buyer and seller are often less familiar with each other. Distance and a general lack of available credit data make transactions more uncertain. Therefore, firms doing foreign business often seek the services of an intermediary such as a bank to help prepare necessary documents.

Two types of international trade credit are available: credit arranged on an open account basis and credit arranged on the foreign collections basis. Both types need documents, but the **open account basis** is less complex: The exporter sends the merchandise and accompanying documents to the importer; the importer pays when the merchandise arrives. This method, of course, requires a great deal of trust.

The **foreign collections basis** differs from the open account in that a bank helps prepare documents and aids in transmitting payments, usually with the use of letters of credit. As discussed in Chapter 10, letters of credit contain bank promises to the exporter to make payments for the importer under specific conditions.

Documents may be required even when traders do not use credit. There are two types of foreign trade documents: negotiable money paper and commodity paper. Money paper requires financial payment; commodity paper requires payment in goods or services.

Many kinds of negotiable money paper are currently being used. The promissory note and several forms of a "draft" note are the two most frequently used. The promissory note states that a promise is being made to pay a fixed amount at a specified time. It is especially popular with businesspeople involved in long-term projects because it reduces the paperwork when there are several subsequent shipments. Terms are set in advance. When each shipment is made, the same terms can be used.

The draft, often also called a *bill of exchange,* is used more often than the promissory note. It differs from a promissory note in that a bank or some other third party can be named as the recipient of the funds. Such a note permits the exporter to use the draft as a form of collateral for a loan, since the bank can be named as the recipient.

Several types of drafts exist. Clean drafts are basically foreign accounts receivable for sales made on an open account basis. The sight draft requires immediate payment on delivery of the merchandise. Acceptance drafts permit a period of time before the payment is due. The importer simply signs his or her name, the date, and the word *Accepted* on the draft when it arrives. Banker's drafts and bank money orders are other forms of negotiable money paper that may be used in trade.

Commodity paper is used less frequently than negotiable money paper, but many importers still use it. Two negotiable types of commodity paper include the bill of lading, which is a carrier document, and the warehouse receipt, which is a storage document.

Both money and commodity paper can be used as negotiable instruments since the terms must be agreed to by both parties, are considered as proof of ownership, and can often be sold or used as collateral for short-term bank loans. If the documents are sold, they are usually sold at a discount. This, in fact, is similar to selling domestic accounts receivable to factoring companies.

Commercial Banks

All of these new terms, documents, and methods may scare off potential international businesspeople, but they should not. Banks are quite willing to take care of the paperwork related to the credit, billing, and collection of payments for international trade. No firm should be intimidated by the different documents required. Most large banks maintain experienced staffs and establish reasonable charges for their expertise.

Commercial banks are actually very important in international business. Not only do they provide many services, but also they are the single most important external source of international short-term financing. The specific types of funds and services offered vary from country to country so most MNCs use more than one bank. However, MNCs usually coordinate all their banking activities through a large bank in their home country (country of the parent company). The banking network might seem complex at first, but it need not be since many countries' banking practices are similar and many of the financial documents are almost internationally standardized.

Banks also provide lines of credit and commercial loans. They use drafts and are involved in trade credit. They also can permit the use of overdrafts (writing checks beyond deposits) – one of the major forms of short-term credit outside the United States. In fact, most non-U.S. banks provide a broader range of services than banks are permitted to offer in the United States. They lend more long-term money and are involved in investment banking. More financing is unsecured, and banks buy or sell (at a discount) trade documents more often. Discounting costs vary, but banks in most developed countries have efficient means to handle the entire process.

The Eurocurrency Market

The international money market comprises more than just new credit instruments and expanded banking services. New kinds of money are also available. Each country has a currency, and developed countries also have Eurocurrencies. **Eurocurrencies** are moneys deposited outside the control of the country of origin. U.S. dollars deposited in any European bank, for example, are called **Eurodollars**. British pounds deposited in the United States are called *Eurosterling* or *Europounds.*

Other names for portions of the Eurocurrency market have been established. It is also possible to refer to *Asian currencies* or *Asian dollars* to identify foreign moneys or dollars deposited in Asia. Such names refer to classes of money outside the country of origin, but it should be remembered that all such groupings are really subsets of the vast money market generally known as the *Eurocurrency market.*

The Eurocurrency market is well organized, very efficient, and extremely large. It is also very popular. One reason for its popularity is the ready availability of its money, often at lower interest rates than those prevailing elsewhere. Local governments do not place reserve requirements on foreign currency deposits, so interest rates to borrow these funds can be low. From the point of view of businesspeople, such currencies therefore are desirable. Governments would prefer more controls but agree that Eurocurrencies are important for international business. Economists worry that a credit failure may set up a chain reaction of other failures, but few recommend that Eurocurrencies be eliminated.

Supply and demand conditions determine prevailing interest rates for Eurocurrency loans. The rates and terms are published daily in many leading financial papers, but if a businessperson is interested in considering such a loan, all he or she needs to do is call a bank.

Long-Term Financing

Companies are permitted to issue stock or bonds in most of the countries in which they operate. A few countries (primarily the communist countries), however, prohibit this, and some simply do not have large enough capital markets to meet the needs of firms. The number of such countries, though, is declining, and many countries are now actively encouraging MNCs to enter their stock and bond markets.

Just as in other areas of corporate finance, differences exist between long-term foreign financing and domestic long-term financing. For example, although most stock certificates in the United States are registered, most shares in Europe are **bearer shares** – the issuing firm does not maintain a list of stockholders and must wait for stockholders to request dividend payments. Preferred stock is less popular outside the United States than it is in the United States.

Practices concerning voting power also differ. Voting is sometimes weighted based on the length of time the stock has been owned. Naturally, in countries that practice this system, it is harder to attract interest in new shares.

The average sale of stock is often larger in Europe than in the United States, because a larger proportion of issues is purchased by financial institutions. In fact, most European banks purchase stock for inclusion in their own portfolios (an act not permitted in the United States). Selling stock that a person does not own (*short selling*) is prohibited in many countries. Although this does not automatically affect the MNC, it tends to reduce investor interest in equity markets and thus limits the volume of transactions. Fewer daily transactions may result in a less stable market.

Each market establishes its own set of requirements for listing firms and sets fees for listing a firm's stock. Because these charges can be rather substantial, most MNCs list only in the countries in which they are the most active.

Another differing aspect of foreign business is the practice of companies paying a higher percentage of earnings in dividends. Although most Canadian and U.S. investors prefer capital gains to dividends, many other investors seem to prefer dividends to capital gains. This difference is exaggerated because many foreign firms report only enough earnings to pay the dividend that the firm wants to declare (the rest of their earnings are often reported as "reserves" for possible expenses later). To avoid possible problems or misunderstandings, at the onset of its business dealings the MNC should explain its reporting and dividend policies. Naturally, if the company adopts the policy to retain earnings, the firm might still have problems in issuing shares because this policy is not common in most countries.

There is also the option of raising money in a third country. The issue is likely to be denominated in the third country's currency; therefore, a different set of currency risks is encountered. Choosing the country in which to obtain funds can be as important as deciding which type of funds to use or for what project the funds will be used. Regardless of the choice, however, other capital markets are not as large as the U.S. market; it is more difficult to raise large sums without paying higher costs in these markets.

Rather than issue securities in only one country, a firm may choose to issue Eurobonds. In general, **Eurobonds** are bonds issued (often in Europe) in a currency other than that of the local market. An issue can be sold in many different countries, but it is usually denominated in the currency of only one country. Hence, the geographical market of a Eurobond is much wider than one country. Eurobonds can be denominated in almost any currency; however, most are denominated in the strong currencies of developed countries. They can also be stated in terms of the European currency unit (ECU). The ECU is an artificial currency determined by a formula based on other currencies.

Eurobonds have many benefits compared to single nation bonds. Some governments place fewer restrictions on Eurobonds, and disclosure requirements are sometimes less stringent. The size of the issue can be larger so the unit costs of issuance can be lower. Additionally, Eurobonds allow added flexibility. A firm can choose the currency in which it wishes to make payments. The choice, however, affects the marketability of the issue. For example, if a U.S. company wants to sell a bond in Japan but states the interest payments in U.S. dollars, the Japanese will pay less for the bond if the dollar is expected to decline against the Japanese yen. However, if the bond promised to pay interest in a stronger currency, the Japanese would be willing to pay a higher price for that bond.

Derivatives

In recent years, many new approaches to financial management have been developed. For example, rather than buying or selling a currency or commodity, a firm can now enter into an agreement to buy or sell the future change in almost any asset's value. These "derivatives" can remove or reduce some risks but might also increase others.

There are hundreds of different derivatives. Some are very simple, but others are very complex and risky. Companies need to know what they are doing and have good controls in place before entering derivatives' markets; otherwise, they risk disasters. Procter & Gamble (U.S.), for example, lost $157 million on two leverage swap contracts in 1994. Allied-Lyons (U.K.) lost $273 million in 1991 on foreign exchange options. Codeleo (Chile) lost $660 million in 1993 using derivatives. These are small losses, however, compared to the losses in Japan by Showa Shell Sekigu of $1.05 billion in 1993 and Kashima Oil's $1.45 billion in 1994. Most dramatic was the estimated loss of perhaps as much as $1.3 billion (estimates vary) by Barings Bank (U.K.) in 1995, which forced it to declare bankruptcy. Not all firms lose money, of course. Even those that do lose usually have recovered it in other transactions. Nevertheless, the risks are real and care must be taken.

Development Banks

Although many financial institutions lend money and capital to businesses, some institutions are unique to international business. These institutions are of special interest to companies because of the services they provide. The most important of these specialized institutions are known as **development banks,** which operate as nonprofit organizations for the sole purpose of aiding economic development. They do this by lending at very favorable terms.

The International Bank for Reconstruction and Development (IBRD), better known as the World Bank, is the best known development bank. The International Development Association (IDA) and the International Finance Corporation (IFC) are affiliated with IBRD. Most of the loans from IDA are made to the poorer nations for use in major economic projects such as power plant or highway construction, agricultural development, or communication systems. The loans are granted with very favorable terms, and as a result, IDA loses money. The IFC lends to the private sector on very favorable but somewhat more realistic terms. It funds projects such as the construction of manufacturing plants.

There are several other development banks. Some are regional in scope; others are national. The Inter-American Development Bank is a well-known regional bank. Although it has experienced more political problems than the World Bank, it is widely known for its work in Latin America.

National banks also attract and issue capital for projects deemed worthwhile for development. Some of these banks are more successful than others. As a general rule, the less favoritism shown and the more strictly the loan is tied to expected economic contribution, the more successful is the bank. In most cases, however, the firms receiving the loans have benefited (even if the country has not); therefore, any company considering a project that might be deemed "economically beneficial for the development of the country" should remember that it might be eligible for a loan from the host country's development bank.

Investment Bankers

Investment bankers play an important role in the flotation of international equities and bonds. Governments and private firms depend on investment bankers not only for their expertise in the flotation of securities but also for their expertise in such diverse areas as leasing, balance-of-payments problems, monetary fluctuations, intricate international taxation considerations, broad fluctuations and differentials in interest rates, devaluations, revaluations, and domestic limitations on the capital markets.

The term **investment banker,** while apparently referring to one person, often really refers to an underwriting syndicate. The individual investment banker cannot risk his or her existence on the success of a single firm's securities. The syndicate is a combination of many investment houses that share the risks of issuance. An additional advantage of syndication is that the individual security can be sold in a much larger market area. The most important function of investment bankers is their assistance in the sale of bonds. This assistance begins long before the actual flotation of the bond issue. The investment banker can create a package for the client that consists of alternatives that have been chosen to meet the needs of both the market and the issuer.

Another role of the investment banker is to arrange equity financing. The investment banker may either acquire the issue outright or agree to sell it. Naturally, the more services provided or the greater the amount of risks taken, the more the banker will charge. The investment banker often seeks a private placement for the securities of a small firm without the prestige or capital base with which to support a public stock or bond flotation. The investment banker arranges a private placement of the securities with a pension fund or insurance company in return for a finder's fee. Insurance companies and pension funds circumvent the market and thus avoid some of the costs associated with the public funds market.

Although the primary role of the investment banker is to serve as an intermediary between firms requiring capital and people wishing to invest funds, the role is beginning to expand into such areas as locating joint-venture partners, providing research reports, leasing, trading in international money markets, and maintaining inventories of many currencies, bonds, and equities. Smaller firms often do not possess the managerial or financial capability to search for a partner in a joint venture or develop a foreign market without the valuable experience and contacts of the international investment banker. The banker can locate a suitable partner, acquire the requisite funds, and assist the firm in the introductory phases of the new venture. These counseling and other intelligence services are proving to be very profitable for investment bankers, since they already possess the necessary information and contacts.

Capital Budgeting

The capital budgeting of a multinational firm involves the same techniques a domestic firm employs. These techniques, though, must be applied in conjunction with a careful consideration of the many additional variables, risks, and constraints inherent in the international environment. The MNC, however, must determine how all these risks, constraints, and new variables are to be absorbed into the capital budgeting process.

Inexperienced managers often consider offsetting the added risks of international business by setting a discount rate for foreign projects higher than the firm's weighted average cost of capital. Sometimes the rate applies to all foreign countries, but often firms cluster groups of countries and set one rate for one group and other rates for other groups. When using either of these methods, the obvious problem is that the firms have failed to realize that each country is unique. To solve this problem, some companies try to set a discount rate for each country. However, even this method is flawed because it assumes that all the extra risks, constraints, and new variables are uniform within the country. In reality, even within a country, risks vary over time and depend on each situation. Attempts by a firm to simplify the process by setting a generalized discount rate generally decrease the reliability of the resultant calculations.

A better approach for a company is to rely on basic financial management techniques that independently examine every cash flow. Each cash flow must be adjusted for time and risks. This same procedure is used in both international capital budgeting and domestic capital budgeting (the system is known as *using certainty equivalents*). Basically, the only difference between the two types of capital budgeting is that, in international capital budgeting, more risks must be accounted for when discounting the cash flows.

Let us consider a simplified example that illustrates the mechanics of international capital budgeting. Suppose an Australian company could invest in country X but was told that it must sell the investment back to the host country's government after five years. The resale price would be the original investment price. The best investment opportunity requires 1,000,000 pesos and it might return 200,000 pesos per year (the peso from country X is currently worth A\$1); however, the peso is expected to continue losing value against the dollar, so it is necessary to discount the peso cash flows by 10 percent per year since all projects must be valued from the point of view of the parent company (and its currency). The biggest problem is that, in two and one-half years, a change of leadership in country X is expected. Although it seems that current political risks reduce expected cash flows by only 5 percent, the new government is expected to take tougher stands and reduce cash flows by 20 percent. If the risk-free rate is 8 percent and the business project risk for each cash flow is 4 percent, then the assessment of the opportunity could be set up and computed as follows:*

$$PVR - PVC = NPV$$
$$PVC = \$1,000,000$$
$$PVR = \sum_{1}^{5} PVR_i$$

$$PVR_i = R_i \frac{1}{(1 + rf)^i} \frac{1}{(1 + fx)^i}(1 - pr_i)(1 - br_i)$$

PVR = present value of revenue
PVC = present value of costs
NPV = net present value
R_i = possible peso flow in year i
rf = risk-free discount rate
fx = discount rate for foreign exchange adjustment
pr_i = political risk discount for year i
br_i = business project risk discount for year i

(Note that the political and the business project risks are not compounded over time but are simply presented as discounts for the year.)

$$
\begin{aligned}
PVR_1 &= 200,000(0.926)(0.909)(0.95)(0.96) = \$153,532.28 \\
PVR_2 &= 200,000(0.857)(0.826)(0.95)(0.96) = 129,117.67 \\
PVR_3 &= 200,000(0.794)(0.751)(0.80)(0.96) = 91,590.76 \\
PVR_4 &= 200,000(0.735)(0.683)(0.80)(0.96) = 77,107.97 \\
PVR_5 &= 1,200,000(0.681)(0.621)(0.80)(0.96) = \underline{389,745.56}
\end{aligned}
$$

$$\sum_{1}^{5} PVR_i = \qquad\qquad\qquad PVR = \$841,094.24$$

therefore,

$$NPV = \$841,094.24 - \$1,000,000$$
$$= (\$158,905.76)$$

---

*It should be noted that there are many unresolved issues concerning international capital budgeting. The example presented tends to simplify the problem. Actual risks and discount rates, for example, are hard to separate or quantify, so lumped approximations frequently are made. The example, therefore, is useful for creating awareness of the many relevant variables but may not be possible or perhaps even desirable to implement in the real world.

Obviously, the risks are too high to warrant this investment.

In summary, the concept of international capital budgeting is simple: Discount each cash flow by each of its perceived risks. The mathematics is often cumbersome, but it is well worthwhile.

This procedure not only enables firms to evaluate and compare projects within a country, it also permits them to evaluate and compare alternatives anywhere in the world. No other system does this as accurately. Without such a system, multinational corporations would not know where to allocate financial resources best.

Summary

Many mistakes have been committed by firms engaging in international business. One of the reasons that international managers blunder is that they sometimes forget they are facing more risks than their domestic counterparts. International financial managers must deal with the added risks of expropriation, discrimination, and foreign exchange rate fluctuations.

The foreign exchange rate risk is of greatest concern to the international firm. Currency values are constantly changing and can greatly influence the cash flows of a company. To minimize risk, a firm must try to anticipate exchange rate changes and then take appropriate action. Exchange rate forecasting requires knowledge of economics and politics. Inflation, speculation, and political events are some of the most important variables that influence currency values. Computer models have been developed to aid in exchange rate forecasting, but unfortunately none is a perfect forecaster.

A company may take many courses of action when attempting to reduce its net exposure. Most alternatives involve maintaining assets in strong currencies and holding liabilities in weak currencies. These strategies, however, are not cost free. The firm's real challenge, therefore, is to optimize its strategy.

International business is not without its rewards. In fact, foreign operations are generally more profitable than domestic operations. Although added risks are involved in international business, many intermediaries and specialized documents now exist that can aid in the reduction of these risks. Investment bankers and development banks are often able to locate or provide funds at attractive prices. Eurocurrency and Eurobond markets also enable a firm to raise money rather easily. Furthermore, documents have been created by banks that can reduce or eliminate at least some trade risks.

Capital budgeting for international operations is more complex than for domestic projects, but it is manageable. The added risks must be acknowledged and adjusted for, but the evaluation techniques used are similar to those techniques used domestically.

MINI-CASE
A Question of Foreign Exchange Rates

The following situation involves different currencies. Please read the brief description and respond to the questions.

A small Australian company has contracted to purchase 100,000 toys for £3.50 each from a British company. The Australians have agreed to pay in sterling. The Australians have also agreed to sell the toys to a U.S. company for US$5.50 per toy. The Australian company has agreed to accept U.S. dollars but plans to convert these revenues to Australian dollars. The Australian company estimates its marginal costs (warehousing, travel, and so on) as A$0.75 per toy.

Exchange rates at the time of signing the agreements are as follows:

A$1 = US$0.80
A$1 = £0.66

Discussion Issues

1. Is this a good deal for the Australian company? Why or why not?
2. What impact would a devaluation of the U.S. dollar relative to the Australian dollar have on the Australian company's profits? What impact would a revaluation upward have?
3. What impact would a devaluation of the British pound relative to the Australian dollar have on the Australian company's profits? What impact would a revaluation upward have?
4. What impact would a devaluation of the British pound relative to the U.S. dollar have on the Australian company's profits? What impact would a revaluation upward have?
5. If exchange rates changed to the following, what impact would this have on the Australian company's profits?

A$1 = US$0.90
A$1 = £0.57

6. What could the Australian company do to minimize its exposure to exchange-rate losses?

Discussion Questions

1. What are some important risks that international financial managers face that domestic managers do not?
2. Should a company refuse to invest in a foreign country if another company there has a higher rate of return? Why or why not?
3. What are some of the causes of foreign exchange rate fluctuations?
4. How can a firm reduce its foreign exchange risk?
5. Should MNCs list stock in every country where they do business? Why or why not?
6. Why might a firm want to issue a Eurobond?
7. Why might a firm want to borrow from a development bank?
8. Why might a firm use an international investment banker?

Assignments

1. If the British pound was worth US$1.5000 but has appreciated by 10 percent, what is it worth now?
2. If the French franc is worth US$0.2000, how many French francs is the U.S. dollar worth?
3. In the capital budgeting example, suppose that the risk-free rate were 5 percent and that you believe that political risks with the new government will be 10 percent. (Nothing else changes in the sample problem.) Would you now accept the project? Why or why not? What is the net present value?

Selected References

Adler, M., and B. Dumas, "Exposure to Currency Risk: Definition and Measurement," *Financial Management* (Summer 1984), pp. 41–50.

Aggarwal, R., and L. A. Soenen, "Corporate Use of Options and Futures in Foreign Exchange Management," *Journal of Cash Management* (November–December 1989), pp. 61–66.

Agmon, T., "Capital Budgeting and Unanticipated Changes in the Exchange Rate," *Advances in Financial Planning and Forecasting* 4, part B (1990), pp. 295–314.

Aliber, R. Z., *Handbook of International Financial Management* (Homewood, Ill.: Dow Jones-Irwin, 1989).

Ang, J. S., and Tsong-Yue Lai, "A Simple Rule for Multinational Capital Budgeting," *Global Finance Journal* (Fall 1989), pp. 71–75.

Batten, J., R. Mellor, and V. Wan, "Foreign Exchange Risk Management Practices and Products Used by Australian Firms," *Journal of International Business Studies* (Winter 1993), pp. 557–573.

Belk, P. A., and M. Glaum, "The Management of Foreign Exchange Risk in UK Multinationals: An Empirical Investigation," *Accounting and Business Research* 21, no. 81 (1990), pp. 3–13.

Bishop, P., and D. Dixon, *Foreign Exchange Handbook: Managing Risk and Opportunity in Global Currency Markets* (New York: McGraw-Hill, 1992).

Booth, L. D., "Hedging and Foreign Exchange Exposure," *Management International Review* 22, no. 1 (1982), pp. 26–43.

Booth, L., and W. Rotenberg, "Assessing Foreign Exchange Exposure: Theory and Application Using Canadian Firms," *Journal of International Financial Management and Accounting* 2, no. 1 (Spring 1990), pp. 1–22.

Buckley, A., *Multinational Finance,* 2nd ed. (London: Prentice-Hall International, 1992).

David, E., J. Coates, P. Collier, and S. Longden, *Currency Risk Management in Multinational Companies,* Research Studies in Accounting (London: Prentice-Hall International, 1991).

DeRosa, D. F., *Managing Foreign Exchange Risk* (Chicago: Probus, 1991).

Eiteman, D. K., A. I. Stonehill, and M. H. Moffett, *Multinational Business Finance,* 7th ed. (Reading, Mass.: Addison-Wesley, 1995).

Giddy, I. H., *Global Financial Markets* (Lexington, Mass.: D. C. Heath, 1994).

Glaum, M., "Strategic Management of Exchange Rate Risks," *Long Range Planning* 23, no. 4 (1990), pp. 65–72.

Grabbe, J. O., *International Financial Markets,* 2nd ed. (New York: Elsevier, 1991).

Grant, R., and L. A. Soenen, "Conventional Hedging: An Inadequate Response to Long-Term Foreign Exchange Exposure," *Managerial Finance* 17, no. 4 (1991), pp. 1–4.

The Guide to Export Finance 1988 (London: Euromoney Publications, 1985).

A Handbook on Financing U.S. Exports, 5th ed. (Washington, D.C.: Machinery and Allied Products Institute, 1988).

Heckman, C. R., "Measuring Foreign Exchange Exposure: A Practical Theory and Its Application," *Financial Analysts Journal* (September–October 1983), pp. 59–65.

Holland, J., *International Financial Management,* 2nd ed. (New York and Oxford: Basil Blackwell, 1992).

Investing, Licensing, and Trading Conditions Abroad (New York: Business International, updated regularly).

Jorion, P., "The Exchange-Rate of Exposure of U.S. Multinationals," *Journal of Business* 63, no. 3 (July 1990), pp. 331–345.

Kerkvliet, J., and M. H. Moffett, "The Hedging of an Uncertain Future Foreign Currency Cash Flow," *Journal of Financial and Qualitative Analysis* 26, no. 4 (December 1991), pp. 565–578.

Kubarych, R. M., *Foreign Exchange Markets in the United States,* rev. ed. (New York: Federal Reserve Bank of New York, 1983).

Lessard, D. R., "Evaluating International Projects: An Adjusted Present Value Approach," D. R. Lessard, ed., *International Financial Management: Theory and Application* (New York: Wiley, 1985), pp. 570–584.

Lessard, D. R., "Global Competititon and Corporate Finance in the 1990s," *Journal of Applied Corporate Finance* (Winter 1991), pp. 59–72.

Levi, M., *International Finance: Financial Management and the International Economy,* 2nd ed. (New York: McGraw-Hill, 1990).

Luehrman, T. A., "The Exchange Rate Exposure of a Global Competitor," *Journal of International Business Studies* (Second Quarter 1990), pp. 225–242.

Madura, J., *International Financial Management,* 3rd ed. (St. Paul, Minn.: West Publishing, 1992).

Masson, D. J., "Planning and Forecasting of Cash Flows for the Multinational Firm: International Cash Management," *Advances in Financial Planning and Forecasting* 4, part B (1990), pp. 195–228.

Maxwell, C. E., and L. J. Gitman, "Risk Transmission in International Banking: An Analysis of Forty-eight Central Banks," *Journal of International Business Studies* (Summer 1989), pp. 268–279.

Moffett, M. H., and J. K. Karlsen, "Managing Foreign Exchange Rate Economic Exposure," *Journal of International Financial Management and Accounting* 5, no. 2 (June 1994), pp. 157–175.

Moffett, M. H., and A. Stonehill, "International Banking Facilities Revisited," *Journal of International Financial Management and Accounting* 1, no. 1 (Spring 1989), pp. 88–103.

Nance, D. R., C. W. Smith, Jr., and C. W. Smithson, "On the Determinants of Corporate Hedging," *Journal of Finance* (March 1993), pp. 267–284.

Oxelheim, L., and C. Wihlborg, "Corporate Strategies in a Turbulent World Economy," *Management International Review* 31, no. 4 (1991), pp. 293–315.

Pringle, J. J., "Managing Foreign Exchange Exposure," *Journal of Applied Corporate Finance* 3, no. 4 (Winter 1991), pp. 73–82.

Ricks, D. A., *Blunders in International Business* (Cambridge, Mass.: Blackwell Publishers, 1993).

Ruesch, O. J., "Protecting Your Profits with Foreign Exchange Procedures," *Journal of European Business* (May–June 1992), pp. 34–36.

Shapiro, A. C., *Multinational Financial Management,* 4th ed. (Boston: Allyn and Bacon, 1992).

Smith, R. C., and I. Walter, *Global Financial Services: Strategies for Building Competitive Strengths in International Commercial and Investment Banking* (New York: Harper Business, 1990).

Soenen, L. A., and R. Aggarwal, "Corporate Foreign Exchange and Cash Management Practices," *Journal of Cash Management* (March–April 1987), pp. 62–64.

Soenen, L. A., and J. Mandura, "Foreign Exchange Management – A Strategic Approach," *Long Range Planning* 24, no. 5 (October 1991), pp. 119–124.

Solnik, B., *International Investments,* 2nd ed. (Reading, Mass.: Addison-Wesley, 1991).

Srinivasan, V., and Y. H. Kim, "Payments Netting in International Cash Management: A Network Optimization Approach," *Journal of International Business Studies* (Summer 1986), pp. 1–20.

Srinivasan, V., S. E. Moeller, and Y. H. Kim, "International Cash Management: State-of-the-Art and Research Directions," *Advances in Financial Planning and Forecasting* 4, part B (1990), pp. 161–194.

Stoll, H. R., and R. E. Whaley, *Futures and Options: Theory and Applications, Current Issues in Finance* (Cincinnati: South-Western, 1993).

Venedikian, H. M., and G. A. Warfield, *Export-Import Financing,* 2nd ed. (New York: Wiley, 1986).

Wyatt, S. B., "On the Valuation of Puts and Calls on Spot, Forward, and Future Foreign Exchange: Theory and Evidence," *Advances in Financial Planning and Forecasting* 4 (1990), pp. 81–104.

CHAPTER 12

Marketing Management in International Companies

LEARNING OBJECTIVES

After reading this chapter, you should be able to

▶ Define *marketing* and explain its role in the organization.

▶ Discuss the advantages and disadvantages of a standardized, global approach to marketing and of an adapted, differentiated approach.

▶ Explain the role of communication in international marketing.

▶ Identify the forms of research that provide information for marketing decisions and discuss these from an international perspective.

K E Y   T E R M S

▶ Marketing standardization

▶ Marketing adaptation

▶ Marketing communication

▶ Backtranslation

▶ Consumer panels

T H O U G H T   S T A R T E R S

▶ Canadians are told: "Expanding south? Remember the U.S. is a foreign market. Expect the unexpected (naturally), plus rough competition, regional skews, xenophobia and (possibly) litigation. Then go!"

(Challenges 1989)

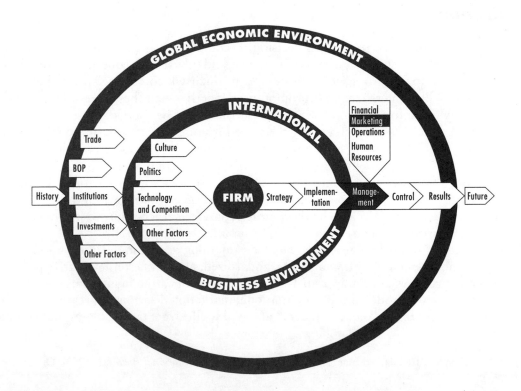

▶ *Mad* magazine published its 300th issue in 1990. It is the oldest U.S. humor magazine and has a circulation of about 1 million in North America and 400,000 in foreign countries. After operating for 38 years, its record includes the following. It

- ▶ has been profitable since its fourth issue
- ▶ has no advertising, no market research, no precise circulation numbers, no phone number listed under its own name, no particular effort to add subscribers
- ▶ publishes British, Dutch, Brazilian, Australian, Chinese, and four Scandinavian editions
- ▶ is the biggest humor magazine in Germany but failed at least three attempts at a French edition
- ▶ pays freelancers on the spot; gives 12 staffers and most contributors a lavish, all-expense-paid vacation each autumn; sent the entire staff to Haiti one year to persuade the sole subscriber there to renew.

(Globe and Mail *1990*)

▶ Although many third-world shoppers buy it as a symbol rather than a drink, Coca-Cola probably does qualify as a global brand: It is so well known that only a purist would call it anything else. That has taken a century of marketing. Who else has managed it? In Landor Associates' recent survey of brand power in Europe, Japan, and America, no other brand name came in the top 50 brands in all three areas.

(The Economist *1989, p. 99*)

Introduction

Marketing policies are basic to a firm's decision to commit resources. These policies include, among others, decisions regarding what is going to be sold (physical product), to whom (customers), for how much (price), over what period and through which channels (distribution), and how the product will be merchandised (promotion). Underlying all these decisions is a research process that provides information on which the decisions can be founded.

The issues that need to be analyzed are the same for domestic and international companies, but an international company faces environments that may vary widely, and these variations can affect its decisions. Marketing is universal in the sense that it is a function performed everywhere, but the experience of marketing differs from location to location. The effective company tries to exploit both the similarities and differences that are found among various locations: "Think global and act local has become the consensus," according to Jacques Blanchard of Novaction, a Paris-based consultancy (*The Economist* 1989, p. 101).

This chapter begins by defining *marketing* and examining its role in the international organization. The advantages and disadvantages of standardized, global marketing relative to adapted, differentiated approaches are considered. The role of communication in international marketing is then examined, and a model to guide international marketing decisions is presented. Throughout, specific examples of marketing blunders* are used to illustrate the problems that companies

---

*Many of these blunders are adapted from D. A. Ricks, *Blunders in International Business* (1993). Others are from the authors' personal experiences.

International business is fraught with unexpected events. Fortunately, some of these surprising occurrences prove to be advantageous to the multinational corporations involved. For example, a U.S. firm selling feminine sanitary napkins in South America suddenly experienced a major surge in sales. The company was naturally delighted, although a bit startled, when it discovered that the sales boost was prompted by local farmers who were buying the napkins to use as dust masks. No less surprised was the U.S. company that sold toothbrushes in South Vietnam during the late 1960s. It too experienced an unexpected increase in sales. Years later the company learned why: The Vietcong had bought the toothbrushes for weapon cleaning.

(Ricks 1993, p.1)

may encounter as they move from one country to another. These blunders also illustrate the value of learning the lessons discussed.

The Role of Marketing in International Companies

The task of international marketing is often far more difficult and riskier than many firms expect. This is due primarily to the number of uncontrollable variables that influence the effectiveness of international marketing policies. The complexity of the international marketing environment has resulted in a number of blunders by international companies. A company is said to have blundered if it makes a costly or embarrassing decision when such a result was foreseeable and avoidable. Although blunders have been made in every functional area of business, the most visible have been experienced by companies while trying to market their products and services.

Marketing Defined

A company that cannot sell its product or service has no reason to exist. Marketing concerns efforts to ensure that a company's products or services will be sold; "the essence of marketing is creating customer value that is greater than the value created by competitors" (Keegan 1989). This means that effective marketing involves a thorough understanding of what a company can offer and what customers want or need. Successful marketing is customer driven; it begins and ends with the customer. To achieve this customer orientation, marketing is based on understanding both a company's internal and external environments (i.e., internally, what the company can offer and, externally, what the customer wants).

Competitive strategy decisions are developed in terms of a company's internal strengths and weaknesses relative to external opportunities and threats. This essentially means that marketing flows from a company's competitive strategy. Marketing is the process by which the organization's strategy is achieved. The role of marketing is often thought of as the lifeblood of the organization because ineffective marketing can destroy a company when all other parts of the organization are functioning well.

Domestic and *international marketing* can be defined in the same way. The difference between the two occurs because of the differences in the external environment faced by an international company. These differences from one country to another can be in competition, customs, buying power, education, geography, politics, regulations, and religion, to mention only a few. Such differences influence what is acceptable and appropriate in terms of marketing activities. These varied external factors mean that internal strengths and weaknesses may be assessed differently in relation to different locations. Examples of these factors follow.

▶ A strong product or service in a mountainous environment (e.g., well-recognized downhill skis) might be useless, and therefore no longer a strength, in a geographically flat location.

▶ Control of a distribution system (e.g., an efficient trucking fleet) that would be a strength in one location may not be transferable to another where roads are less common.

▶ A product facing a saturated domestic market would be characterized as a weakness at home, but this same product may face a growth market in another location and become a strength.

The Simmons Co., a marketer of quality beds, might never have taken the plunge to expand to Japan if it had known the magnitude of the problems it would encounter. With numerous successful overseas ventures under its belt and confident of its product, the Simmons Company set out in the early 1960s to manufacture mattresses in Japan. Four years later, the company was still experiencing substantial losses in Japan. Several complex problems plagued its operation. Although aware of many of the difficulties in the Japanese market, the company had underestimated the degree of complexity present in the Japanese environment. Several complex problems plagued its operations. From the start, Simmons had realized that it would face several obstacles. Not only do most Japanese still sleep on futons (a type of floor mat), but also the complex and unusual Japanese distribution system could be quite confusing. The fact that an oligopolistic group of local manufacturers historically vied for control of the limited market complicated matters further. However, because the firm strongly believed in its product and know-how, Simmons Tokyo (later Simmons Japan) was organized in October 1964. Entry into the market timed to coincide with the Tokyo Olympic Games when the demand for beds would rise sharply over a short period of time. Early production progressed smoothly, but problems developed later. Among the difficulties the company encountered was its choice of a sales force. Because of the existence of social class differences and subtle language styles, the salesmen were most effective only if they and the client were of the same class. The initial sales force, therefore, had to be rigorously screened. None of the salesmen had ever slept on a bed. How could they be expected to endorse Simmons's product? Simmons also learned that it had overpriced its beds by as much as $60 above domestic prices. Even the distribution system proved baffling since everyday conduct and favors were often intertwined. A customer might engage in business with a supplier to whom he owed a favor regardless of the price difference, and this became a tangled network of complex relationships. Since no Japanese wished to lose face, Simmons also discovered that trying to operate outside of this established system was quite difficult. Finally, Simmons made an unfortunate choice regarding advertising media. The company chose print media and concentrated its distribution in the Tokyo area even though television is generally the most effective and penetrating advertising medium in Japan.   (Ricks 1993, pp. 112–113)

Marketing Standardization versus Adaptation

Marketing standardization is described as using essentially the same marketing approaches on a global scale. **Marketing adaptation,** in contrast, suggests changing part, or all, of one's marketing approaches to fit conditions in various local markets. The international firm, under appropriate conditions, can employ a global marketing approach. Such an approach essentially uses a standardized approach to marketing in all, or most, countries where the product or service is available.

A globally standardized approach to marketing has many advantages for the international company. It is an efficient means to deal with a variety of markets. The company that can employ this approach successfully eliminates many of the difficulties associated with adaptation and change to fit into a local market. Such a firm has a product or service that is basically the same everywhere, its use is consistent around the world, and one message can convey its appeal in spite of cultural and national differences.

Levitt (1983) points out that the efficiencies achieved by a global marketing approach can be translated into cost savings that can be passed on to customers in terms of lower world prices, which, in turn, gives the global marketer a competitive edge. Certain products – steel, chemicals, petroleum, cement, agricultural commodities and equipment, computers, semiconductors, electronic instruments, pharmaceuticals, and telecommunications – are generally standardized, but standardization is not necessarily confined to raw materials or high-tech and industrial products. The success of McDonald's around the world, Coca-Cola in the Middle East, Pepsi-Cola in the USSR, rock music, Rambo movies, Revlon cosmetics, Sony televisions, and Levi jeans everywhere indicates that some products have the potential to appeal to people in widely different countries and cultures.

> A powerful force drives the world toward a converging commonality, and the force is technology. It has proletarianized communication, transport[ation], and travel. It has made isolated places and impoverished peoples eager for modernity's allurements. Almost everyone everywhere wants all the things they have heard about, seen, or experienced via the new technologies.
>
> The result is a new commercial reality – the emergence of global markets for standardized consumer products on a previously unimagined scale of magnitude. Corporations geared to this new reality benefit from enormous economies of scale in production, distribution, marketing, and management. By translating these benefits into reduced world prices, they can decimate competitors that still live in the disabling grip of old assumptions about how the world works. (An excerpt from "The Globalization of Markets," by Theodore Levitt, *Harvard Business Review* [May–June 1983])

There is no question that global standardization in marketing can provide advantages to the international company, and there are examples of success in using such an approach. However, difficulties are associated with standardization because cultural and national characteristics in different locations can make it impractical. The issue for the international company is to identify when standardization is appropriate, when adaptation is needed, or when a complete change is the best choice. Two approaches for making this decision are market grouping and limited adaptation.

International Market Grouping

To take advantage of the benefits of standardization without committing marketing blunders, it may be possible to identify groups of countries that can be served by a standardized marketing

Tourism is an important sector for many countries which can capitalize on their natural beauty, famous monuments, unusual features, or myth. Since tourism promotes exports, brings foreign exchange, and creates employment, some countries go to great lengths to conceive and to implement original ideas to attract tourists.

The Scandinavian countries have done this by building on the myth of Santa Claus. Taking advantage of their proximity to the North Pole, an abundance of snow, and a large reindeer population, they compete with each other to be the true home of Santa Claus. Denmark had a head start when a 1932 Walt Disney cartoon put the workshop of Santa Claus in Greenland; subsequently, children began to send letters to him there. Sweden has established a Santa Claus amusement park near Mora, which attracted 100,000 visitors in 1986 (the entrance fee: $6.75 for adults, half for children). A business group in Mo I Rana, near the Nordkap, Norway, is planning to make this village the home of Santa Claus.

So far, however, Finland seems to be making the [strongest] running. International publicity through television, radio, the press, personal visits by Santa Claus to many countries, and a special post office address (which guarantees personal replies from Santa Claus) have elicited a growing response. Joulumaa (Christmas Country) in Rovaniemi, the capital of Finnish Lapland (the part of Finland that falls within the Arctic Circle), is the centre of attraction. The current Santa Claus village was visited by about 300,000 tourists in 1986. Hotels, restaurants, crafts, polar safaris, and skiing thrive on them. The village has been so successful that plans are under way for a much bigger one. More attractions and better facilities will certainly increase its international competitiveness.

The Santa Claus project is sponsored by the provincial government in Lapland, the Finnish Tourist Industry and Travel Boards, the Finnish Foreign Trade Union, the Finnish Broadcasting Company, and Finnair, which has been proclaimed "Santa Claus's official airline." However, the idea has been so lucrative that, in 1984, a British tour operator began offering a Christmas day tour to Santa Claus land on Concorde, operated by another transnational airline, British Airways. The thought of visiting Santa Claus by Concorde is obviously irresistible to many: By 1987, the number of Concorde flights had increased to four, with 400 believers making the trip. Two transnational shipping lines, Viking Line and Silja Line, combine cruises to Stockholm with tours to Santa Claus land. Santa Claus land is furthermore served by Hertz, Avis, Budget, and Europecar. In line with the dismal state of statistics on services, no systematic time series data exist on the extent and pattern of presents received by the faithful.

What is clear, however, is that Santa Claus land has been firmly integrated into the transnational travel-tourism complex. The Santa Claus example shows how a country can successfully create a competitive advantage in order to promote its tourism industry. Another example is theme parks, through which imaginary characters are exploited nationally and internationally. Children's literature offers many ideas for countries (and particularly developing countries) to corner – alone or together with transnational service corporations – lucrative myth-market niches. Where will be the home of Ali Baba, Robinson Crusoe, or Aladdin? Which island will become Treasure Island?

(United Nations Centre on Transnational Corporations 1988)

approach for certain products. The United Nations provides information on a large number of countries. It is possible to group these countries in terms of a number of characteristics (e.g., economic, geographic, climatic, cultural, political) and then develop a standardized marketing approach for countries grouped together on the basis of certain key market factors.

The method chosen for grouping countries depends on the product or service to be marketed. The idea is to try to identify those locational factors that would require adaptation of the firm's marketing approach. If, for example, the product is one that would be marketed differently under different climatic conditions, then climate is a primary concern; if it is a product that would have to be altered to fit different income levels, then income is important.

Market grouping also can identify a group of countries in which a product or service can be marketed in much the same way as it is in the home market. Jain (1987, p. 348) suggests the following:

1. Develop a market taxonomy for classifying world markets.
2. Segment all countries into groups on the basis of the dimensions of the market taxonomy.
3. Determine theoretically the most efficient means of serving each market.
4. Choose the group whose requirements fit best with the characteristics of the product or service to be marketed.
5. Examine real-world constraints and factor these into the marketing plan.

This approach distinguishes those countries for which standardized marketing is suitable from those for which it is not. This distinction can help a firm reap the advantages of standardization with relatively little risk. Even with this system, however, care should be taken with regard to names, translations, colors, and all of the other marketer's pitfalls that will be discussed in this chapter.

Limited Adaptation

A marketing strategy can be changed from one location to another in several ways. Among others, it is possible to adapt or change the product itself for a new location. Alternatively, the product itself may remain the same but its use can be adapted or changed, the message used to sell a product may be adapted, or the message can remain constant while the method of selling (media, distribution, and so forth) changes. To take advantage of the benefits of standardization without risking the pitfalls of marketing blunders, a firm can analyze the various facets that make up its marketing strategy and identify those that can be standardized and those that are likely candidates for change.

Some products are likely to be better candidates for standardization than others. Products in specialized niches can be good candidates for standardization – luxury products such as Rolex watches probably appeal to the same aficionados for the same reasons worldwide. Industrial products are also often good candidates for standardization – factories are interested in the same qualities in their ball bearings no matter where in the world they are located. Some markets around the world (i.e., the youth market) share certain characteristics and products – rock and roll music and blue jeans seem to fit this category – so that appeal to these markets can be standardized. Although standardization of some aspects of the marketing mix may be possible, it is unlikely that total standardization will be possible; therefore, some adaptation is usually required.

Even where products appear to be good candidates for standardization or where certain facets of the marketing strategy seem right for standardization, the marketer should not overlook the possibility of local variations. Standardization should be used cautiously, and the benefits are most likely to be reaped by those who do their local homework carefully before adopting a standardized marketing strategy.

Although global marketing and standardization provide advantages to the international company, this approach can also lead to difficulties. Marketing, as noted earlier, is the major means of communication between the organization and the public, particularly its customers. A look at the communication process, from an international perspective, indicates the "noise" that can make standardization impractical.

Communication in Marketing

The communication process is usually pictured as including a sender who transmits a message, a medium that carries the message, and a receiver who receives a message. Good communication is said to have taken place when the receiver ends up with the same message that the sender began with, and the receiver provides feedback that allows the sender to judge the accuracy of the communication that has taken place. In the case of **marketing communication**, one can view the firm as both sender and receiver in the communication process. The firm begins the communication process as a receiver who receives messages about customer wants and needs. These messages must be clearly understood if the firm is to meet customers' expectations. The firm is also the sender in the communication process because it has certain messages to convey to its customers. It conveys these messages through its marketing activities. If communication is good, the targeted customers will view the product or service positively and purchase it, thus providing the desired feedback. If communication is not good, sales will be lower than they could have been.

The good marketer recognizes these roles that the firm plays and is proactive in each role. First, the firm "listens" actively to the marketplace to determine what potential customers are communicating. Second, the firm carefully encodes its message, chooses an appropriate medium, and transmits the message to potential customers in a way that is sensitive to their needs and wants. Finally, the firm seeks feedback from customers. It does not simply accept sales figures as indications of good or bad communication; rather, it finds additional ways to determine its level of success.

Noise Interference

Difficulties arise because of noise in the communication system that distorts the message. *Noise* is used in this context to indicate anything that interferes with the communication process. When noise occurs, the receiver ends up with a different message than the intended one. Noise occurs for a variety of reasons and at a variety of points in the process. It may be physical, emotional, or psychological. Physical noise makes messages difficult to hear, and see (at the extreme, printed messages to the blind or spoken messages to the deaf). Emotional and psychological noise occurs because of predispositions in either the sender or receiver. This type of noise makes it troublesome either for the sender to develop and transmit an accurate message or for the receiver to pick up and understand the desired message. Noise can occur because the medium chosen for a particular message is inappropriate (again, print aimed at blind consumers or radio for the deaf).

Some noise occurs in any communication process, but it is particularly evident in international marketing because of the differences that exist between the domestic market with which the firm is most familiar and the foreign market. These differences often distort the message that the firm is trying to send to customers.

Generally, if the sender and receiver are alike, communication is relatively easy (identical twins who have always lived together usually have little difficulty communicating with each other), but the more dissimilar the sender and receiver, the more difficult communication becomes. This is because people tend to assume that others react as they themselves do, and they communicate from this viewpoint. The international marketer is usually communicating with customers who differ from those in the home country; therefore, communication can be complex. This complexity often makes standardization impractical. The following section elaborates on the complex issues of translation faced by the international marketer.

Translation Issues in Marketing

As discussed in Chapter 6, language provides an important means of communication. Precision in language is critical in the marketing process, and other factors such as the tone and pitch of the spoken word, pronunciation, misspelling, and even the choice of a word in the same language (American English to British English, for example) can affect the message consumers receive. The following are international marketing blunders resulting from the language barrier.

Companies have been known to promote their products in the wrong language. In Dubai, for example, only 10 percent of the population speaks Arabic. The remaining 90 percent originate from Pakistan, India, Iran, or elsewhere. Several European and American firms, however, have assumed that all Middle Eastern countries are populated primarily with Arabic-speaking people and so have promoted products only in Arabic.

Translations also lead to difficulties. An automobile manufacturer promoted its product as one that "topped them all"; unfortunately, in French Canada, this became "topped by them all." A battery described in the United States as "highly rated" became "highly overrated" in Brazil. Some translations are both humorous and embarrassing. Otis Engineering found that its sign that was supposed to say "completion equipment" in Moscow actually said "equipment for orgasms." A sign in a Saudi Arabian laundry included the item "lady's shirt" with the *r* omitted. In Tokyo, a hotel's laundry instructions included the following: "The flattening of underwear with pressure is the job of the chambermaid. To get it done, turn her on."

Even with the proper words, translation problems can arise. Missionaries in Africa discovered that *tones* and *pitches* can also be important. The Igbo people of Nigeria had been taught to sing the second verse of "Oh, Come All Ye Faithful." They were thought to be singing "Very God, begotten not created," but the actual meaning when the words were sung was "God's pig, which is never shared." Another hymn's words, "There is no sorrow in heaven," came out "There is no egg on the bicycle" because of the musical tones.

Problems with meanings even occur when English is the common language. A U.S. company in Britain decided to use its U.S. commercial, "You can use no finer napkin at your dinner table," in Britain. The word *napkin* in Britain usually means diaper, so the firm was unknowingly advertising "You can use no finer diaper at your dinner table." The Brits found the ad entertaining, but it could hardly have been expected to boost sales greatly.

Several of these blunders illustrate that even the smallest translation error can greatly affect the intended message and the market's reaction to that message. Occasionally, just one seemingly insignificant letter can change the entire context of the copy. One international corporation had its annual report translated into Spanish. In the sentence "Our vast enterprise achieved record sales, . . ." the word *vast* was translated as *"basto."* The actual Spanish word is *vasto,* but people often are confused because *b* and *v* are pronounced similarly. Due to this apparently minor error, the sentence read "our crude and uncultured enterprise achieved record sales, . . ."

A second set of translation blunders involves slogans that convey more than one message. The Parker Pen Company used its American condensed promotional slogan, "Avoid embarrassment – use Parker Pens," in Latin America, but, unfortunately, the Spanish word for embarrassment is also used to indicate pregnancy, so the Parker Pen Company was unknowingly promoting its pens as contraceptives. Another company promised that its toothpaste would make its customers more interesting, but in some Latin American countries, interesting is another euphemism for pregnant.

Translations play a key role in all aspects of international business, particularly in the area of marketing; thus, accuracy is of utmost importance. A company can be hurt by one faulty translation. The previous examples illustrate the need for caution in the translation and interpretation of messages: Exact wording should not always be translated literally; rather, the meaning of a word or phrase should be translated. To improve translation and avoid problems, a firm can take several steps. These include selecting an effective translator, using a technique known as backtranslation, and getting local input.

Selection of a Translator

A good translator eliminates much of the worry regarding mistakes in translation. Finding and keeping a good translator is not always easy. It is not enough that the translator has studied the language and can speak and write in the foreign language in a grammatically correct manner. The translator needs to be intimately familiar with the second language and to understand its nuances, colloquialisms, slang, and idioms. In addition, the translator should

▶ Have access to a library of reference books dealing with the appropriate subject and industry
▶ Understand required technical terms or be able to learn them
▶ Have access to experts in various appropriate fields, such as law, medicine, economics, and so on
▶ Have recently been in the country where the translation will be used (even a native loses track of slang and idioms after being away from home for a period of time).

Backtranslation

As discussed in Chapter 6, **backtranslation** requires that one individual translate the message into the desired foreign language and another party translate the foreign version back to the original language. This allows the original version of the message to be compared with the backtranslated version. If there is a discrepancy, changes are made until the backtranslated version closely matches the original version. This approach is time consuming and expensive, but the result is worthwhile because the company will have increased its confidence that it will not blunder.

Local Input

Local input is invaluable in assessing the appropriateness of a marketing campaign, particularly in terms of translation. Locals familiar with their slang and unusual idioms react to proposed promotions and represent other locals. Even when a company has hired the best translator available, one who is very familiar with both languages, and has gone through the backtranslation process, it is important to get input from representatives of the target market to minimize the possibility of mistakes. The next box shows that even animals are not immune from the problem of foreign languages.

A Model of the Marketing Communication Process

The marketing process is usually described in terms of the activities companies undertake to relate to markets. The model of the marketing process presented in Exhibit 12.1 illustrates the major aspects of marketing in the context of the communication process. This model identifies the various communication processes that occur when a firm develops an effective marketing approach. These activities are examined in more detail, in the international context, in the following discussion. The focus of this discussion is on the complexity of the international marketing environment and the aspects of this environment that can affect a firm's marketing strategy and tactics.

Marketing Research Activities

Communicating effectively with the customer, especially in a foreign market, is a challenge to marketers. To make marketing decisions, the marketing manager needs information about the customer, the product, and the competition, as well as the availability and effectiveness of various other aspects of the marketing mix. Often this information is not immediately available in the form the marketer would like, and data must be gathered and analyzed. Marketing research can provide this information.

Marketing research can take many forms. The following is a discussion of the most common forms of research that provide needed information for marketers, both domestic and international.

Analysis of Published Material

Published material often supplies a great deal of data that are useful in making marketing decisions. Using published information is a relatively inexpensive form of research, and many

Translating Can Be Beastly

Every dog may have its day, but whether it has the "bow-wow" depends on the country it lives in and the "language" it speaks. The French pup says "oua oua," but its Japanese counterpart barks out "wan wan," and in Italy the canine chorus is made up of cries of "bau bau." Dogs in Spain say "guau-guau," in Korea "mong-mong," "vovvov" in Norway, and "hav hav" if their dog houses are located in Istanbul.

Animals, it seems, speak in dozens of "foreign languages" just like people; and just like human languages, sometimes their sounds are similar and sometimes not at all alike.

Cats say "meow" in America, and their Polish cousins sound pretty much the same when they "miau," as do felines in Holland who "miauw," in Yugoslavia who "mijau," in France who "miaou," and you'd think a Siamese kitten had English lessons when you hear him "miew." But you may need a translator to help you pet your pussycat in Sweden or Indonesia, where "cat-ese" comes out as "jama" and "ngeong," or in Japan, where "nyaw" is what you'll hear.

If you're out for a ride, don't be surprised when your foreign-born mount refuses to "neigh" and tells you instead "hi-hi" (France) or "hii" (Spain). Down on the farm, hens don't "cluck" in most other countries, either. The three French hens who arrived on the third day of Christmas are more likely to be saying "glouk-glouk." Chickens who completed Spanish 101 will, of course, run around the barnyard with a "cloc-cloc" here and a "cloc-cloc" there.

Naturally, this onomatopoeic phraseology represents what the animal sounds like to the listeners' ears. Clearly, many of us hear things pretty much the same way; but not all of us do. (Ricks 1993, p. 86)

According to Kellogg, roosters around the world also say different things in the morning. In English they say "cockadoodledoo," in Danish "kykkaliky," in French "cocorico," in German "kikeriki," in Greek "kikipikou," in Italian "chichirichi," in Russian "kykapeky," and in Spanish "quiquiriqui." (Kellogg's Corn Flakes Cereal box)

There are numerous examples of English signs in non-English countries that illustrate the difficulties of translation. For example,

▶ In a Copenhagen Airline Office – "We take your bags and send them in all directions"
▶ In a Bangkok temple – "It is forbidden to enter a woman even if a foreigner if dressed as a man"
▶ In Germany's Black Forest – "It is strictly forbidden on our Black Forest camping site that people of different sex, for instance men and women, live together on one tent unless they are married with each other for that purpose"

Imagine what attempts in English-speaking countries to communicate in other languages really say!

Source: e-mail over the Internet.

companies begin their marketing analysis by examining these materials to provide background information and current data to help determine what additional research is needed. Published information of a wide variety is often available, including population demographics (e.g., rural versus urban, age and sex, income levels, literacy, educational attainment), information on companies operating in the country (e.g., size, products and services, locations), and information on trade and investment (e.g., imports and exports, trading partners, foreign investment). The following are major sources of such information:

EXHIBIT 12.1
**The Marketing
Communication
Process**

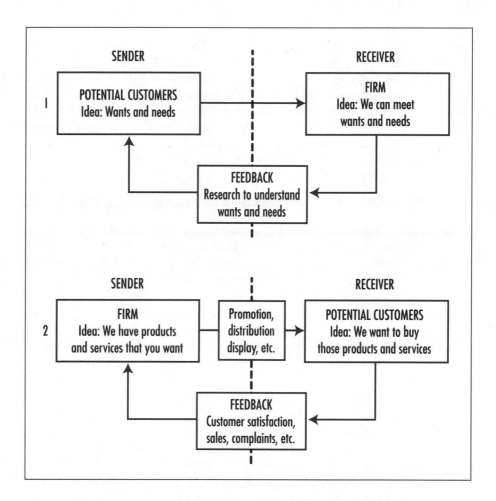

- ▶ International statistics published by international organizations such as the United Nations, the World Bank, and the International Monetary Fund
- ▶ National statistics compiled by local governments
- ▶ Local statistics compiled by foreign governmental or nongovernmental organizations such as the U.S. Agency for International Development (AID), Canadian International Development Agency (CIDA), Planned Parenthood, and the Red Cross
- ▶ The National Trade Data Bank and information available on the Internet and the World Wide Web
- ▶ Local and foreign statistics compiled and published by industry associations, banks, insurance companies, and so on
- ▶ Newspaper and magazine articles.

The same basic types of information are usually available around the world; however, in an unfamiliar international environment, knowing where to look for needed material and being able to understand its presentation and evaluate its accuracy may be difficult. Information can be stored in different places and formats. For example, computer systems, public libraries, private libraries, business libraries, royal libraries, government offices, schools, and universities all store information. Information can also be presented in unfamiliar ways; foremost, of course, is the issue of language and translation. In addition, different units of measure, different cost structures, and different methods of calculation may be used in various countries. For example, in the United States, 1 billion is 1,000,000,000; in the United Kingdom, it is 1,000,000,000,000; turnover in the United States is a ratio of two numbers – usually sales:inventory – while in Europe it refers to profitability; in the United States, 05/10/97 means May 10, 1997, while in Canada and Europe it means October 5, 1997.

Even when the needed information has been found and understood, it is still necessary to decide how accurate it is. When information is provided in concrete numbers, there is a tendency to equate precision with accuracy, but the two are not necessarily the same. Much of the information presented in published sources in fact is based on estimates, best guesses, dreams, and aspirations, or in the worst case, it may be intended to mislead. In the well-known environment of the home country, the researcher can often spot possible inaccuracies based on familiarity and personal experience, but this is not the case in unfamiliar environments. For example, a marketing consultant was investigating the trends in wine consumption in a small Caribbean country. According to the government's published statistics, imports of wine had decreased substantially over the past five years, suggesting a corresponding decrease in consumption. Fortunately, the consultant did not stop there but interviewed local hoteliers, restaurant owners, and bartenders. They all concurred that wine had become much more popular in recent years and that consumption had increased substantially. Discussions with a knowledgeable customs agent cleared up the apparent contradiction. It seems that when wine became more popular, smugglers began to bring it into the country illegally to avoid the tariffs and excise duties. This meant that wine coming into the country had increased, but this fact was not reflected in the official numbers.

To overcome difficulties in accessing and understanding information in foreign locations, the researcher should be innovative, persistent, and cautious: innovative in terms of considering new places to find information and ways to understand it; persistent in terms of gaining access to the information and obtaining explanations of how it is compiled; cautious in terms of accepting and interpreting the information provided.

Although it is true that the same sources of data may be available for many parts of the world, these sources may not include much data for many other places (particularly the less developed countries). In this event, published material will not be helpful and the researcher will have to rely on other methods for gathering information.

Surveys and Interviews

Surveys are designed to get opinions on a limited set of issues from a representative group of people. Surveys can be conducted by mail, by telephone, or in person. They can ask either closed- or open-ended questions (closed having a specific response set, open leaving the response up to the respondent). Interviews are conducted by telephone or in person. They are usually designed to get precise opinions from a relatively small number of people. Interviews also can involve closed- or open-ended questions.

Surveys and interviews are conducted by companies in both domestic and foreign markets to provide information that is not currently available from published sources. They might be used, for example, to identify customer needs and preferences, to assess perceptions of particular products, to estimate price elasticities, or to gauge reactions to a promotional campaign. Surveys and interviews can provide company-specific information that is not available elsewhere, and they can be tailored to provide specific information of relevance for a particular marketing decision.

The design and administration of surveys and interviews are critical to their success. They should be designed so that chosen respondents are willing to respond and questions elicit answers that are meaningful and useful to the researcher. Surveys and interviews should be administered in ways that are acceptable to respondents and that provide information that is reliable (credible) and valid (legitimate). Designing and administering surveys and interviews that fulfill these requirements and therefore are effective is difficult even in a familiar environment; it is more complex in a foreign one.

In North America, surveys and interviews are relatively commonplace, and their design, administration, and response are fairly well understood. In other countries, they may be quite unusual. This lack of familiarity can introduce biases into the research process; therefore, surveys and interviews must be used with caution in new locations. Some points to be considered by the international researcher follow.

The researcher needs to consider the most effective means of administration. For example, if the mail service is unreliable or unusual then it may not be effective for a survey; if only the wealthy or elite have access to telephones, the surveys may be useful only for gathering specific types of information; if approaching people for personal interviews is considered impolite, it may be difficult to use this format.

The researcher should determine who can best conduct a survey or interview. For example, age, gender, education, race, and other characteristics can influence a respondent's willingness to respond at all as well as the genuineness of thoughts that he or she will volunteer. The status of the administrator relative to the respondent (e.g., gender, age) may reflect these factors and can result in responses that are either positively or negatively biased.

The researcher should consider whether responses are likely to reflect authentic beliefs, attitudes, preferences, and so on. In some countries, for example, responding as an individual may be difficult because people may be accustomed to discussing issues with others before reaching a decision; if these people are asked to respond individually, they will likely respond as they think others would. In this case, the researcher may choose to rephrase questions in this way or to have a group discussion of the issues. In some cultures, people are uncomfortable giving negative answers because this might offend the questioner; they will likely respond to all questions in a relatively positive manner. In this case, the researcher might provide a scale or ranking mechanism to get meaningful information.

The researcher needs to examine the meaning of the questions asked in the context of the local environment. For example, a question about the attractiveness and potential future use of a product depends on familiarity with the product and previous use of similar products. Responses may reflect a culture's general acceptance of change, understanding of technology, perception of the company doing the survey, and willingness to respond openly to questions. These biases need to be understood in order to interpret research results meaningfully.

A classic example involves one of the oldest U.S. fast-food companies. This firm, having gained a great deal of domestic experience, decided to open overseas outlets. Sophisticated techniques were employed by the management, and the possible location sites were narrowed down to three addresses in Hamburg. Careful "traffic counts" were undertaken to determine the best location, and the most frequently passed site was then purchased. A store was built, but sales were surprisingly slow. Was the traffic count in error? No. In this case, while it was true that great numbers of people were passing by the location, hamburgers were not foremost on their minds – they went by the hamburger site only because a major bordello was located next door.

McDonalds's also chose an inappropriate location when it first expanded into Europe. The company opened an outlet in a suburb of Amsterdam but soon learned that to attract adequate local traffic, the store should have been downtown. Once the company moved into town, sales immediately improved.

(Ricks 1993, pp. 136–137)

Experimental Studies

Experimental studies are designed to test the impact of one particular variable on some other: One variable is changed and its effect on some other variable is examined. These studies are usually limited in scope and seek to control as many external factors as possible in order to focus on one item. For example, a company examining the effect of a change in product color on customer purchases could vary the color of its product and examine customer purchases relative to the changes in color. A wide range of experimental approaches can be used, including taste tests, blind comparisons of products, limited market introduction of a product, testing packaging, advertising, media, and so forth in a restricted environment. This type of research is appealing because it allows the company to get actual reactions to specific stimuli. To be effective, however, the environment must be very well understood because unexpected situational factors can have a major impact on the results of an experiment. Some examples of these factors follow.

A blind taste test (i.e., one in which the respondents do not know which product is which) comparing two products may be influenced by the color associated with the options. Certain colors are more attractive in some locations than others, the people tend to choose the option that is more colorfully attractive when they are uncertain or otherwise indifferent. This means that results of these tests are questionable unless the researcher is aware of these possible confounding effects and has controlled for them (e.g., by alternating the use of various colors).

Limited introduction of a new product can be influenced by extraneous events occurring in a particular location. In a country in which most of the population celebrates the Christian Lenten season by abstinent behavior, the pre-Lenten festivities are usually lavish and extravagant carnival celebrations. Therefore, many products tested in the pre-Lenten period are likely to appear to be popular but may fail in year-round markets.

Taste tests can be influenced by what people take for granted about the product being tested. Taste tests by Knorr, a Swiss food company, of its dry soups in the United States indicated interest, but sales were low when the product was introduced. The respondents had not realized that the product being tested was a dry soup that would take considerable preparation; consumers liked the taste and responded on that basis only. The market test had overlooked the U.S. tendency to avoid dry soups.

Consumer Panels

Consumer panels are made up of a group of consumers who give their opinions on various aspects of the marketing approach. This type of research relies on the reasoned judgment of a group of people selected to represent typical consumers. Companies may employ individuals or families they believe are representative of their customers to test and react to various marketing strategies and tactics, including products, packaging, media, advertising, distribution, price, and so on. Some companies also organize focus groups, consisting of a group of selected people brought together for the special purpose of testing and reacting to specified proposed marketing strategies and tactics.

Consumer panels can provide particularly useful information if the firm is confident that the information it is receiving is reliable and representative; that is, the panels provide information that is realistic and they are made up of people who are actually typical consumers. Even domestically this may be difficult to evaluate; however, in the familiar domestic environment, the market researcher has a fair degree of confidence in the chosen consumer panel. In a foreign environment, it can be difficult to obtain support from people who would be willing to act in such a capacity and much more difficult to assess whether those who do agree in fact are representative and will provide frank information in the company of others.

Customer Profile

When deciding whether to offer a particular product or service, firms must understand potential customers' needs and wants. To understand them, the firm's research should include a profile of the customers to whom it expects to appeal. The customer profile should include consumers' lifestyles, economic constraints, values, attitudes, tastes, differences in what they buy, when they buy, where they buy, and who makes the decisions.

Consumers' lifestyles may vary within a country and among countries. Firms must consider this fact particularly before entering an international market. "It is the international differences in buyer behavior, rather than the similarities, which pose stumbling blocks to successful international marketing. Thus the differences must receive disproportionate attention from the marketer" (Terpstra 1988).

Another company tried to market aerosol-spray furniture polish in one of the less-developed countries. Analysis of the local average income levels suggested that the surrounding population could afford the product. This type of data, though, can be misleading when most of the wealth is concentrated and owned by a few. Therefore, average income levels can erroneously indicate that many people in a population can afford the product. In this particular case, only a few individuals could afford the "luxury" of an aerosol-spray polish. Even they, however, were not very interested in the product; they did not believe in such labor-savings devices for their servants.   (Ricks 1993, p. 138)

Managers have made many mistakes because they failed to realize that these factors differ from country to country. Because of these differences, companies may need to adapt their products to allow for these different factors. Such adaptations may take place in the product itself: its taste, style, package, or price; its promotion; or its distribution method.

Promotion

The appropriate promotion of products should be determined in light of local conditions; for example, the media available for promotion, the need to reach local target markets, and the ability to be understood by and appeal to that market.

Product promotion has probably caused the most corporate headaches in the field of marketing. The old adage "if something can go wrong, it will" seems especially true for promoters. This is probably because promotion, of all aspects of marketing, is most dependent on cultural understanding for effectiveness. The promotional mix, the media employed, timing, images, and names, among others, all contribute to an effective promotional campaign. Achieving the optimal mix of these is complex in any situation, but it is far more complex in an unfamiliar one. Mistakes here are very dramatic and particularly effective in illustrating the problems and complexities of international promotional efforts. The following are some problems that the marketer may encounter in designing a promotional campaign.

If a theme works exceedingly well in one country, the firm naturally would like to use it elsewhere. This can be ineffective, however, because good themes are often culturally oriented. Consider the very popular and successful Marlboro cigarette advertisements. The Marlboro man projects a strong masculine image in America, but not everywhere – attempts to use it were unsuccessful in Hong Kong, where the totally urban people did not identify at all with horseback riding in the countryside. Philip Morris changed its ad to reflect a Hong Kong-style Marlboro man. He is still a virile cowboy, but he is younger, better dressed, and owns a truck.

Failure to recognize local weather conditions can also foul up a multinational's promotional campaign. One firm, for example, which tried to use a typical U.S.-type radio advertisement to promote its swim suits in Latin America, boasted that one could wear the suit all day in the sun and it would not fade. The local Latins, however, were unable to understand the point because the weather is always too hot to stay in the sun for very long.

The message may be right but in the wrong place. One company rented space beside the road leading from the airport into Buenos Aires with the message, appropriately translated, "with [brand name] you'd be there already." The problem here was that the message was written on a cemetery wall.

Symbols or logos have caused headaches for companies as well. One firm used a large deer as a sign of masculinity in Brazil, but one Brazilian street name for a homosexual is deer. Another firm used an owl in its Indian promotion, but in India the owl is a symbol of bad luck.

Determining What to Adapt

When marketing at the international level, a firm must decide not only what product to sell but whether the product must be adapted to particular markets to meet consumer needs. Necessary adaptations may affect the physical characteristics of a product (its taste, style, or packaging), its price, or the way it is distributed. The following sections discuss these aspects of the market mix.

Physical Product

Some products require substantial technical modification to work in new locations. If the electrical current available is different or if measurement systems differ, then products must be adapted to conform to local conditions. A British firm, for example, experienced difficulty selling in Japan until it remodeled its product 1/16 inch to conform to Japanese specifications. Such modifications may be costly to the company and can affect the profitability of a particular product in a particular location; therefore, it is important that the firm conduct the proper research to be able to assess the need for such adaptations before deciding to enter a new market.

General Motors of Canada likewise experienced major technical problems with one of its cars in Iraq. It shipped 13,500 Chevrolet Malibu automobiles there only to discover that the cars were mechanically unfit for the hot and dusty climate. Iraq refused delivery of the remaining 12,000 autos that had been ordered until GM modified the vehicles so that they would work reliably. GM tripled its number of engineers and mechanics in Baghdad, but by the time the company figured out that supplementary air filters and different clutches would eliminate the mechanical failures, it began to encounter political problems. Twelve thousand automobiles specially designed for desert driving were then left collecting snow in Canada while GM waited for the political dust to settle.   (Ricks 1993, p. 22–23)

Some modifications may be relatively simple. Companies have found, for example, that filter-tipped cigarettes do not sell well in the less-developed countries. Consumers are less aware of the health risks and, with relatively low life expectancy, the threat of lung cancer is not a major concern. Filters therefore are seen as unnecessary additions that add to the cost and detract from the taste. In such cases, the only modification needed may be removal of the filter with an accompanying reduction in price.

Taste

One physical variable of a product that often requires modification is taste. Even the famous McDonald's hamburger has had to be modified to appeal to consumers in different parts of the world. Often all that is required is a subtle change, but, without this, sales may slump. The change may reflect a local preference for sweetness, saltiness, or spiciness. It seems that even minor taste variations can affect the way people respond to a product.

Among products affected by variation in taste preferences are cigarettes, which are generally blended to suit local tastes; soft drinks, which are usually modified for various locations; soups, which often have to be adapted; and coffee, which may have to be blended differently for different locations.

Style

Style is another important aspect of the market mix that can influence consumer choices. Failure to reflect local style can cause consumers to reject a product. In the 1960s, for example, Ford introduced "American" features into its European cars and found that sales slumped; once they returned to cars produced to reflect European styling preferences, sales improved in response.

Reactions to colors and objects can also differ. The same color or object is often interpreted very differently in various parts of the world:

▶ Green is popular in many Moslem countries but is associated with disease in some countries with dense, green jungles.
▶ Black signifies death to Americans and many Europeans, but in Japan and many other Asian countries white represents death, in Latin America purple is associated with death, and along the Ivory Coast death is signified by dark red.
▶ Pink is seen as the most feminine color in North America, but much of the rest of the world considers yellow to be.
▶ White lilies are used for funerals in many countries with a British influence, but in Mexico they are used to lift superstitious spells.
▶ Yellow flowers represent death or disrespect in Mexico, but in France and the Soviet Union they signify infidelity.
▶ The scythe or sickle is associated with death in Europe but represents the state in communist countries.
▶ Dogs and cats are thought of as pets in North America, but in the Far East they are not kept in the house and often are regarded as food.
▶ The number 13 is superstitiously avoided in North America; Japan's mystic number is 4 because the word *four* in Japanese also sounds like the Japanese word for death.

Clearly, these examples indicate that the color of a product as well as methods used to present the product to the consumer can have a critical impact on how the product is viewed and consequently whether it is accepted. To avoid costly mistakes and the wasted time involved in changing products after the fact, companies should invest the time and money prior to product introduction to research these product-specific factors.

Packaging

In many markets, the product may be quite acceptable but still may not sell well if housed in an inappropriate package. Packages play two key roles for a product: They protect the product and they promote it. Packages that require long-distance shipping must be capable of withstanding the journey. Many companies have exported their products only to experience the return of crushed and partially empty containers. Others have tried to ship perishable goods via means requiring months for delivery. Still others have placed goods in packages unable to withstand moisture, extreme cold, high heat, or other unique conditions. In some climates, packages must be specially designed to ensure product survival. Quaker Oats, for example, uses special vacuum-sealed tins to protect its products in hot and humid countries.

Local storage conditions also vary, and the package must be an appropriate size and shape for effective storage. Coca-Cola tried to introduce the two-liter plastic bottle in Spain but discovered that few Spaniards had refrigerator doors with compartments large enough to accommodate a bottle that size.

Containers occasionally embarrass a company. U.S.-made medical containers drew a great deal of unwanted attention when they were used in Great Britain. The containers carried the instructions "Take off top and push in bottom." This message, considered harmless in the United States, bore sexual and humorous connotations for the British. Even something as innocuous as the wrapping used for shipment can cause problems. A New York exporter wrapped products destined for an Arab country in local newspapers; the Arab customer was arrested and the goods confiscated when an Arab customs inspector found the wrappings were Jewish newspapers.

Packaging changes in response to physical conditions of shipping and storing should be relatively easy to identify. Package modifications that are required to enhance a product's appeal to the consumer may be more difficult. These promotional modifications can be minor or fairly complex, but they are often critical for acceptance in foreign locations. The task of deciding on what modifications are needed is not an easy one but one that should not be overlooked.

Price

The appropriate prices of products should be determined in view of local conditions. Product prices should reflect the economic conditions of the country, the income level of the target market, the "normal" price of similar products, and the use to which the product is expected to be put. Companies price their products using a variety of factors, including costs, competitors' prices, image, and target market. The same factors are used to determine prices in foreign locations. The key is not to assume that the price charged at home should be the price charged in other locations, but to expect and assess the differences.

Costs are likely to differ from one location to another because of real differences in costs of inputs, transportation, promotion, and so on. The likely final cost of a product when it reaches the customer should be estimated and carefully assessed before deciding to introduce a new product; if the required cost is too high, the product is unlikely to be successful.

The difficulty in foreign locations is in anticipating all of the costs when the firm is not familiar with doing business in that environment. Setting an appropriate price for a product is often more difficult than it appears. If only one otherwise insignificant detail is overlooked or misjudged, trouble can develop. Consider the experience of one company trying to market cans of luncheon meat. To beat the prices of its competitors, the firm cut its prices slightly and rounded them off to easy-to-record numbers (e.g., $2.50). Sales were slow until the company discovered a local custom: Shopkeepers and salespeople knew that customers would not request the small change due when prices were not rounded (e.g., if the price was $2.69, the customer would pay $2.75). The higher-priced competitors' products, in effect, carried a "tip" for the salesperson, who therefore promoted those products.

Price negotiation can also prove to be tricky. If the company negotiators are unaware of local customs, inappropriate prices can result. This is best illustrated by examining the American and Japanese negotiation processes. As discussed in Chapter 10, American managers are accustomed to time-pressured decision making and are often given the authority to make final decisions; Japanese managers, on the other hand, prefer to negotiate more slowly and tend to make decisions by group consensus. In price negotiations involving American and Japanese negotiators, the American may quickly suggest a price, usually not the best one. When the Japanese do not respond immediately, the American interprets this as a negative response to the suggested price and offers a better one. When the Japanese still hesitate, the American may again change the price. The Japanese are not hesitating because the price is unacceptable, but the American who misinterprets silence ends up with a suboptimal price.

Exchange rates add another complexity to the task of setting prices. Companies can lose money because they have stated prices in a currency that has fluctuated. Similarly, failure to identify and analyze inflationary factors has hurt a number of companies. A German company, for example, agreed to a substantial Algerian construction contract. The price was set in Algerian currency and was fair at the time of the commitment, but due to inflation, local costs rose dramatically during the life of the contract. Unfortunately, the firm had failed to include protective price escalators in the original contract, and the Algerian partner made payments in the Algerian currency, which had declined in value. This double-barreled event cut out all of the company's expected profits and actually cost the firm millions of dollars.

Distribution

The methods used to get a firm's product from the production facility to the final customer or consumer can vary widely from one location to another, as discussed in Chapter 10. Distribution systems can vary for a number of reasons, including the following:

▶ Physical environmental factors – In remote areas delivery by small air cargo planes may be most appropriate; however, delivery by trucking systems to major cities may be better than air transportation

▶ Social customs – In some societies the Avon lady calling unexpectedly is acceptable; in others, it would be considered a breach of etiquette. (Note that Avon has found its "door-to-door" approach does work by boat along the Amazon).

▶ Availability of services – Where a good postal service exists, mail order is popular, but in its absence, mail order makes little sense

▶ Tradition – Where it is common to use intermediaries between the manufacturer and retailer, it is difficult to avoid such agents, even if they seem to add an unnecessary layer for a particular product.

The delivery systems to which we are accustomed at home often seem so obvious that it may be difficult to recognize that totally different systems may be required in other locations. An effective delivery system is a key aspect of getting a product to the customer, and companies cannot afford to overlook this aspect of their marketing mix.

Calculated Risks in International Marketing

Much of the previous discussion focuses on the firm's need to understand its international markets and adapt to them. This understanding and adaptation should not be interpreted as

A U.S. company discovered the importance of understanding the host's distribution system when it entered the Japanese market. Hoping to achieve optimum market penetration, the firm selected the best distribution networks of its Japanese partner and set up a single-level system of wholesalers. Even though the product sold well through the channels where distribution was achieved, market penetration was short of expectations because the needed national coverage was not available. Although the original decision to use the partner's best distribution networks appeared wise, the firm had failed to realize how numerous and diffuse the Japanese retail outlet networks are.

Another U.S. company experienced difficulties introducing its products in France. It tried to market its line of cosmetics through a chain store to achieve maximum market exposure while holding down marketing and distribution costs. In France, perfumers, small local retailers specializing in cosmetics, are traditionally considered the opinion makers, and the public relies heavily on the opinions of these perfumers. When the company bypassed them, the American company angered the perfumers to the extent that they discredited the American product and damaged the manufacturer's reputation in France.

Cigarettes in the United States are sold solely in packages but in many other countries they are sold one at a time. The retailer in such countries wants to receive the cigarettes in bulk, not in the smaller packages that would be appropriate in America. (Ricks 1983)

meaning that international firms should not try marketing approaches that are new to a particular location. International marketers often have the advantage of being familiar with alternative approaches, and they may be successful by using distinctive tactics. For example, Avon has found that its door-to-door sales force has been particularly effective in some locations, essentially because this tactic is an innovative distribution system. Innovative tactics need to be recognized as such. They should be used intentionally, based on a logical analysis of the situation and a recognition of the risks involved.

Effective international marketers benefit from the advantages of being international while avoiding the potential pitfalls of communicating in unfamiliar environments. It is important to recognize that the domestic marketer is often part of the marketplace; therefore, assumptions about the marketplace can be made with relative safety. In the international arena, assumptions about the marketplace are more likely to be incorrect, and hence, the risk associated with making them increases. Effective international marketing decision making recognizes the risks, evaluates them, and takes those risks only when they seem worthwhile.

Copeland and Griggs (1986) offer the following advice to American marketers in foreign countries:

▶ Ancient differences in national tastes or modes of doing business are not disappearing.
▶ Even on a clear day, you cannot see Belgium from New York.
▶ Sell to the customer (who is not always obvious).
▶ Identify national goals and promote national pride.
▶ Get local help in unfamiliar territory.
▶ Make personal contacts.
▶ Sell yourself before your products or services.
▶ Admit to being an American but one who is interested in the local culture.
▶ You may decide to adopt or ditch the local style, but you had better know what it is.
▶ Appeal to the right needs with the right benefits.

▶ Reflect the right values in advertising.

▶ Colors and symbols have meaning, often not the ones you think.

▶ A rose by any other name will not sell so well.

▶ Watch out for restrictions and practical problems.

Summary

International marketing activities present a major challenge to the international firm. There are opportunities to be taken advantage of and pitfalls to avoid. On the one hand, there are opportunities in terms of the potential for at least some global standardization as well as those presented by the unique character of different locations. On the other hand, the different nature of the foreign environment means that communication can be difficult, and it is easy for the firm to blunder under these conditions. This chapter includes a variety of blunders involving marketing activities. These serve to illustrate how important it is to pay careful attention to international marketing activities.

MINI-CASE
**How May We
Serve You?** ▶

Jean Marie has been with IFM for 10 years. During his time with the firm, he has seen sales go from $25 billion to $54 billion, all through internal growth except for two acquisitions, which together added about $10 billion in sales. Because he has been director of marketing in the French country operation for the past three years, he takes some pride in thinking that his market instincts have served him and IFM well. It was well known when he took over the French operation of this large multinational consumer products and food conglomerate headquartered in Zurich that the French market was the most challenging because of competitors like BSN. His desire for challenge and his desire to see IFM overtake its competitors in Europe made the job in France that much more appealing. In three years, Jean Marie had turned the French market around and IFM had increased its presence in four major product groups by more than anyone thought possible. As a consequence of his success, he was ready to take on another challenge. His desire coincided with the unexpected resignation of the vice-president in charge of personnel for all European operations.

The European operations represent more than 75 percent of IFM's sales worldwide. Unfortunately, its percentage of the total turnover is less than 50 percent. Therefore, while he was doing well in France, in terms of both sales and turnover, IFM in Europe was gaining only in terms of sales. His evaluation of the situation and what was happening in Europe convinced him that the personnel job would be not only the most challenging job he could have but also the most important to the firm. His 10 years of marketing experience in the United States with a major consumer products company combined with his 10 years with IFM persuaded him that, unless the firm focused even more on high-quality service, it would not increase turnover. He knew that high-quality service meant higher margins. He also knew that moving all their products and services upscale had great implications for personnel management. However, only one other person saw the situation the same way. The other person was the director of personnel in the firm's Spanish operation. This was largely due to the fact that personnel had always played a very minor role in the operations of the firm. Neither headquarters nor country managers thought personnel could do much for them – it never had done much other than take care of the payroll.

Jean Marie was determined to apply his marketing savvy to the personnel area. Thinking that personnel could market products and services just like the firm did, he reasoned that all he had to do was to ask the customers what they wanted and then provide them with goods and services that gave them real value. This is what he wants to see happen in his own operation and in the country operations. He is just not sure exactly where to start or what to do.

Source: Randall S. Schuler, research professor, Stern School of Business, New York University; used with the author's permission.

Discussion Issues

1. What products and services does a personnel department have that it can market to the company as a whole?
2. In a company operating in a variety of countries in Europe, can these personnel products and services be standardized for all country operations, or do they need to be adapted for each operation?
3. Identify three European countries and find specific information on these countries to illustrate the possibilities for standardization or the need for adaptation.

Discussion Questions

1. How are international marketing activities likely to differ from domestic marketing activities?
2. What are the major challenges faced by international marketers?
3. Why is research vital to the marketing process in international companies?
4. What problems are encountered most often in advertising in foreign locations? Discuss how these can be resolved.

Assignments

1. Select a product that is currently marketed in your domestic market. Now select a foreign country in which to market this product. Develop a marketing plan for this product in the foreign location: Consider product, packaging, price, distribution, and promotion.

2. In groups of four to six students, select a product and foreign country as in Assignment 1. Develop an advertising campaign for this country, including billboards, magazines, newspapers, radio, and TV, as appropriate. The group should produce actual advertisements and illustrate why they are appropriate for the country selected, as well as how they differ from advertisements in the domestic market.

3. Find advertisements for the same product for several different countries and identify the similarities and differences among them. Explain how these relate to characteristics of the countries.

4. In groups of four or five, select a product that the group believes could be marketed using largely standardized approaches around the world. Discuss the characteristics of the product that allow for standardization.

Selected References

Buzzell, R. D., and J. A. Quelch, *Multinational Marketing Management* (Reading, Mass.: Addison-Wesley, 1988).

Challenges, Ministry of Industry, Trade, and Technology, Toronto (Summer 1989), p. 22.

Copeland, L., and L. Griggs, *Going International – How to Make Friends and Deal Effectively in the Global Marketplace* (New York: Random House, 1985).

The Economist (December 24, 1989).

Globe and Mail, "Social Studies" (November 15, 1990), p. A24.

Jain, S. C., *International Marketing Management* (Boston: PWS-Kent, 1987).

Keegan, W. J., *Global Marketing Management* (Englewood Cliffs, N.J.: Prentice-Hall, 1989).

Lane, H. W., and T. Hildebrand, "How to Survive in U.S. Retail Markets," *Business Quarterly* (Winter 1990), pp. 62–66.

Levitt, T., "The Globalization of Markets," *Harvard Business Review* (May–June 1983).

Light, W. F., and J. W. Brown, "Competing Successfully in the International Marketplace," in H. W. Lane and J. J. DiStefano, *International Management Behavior* (Toronto: Nelson Canada, 1988), pp. 70–80.

Phatak, A., *International Dimensions of Management* (Boston: PWS-Kent, 1987).

Ricks, D. A., *Big Business Blunders – Mistakes in Multinational Marketing* (Homewood, Ill.: Dow Jones-Irwin, 1983).

Ricks, D. A., *Blunders in International Business* (Cambridge, Mass.: Blackwell Publishers Inc., 1993).

Stanton, W. J., *Fundamentals of Marketing* (New York: McGraw-Hill, 1978).

Terpstra, V., *International Dimensions of Marketing* (Boston: PWS-Kent, 1988).

United Nations Centre on Transnational Corporations, *Transnational Corporations in World Development – Trends and Prospects* (New York: UNCTC, 1988).

CHAPTER ▼ 13

Operations Management in International Companies

LEARNING OBJECTIVES

After reading this chapter, you should be able to

▶ Distinguish between goods and services and discuss their role in the global business environment.

▶ Identify and discuss the main operational decisions facing international companies.

▶ Describe the operations function in an international company.

KEY TERMS

- Goods
- Services
- MFN treatment
- Procure
- Degree of vertical integration
- Make versus buy trade-offs

- Location of suppliers
- Just-in-time inventory systems
- Location of facilities
- Concentrated production strategy
- Dispersed production strategy
- Logistics networks

THOUGHT STARTERS

- In Grand Rapids, Larry Bratschie, marketing executive for a large manufacturer of office furniture, once hosted a key group of Japanese customers. Knowing that the Japanese were great gift givers, Bratschie purchased silver pocket knives for each guest. He had them carefully wrapped Japanese-style (pastel colored paper, no bows) and positioned at each place at the dining table. As the Japanese opened their gifts, each guest suddenly went mute.

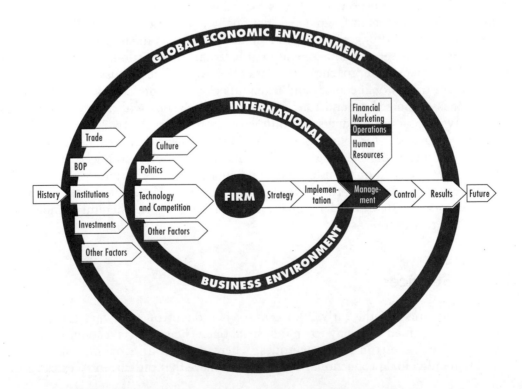

Each carefully set the knife back in the gift box and stared stiffly into the distance. As the guests left the dinner table, the gifts remained behind, untouched. Later, Bratschie learned that in the Japanese culture the act of presenting a knife as a gift can be a symbol of suicide.

(Axtell 1990, pp. 1–2)

Introduction

The purpose of this chapter is to examine operational decisions from an international perspective. Operational decisions can be either strategic or tactical: "big" strategic decisions regarding plant locations, size of facilities, and so on; "small," or day-to-day, tactical decisions regarding production schedules, delivery timetables, and so on.

As a result, operational management sometimes takes a long-term view and at other times a short-term view. Strategic operational decisions often lock a company into a particular arrangement for many years, but tactical operational decisions need to be made quickly with the current situation as the paramount consideration. This dual nature of operational management needs to be kept in mind throughout the discussions in this chapter.

Managers of international companies often face another dichotomy when making operational decisions. They must make a trade-off between a global perspective and a multinational perspective. The global perspective leads companies to consider the availability and costs of resources around the world in order to choose optimal sites for operations and results in pressures for unified, globally rationalized operations. The multinational perspective leads companies to tailor operations to fit the unique aspects of various locations and to adapt company operations to local requirements and results in fragmented, nationally adapted operations. Both approaches have advantages and disadvantages that depend on the individual company, industry, and market characteristics, as well as the available operational locations. International companies combine the unified and fragmented approaches in a variety of ways. The discussions in this chapter focus on how these operational choices and trade-offs can be made.

This chapter is organized around four major topics. It begins with a discussion of goods and services as two classes of products and differentiates between the two. This is followed by a discussion of procurement (or sourcing) decisions. Procurement decisions are those about the source, timing, and means of obtaining needed inputs. This section is followed by a discussion of production issues focusing on location, type, and coordination of facilities. The final section deals with delivery of the finished product to the customer and logistical networks as they apply to the entire operational system. The diagram presented in Exhibit 13.1 is helpful in understanding the framework for this chapter.

Goods and Services

The industrial revolution of the early 20th century is thought of as having transformed the world from a craft-oriented economy to an industrial one. The industrial economy is described as producing physical goods in large quantities, whereas the craft economy had focused on small-scale, often individual production. Many people believe that the current Western economy

EXHIBIT 13.1
Operational Flows

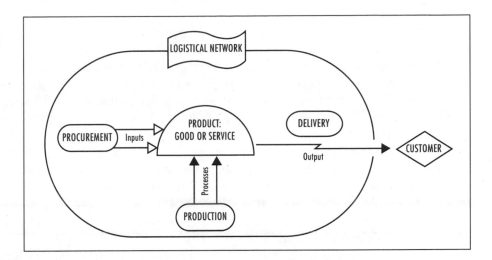

is a postindustrial one, often described as a service economy, devoted to providing intangible benefits or services. This section of the chapter defines goods and services and their relationship and considers the role of services in international business. The distinction between goods and services is identified because procurement, production, and delivery decisions can often differ depending on whether the decisions relate to a good, a service, or a combination of goods and services.

Products are defined here broadly as a firm's salable outputs. These can be anything including nuts and bolts, high-tech scientific equipment, over-the-counter medicine, managerial know-how, technology, and energy. One way to differentiate among such an array of products is to categorize them as goods or services. This distinction is used in this chapter. When reference is made to *products,* the term includes both goods and services. Where a distinction is made, one or the other category is referred to specifically.

Goods are defined here as physical products, **services** as intangible products. Some examples of goods and services serve to illustrate the differences and relationships between the two.

Services often accompany goods. If you buy a washing machine, you may also buy a service contract that guarantees that you will be provided with maintenance and repair on the machine. In this case, the washing machine is a physical product that you can see and touch; therefore, it is a good. The service contract is intangible and its specific form is not easily identifiable; therefore, it is a service.

Services may compete with goods. You can choose to purchase your own computer or you can pay for a computer service to fill your computer needs. In this case, the computer is the good and the computer service is a service.

Some services are by their nature distinct from goods. Accounting and financial services fall into this category. The services of an accountant or financial adviser have no attendant good associated with them.

The difference between goods and services is not always clear because they can be closely connected; for example, a haircut is generally thought of as intangible and thus a service, but it can also be thought of as resulting in a physical product, the finished hairstyle. Nevertheless, a haircut is usually classified as a service. The individual and personal character of service products is often one means to classify services.

This individual, personal nature of services is very important in the international context. By their very nature, expectations regarding good service are quite likely to differ from one location to another because of national and cultural characteristics. Expectations regarding service characteristics as well as service levels both may differ from location to location. Service characteristics refer to the attributes of the service; service level refers to the quality of service performance. For example, a service contract for a washing machine might include regular maintenance, emergency repair, and replacement of faulty parts; these would be the characteristics of the service. Service level would focus on the timing and quality of the maintenance, repairs, and replacement.

These examples also can be used to illustrate how services are likely to differ because of national and cultural variations.

In the case of the washing machine and the service contract, the machine (physical good) may have to be modified for use in different countries, but the physical nature of the modifications means that they can be objectively identified. The service (intangible good) that is expected and accepted, because of national and cultural characteristics, tends to be more subjective, and therefore, the modifications may be more difficult to identify. For example, in some locations, a lone serviceman may be allowed into the home to service the machine, and in others not. In some locations, a woman as serviceperson would be welcomed, in others not. In some locations, immediate service would be expected, in others not.

In the case of the computer and computer service, the computer (physical good) will be relatively similar from one location to another except for technical changes; the computer service (intangible good) that is appropriate may differ significantly in various locations. For example, in some locations a computer service might provide basic output of raw data for the customer's analysis; in others a complete analysis and discussion of data may be more appropriate. In some locations computer service is extremely sensitive and confidential; in others information is largely public knowledge.

In the case of accounting services, the accepted accounting principles and procedures may vary from country to country, depending on local legislation, regulations, and culture. Following the particular country's accepted practices is inherent to the success or failure of the service. For example, some accounting procedures used for American firms are not acceptable for British firms, and their use in the United Kingdom would make the service totally undesirable from the British perspective.

Services are an increasingly important component of the world's economy, and trade in services increased dramatically through to 1990 as illustrated in Exhibit 13.2. This fact is very important to the multinational firm because, as the previous examples illustrate, services are subject to the impact of cultural and national variations. Trade in services is expected to increase further with the implementation of the General Agreement on Trade in Services (GATS). The GATS is summarized in Exhibit 13.3.

Although goods and services differ in some respects, decisions regarding their procurement and delivery are often similar. The following discussion examines these decisions as they relate to both sets of products. The term *product* is used throughout to refer to both goods and services.

EXHIBIT 13.2   **Another Sort of Trade**

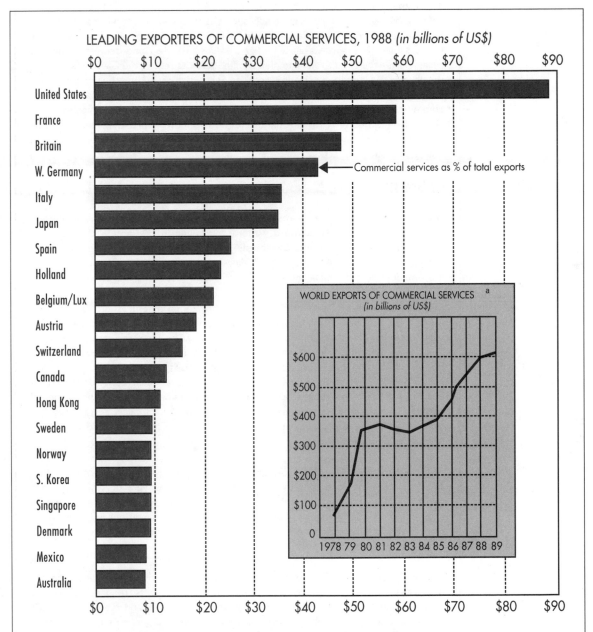

LEADING EXPORTERS OF COMMERCIAL SERVICES, 1988 *(in billions of US$)*

Commercial services as % of total exports

WORLD EXPORTS OF COMMERCIAL SERVICES
(in billions of US$)

EXHIBIT 13.3
The GATS

The General Agreement Trade in Services (GATS) is the first multilateral, legally enforceable agreement covering trade and investment in the service sectors. The GATS also provides a specific legal basis for future negotiations aimed at eliminating barriers that discriminate against foreign services providers and deny them market access. Given the breadth and complexity of the services sector, the GATS provides for the progressive liberation of trade in services. Successive rounds may be commenced at five-year intervals to allow improvements in market access and national treatment commitments and to allow liberalization of most-favored-nation exemptions. The GATS also sets out terms for negotiation of several framework provisions that currently contain no substantive disciplines such as subsidies, government procurement, and emergency safeguard actions.

Key Provisions

Framework. The principal elements of the GATS framework agreement include most-favored-nation **(MFN) treatment**, national treatment, market access, transparency, and the free flow of payments and transfers. The rules embodied in the framework are augmented by sectoral annexes dealing with issues affecting financial services, movement of personnel, enhanced telecommunications services, and aviation services.

Schedules. Schedules of commitments include horizontal measures such as commitments regarding movement of personnel and service providers. The schedules also include commitments in specific sectors, such as professional services (accounting, architecture, engineering), other business services (computer services, rental and leasing, advertising, market research, consulting, security services), communications (value-added telecommunications, couriers, audiovisual services), construction, distribution (wholesale and retail trade, franchising), educational services, environmental services, financial services (banking, securities, insurance), health services, and tourism services. Maritime and civil aviation commitments were also scheduled by a small number of countries.

National Treatment. The GATS contains a strong national treatment provision that requires a country to accord to services and services suppliers of other countries treatment no less favorable than that accorded to its own services and services suppliers. It specifically requires GATS countries to ensure conditions in the domestic market against foreign firms in scheduled services sectors; that is, those listed in its schedule of commitments.

Market Access. The GATS also includes a market access provision that incorporates disciplines on six types of discriminatory measures governments frequently impose to limit competition or new entry in their markets. These laws and regulations – such as restrictions on the number of firms allowed in the market, economic "needs tests" and mandatory local incorporation rules – are often used to bar or restrict market access by foreign firms. A country must either eliminate these barriers in any sector that it includes in its schedule of commitments or negotiate with its trading partners for their limited retention.

Additional Provisions. For service companies that benefit from sectoral commitments, the framework also guarantees the free flow of current payments and transfers. The provision on transparency requires prompt publication of all relevant measures covered by the agreement. The GATS allows countries to enter into free trade arrangements with other countries and to establish mutual recognition agreements for licensing, qualifications, or standards. Disputes over barriers to trade in services will be settled under the new strengthened rules of the Dispute Settlement Understanding.

The GATS also recognizes the right to regulate or introduce new regulations. Exceptions to the GATS are provided for national security, safety, human, animal and plant life or health, prevention of fraudulent practices, protection of privacy, and measures taken pursuant to tax laws.

Subject to negotiations, specific laws or regulatory practices may be exempted from MFN treatment, by listing them in an annex provided for that purpose. This mechanism allows countries to preserve their ability to use unilateral measure as a means of encouraging trade liberalization.

Source: Information provided by Michael P. Ryan, Georgetown University School of Foreign Service, at a workshop of Historically Black Universities and Colleges. June 1995, St. Kitts.

Procurement Issues

To provide a product, a firm needs to **procure,** or obtain, certain inputs. These inputs include raw materials, labor, and energy, among others. The firm must decide on the best source for these inputs, the most effective means to obtain them, and the timing of acquiring them. The international firm's objective is to obtain the best inputs from around the world to produce components and products efficiently. The firm must consider two major issues relative to the source and means of inputs: the degree of vertical integration desirable and the national origin of inputs and their suppliers. Each of these aspects will be discussed in terms of the trade-offs associated with various choices. A discussion of supply timing issues then follows.

Degree of Vertical Integration

The **degree of vertical integration** refers to the degree to which a firm is its own supplier and market. The focus in terms of procurement is on the supplier side. In effect, therefore, decisions regarding vertical integration are **make versus buy trade-offs** or decisions. At one extreme, a firm can seek to make all of its own inputs and be its own supplier. At the other extreme, it can choose to buy virtually all the inputs it needs and rely on others as suppliers. Partial integration is also possible, with some inputs bought and others made.

In simple terms, a major benefit of making inputs (backward integration), is the degree of control that is maintained over inputs (in terms of costs, quality, timeliness, etc.); some of the main drawbacks are the investment and expertise needed to provide these inputs. One benefit of buying is the ability to choose among suppliers and avoid the risks associated with the suppliers' businesses; one drawback is the reliance on others for needed inputs. Of course, other benefits and drawbacks might be evaluated, but these examples give the reader some understanding of the kinds of trade-offs that exist. The trade-offs associated with this decision are summarized in Exhibit 13.4.

EXHIBIT 13.4
Some Make versus Buy Trade-Offs: (In-Sourcing versus Out-Sourcing Trade-Offs)

	Make	**Buy**
Advantages	Control over costs	Choice among suppliers
	Control over quality	Avoid their business risks
	Control over delivery	No additional investment
	Not competing for supply	No need to learn about a new
	Develop new expertise	business
Drawbacks	Increased investment	Reliance on outsiders
	Need for expertise	Need to compete for supplies
	Need for management	Supplier may go out of business
	May be inefficient	
	Overspecialization	

The make versus buy decision is complex in an international company because it must be made relative to both the company as a whole and each of its subsidiaries. Some of the complexities are examined in the following discussion.

Most simply, three make versus buy options can be considered:

1. A subsidiary can be vertically integrated itself; that is, it makes its own inputs.
2. A subsidiary can be vertically integrated with other parts of the company; that is, it purchases inputs from other subsidiaries or the parent.
3. No backward integration occurs; that is, supplies are obtained outside of the company.

These are clear-cut options that will be considered here for the sake of simplicity. The real world is not likely to be as simple as this, and many possible variations and combinations can be found.

Each of these options can have quite different consequences for the subsidiary, its associated subsidiaries, and the company as a whole. The following simple example illustrates some of these consequences.

Consider a Brazilian wire producer with one subsidiary in Jamaica that assembles printed circuit (PC) boards and a second subsidiary in the United States that produces the wire used in the PC boards. The Brazilian company has the choice of supplying the Jamaican subsidiary with wire from the U.S. subsidiary, its Brazilian headquarters, or from external sources. The decision has consequences for each of the parties and the "best" decision can be different for each party in relation to its particular objectives.

The Jamaican subsidiary probably wants a stable and cost-effective source of supply, the U.S. subsidiary likely wants sales at the best price that it can obtain, and the Brazilian parent wants to maximize its overall returns while minimizing its exposure to risk. The difficulty is that these objectives may be achieved in different ways, with different benefits or drawbacks for the various entities, as the following illustrates:

▶ The Jamaican subsidiary may want to purchase wire from the U.S. subsidiary because of its quality and availability, but the U.S. subsidiary may be able to get a better price elsewhere.

▶ The Brazilian parent may choose to sell wire to the Jamaican subsidiary at a high price to maximize profits in Brazil, but the Jamaican subsidiary might prefer to purchase inexpensive local wire to maximize its local profits.

▶ The U.S. subsidiary may want to sell to the Jamaican subsidiary because this gives it a known and captive market, but the Jamaican subsidiary might prefer to have the flexibility of buying wire outside the company to get the best possible price and quality.

These are only a few of the possible conflicts that can arise in such a situation. To complicate the decision further, more than just dollar expenditures and returns should be considered. The decisions have political implications as well. For example, guidelines and regulations in many countries encourage or specify the use of local suppliers or give preference to suppliers from favored trading partners. All of these considerations must be balanced in making the final choice.

In addition, as discussed in Chapter 7, the company's political risk management strategy may promote or discourage the use of certain suppliers. This has to be factored into the decision as well. In the situation described, the Jamaican government may encourage the use of local suppliers, the U.S. government may have incentives associated with exports to the Caribbean, and the Brazilian parent may believe it can minimize its political risk exposure if it controls supplies to Jamaica from Brazil. Decisions made in terms of the political situation in one location can also have negative repercussions at home and elsewhere. For example, if the Brazilian parent obtained some of its raw materials from Cuba, and these in turn became components in the PC boards assembled in Jamaica and shipped to the United States, this indirect association with Cuba could have negative consequences for the U.S. subsidiary selling in the United States.

The example used here is a rather simple one, involving only three locations and one input. For international companies the situation can be far more complex, involving a large number of locations, inputs, and potential suppliers.

The Body Shop was founded in England in 1976. It is now an international company producing, distributing, and selling skin and hair products in Canada, Europe, Japan, and the United States, as well as elsewhere in the world. The company sells itself as, foremost, an ethical company. Margot Franssen, president of the Body Shop Canada (in a talk to the Canadian Association of Women Executives in Toronto, September 13, 1989) explained that the products are biodegradable and have not been tested on animals; they are sold in refillable and recyclable containers; the company operates with a nonexploitive approach.

The company identifies ingredients currently used in many Third World countries as beauty products and incorporates them into its products. Worldwide operations and the unique approach have led to an interesting supply system. The system has included the following:

▶ work with the World Bank to obtain raw ingredients from countries where their purchases will do the most economic good
▶ establishment of two Body Shop boys' towns in India for destitute children; the children make Body Shop foot rollers and grow bananas for banana hair conditioner and are paid a "first world price to third world children"
▶ purchase and operation of a previously abandoned soap factory in a Scottish town to provide employment where little had existed
▶ a project with New Brunswick native Indians to provide gift baskets and thus alleviate a 95 percent unemployment rate.

Clearly, it is difficult to reconcile the varied objectives and views that are likely to have an impact on an international company's choice of suppliers. One approach is to consider the problem initially from the overall corporate efficiency point of view and then develop a procurement model based on costs and efficiencies. This model can be used as a basis on which to build. Final decisions can be adjusted based on national and political characteristics as well as local, regional, and headquarters' objectives and management preferences. In this way, the trade-offs can be clearly identified and the drawbacks estimated and compared with the benefits.

Overall, the international firm's aim is to obtain inputs from around the world in an efficient manner. The firm wants to ensure that inputs of a desired standard are available when needed and at a competitive cost. International firms have many supply options available to them; this can give them a competitive advantage. At the same time, the variety of options increases the complexity of the procurement decision. This complexity means that the most efficient procurement decision is not always practical. The procurement decision in an international company, therefore, often is a combination of objective programming models and subjective judgments.

National Origins

The vertical integration decision necessarily involves decisions regarding **location of suppliers**, as the previous examples showed, as well as other considerations. In selecting suppliers, whether internal or external, international companies can often choose among suppliers from different nations. This provides both opportunities and difficulties.

Opportunities arise because the firm has a large base of suppliers from which to select. Suppliers from different locations may offer variations in quality and service; therefore, the firm may be able to match suppliers to its specific needs more exactly than if it were limited to suppliers from the same country of origin. These variations in quality and service can also be the cause of difficulties because the quality or service offered by suppliers in foreign locations may differ from the company's expectations. Prior to selecting a foreign supplier, the firm must be sure that it has thoroughly investigated the foreign firm's ability to provide the desired inputs.

Specifications and regulations are also part of this decision. Variations in national standards can be an important consideration in choosing a supplier. The supplier must comply with its local standards, which may not correspond with the requirements for another location. National origin of suppliers can have political and social implications as well. Certain countries may be looked on unfavorably and any association with suppliers in those countries can have negative repercussions. The following illustrates these points.

The United States does not use the metric system of measurement while most other countries do – this causes numerous complications for companies that must convert inches to centimeters, gallons to liters, Fahrenheit to Celsius, and so on. The conversion can be crucial when dealing with parts that must fit with precision.

Consumer boycotts have often been organized against a company's products because the company uses inputs that originate in a foreign location that is viewed negatively by consumers.

Moving products from one country to another can mean moving them through additional countries. This movement complicates the procurement issue because these other countries' political relationships, regulations, and dependability must all be taken into account. Even relatively minor problems that occur in an intermediary country can disrupt an otherwise

Canadian consumers wanting to take advantage of lower car prices in the United States can run into difficulties because U.S. cars do not comply with Canadian standards.

▶ Americans accept passive seat restraints (e.g., air bags or automatic seat belts), while the Canadian government requires active restraints (seat belts that the user straps on).
▶ Canada requires an anchoring point for baby (jumper) seats; the United States does not.
▶ The two countries have different requirements for bumper strength.
▶ Canada requires daytime running lights (i.e., headlights that turn on with the ignition), but the United States used to require headlights that could be turned off. (The use of headlights was actually illegal in certain circumstances in the United States, such as in the tunnel between Detroit and Windsor.)

efficient and effective procurement system; therefore, the potential impact of third countries in transactions should be carefully examined in making sourcing decisions.

Problems arising in intermediary countries can be particularly difficult to deal with because both the supplier and the buyer may be unfamiliar with the third country. Companies are generally reasonably well versed in terms of the environments in their home country and thus are well equipped to operate in this environment and solve problems as they arise. It is much more difficult to find solutions to problems in an unfamiliar environment. If a Polish supplier of raw materials is selling to a French company, each partner in the transaction operates in both a familiar environment and an unfamiliar one. For the Polish firm, the Polish environment is familiar and can be dealt with reasonably effectively. The firm also faces an unfamiliar environment in France and probably relies on its French partner to deal with that environment. The reverse is true for the French company, which relies on its partner in the unfamiliar Polish environment and is more effective in its home environment of France. If the transaction is complicated by the need to ship the materials through a third country, such as Germany, neither the Polish nor the French company is on home ground and both may find that problems in this third country are particularly difficult to solve. They cannot rely on their instinctive know-how or on established patterns. In this situation, the companies need to turn to other parties with the needed expertise in the third country or to develop the expertise themselves. This necessity adds to the cost of doing business together.

A company in the United Kingdom publishes a magazine with contributors from around the world. Articles from contributors are supplied electronically. For a contribution from Hong Kong to reach the publisher, it must pass through communication lines located in a variety of countries. The success of this supply system depends to a large extent on the intermediary countries that allow the use of their facilities for the communication.

Many Canadian companies rely on inputs from Mexican border factories – products are produced in Mexico and shipped across the United States and into Canada. This supply system works very efficiently much of the time but can be affected by factors outside the control of either the Mexican supplier or the Canadian buyer; for example, U.S. government regulations regarding the transportation of certain materials may cause problems.

The most efficient supply route from Syria to Iran might be through Iraq, but during periods of war between Iran and Iraq, such a supply route is clearly impractical.

Timing Issues

The timing of shipments and of receipt of supplies is also an important consideration. It is essentially an inventory issue, and companies can choose to maintain needed inputs in minimal stocks, in large stocks, or in amounts in between. The trade-offs relate to shipping costs, carrying costs, and risks of being out of stock of needed items. All companies face these issues, and inventory models have been designed to identify optimum inventory levels.

International companies find that the situation is more complex, however, because of the necessary border crossings. These border crossings can lead to unanticipated delays in transporting products that cannot always be factored into the inventory equation. The following is an example of the potential difficulties.

Many U.S. and Canadian auto plants adopted a **"just-in-time" inventory system** in the late 1980s. This system relies on suppliers getting parts to the plants just in time to be used by the plant. In essence, the auto manufacturers do not keep any inventory on hand. This system is very cost efficient, and because of the trade agreements between Canada and the United States, parts suppliers in both countries are used, and parts cross the Canadian-U.S. border regularly. In 1990, Canadian independent truckers established a blockade of major border crossings on several occasions to protest Canadian trucking regulations. As a result, the auto plants had no just-in-time delivery of parts and several were forced to shut down for several hours and even days until deliveries resumed.

Nigeria though, probably experienced the largest purchasing blunder. Due to increased oil revenues that resulted from the sharp rise of oil prices in the mid-1970s, Nigeria began to initiate major modernization programs. An economically minded bureaucrat decided to purchase, mostly from other countries, the total amount of cement needed to construct all of the new buildings being planned. Soon the cement began to arrive by the shipload. The dock workers were unable to unload the cement as fast as it arrived, so the ships were forced to await their turn for unloading. Within weeks, there were so many shiploads of unloaded cement that someone computed the length of time required to unload all of the ships. Even with an expanded dock in Lagos, it was discovered that the 20 million tons of cement could not be fully unloaded for 40 years! Much of the cement had to be dumped overboard; the cost to hold the ships until unloading was greater than the cost of reordering the cement.   (Ricks 1993, pp. 108–109)

The efficient management of supply networks can contribute greatly to a company's ability to compete internationally; however, the previous discussion illustrates some of the complexities inherent in such a network. Designing and managing an effective international supply network require both science and subjective judgment. Scientific linear programming models can be used to identify optimum solutions and to serve as the basis for establishing a supply network. To function in the real world of national boundaries, however, these solutions may need to be modified based on human judgment, which is often subjective in nature. A globally efficient sourcing network means that the international company is functioning as a global citizen in essence, but this network may not fit with the rest of the world, where local concerns can be paramount. International companies are faced with the need to find a balance between global and local needs.

Fruehauf, a U.S. truck manufacturer, sold truck bodies to a French firm through its French subsidiary. The French firm then finished the trucks and sold them to the People's Republic of China. The U.S. government took action against Fruehauf for selling trucks to China, then an outlawed destination. Consequently, this U.S. behavior caused the French government to seize control of Fruehauf's French subsidiary. France believed that Fruehauf had to honor its contracts – even if it meant selling parts that eventually ended up in China, an acceptable destination to the French. Not only did Fruehauf lose money, but the company became the unwanted center of a highly charged, public debate in France concerning the role of America and its firms in France. At that point, it was clearly a no-win situation that would take years to overcome.

(Ricks 1993, p. 130)

Production Issues

The previous discussion focused on acquiring inputs needed for a product. We now focus on decisions related to converting inputs into final product; that is, on the locations and types of production facilities, as well as on coordination among these facilities. We'll review different operational strategies that firms can choose and the cost/benefit trade-offs associated with these strategies. The specific choice of a location for facilities, the design of the facilities, and the coordination among facilities are examined.

Location of Facilities

Facilities can be located to take advantage of inputs or of markets and can be concentrated or dispersed. The trade-offs between these choices in location of facilities are discussed in the following sections.

Input versus Market Locations

If sources of inputs are relatively near major markets, then a production facility can be located convenient to both. For many international companies, however, markets and sources are not near each other because inputs can come from around the world and markets may be in varied parts of the world. The major factor that determines the appropriate location of facilities relative to inputs and markets is the ease with which inputs and finished goods can be moved from one location to another. This depends on factors such as mobility, size and weight, ability to withstand transportation, and need to preserve freshness. These factors should be examined relative to inputs as well as intermediate and finished products to select appropriate locations for production facilities. The following illustrate some of these considerations:

▶ Printed circuit boards are often assembled by unskilled labor in countries where labor costs are low. It is often difficult to move people around the world, and if labor is an important input into a product, facilities are generally located close to the source of the needed labor.

▶ Wire, beads, coils, and so on used to produce electronic parts are small and easy to transport around the world, as are the finished parts. Companies that assemble these parts often have their facilities located near labor sources but remote from other inputs and markets.

▶ Precision scientific equipment often cannot be moved once it is assembled because movement can affect the delicate balance needed for accuracy. Companies that provide such equipment need to have at least some facilities located near their customers.

▶ Produce retains its freshness for only a limited period. Companies that use such produce tend to locate their facilities close to the source of supply. Many companies that can fruit and vegetables are located in small farming communities, where fresh produce can be brought to the factory within hours of harvest.

▶ Harvesting fresh produce in some developed countries relies on unskilled, low-cost labor, which may be unavailable locally. The growing location cannot be changed easily; therefore, seasonal labor is brought from other locations in spite of the difficulties associated with such movement of people.

▶ Automobile components are smaller and cheaper to transport than completed automobiles. Components may be produced in a variety of locations to take advantage of local conditions and shipped to a point near major markets for assembly.

▶ Precious stones for jewelry must be obtained in locations where they are available, but they may be shipped to other locations for cutting, polishing, and setting and to still other locations for sale where the major markets exist.

A U.S. food processor attempting to combine the advantages of a fresh source of supply with ease of shipment to markets illustrates the difficulties inherent in these decisions.

One U.S. food-processing company built a pineapple cannery at the delta of a river in Mexico. Since the pineapple plantation was located upstream, the company planned to float the ripe fruit down to the cannery on barges. To its dismay, however, the firm soon discovered that at harvest time the river current was far too strong for barge traffic. Since no other feasible alternative method of transportation existed, the plant was closed. The new equipment was sold for a fraction it its of original cost to a Mexican group that immediately relocated the cannery. A seemingly simple navigation oversight proved quite expensive to the firm.

(Ricks 1993, p. 16)

Consider the earlier example of a Brazilian firm with a subsidiary in Jamaica and sources of raw materials in both Brazil and the United States. This company is likely to be selling its finished printed circuit boards to a computer company in the United States. Initially it might seem inefficient to locate the main facilities in a third country that is not near either its sources of physical inputs or its markets. Clearly, however, the main consideration in this situation is the availability of relatively inexpensive labor in Jamaica. The additional costs associated with transporting materials to Jamaica and finished goods to the United States are offset by the savings in labor costs. The specific choice of Jamaica, rather than another low labor cost country, would be based on an assessment of the actual transportation costs, the reliability of transportation, and other benefits and risks associated with alternative locations.

Concentrated versus Dispersed Production Strategies

A **concentrated production strategy** implies a small number of facilities in a few locations; a **dispersed production strategy** implies a large number of facilities in many locations. Companies can produce all their products in one location and supply all markets from this location; they can locate plants strategically in a variety of locations, each for a certain market; or they can produce in each market for that market only. These choices form a continuum, with varying degrees of concentration or dispersion in between. The following discussion examines the two extreme choices. Each strategy has benefits and disadvantages.

The benefits of a concentrated approach are efficiency and standardization. A concentrated strategy with one, or a few, production facilities means that larger quantities are produced in these facilities and efficiencies of scale result in a lower per-unit cost. This strategy usually allows for standardized production processes and procedures, which result in a simplified administrative system. A concentrated strategy, in some ways, therefore, is easier to establish and operate.

The disadvantages of a concentrated strategy from a logistical view mean that inputs must be transported to central facilities and final products moved from these facilities to markets. This can add time, expense, and complexity to the production system. The efficiencies and simplicity associated with concentration can be dissipated due to these countering inefficiencies and complexities. The degree to which these offsetting pressures will influence a particular company depends on the specifics of the product and production processes. If inputs and markets are relatively concentrated, and adaptations are not needed, concentration of production facilities will likely be attractive. If inputs or markets or both are dispersed, or adaptations are needed, concentration of production facilities will be less attractive.

From a national or cultural view, noneconomic considerations could counter the benefits of centralization. It can be politically beneficial to engage in local production for some markets and politically unwise to do so in others. A concentrated strategy also means that the company relies on one, or only a few, locations for its production. If these locations should become less attractive for some reason (a negative change in exchange rates, government, employee attitudes, and so on), it can be difficult to shift operations quickly to other locations. If sources of inputs and markets are not politically sensitive and are seen as relatively safe, a concentrated strategy will be attractive. If the reverse is the case, a concentrated strategy will be less attractive.

The benefits of a dispersed production strategy are adaptation and flexibility. When inputs from suppliers in different countries vary, or products have to be adapted for different markets, standardization is no longer an advantage. In this situation it can be more effective to have production facilities in a variety of locations. The dispersion allows the company to take advantage of the opportunities offered by different sources of supply and to cater to the needs of different markets. This strategy can also provide more flexibility, because production can be increased or decreased at different locations as circumstances change. If a location becomes less attractive (because of, say, a negative change in exchange rates, government, or employee attitudes), production can be decreased and the difference made up in another location. This strategy means that the company is less dependent on any one location. In addition, a growing trend appears to include smaller production runs at facilities closer to the user to allow customization of the product for a particular buyer's needs.

The negative aspects of a dispersed production strategy are possibly higher per-unit costs associated with smaller production quantities and greater administrative complexity because of the need to manage multiple facilities. These disadvantages must be weighed against the benefits. The appropriate choice depends on the specific product, production processes, and sources of supply and markets.

Firms that produce a standardized product for a region or the entire world market may adopt a rationalized production system. Such a system has each plant specialize in a particular component, which it provides to the final assembly. This system allows each plant to produce larger quantities and benefit from economies of scale and efficiencies of standardization. Such a system needs to be carefully coordinated because the final product depends on each subsidiary facility providing the appropriate quantity of components of an acceptable quality and at the expected time; consequently, the system is only as strong as its weakest link.

Types of Facilities

The appropriate design for facilities often differs depending on a firm's choice of production strategy. Centralized strategies call for large, efficient, standardized, and probably automated designs. Dispersed strategies result in facilities that are smaller with each perhaps unique in design to meet the special needs of a particular location and product adaptation.

The distinctive characteristics of any location selected need to be considered prior to designing the facilities for that location. These characteristics may be climatic, cultural, physical, or governmental, among others, as the following illustrates.

Different climatic conditions can affect the appropriate design of facilities. In the tropics, particularly in developing countries where air conditioning is expensive and unusual, facilities need to be designed to take advantage of cool breezes. An unfortunate example of a design that fails to do this is a hospital in a small Caribbean island designed by a Canadian architect. The building does not face in an appropriate direction, so there is little air circulation; combined with a black roof, temperatures often soar to well over 100 degrees even though the outside temperature is only 80 degrees. Locals joke that the Canadian thought he was designing a hospital to be warm in Canada's north. Unfortunately, patients are often too uncomfortable to consider it a joking matter.

Different cultural conditions can affect the appropriate design of facilities. In certain Moslem countries, men and women are not permitted to work together; hence, facilities have to be designed so that those tasks likely to be done by women can be performed in an area separate from those likely to be done by men.

Different physical characteristics of people have to be taken into account in designing appropriate facilities. People in the Far East are, on the whole, relatively short in comparison with North Americans. Facilities (e.g., table and chair heights, machine switches) that are comfortable for North American employees would likely be unsuitable for employees in the Far East.

Government regulations can affect the appropriate design of facilities. Some countries require that employers provide separate toilet facilities for male and female employees; in other locations this would be considered wasteful and unnecessary.

Logistics

The means by which inputs get to the production site and the product gets to the customer is referred to as the logistics network or system. Logistics networks can range from the very simple to the incredibly complex. When inputs are close to production facilities and production takes place near the market, logistics are likely to be relatively simple. When production is distant from both sources of supplies and markets, the network is likely to be more complex.

The issues associated with international transportation of finished goods from production site to market are essentially the same as those discussed relative to the transportation of inputs to production facilities. It is important to recognize, however, that the specific regulations and requirements that apply to finished goods may be different from those that apply to raw materials, components, and so on.

The relationships between the supplier, the producer, and the buyer are important to the logistical system. Good relationships encourage relatively smooth movements of supplies and products, whereas bad relationships can have a major impact on this flow.

An example given earlier indicates some logistical complications. The Soviet Union built a large, expensive steel mill for India. Only afterward did it discover that the mill had been located in an area with inadequate transportation facilities. The steel mill was intended as a showplace for Soviet propaganda purposes, but it became an embarrassment instead.

The development of reliable, efficient, low-cost transportation methods such as bulk ocean carriers and air cargo planes has made it possible to move both intermediate goods and finished goods around the world relatively easily. This has increased the flexibility that companies have in selecting sites for their production facilities.

Companies in developed countries have come to take for granted the existence of reliable and effective transportation systems, but in reality, they do not always exist or function as international companies would like. In many remote parts of the world, and in the less developed countries, transportation can be inefficient and unreliable. Logistical systems, like rationalized production systems, are only as good as their weakest link. It is important, therefore, that companies examine the details of planned logistical systems to identify the potential problems and bottlenecks. The increased flexibility offered by improved transportation has made logistical networks an integral part of doing business internationally; such networks can be designed and costed by trained technicians so that global companies can make efficient choices. These networks are effective only if all aspects fit together and run smoothly. Beautifully designed systems can turn into nightmares when one aspect ceases to work as it was intended. Delays and problems are common to all transportation situations, and logistical networks need to include enough slack to accommodate these delays and potential problems.

Summary

Operational decisions are, in many ways, similar to foreign investment decisions. The initial foreign investment decision involves the same considerations as ongoing decisions regarding procurement and delivery. The decisions are often different, however, because investment decisions are strategic, whereas operational decisions can be both strategic and tactical. The chapter began with a discussion of the differences between goods and services. This distinction was examined because of the increasing importance of services in world trade and because the word *product* is used throughout the chapter to refer to both goods and services. The chapter then considered operations from the supply or procurement side and from the production side. The supply side was discussed in terms of procurement of needed inputs. The production side was discussed in terms of locating and coordinating facilities. Finally, logistical networks were examined.

Throughout, the cost/benefit trade-offs inherent in various choices were examined. Operational decisions always involve trade-offs, and the effective international company recognizes these and seeks to find the optimum balance. Operational decisions must be made in the context of the overall international environment. Throughout this chapter, the suggestion was made that firms begin with models intended to design efficient systems and then temper the results of these models with more subjective judgment about the political and cultural realities of the world.

This chapter is intended to give students an overview of operational decisions. Detailed models and advanced planning techniques are not examined here, but students should be aware that they exist and that international managers make extensive use of them in designing effective operational systems.

MINI-CASE
The Global Competitive Growth Strategy of Credit Lyonnais

Credit Lyonnais (CL) is undertaking a global competitive growth strategy aimed at increasing its profitability and market share. Because the New York branch is instrumental in this strategy, Credit Lyonnais's new objective is the rapid penetration of the U.S. corporate and investment banking markets.

The New York branch, established in 1971, is considered a recent development in CL's 125-year history. The branch management is composed of French expatriates who know the policies and politics of the head office but very little of the U.S. market and business culture. Selection of American managers is based on the applicant's ability to adapt to the French corporate culture (and know the French language) more than on market expertise and job fit. A French-based patriarchal management philosophy excludes U.S. managers from career paths traditionally available only to French nationals. This selection policy has been encouraged by CL's long-standing nationalization by the French government.

The recent denationalization of financial and other institutions in France is having a profound impact on CL's centralized policies and objectives. The trend now is to decentralize and allow more autonomy throughout the global branch network. CL must decide how to implement this policy in its New York branch.

Source: Randall S. Schuler, research professor, Stern School of Business, New York University; used with the author's permission.

Discussion Issues

1. Evaluate the advantages and disadvantages of centralization and decentralization of CL globally.
2. Is decentralization a good idea for the New York branch? Explain why or why not. How is decentralization likely to change CL's staffing policies?
3. Find information on an international bank and identify its global structure.

Discussion Questions

1. What is the distinction between goods and services? Give examples of each.
2. How might the increase in regional trading blocks influence international operational decisions?
3. How is the increased role of services in the global economy likely to influence operational decisions?

Assignments

1. Select an international company to research. Identify the company's main markets and sources of supply and describe its operational structure.

2. Select a product to investigate. Identify the distribution system associated with it in a variety of countries. Discuss the similarities and differences in the distribution systems.

3. Select a product to investigate. Identify the major inputs into it and identify suppliers around the world of these inputs.

Selected References

Axtell, R. E., *Do's and Taboos of Hosting International Visitors* (New York: John Wiley & Sons, 1990), pp. 1–2.

Boddewyn, J. J., M. B. Hallbrich, and A. C. Perry, "Service Multinationals: Conceptualization, Measurement, and Theory," *Journal of International Business Studies* (Winter 1986), pp. 41–58.

Cohen, M. A., M. Fisher, and R. Jaikumar, "International Manufacturing and Distribution Networks: A Normative Model Framework," in K. Ferdows, ed., *Managing International Manufacturing* (Amsterdam: North-Holland, 1989).

Dunning, J., *International Production and the Multinational Enterprise* (London: George Allen and Unwin, 1981).

Dunning, J., "The Eclectic Paradigm of International Production: Restatement and Some Possible Extensions," *Journal of International Business Research* (Spring–Summer 1988), pp. 1–32.

The Economist (September 22–28, 19XX), p. 36.

Foulkes, F. K., and J. L. Hirsch, "People Make Robots Work," *Harvard Business Review* (January–February 1984), pp. 94–102.

Garvin, D. A., "Quality on the Line," *Harvard Business Review* (September–October 1983), pp. 64–75.

Kotabe, M., and G. S. Omura, "Sourcing Strategies of European and Japanese Multinationals: A Comparison," *Journal of International Business* (Spring–Summer 1989), pp. 113–130.

"The Latest Business Game," *The Economist* (May 5, 1990), p. 16.

Mascarenhas, B., "The Coordination of Manufacturing Interdependence in Multinational Companies," *Journal of International Business Studies* (Winter 1984), pp. 91–106.

Mefford, R. N., "Determinants of Productivity Differences in International Manufacturing," *Journal of International Business Studies* (Spring–Summer 1986), pp. 63–82.

Myers, P., "Free-Trade Agreement Distorted in Auto Industry," *The Bottom Line* (June 1990), p. 20.

"Playing Hard to Get," *The Economist* (June 30, 1990), p. 69.

Poynter, T. A., and A. Rugman, "World Product Mandates: How Will Multinationals Respond?" *Business Quarterly* (October 1982), pp. 54–61.

Prahalad, C., and Y. Doz, *The Multinational Mission: Balancing Local Demands and Global Vision* (New York: The Free Press, 1987).

Ricks, D. A., *Big Business Blunders* (Homewood, Ill.: Dow Jones-Irwin, 1983).

Ricks, D. A., *Blunders in International Business* (Cambridge, Mass.: Blackwell Publishers, 1993).

CHAPTER ▼ 14

Human Resource Management in International Companies

LEARNING OBJECTIVES

After reading this chapter, you should be able to

▶ Discuss the importance of people to various management processes and functional areas.

▶ Identify the advantages and disadvantages of various groups of personnel and discuss the mix of personnel from an international perspective.

▶ Explain how international firms can effectively select and train personnel around the world.

▶ Discuss the challenges associated with expatriate assignments.

▶ Discuss the special considerations involved in managing a cross-cultural work force.

KEY TERMS

▶ Management process
▶ Functional areas
▶ Parent-country nationals (PCNs)
▶ Host-country nationals (HCNs)
▶ Third-country nationals (TCNs)
▶ Ethnocentric staffing approach
▶ Polycentric staffing approach
▶ Geocentric staffing approach
▶ Mentoring

▶ Environmental briefing
▶ Cultural sensitivity training
▶ Critical incidents and cases
▶ Dual-career couples
▶ Overseas bonuses
▶ Hardship premiums
▶ Moving allowances
▶ Culture shock
▶ Repatriation

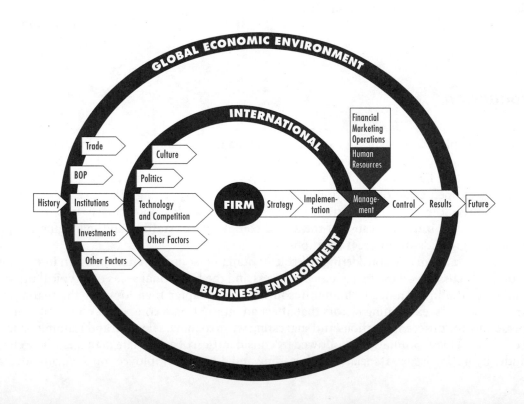

T H O U G H T   S T A R T E R S

▶ After traveling 7,000 miles, an American walks into the office of a highly recommended Arab businessman on whom he will have to depend completely. What he sees does not breed confidence. The office is reached by walking through a suspicious-looking coffeehouse in an old, dilapidated building in a crowded, non-European section of town. The elevator, rising from dark, smelly corridors, is rickety and equally foul. When he gets to the office itself, he is shocked to find it small, crowded, and confused. Papers are stacked all over the desk and table tops – even scattered on the floor in irregular piles.

   The Arab merchant he has come to see had met him at the airport the night before and sent his driver to the hotel this morning to pick him up. But now, after the American's rush, the Arab is tied up with something else.

(Hall 1960, p. 87)

▶ Most of the Saturday shoppers at Janss Mall in Thousand Oaks, California, guessed they were seeing some kind of initiation rite. Eight men and two women took turns standing at attention outside Von's supermarket and shouting a song to a stern-faced man 75 feet away. . . .

   The shoppers had witnessed one of the critical tests in the first U.S. class conducted by Kanrisha Yosei Gakko, a renowned Japanese management training school. Known as "hell camp" for salespeople and managers, the school requires students to sing a "sales crow" song – so named because the singers are supposed to sound like cawing crows – in a public place to break down their inhibitions.

(Time 1988, p. 55)

Introduction

This chapter explores the issues associated with managing human resources in an international company. People are often considered an organization's most important resource because virtually everything that happens in an organization depends, to some extent, on people. People either make things happen in an organization or stop them from happening. Effective management of human resources therefore is important in any organization. It is particularly important to the international organization because of the added complexity of staffing and managing people of different backgrounds in different locations.

   This chapter begins by considering the role of human resources in managing an international company; a discussion on the management process and the functional areas of a typical organization indicates the importance of human resources. The chapter then looks at the management of human resources, examining factors that affect an international company's choice of managers and personnel for different locations and suggesting ways to make selection and training processes most effective. This examination is followed by consideration of expatriate managers. The chapter concludes by noting issues associated with leading and directing employees on a worldwide basis.

The Role of Human Resources in International Companies

The importance of human resources in international companies can be seen by considering the process of management and the functional areas of an organization. The following brief discussion demonstrates the need for effective human resource management throughout an international company.

The Management Process

The **management process** is often described as consisting of planning, organizing, staffing, directing, and controlling. This management process takes place in both the international company and the domestic one, but there are additional dimensions to consider in the international firm; some of these additional dimensions, as they relate to the international management of human resources, are discussed next.

The management process begins with planning; plans are necessary so that the organization knows where it is going. People make these plans. The capacity for making decisions that form the basis of an organization's plans is unique to people. The role of people in the planning process of both domestic and international companies is critical. Because the international company interacts with many different groups of people at home and at other locations, people who speak various languages and have different customs, cultures, and expectations, those making the company's plans must be aware of and sensitive to these facts and include them in their decision making. Developing plans that are acceptable to such different groups relies on input from a variety of people who are familiar with these varying expectations. Further, coordinating information and analyses from around the globe and interpreting the interplay of worldwide events, while facilitated by electronic data transmission and analysis, can best be accomplished by people with international understanding.

Organizations typically are broken into functional units (e.g., marketing, finance, and production) that group together similar work activities. These units are usually identified in terms of the tasks associated with them rather than the people who will fill the positions within the unit. This focus on work activities is somewhat misleading, however, because positions in fact are staffed with people. It is particularly important to remember this human side of an international organization's structure, because this will influence the design. The particular configuration of tasks and positions that is appropriate in one location may not be appropriate in another. Different work values in different locations often have to be considered in an organization's design.

A precarious balance seems to exist between the number of foreign and U.S. managers needed for a successful operation. At one extreme, Imperial-Eastman experienced problems by relying too heavily on inexperienced local managers. General Electric, at the other extreme, encountered troubles by placing and retaining U.S. employees in most managerial positions. In some cases, because the U.S. employees were unfamiliar with the local business practices, they unknowingly nullified the firm's ability to compete with local businesspeople.

The staffing aspect of management deals specifically with the allocation of the organization's human resources. People must fill various positions for the organization to accomplish its goals, and unless people are properly allocated, the organization cannot be effective and successful. The international company, because it is international, must manage people from different national and cultural backgrounds. Such a company must allocate people from a variety of countries to positions in particular countries; hence, the staffing process is complex and must take into account the differences that exist in various locations.

> An American manager who understood little German was sent to West Germany to discuss marketing plans with the local German subsidiary managers. The local managers, however, spoke little English. Both sides tried to understand each other, but neither nationality did very well. Eventually, they parted thinking that all were in agreement. It was later discovered that during the meeting important points were overlooked, and the company subsequently lost numerous sales opportunities.

Directing involves enabling people to work toward the goals that the organization has identified for them to accomplish. Effective direction of people involves understanding how to motivate them. The process of directing people in different locations is complex. People in various countries are motivated by diverse needs, expect various rewards, are disciplined in different ways, and experience different but acceptable leadership styles. This means certain behaviors may be unique to a specific location and vary from place to place. An international company can be successful only if it understands the people who constitute its international human resources and can direct them effectively.

> A Bata Shoe Company executive tells the story of a subsidiary in which women workers who came to talk to their male supervisors would sit on the floor, facing the wall, with their backs to their supervisor. Suddenly, it was clear that the question of how to communicate effectively could no longer be answered in traditional Western terms.

An organization's control systems may appear to have little relationship to people; some systems may be based on mechanical performance measures that simply report variances. These systems have been developed by people, however, and rely on people to operate them. No control system can work unless the proper information, which is usually provided by people, is available as input. Even more important, controls are useful only if they cause changes to occur when variances are evident. These changes occur only when people pay attention to the control systems and are willing to change in response to them. People around the world react differently to control systems; so, the international company should design and implement control systems with this in mind. Many companies have found that the control systems effective in North America cannot be transferred to other locations because people in the foreign locations cannot, or will not, comply with the requirements of the system. It is often more effective to design a new system with input from local personnel rather than try to force the parent system on an unwilling foreign location.

> To realize substantial cost savings, a U.S. company planned a massive cost-reduction program that involved the layoff of a significant number of employees. It was fortunate for the company that, prior to the initiation of the program, it learned that layoffs based on these grounds were highly unacceptable in the host country. Since much of the firm's business involved agencies of the host government, this action would surely have evoked great unhappiness, and the government agencies would have been pressured to place their orders with other suppliers.

The Functional Areas

The importance of the effective management of human resources in an international company is illustrated by looking at some typical **functional areas** (activities) in international companies.

The operations area is responsible for producing the goods or services that the company provides. Although work in today's world is becoming more automated, people still form the basic unit that produces the goods or performs the services. Therefore, effective management of operations should seek to use human resources effectively. People around the world have varied skills and expertise that may be used for different aspects of the production or service process; in fact, the international company often seeks such variations to improve its operations. Choosing locations for operations around the world should involve a consideration of the skills, expertise, culture, language, and so on of the people in each location being considered.

> One executive told a story of visiting his company's factory in rural India only to find the workers squatting as they worked. He immediately arranged for tables and benches to be provided to make them more comfortable. The next time he visited, the workers were still squatting to work, but now they were doing so up on the tables.

The marketing and sales area is responsible for ensuring that the company's products or services are available to its customers. The success of this area depends, to a large extent, on understanding what the customer wants and needs and being able to demonstrate that the company provides products or services that match these wants and needs. Understanding people is crucial for effective marketing and sales. Developing such knowledge is particularly challenging in an international company because wants and needs are likely to differ according to locations, and methods to attract and persuade the customer are likely to vary from place to place.

> To some groups, the display of certain parts of the body generally believed harmless proves to be offensive. One American shoe manufacturer promoted its product through photos of bare feet. Although many people would consider the ad harmless, people in Southeast Asia, where the photos were shown, consider exposure of the foot an insult.
>
> Mountain Bell experienced a similar problem when one of its promotional photos depicted an executive talking on the telephone with his feet propped up on his desk. The photos, seen by Middle and Far Easterners, were considered to be in poor taste. To them, the display of the sole of the foot or shoe is one of the worst possible insults.

International companies find it particularly important to consider cultural differences in their marketing and sales activities, and understanding cultural differences, essentially, is understanding people in different locations.

The public relations area involves the company's external relationships, specifically managing its interactions with various external constituencies, including the government, the public at large, potential customers, and suppliers. The role of the public relations group is to ensure that the company's activities are portrayed in a way that is beneficial to the company's image. Clearly understanding how people view various company activities is very important in accomplishing this goal. Public relations may be particularly important for an international company because certain activities can be viewed positively in one location and negatively in another. The international company's public relations group has the complex task of ensuring that its numerous constituencies are all pleased, or at least not dissatisfied, with the company's activities. To accomplish this, sensitivity to the opinions of people in different locations is vital.

Accounting and finance information monitors the company's past performance and projects and plans future performance to ensure its continuing viability. Accounting and finance functions involve nonhuman resources. However, the responsibility for performing these functions – monitoring and planning the allocation of financial resources – rests with the company's human resources. An international company must follow accounting standards and procedures that may vary from country to country and must react to financial opportunities and problems, which also may differ from one location to another. People who can understand and comply with different accounting practices, as well as those who can understand and manage different financial situations, are of particular value to international companies.

> A story is told of an American executive in France who received a call from his foreign exchange buyer to say that the U.S. dollar had risen dramatically relative to the French franc. He was upset by the news and said "Aw, Sh--!" and then hung up. To his horror, the buyer called back a short while later to say that he had purchased a large quantity of U.S. dollars because he thought that the executive had said "*achette*," the French word for "buy."

Managing Human Resources in International Companies

The previous discussion demonstrates the pervasive importance of people to an international company's success. An essential part of managing an international company's human resources is deciding which people will be effective in each location. This management function is discussed in terms of the advantages and disadvantages of staffing subsidiaries with parent-country nationals, host-country nationals, or third-country nationals. Selecting and training personnel for specific jobs and locations are also important; these functions are discussed in terms of the factors that affect these human resource decisions and the guidelines for effective selection and training in the international context.

Choice of Personnel

An international company that operates in several foreign locations has essentially three types of people available for any position. These are parent-country nationals (PCNs), host-country nationals (HCNs), and third-country nationals (TCNs). The choice among them is not left entirely to the company because most countries have regulations restricting the numbers and types of foreigners allowed to work locally. Companies frequently rely on HCNs for lower-level positions (except in countries where menial work is performed by foreign workers in the host country) but may favor PCNs and TCNs for certain technical or managerial positions. The following discussion examines each of these groups separately and identifies the advantages and disadvantages generally associated with staffing with individuals from each group. The particular advantages or disadvantages of interest to a specific company depend on the nature of the foreign subsidiary in question as well as its location.

PCNs

The benefits and drawbacks associated with employing **parent-country nationals** in a foreign location are presented in Exhibit 14.1. The most important advantage of PCNs appears to be their familiarity with the parent company's way of doing things; the most critical disadvantage is their lack of awareness of local cultures.

HCNs

The benefits and drawbacks associated with choosing a **host-country national** for a foreign location are presented in Exhibit 14.2. The most important advantage to HCNs appears to be their local knowledge; the critical disadvantage is their lack of expertise and familiarity with the parent company.

TCNs

The benefits and drawbacks associated with choosing a **third-country national** are summarized in Exhibit 14.3. The most important advantage of using TCNs appears to be the effectiveness of getting the best person for the job; the disadvantage is the need to adapt to both the local environment and the parent company.

The Right Personnel Mix

Most companies use a mix of PCNs, HCNs, and TCNs for management and technical positions. This mix depends on the benefits and costs of each group in a particular location. Local attitudes toward different groups, the need for local knowledge, and the availability of people with the needed expertise are often major factors in the decision.

> Choosing the right person for the job is complex. Having managers with the appropriate attitudes and who speak the language does not assure a successful performance. Raytheon hired Italian-Americans to manage operations in Sicily but found that the strategy was not as effective as hoped. In this case, the trouble lay in the origins of the managers. Because their family ties were with the mainland, not with Sicily, they were not trusted or accepted.

If local personnel are available, companies often favor HCNs because this policy reduces the foreign image of the company and provides local know-how. This choice is particularly appropriate where locals have negative attitudes toward foreigners. In contrast, where foreigners are admired for their expertise, locals lack appropriate training, and local know-how is relatively unimportant, companies favor PCNs or TCNs. North American firms increasingly are turning to HCNs who have been trained in North American business schools, and who therefore combine the benefits of being managers who are HCNs with North American training.

EXHIBIT 14.1
Staffing with PCNs

Benefits

PCNs are often favored for top management positions in subsidiaries because the parent company associates a certain sense of control with having someone from the head office in the foreign location.

They may have particular expertise or knowledge that is needed in a particular subsidiary.

They are familiar with the way things run at home and are expected to ensure that operations at the subsidiary conform to expectations at the head office.

Communication between managers at the head office and the subsidiary's manager may be easier because they speak the same language and understand how communication normally takes place within the company.

Employing PCNs may be seen as enhancing the foreign image identified with the parent company or country.

PCNs may be a neutral choice when racial or ethnic tensions exist among local groups in the host country.

Foreign assignments provide international experience for prospective senior executives.

Foreign assignments provide opportunities for increased responsibility and opportunities for managers to prove themselves, sometimes at little risk to the company as a whole.

Foreign assignments can provide an opportunity to reassign a manager who is not performing well at home (although we would not advocate this approach, it is one that some companies use).

Drawbacks

The cost of sending a manager from the home country to a foreign location is high.

If the PCN is not successful, the cost to the company can be higher than if an HCN were used.

Having a PCN in the top management position emphasizes the foreign image of the subsidiary. In some locations, this may not be desirable if foreigners are viewed negatively.

Communication between the PCN and local employees may be poor.

Communication between the PCN and local groups (government, suppliers, customers, and so on) may be poor.

The PCN may not understand the local culture.

EXHIBIT 14.2
Staffing with HCNs

Benefits

HCNs are familiar with the host culture and host environment.
They provide ease of communication with host employees.
Communication with local groups, including the government, suppliers, and customers should be easier for HCNs.
Hiring HCNs enhances the local image.
Local requirements are met by hiring HCNs.
Costs related to hiring HCNs are usually relatively low.

Drawbacks

Qualified and experienced locals may not be available.
The cost of training may be high.
Communication between headquarters and the subsidiary may be difficult.
HCNs may not understand or appreciate parent policies and procedures.
The potential for conflict exists between loyalty to the company and loyalty to the country.

EXHIBIT 14.3
Staffing with TCNs

Benefits

Using TCNs takes advantage of the best person for the job on a global scale.
It prevents the company from developing either a host-country or a parent-country image and projects a truly international image.
It provides opportunities for personnel throughout the company to gain international experience.

Drawbacks

Communication with both the parent company and local groups may be difficult.
Cultural adaptation may be difficult.
It can emphasize the foreign image of the company.
The "best person for a job," in terms of expertise, may not be appropriate for the specific location due to racial, ethnic, religious, or other such reasons.
The costs are relatively high.

Companies that favor PCNs for important positions have been described as ethnocentric, those that favor HCNs as polycentric, and those that favor TCNs as geocentric.

An **ethnocentric staffing approach** means that the company essentially believes that parent-country nationals are better qualified and more trustworthy; therefore, wherever possible, it prefers to staff with PCNs. A **polycentric staffing approach** means that the company essentially believes that locals know the local environment better; therefore, wherever possible, it prefers to staff with HCNs. A **geocentric staffing approach** means that the company believes in a policy of staffing with the person best suited for the job, regardless of national origin; therefore, wherever possible, it ignores national origin in its staffing decisions and encourages the movement of all personnel among all locations.

The choice of personnel is also a function of a company's stage of development and types of operations. Some examples follow.

If a company needs to maintain tight control over a subsidiary, it may adopt an ethnocentric staffing policy and favor PCNs for positions that exert control. Most joint ventures in China have PCNs in top management positions; for example, the Beijing Jeep joint venture involving Chrysler has stationed U.S. nationals in China from the beginning of the venture.

If a company has developed confidence and trust in local management, it generally adopts a polycentric staffing policy and favors HCNs for most, if not all, positions. For example, many U.S. companies in Canada employ Canadians at the top management level. Chrysler Canada's president has typically been a Canadian.

If a company is concerned about specific expertise, it tends to adopt a geocentric staffing approach and chooses the best person for the job, regardless of nationality. This is often the case when technical expertise and reputation are recognized globally, as in the case of the famous oil fire-fighting specialist Red Adair.

The Product Life Cycle Model and Human Resource Choices

The product life cycle model of international business was discussed in detail in Chapter 5. The stages of the product life cycle model can be helpful in making appropriate staffing choices. The three stages of international development are discussed as they relate to staffing choices.

Stage 1 of the product life cycle describes a company that produces essentially for the home market. Response to the home market needs is very important. A company at this stage of international development might follow an ethnocentric staffing policy, because PCNs can best understand and react to the home-market needs.

Stage 2 of the product life cycle describes a company with a focus on a variety of foreign markets. This type of company produces close to these markets and responds to the needs of each market separately. A company at this stage of international development might follow a polycentric staffing policy, because HCNs can best understand and react to their own market needs.

Stage 3 of the product life cycle describes a company with a global focus. This type of company produces a relatively standardized product in a limited number of locations and for a worldwide market; efficiency is its major concern. A company at this stage of development might follow a geocentric staffing policy, because choosing the best person for a particular position regardless of nationality is generally the most efficient choice.

Companies do not necessarily progress from stage 1 through stage 2 to stage 3; therefore, their staffing policies need not follow a progression. Rather, a company can assess its operations relative to the three stages and institute a staffing policy that is appropriate for its type of business. In addition, a company may well have some subsidiaries in all stages of development and therefore may find it appropriate to have different staffing policies for different locations.

Selecting and Training Personnel

This discussion focuses on the specific issues associated with selecting and training individuals for particular jobs and locations. The selection and training process is very important if an international company's personnel are to be successful.

A person should be selected for a particular position based on his or her identified ability to perform effectively in that position; training should then be tailored to the individual's needs. This means that the expertise necessary to perform in a particular position is always required. The particular nature of an international company, however, requires that other abilities also be considered. An HCN needs to understand the way the parent company operates, be able to relate to its culture, and communicate with it and other subsidiaries. A PCN needs to understand the local subsidiary culture and interact and communicate with locals. A TCN needs to be able to relate to both the parent and the subsidiary and interact and communicate with both groups.

If a company chooses an HCN to manage its foreign operations, a major concern in the selection and training process should be that the HCN interacts well with the parent. Many companies find it helpful to seek out HCNs who have been educated or trained in the parent country because they will be relatively familiar with norms in the parent country. Also, HCN managers can spend time at the parent company learning about its operations and understanding its culture.

If a company chooses a PCN to manage its foreign operations, a major concern in the selection and training process should be the person's ability to adapt to the foreign environment. Characteristics of those who adapt successfully include flexibility, emotional maturity, and cultural empathy.

If a company chooses a TCN to manage its foreign operations, a major concern in the selection and training process should be the knowledge of both the parent and foreign cultures and the ability to adapt to both. Companies often develop a small cadre of international managers who have experience in a wide variety of locations and are willing to go wherever they are needed; these managers tend to be very flexible and adaptable and fit into foreign environments easily.

Expatriate Managers

No matter what general staffing policy a company has adopted, it usually has at least some PCNs who serve in foreign positions, generally at the managerial level. The success of these expatriate managers is often very important to the company's overall success.

An effective expatriate manager must possess special abilities and traits if he or she is to avoid blundering. Among the most important characteristics are:

1. an ability to get along well with people
2. an awareness of cultural differences
3. open-mindedness
4. tolerance of foreign cultures
5. adaptability to new cultures, ideas, and challenges
6. an ability to adjust quickly to new conditions
7. an interest in facts, not blind assumptions
8. previous business experience
9. previous experience with foreign cultures
10. an ability to learn foreign languages.

(Ricks 1993, pp. 96–99)

To understand the importance of ensuring expatriate managers are effective, consider the possible indirect costs of failure (failure meaning that the managers return before expected or do a poor job in their overseas assignments):

▶ Foreign government contacts may be alienated.
▶ Foreign suppliers, creditors, and customers may be lost.
▶ Foreign contracts may be lost.
▶ Foreign operations may be inefficient.
▶ Foreign employees may be alienated (resulting in labor problems).
▶ The company's international reputation may be damaged.
▶ The manager's self-esteem will be damaged; this can result in poor performance as well as stress-induced illnesses once back home.
▶ Other potential expatriates and their families may be less willing to undertake foreign assignments.

Sometimes the failure to understand cultural differences can have serious consequences. Consider the following example.

An American manager working in the South Pacific had foolishly hired local natives without regard to the traditional status system of the island. By hiring too many of one group, he threatened to change the balance of power and traditions of the people. The islanders talked over this unacceptable situation and independently came up with an alternative plan. But it had taken them until 3 A.M. to do so. Since time was not important in their culture, they saw no reason to wait until morning to make their suggestions known to the American. They casually went to his place of residence; their arrival at such a late hour caused him to panic. Since he could not understand their language and could not imagine that they would want to talk business at 3 A.M., he assumed that they were coming to riot – or worse, so he called in the Marines! It was some time before the company was able to get back to "business as usual."

The incremental cost (i.e., that over and above the amount incurred if the position were staffed locally) of sending an expatriate manager to a foreign location is in the vicinity of $200,000. This cost, added to the indirect costs identified already, suggests that the expatriate decision cannot be taken lightly.

Recent literature on the expatriate process has related the degree of success in international assignments to the parent company's selection, training, support, and repatriation of foreign assignees. Tung (1988b) discussed these issues in terms of U.S., Japanese, and European companies. First, it appears that U.S. companies have expatriate failure rates of 10–20 percent compared with less than 5 percent for European and Japanese companies. Tung attributes this difference to the longer-term orientation of the Europeans and Japanese, and that they appear to pay more attention to the overall qualifications of candidates for foreign assignments and have rigorous training programs and comprehensive support systems. Some of Tung's conclusions regarding effective expatriation follow.

Short stints of two to three years in a foreign locale are not conducive to high performance. The longer-term orientation of the Europeans and Japanese is reflected by assignments that typically last five years. U.S. expatriates appear reluctant to accept extended assignments because of concerns that they will be passed over for promotion at home.

U.S. firms overemphasize technical competence relative to relational abilities. Technical competence is an important factor in the overall determination of success; however, relational abilities appear to increase considerably the probability of successful international performance.

Training consisting largely of an environmental briefing is usually inadequate. This approach does not equip the assignee for the extensive contact with the local community necessary in most foreign assignments.

Support systems are necessary for successful expatriate assignments. **Mentoring**, a process whereby an expatriate is paired with a superior at corporate headquarters who acts as a sponsor and provides a support system for the expatriate, is suggested.

The Role of Careful Selection

It is possible to make the foreign assignment selection process an ongoing one. Candidates who have an interest in serving in foreign locations are identified and assessed in terms of their general suitability for foreign assignments. This general assessment considers each candidate's apparent adaptability, flexibility, openness to other cultures, and reasons for applying for a position in a foreign country. A candidate who appears to be generally suitable is considered in more detail as specific opportunities arise. The candidates judged to be less suitable receive suggestions for improvement (e.g., courses to take, books to read, language instruction).

If this procedure is followed, the company has at hand a list of candidates to consider when particular opportunities arise in foreign locations. Candidates should be assessed first in terms of their job-specific expertise. Those who have the necessary expertise then are contacted to determine whether they are interested in the particular position (the potential candidate is encouraged to discuss this question in detail with family members before responding). Those candidates who are interested and whose families are supportive are then assessed in terms of their psychological ability to adjust to the new location. Those who are judged best able are then assessed in terms of their country-specific knowledge (e.g., knowledge of the language).

This assessment involves a variety of methods. The job-specific expertise is judged by prior performance, experience, and training. Psychological tests and superior and peer evaluation are used to determine psychological ability. The country-specific knowledge is based on self-reports. Each step in the evaluation represents a hurdle for the prospective candidate to pass; unsuitable candidates are identified and eliminated from the process at appropriate stages.

The final step in the selection process involves a series of personal interviews of the candidate and his or her family. These interviews can be most effective when others who have served in the same or similar foreign locations conduct them. They can identify potential problems and give the candidate and family members the opportunity to obtain a realistic preview of what life in the foreign country is really like. In some cases, the chosen candidate and family may be given an opportunity to visit the foreign site before a final decision is made.

The discussion of this process has not mentioned the issue of eliminating candidates on the basis of gender, religion, race, and so on, because, from the North American view, it is not appropriate to discriminate on this basis. However, these issues must be acknowledged in situations where they may cause problems. For example, a woman in Saudi Arabia or a Muslim in Israel will likely face difficulties associated with sex, race, or religion, respectively. In reality it may be against the regulations in the foreign location to have people of a certain gender, religion, or race performing particular duties. This could make it difficult, if not impossible, for the person to perform effectively. In such situations, the candidate and the company should acknowledge and realistically assess the potential difficulties.

The Role of Careful Training

After being selected for a particular assignment, the candidate and family members should go through a training process. The intent of this training, for which a variety of training methods are available, is to ensure that adjustment to the new environment is quick and smooth. The methods range from relatively superficial country briefings to in-depth environmental experiences. The type of appropriate training depends on the candidate's previous experience and the degree of similarity or dissimilarity between the home country and the host country, as well as the length of stay, type of position, and the required degree of integration into the community.

The cost of extensive, in-depth training is high; therefore, the company wants to use this type of training effectively. If a Canadian who has previously worked in the United States is going to manage a subsidiary there, then minimal training may be needed. In contrast, an American who has lived only in the Midwest of the United States, has traveled very little, and is going to manage a subsidiary in the People's Republic of China probably requires extensive training.

Research suggests that appropriate training of expatriates and their families improves their success rates (e.g., Earley 1987). Given the costs associated with an expatriate's failure, it seems that international companies should consider training as an integral part of the expatriation process. The aim of a cross-cultural training program is to increase individuals' sensitivity to their own and other cultures, to promote acceptance of cultural differences, and to provide understanding of a specific culture.

The Manager

Training for the manager should focus on job-related issues, including

- ▶ Economic, political, and legal environments
- ▶ Government policies and regulations
- ▶ Management practices (including labor relations, hiring and firing, religious holidays, and so forth)
- ▶ Relationship of subsidiary to the rest of the company
- ▶ Specifics of the job (including reporting relationships, time frames, objectives, and so forth).

The Manager and Family

Training for the manager and family should focus on relationship issues, including

- ▶ Language training (at least an elementary knowledge of the local language to allow some basic communication on arrival)

▶ Area training (including history, religion, culture, and so forth)
▶ Practical training (including currency, food, dress, climate, specific customs, and so forth).

The following training methods can be used:

1. **Environmental briefing** consists of a short briefing by someone with knowledge of the foreign environment. This usually includes readings, films, lectures, and discussions. This training approach is specific to one location and gives general information.
2. **Cultural sensitivity training** consists of a variety of interactions with people of other cultures. The aim is to increase individuals' sensitivity to cultural differences by allowing them to develop a better understanding of why people behave in different ways. This training approach is not location specific and focuses on relationships rather than specific information. A particular form of this training approach is the cultural simulation, in which real or imagined cultures are simulated and participants interact with people who exhibit different cultural behaviors.
3. **Critical incidents and cases** consist of a variety of simulated real-life episodes that are location specific and involve interactions between people of different cultural backgrounds. The trainee assesses and responds to different situations, and these responses are evaluated and discussed. The aim is to increase sensitivity to locational differences and to focus on specific issues that may arise in a particular location. This approach can focus on location specifics as well as general cultural sensitivity.

The Role of the Family

It appears to be particularly important that the family be included in the training process because its inability to adjust to a foreign location has been cited by American expatriates as the greatest cause of failure in foreign assignments. The family often has a more difficult time adjusting than the expatriate manager.

It is not surprising that the family of an expatriate has a particularly difficult time adjusting to overseas conditions. Managers have jobs that keep them busy most of the day. Work puts them in a position to meet and interact with locals; other expatriate managers may provide a support system, and new managers can rely on expatriate as well as local managers for advice regarding local customs. Family members are not so fortunate. They are often on their own with little to do and have no easy way to meet locals and no support systems. Further, the spouse often has the responsibility of dealing with unfamiliar foods, shops, transportation, and so on.

To overcome the difficulties that families face in unfamiliar surroundings, companies can ensure that the family is included in planning the expatriate assignment process. A realistic preview of the foreign location prepares the family; training in host-country culture helps the family adjust; support groups, specifically aimed at the family, ensure that they adapt to the new environment.

The Role of the Spouse

The role of the spouse in foreign assignments is an issue of increasing importance for North American companies. In the past, the traditional expatriate manager was a man, and his wife and family were generally willing to accompany him to the foreign location if it was beneficial to his career. This is no longer automatically or necessarily the case. First, although the majority of expatriates are still men, companies are increasingly seeking women for these positions. Second, wives often have their own careers and are unwilling to give them up for the benefit of their husband's career. This is further complicated because many countries specifically prohibit spouses of foreign assignees from working.

Women Expatriate Managers and Dual-Career Couples

Companies in the past had few women in foreign assignments for a number of reasons. First, not many women in the home office were at a level at which they would be eligible for most foreign assignments. Second, many companies believed that it would be difficult for women to undergo some of the hardships associated with foreign assignments. Third, companies assumed that women would not be accepted as managers in countries where local women did not hold such positions.

In the 1980s, only about 3 percent of expatriates were women, according to Adler (1984). This situation is changing, however. More women are now in eligible positions, and pressure for equality in the workplace, including in foreign assignments, is increasing, particularly when foreign assignments are seen as a stepping stone to top-level positions. Women want access to these assignments. They are willing to undergo the hardships associated with foreign assignments and believe that they are equally capable of undertaking them. Most important, research (e.g., Adler 1988; Jelinek and Adler 1988; Moran 1986) suggests that women are good expatriate managers and that foreign women are accepted as managers, even in countries in which local women do not hold such positions – they are seen, in a sense, as a third sex.

Women may actually be particularly effective in some foreign assignments (Adler 1991). Research suggests that women are sometimes more sensitive to cultural differences than their male counterparts, that they may be treated with deference in some locations, and that they can sometimes gain access to locals when men cannot. Although this does not suggest that companies should send only women on foreign assignments, it does suggest that women should be considered for any foreign assignment where they have the necessary expertise.

The **dual-career couple** is an emerging issue, and currently companies are trying a number of different approaches to overcome the problem it poses in expatriate assignments. Interviews with personnel managers in international companies suggest a number of options:

▶ A reduction in the number of expatriate managers
▶ The need for added bonuses to entice the spouse to leave her or his current career
▶ Providing a means for the spouse to continue her or his career in the foreign location.

The dual-career issue becomes particularly important when considering women expatriates because these women ususally have spouses with careers of their own. North American society has encouraged equality in the workplace between women and men, but in general it is still more difficult socially for men to accept the subordinate work role or the homemaker role. Such roles are very often necessary when a man accompanies his wife on an expatriate assignment. International companies need to give careful thought to this if they want to make the best use of their human resources in international assignments.

Interviews with directors of human resource management in the United States (Tung 1988a) and Canada (Punnett 1989a) suggested that the issue of women expatriates and the management of dual-career couples in a global environment is seen as a major challenge for international companies in the 1990s. Companies to date have used less than optimal approaches to dealing with this issue. For example, some companies have opted to hire host-country or third-country nationals rather than home-country nationals to avoid the issue; others have avoided it by selecting single candidates; still others have essentially ignored the issue by adopting a hands-off policy because it is a personal matter. These approaches are less than optimal because they may result in managers who are selected for reasons other than their management ability.

Proactive approaches can be more useful in facing this challenge. The following options can be considered by international companies.

Counseling dual-career couples prior to an expatriate decision allows a couple to assess the impact of an international transfer on both parties and make an informed decision. The foreign situation often is largely unknown to the expatriate and spouse, and therefore they are not equipped to evaluate the impact without expert advice and counseling.

If work in the foreign location is permitted, support can be provided in finding employment and networking for the expatriate's spouse. The employment systems and practices are likely to vary from those at home, and help from someone familiar with the environment makes the transition much easier.

Some companies have found that it can be beneficial to provide a job for the spouse within the organization in order to transfer the desired candidate. This option may have merit in situations where other possibilities are limited.

Other support, including providing computer or other equipment to allow the spouse to work at home, funds for further education, or support for research projects related to the spouse's career, can also be helpful. These are all relatively low-cost approaches that allow the spouse to undertake productive and career-oriented activities in situations for which employment may be impractical.

The aim of such approaches, from the international firm's perspective, is to ensure that women and dual-career couples are not systematically precluded from expatriate assignments. This is only partially to avoid discrimination. More important, it is to ensure that the firm is able to select the best person for a foreign position and encourage that person to be successful.

The Role of Compensation

In addition to the complex process of selecting the right individuals for foreign positions, training those individuals and their families, and implementing systems designed to ensure their success, the company should design an acceptable compensation package for the expatriate. A number of options are available; in a general sense, companies can choose one of the following approaches.

Ethnocentric Compensation Approach

This approach essentially relates compensation to what the manager would receive at home (i.e., compensation remains what it would be if the manager were working in the home country). The problem with this approach is that expatriates may be worse off if the cost of living abroad is higher than at home or negative tax differentials exist; they may benefit if the reverse is the case. To offset any negative impact, various allowances may be added to the base compensation package.

Polycentric Compensation Approach

This approach establishes compensation based on local norms and, therefore, different compensation packages for different locations. This approach offers managers compensation comparable to that earned by local managers. Because norms for salary levels and mixes (i.e., bonuses, profit sharing) can vary widely from one location to another, some locations are more attractive than others. Some companies make additional payments to the expatriate manager to offset the differential, but these payments remain at the home office until the expatriate returns. This means that the expatriate is on a par with locals while in the local community although he or she is actually receiving more than the local counterpart.

Geocentric Compensation Approach

This approach establishes worldwide compensation packages. Managers at the same level, no matter the location, receive the same compensation. This approach eliminates questions regarding changes in compensation when managers move from one location to another. The difficulty with this approach is that the cost of living varies from country to country and tax differentials and different norms exist. Therefore, rather than providing equity across national boundaries, this approach may make some locations more attractive than others. To offset this factor, compensation can be uniform except for allowances for cost of living and tax differentials. This approach means that compensation for the company's managers will be generally equivalent, but they may be out of step with managers from other companies in the same location.

Bonuses, Premiums, and Allowances

Clearly, the choice among compensation options is not easy. Most companies end up with a complex mix of all of the preceding. U.S. companies tend to recognize that some hardships are associated with a foreign assignment and that the executive should receive extra compensation for undergoing them. In addition, there is a general belief that the executive and family should not suffer a negative change in lifestyle from accepting a foreign assignment. These two beliefs have resulted in a variety of bonuses and allowances that are often included in the overall compensation package for an expatriate assignment. The most common of these are outlined in the following.

Overseas bonuses are premiums paid in recognition of the inconveniences associated with a move to any foreign location. Usually a lump sum payment, these premiums may be paid at home or in the foreign location. They may be calculated as a percentage of salary or be a fixed sum for all expatriates. The options are numerous, and in some cases they are negotiable.

Hardship premiums are additional payments in recognition of the hardships associated with certain locations. These are usually established as a percentage of the base salary.

Moving allowances are usually paid by companies to cover all of the costs associated with a move to a foreign location. The allowance usually includes transportation, moving household effects, and hotels and meals while traveling. It sometimes includes the costs associated with selling or renting the employee's house.

Housing allowances allow expatriates to live in houses equivalent to those at home or equivalent to those of local managers. These allowances are usually based on the idea that the expatriate should not spend more than a certain percentage of her or his salary on rent; therefore, some companies cover any rent in excess of these amounts.

Education allowances allow the children of expatriates to attend schools equivalent to those at home and to be taught in the home language. U.S. companies usually cover the costs associated with children attending "American" schools, either those operating in the foreign country or private schools in the United States.

Travel allowances allow the expatriate and family to visit home regularly. The company usually covers all expenses associated with a trip home once a year; often the company offers leave, in addition to normal vacation time, for a trip home to the parent company.

Health allowances ensure that the expatriate has access to health care and facilities equivalent to those available at home. These are usually in the form of health insurance that covers the cost of all needed medical care and travel to receive such care.

Additional allowances may be included, depending on the particular company and location. These include car allowances, club memberships, foreign travel, and so on.

The Issue of Culture Shock

Even people who are well prepared for foreign assignments are likely to suffer a form of disorientation when they face the reality of the foreign location. This is generally referred to as **culture shock.** Culture shock occurs when an individual faces an unfamiliar set of assumptions and behavioral cues and finds that his or her traditional frame of reference seems inadequate.

People arriving in foreign locations often go through a phase of enrapture when the differences are seen as new and exciting, and they are anxious to explore the new sights and experiences (this is essentially a "tourist" phase). Unfortunately, the reality of new experiences, over a period of time, often becomes less pleasant. People who experience difficulty interacting in the local environment then begin to focus on the negative aspects of the situation and see the local environment and people in negative, even hostile, terms. The successful expatriate overcomes this by accepting the differences and adapting her or his behavior to the new surroundings. The unsuccessful expatriate does not adapt but withdraws and tries to change the behavior of others.

It is helpful for expatriates to know that most people experience some culture shock when they travel to foreign locations. The expatriate should not try to avoid such feelings; rather they should be expected and managed in a positive way. It is particularly helpful for expatriates to have a support group of some kind with whom they can talk freely about these feelings. It is also important for expatriates to recognize that the process of moving to a foreign location is stressful and that managing stress in a positive way will greatly contribute to their success.

In the People's Republic of China, Caucasians are unusual and local people often stop to stare at foreigners. One visitor to China found herself the object of even greater than usual attention when a chimpanzee at a zoo also seemed to find her unusual. She soon found that a crowd had gathered to stare, point, and laugh, at her and the chimpanzee.

Another expatriate in the PRC reported getting angry at a crowd staring at him trying to buy some bananas in a market. His reaction was to shout at the crowd to leave him alone. The crowd thought this enormously funny, and his reaction drew an even larger crowd.

The Problem of Repatriation

The expatriate process is not complete until the expatriate has returned home and adjusted successfully to the parent country and the parent company. A major difficulty here is that once an expatriate family has successfully adjusted to life in a foreign environment, it often finds returning home difficult.

Very often, the expatriate and family experience a culture shock on returning home that is similar to the one they experienced when arriving in the foreign location. This can be difficult to deal with because it may be totally unexpected. In fact, the expatriate and family are probably looking forward to getting back to what they remember as normal life; therefore, it is particularly disconcerting when "normal" life now appears strange. To readjust successfully, people returning after an extended stay in a foreign country need to be conscious of the problems they may encounter, need to be briefed about the situation at home, and need support on reentry to help them adjust; in short, they need effective **repatriation**

The problems of reentry have often been ignored in the past. Many expatriates have apparently found that the saying "out of sight, out of mind" applies in the case of foreign assignments. Many are out of touch with what is happening in the home office while they are away, and they return with no clear idea of what their new positions at home will be. Often the company has no clear idea of what it expects of the returning expatriate. This is particularly demoralizing when one realizes that the expatriate has probably been in a top foreign position and is looking forward to putting the experience and knowledge gained there to work at home.

Some companies have adopted a mentoring system to avoid some of these problems. As previously mentioned, the concept is that a senior manager in the home office becomes the sponsor of the expatriate manager. The mentor's responsibility is to ensure that the expatriate manager is kept informed of the company's activities at home and that an appropriate position is waiting for him or her upon return. This approach seems to have worked well for those companies that have adopted it.

In addition, companies can ensure that the expatriate and family come home regularly, that they have access to news from home, and that they are provided with videos and other entertainment from home on a regular basis. The idea is not to inundate them with home-country media but to give them a continuing sense of home.

Managing a Cross-Cultural Work Force

Staffing international positions and training individuals to relate to both host-country conditions and parent-company culture is just the beginning of the challenge in managing human resources in an international company. The entire management process must consider the different cultural characteristics of different locations. Chapter 6 described the cultural environment of international business. All of the factors discussed in that chapter should be considered to manage a cross-cultural work force effectively. In addition, international firms need to understand the role of unions in various locations.

The international company is torn between the need for integration and the need for fragmentation in all of its operations, but particularly in its management of human resources. The company sometimes needs global approaches to make its operations efficient and use its human resources effectively. At the same time, the cultural differences apparent in different locations dictate a policy of adapting management approaches for different locations.

Most companies employ a mix of standardization and adaptation. Policies and procedures are standardized that seem to be acceptable in most locations or that for technical reasons must be standard. Policies and procedures are adapted that seem to cause difficulties in different locations. Although it is easy to make a statement about combining standardization and adaptation, in reality it is very difficult to develop this mix. In fact, successful companies seem to develop an appropriate mix, partly by intuition, partly by trial and error. International experience seems to be the best pragmatic guide regarding what can be transferred and what cannot.

A U.S. firm in Spain had the following problem: The home office had a tradition of holding company picnics for management and workers to mingle with ease in a comfortable environment. The firm tried to import its company picnic into Spain and, to highlight management's "democratic" belief, the U.S. executives dressed as chefs and served the food. However, the picnic failed to help elicit the desired rapport between the U.S. managers and the Spanish workers. In fact, it was a most awkward affair; the lower-level staff clung together and did not want to be served by their superiors. When an executive approached their table, everyone stood up. Spanish attitudes of class distinction and social groups prohibit casual mixing and socializing of workers with executives.

An American textile manufacturer had to close the Robert Arundel textile machinery plant in Stockport, England, after a year-long struggle to change production methods, including the customary afternoon tea break, failed.

The behavior of people in organizations is determined by a variety of factors including their cultural values. Managers cannot expect the management practices that are effective at home necessarily to be effective in other locations. Effective management of a cross-cultural work force in an international firm relies on sensitivity to cultural variations and the ability to adapt to these variations.

Of particular importance to effective cross-cultural management is the status of trade unions in a particular country. Unions can play substantially different roles from country to country. In the United States, for example, membership in trade unions declined from 31 percent of the work force to 17 percent between 1970 and 1989. However, outside the United States, the percentage of worker membership in unions rose from 48 percent in 1970 to 55 percent in

1989. Effective managers recognize the need to assess the union environment of the local country and consider the situation in their decision-making process. Some of the management issues related to unions are the following.

The union-management relationship can differ from country to country. In Japan, for example, company unions often work closely with management, but in the United Kingdom, militant industrial unions are more likely to be in conflict with management.

The legal framework affecting management-union relationships can differ from country to country. In the United Kingdom, for example, few regulations govern union activities, but in the United States, the legal union framework is detailed.

The effect of union input on company decisions varies from one country to another. For example, codetermination in Germany by law gives unions a 50 percent representation on boards of directors; such representation occurs in the United States only if the company and the union(s) so choose.

The loyalty of union members differs from country to country. In Europe, for example, unions are associated with political parties and primary loyalty is to the affiliated party; in the United States they are often organized around trades or industries; in Japan unions are company unions.

Union demands can differ from country to country. For example, in some locations increased wages are a priority, while in others it is fringe benefits or job security, and in still others it is participation in decision making.

Multinational labor activity has increased with the internationalization of business. National unions have attempted to coordinate activities and share information with unions in other countries. The convergence in industrial relations around the world has not yet materialized, however, and to some degree, internationalization has instead polarized the different objectives of unions in various locations.

It is beyond the scope of this book to explore management-union relations in detail. These brief comments are intended to alert students to the need to investigate this issue as part of the international human resource management process.

On the consultation front, one of the most important bodies in Japan is the Sanrokon, or industry and labor conference. This group of 32 prominent labor, employer, and governmental leaders meets monthly to discuss critical economic and labor issues. An implicit objective is to ensure that when bargaining comes, there are as few destabilizing surprises as possible, that the bargaining parties know the relevant economic facts and are aware of each other's problems and needs. The body is chaired by a prominent neutral. The minister of labor attends all meetings, the prime minister attends at least once a year, and the group receives regular reports from the head of the Economic Planning Agency.

In Austria, wage bargaining is tied to price determination, tax policy, social legislation, and so on. Mechanisms to effect and, in some cases, force a coherent approach to collective bargaining and public policy formulation are present, in varying degrees, in Sweden and West Germany as well. In North America, such connections are haphazard, if they exist at all.   (Armstrong 1990)

Summary

This chapter began with a consideration of the role of human resources in international companies, particularly the management process from an international perspective. This was followed by a discussion of some typical functional activities in international companies. This discussion was intended to demonstrate the importance of human resources in international companies. The human resource mix in an international context was examined, including advantages and disadvantages of parent-country nationals, host-country nationals, and third-country nationals. The selection, training, and repatriation of expatriates were discussed from the perspective of the unique issues associated with sending personnel to foreign locations. Assigning women to expatriate managerial positions; recognizing the problems encountered by spouses, families, and dual-career couples; and dealing with culture shock were presented in the discussion of expatriate managers. The chapter concluded with a brief look at managing a cross-cultural work force.

As this chapter's discussion indicates, managing human resources in an international company is a complex process and one that is important throughout the organization. The complexity of the process, combined with its importance, means that international companies must pay careful attention to their human resource practices if they are to be successful.

MINI-CASE
An American Expatriate in the People's Republic of China

Background

Jane Kent is a sixty-three-year-old businesswoman from Michigan who chose early retirement at sixty in order to embark on a three-year stint in China, teaching English to Chinese university professors. The opportunity to go to China came by chance when she gave two professors a ride from Michigan to Washington and one of them invited her to come to his university. She accepted the invitation in 1986 and went to China with no formal preparation.

Prior to her extended stay in China as a teacher, Jane had visited as a tourist. She had lived in Japan immediately following World War II with her husband, who was in the Air Force, and had traveled and lived throughout the United States.

Comments

In May 1989, Jane described her stay in China as a "love affair": "I have fallen in love with the Chinese," she said, and then qualified this with "but not with China." The tragic events of the massacre of students in June 1989 make this statement particularly relevant.

Jane appeared to be the classic successful expatriate. She was enthusiastic and committed, described her experience in glowing terms as "rewarding," "fulfilling," and "exciting," and she believed that she was doing something really worthwhile. Perhaps more indicative of real success, her Chinese students and friends did not want her to leave and believed that she belonged in China.

Jane acknowledged encountering all kinds of difficulties during her three years in China. She told stories of strange foods: "I'm sure I've eaten dog, but I don't ask"; of never-ending train rides on dirty trains: thirty-six hours from Hong Kong's New Territories to Wuhan, a distance of only about 600 miles; of difficulty breathing the polluted air: "jogging is bad for the health"; of odd Chinese remedies when sick: "One student caught and cooked a snake to cure my flu"; of teaching in unheated buildings on cold winter days: "If there were one thing I would like to give to the people in Wuhan, it's heat." These events do not seem to have had any negative impact; rather, she talked of how much she has learned and how much more she appreciates what one has in North America.

The real culture shock for Jane may be that of reentry. Already on trips home, she has found it difficult to relate to how people "at home" behave; for example, she was shocked by the wastage of food that she would have been pleased to have had in China.

Asked why she thought she had been able to adjust so well to a totally foreign environment, she gave several answers:

> "It seemed like fate, I was destined to come; everything in my life just fell into place so that it was the appropriate thing to do."
>
> "I have always been a gypsy and moved around a lot; to me, home is wherever you lay your head."
>
> "I don't impose my Western ideas on China; the biggest problem that people face is an inability to separate West from East. They insist on imposing a Western view and concepts of what's right on the Chinese, and these expectations lead to disappointments, which are hard to accept."

Conclusions

Jane was a "good American," in contrast to the arrogant, ethnocentric "ugly American," whom one sometimes still encounters in foreign locations. Her comments show that expatriates can, and do, benefit from foreign experiences, as well as provide benefits for others. The challenge for companies and expatriate managers is to ensure that more people have a successful experience like Jane's.

Source: Interviews conducted in Wuhan, People's Republic of China, May 1989.

Discussion Issues

1. What factors contributed to Jane's apparent success as an expatriate?
2. What lessons could an international company learn from Jane's experience?
3. Identify some recent events that have occurred in the People's Republic of China. If you were an expatriate in China, how do you think you would react to those events?

Discussion Questions

1. Using your home country as an example, discuss the relative benefits and drawbacks of using PCNs, HCNs, and TCNs in that country (e.g., if you were born in the United States, you would consider a foreign company operating in the United States and HCNs would be U.S. citizens, PCNs would be from the foreign company's home, and TCNs would be other non-U.S. citizens).

2. What is the relationship between the need for expatriate training and cultural differences?

3. Assume that you accompany your spouse on an expatriate assignment where you cannot work; what would be your feelings about this situation?

Assignments

1. In groups of three or four, identify the issues that you would find most important if you were making a decision to accept or reject an expatriate assignment. Why are these particularly important to you?

2. Select a country to research in the library. Based on the information that you find on the country, discuss aspects of management style that would be effective or ineffective in that country.

3. Identify a company with subsidiaries in several different countries. Identify the company's mix of PCNs, HCNs, and TCNs in two or more of the subsidiaries. Discuss how this mix relates to the company and its operations in the host country.

Selected References

Adler, N. J., "Women as Androgynous Managers: A Conceptualization of the Potential for American Women in International Management," *International Journal of Intercultural Relations* 3, no. 4 (1979), pp. 407–436.

Adler, N. J., "Reentry: Managing Cross-Cultural Transitions," *Group and Organization Studies* (1981), pp. 341–356.

Adler, N. J., "Women in International Management: Where Are They?" *California Management Reviews* 26, no. 4 (1984), pp. 78–89.

Adler, N. J., Address to Conference on Research for Relevance in International Management (Windsor, Ontario, 1988).

Adler, N. J., *International Dimensions of Organizational Behavior* (Boston: PWS-Kent, 1991).

Armstrong, T., "Industrial Relations Japanese-Style," *Challenges* (Winter 1990).

Bass, B. M., "Leadership in Different Cultures," in B. M. Bass (ed.), *Stogdill's Handbook of Leadership* (New York: The Free Press, 1981), pp. 522–549.

Briggs, N., and G. Harwood, "Training Personnel in Multinational Business," *International Journal of Intercultural Relations* 6 (1982).

Brown, R., "How to Choose the Best Expatriates," *Personnel Management* (June 1987), p. 67.

Business International Corporation, Worldwide Executive Compensation and Human Resource Planning (New York: Business International Corporation, 1982).

Business International, "India; Limited Avenues to an Unlimited Market" (1985).

Copeland, L., and L. Griggs, *Going International: How to Make Friends and Deal Effectively in the Global Marketplace* (New York: New American Library, 1985).

Dunbar, E., and M. Ehrlich, "International Human Resources Practices; Selecting, Training, and Managing the International Staff: A Survey Report," *The Project on International Human Resources* (New York: Columbia University Teacher's College, 1986).

Earley, P. C. "Intercultural Training for Managers: A Comparison of Documentary and Interpersonal Methods," *Academy of Management Journal* 30, no. 4 (1987), pp. 685–698.

Grove, C. L., and I. Torbiorn, "A New Conceptualization of Intercultural Adjustment and the Goals of Training," *International Journal of Intercultural Relations* 9, no. 2 (1985), pp. 205–233.

Hall, E. T., "The Silent Language in Overseas Business," *Harvard Business Review* (May–June 1960), p. 87.

Haque, M. R., "Western Institute and Research Centre," in O. H. M. Yau, E. F. K. Yu, and A. C. K. Ko, eds., *Compendium: First Conference on Case Method and Research on Asian Business Management* (Kowloon, Hong Kong: City University of Hong Kong, Department of Business and Management, 1995).

Heller, J. E., "Criteria for Selecting an International Manager," *Personnel* (May–June 1980), pp. 47–55.

Howard, C. G., "Out of Sight – Not Out of Mind," *Personnel Administrator* (June 1987), pp. 82–90.

Illman, P. E., "Motivating the Overseas Workforce," *Developing Overseas Managers and Managers Overseas* (1980), pp. 107–113.

Jeannet and Hennessey, *Global Marketing Strategies* (Boston: Houghton Mifflin, 1995).

Jelinek, M., and N. J. Adler, "Women: World-Class Managers for Global Competition," *Academy of Management Executive* (February 1988), pp. 11–20.

Laurent, A., "The Cultural Diversity of Western Conceptions of Management," *International Studies of Management and Organization* (Spring–Summer 1983), pp. 75–96.

Mendenhall, M., E. Dunbar, and G. Oddou, "Expatriate Selection, Training, and Career-Pathing: A Review and Critique," *Human Resource Management* (Fall 1987), pp. 331–345.

Mendenhall, M., and G. Oddou, "Acculturation Profiles of Expatriate Managers: Implications for Cross-Cultural Training Programs," *Columbia Journal of World Business* (Winter 1986), pp. 73–79.

Moran, R. T., "Forget about Gender, Just Get the Job Done," *International Management* (March 1986), p. 72.

Ondrack, D., "International Transfers of Managers in North American and European MNEs," *Journal of International Business Studies* (Fall 1985), pp. 1–19.

Phatak, A., *International Dimensions of Management* (Boston: PWS-Kent, 1983).

Prahalad, C. K., and Y. Doz, *The Multinational Mission* (New York: The Free Press, 1987).

Pulatie, D., "How Do You Ensure Success of Managers Going Abroad?" *Training and Development Journal* (December 1985), pp. 22–24.

Punnett, B. J., "International Human Resource Management," in A. Rugman, ed., *International Business in Canada* (Toronto: Prentice-Hall Canada, 1989a), pp. 330–346.

Punnett, B. J., *Experiencing International Management* (Boston: PWS-Kent, 1989b).

Ricks, D. A., *Blunders in International Business* (Cambridge, Mass.: Blackwell Publishers, 1993).

Ronen, S., *Comparative and International Management* (New York: John Wiley & Sons, 1986).

Thomas, T., "Change in Climate for Foreign Investment in India," *Columbia Journal of World Business* (Spring 1994).

Time (March 7, 1988), p. 55.

Tung, R., "Human Resource Planning in Japanese Multinationals: A Model for U.S. Firms?" *Journal of International Business Studies* (Fall 1984), pp. 139–149.

Tung, R., "Expatriate Assignments: Enhancing Success and Minimizing Failure," *Academy of Management Executive* (May 1987), pp. 117–126.

Tung, R., *The New Expatriates: Managing Human Resources Abroad* (Cambridge, Mass.: Ballinger, 1988).

Tung, R., "Career Issues in International Assignments," *Academy of Management Executive* (August 1988), pp. 241–244.

Zeira, Y., and M. Banai, "Selecting Managers for Foreign Assignments," *Management Decision* 25, no. 4 (1987), pp. 38–40.

CHAPTER ▼ 15

Control Issues in International Companies

L E A R N I N G   O B J E C T I V E S

After reading this chapter, you should be able to

▶ Explain the role of controls in an international company.

▶ Discuss the attributes of an international control system.

▶ Discuss the effectiveness of an international control system.

▶ Identify different types of controls and evaluate them from an international point of view.

▶ Describe different types of international corporate structures and relate these to organizational strategy and control.

K E Y   T E R M S

▶ Complexity of internal and external environments

▶ Attributes of effective control

▶ Control activities

▶ Performance evaluation

▶ Development of international companies

▶ Export division

▶ International division

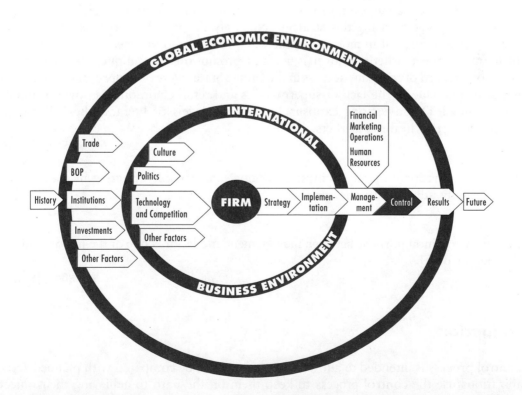

- ▶ Accounting and auditing controls
- ▶ Plans
- ▶ Policies
- ▶ Procedures
- ▶ Bureaucratic control systems
- ▶ Corporate culture control systems
- ▶ Centralization
- ▶ Information systems

- ▶ Global functional structure
- ▶ Global product structure
- ▶ Global area structure
- ▶ Multidimensional structures
- ▶ Matrix structures
- ▶ Coordinating committees
- ▶ Hierarchy
- ▶ Responsibility and authority

T H O U G H T   S T A R T E R S

▶ A U.S. consumer products firm developed a plan to create a world structure of subsidiaries through the acquisition of similar companies located in both developed and developing countries. Through these subsidiaries, it hoped to form a worldwide market for its products. Small- and medium-sized companies in Europe, Latin America, and Japan were purchased within a three-year period. Special efforts were made to add the U.S. products to the existing lines of the acquired companies, since the consumer goods available through the foreign companies were different from those in the parent's line. However, the U.S. company ran into several problems using this strategy. Not only did it fail to consider the tastes of its potential customers, but in most cases, the U.S. products did not meet foreign requirements. Furthermore, the marketing, advertising, and promotional techniques that had produced such a long record of company success in the United States were not appropriate for the foreign environments. Due to the lack of supermarkets and retail chain outlets, lower standards of living, limited TV advertising exposure, and lower levels of literacy, the U.S. techniques proved ineffective in these markets.

(Ricks 1993, pp. 117–118)

▶ Effective international managers must be chameleons capable of acting in many ways, not experts rigidly adhering to one approach.

(Adler 1990, p. 171)

▶ Creating a common purpose between management and labor is one of the major issues facing all of us [at Bata].

(Bata 1990, p. 285)

Introduction

The control process is intended to allow actual activities to be compared with planned activities. Organizations use the control process to keep them on the path to achieving their objectives.

Planning and controlling therefore are closely linked. The planning process sets forth the strategies and goals of the organization and defines the means to attain them. The control process measures progress toward goals, identifies any deviations in the progress, and attempts to identify the causes of the deviations. The control process alerts management when corrective action is needed or when strategies and goals, or the means to attain them, need to be reevaluated.

Control is fundamental to effective operations in any organization because it keeps the enterprise within a manageable range of planned results. It is of particular importance in international firms because of the complexity of their operations and the physical and cultural distance between the various parts of the organization. The international business, operating in a variety of locations around the world, easily can find its varying operations acting on their own with little regard for the objectives of the enterprise as a whole. A good control system can help minimize the degree to which this occurs.

Control systems consist of a variety of measures that are designed systematically to evaluate actual performance relative to desired or planned performance. Numerous methods can be used to perform this evaluation, and international and domestic firms may use the same method(s). Choosing the best control methods for an international firm can be more complex than for a domestic firm because of the cultural and national differences that exist at the international level. An international firm's control systems need to be designed so that they are compatible with all of the cultural and national requirements in different locations.

This chapter considers the issues associated with the control process and control systems from an international company's perspective. It begins with a general discussion of the need for, and importance of, international controls and the characteristics of effective control systems. Accounting and auditing controls are then identified and considered. This is followed by a discussion of plans, policies, and procedures as international control mechanisms. Additional dimensions of control are then examined: first, bureaucratic controls are compared with corporate culture control; then issues of centralization and decentralization of control are examined. Information flows are considered next, and their importance in effective international control is discussed. Managerial performance evaluation and some of the complexities associated with evaluation on a global scale are reviewed. In the final sections of the chapter, organizational structure and its relationship to effective control systems are discussed, and some overall conclusions are presented.

The Importance of Controls

Controls increase in importance as firms increase in internal complexity and face increasingly complex external environments. In addition, control is particularly relevant when a substantial degree of delegation of authority is required and where the environment changes frequently. These factors contribute to the need for a formal system of controls to ensure that the firm is moving in the desired direction.

A complex internal environment that involves substantial delegation of authority provides many opportunities for individuals or groups to act in ways that are not consistent with the organization's goals, either intentionally or unwittingly. An effective system of controls limits the likelihood of this happening by measuring deviations from plans and alerting managers to them. A **complex external environment** that is changing can make it difficult to achieve desired targets, but it also can provide new and unforeseen opportunities. An effective system of controls identifies deviations so that timely corrective action can be taken or goals can be changed to be able to take advantage of new opportunities.

Characteristics of an Effective Control System

International business, by its nature, embodies the following characteristics. Companies are complex internally because of differing activities in locations around the world. Authority must be delegated to managers in foreign locations. The external environment is complex because of varying cultural and national characteristics, and the overall environment is likely to be changing constantly because changes in any location can affect operations in other locations. In addition, shifting currency relationships can alter an international enterprise's priorities and choices. The nature of international business, therefore, underscores the need for effective control systems in international companies.

The international firm operates in distant countries with diverse and changing environments and relies on people of many nationalities to achieve its plans. This complexity emphasizes the need for control to an even greater degree than in a domestic counterpart, and also makes achieving effective control more difficult.

To design a good international control system, several **attributes of effective control** systems should be considered. Seven characteristics are identified here and discussed with an international emphasis.

Accuracy

Information clearly must be accurate if it is to identify whether actual performance conforms with expected performance. Inaccurate information can lead to a false sense of security or corrective action where none is needed. What is measured and how it is measured therefore must be clearly defined in an effective control system.

For measurements to be accurate, standards of measurement – "how to measure" – must be clearly stated. This standardization is particularly important in international operations because different groups or different people may follow various standards. The head office must attempt to avoid problems, for example, that would result if some subsidiaries consider a report of exact expenditures to be in round numbers but others interpret this to mean amounts in the exact dollar and cents. Headquarters may need to specify the currency in which its subsidiaries are to forecast their budgets. The failure to use a standard currency could result in a subsidiary reporting the budget in local currency but the headquarters budgeting the needed amounts in U.S. dollars.

In addition, systems of measurement vary and particular measurement approaches may be unfamiliar to some people. This means that what is measured and how it is measured may have to be defined differently for different locations. Before selecting a system of measurement for a particular location, a preliminary trial is often appropriate to ascertain if there are problems associated with its use.

Timeliness

Information is useful only if it is available in time for managers to take corrective action or make appropriate changes in strategy. Information that is late can result in inappropriate responses or none at all. The timing of measuring results and the speed with which they are reported therefore are key aspects of an effective control system.

Timeliness can be difficult to achieve in international companies because of geographic distance and cultural and national differences. Delays in getting information may be due to the physical distance that the information has to travel (e.g., mail delays, telephone delays, airline delays). These delays may be further complicated by the location of various offices in different time zones, which means that various parts of the enterprise are open for business at different times.

Delays may also result from cultural attitudes relating to time matters or because of local restrictions and regulations. For example, Latin Americans are often described as paying little attention to time as illustrated by the "mañana" attitude of putting off until tomorrow what does not have to be done today. Apparently, this attitude toward time is reflected in public clocks in the United States and various Latin American countries; U.S. clocks are significantly more accurate than those in Latin America.

Decisions regarding when information is measured and how it is reported should consider these potential delays to ensure timeliness. Many iterations of the process may be needed to work out appropriate time frames.

Objectivity

Information must be as objective as possible to be useful in indicating corrective action; that is, information should reflect observable facts as much as possible rather than be limited to personal descriptions and opinions. Personal opinions may be biased, either consciously or unconsciously, and can affect the accuracy of information. Wherever possible, therefore, objective measures are preferred. When subjective measures are needed because of the nature of the information, the possibility of bias should be examined.

Objectivity may be difficult to ensure internationally because perceptual biases are likely to exist and influence even seemingly objective measures of performance. For example, a particular percentage increase in sales might be considered "substantial" in one location and only "moderate" in another. Cultural and national differences can make identifying when and how information may be biased particularly difficult. Special care should be taken to identify measures of performance that are not easily influenced by personal opinions and to evaluate the information provided for possible inaccuracies.

Acceptability

A control system works only as well as the people who maintain it. If a system is unacceptable to the members of the organization, they may ignore or sabotage it or comply with it unwillingly. In such cases, the information provided is likely to be inaccurate, untimely, and subjective. A good control system, therefore, is designed with the users in mind.

Designing such a system may be complex in an international company. Because of cultural and national differences, what is acceptable in one location may not be in another. For example, written reports may be normal in North America but unusual in a country in which literacy is low or where paper is scarce. International control systems may have to be tailored to the specific needs of different locations in order to be accepted and thus useful. If this is the case, the international company faces the challenge of finding ways to make the different forms of information comparable.

Clarity

Information is useful only if it is clear and understandable and can be readily interpreted by those who use it. Information that is unclear is frustrating and annoying, can be misunderstood and lead to mistaken actions, or may be ignored. Ensuring that the information provided by a control system is clear is therefore an important aspect of designing an effective system. This can be complex on the international level.

The ways to collect and report information may vary from one place to another. What may be clear and easy to understand in one location may be virtually incomprehensible in another location. The following are some examples:

- ▶ One system can report all sales and costs as total figures, but another may break them down item by item.
- ▶ Sales and costs can be reported as currency amounts or as percentages.
- ▶ Budgets can be in currency amounts or expressed as percentages.
- ▶ Amounts may be expressed in local or headquarters currency, U.S. dollars, or some combination of currencies.

An effective international control system must be designed to overcome these variations, either by translating information into appropriate formats or by training people to understand a standard format. In some cases, both translation and training may be required.

Cost Effectiveness

A good control system needs to provide greater benefits than the cost of implementing and maintaining it. Benefits include improved management decisions based on the information the system provides. The system should also be compatible with the organization; that is, the effort required to maintain the system should be reasonable. If the costs in terms of employees' time and effort are excessive, there is no gain from the system; therefore, these costs should be carefully evaluated. These costs are not always obvious because of the complications associated with such systems. The system therefore may require modifications over time as the costs become clear and a realistic cost/benefit evaluation can be made.

Relevance

An effective control system is designed to be relevant given a firm's unique characteristics. Information about performance areas that are important to the firm's overall success should be identified. The information can be derived from the firm's normal work patterns without disrupting operations.

Each international firm can have vastly different operations around the world, and the appropriate controls are likely to vary from one location to another as a result. At the same time, an international company is concerned with controlling its overall operations. An effective international control system incorporates a delicate balance between standardization and adaptation. Such a system adapts to local needs as required but still maintains an overall view of the company.

Designing a control system involves the following activities:

► Determining desired final results
► Identifying interim results that will lead to desired final results
► Establishing standards for interim results
► Collecting data and comparing with standards
► Identifying causes of deviations
► Taking corrective action
► Comparing actual results with expectations
► Reviewing plans and goals for the next cycle.

Although this list may indicate that the control system has a beginning and end, it is really a continuous system because actual results at any stage can lead to changes in plans or activities, and shorter-term results modify or change longer-term plans. In addition, the control system itself constantly is monitored for effectiveness and can be modified or changed to increase its usefulness.

Control Mechanisms

Various mechanisms of the control process are available to enable organizations to reach their goals in specified ways. These mechanisms include accounting and auditing controls, plans, policies, and procedures.

International Accounting and Auditing Controls

Accounting and auditing controls are a fundamental aspect of any company's control system. These controls are designed to measure the financial results of activities over a period of time and identify and evaluate resources at a particular point in time. These financial controls allow managers to compare actual results with anticipated ones.

Accounting information is historical in nature. It is based on activities that have already occurred; that is, it documents past performance. It reports an organization's assets, revenues, and inflows of money and its liabilities, costs, and outflows of funds. The basic purpose of accounting information is to provide a picture of the firm's financial position so that its managers can evaluate and monitor its financial performance. As such, accounting systems are clearly control systems. Their function is the same in an international company as in a domestic company; however, this function is much more complex because accounting procedures and standards vary around the world.

An audit checks or verifies the information provided by accounting statements. The audit, which determines whether operational and financial controls are being followed, provides information intended largely to serve the shareholders. Audits focus on the reliability and validity of reported financial information. An audit, therefore, is essentially a control mechanism to check on the firm's control systems. Audits are used for the same purpose worldwide, but as with accounting, procedures and standards can vary widely around the world.

It is beyond the scope of this text to discuss international accounting and auditing in any depth. The following points are presented, however, to illustrate some of the complex issues encountered relative to international accounting and auditing controls.

Legal requirements for reporting financial information can vary from country to country. This variation may be in terms of the specific information that a firm is required to document, the timing of information gathering, or the public availability of such information. The international company must comply with different regulations in different countries. At the same time, it needs to ensure that it has access to the information it requires to make informed decisions.

Cultural differences can result in different attitudes toward the collection and documentation of financial information. These differences influence the ease with which information can be obtained and sometimes its reliability. For example, in some Asian countries, asking for proof of someone's statement is insulting because it implies that the person could be dishonest; this cultural element makes it difficult to obtain objective evidence to corroborate stated assertions.

Business practices that differ from one location to another make uniform accounting practices impossible. The same information simply may not be available in different locations. For example, canceled checks are normally returned to the issuer in some countries but in others they become the property of the bank. Similarly, receipts can be difficult to obtain in countries where they are infrequently required.

Activities illegal according to some laws create difficulties. In some countries, it may be normal to engage in black market or unreported activities of various kinds. By their nature, these transactions will not be formally reported in those countries by local managers. In the United States, however, the Foreign Corrupt Practices Act (FCPA) requires that all transactions, including illegal ones, be reported; the FCPA makes such activities on the part of a U.S. company or U.S. national illegal, no matter where they occur. Other countries have similar legislation.

Communication difficulties can be numerous. These difficulties range from different spoken and written languages to mail delays and inadequate telephone service to different time zones with little effective overlap. Any of these can make gathering accounting and auditing information very complex, particularly when the information purports to be for a specific point in time.

International companies often have peculiar financial information needs that differ from their domestic counterparts. Financial information often is required on a country, regional, and global basis. Performance in each distinct location may need to be assessed as well as the impact of performance in one location on other locations. Finally, performance of all locations must be integrated to judge the international company's total performance. Performance at all levels is partially a function of allocated costs between units, or from the parent, but currency fluctuations can make performance appear better or worse than it actually was. Exhibit 15.1 presents some of the complexities associated with measuring subsidiary performance.

Control through Plans, Policies, and Procedures

A company uses plans, policies, and procedures as part of its control system to ensure that activities throughout the organization conform to its expectations and accepted standards. These elements of the control system are discussed from an international perspective.

EXHIBIT 15.1   **Evaluating Subsidiary Performance**

The following situation, describing a subsidiary's performance, illustrates the complexity of evaluating performance internationally, even with very simple assumptions. Consider a U.S. multinational company with a joint venture subsidiary that assembles electronic components: The components are sold to other affiliates, and payments are made in varying currencies; assembly materials are provided by headquarters and billed to the subsidiary in U.S. dollars; services are provided by headquarters and the local partner as needed.

	Budget Local $	Actual Local $	Foreign Exchange Effect	Under Local Control
Net sales	1,000,000	1,200,000)	varied	no
Less				
Materials	400,000	540,000)	100%	partly
Direct labor	200,000	300,000)	0%	yes
Import duties[a]	—	90,000)	0%	
Depreciation	50,000	50,000)	0%	partly
	650,000	980,000)		
Gross Profit	350,000	220,000)		
Administrative expenses				
Management expenses	200,000	230,000)	60%	partly
Staff expenses[b]	75,000	100,000)	50%	partly
Other expenses	75,000	100,000)	0%	yes
	350,000	430,000)		
Net profit/(loss)	—	(210,000)		

[a]A request is being considered for a refund of import duties.
[b]$50,000 consultation fee to local partner, $50,000 services from headquarters.

Plans and Control

As noted previously, planning and control are closely linked. The firm's **plan** is the yardstick by which it measures success or failure. Achieving planned objectives is interpreted as success; failing to achieve them must be explained by those responsible for the results.

International firms frequently have long-term strategic plans stretching 10, 20, or more years into the future; these plans guide their activities. They also have shorter-term business plans for the immediate future that serve as a very specific guide for the activities of each unit of the organization. These short-term plans often are accompanied by budgets and serve primarily as control mechanisms.

These plans incorporate specific objectives and goals as well as time frames for achieving them. Typically, objectives and goals are stated and measured in terms of profitability, market share, sales growth, levels of expenditure, production volumes, quality levels, employment levels, investments, and other similar items. These measures are identified for the company as a whole and for individual units. The degree of autonomy and authority in various locations is often identified as well as a budget allocated for each unit. This budget may be allocated to specific activities within a given unit.

Performance related to the stated plans can be measured at predetermined intervals and actual achievements compared with those projected. The plan and periodic measurements of results function as a control system. If actual results differ from those needed to achieve the plan, corrective action can be taken in a timely manner.

Short-term plans of this type are developed specifically for each unit or location, and therefore the differing characteristics of each can be taken into account. These plans are usually best developed with input from top management, regional managers, and managers at the local level. Such development ensures that all viewpoints are represented and that all levels have agreed to the specific objectives and goals identified in the plan. Top management provides the global view of the international firm and ensures that a particular unit's activities contribute to the firm's global objectives. Regional managers are acutely aware of the interactions among units at the regional level and can ensure that the activities of various units contribute positively, where possible, to regional performance and do not negatively affect other units. Local managers are likely to be best informed about local conditions and able to decide whether the plan is or is not possible given the local environment.

Policies and Procedures and Control

Management establishes policies and procedures to channel the thinking and behavior of organization members so that they are consistent with organization objectives. Policies and procedures thus act as a control over organizational activities. A **policy** is a general guideline that directs decision making. A **procedure** is a detailed set of instructions for carrying out a series of activities that occur regularly.

There are advantages to standardizing policies and procedures on a worldwide basis. Such standardization ensures that all units follow similar practices, which facilitates communication, coordination, and transfers of personnel, resources, and services among units, as well as contributes to a uniform global image. The use of standardized policies and procedures throughout a global business reduces confusion and simplifies the control process for headquarters.

Standardizing policies and procedures also has disadvantages, particularly in an international setting. This is partly because units of the organization may be involved in quite different businesses and may be organized in varied forms. In addition, the contrasting customs and regulations associated with different cultural and national environments often militate against the use of standardized policies and procedures. North American management relies on accurate and precise control information, and its lack often leads to the imposition of tighter controls through standardized policies and procedures. What may be needed are not tighter controls but different forms of policies and procedures that are acceptable locally and reflect local laws, customs, and practices. In this situation, appropriate controls may need to be developed for each unit of the organization. Of course, this lack of standardization complicates the process of communication, coordination, and transfer and generally makes the control process more complex and varied. International managers must become accustomed to managing in this multifaceted environment.

Additional Aspects of International Control

In addition to the choices among varied control mechanisms (e.g., plans, procedures, policies) available to international organizations, control systems can vary in other aspects. Two aspects of control, bureaucratic versus corporate culture and centralization versus decentralization, are considered here.

Bureaucratic versus Corporate Culture Control

Bureaucratic control systems are those that rely on formal, explicit stipulations regarding expected levels of performance and acceptable activities and behaviors. Several of the control mechanisms discussed previously fall into this category. These mechanisms tend to be relatively rigid and quantitative.

Corporate culture control systems rely on more qualitative and personal means to maintain control. International firms that emphasize control through the establishment of a global corporate culture deliberately seek to institute a similar corporate culture in all units worldwide. This culture is achieved by carefully selecting and training personnel and frequently making international transfers of key personnel. Key managers from the head office take its culture with them to units around the world, and key managers from foreign locations spend time at the head office to learn and absorb its culture.

The choice between bureaucratic and corporate culture controls is not an either/or choice. Most international firms employ a mix of the two. The particular mix depends on the company's operations and country of origin. U.S.-based international companies historically have favored bureaucratic controls; Japanese and European firms have been more likely to use the corporate culture approach.

Centralized versus Decentralized Control

International control systems also vary in terms of the degree of centralization associated with the system. **Centralization,** in this context, refers to the degree of control that corporate headquarters (the parent) maintains relative to the degree of control allocated to the subsidiary units of the organization. Headquarters of highly centralized international companies maintain a high degree of control; decentralized companies give more freedom to subsidiary units.

Note that the degree of centralization refers here to the international organization as a whole; it does not consider centralization or decentralization at the local level. It is possible that an international firm, as a whole, is described as decentralized because each subsidiary unit makes its own plans and selects its own controls. Individual units might themselves be centralized if decisions are made and controls enforced by one or a few individuals within that unit.

International companies seek a mix of centralization and decentralization that suits the specific firm and the management styles of its leaders. Many factors influence this control decision, and the degree of control retained by headquarters varies from firm to firm. Among the major factors influencing this decision are the following:

1. Industry – Certain industries tend toward centralized controls because they require product consistency (e.g., the pharmaceutical industry) or because they can achieve substantial economic advantages through standardized and harmonized global operations (e.g., the oil and gas industry).
2. Type of subsidiary – Certain types of subsidiaries are amenable to central control; others need to be decentralized to adapt to local conditions. In general, manufacturing subsidiaries are more likely to be centrally controlled to allow for product standardization, but marketing subsidiaries may be decentralized to reflect local market characteristics. Joint ventures and local participation may limit the degree of central control that is acceptable.
3. Function – Certain functional areas of international firms tend to be centrally controlled but other areas are controlled by the subsidiary units. Financial controls are usually centralized; local human resources are usually controlled at the subsidiary unit level. Research and development is usually centrally controlled; public relations may be locally controlled. Marketing may combine global product programs with local execution.
4. Parent philosophy – Some companies believe in centralization; others find that decentralization is more effective. This philosophy is often related to the company's business and its previous international experience, as well as the management style of its chief executive officer. Global firms are more likely to be centrally controlled; multidomestics may be more decentralized. Frequently, the greater the degree of interdependency among units, the greater is the need for central coordination and control.
5. Parent confidence in the subsidiary – The more confidence that a parent has in the subsidiary's management, the more likely it is to decentralize controls. Confidence is likely to develop over time; therefore, controls may be more centralized initially but become more decentralized later on.
6. Cultural similarity – Cultural similarity affects centralization because people tend to trust others who express similar cultural values and attitudes. Units that are culturally similar to the parent therefore may be given more freedom. Alternatively, if a unit is very dissimilar culturally from the parent, the decision may be made that it needs more control.
7. Firm-specific advantage – Firms generally want to maintain centralized control over those factors that contribute substantially to their competitive position. If a company's technology is its main advantage, it is likely to control technology centrally. If its training of employees is a key strength, it is likely to control training centrally.

The task for international executives is to find the appropriate balance between headquarters's control and subsidiary units' freedom. Too little central control can result in an ineffective system, but too much central control inhibits local initiative and development. The right balance depends on the firm and its particular subsidiaries. The degree of centralization maintained by an international firm often varies from one subsidiary unit to another. A firm's philosophy, relative to centralization, may change over time as it experiences varying reactions to, and results from, centralization or decentralization. A firm's business changes over time, and this also influences its choice of control techniques. Centralization versus decentralization choices, therefore, continually are reevaluated.

Information Systems as Part of Control Systems

The proper flow of information from headquarters to subsidiaries, from subsidiaries to headquarters, and between subsidiaries is instrumental in the effectiveness of the control system. Designing an effective information system is therefore an integral aspect of designing a control system. A good **information system** provides information that is understandable and usable.

While information systems are an important part of any company's control system, they are critical for the international company. Because of the physical and cultural separation between units of the organization, clear information is vital to the maintenance of control throughout the organization. Of course, this separation also makes the design of an effective system a major challenge. An international company's system may have to be understandable to and usable by people who work in different countries, speak different languages, have different literacy levels, and view their information needs differently.

The specifics of each information system differ depending on the organization's needs; however, to design an effective system, an organization should consider the following questions:

1. What information is needed? – The precise information needed at the various levels in the organization must be identified and systems put into place to accumulate the data required to provide it.
2. Who will accumulate the data? – Responsibility must be assigned for data collection and the needed authority delegated to an area or person to ensure that the data can be collected.
3. Who will receive the data and information? – People need to receive only information that relates to the decisions that they have to make or to which they contribute. Only relevant information should be supplied to appropriate people. The determination of who are the appropriate people to receive specific information might vary from manager to manager, depending on the style of management and the location.
4. What form will the information take? – Raw data often must be transformed into more meaningful information; responsibility and authority for this task need to be defined and allocated. Data must be converted to information that supports decision making. User input is particularly important in deciding on the format for presenting information so that it is in a form that the receiver can use and understand.
5. When will information be available? – Information is useful only if it is available in a timely manner. Identifying and reducing the time lag between an event and the availability of information describing it therefore are very important.

These questions need to be asked when any information system is being designed; they are particularly relevant to the international system. The complexity of the international firm, because of the geographic and cultural distances between units and the varying regulations applying to each, affects the answers to all of these questions; therefore, the answers must be thought through carefully. Because of the complex nature of an international organization, its effective information flow may have to evolve over time.

Performance Evaluation

An important purpose of any control system is the evaluation of people's performance. People within the organization are expected to perform certain activities and achieve certain results. To ensure that these activities are adequately performed and that objectives are reached, the performance of employees is reviewed and evaluated periodically in most organizations.

From a control perspective, the focus is frequently on evaluating managers of subsidiary units to determine whether the units are accomplishing expected results. In a U.S. noninternational firm, managers typically are evaluated on the basis of growth in sales, market share, and profits. Managers of various domestic groups (e.g., product groups) are often evaluated comparatively on these variables.

Effective **performance evaluation** focuses on factors within the scope of control of the person being evaluated. Because managers may sometimes have little control over the results of their units, evaluation can be more difficult in an international firm. In a global company, many decisions made at the regional or headquarters level have an effect on subsidiaries' performance. The following are types of decisions for which managers may have little control:

▶ Prices for transfers of goods or services among corporate units often are not determined by the subsidiary. Profitability and costs therefore may be beyond the subsidiary manager's control.

▶ Sales to other corporate units often are not a function of the market but are determined by corporate requirements. Sales and market share therefore may be outside the subsidiary manager's control.

▶ A subsidiary may be established for strategic or tactical reasons relating to global returns rather than the subsidiary's returns. The subsidiary manager therefore has little control over sales, costs, or profits.

▶ Sudden and unexpected changes in local government policy may affect a subsidiary's performance. If the local manager had no reason to expect these changes, he or she cannot be held responsible for the results associated with them.

▶ Environmental changes that affect economic factors such as currency values, inflation rates, and levels of exports or imports may be unpredictable. A local manager cannot be held responsible for results stemming from these economic impacts.

Evaluation of subsidiary managers should be based on performance that is within their control. This often means a goal-based evaluation system as opposed to one based largely on financial performance. A goal-based evaluation system is similar to a plan, as described earlier.

Such a system establishes goals for the subsidiary that are agreeable to the subsidiary manager as well as to regional and headquarters' managers. Performance is then measured in relationship to goal achievement.

The goal-based approach focuses on results that can be attributed to the manager's activities at the subsidiary level. The critical factor is to identify and distinguish controllable factors from uncontrollable ones. Financial goals form part of the evaluation, but nonfinancial goals (e.g., those reflecting government relations, employee satisfaction, communications with other subsidiaries) are included as well.

Organizational Structure and Control

The structure of an organization is fundamental to the organization's ability to achieve its goals effectively; therefore, structure provides a framework for control for the firm. The structure of the organization ensures that the work to be performed is identified and broken into manageable units, that these units are meaningfully related to each other, and that desired communication among them can take place.

Organizations need a defined structure to facilitate the accomplishment of their chosen strategy. Designing the formal structure of an organization can be thought of as similar to designing the structure of a building. A building's structure depends on its purpose. It functions well when its structure is appropriate for its purpose: A hospital needs to be different from a school, which, in turn, must be different from a home. In much the same way, organizations can be structured differently to accomplish varied purposes. An organization that is primarily a distributor has a different structure from one that focuses predominately on research. This is true of domestic organizations as well as international ones. International structures are further differentiated by the need to standardize or adapt various aspects of the organization and its outputs around the world. Although organizations have unique structures, there is a structural development typical in North American companies. This structural development is examined in the next section.

Typical Structural Development of North American International Companies

Although organizations have unique structures, a study by Stopford and Wells (1972) suggested that U.S. international companies develop according to a predictable pattern. First they establish an export division; then an international division; followed by a global functional, product, or area structure; and finally a global matrix. This pattern of development reflects the experience of U.S. firms during the 1970s and is illustrated in Exhibit 15.2.

Although the four structural patterns are discussed sequentially, companies do not necessarily follow this progression. Many firms, for example, retain export or international divisions for a long period. Others move rapidly to a global product or area structure. The specific pattern a particular firm follows depends on its strategy and environment.

EXHIBIT 15.2
**Structural
Development**

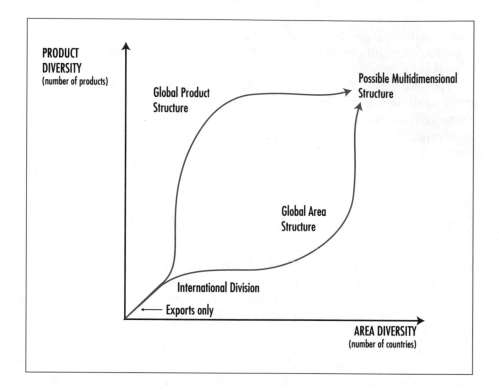

Many companies do not seek export opportunities but, as discussed in Chapter 9, decide to take advantage of fortuitous ones. Such opportunities generally occur when the organization is approached by an outside party to supply a specific product to a particular foreign market. Most companies consider such an opportunity as a temporary situation. In such cases, there is little need for a formal, permanent adjustment to the company's structure. The only requirement is that the fortuitous exports be taken care of in a timely and efficient manner.

Export Division

Many companies do not seek export opportunities but, as discussed in Chapter 9, decide to take advantage of fortuitous ones. Such opportunities generally occur when the organization is approached by an outside party to supply a specific product to a particular foreign market. Most companies consider such an opportunity as a temporary situation. In such cases, there is little need for a formal, permanent adjustment to the company's structure. The only requirement is that the fortuitous exports be taken care of in a timely and efficient manner.

In many instances, fortuitous opportunities lead firms to recognize the profit in such transactions and to change their strategies to seek exports intentionally. Once they develop intentional export strategies, companies are more likely to make formal, permanent adjustments to their organizational structures. Such adjustments often result in the creation of export divisions, which coexist with the traditional organizational structure. The new division can be added to either a functional or divisional structure as illustrated in Exhibit 15.3.

The choice of delegation between marketing and operations is an interesting one. Viewing the export function as a marketing function indicates that the company focuses on selling its product in foreign markets. Considering the export function as an operations function indicates a concern with allocating production for exports but with little focus on selling in these markets. The first may lead to a greater emphasis on developing foreign markets. The second may by more appropriate when modifications in the product are necessary to make it appropriate for foreign markets.

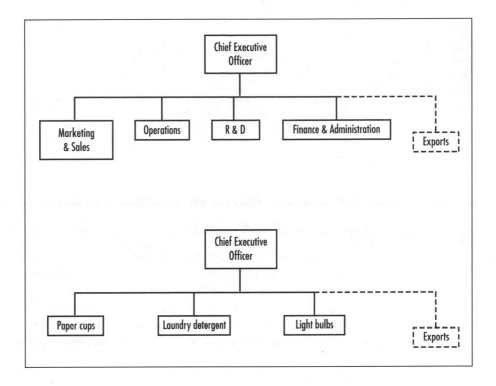

EXHIBIT 15.3
Adjustment to Organizational Structure, Adding Export Division

In either structural choice in Exhibit 15.3, although exports may appear to be on a level with other important functional or divisional priorities, this is often not the case in reality. At this stage of organizational development the firm's exports may receive a lower priority than other organizational considerations. Therefore, the main priority of an organization structured with an export division is still domestic.

The focus on an organization structured in divisions is primarily on the product in a domestic context (or on a particular region, in a regionally organized company), and less attention is likely to be paid to the export context. Executives in this situation see little need to develop expertise in foreign markets. This position is appropriate for a company that is almost fully occupied by domestic interests. When a company's strategy recognizes foreign opportunities but is not currently anxious to pursue them, an export division is often appropriate.

International Division

Many companies move to the structure of an international division as foreign opportunities become more interesting from a strategic point of view. The structure of the international division implies a change in strategic focus to an increased emphasis on international opportunities. This shift in focus results in a conscious intent to seek not only exports but also other international involvement. A typical international division structure is pictured in Exhibit 15.4.

International divisions generally are on the same level as other corporate divisions. This approach concentrates the international expertise in the company and implies a fair degree of power for the international division. In many cases, however, international opportunities in

EXHIBIT 15.4
Adjustment to Organizational Structure, Adding International Division

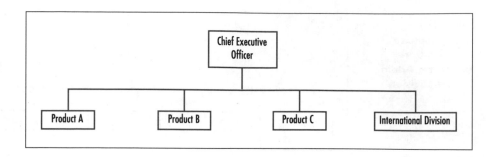

actuality may remain relatively less important than domestic ones – in effect, these opportunities are separated and somewhat isolated and may be deferred in favor of their domestic counterparts when corporate trade-offs are required.

The international division structure increases the focus on international opportunities, but the international division is responsible for all product groups marketed or produced outside the domestic area. This generally means that intensive development of international opportunities is difficult because of the need to coordinate international requirements with domestic divisions and functional activities. Product development, research, and marketing resources are often scarce for the international area. The focus of such firms remains on domestic interests and opportunities.

Many companies establish an international division and retain this structure for an extended period of time. This structure is appropriate for a company that recognizes its international opportunities but knows that they require specialized attention and believes that there are better domestic opportunities yet to be exploited. This structure is an intermediary stage between the essentially domestic company and the international company.

Global Division

The structure of a global division can take essentially the same forms as domestic ones except that the global structure's strategic view is the entire world rather than the domestic one. A global area structure – for example, like that in Example 15.5 – illustrates this international focus. In this structure, the world as a whole is divided into geographic areas, and domestic interests are only one of the firm's many interests.

EXHIBIT 15.5
A Global Area Structure

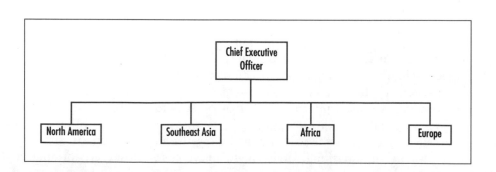

Similarly, a global product structure is identical at the top level to a domestic product structure, but each product has a foreign as well as domestic mandate. A global functional structure is similar to that in a domestic company, but functional responsibilities are worldwide.

A global structure becomes appropriate when global opportunities and interests become as important as domestic ones. This can become apparent in several ways.

▶ International sales or profits are increasing faster than domestic ones.
▶ International sales account for 50 percent of total sales.
▶ The international division is as large (in terms of investment, employees, assets, or other appropriate measure of size) as the largest domestic product division.
▶ International experience and expertise have been developed by top executives.

The three primary types of global structures identified are discussed in terms of advantages and disadvantages.

1. A **global functional structure** is typical of extractive industries (e.g., mining, oil, and gas) in which the need for functional know-how is paramount to success and functional expertise is appropriate on a worldwide basis. For example, oil exploration and refining tend to be the same around the world, and oil companies depend extensively on this expertise; this means that a global functional structure is appropriate for extractive companies.

    On the other hand, global functional structures tend to be cumbersome and ineffective for firms with multiple products. Functional needs and production processes tend to differ and require different expertise from product to product. As discussed in Chapter 13, production processes tend to vary and require different expertise from product to product and region to region. Similarly, marketing differs from product to product and region to region, as discussed in Chapter 12. These differing needs lead many companies with different product lines to adopt a global divisional structure focused around products or geographical areas.

2. A **global product structure** is typical of companies with a varied product line of individual products that can be made and marketed in a similar fashion around the world. The varied product line suggests differentiated technologies and end users for each product line but global standarization within product lines. For example, a company that produces and sells calculators and coffee beans would likely find that these two products need separate expertise to produce and sell, but that the production and sales of each is the same globally.

    The global product structure allows the company to focus on the differing needs of each of its product groups and to put primary emphasis on serving those product needs. It encourages the company to overlook regional and cultural differences and may thus create problems. This structure can also lead to duplication of corporate activities and consequent inefficiencies within regions. In the preceding example, the company could have separate facilities for calculators and coffee beans in the same location, and these facilities might duplicate each other in some ways.

3. A **global area structure** is typical of companies with relatively narrow product lines that need to be differentiated regionally. The narrow product line suggests that all items require essentially the same production expertise but that in different regions the same product has varied uses and needs to be distributed and marketed differently. For example, a company that produces and markets bicycles and small wagons uses the same technology for each

product around the world but finds that their uses and appropriate marketing practices differ depending on region. Bicycles need to be marketed as a recreational vehicle in some areas and as a primary means of transportation in others. Similarly, wagons might be considered toys in some areas and work tools in others.

The global area structure allows the company to focus on regional differences and integrate facilities regionally. It optimizes operations in any region and allows the company to develop approaches that are consistent with regional conditions. At the same time, this structure encourages a focus on areas rather than products. This means essentially less focus on product groups and their needs; therefore R&D may be duplicated, and products developed in one area may not be introduced in other areas. Overall, the area focus may discourage a globally integrated approach to operations.

In the case of bicycles and wagons, in a global area structure, the company would likely produce and market both products in every region. Insofar as production and marketing require similar expertise, this approach would be effective, but it becomes less effective if this is not so. If, for example, wagons are sold as toys for children and bicycles are sold as transportation for adults, then the marketing approaches might be quite different. Some of these structures are illustrated in Exhibit 15.6, Parts 1 and 2.

Global structures can be a mixture of functions, product groups, and geographic regions, depending on the company's global strategy. A mixed possibility is illustrated in Structure 1 of Exhibit 15.7.

Multidimensional Structures

The need to coordinate functional, product, and area needs leads to trade-offs and modifications in the organizations. The choices may not be simple and straightforward. A company may have some product lines for which a functional structure seems appropriate, others for which a product structure might be the best choice, and still others for which an area structure might be preferred. In addition, more than one priority – function, product, or area – may exist at the same time. This situation has led to multidimensional structures that attempt to give equal weight to more than one organizational activity or to coordinate action among activities.

The **global matrix structure** is one such multidimensional structure. The most common global matrix combines product and area priorities. This structure gives the company a focus on its product groups and the associated efficiencies at the same time as acknowledging the need for differentiation among different geographic areas. This is illustrated in Exhibit 15.6, Part 2.

Another multidimensional structure is the **coordinating committee**. In a global product structure, an area committee provides input and advice to product decisions regarding regional needs. In a global area structure, a product committee provides input and advice to area decisions regarding product needs. These are illustrated in Structures 2 and 3 of Exhibit 15.7.

Other Structures

The preceding discussion focused on organizational structures likely to occur in North American international companies; it is important, however, for North American managers to realize that

EXHIBIT 15.6   **PART I** International Structures

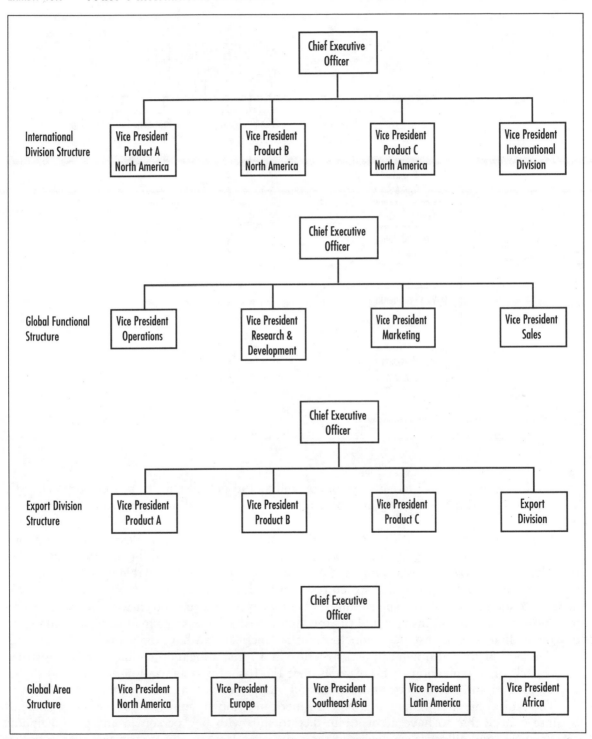

EXHIBIT 15.6   **PART 2 International Structures**

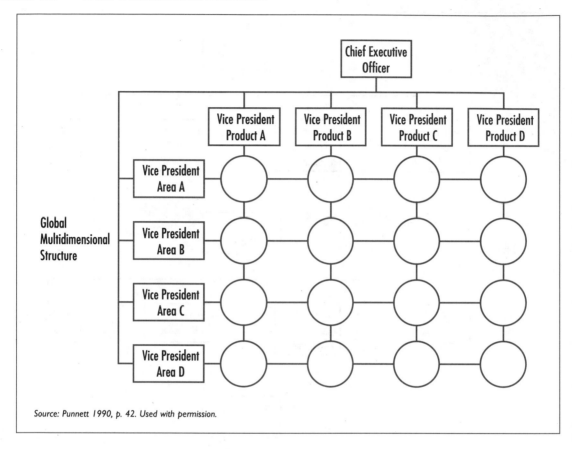

Source: Punnett 1990, p. 42. Used with permission.

other cultures may have different ways of controlling through systems of power, responsibility, and authority and that organizations therefore can be structured in different but equally valid ways.

The concept of a formal structure appears to some extent to be a Western organizational concept. In some countries, the hierarchy, responsibility, and accountability can be implicit and flexible. This approach gives a company flexibility that is often not available in more structured organizations. The lack of formal structure is frustrating to a foreigner, however, because it is difficult to identify who has responsibility and authority for particular decisions and who reports to whom. In fact, in an unstructured organization, these relationships may change from day to day depending on circumstances, which a North American can have difficulty interpreting.

The lack of formal organizational structure in a foreign location should not be construed as the lack of organization. It means only that the basis for organization is not what one is accustomed to and needs to be understood and interpreted within the cultural environment.

The typical hierarchy found in a North American company may not be found elsewhere. It is quite conceivable to have a corporate dictatorship with one person in charge, no middle management, and all other employees at the same level. It is equally conceivable that power at

EXHIBIT 15.7
Some Alternative Structures

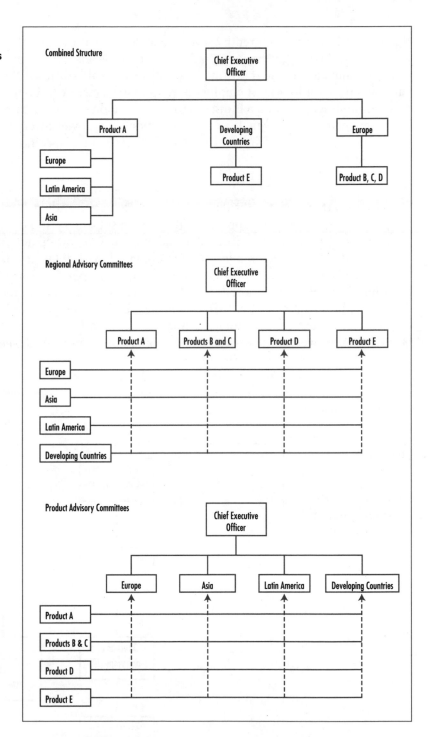

Combined Structure

Regional Advisory Committees

Product Advisory Committees

the top level might be shared by several people, or that the middle management level (in North American terms) might be very "fat" while other levels might be "thin."

Communication and reporting relationships can also differ. Top management can communicate directly with low-level employees. Top management can be made up of several individuals who communicate with each other and then have one of them communicate with lower levels. Top management can wait for communication from lower levels and then respond.

Particular structures have been identified with some specific countries. A few of these are described briefly.

1. European companies tend to use a national subsidiary, or mother-daughter, structure. This structure treats each subsidiary as a separate entity and each subsidiary reports directly to top management. This approach allows each subsidiary substantial autonomy. A drawback of this approach is the difficulty of adequately integrating activities.
2. Centrally planned economies, such as China's, have organizational structures that interweave various levels of government with the industrial organization. Laaksonen (1988) identified administrative systems and levels of management in Chinese management systems as depicted in Exhibits 15.8 through 15.10. This can result in the government administrative structure linked with enterprise management as depicted in Exhibit 15.10.
3. A matrix government organization that might be used in developing countries (Kiggundu 1989) is pictured in Exhibit 15.11.
4. A comparison of Chinese, European, and Japanese companies presented by Laaksonen (1988) suggests variations in power at different levels in the organization as shown in Exhibits 15.12 through 15.14.

EXHIBIT 15.8
Hierarchical Appointing Structure, Chongqing Rubber Factory, China

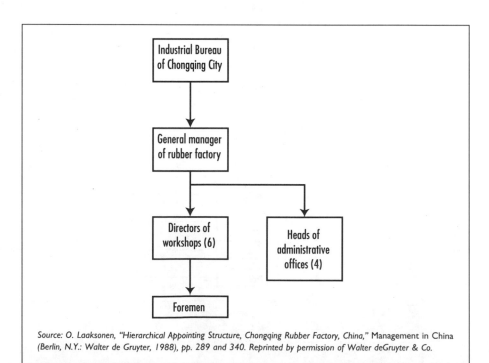

Source: O. Laaksonen, "Hierarchical Appointing Structure, Chongqing Rubber Factory, China," Management in China (Berlin, N.Y.: Walter de Gruyter, 1988), pp. 289 and 340. Reprinted by permission of Walter deGruyter & Co.

EXHIBIT 15.9
Government Administrative Structure Linked with Chongqing Rubber Factory

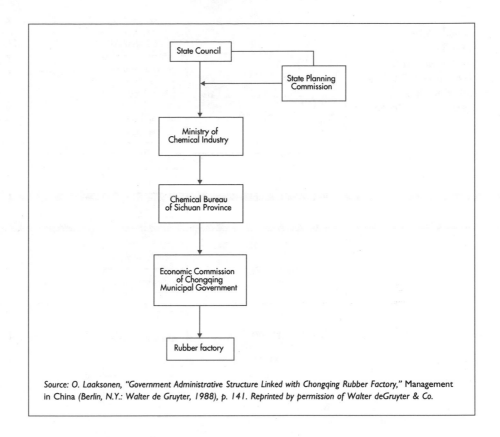

Source: O. Laaksonen, "Government Administrative Structure Linked with Chongqing Rubber Factory," *Management in China (Berlin, N.Y.: Walter de Gruyter, 1988), p. 141. Reprinted by permission of Walter deGruyter & Co.*

Effective Controls

An organization's structure to a large extent determines the type of control system that will be effective for it. A structure that is appropriate for the organization's strategy facilitates the implementation of appropriate controls. The structure of the organization also influences the direction and flow of information.

A control system therefore must be designed in the context of the overall organization's structure. The organization's structure evolves as the firm's strategy evolves, and control systems need to change to be compatible with the evolution.

Because international firms face complex issues in terms of designing both an appropriate structure and an effective control system, the two must be carefully constructed if they are to be complementary and contribute to the overall effectiveness of the organization. An international firm may occasionally achieve its chosen strategy by chance, but it needs to rely on careful planning to be successful consistently. Effective design of international organization structure and control systems enables the international firm to control its own destiny rather than to rely on chance.

EXHIBIT 15.10
**The Two
Administrative
Structures Guiding
the People's
Republic of China**

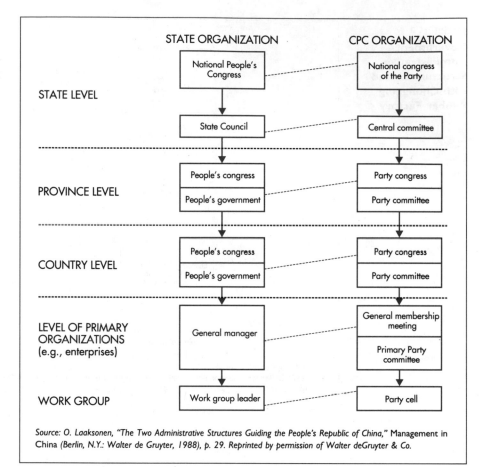

Source: O. Laaksonen, "The Two Administrative Structures Guiding the People's Republic of China," Management in China (Berlin, N.Y.: Walter de Gruyter, 1988), p. 29. Reprinted by permission of Walter deGruyter & Co.

EXHIBIT 15.11
**A Matrix
Government
Organization
(Africa)**

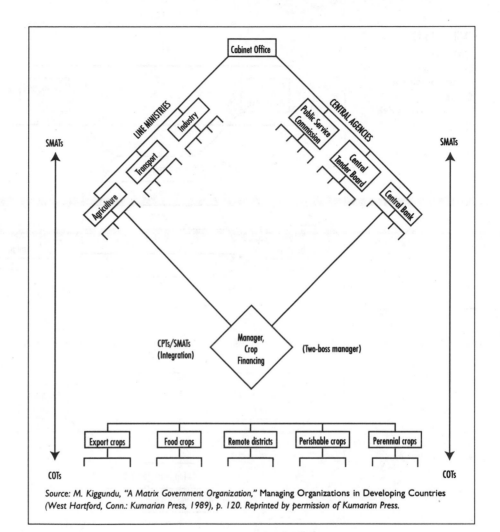

Source: M. Kiggundu, "A Matrix Government Organization," Managing Organizations in Developing Countries
(West Hartford, Conn.: Kumarian Press, 1989), p. 120. Reprinted by permission of Kumarian Press.

EXHIBIT 15.12
Chinese Management in Cross-National Context: Comparison with Europe

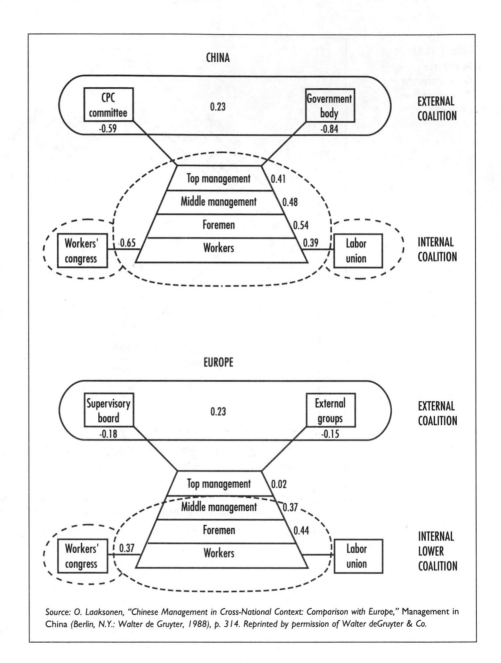

CHINA

CPC committee
-0.59

0.23

Government body
-0.84

EXTERNAL COALITION

Top management   0.41
Middle management   0.48
Foremen   0.54
Workers   0.39

Workers' congress   0.65

Labor union

INTERNAL COALITION

EUROPE

Supervisory board
-0.18

0.23

External groups
-0.15

EXTERNAL COALITION

Top management   0.02
Middle management   0.37
Foremen   0.44
Workers

Workers' congress   0.37

Labor union

INTERNAL LOWER COALITION

Source: O. Laaksonen, "Chinese Management in Cross-National Context: Comparison with Europe," Management in China *(Berlin, N.Y.: Walter de Gruyter, 1988), p. 314. Reprinted by permission of Walter deGruyter & Co.*

EXHIBIT 15.13
**Comparison of
Influence
Structures
between China,
Europe, and Japan**

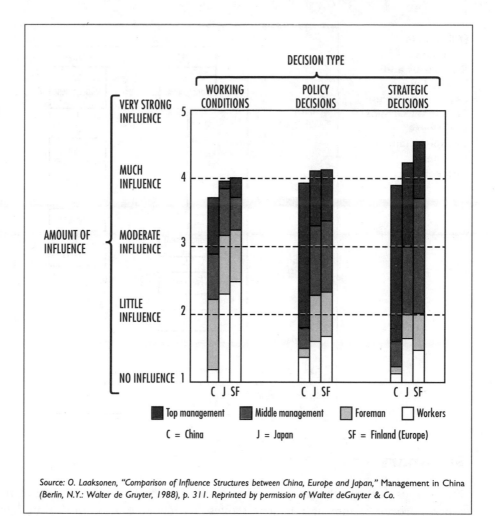

Source: O. Laaksonen, "Comparison of Influence Structures between China, Europe and Japan," Management in China (Berlin, N.Y.: Walter de Gruyter, 1988), p. 311. Reprinted by permission of Walter deGruyter & Co.

EXHIBIT 15.14
Influence Structures and Power Distance between Different Personnel Groups in Chinese, European, and Japanese Enterprises

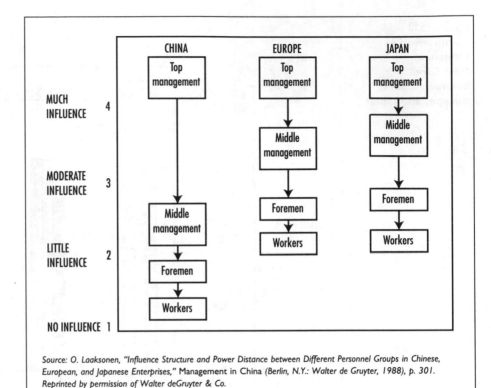

Source: O. Laaksonen, "Influence Structure and Power Distance between Different Personnel Groups in Chinese, European, and Japanese Enterprises," Management in China (Berlin, N.Y.: Walter de Gruyter, 1988), p. 301. Reprinted by permission of Walter deGruyter & Co.

Summary

The purpose of this chapter is to alert readers to the factors that need to be considered in the control process in international companies. The chapter does not deal in depth with issues such as accounting or auditing practices; rather, it gives a general overview of the international control process. Control is an important aspect of effective management because it helps ensure that the enterprise achieves the goals it has identified.

Effective control systems are particularly important to the management process in companies that face complex internal and external environments. International companies clearly fall into this category and, therefore, must pay close attention to the control process.

The internal and external environments of international firms make control particularly important for these companies, but the complexity of these environments also means that designing and implementing an effective control system in these companies can be difficult. The chapter identified and discussed some of the major factors influencing the effectiveness of international control systems.

This chapter examined specific international control mechanisms as well as variations in control systems. It also considered information systems, performance evaluations, and organizational structure as integral aspects of achieving international control.

The chapter concludes the major portion of the text. It seems appropriate to conclude with issues of control because these issues, in effect, lead back to all the other issues covered in the text. Control systems tell the international firm how well it is doing in meeting its objectives and achieving its chosen strategies. Results of the control system can indicate where better understanding of the global environment is needed, they can suggest when political and cultural factors need to be reexamined, and they pinpoint firm-specific decision-making and functional areas that need improvement.

Managing an international business effectively, like managing any business, depends on a thorough understanding of the internal and external environments of the firm and the opportunities and risks posed by the interaction of these environments. The management process in an international company is particularly germane to its effectiveness because of the complex internal and external environments it faces. A sound control system gives the company command over information that improves this management process.

MINI-CASE
Queen Island
Telco

Queen Island is a small independent island country in the tropics. Its population is 2,500,000, and half the population lives in or near the capital city of Port Elizabeth. Culturally, Queen Island is a mixture of people of African, Indian, and Chinese heritage. There are a few aboriginals on the island. Queen Island is a former British colony and retains most of the laws and institutions even after 27 years of independence. Its economy is strong, based on ample natural resources and some tourism, and the political climate has stablized after some racial unrest a decade ago.

The Telephone Company

In 1994, Queen Island Telephone Company, or Telco as it is referred to, is nearing completion of a long awaited major overhaul of its structure, services, and position in society. It is now preparing for the 21st century, and the effects of mushrooming multimedia applications and the "information highway." Although these developments are dramatic from the point of view of the customer, Telco officials feel that current technology will be sufficient to meet the technical requirements of widespread and growing use of sophisticated personal computers: The challenge will be to meet the volume demands.

Telco's history is a colorful one. As was the case of most capital intensive utilities of the 1950s, the company began as a department of government, in this case the colonial government. When independence was achieved, there was some pressure to establish Telco as a state corporation, but the political agendas delayed this move. The deputy minister with responsibility for Telco was also elected mayor of Port Elizabeth, and with the burgeoning demand for telephone services in the new country at a time of some prosperity, he found himself besieged with requests for preferential treatment from friends and political leaders. In addition, because the work force was large and relatively unskilled, contracts for expansion of services were labor intense and therefore became political decisions as well.

Before long, the public complained that telephone service in Port Elizabeth was demonstrably superior than in the rest of the country, and that one had to wait for six months to have a business line installed – unless you knew someone. Even then, service reliability was poor, and out-of-service time was frequently greater than in-service time. Telco had become a high profile political issue. The civil service, anxious to avoid complicity, arranged for competitive bids for all development, maintenance, and supply contracts and awarded them strictly on a low-cost basis. As a result, incompatible systems were installed and "jerry-rigged" to fit. They worked poorly, and system performance became a scandal itself. Telco managers claimed that they were embarrassed to be introduced socially as connected with Telco, and general morale was poor.

Change was inevitable, and according to rumor, was triggered when the prime minister experienced the poor service first hand. The prime minister, who had led the independence negotiations, was a popular and strong figure, able to make changes happen. The rumor described him as attempting to call his executive assistant, only to find a third party on the line, participating in the conversation. Fortunately, the third party was a former colleague of the prime minister who later said that he was innocently attempting to make a call when he found himself party to the prime minister's call. In any case, the prime minister was reported to have torn the telephone from the wall, handed it to his driver with instructions to "Throw this thing as far as you can into the sea!" and swore, "It's time to do something about this – telephone company."

Although referred to as the *telephone company* at the time, it was still a government department. The first step, therefore, was to convert the department to a state corporation and assign the appropriate subsidy program. Next, in 1988, with the help of a regional development bank and government funding from Canada, Telco arranged for a massive upgrade in technology, standardizing on Northern Telecom equipment and commissioning Bell Canada International (BCI) to assist in implementing the necessary operating and administrative procedures. BCI was asked to train Telco personnel in the appropriate supervisory procedures as well. This was a massive undertaking, which was scheduled to span five years.

The change did not mark the end of Telco's challenge. In 1991, Queen Island was hit by a major recession as the price of its main natural resource, the rare metal krypton, fell dramatically, due to a UN trade embargo against its major customer. While some international financial support was made available, Queen Island was forced to devalue its currency by almost half, and unemployment rose dramatically. Telco's operating subsidies were slashed by the government, and it was mandated to operate as a private sector concern, raising funds on the open market and earning profits to support its activities and future capital requirements. The BCI contract would be protected, however, and the modernization program would continue, partly supported by increased CIDA funds.

Telco's Management

Telco's executive team was strengthened substantially in 1987 in connection with the BCI contract. The country's leading executives helped the government search for and attract several highly talented and technically trained managers to take up the challenge of converting a failing, inefficient, and outdated telephone company into a modern, efficient telecommunications provider to take the country into the next millennium. All were Queen Islanders employed by telecommunications firms in Canada, the United States, and the United Kingdom. The following illustrates the results of this international recruiting effort:

▶ Ivan MacLeod – 45 years old, Ph.D. in electronics engineering from California Institute of Technology, specialist in advanced electronics, consultant to defense companies working on inertial guidance and secure communications, located teaching in a Canadian university; hired as executive director for Telco.
▶ James Samson – 27 years old, electrical engineer with MBA from Stanford University, working in the systems development department of a California telecommunications company; hired as general manager, Marketing, for Telco.
▶ Muhammad Aile – 34 years old, mechanical engineer, working as a project manager with Ohio Telephone, previously with the British Post, managing special projects implementation; hired as general manager, Projects, for Telco.
▶ Arthur Chan – 38 years old, chartered accountant, formerly controller, Alberta Telephone, in Canada; hired as general manager, Finance, for Telco.
▶ George Marlowe – 42 years old, degrees in business administration and public administration, working as manager of Employee Benefits, British Columbia Civil Service Commission; hired as director of Human Resources for Telco.
▶ Jim Hardcastel – 57 years old, 25 years' experience in British Post Office, Telecommunications Division, various positions in telephone operations and network development, record of steady rise in organization, extensively trained in in-house programs, excellent record of achievement; hired as general manager, Telephone Operations, for Telco.

Dr. MacLeod was able to assemble a strong management team and encountered little resentment from the preexisting managers in the light of the demonstrable strength and breadth of this group of returning nationals. The more competent of the long time Telco managers welcomed an opportunity to be a part of the change. The diagram in Exhibit 15.15 summarizes the current Telco organization.

Dr. MacLeod was concerned about the future of Telco, now that the current modernization program was nearing completion. The task force style organization might not be appropriate for sustaining quality service, and public confidence in Telco's abilities consistently to perform well over time was still fragile. If Telco was to survive financially, it would have to be able to command a reasonable price for its services; the public would not tolerate a return to the Telco of old. He wondered whether his high-priced executive team would respond to the Telco of old. He wondered whether his high-priced executive team would respond to the more routine operations after the contract work was finished. Would the unions continue to support the company after the glamor (and overtime) of rapid development receded as the organization focused on maintaining the system by upgrading at a more measured pace?

EXHIBIT 15.15   Queen Island Telephone Company Ltd. Chain of Command

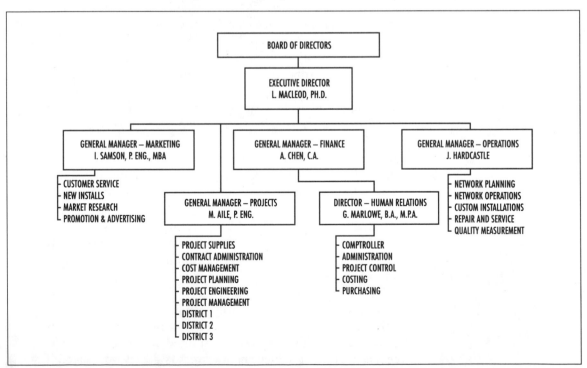

He considered calling for consulting help, but had little experience with consultants and viewed them with skepticism. In addition, he was concerned about his leadership if he were to seek outside help. He decided to discuss Telco's strategy with his executive team and began preparing material for the group to consider.

Source: Case prepared by Donald M. Wood, Eureka Management Consultants. Used with the author's permission.

Discussion Issues

1. How appropriate is Queen Island Telco's current organizational structure? What changes would you suggest in the company's structure?
2. Discuss the advantages and challenges associated with Telco's executive staffing decisions.
3. Identify and discuss control issues that Telco must manage effectively to be successful in the future. If you were in the Executive Director's position, what actions would you take to ensure success?

Discussion Questions

1. Using the characteristics identified as important to effective control (accuracy, timeliness, etc.), develop examples of how these might differ from one location to another. How might these differences likely affect the control process?

2. Using Hofstede's cultural dimensions of individualism, power distance, uncertainty avoidance, and masculinity (see Chapter 6 for a description), what influences might culture have on control systems? Discuss.

3. Identify some recent developments in technology and communication. How might these influence international information systems?

Assignments

1. Identify and discuss recent developments in the standardization of global financial reporting.

2. Interview an international company in your area and identify various aspects of its international control system (e.g., accounting and auditing, plans, policies and procedures, performance evaluation, structure).

3. Identify a recent world event that you believe will affect international business. Explain how this event will relate to international control issues.

Selected References

Adler, N., *International Dimensions of Organizational Behavior* (Boston: PWS-Kent, 1990).

Baliga, D. R., and A. M. Jaeger, "Multinational Corporations: Control Systems and Delegation Issues," *Journal of International Business Studies* (Fall 1984), pp. 25–40.

Bata, T. J., with S. Sinclair, *Bata, Shoemaker to the World* (Toronto: Stoddart, 1990).

Brooke, M. and H. Remmers, *The Strategy of Multinational Enterprise* (London: Pitman, 1978).

Bruce, R., "U.K. Working on Radical Changes to Financial Reporting," *The Bottom Line* (December 1990), p. 6.

Cray, D., "Control and Coordination in Multinational Corporations," *Journal of International Business Studies* (Fall 1984), pp. 85–98.

Daniels, J. D., R. A. Pitts, and M. J. Tretter, "Strategy and Structure of U. S. Multinationals," *Academy of Management Journal* 27, no. 2 (1984), pp. 292–307.

Doz, Y., and C. K. Prahalad, "Headquarters Influence and Strategic Control in MNCs," *Sloan Management Review* (Fall 1981), pp. 15–29.

Doz, Y., "Patterns of Strategic Control Within Multinational Corporations," *Journal of International Business Studies* (Fall 1984), pp. 55–72.

Egelhoff, W. G., "Strategy and Structure in MNCs: A Revision of the Stopford and Wells Model," *Strategic Management Journal* 9, no. 1 (1988), pp. 1–14.

Kane, M., and D. Ricks, "The Impact of Transborder Data Flow Regulations on Large United States-based Corporations," *Columbia Journal of World Business* (Summer 1989).

Kiggundu, Moses N., *Managing Organizations in Developing Countries: An Operational and Strategic Perspective* (West Hartford, Conn.: Kumarian Press, 1989).

Laaksonen, O., *Management in China* (New York: Walter de Gruyter, 1988).

Prahalad, C., and Y. Doz, *The Multinational Mission: Balancing Local Demands and Global Vision* (New York: The Free Press, 1987).

Punnett, B. J., *Experiencing International Management* (Boston: PWS-Kent, 1990).

Ricks, D. A., *Blunders in International Business* (Cambridge, Mass.: Blackwell Publishers, 1993).

Samiee, S., "Transnational Data Flow Constraints: A New Challenge for Multinational Corporations," *Journal of International Business Studies* (Summer 1984), pp. 141–150.

Selig, G., "A Framework for Multinational Information Systems Planning," *Information and Management* (June 1982), pp. 95–115.

Stopford, J. M., and L. T. Wells, *Managing the Multinational Enterprise* (New York: Basic Books, 1972).

Stueck, W., "Pacific Rim Accounting Conference Stresses Ethics, Controls, and Corporation," *The Bottom Line* (December 1990), p. 19.

"Thought Control," *The Economist* (July 7, 1990), p. 68.

The Changing World of International Business

THOUGHT STARTERS

▶ The face of earth is changing. New names are being etched on maps. Old bonds are being broken. And regional pacts are altering age-old trading patterns.

(National Geographic Society 1990)

▶ A series of political and economic developments in the last half of 1989 will have a major impact on international business for the 1990s, and probably well into the 21st century.

(Coplin and O'Leary 1990)

▶ Three or four things will happen during 1996 that will help to shape the way the world goes for the next 15 or 20 years, and maybe even longer. An American election. . . . A Russian election. . . . A constitutional conference of the European Union. . . . And, probably, the long-drawn-out dying of Deng Xiaoping. . . . By the end of 1996, putting together the first tentative answers to those four questions, the world should be able to look into the future more clearly than it can now.

(The Economist 1996, p. 19)

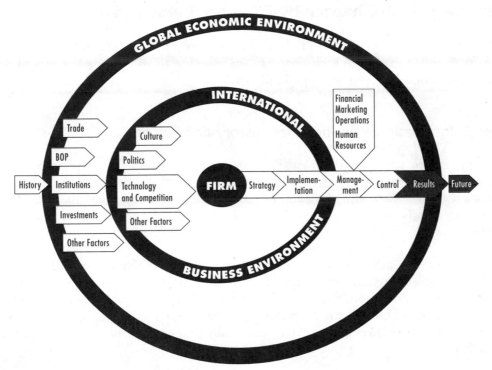

Introduction

Companies operating in today's global environment need to be constantly aware of the changes occurring around the world. Events in any area of the world can have an impact on business nearby, as well as on the other side of the globe. The world can change rapidly to present international firms with new opportunities and risks at home and abroad.

The purpose of this chapter is to reinforce the need for global awareness in international firms and to illustrate the impact of changes in the world on particular aspects of international business. The discussion in this chapter relates some recent events to doing business internationally. The focus is on the need for decision makers to monitor occurrences around the world constantly. Because the world is dynamic and frequently changing, many of the situations mentioned here will have changed, possibly dramatically, since the book was completed. Students should recognize these changes and examine more recent incidents and events of interest, and consider their potential impact on various facets of international business.

Throughout the text the authors have related theories and concepts to management practice, the real world, and current events. The dynamic nature of the world means that current events inevitably soon become dated; therefore, the emphasis in the text has been on the interrelationship of events and various aspects of doing business internationally rather than simply on the events themselves. This chapter turns students' attention to events.

Recent Events: A Chapter-by-Chapter Perspective

The following sections reflect concepts from the previous chapters and relate specific current events to the subject matter of each chapter. The intent is to use selected events to illustrate their impact on doing business internationally.

Chapter 2. International Business: Its History and Future

Many events in the late 1980s and early 1990s have significant historical importance. The reunification of Germany, the countries of Eastern Europe overthrowing their communist governments, the invasion of Kuwait by Iraq and the response by other countries, and the release from jail of the African National Congress leader Nelson Mandela are all part of the historical evolution of the world. Consider the impact of such historical events on the cartographers of the world.

The National Geographic Society released a redrawn map of the world in 1989, but within a year it was obsolete in some ways and would need to be drawn again. The reunification of East and West Germany meant that one country instead of two would appear; the decision by the people of Burma to rename the country meant changing its name on the map to Myanmar.

More recent events also contribute to a continually changing world make-up. Among others are the following:

▶ China is on the verge of absorbing Hong Kong in 1997 and has reaffirmed its intention of reuniting with Taiwan.
▶ Elections were held in Palestine in early 1996.
▶ Australia has strengthened its ties in the Pacific region and is seeking to establish itself as a Pacific nation.
▶ The separatist movement in the Province of Quebec (Canada) strengthened and a referendum on separation was narrowly defeated in late 1995.
▶ Peace talks in Ireland renewed hopes that issues associated with partition in Ireland might soon be resolved.
▶ Tensions between the Hutu and Tutsis in both Burundi and Rwanda remained high.
▶ The former Yugoslavia's violent breakup brought NATO into a new role and established a new type of international "peace-keeping" force.

Such events can have either a positive or a negative impact on international business decisions. Some imply greater assurance about world, regional, or country stability; other events imply more instability and reason for concern. Managers in international firms have to assess the impact of world events in terms of their own companies, and factor these events into their decisions.

The Economist (1996, p. 19) posits two extreme futures. One future is nationalistic, including a withdrawn America, Europe absorbed in constitutional debates, Russia led by the nationalist Zhirinovsky, and China dedicated to reestablishing a Chinese face. The result could be violence and even war. The opposite future involves a resurgent America with international commitments and European powers happy to work alongside, combined with cooperation of the United States and Europe with Russia and China. This future, according to *The Economist,* suggests "democracy's century." Neither of these extremes is really likely, but they highlight how the world's future, and thus the future of international business, can be influenced by relatively few events.

Chapter 3. International Trade Issues

World events can have a definite impact on the degree and direction of trade. Consider the following.

► China will absorb Hong Kong in 1997. In spite of promises to maintain Hong Kong's way of doing business, many Hong Kong businesspeople have established optional bases. Australia and Canada have been popular relocation countries. In time, some Chinese markets currently supplied through Hong Kong may be supplied from other locations, such as Australia and Canada.

► The North American Free Trade Agreement (NAFTA), which includes Canada, Mexico, and the United States, has resulted in increased trilateral trade. Talks are under way that may lead to including Chile in the agreement, and other Latin American and Caribbean countries want to join. This suggests a likely increase in trade among all the countries of the Americas in coming years.

► South Africa dismantled apartheid, and Nelson Mandela's ANC party consolidated its power, in the context of conciliation toward white South Africans. Newly reopened opportunities in South Africa were eagerly embraced by firms that formerly had to disregard these opportunities for ethical and political reasons.

► Establishment of the World Trade Organization as a permanent body devoted to world-wide trade liberalization suggests broad-based support for the tenets of free trade. This supports the expectation that markets will become even more open in terms of exports and imports.

Chapter 4. Balance of Payments and International Monetary Systems

World events have an impact on countries' external balances and on various international financial institutions. The following examples illustrate this impact:

► In early 1996, Jacques Delors, the former president of the European Commission, told a French newspaper that it would be difficult for the European Union to achieve monetary union within the agreed timetable – several European countries are not likely to meet the criteria for union and the United Kingdom may opt out. A delay in the monetary union means individual European currencies may encounter increased speculation.

▶ A number of former communists have regained power in Eastern Europe. Many of the Eastern European countries have not yet established stable market economies following the collapse of communism. The results of the recent elections lead to doubts as to whether communism has been truly abandoned and market economics embraced. These doubts in turn diminish Western business interests in this region.

▶ The U.S. currency became the currency of choice for transactions in Russia, but the appearance of counterfeit $100 bills caused concern in Russia that $100 bills would be replaced and therefore the old ones would become valueless. This illustrates that currencies are no longer wholly under the control of the issuing government.

▶ The collapse of the Barings Bank, combined with massive losses by a Japanese bank and a variety of other similar events, provided evidence that individuals trading on the foreign exchange markets could have a real impact on the value of targeted currencies. Speculation, which had previously been seen as a minor influence on currency values, became a major concern for the international monetary system.

▶ Debt-for-equity swaps between countries with heavy international debt burdens and foreign investors took an environmental-ecological twist; for example, exchanging debt for rain forest acreage in Brazil. This trend was supported by the World Bank's decision to include environmental impact in its evaluation of development programs.

▶ Global warming was thought to have raised the temperature of tropical waters by a slight fraction. This fractional change was blamed for killing coral reefs in some tropical waters. The disappearance of these coral reefs, in turn, could have a disproportionate effect on fish stock elsewhere, as well as a detrimental impact of the tourist industry in the tropical locations. Fish imports and exports would likely be affected along with the flows of currencies associated with tourism.

▶ The close referendum results in Quebec forced Canadians to consider issues that would have to be resolved if Quebec separated; in particular, would Quebecers continue to use Canadian currency or would they need to create a separate currency? Using Canadian currency would tie together the two hypothetical countries (Quebec and Canada) and give Canada substantial economic influence in a sovereign Quebec.

Chapter 5. World Investment Flows

Many events around the world have an impact on the degree and direction of foreign direct investment. Some examples follow:

▶ Pools of risk capital have been established in North America for investment in specific foreign locations. The capital for these funds is typically raised from recent immigrant families who want to invest in their former home countries – for example, immigrants from Poland directing investment to Poland, immigrants from Guyana directing investment to Guyana, and so on.

▶ The Australian Foreign Affairs Minister visited Cuba in 1995 in an effort to strengthen economic and political ties between the two countries. He expressed optimism regarding Australia's economic role in Cuba, especially in the mining industry, where Australia's Western Mining was negotiating a nickel mining joint venture. In contrast, the United States continued its economic embargo of Cuba. Because U.S. firms could not invest in Cuba, investment flows were likely to be supplied by other countries, such as Australia.

▶ The imminent unification of Hong Kong with the People's Republic of China, scheduled for 1997, influenced global investment patterns. Some investors chose to disinvest in Hong Kong and increase their investments in countries such as Singapore, from which they could serve the PRC.

▶ Environmental issues continue to concern people around the world. Some people select their portfolio investments to reflect their environmental concerns. "Green" issues have even become an integral part of the global investment picture, with the establishment of "green" investment funds.

▶ Serious anticorruption actions, in countries as varied as India, Mexico, South Korea, and Sweden, during 1995 and 1996, suggested a tougher stance toward illegal business activities. For some investors, this made these countries more attractive as potential sites for doing business.

Chapter 6. The Cultural Environment of International Business

Many news events can be explained in cultural terms, and these culturally based events often have major implications for business decisions.

▶ In late 1995, a senior Japanese official made a statement that Japan's colonial rule of Korea, from 1910 to 1945, had had a good side. The Korean reaction was predictably negative. This cultural clash between the Japanese and Koreans exacerbated the existing resentment that Koreans feel for Japanese businesspeople. In turn, antipathy to the Japanese results in South Korea encouraging U.S. business interests.

▶ The Israeli prime minister, Yitzhak Rabin, was assassinated by an Israeli student opposed to peace with the Palestinians. This event underscores the cultural conflicts that are found around the world. These cultural conflicts deter international business when they contribute to instability for businesses. Interestingly, in this specific situation, Shimon Peres succeeded Mr. Rabin and promised to continue the peace process. The apparent success of the peace process suggests the region will likely be more stable in the immediate future; thus, contributing to greater business interest in the region.

▶ The war in Bosnia (the former Yugoslavia) was based on cultural conflict and continued throughout 1995. This meant that Sarajevo, a city that once served as the site for the Olympics and was considered by many to be the cultural capital of the region, became a war-torn shambles. Essentially this war made the former Yugoslavia of no interest to businesses, except for those opportunistic few who see advantages in high-risk situations.

▶ The breakup of the Soviet Union in the late 1980s resulted in a variety of new countries, which were culturally based. These countries have exhibited a wide variety of political patterns. One country that looks positive for Western businesses is Georgia. Edward

Shevardnadze was reelected in 1996 with about 70 percent of the vote in a large turnout. Shevardnadze is pro-business, pro-market reforms, and pro-Western – all positive attributes from the perspective of Western businesspeople.

▶ South Africa is a country that has been plagued by cultural and racial conflicts for decades, yet postapartheid South Africa appears to be attracting substantial international business and is seen by many as Africa's best investment location. Nelson Mandela is seen as the basis for this positive business climate. Elections in late 1995 left Mandela's ANC party stronger than ever, and consequently, South Africa is once again being considered seriously by many firms.

Chapter 7. The Political Environment of International Business

Political events are almost always newsworthy, and at the same time, these events very often have significant implications for international business decisions. Consider the potential impact of the following events:

▶ The volatility of world events – war betwen Russia and Chechnya; Australian boycotts of French products; terrorism from Sri Lanka to the United States; elections in Palestine, South Africa, and Taiwan; economic growth in Asia – both positive and negative, accents the need for appropriate policies for effective risk management in this dynamic environment.

▶ In Mexico, the almost one-party government of the PRI suffered state and local election losses in 1995. This was attributed to political and financial scandals and the collapse of currency values earlier in 1995 as well as the continuing unrest in Chiappas. Overall, investors reacted cautiously to Mexican business opportunities because of increased uncertainty.

▶ The People's Republic of China conducted military exercises near Taiwan and vowed to revoke local elections in Hong Kong. The Chinese government also said that Hong Kong would keep its way of life after the 1997 takeover. These contradictory messages left many international businesses unclear as to Chinese opportunities. The continued growth in the Chinese economy, combined with China's large and still untapped internal market, meant that China remained very attractive to foreign companies. These companies were cautious, however, because of questions as to what the future would bring for businesses in China.

▶ The Quebec population narrowly voted against separating from Canada, in a referendum held in late 1995. The closeness of the vote was a surprise to many English-speaking Canadians and highlighted the need for political changes in Canada. Following the vote, the complexity of the separation question became evident; for example, native Canadians in Quebec stated unequivocally that they would remain in Canada if Quebec separated, and the Quebec government said Canada was not a real country and could be divided whereas Quebec could not be. The impact on international businesses was mixed, at least initially. Some businesspeople saw the vote against separation, however close, as positive; others felt that the continuing debate represented an uncertain situation.

▶ The Bosnian political situation was unclear in early 1996. Peace was at last a possibility, but the reality of war crimes was affecting the peace process. In March 1996, the best that could be said of the former Yugoslavia, from a business perspective, was that if the Dayton Peace Accord was successfully implemented, there might be opportunities. These opportunities were hardly seen as worth considering immediately.

▶ Peace in Northern Ireland also appeared to be a possibility in early 1996, but this was marred by the Irish Republican Army's unwillingness to begin laying down arms. The United States played a major role in bringing the situation to a potential peace. The U.S. government's interest in Ireland reflected a strong general interest in Ireland on the part of a number of U.S. citizens and businesses. Many U.S. firms could use Ireland as an entry into the European Union, but the continued problems with the North diminish this interest in doing business from an Irish base.

▶ The strength of Nelson Mandela's ANC party in South Africa boded well for business in South Africa. South African businesses were expanding, and foreign businesses were again seeing South Africa as a good place to invest. The previous sanctions against South Africa, which resulted in disinvestment there, actually created pent-up opportunities. Domestic firms were anxious to access technologies and intellectual capital from outside of South Africa.

Chapter 8. The Competitive and Technological Environment

Recent technological developments around the world have had an impact on international business and international competition. The following points illustrate some of these developments and their impact:

▶ The expression *surfing the 'Net* became commonplace in the mid-1990s, indicating the rapid acceptance by many people of the Internet and access to the World Wide Web. The Internet had been used almost exclusively by academics and the military until private firms began offering inexpensive access to the 'Net to businesses and individuals. The upsurge in access to the Internet, around the world, provided easier communication for international firms, allowing instant linkages between subsidiaries virtually anywhere on the globe and vast increases in international information exchanges. Many people see the Internet as providing a means for entrepreneurs in developing countries to find partners in other locations, thus increasing their potential contribution to international business.

▶ The Indian government promoted certain locations in India as new Silicon Valleys, and the place to invest in high technology industries. Highly trained Indian technicians are available at a much lower cost than their counterparts in Europe or North America. Many have been trained in the West and have returned to India to take advantage of anticipated economic growth.

▶ France conducted nuclear tests in the South Pacific in late 1995 and early 1996. The rest of the world was dismayed by these tests, and the Pacific nations demonstrated against them. One impact of these tests was to reinforce Australia and New Zealand's status as Pacific nations. Australia, in particular, is making efforts to change its image as an Anglo or European country and participate more directly in the growing economies of South East Asia.

▶ A promising development in waste water treatment is the use of plants to purify and aerate the waste. Several experimental projects have successfully used waste as food for plants and snails and created an attractive greenhouse environment while managing the waste in an environmentally friendly manner. These projects may be extended to parts of the world where sewage disposal is a major environmental problem, providing substantial benefits both to the providing firms and the receiving countries.

▶ The 1990s brought a realization that the biodiversity of the tropical rain forests could be an important asset for humankind. Most important, from a business perspective, major pharmaceutical firms saw this diversity as the potential base for developing a range of new products. Consequently, these firms took steps to preserve the forests and conserve the diversity. This was in contrast to multinationals that had contributed to the destruction of the rain forests to establish plantations, mining, and so on.

Chapter 9. Going International: Strategic Decisions

Firm-specific decisions regarding where to invest, and what form that investment should take, are affected by world events. Some decisions that may be attributed to recent events follow:

▶ Canada, Mexico, and the United States signed a free trade agreement (NAFTA). Canada and the United States were already each other's major trading and business partners, and Mexico and the United States were also substantial trade and business partners. In contrast Canada and Mexico had previously done relatively little business together. Some surveys of Mexican businesspeople suggested that they saw Canadian businesses as particularly attractive partners in the new regional trading bloc. The NAFTA, therefore, seems likely to increase business partnerships, and trade, among all three countries, but disproportionately between Canada and Mexico.

▶ Taiwanese investors have sought investment opportunities outside of Taiwan. In the past decade a substantial portion of this investment went to the People's Republic of China. In turn, this contributed to China's economic growth. Tensions between Taiwan and the PRC increased in 1996. Apparently in response to Taiwan's democratic elections, the PRC marshaled troops for war games in the province opposite to Taiwan. This show of troops, combined with threats of invasion, had a negative effect on the Taiwanese stock market. The downturn in the stock market and the heightened tensions, ironically, could result in declining Taiwanese investment in the PRC.

▶ The disintegration of the Soviet Union and the move from centrally planned economies to market economies in Eastern Europe opened new trade and investment opportunities for Western firms. These opportunities were seen as especially attractive to businesspeople with family and cultural ties to the Eastern European countries. The change to market economies has not been smooth, and many countries have reelected "former communists" in their recent elections. In sum, some firms have taken advantage of the opportunities in Eastern Europe, but many are viewing the region with caution, taking a wait and see attitude before committing major resources to the region.

▶ The Japanese yen's continuing strength, high Japanese labor costs, and sluggish domestic sales contributed to Japanese automotive firms' choices in terms of implementing strategies. These firms increased overseas production substantially – according to *The Economist* (February 10–16, 1996, p. 59) in 1995 Honda became the first Japanese car company to produce more cars abroad than at home – and as a result exports declined as a percentage of total sales.

Chapter 10. Implementing International Strategic Decisions

The way international firms choose to implement their global strategies is often a function of events taking place around the world. Examples of such choices of recent implementation follow:

▶ The Republic of Ireland is a member of the EU and has experienced the highest rate of growth of any EU country since 1985. Ireland has sought to attract non-European investment by portraying itself as an effective gateway into the European Union. The instability associated with the conflict over Northern Ireland has served to dampen interest in Ireland as a place for investment. Peace in the North may be established at last in 1996, but the Irish Republican Army's bombing of Canary Wharf in London in February 1996 left investors questioning whether peace would ever be a reality. Ireland's hopes for major foreign inflows of investment will likely materialize only if there is a peaceful resolution of the Northern Ireland conflict.

▶ Vietnam has been sending mixed signals about its openness to foreign investment. On the one hand, the government insists it wants investment and contact with other countries. On the other hand, the government has instituted a cultural purge; this included burning pornographic magazines and calendars and crushing videos, as well as ensuring that banned pre-1975 Saigon music was not played and covering foreign brand names such as Carlsberg, Panasonic, and Pepsi. This inconsistency clearly affects how foreign firms choose to do business in Vietnam. The demand for foreign products suggests that firms will continue to sell these products as long as their sale is profitable. The antiforeign sentiment in the government suggests that there will be little substantial investment and foreign firms will structure their Vietnamese operations so that they can withdraw easily and suffer minimal losses if rapid withdrawal is necessary.

▶ Some firms in the United States, with subsidiaries in Canada, reorganized in response to the North American Free Trade Agreement. Reorganization took the form of adopting a regional focus and structure. For their Canadian subsidiaries, this meant less autonomy and fewer decisions regarding research and development, operations, and investment made in Canada.

▶ The news from many African countries was negative – ethnic violence in Rwanda and Burundi, continued unrest in Angola and Somalia, executions in Nigeria. In contrast, the news from South Africa was relatively positive – the dismantling of apartheid moved ahead and Nelson Mandela's African National Congress Party was reelected with a strong majority. For firms that see Africa as a whole as a potentially attractive business opportunity, this situation suggested using South Africa as the gateway into the continent.

Chapter 11. International Financial Management

Decisions regarding financial management in international companies are also affected by current events. The following are some possible reactions to recent events:

▶ "Derivatives" made big news in 1994 and 1995 when they played a role in both the collapse of Britain's oldest merchant bank, Barings, and the bankruptcy of Orange County in California. In 1994, other firms had been negatively affected by derivatives trading: Procter & Gamble had announced losses of more than $100 million on interest-rate derivatives, Gibson Greetings had similar losses of $20 million, and the German firm Metallgesellschaft came close to bankruptcy because of its oil-derivatives trading strategy. Non-financial managers in international firms reacted by asking why their firms would use such strategies. While there may be situations where these tools to manage risks are beneficial and justified, the disaster and near disaster stories should encourage international managers to pay closer attention to financial risk management and make careful judgment regarding the use of derivatives.

▶ A growing number of Hong Kong firms, concerned about the impact of the impending reunification with the PRC, moved their head offices overseas. Bermuda and the Cayman Islands were among the beneficiaries of this move, because of the tax benefits and political isolation available in these locations. These firms continued to do business in Hong Kong, the PRC, and elsewhere in the region as they had previously, but profits accumulated in the new headquarters' location.

▶ United States' international firms could rest assured that the American currency would be readily accepted almost anywhere as the following illustrates. The Vietnamese government decreed that all financial transactions within the country must be in Vietnamese currency, the Dong, not the more popular American dollar. The Vietnamese complied for a brief period, but the dollar is considered stable and valuable, and soon transactions in the dollar again became the norm. The Federal Reserve Bank announced that it would be replacing old $100 bills with a new bill that was harder to forge. This was in response to recognition that a large number of extremely well-forged $100 bills were in circulation. The reaction in Moscow was panic, because there, as in other places, the American dollar is the preferred currency for daily transactions. Muscovites thought their old $100 bills would be worthless, but they were reassured that these could be exchanged for new bills.

▶ Canada decided to replace its $2 bill with a coin in February 1996. This would pose a difficulty for businesses in U.S. border states, who typically accept Canadian payments easily. The difficulty is that slot machines, tills, and the like are not equipped to accept $2 coins. Many of these businesses, not long ago, had retooled to accept the Canadian $1 coins introduced in the 1980s.

Chapter 12. Marketing Management in International Companies

Current events open and close markets for international firms in addition to influencing the way markets are approached. Some considerations follow:

▶ In the 1990s, Australia has been seeking to establish itself more firmly as a Pacific nation. On the surface, this might suggest that one could market to the Pacific nations, including Australia, in a similar way. Culturally, however, Australia retains many of the "Anglo" cultural values, including emphasis on individualism, that are substantially different from the typical Asian values. Marketers in international firms will need to distinguish between what makes Australians "Asian" and what makes them "Anglo."

▶ Changes in South Africa with the dismantlement of apartheid suggest that South African blacks will represent a major new market as they adjust to new freedoms. Many outsiders may make the mistake of seeing South Africa as one market. In fact, there are clear cultural differences among the major tribes. This suggests that successful marketing in South Africa may depend on addressing a variety of separate markets.

▶ The idea of a "greater China," which includes predominantly Chinese countries such as the People's Republic of China, Hong Kong, Taiwan, and Singapore, was being promoted in the mid-1990s. To the extent that the ethnic Chinese in all these locations, as well as in Chinatowns around the world, share certain values, marketers in international firms may be able to target these "Chinese markets" as a relatively homogenous whole.

▶ The formation of regional trading blocs, such as North America, the European Union, and the ASEAN countries, encourages regional marketing approaches. These blocs should adopt uniform policies regarding such things as advertising content, and marketers can expect a certain amount of regional standardization. At the same time, these blocs often include very diverse peoples and cultures, and adaptations in marketing are still likely to be necessary.

▶ Canadian firms are more likely to find themselves marketing to Mexico following the North American Free Trade Agreement of 1995. This is an unfamiliar market for Canadians, who have previously done very little business with Mexico. Mexicans are industrious and hard working in contrast to the indolent stereotype that may be held by people unfamiliar with Mexico. Canadian marketers need to be very careful to avoid any hint of the stereotype in their Mexican marketing efforts.

▶ Cultural conflicts based on race, religion, ethnicity, language, and other such factors were widespread in 1995. Conflicting values were expressed by a variety of groups, including Croats, Moslems, and Serbs in Bosnia; the Hutu and Tutsi in Africa; the East Timorese in Indonesia; French and English Canadians; native peoples in Australia, Mexico, New Zealand, and North America. These expressions of cultural conflicts, which in some cases involved genocide and war, underscore the importance to many people of factors such as race and religion. A goal of international firms often is to find ways to standardize their marketing efforts, but these cultural conflicts clearly indicate that the world is not one global village where such standardization will always be successful.

Chapter 13. Operations Management in International Companies

Operational decisions may also vary depending on current events. Companies may select different operational sites and structures to respond to a changing world. Some possible responses to recent events include the following:

▶ The formation of regional trading blocs gives rise to centralized operations organized on a regional basis. These blocs favor centralized regional operations because economies of scale often can be achieved by serving an entire region from one location within a free trade zone. Serving the region from outside the zone may be prohibitive because of regional trade barriers. Decisions to centralize based on regional trading blocs can also result in changes in transportation and distribution patterns.

▶ The People's Republic of China has created a series of "special economic zones" (SEZs) along the Pacific coast. Creation of these zones encourages foreign ventures to locate in these regions. Without the SEZs, the foreign firms might have chosen to locate elsewhere to take advantage of a particular population base or source of supply.

▶ Establishment of the North American Free Trade Agreement eliminated many of the advantages of the Mexican *maquiladoras*. The lowering of trade barriers between Mexico and the other two countries meant that factories throughout Mexico can have many of the same advantages formerly restricted to the *maquiladora* zones.

▶ The ease of communication around the world was dramatically increased with the widespread use of the Internet, combined with cellular telephones and fax machines. These communication devices make it feasible for businesspeople to operate from just about any corner of the world. Locational decisions consequently became much more flexible than formerly. The sailor running a global business from a yacht in the Caribbean may become a reality with these technologies.

▶ The referendum in Quebec in late 1995 left serious doubts as to whether Quebec would remain a part of Canada. The possibility of a sovereign Quebec had locational implications for Canadian international firms as well as non-Canadian firms doing business in Canada. Canadian firms headquartered in Quebec discussed moving their headquarters outside, and non-Canadian firms also preferred locations outside of Quebec.

▶ The United States budget stalemate of early 1996 shut down government offices. Some U.S. businesspeople found themselves unable to travel because they lacked travel documents, and business agreements were delayed because of export licenses, permissions, and so on. Some of these delays may have resulted in lost business, which may have been diverted to other locations.

▶ The strength of the Japanese yen meant that production costs in Japan remained relatively high. Japanese firms increased their production outside of Japan to take advantage of relatively lower costs. This left Japan with an overcapacity in some of its domestic plants.

Chapter 14. International Human Resource Management

Human resources and decisions about people are very often affected by events around the world. Some recent events that will affect these decisions follow:

▶ Bombings were the preferred weapon of terrorists in the mid-1990s. Bombs at the World Trade Center in New York and a federal building in Oklahoma City showed that the United States was not immune to this form of terrorism. In January and February 1996, other attacks included a Tamil Tigers' bomb in a main street in Colombo, Sri Lanka; Irish Republican Army's bombs in London; and a bomb in a luxury hotel in Bahrain placed by the Islamic Front for the Liberation of Bahrain. These random attacks, by a wide variety of terrorist groups, make travelers cautious. For many international firms, the safety of their employees is a major concern when acts of these kinds occur unexpectedly. Some companies want to provide training for their international managers in dealing with terrorism, and consequently, a new industry has developed to provide such training.

▶ Women leaders have made the headlines in Asia; for example, Ahn San Su Chih in Myanmar, Chandrika Kumaratunga in Sri Lanka, Benazir Bhutto in Pakistan. At the same time, in many locations around the world statistics show a continuing increase in the number of women entering the work force. On the surface, these events suggest that selecting personnel for overseas assignments should be easier. Firms should have less concern about sending women overseas, and they have a larger pool from which to select because they can consider both men and women as potential candidates. The reality may be more complex, because it still is difficult for women to move freely in many parts of the world and they face constraints in terms of permissible activities. Further, there is some evidence in North America that women are rethinking the relative roles of career and family in their lives; some women may not be willing to risk the negative impact that an international assignment could have on their families.

▶ Many students from the People's Republic of China remained in Australia, Canada, Europe, and the United States, following the Tiananmen Square massacre in 1989. These students were often among the brightest of China's students, selected to study abroad. Many continued their educations, and by 1996, they constituted a well-educated group interested in making business links with China. Their knowledge of Chinese languages combined with fluency in English, as well as familiarity with business practices in the East and the West, gave them a competitive edge. Western companies were finding this group of former Chinese nationals valuable in addressing opportunities in China.

▶ Chile was reported to be the next country to join NAFTA. Chile's GDP growth has grown steadily since 1990, and reached 8 percent in 1995. This suggests that Chile will represent a substantial potential market for companies from North America. In turn, this will mean considering staffing operations in Chile and potentially sending North American managers to Chile. Unfortunately, the downside of economic growth has been an increased inequality in income distribution, at least up to 1994. This also has to be considered in assessing the Chilean market, and expatriates from Canada and the United States may find poverty in Chile is unexpectedly widespread.

▶ The European Union has progressed to the stage that people move freely from one country to another and residents of any country within the union can work throughout the union. This increased labor mobility facilitates selection of employees on a regional, rather than a country, basis. Cultural differences, as well as language differences, remain a barrier to employee transfers from country to country.

Chapter 15. Control Issues in International Companies

International controls that are well designed help firms react to global events in a competent and effective manner. Controls should be designed to fit the current environment; therefore, they may be altered in relation to recent events. Some possible implications of recent events for international companies follow.

▶ The collapse of Barings Bank in 1994, because of one individual's speculative activities, and other similar events, such as the major losses suffered by the Japanese Daiwa Bank in 1995, illustrated the potential impact of one individual on a firm's investments around the world. These incidents highlighted the need for effective controls in firms to ensure that risky, speculative activities cannot proceed unnoticed.

▶ Environmental concerns became headline news in the 1990s. Concerns ranged from increased skin cancer due to ozone layer depletion to the loss of biodiversity due to deforestation. In response, consumers were taking a closer look at the operations of the companies whose products they might purchase. Some firms instituted control systems to ensure that their operations, no matter where they were located, could be described as "environmentally friendly."

▶ The establishment of accounting standards accepted throughout the European Union simplify the collection, reporting, and consolidation of information among these countries. Firms find it easier to keep records that are consistent from country to country. This means operational information is easier to compare and control.

▶ Improved electronic communication systems can support the provision of timely reports and other control information. For example, electronic file transfers mean that inventories can be counted in Nairobi or Bangkok and reported immediately to London or New York.

▶ Human rights concerns were raised by many activist groups. The issue of child labor caught the attention of people in the more developed countries. Some firms that do business with countries where child labor was considered a problem needed to consider the implications. One possibility was to implement control systems to ensure that any products purchased in these countries did not come from factories using child labor.

Summary

International business takes place in a dynamic environment, because the world is ever changing. Effective international managers want to be constantly aware of the changes occurring around the world in order to understand and assess their potential impact on business. This chapter focused on selected events in the 1995–1996 period to illustrate the impact of current events on various facets of the international business process. Students can use this discussion as a model for investigating other, more recent events and as subjects for research papers linking the real world of international business to the principles and concepts of international business and management.

Selected References

Bata, T. J., with S. Sinclair, *Bata, Shoemaker to the World* (Toronto: Stoddart, 1990).

Coplin, W. D., and M. K. O'Leary, "1990 World Political Risk Forecast," *Planning Review* (March–April 1990), p. 42.

The Economist, "Why 1996 Matters" (January 27–February 2, 1996), p. 19.

Globe and Mail, "Torture Common in Myanmar, Amnesty Says" (November 7, 1990), p. A13.

National Geographic Society, advertisement for *National Geographic Atlas of the World,* 6th ed. (November 1990).

CASE ▼ I

Queensland Minerals Limited

Don Jackson, vice president of the Metals Division of Amcon Corporation and the manager of the company's worldwide toranium business, put down the telephone with a smile. He had just learned that the company's recently expanded toranium smelter in Pittsburgh had successfully met all of its emission and economic targets for its first six months of operation. Pittsburgh's performance was good news for the Metals Division as it was the first full-scale test of the division's new Micron refining process, and it appeared to be an unqualified success.

Jackson's smile grew particularly broad as he considered Amcon's plans for a major expansion of Queensland Minerals. Located in Australia, Queensland operated the world's largest toranium mining and smelting operation and was equally owned by Amcon and Victoria Heavy Industries (VHI). In the past, Jackson had had difficulty convincing VHI that Queensland should be expanded, but with the low emission levels and energy savings offered by the Micron process, he thought that he should now be able to carry the day.

The Parent Companies

Amcon Corporation and Victoria Heavy Industries were among the world's largest natural resource companies. Approximately the same size, the two companies competed around the world in a variety of markets. They also frequently cooperated. Although the Queensland venture was their largest alliance, Amcon and VHI worked together in a variety of joint exploration ventures in remote corners of the world.

Amcon had been founded by an American prospector whose extravagant ways and propensity to gamble on unproven mineral deposits had brought the company to the point of bankruptcy more than once. After one particularly harrowing experience, disgruntled shareholders united to eject the entrepreneur and hire professional managers with a mandate to bring more discipline to the organization. Amcon subsequently developed an industry-wide reputation for sound financial management practices, and for always having its homework done. VHI, on the other hand, often reminded Amcon managers of their own company in its earlier days. Amcon managers saw their VHI counterparts as less disciplined than themselves, and operating with a greater degree of autonomy than would be possible in Amcon. Whether these generalizations were true or not, what was evident for all to see was that Amcon and VHI were the two most profitable companies in the industry, and the rivalry between them was high.

As indicated in Exhibit 1, both Amcon and VHI had a Metals Division, and in each company, this division accounted for more than 50% of total revenue and profit. Don Jackson and Sam Ziff ran the toranium business in their respective companies, and each had prime responsibility for Queensland Minerals.

Queensland Minerals

Queensland Minerals was believed to be the lowest cost toranium-producing facility in the world. Its profits were of major importance to the Metals Divisions of both Amcon and VHI.

Although each parent owned 50% of Queensland, the venture agreement called for VHI to operate the company, which it had done since the birth of the alliance eight years earlier. In practice, this meant that the venture was staffed and managed on a day-to-day basis by VHI. The board of directors, which contained four members from each parent company, met quarterly to review performance and approve the annual operating and capital budgets. Don Jackson was on the board, along with John Pitman, the president of Amcon's Metals Division, Len Major, the vice president of finance from Amcon Corporation, and David Ringwood, the president of Amcon's Australian subsidiary.

Queensland's outlook was promising, as demand for toranium was growing, particularly in Japan, and in the opinion of Jackson, expanding the output of the facility had been a viable economic proposition for the past four years. VHI had resisted Jackson's continued recommendations for expansion, however, arguing that the environmental issues were too great and expansion would never be approved by the government. To make matters worse, a request for permission to expand would focus the attention of environmental groups on the operation. When the Micron process was first completed Jackson had tried to convince Sam Ziff that the time was right for expansion. Although Ziff had seemed to favor the idea, he had come back with the comment that his fellow managers wanted to see Amcon first use the process in one of their own smelters, to make sure that it really worked: Now, two years later, Jackson had the evidence that he needed, and the time for the long overdue expansion in Australia had arrived.

**EXHIBIT I
Queensland
Minerals Limited
Partial
Organization
Charts**

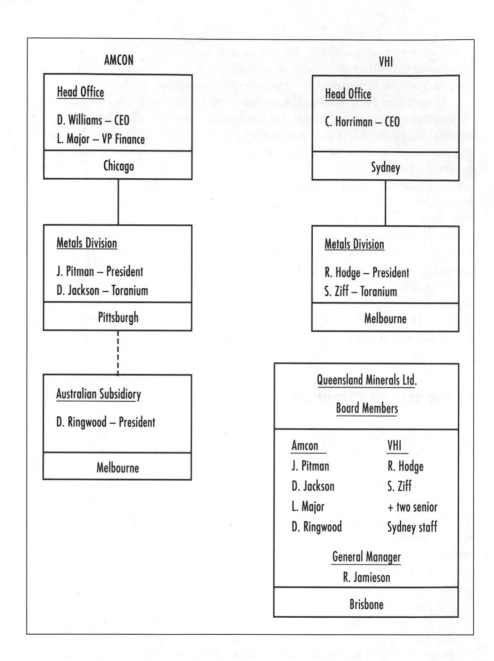

Arrival in Melbourne

Two weeks later, Don Jackson was in Melbourne, meeting with David Ringwood.

Don Jackson: As I told you over the phone, David, the Pittsburgh expansion has gone according to plan, and we are now in a position to make a solid proposal to VHI and Queensland for a 30% expansion of the Queensland mining operation and the smelter. I would like Ralph Samson (a Pittsburgh-based staff analyst) to work with one of your people to update the numbers on the project, but I don't believe that will take very long. The projected return on investment for the expansion will be higher than any other project that we have in the pipeline, and I would guess that will be true for VHI as well. I think we should plan to make a proposal to them in about a month. My feeling is that we should target Jamieson (Queensland Minerals' general manager) and his management team first, and then let them sell it to VHI's Queensland board members. Meanwhile I will get Pitman and Major up to speed so they know what we are pushing for. Does this sound OK to you, David?

David Ringwood: I don't think that this is going to be as simple as that, Don. I know that, historically, VHI executives have always said that they did not want to expand Queensland because of the environmental issues, but now there is a lot more to it than that. As you know, for the past two years, VHI have been trying to expand one of their coal mines in Northern Australia, and they are now in the middle of an acrimonious dispute regarding aboriginal rights and sacred ground in the outback. The last thing that they want is to present the Australian government with another expansion proposal, no matter how environmentally improved it is.

I have proposed that I talk directly to the government to explain the benefits of the Micron process, but VHI does not want me to. They have made it clear that this is their country, and they do not want us wandering the halls of power interfering in their existing relationships.

Anyway, Don, even without this problem, I would argue that Jamieson is having so much difficulty operating the mine at current levels, that we should not push for expansion right now. Since VHI reorganized their Metals Division a year ago to make it "meaner and leaner" the efficiency of Queensland has been falling steadily. Remember that discussion at the last board meeting about the fact that operating costs have risen from $45 to $48 per ton over the past six months. I think that we are going to see that trend continue, unless we get some changes made.

What seems to be happening is that the VHI Metals Division staff backup that Jamieson's people had relied on is no longer there, and it is making a difference – although they will not admit it. I am trying to get Jamieson to take more Amcon people into his operation – we have six in there at the moment – but they see our people as meddling in their affairs. Jamieson has made it clear that *they* are the operators, and the operation is theirs to run.

Don Jackson: Yes, I remember the cost discussion, but didn't Jamieson explain that costs were rising because they were now taking material from a more difficult area of the mine. . . . they have done the "easy stuff" was the way I think he put it.

David Ringwood: That's what he said, but it is only partly true. The real problem, which I have learned from the engineers that we have in Queensland, is that Jamieson has a couple of supervisors two levels below him that are doing a poor job and need to be replaced. Of course no one will listen to their opinion. I even brought the matter up with Ziff, privately, but got nowhere. He says that issues like that are not the concern of the board. In his view, Jamieson is making good money, and the way prices are going, he is going to make even better money. He says it's not our job to tell him how to manage his people. I think that we had better bring the issue up at the next board meeting . . . and I think, Don, that this definitely has to take precedence over the expansion issue.

Don Jackson: David, I appreciate that we have to keep on top of Jamieson with respect to the existing operation, but this expansion *has* to happen. Williams and Pitman are both counting on it, and that means my head is on the line. Everyone knows that the Micron process is a winner, and I can't just go back and say that the Australians don't want it. That's not good enough. Anyway, if we don't move very soon, I am sure that Torcan, our Canadian competitor, is going to expand their mine in Ontario. I want to forestall that if I can, by announcing our own expansion.

I understand that VHI has some problems with their coal mine expansion, but Sam Ziff has not said anything to me to the effect that this will hold up the expansion of Queensland. I'll discuss the issue with him tomorrow.

Meeting with Sam Ziff

The following morning Don Jackson met with Sam Ziff in Ziff's Melbourne office, which was about two blocks from the office tower in which Amcon's Australian head office was housed. Ziff said that he was delighted to learn of the success of the Micron process, but explained that while he fully supported the expansion of the Queensland operation, the timing was not ideal.

I understand your impatience, Don, but please bear with us on this. We have a number of sensitive negotiations under way with the government at the moment, and adding one more might well destroy what is already a very shaky situation . . . and both our companies would be losers if that happened. Remember that we have 20 years of reserves in the Queensland mine, and a year or so here or there is not going to make much difference in the overall success of the project. In fact the way toranium prices are moving up . . . and are likely to continue to increase . . . selling our output later at a higher price might not be a bad idea.

Later the Same Day

Later the same day a very frustrated Don Jackson was back in David Ringwood's office discussing the situation with Ringwood and Peter Harper, a mining engineer who had been working for Queensland for a year, although he remained on the payroll of Amcon Australia.

Don Jackson: I cannot believe these people! Who does Ziff think he is, saying that the timing is "not ideal!" He has known for two years that this was coming. Did he hope that the Micron process would fail? Pitman is going to have my head.

David Ringwood: I think that you should give up on the expansion for the time being, Don. VHI will not give in on this one, no matter how high you go up the ladder. They have too much at stake, and for them the expansion of Queensland is not a major issue. Did you tell him that Jamieson needs to fire a couple of people?

Don Jackson: I decided not to get into it. Ziff and the other VHI directors give Jamieson a very free hand . . . so there did not seem to be much point. They simply do not control things as tightly as we do. Unfortunately that 15-page agreement that we signed ten years ago to establish this venture does not help much. If we were doing this deal today we would have 200 pages, and a lot more disclosure and control!

David Ringwood: Well, maybe it is time for a change in the agreement. I have been thinking for some time that our lives would be a lot easier if we operated the Queensland venture ourselves. If we were the operator, we could solve these immediate production issues, and we could influence the timing of the expansion as well. Given the Australian government's attitude to foreign investment, I don't think that we should try for 51% ownership, but we should be able to keep the ownership at 50% and have us as the operator. What do you think, Peter?

Peter Harper: I think that would be great. Trying to influence Queensland managers from positions like mine inside the venture is hopeless. We do our technical homework and sometimes they use it, but more often they ignore it. We don't usually get invited to the meetings where the decisions are made, and we only find out afterwards if our arguments carried the day.

If we were the operator, we could end the constant frustration and wasted effort that this relationship currently involves. Time after time we have done our homework and they have not, and time after time they ignore us. I don't just mean me, Don; I am thinking of your lack of results with Ziff a couple of years ago, and I could quote lots of other examples. We are always right, and we can prove it, but they don't care! I don't know how to get them to listen.

I have tried to get them to accept more of our engineers – after all, we are not costing them anything – but it is pretty clear that we have reached the limit. They see us as Amcon spies who add some value, but are often more trouble than we are worth, because of what we report back to you guys. As operator, we could really clean this place up.

Don Jackson: Do you two think that this is realistic? Why would VHI give up being the operator? There is a lot of pride involved here. If the positions were reversed, we certainly would not yield. What arguments could we use? Having said that, I do think that you two are right. Maybe it is time for a fundamental change in this relationship. Setting aside a move to us as the operating partner, we have three choices. (Moving to flipchart:)

1. We buy out VHI's interest.
     Would they sell?
     Would the government let it happen?
     Would Pitman and Williams go for it?
2. We sell our interest in Queensland.
     Would they buy?
     Could we get a good price?
     Would Williams and Pitman go for it?
3. Establish a new 50-50 management structure.
     Would it work?
     Could we sell the idea to both sides?

What I mean by the third alternative is that we would change the management structure to reflect the fact that we are equal partners in this venture. So far, they have dominated everything.

What if we changed the arrangement so that half of Jamieson's management team were our people? We could also supply half the engineers, half the operating people, and so on. Then we could influence the operating issues and the strategic stuff, like this expansion. This makes a lot more sense than trying to influence them from the outside, as we are at present. The board would also start getting better information. At the moment Jamieson tells us whatever he wants to. I never feel that we get the full picture.

I think that this last alternative is the best. David, will you help me work up a proposal for Pitman on this?

CASE 2

Labatt Breweries of Europe

At the start of May 1989, Labatt Breweries of Europe, London-based unit of Toronto's John Labatt Limited, was in the final stages of negotiations to purchase Italian brewers Birra Moretti, SpA, and Prinz Brau Brewing Company. Adam Humphries, finance chief for LBOE, recalled, "Moretti and Prinz were seen as strategic acquisitions to enable Labatt to start the process of becoming a key player internationally and, specifically, in the Italian and European beer markets." Acquisition team leader John Morgan added, "And they were priced right." Both purchases were set to close by the middle of the month, although just-discovered irregularities at Prinz gave Labatt the apparent right to abort that deal, if not both.

Background

John Labatt Limited had two principal divisions, Labatt Brewing Company, headed by life-long brewer Sidney M. Oland, and Labatt Food Company, headed by George S. Taylor, a former finance specialist. Brewing had fiscal year 1989 (ending April 30) earnings before interest and taxes (EBIT) of C$158 million on sales of C$1.8 billion.* The Food Company's EBIT was C$106 million on sales of C$3.6 billion. About 15 percent of Food Company revenue came from "other investments," which included a Canadian sports broadcaster, an agricultural biotechnology company, and 45 percent ownership of the Toronto Blue Jays baseball club. Labatt had begun exporting its beer to England in 1982 and formed LBOE in 1987. Oland explained his strategy:

*The exchange rate as of March 31, 1989, was C$1 = US$0.8378.

By Arthur Sharplin, Institute for International Business Studies, NEOS Consortium MBA, Pordenone, Italy, and Waltham Associates Inc., Austin, Texas. Management assisted in the research for this case, which was written for research purposes and to stimulate scholarly discussion. Special thanks go to Richard Beveridge, Yasmin Ferrari, Adam Humphries, William G. Bourne, Sidney M. Oland, and John Morgan as well as to the editor and anonymous reviewers for the *Case Research Journal*. Faculty members in nonprofit institutions are encouraged to reproduce this case for distribution to their students without charge or written permission. All other rights reserved jointly to the author and the North American Case Research Association (NACRA). Copyright © 1995 by the *Case Research Journal* and Arthur Sharplin.

We had won the battle in Canada. We were making lots of money in Brewing and had to decide what to do with it. We surveyed the world looking for good places to invest. England was our first choice, mainly because of the language. Spain and France came next. But Italy was within our sights.

Humphries, a young Englishman who had moved up from Labatt's U.K. operation to LBOE, added, "Labatt's comfortable domestic market position [42.3 percent in 1988] was under threat from the U.S.-Canada free trade agreement, and the diversification process outside brewing was not going well."

In fact, the U.S. was preparing a formal complaint against Canadian brewers under the General Agreement on Tariffs and Trade (GATT). A Canadian newsmagazine soon concluded,

The stage is set for cheap, tariff-free brew from the United States to flood Canada. . . . For the past sixty years, the domestic brewing industry has been governed by a host of interprovincial barriers that have angered foreign competitors. A particular sore spot is the time-honored rule forcing companies to brew beer in every province where they want to sell their brands. The result is a fragmented Canadian industry that has spawned many small, inefficient plants at a time when breweries in other countries have been producing cheaper beer by building huge megabreweries and consolidating smaller plants.[1]

Labatt, for example, had twelve breweries strung across Canada. The import threat intensified Labatt's competition with Molson Companies Ltd., which had merged its beer operations with Carling O'Keefe Breweries of Canada Ltd., giving Molson a 53 percent domestic share. But Oland pooh-poohed the impact of the Molson merger, saying, "Our weaker competitor combined with our weakest one." In the meantime, Canada's beer consumption declined from 86 liters per person in 1981 to 80 liters in 1989.[2]

Labatt sold several businesses in 1988, ostensibly due to their lack of "strategic relevance." According to Morgan, another reason for the divestments was pressure from Brascan Ltd. to "maximize cash coming up [Labatt's] corporate chain." Brascan, owner of 42.3 percent of Labatt's outstanding common stock, was part of the troubled Peter F. and Edward F. Bronfman financial empire (headquartered in Toronto but with interests worldwide). Labatt's twenty-three directors included Peter Bronfman and two Brascan executives. In the winter of 1989, a new director slot had been added, filled by Dr. Maurice J. LeClair, vice chairman of Canadian Imperial Bank of Commerce, who also joined Labatt's audit committee. And Edwin A. Goodman, a director for 23 years and a business consultant, resigned and was replaced by Melvin M. Hawkrigg, Chairman of Trilon Financial Corporation. Morgan said Labatt was being "actively marketed" during this period, although Oland disputed that. "Actually," Oland added, "Our plan was to separate the company into brewing and entertainment divisions, both publicly traded. Labatt would own 51 percent of Brewing and 50 percent of Entertainment."

Seeking Major European Acquisitions

As Oland had instructed, Morgan pushed forward in Europe. The U.K. operation was shifted from importing to "toll brewing," employing regional brewers with excess capacity to brew the beer. The product was then marketed through joint venture arrangements. Morgan said Labatt's U.K. sales had expanded rapidly, characterizing the move as "the most successful lager launch ever in the U.K."

In early 1988, Michael Hurst, a marketing executive from Labatt Canada, was transferred to LBOE as vice president, Marketing. And in September that year, Humphries recruited Richard Beveridge, a recent graduate of the London Business School, as financial analyst.

Humphries said, "There was a window of opportunity to take a major position in Europe." He continued:

> Our first choice was Grand Met's brewing assets, mostly in the U.K. But we were offering cash, and Grand Met opted for a swap-type arrangement with another partner. We then looked at opportunities in Germany and Switzerland. When that seemed a dead end, we turned to La Cruz del Campo in Spain, but that deal wasn't ready to do either.

The Grand Met sale was valued at US$600 million. La Cruz del Campo was acquired by London-based Guinness PLC in 1990 for US$1.15 billion. One former LBOE official said "pussyfooting" by recalcitrant Labatt directors had nixed the deals for the Canadians. Humphries acknowledged, "At corporate there were those who saw European expansion as risky and who needed to be convinced." But Morgan disputed the pussyfooting charge, saying, "Brascan's cash needs were the reason."

Turning to Italy

In the second quarter of 1988, the team turned its full attention to Italy. Humphries said, "It was important at the time to show results, and Moretti and Prinz were the only acquisitions which seemed doable." The acquisition team believed that Italy offered the following advantages:

1. It was one of the few growing beer markets in the world, averaging 2.5 percent annual growth over the previous 10 years.
2. It was ripe territory for branding, image-building strategies.
3. Operations could be distribution driven, through relations with small vendors.
4. The beer target group (male 18 to 35) was growing.
5. Italy had one of the lowest per capita beer consumption rates in Europe.

Morgan said that these characteristics were similar to those that had preceded "the growth of beer in Canada." However, data then available from Assobirra, the Italian brewing industry association, revealed that all the growth in beer consumption in Italy noted above had occurred before 1986. And what Assobirra labeled the "formative beer drinking category," the 15 to 34 age bracket, was projected to peak at 18 million in 1990 and fall to 16 million in 2000. Italy's population in 1989 was 57.5 million.

Italy's Beer Industry

In Italy, 5000 or so "concessionaires" took large shipments of beer from brewers and delivered it to tens of thousands of small retailers. Concessionaires usually represented only one brewer and were given specific territories. They paid brewers deposits on bottles and crates and collected similar deposits from retailers. Brewers installed and serviced draught equipment, further tying retailers and concessionaires to brewers. Assobirra administered a cooperative advertising program, which used television, radio, and posters to advertise the beer category.[3]

Table 1 provides statistics on beer drinking for selected European countries. According to Humphries, it was widely assumed that Italian beer consumption would grow to at least match that of Spain, Portugal, or France, if not of other European countries. The assumption was buttressed by the continuing decline in wine sales in Italy, which was believed to mean that Italians were switching to beer.

Table 2 shows estimated shares of Italian beer production for all nine significant producers in 1988. About 2 percent of production was exported that year, up from about 1 percent in 1980 (imports were about 18 percent of consumption in the late 1980s). Peroni and Dreher had six plants each, Prinz and Poretti two each, and the others one each.

TABLE 1   1988 Per Capita Beer Consumption and 1980–1989 Growth in Per Capita Beer Consumption for Selected European Countries

	1988 Liters/Capita	1980–89 Growth (%)
Belgium/Luxembourg	121.0	−12.0
Denmark	125.2	−2.6
France	38.9	−7.9
Holland	86.0	1.4
Ireland	109.0	−25.8
Italy	24.2	30.5
Portugal	47.0	n/a
Spain	66.8	n/a
UK	110.5	−5.7
West Germany	118.0	−1.9

Source: Databank SpA.

TABLE 2   Estimated 1988 Market Shares of Major Italian Brewers

Brewer	Market Share (%)
Peroni	38
Dreher	31
Poretti	9
Interbrew	7
Forst	6
Moretti	4
Prinz	3
Castelberg	1
Menabrea	1

Source: Assobirra.

Multinational companies bought up most of the Italian brewing industry during the 1980s. Foreign ownership of the top four brewers in 1988 was as follows:

Dreher – Heineken, Dutch brewer (100%)
Interbrew – Stella Artois, Belgian brewer (100%)
Peroni – BSN Danone, French food group (% not known)
Poretti – Carlsberg, Danish brewer (50%)

Sidney Oland said brewing was distinguished from other process industries by the need for sanitation and temperature control. "In fact," said Oland, "in brewing, we don't *make* beer. God does. And you know He never does the same thing twice. We just try to provide an environment which dampens the natural variations." Exhibit 1 describes how beer is made.

Moretti and Prinz

Moretti was headquartered in Udine, northeast of Venice, and Prinz in Crespellano, near Bologna (see Exhibit 2). Each had a brewery at its headquarters and Prinz had a southern brewery, in Baragiano. Moretti's annual brewing capacity was 450,000 hectoliters (a hectoliter is 100 liters, or 26.4 U.S. gallons) and Prinz's was about 700,000 at Crespellano and 75,000 at Baragiano. Moretti was financially weak in 1989 but was still owned by Luigi Moretti, whose family had founded the brewery in 1859. Beveridge said the brewery had "a strong brand image, stable sales, and a well-established distribution network in northern Italy." It had agreed to stay out of southern Italy for 10 years in connection with an asset sale in mid-1980. Moretti's brewery, near Udine's central traffic circle, was operating near capacity, and cars in the area were often

EXHIBIT I
How Beer Is Made

A modern brewery at first glance appears to be a simple process plant, consisting mainly of stainless steel tanks, hoppers, dryers, filters, pumps, and so forth, connected by pipes and valves. Temperatures, pressures, and product chemistry are tightly controlled throughout, and the system is sealed off from the atmosphere. An on-site laboratory uses spectrographic analysis and chemical methods to test raw materials and to check the product at various points. Brewery products are also tasted regularly. Few workers are required and only an occasional technician may be observed taking a sample, recording data, or adjusting machinery.

Primary raw materials for brewing beer are water, barley malt (which provides starch for conversion to alcohol), about a fourth as much of other cereal grain (such as rice or corn), a much smaller amount of hops (which impart bitterness and aroma), and yeast (to promote fermentation). The cereals and hops are cooked in large steam-jacketed kettles to produce wort, an amber sugar solution. This takes from 2.5 to 3.5 hours, allowing 7 to 9 batches per day. The residue is usually sold as animal feed.

The wort is fermented in large tanks for about 4 days and the resulting beer aged for about 16 days. Product characteristic – color, taste, alcohol content – are varied by adjusting the variety and amount of malt, grain, and hops used and by modifying the fermentation and aging regimens.

EXHIBIT 2
Map of Italy

dusted with a sticky, white substance coming from the brewery's brew kettles. In the headquarters building were a restaurant and bar. Local citizens often gathered there to socialize and consume a special unfiltered, nonpasteurized draught brew sold nowhere else. There was also a museum containing memorabilia, pictures, and films from Moretti's 130-year history. Oland recalled:

> The essential attraction of Moretti was that you had a good brand which had been constrained to a small area of Italy for legal, financial, and other reasons. That area happened to be home to most of Italy's military. Young soldiers would learn to like Moretti beer, then not be able to find it when they got back home.

Prinz was virtually bankrupt in 1989, and had been since its purchase for L1000 (about US$1.00) by an Italian prince and another investor in 1985. Prinz leased its breweries but had the right to purchase them in the event that the company was sold. Most managers and many experienced operators and administrative people had left Prinz, and the company's distribution system was collapsing. According to Beveridge, the scant crew "made beer whenever suppliers could be talked into shipping raw materials and then attempted to sell the product." Oland added, "Prinz offered a chance to buy capacity very cheaply."

Making the Deals

Morgan and his team contacted the respective owners, set up confidentiality arrangements, and obtained data thought necessary to value each company. Few executives in domestic Italian firms spoke English and even fewer workers did. No one on the acquisition team spoke much Italian, and most information and conversation had to be translated. Despite this, the team was able to prepare a report, including financial data and valuation estimates, and dispatch it to Oland.

In August 1988, Oland traveled to Udine and met with Luigi Moretti. Oland recalled, "The final negotiation took just a day. This was actually the second time I had met Moretti. The first was just a 'beauty contest,' to get acquainted." Humphries said the two were initially far apart on price but quickly came to terms "at a price at the top end of the team's recommended maximum." He added, "Sid started high, which was a surprise, but this removed the block in negotiations, which could have dragged on for some time. And we were just very pleased to have the deal done." Oland confirmed Humphries's account in general, but said the deal was hardly "done" at this point. Oland added, "I put a great deal of weight on the financial projections and present value analysis the acquisition team had done. And the final price was in their recommended range – barely so, but within the range." The price for Moretti was never disclosed but was estimated by outsiders at US$75 million, including assumption of specified liabilities. One observer said Luigi Moretti asked that the price not be disclosed because, "In Sardinia [where Moretti vacationed], you let people know how much money you have and you end up with a sack over your head."

In September 1988, the team began negotiations with the owners of Prinz. In November that year, Morgan, Humphries, Hurst, and Beveridge flew to Canda to seek board approval to buy Moretti alone or to buy both Moretti and Prinz. Beveridge recalled, "We could never make a Prinz-only acquisition work in our model, at any purchase price." According to Oland, the combined operation was projected to become profitable "on an EBIT level" in the third year after acquisition. The board of directors gave authority to buy Moretti and Prinz, but not to buy either one alone. Oland said the board's consideration of this "was not controversial."

In December 1988, a letter of intent was signed with Moretti, subject to *due diligence* (audits ordinarily employed to verify seller representations). A purchase price for Prinz, estimated at US$25 million, was agreed upon in February 1989, also subject to due diligence. Oland said the cost of new construction would have been about US$150 per hectoliter of capacity, and the real cost of the Prinz capacity was about US$30 per hectoliter.

How Bad Can It Be?

The Moretti deal was ready to close by April, but delay was necessary because of concerns about problems discovered at Prinz during the due diligence audits. Beginning in early 1988,

Prinz had apparently inflated its sales figures, failing to account for returns, billing some product that would not be delivered until later, and even delivering presold production, for cash, to different customers than those who had initially ordered and paid for it. In December 1988, Prinz's recorded sales began to plummet. By May 1989, prepaid customers were threatening to sue, and unpaid suppliers were refusing to ship. Beveridge recalled,

> The principals had a severely inflated sense of their own, and their company's, worth. Most of the good managers had left Prinz long before, and there wasn't enough of an information system in place to allow auditing. Beyond the standard financial reports submitted to the government and accumulated by industry analysts, we simply did not trust any information we were given. At one point, the Labatt team was even locked out of the brewery. They just stayed holed up in their hotel for days. All the "Italian" negotiating tricks were used against us.

No one on the acquisition team had even seen the Baragiano brewery. Oland said he wanted to go himself, but government officials in Baragiano would not permit it. "Kidnapping," said Oland. "They were afraid I would be kidnapped." An Oland aide finally was flown from Canada to Baragiano and back the same day on the prince's private jet. "He was the only Labatt employee to see the brewery," said Oland.

During the first week of May 1989, Oland was briefed on the situation at Prinz. He remarked, "Okay, fellows, how bad can it be? Does it justify canning both deals?" It was then explained to an increasingly impatient Luigi Moretti that neither deal could be done without the other. Beveridge said this increased the pressure on the acquisition team to make a quick decision, because he felt the Prinz owners would ruthlessly exploit their position if they were to learn of the linkage with Moretti.

References

1. John DeMont. "A Global Brew." *Maclean's*, vol. 102, no. 30 (July 24, 1989), p. 28.
2. Deirdre McMurdy. "Brewing Struggle." *Maclean's*, vol. 104, no. 7 (February 18, 1991), p. 39.
3. Canadean Ltd. *The Beer Service Basic Report: Italy*. Basingstoke, Hants, U.K.: Canadean Ltd., 1992, sec. 8.

CASE 3

Teléfonos de Mexico: The Privatization Decision (A)

"Privatization will be the means for realizing the commitment to modernize Teléfonos de Mexico . . ."

President Carlos Salinas de Gortari, September 1989

On September 18, 1989, nine months after assuming office as president of Mexico, 40-year-old Carlos Salinas de Gortari announced at the annual meeting of the telephone workers union (STRM) that the state-owned telephone company, Teléfonos de Mexico (Telmex), would be privatized. The announcement came as a surprise to many Mexicans, since Telmex was one of the largest state enterprises and there had been no talk of privatizing it earlier. However, the leader of the STRM, Francisco Hernández Juárez, knew the announcement was forthcoming and had already agreed to support it. Indeed, in April 1989, his union had made several concessions while renegotiating its labor agreement with Telmex, paving the way for privatization. At the September meeting, the workers voted unanimously to support the government's decision.

Jacques Rogozinski (Ph.D. Economics, University of Colorado), Director of the Office for Privatization of State-Owned Enterprises in the Ministry of Finance, had primary responsibility for organizing the Telmex privatization. For more than 6 months prior to Salinas's announcement, he and a select group of colleagues from the Ministry of Communications, the Ministry of Transportation, the Ministry of Commerce and Industry, and Telmex had been studying the matter. Yet, three months after the president's announcement, in December 1989, they remained divided on

By Ravi Ramamurti of Northeastern University. This case was written with the cooperation of management, based on published information and field research in Mexico, solely for the purpose of stimulating student discussion. Partially supported by the Harvard Institute for International Development. Produced originally for use at the 1992 Harvard University Public Enterprise Workshop. All events and individuals are real. Faculty members in nonprofit institutions are encouraged to reproduce this case for distribution to their own students, without charge or written permission. All other rights reserved jointly to the author and North American Case Research Association (NACRA). Copyright © 1993 by the *Case Research Journal* and Ravi Ramamurti. Videotapes are available from the Videocase Center, College of Business Administration, Hayden 313, Northeastern University, Boston, MA 02115.

many issues. There were different points of view on whether Telmex should be divided before privatization, whether it should be permitted to diversify, how much equity ought to be given to workers, what role foreign capital ought to play in Telmex, how buyers might be found, and whether its monopoly rights ought to be preserved after privatization, and, if so, for how long.

Rogozinski was scheduled to discuss these and other issues the following Monday with his boss, Finance Minister Pedro Aspe Armella (Ph.D. Economics, MIT), who expected the Telmex privatization to be concluded within a year of the president's announcement, that is, by September 1990.

The Telecommunications Industry

Technology

A telecommunications system consists of three parts: customer-premise equipment, such as telephones and private branch exchanges (PBXs); transmission equipment, such as the cables connecting individual phones to the local exchange or lines connecting exchanges to one another; and the exchanges themselves, where telephone calls are completed by linking one telephone to another.

Over the years, technological change had affected all three parts. Exchanges that relied on human operators to complete phone calls were replaced first by electromechanical switches, then by electronic exchanges in which computers managed the network, and, most recently, by digital exchanges. With each successive technology, the telephone system's quality, reliability, versatility, and cost-effectiveness improved.

Initially, all transmission – local and long distance – was via copper wires or cables that physically tied the system together. In more recent years, fiber-optic technology had permitted far greater amounts of information to be transmitted in a single cable and with far greater reliability than ever before. In addition, alternative methods of transmission, such as microwave and satellite systems, had become available. Like mobile (cellular) telephones, satellite and microwave systems did away with cables and wires and were therefore more economical; they found extensive use in long-distance transmission. Yet even in the 1990s, in most countries the local network – which connected phones to the nearest exchange – relied almost entirely on wires and cables. Industry experts believed that the day was not far away when wires and cables could be done away with altogether, and everyone could own a portable phone.

Finally, the choice of customer-premise equipment had broadened from the "plain old rotary telephone" to products such as push-button telephones, fax machines, answering machines, and networked computers.

Another trend affecting the telephone industry was the growing interdependence between the technologies for communication and computing. Business users, such as banks, retail outlets, and multinational companies, demanded an integrated solution for their computing and communication needs so that they could freely input, transmit, and process messages of all kinds – voice, text, data, and images – within a dispersed but interconnected computer system. (The term "telecommunications" referred to a system that could handle the full range of messages mentioned rather than just voice messages.) Telephone companies around the world were straining – and, in some cases, failing – to satisfy these emerging needs.

Industrialized countries undertook massive investments to convert to digital systems increasingly linked by fiber-optic cables. Developing countries, on the other hand, were torn between extending basic service to a wider segment of the population and offering modern systems for business users. One common solution was to create a digital system on top of the traditional network to serve business customers. Another was to permit large users to bypass the existing network through satellite-based communications.

Deregulation and Privatization

In the early 1980s, the telephone system was state-owned in most rich and poor countries. Even among the exceptions to this rule, such as the United States, Barbados, the Dominican Republic, Hong Kong, and Puerto Rico, governments tightly regulated the private phone companies. However, in the 1980s, several countries began to deregulate and/or privatize the telecommunications industry.

The deregulation trend had been led by the United States, where privately owned AT&T (known more commonly as the Bell system) had monopolized the sector for decades. In 1968, the Federal Communications Commission (FCC) allowed customers to connect non-Bell phones to the system for the first time. A year later, the FCC allowed alternative long-distance microwave carriers to interconnect with AT&T's network, though only for private use. In the late 1970s, a company called MCI fought and obtained the right to convert its private-line, microwave network into a public service that would compete with AT&T in the long-distance business. Finally, in 1984, AT&T and U.S. regulators reached an agreement to break up the Bell system into eight parts. Seven of these, the so-called Baby Bells, would offer local service in the assigned regions but would be barred from long-distance service (outside their territories), equipment manufacture, and enhanced information services, such as voice mail or electronic yellow pages. The regional companies would be regulated by state-level agencies on matters such as pricing, quality of service, etc. The eighth company, to be called AT&T, would offer domestic and international long-distance service, manufacture equipment, and retain control over the world-famous Bell Labs. In addition, the new AT&T would be permitted to diversify into other businesses, including computers, from which it had been barred in 1956.[1]

By 1990, these measures had resulted in a sharp fall in long-distance rates in the United States, a rise in the rates for local service (which had previously been cross-subsidized by long-distance charges – paid mostly by businesses), a wider choice of telephone equipment for the regional Bells as well as for telephone users (cordless telephones, fax machines, etc.), and access to new voice and data services for business customers. The two biggest rivals of AT&T in the domestic long-distance business, MCI and Sprint, had garnered small but significant shares of that market by 1990.

The most celebrated case of privatization probably occurred in the United Kingdom in 1984, when Prime Minister Margaret Thatcher sold 51 percent of British Telecom (BT) for 3.9 billion British pounds through a global stock offering, the largest of its kind until then. The government appointed a new chairman and president for the company – both from the private sector – before privatization. No single investor, British or foreign, was permitted to own more than 15 percent of the voting stock, while the government retained a "golden share" (worth only 1 British pound) that gave it the right to appoint some directors and approve changes to the company's charter. Simultaneously, the government permitted another long-distance company to compete with BT but barred additional competitors for the next 7 years. Under the license granted to BT, the company was permitted to continue offering other local and long-distance service, to manufacture equipment, and to offer enhanced information services. BT was also permitted to raise its prices periodically for a basket of services by the rate of inflation (as measured by the retail price index) less 3 percent. A new, independent agency, Oftel, was created to regulate the telecom industry.

In 1985, Japan sold a minority share in its state-owned company, NTT, but barred foreigners from participating in the sale. The government's share was supposed to fall eventually to 33 percent. The new law ended NTT's legal monopoly over telehpne service, but no serious competitor had emerged by 1989. Elsewhere in the industrialized world, the New Zealand government was expected to sell 49.9 percent of its telephone company to two Baby Bells, Bell Atlantic and Ameritech, for over US$2.0 billion, and planned to divest the rest of its shares through an international stock offering in 1991.

Toward the end of the 1980s, the idea of privatizing telecommunications firms had gathered steam in the developing world. Several countries were turning their telephone departments into joint stock companies. Others, like Malaysia and Fiji, were planning public stock offerings. Several small countries had sold big blocks of shares to foreign telecommunications firms: France Cable et Radio, a subsidiary of state-owned France Telecom, owned between 25 and 48 percent of the shares of telecommunications firms in many francophone nations in Africa, while Cable and Wireless of the U.K. held similar positions in former British colonies. In Latin America, Chile privatized its telephone company in 1988, while Argentina, Mexico, and Venezuela were in the process of doing the same. Chile had two state enterprises in the telephone sector, one devoted to local service (CTC) and the other to long-distance service (ENTEL). Fifty-two percent of CTC was sold to an Australian group with no experience in the telephone business, while 30 percent of ENTEL was sold to a consortium consisting of the Spanish state-owned telephone company, Teléfonica, together with Chase Manhattan Bank. Argentina, on the other hand, was reportedly planning to divide the telephone company along geographical lines (north and south), with a third company for long-distance service that would be jointly owned by the two regional companies. The capital city of Buenos Aires, in which almost two-thirds of the telephone lines were installed, was to be divided equally between the regional companies.

In most developing countries, the state-owned telephone company or agency was unable to keep up with demand: waiting times of 2 to 10 years for new connections were not unusual. Rumor had it that it cost US$2000 to US$3000 under the table for a connection in downtown Bangkok, while in Indonesia retiring telephone employees reportedly received not golden watches but a telephone line! While industrialized countries had 40 to 50 telephone lines per 100 persons, developing countries seldom had more than 5 to 10 per 100 persons. In China, the ratio was 1:100, in India 1:160 (with only 1:3500 in rural areas), and in Tanzania 1:500. Further, service tended to be very poor when judged by measures such as the call completion rate or the percentage of lines that were down at any time. At the same time, the telephone companies tended to be overstaffed by developed country standards – in some cases by a factor of 500. (Exhibit 1 contains comparative data on these measures for a few countries, including Mexico.)

State-owned telephone organizations in developing countries tended to be profitable, despite low rates for local service and a considerable amount of underbilling and corruption on the part of employees. Indeed, in many cases surpluses generated by the telephone companies were

EXHIBIT I   **Telephone System Performance, Comparative Data on Selected Measures**

Country	Lines per 100 Population	Workers per 1000 Lines	Waiting Time for Lines, Years	Lines with Failures, %
Mexico	5.2	10	2–3	10
Argentina	9.6	14	22	45
Brazil	5.5	11	na	5
Chile	4.6	8	na	7
Venezuela	7.5	11	8	na
Tanzania	0.2	69	11	na
India	0.5	96	na	13
Indonesia	0.4	50	6	17
United States	51	6.6	few days	less than 1
Japan	40	6.6	few days	less than 1

Source: Various publications.

diverted by governments to other sectors. Some policymakers viewed telephone service as a luxury in the context of poor countries, hence meriting lower priority than sectors such as health, housing, and education. Telephone service was also a capital-intensive proposition, requiring on average US$1000 to US$1500 per new line, with much of that consisting of imported equipment. However, others argued that a good telephone system was essential for promoting domestic commerce, exports, and international competitiveness. They pointed to the example of countries like Barbados and Jamaica that had benefitted from modern telecommunications systems: Barbados had set up an international teleport facility, while Jamaica had set up an office park with an international teleport that provided high-speed, high-quality voice and data links with the United States.

A World Bank report had this to say on telecommunications privatization in developing countries:

> The arguments in favor of some private participation in telecommunications are compelling. Additional financial, technical, and managerial resources – desperately needed in most developing countries – can be provided by private telecom firms. Under increased competitive pressure, private operators of telecom networks can be expected to lower costs by restructuring the work force, introducing new technologies, and procuring components in greater volumes, thus reducing the unit cost of inputs. Commercially minded firms would also increase their responsiveness toward customers and work toward expanding coverage of telecommunications services.[2]

Opponents of privatization argued that telephone companies ought to be government-owned because they were natural monopolies. Technology may have made it possible to create competition in long-distance service, but local service was without doubt still a natural monopoly. Private telephone companies could be counted on to exploit their customers and deny service in remote areas. "Just because governments are financially broke," said one policymaker, "it doesn't mean they should sell their crown jewels at throwaway prices to the highest bidder, including foreigners. How can privatization be a good idea for poor countries when so many rich countries, including France, Germany, Italy, and Spain, have not yet privatized their phone companies?"

The Mexican Economy in 1989

As president of Mexico, Salinas presided over one of the largest economies in the developing world (population 85 million; GNP US$160 billion). It was also one of the richer developing countries, with per capita income of US$1900. Since the adoption of a new constitution in 1917, Salinas's party, the PRI, had dominated Mexican politics. The PRI encompassed almost all segments of Mexican society, including teachers, workers, labor unions under the Confederation of Mexican Workers (CTM), and business interests. Until the 1988 elections, PRI had not lost the presidency nor any of the thirty-one state governorships or sixty-four seats. Elections for president, accompanied by smooth transitions of power, had occurred every 6 years. Presidents were limited to one term, but enjoyed broad powers, including primacy over the legislature and the judiciary.[3]

Like many other developing countries, Mexico pursued a policy of import-substituting industrialization after World War II. In the 1950s and 1960s, GNP and per capita income grew at impressive levels. In the 1970s, Mexico profited from the oil boom, and the new riches led to ambitious public programs under presidents Luis Echeverría (1970–76) and José López Portillo (1976–82). Public spending outpaced the increase in government revenues, leading to fiscal deficits and foreign borrowing. Between 1979 and 1989, Mexico's foreign debt grew from US$40 billion to more than US$100 billion. As oil prices began to fall and interest rates on foreign loans rose, Mexico defaulted on its external debt in August 1982, triggering the global debt crisis. Rich Mexicans, losing confidence in the economy, began to take money out of the country. López Portillo responded by nationalizing the country's large, private banks and instituting exchange controls. Private businessmen, including, of course, the former owners of the big banks, were irate.

Portillo's successor, Miguel de la Madrid Hurtado, a graduate of the Kennedy School of Government at Harvard University, had to administer "hard medicine" to get the Mexican economy back on its feet. He also began Mexico's shift from an inward-looking economy to one that would be more outward-looking. To get the budget deficit under control, he cut subsidies, raised taxes, and reduced public investment in real terms. To open up the economy, he allowed the peso to depreciate, lowered import barriers, relaxed some of the rules governing foreign investment, and made Mexico a signatory of the GATT. He also launched a program of "disincorporating" state enterprises, a term that implied not merely privatization but also the liquidation of enterprises or their transfer from the federal government to state or local governments. Between 1982 and 1988, nearly 600 small state enterprises, accounting for about 10 percent of the state enterprise sector's budget, were disincorporated. These measures began to improve Mexico's balance of payments, but at a high social cost. Real per capita income fell by 40 percent and unemployment hit 20 percent. Inflation remained high (150 percent in 1987) and took its toll on the poor, whose number was believed to have swelled. Meanwhile, the richest 5 percent of the population earned 25 percent of the national income. To contain inflation, de la Madrid convinced workers and private businesses to sign an Economic Solidarity Pact in December 1987, which provided for restrictive fiscal and monetary policies and the reduction of trade barriers. After substantial increases in public-sector prices and utility rates, price controls were also introduced.

In 1987, Carlos Salinas de Gortari, Secretary of Programming and Budgeting, was named the PRI's candidate for the 1988 election. Salinas had never before held elected office. Barely 40 years old, he had a master's degree and a doctorate in political economy from the Kennedy School of Government. Salinas promised to continue the reforms started by de la Madrid.

By the time of the July 1988 election, Mexico's economy was looking far better than at any time in the recent past. Real gross domestic product (GDP) registered its second straight year of growth, inflation was expected to fall to the 50 percent range, the government deficit was less than 10 percent of GDP (compared with a peak of 17 percent in 1982), and both exports and foreign direct investment were on the upswing. On all these measures, 1989 and 1990 were expected to be even better. Nevertheless, Salinas barely won the presidency with 51 percent of the vote in an election marred by charges of fraud. In previous elections, the PRI's candidate had garnered at least 75 percent of the vote.

Within days of assuming office in December 1988, Salinas surprised everyone by arresting the powerful, entrenched leader of the oil workers union (known popularly as "La Quina") and having him replaced with a more acceptable person. Soon thereafter he arrested a notorious drug trafficker and several private businessmen for securities fraud. This earned him the reputation of a tough and determined leader. He also renewed the pact signed earlier between the government, unions, and business groups – this time under the name Pact for Stability and Economic Growth.

Besides continuing many of de la Madrid's economic policies, Salinas pushed harder on trade reform, deregulation of the economy, and privatization. In May 1989, Salinas liberalized the rules governing foreign direct investment, allowing 100 percent foreign ownership under specified conditions, and eliminating government approval for foreign investments under US$100 million. In July, he negotiated a major agreement with international creditors that was expected to reduce Mexico's outflows on foreign debt servicing by US$3 to US$4 billion a year for the next few years. A few months later, he visited the United States to "cement his honeymoon with President Bush," who was reportedly "pleased with [Mexico's] dismantling of protectionist barriers, privatization, and revision of rules for foreign investment."[4] At about this time, the government also announced its desire to enter into a free trade agreement with the United States along the lines of the U.S.-Canada Free-Trade Agreement. Such an agreement would be a major triumph for the Salinas administration and, in the view of some, make his economic reforms irreversible.

The Telmex Announcement

It was in this context that Salinas announced before the telephone workers in September of 1989 that Telmex was to be privatized. Salinas laid out six premises under which the privatization would be carried out:

1. The government would continue to maintain oversight of telecommunications in the country.
2. Telmex would radically improve telephone service for Mexican citizens.

3. The rights of workers would be ensured.
4. The telephone system would be expanded.
5. Telmex would participate in scientific and technical research to strengthen the sovereignty of the country.
6. Majority control of Telmex would remain in Mexican hands.

The president further said that the privatized company would invest US$10 billion between 1989 and 1994 to improve and expand the system.

Two days later, the Secretariat of Communications and Transport (SCT), which supervised Telmex, announced that after privatization the telephone network would be expanded at the rate of 12 percent per year, compared to 6 percent in the recent past. As a result, the current density of 5 lines per 100 people would double to 10 lines by 1994 and quadruple to 20 lines by the year 2000. Specific targets were also announced for the replacement of obsolete exchanges with digital ones, and for the development of new microwave, optical fiber, and satellite systems. The Secretariat of Communications and Transport also announced that workers would participate in the capital of the company, but did not indicate how much. Foreign investors would be allowed to hold up to 49 percent of the privatized company, although no single foreigner, firm, or individual could own more than 10 percent of the total stock. At the time of the announcement, 25 percent of Telmex stock was already in foreign hands and traded in the United States in the over-the-counter market.[5] (Telmex was the only Mexican stock traded in the United States at the time.)

One newspaper noted: "Salinas de Gortari was careful not to provoke a confrontation with the workers this time, in contrast with some previous privatizations. It was significant, indeed, that he chose to make his announcement at a union meeting, where he offered workers a share of the company, and clearly after an agreement had been reached with the usually combative leader of the STRM."[6]

However, the country's political left protested loudly. One influential congressman complained that problems such as low efficiency and underinvestment by state enterprises were "aggravated by the policy of privatization, which preferes to consent to vices and to delay solutions in the public sector, and then uses the consequent loss of prestige to justify privatizing."

The country's business groups cheered the government's decision. On the day following Salinas's announcement, Telmex accounted for fully 40 percent of the shares traded on the Mexican stock exchange. Between the first and last quarters of 1989, Telmex stock had risen from US$0.34 per share to US$0.91 per share.

The Government's Role in the Mexican Telephone Industry

The government first became involved with the telephone sector when it granted concessions to two foreign-owned companies in the late nineteenth century. One firm was started by American investors, the other by the Swedish firm, L. M. Ericsson. Both foreign owners, in fact, were primarily manufacturers of telephone equipment but entered the telephone service business in many foreign markets to promote sales of their equipment. By the early 1900s, each had created a telephone equipment manufacturing subsidiary in Mexico. By 1958, the two telephone service companies had merged under the name Teléfonos de Mexico, and control had moved into the hands of a group of Mexican investors, who owned 73 percent of the stock. Among other things, the government set telephone rates to yield a 12 percent return on equity.

In the mid-1950s, Telmex sought the government's help in raising additional funds for growth and expansion. Unwilling to raise prices, the government agreed that Telmex could give preference in the allocation of new lines to subscribers who bought a stipulated number of shares and bonds issued by the company. (Many new subscribers preferred to sell the Telmex shares and bonds they had been forced to buy, thus spawning the Mexican stock market.)

In addition, the government agreed to impose a telephone tax on users that would be reinvested fully and automatically in Telmex in exchange for bonds yielding a low 6 percent return. Two consequences followed: First, the Mexican controlling group's equity in the company got diluted as subscribers acquired new shares, and, second, Telmex's balance sheet became debt-heavy, as the government continued to accumulate bonds in exchange for reinvesting the telephone tax. To solve the latter problem, in the mid-1960s the government converted its bonds into nonvoting preferred stock carrying a tax-deductible 6 percent dividend.

By 1972 the government's preferred stock represented 48 percent of Telmex's total equity. President Echeverría's government decided that it was time to stop pretending that Telmex was a private company. He decided that the government should convert its preferred shares into voting shares, acquire additional shares in the market, and assume majority control of Telmex. Under the veiled threat that Telmex's license would not be renewed when it expired in 1976, the government got the private shareholders to amend the company's by-laws to create a special class of AA voting shares that could only be owned by the government and which had to represent at least 51 percent of the total equity at all times. The other type, A shares, could be owned by anyone, including foreigners. In August 1972, the government's shares were converted to AA shares and Telmex became a state-controlled, mixed enterprise. In 1976, the Secretariat of Communications and Transportation issued Telmex a new 30-year license.

Although after 1972 the majority of the board's thirteen directors, including the president, were appointed by the government, and the chairman was the minister of communications, Telmex reportedly ran like a private company, at least for the first few years. Many of the government directors were secretaries or senior officials from various ministries; Salinas himself had served as a director of Telmex from 1981 to 1986. For 13 years (from 1974 to 1987), the same individual, Emilio Carillo Gamboa, the son of a highly respected former minister, served as Telmex's president. By the standards of the public sector, Telmex was regarded as a well-run organization, and many of its senior managers were highly qualified.

The practice of coercing new subscribers to buy Telmex shares and bonds continued. In 1988, for instance, a new residential subscriber paid US$475 in installation charges and had to buy over US$500 worth of Telmex stock to get a connection; commercial customers had to pay even more. Over the years, the telephone tax also went up; it was doubled in 1974, but only 50 percent of the new tax was earmarked by the government for reinvestment in Telmex. As the government became increasingly strapped for funds in the 1980s, the telephone tax crept upward and the portion earmarked for Telmex crept downward, reaching 40 percent in 1981 and even less thereafter. In addition, in 1989, customers paid the standard 15 percent value-added tax on their phone bills – which already included the telephone tax. In all, of every 100 pesos that went to Telmex, 60 pesos went to the government in telephone and value-added taxes.

Between 1976 and 1989, Telmex's sales grew in real terms at about 6 percent and the company was consistently profitable. In 1989, the company had sales of US$2 billion and net income after taxes of US$450 million. (See Exhibit 2 for financial data on Telmex.) Although the government was reluctant to raise the price of local service, which affected the average citizen most, it did raise prices for long-distance service, especially international, which mostly affected businesses. (Residential customers accounted for more than 50 percent of local call-minutes billed but only 20 percent of domestic and international long-distance call-minutes billed.) International calling was priced in U.S. dollars rather than pesos, so that Telmex's

EXHIBIT 2 **Telmex Financial Data, 1985–1989 Actuals and Projections for 1990–92 (All Figures in Millions of U.S. Dollars)[1]**

	Actuals					Projections[2]		
	1985	1986	1987	1988	1989	1990	1991	1992
Income Statement Data								
Long Distance								
International	478	515	564	710	907	861	992	1116
National	303	237	309	449	709	1322	1599	1934
Local service	182	116	153	315	442	1131	1331	1566
Other services	31	22	18	25	57	173	241	324
Total revenues	994	890	1045	1499	2115	3488	4164	4940
Net income after taxes	119	113	206	628	450	1068	1431	1773
Balance Sheet Data								
Total assets	3040	3102	3730	5825	6999	7874	9626	11560
Debt and other liabilities	1586	1658	2156	2612	2892	3757	4199	7230
Equity	1454	1445	1573	3211	4107	4117	5427	4330
Sources and Uses of Funds								
Sources								
Cash flow from operations	404	308	385	449	833	1520	1907	2383
Outside financing	452	504	1064	699	638	575	524	256
Total sources	856	812	1449	1148	1471	2095	2431	2639
Uses								
Investment in plant and equipment	576	499	531	746	955	1741	1917	2130
Debt amortization	29	45	73	148	129	92	112	117
Others	251	268	845	254	387	262	402	392
Per Share Data								
Shares outstanding (millions)	4257	4257	4257	4257	4257	4257	4257	4257
Earnings per share (US$/share)	0.06	0.04	0.06	0.16	0.11	0.25	0.34	0.42

[1]Totals may not add exactly due to rounding off.
[2]Projections for 1990, 1991, and 1992 are based on a stock analyst's report and assume that revenue per line will increase from US$450 in 1989 to US$661 in 1990 and US$700 in 1991. The number of lines in service is projected to grow at 10.4 percent in 1990 and 12.1 percent in 1991.

international rates went up automatically as the peso depreciated. By 1988, international calls accounted for only 5 percent of all calls but more than 50 percent of Telmex's revenues. That same year, the monthly rent for a residential telephone was about US$2.40 and local calls beyond the first 150 calls per month were charged less than 1 American cent each. Some local exchanges were not equipped to measure the number of calls made.

High international rates also turned Telmex into a major foreign exchange earner for the country. Since a United States–Mexico call originating in Mexico cost more than twice as much as the same call originating in the United States, the vast majority of United States–Mexico calls originated in the United States, making Mexico a net exporter of telephone service to the United States. In 1989, Telmex received about US$500 million from AT&T at settlement time for this reason. However, Mexico was under pressure from the United States to lower Mexican rates for calls to the United States.

Although Telmex remained profitable and the government helped finance its growth by reinvesting a portion of the telephone tax, the company could not keep pace with the demand for modernization and expansion. In real terms, Telmex's investment was steady through the late 1970s and 1980s; indeed, it had risen significantly from 1987 to 1989. But the waiting list for telephone connections still had 1.5 million names in 1988, which at past rates of expansion would take 3 to 4 years to satisfy even if no new names were added to the list.

Telmex had also invested funds to modernize the system. By 1981, 99 percent of the exchanges were automatic. Since 1982, only digital exchanges had been added to the system, thereby raising the percentage of digital lines from almost zero in that year to 22.0 percent in 1989. Practically all of the exchange equipment was supplied on a turnkey basis by the Mexican affiliates of two companies, Ericsson (Sweden) and Alcatel (France). Telmex first introduced fiber-optic transmission in 1981, but optical fiber accounted for less than 1 percent of the transmission capacity in 1990. In 1988, Telmex introduced an 800 service to calls to and from the United States. In 1989, the company initiated the first phase of a digital overlay network that would encompass the eight largest cities within 2 years and another seventeen cities thereafter. Several large customers, including banks, export-oriented firms, and tourism organizations connected into this network through dedicated private circuits. A research and development center, which employed 160 technicians and held 40 patents, designed improvements to the Telmex network. In 1989, the company also opened the Center for Advanced Telecommunications to work exclusively on digital communications.

Telmex provided domestic long-distance transmission via cable, microwave links, and through geostationary satellites. Part of the microwave network belonged to the Ministry of Communications and Transport and was leased to Telmex. Mexico was linked to North America by microwave and to other countries through international satellites.

Union–management relations were reasonably good, although workers had gone on strike at times. Telmex's work force grew at the rate of 8 percent per annum from 1984 to 1988, while the number of lines added grew at 5 to 6 percent per annum in the same period. In 1989, however, the work force contracted by about 1 percent due to "retirements, voluntary resignations of employees, and by the termination of contracts of temporary employees that did not justify renewals."[7] By 1989, Telmex employed 49,000 persons, of whom 41,000 were unionized. Telmex workers were considered well paid and enjoyed good benefits. The union was believed to have gained influence over the years and, by 1989, had eroded management's authority in several operational areas, such as job rotation and hiring. For instance, in the case of recruitment, management had to choose from within a slate of three candidates proposed by the union.

Readying Telmex for Privatization

Most enterprises privatized by the Office of Privatization had been sold "as is," because that was faster and the government preferred that the new owners decide how to restructure the firms. However, in the case of large companies such as Aeromexico, Mexicana Airlines, and Telmex, the government preferred to restructure before privatization.

Aeromexico, for instance, had been sold in November 1988 after a bitter struggle with the unions. The airline was considered overstaffed, and the government had chosen to close down the company and start a new one that rehired only a third of the original workers. The government cleaned up the company's balance sheet and then sold it to a group of Mexican investors.

In the case of Telmex, the Office of Privatization created committees with representatives from the Ministry of Communications, the Ministry of Commerce and Industry, the Ministry of Finance, and Telmex itself. In addition, the investment banking division of a local bank (Banco Internacional) and an American investment banking firm (Goldman Sachs) were hired to advise on financial issues. Jacques Rogozinski was associated with all the committees. Preparatory work fell into three areas: reorganization of Telmex; legal reforms, including changes to the Telmex license and telecommunications regulations; and financial planning to ensure the sale would be a success.

Corporate Reorganization

Within a month of Salinas's announcement, the Ministry of Finance took over control of Telmex from the Secretariat of Communications and Transportation. This had become standard practice by 1989: firms to be disincorporated were first moved to the Ministry of Finance. Finance minister Pedro Aspe became Telmex's chairman, and Alfredo Baranda García, a former ambassador to Spain, was appointed president with the charge of readying the company for privatization.

The new labor contract signed with the STRM in April 1989 prepared the way for "cleaning up" the company's labor relations. In that agreement, the STRM agreed to sign a single contract for all unionized employees rather than 57 separate agreements as in the past. The union also agreed to reduce the number of job classifications from 500 to only 41 and provided management with the flexibility to introduce new technology. Some observers suggested that Telmex was overstaffed by about 30 percent, but Baranda did not plan to lay off any workers.

Another of Baranda's responsibilities was to move ahead with Telmex's plans for modernization and expansion pending privatization. The company estimated that the expansion goals announced by the government would require investment of US$11 billion between 1989 and 1994 – two to three times the past rates of investment.

Finally, Baranda worked to make Telmex's balance sheet more attractive to private investors by borrowing U.S. dollars (against the settlement charges owned by AT&T for international calls) to buy back some of the company's foreign debt, which was selling in secondary markets at a deep discount.

Legal and Institutional Issues

On the legal front, there were at least two challenges. One was to finalize a revised license agreement for Telmex. The second challenge was to revamp the government's archaic telecommunications regulations to clarify the rules that would govern entry, operations, and competition in the telecommunications sector in the future. Fortunately, the constitution itself would not have to be amended, since it permitted private provision of telephone service, unlike telegraph service and satellite communication, which were reserved for the state. However, Mexico's foreign investment rules limited foreign ownership of telephone service companies to 49 percent.

The task of redrafting Telmex's license opened up a messy set of interconnected issues. Pricing was particularly thorny. Everyone agreed that the heavy cross-subsidization of local service by long-distance service had to end – as it had in the United States. If competition were to be permitted in long-distance, Telmex would be forced to lower those rates, but could the company afford to do that without raising local rates? At any rate, American officials were already forcing down Telmex's prices for calls to the United States, which accounted for more than 80 percent of Mexico's international calling. Then there was the question of how quickly the cross-subsidization should be ended. If Mexican rates were raised to match those in the United States in one swift adjustment, the monthly rent for residential users might have to be increased from US$2.40 to US$15 or US$20, and the charge per local call raised from 1 cent to 8 or 10 cents. How would the public react to such a sharp increase? And might that derail the government's plan to extend the Pact for Stability and Economic Growth with unions and business groups for another stint when it expired in March 1990? A sharp increase in telephone rates could single-handedly add 1 to 2 percentage points to the consumer price index.

On the other hand, the ambitious targets announced by the Secretariat of Communications and Transport for Telmex in September 1989 might not be achievable without higher prices. Financial advisers to the government noted repeatedly that higher prices for telephone service would mean that the government would be able to sell Telmex for a higher price, a point that was not lost on officials from the Ministry of Finance. Indeed, there was under consideration a proposal to revise Telmex's rates as follows starting January 1, 1990:

Raise the monthly rent for residential users to US$3.60
Raise the charge per local call drastically, from 1 cent to 10 cents
Raise rates for an average domestic long-distance call by 55 percent (in real terms)
Lower international rates by 34 percent (in real terms)

To reduce the impact on consumers, however, it was proposed that the telephone tax – one of the highest in the world – be abolished. The combined effect of these changes would be to increase Telmex's annual revenue per line by 47 percent, from US$450 to US$660. The proposal was met with great skepticism by some officials, who feared that it would provide too much of a windfall income for the future owners who might not put it to good use. Another said, "I thought the whole point of privatization was to attract private investment into the telephone sector. If prices can be raised this much, why privatize at all?"

Representatives of the Ministry of Commerce and Industry, on the other hand, were more concerned with the question of deregulation. They proposed, for instance, that the new telecommunications regulations should simplify and liberalize the rules governing the connection of products such as fax or answering machines to the Telmex network. Their most controversial proposal, however, was that Telmex ought to be divided into at least two parts (north and south) before privatization. Even though the two parts would not compete directly, in many ways they might compete indirectly, as in Argentina. Opponents of the idea argued that it might take two or more years to divide Telmex into regional parts. Besides, who would get Mexico City, which had one-third of all the lines in the country? If Mexico City also had to be divided up, might that further worsen service in the capital? Moreover, would anybody want to buy the system in the south, where economic growth and income levels were much lower than in the booming north? Experts brought in by Telmex from the United States argued against breaking up the company, as did the investment bankers, who feared a divided company might not be nearly as attractive to private investors. Officials from the Ministry of Commerce argued that if a geographical break-up was too difficult, a solution might be to divide the firm into a local service company and a long-distance service company, as in Chile.

In the same realm was the question of whether or not to grant Telmex exclusivity in long-distance service for some length of time. Local service had always been open to new entrants, but, as one observer put it, "you would have to be a fool to get into that lousy segment." Domestic and international long-distance service, on the other hand, could actually attract new entrants if opened up. Rumor had it that AT&T and MCI were already exploring opportunities in Mexico. The Ministry of Commerce was impressed by the gains from competition in the long-distance business in the United States and favored the same in Mexico. However, Telmex officials, supported by the financial advisers, argued that the company needed some time – say, 8 to 10 years – to prepare for competition. Britain had restricted competition in long-distance for 7 years, and so had Argentina. Pressing the opposite side, one official remarked: "If Telmex actually invests US$10 billion to modernize and expand the system over the next 5 years, no one will be able to challenge them in long-distance. Telmex will get even more entrenched."

The government's financial advisers introduced an additional issue along the way. Based on discussions with prospective investors in Mexico and abroad, they had discovered a strong sentiment that the microwave system owned by the Ministry of Communications should be sold to Telmex. Investors seemed uncomfortable with the idea that the ministry, which was responsible for regulating Telmex, would in a sense also be a competitor to Telmex if it continued to own part of the national microwave network. The idea was quite fiercely opposed by the Ministry of Communications and by officials from the Ministry of Commerce, who were keen to cut Telmex down to size before privatization rather than strengthen it further.

Another issue dogging the policy makers was whether or not Telmex should be permitted to diversify into areas such as cellular telephone service, value-added service, telephone equipment manufacture, customer premise equipment, computers, and so on, all of which had high growth potential. In 1989, Telmex's nineteen subsidiaries had total revenues of US$56 million and produced telephone directories, yellow pages, and public pay phones, and installed cables and telephone equipment in customer premises. British telecommunications had been permitted to diversify in this manner so long as these activities were carried out by independent subsidiaries without cross-subsidization by the telephone service business. In the United States, the Baby Bells were permitted to offer cellular telephone service but were barred from diversifying into other areas.

Officials from the Secretariat of Communications and Transport were concerned about public service goals that might get ignored by the future management. In particular, they wanted Telmex to quadruple the density of public telephones – from 1 per 10,000 persons to 4 per 10,000 in 1995 – and to ensure that all 10,000 towns in Mexico with 500 or more persons had telephone service by the year 2000. They felt that the revised license ought to stipulate specific targets in these areas as well as measurable targets for quality of service (call completion rates, repair time, percentage of lines down, etc.). And if the targets were missed, the company ought to pay a financial penalty.

Financial Issues

On the financial side, there were at least three sets of issues. First, since the president's guidelines as well as prevailing foreign investment regulations forbade foreign control of Telmex, the company would somehow have to be made affordable to Mexicans. The government was strongly inclined to turn control of the firm over to an identifiable Mexican business group rather than sell shares to dispersed investors. The question then arose, How many business groups could raise the funds necessary to buy Telmex?

The answer would depend in part on the price Telmex fetched. Based on the price of Telmex shares in December 1989, the government's 2.3 billion AA shares (representing 55 percent of the capital), were worth about US$2 billion. On the other hand, in December 1989, the book value of Telmex's assets was US$7 billion. These sums seemed beyond the reach of even the six or seven largest business groups in Mexico. Several experts seemed to feel that no group would be willing or able to assemble more than a billion dollars to buy Telmex. One way around this might be to permit Mexican groups to team up with foreign investors to form a trust in which Mexicans had at least 51 percent ownership. The Mexican-controlled trust might be permitted to buy the government's controlling interest – and this could be taken to mean that Telmex was still under Mexican control. But if the price of Telmex stock doubled in 1990 as it had in 1989, even this approach might not work. It was important for the government to receive multiple bids, so that it could not be accused of giving away the company to the only bidder, yet it was likely that some of the large groups would wait to buy one of the other firms scheduled to be privatized, not Telmex. (See Exhibit 2 for Telmex's projected results for 1990, 1991, and 1992.)

That led to the second set of issues. Would foreign investors want to invest in Telmex? In particular, would foreign telephone companies, which had the technical expertise to improve Telmex, be interested, even though none of them could own more than a 10 percent stake in Telmex? Would they care to be junior partners in a consortium led by Mexican entrepreneurs with whom they had never before done business? To be sure, Mexico had recently done away with the income tax on dividends and capital gains earned by foreign investors, and freed up the repatriation of profits and capital, but could these incentives make up for the restrictions on foreign control that still applied to telephone service? In any case, would U.S. regulators permit the Baby Bells to invest in Mexico? And was it acceptable, from Mexico's standpoint, if telephone companies from France, Spain, or Italy – all of which were government-owned – bid for Telmex? Should the government consider allowing debt-for-equity swaps as a way of enticing foreign investors, especially multinational banks that were holding Mexican debt? And what if some consortiums wanted to buy less than the government's entire 55 percent? Could the government's remaining shares be unloaded on the Mexican stock exchange? Or might they be marketable in foreign stock markets, even though no Mexican company had ever floated shares abroad until then?

Finally, some shares had to be set aside for Telmex workers. How much ought that to be? Should they be sold to the workers or given away? Should the shares be voting or nonvoting? And should workers be given a seat on the board?

Other Issues

A more fundamental question was how to regulate telephone prices after privatization. What rules ought to govern pricing? In the past, the Secretariat of Communications and Transport had approved prices for each service on a regular basis after examining Telmex's costs and assets to yield a "fair rate of return," similar to the method widely used in the United States. Others argued for more decentralized pricing, such as the system used in Britain when British telecommunications had been privatized.

A related but more general issue was whether the Secretariat of Communications and Transport would be able to regulate Telmex effectively after privatization. Did it have the kind of people it needed? Did it have the funding and autonomy to hire good people and keep them? Or would it be no match for the expertise and resources controlled by Telmex? Indeed, executives within Telmex had helped a great deal in the analysis and planning for privatization; could the government count on similar cooperation from the firm when other policy issues affecting the telecommunications section arose down the road? In this context, was it desirable for the government to have one or more seats on the board after privatization? Or should the government retain a "golden share," as the British and Malaysian governments had done?

Sitting in his office in the grand Palacio Nacional in downtown Mexico City, Rogozinski reflected on the status of the Telmex privatization. Over the next 9 months, several policy tangles would have to be sorted out, tough political questions tackled, and a buyer found. There was a lot riding on the Telmex privatization. A successful sale would give the country and Salinas's program a new credibility. That could solidify the mood of optimism building in Mexico, attract additional foreign capital, and lure back the billions of dollars held abroad by rich Mexicans. It might even increase the chances of signing a free-trade agreement with the United States and Canada. Rogozinski took a clean sheet of paper and began making notes for his forthcoming meeting with Finance Minister Aspe.

References

1. U.S. experience based on Richard H. K. Vietor, "Government Regulation of Business," *Harvard Business School Division of Research Working Paper No. 92027*, pp. 45–47.
2. Ambrose et al., 1990, p. 9.

3. See Helen Shapiro, "Mexico: Escaping from the Debt Crisis," Harvard Business School case 390-174.
4. *Latin American Weekly Report*, 10/26/89, p. 7.
5. *Latin American Weekly Report*, 10/5/89, p. 8.
6. *Latin American Weekly Report*, 10/5/89, p. 8.
7. Telmex, *Annual Report 1989*, p. 27.

CASE ▼ 4

The Kalimantan
Paper Project

On April 1, 1988, the syndication departments of Deutsche Handelsbank AG of West Germany, the Metropolitan Bank of New York, and the Kamakura Bank of Japan received telexes from Mr. Ibraihm Hanaffi, a prominent Indonesian industrialist, requesting that each send a team for discussions in Jakarta the following week concerning financing of the Kalimantan Paper Project (the Project), with which they were all familiar. The telex indicated that representatives from the Indonesian Ministry of Finance (MOF) and the Bank of Surabaya would also be present at the discussions. In view of the need to start project construction without delay, the telex continued, each bank should be prepared to offer indicative terms for making funds available to the project, with loan signing to be not later than the end of June. Members of all three banks' teams made phone calls to the Bank of Surabaya (with which all had correspondent banking relationships) and the MOF in Jakarta and to Koenig Neuwinger Deutz AG (KND) of Germany (the favored equipment supplier) to confirm that, indeed, the Project was moving quickly toward financing. Travel plans were made and, around April 7, 1988, the bankers went to Indonesia.

Indonesia: Country Background

Across the expanse of sea between the Indian and Pacific Oceans, the more than 13,000 islands of Indonesia form a 3000-mile archipelago which separates Australia

By Hugh Thomas, Michael G. DeGroote School of Business, McMaster University. The case was written without management cooperation, solely for the purpose of stimulating student discussion. Data are based on field research and secondary sources on several Southeast Asian projects; the location and specific details of this project have been disguised. The author is grateful to Roy C. Smith and Ingo Walter of the Leonard N. Stern School of Business, New York University, under whose direction the original versions of the case were written and in whose classes the case was tested. Faculty members in nonprofit institutions are encouraged to reproduce this case for distribution to their own students, without charge or written permission. All other rights reserved jointly to the author and the North American Case Research Association (NACRA). Copyright © 1993 by the *Case Research Journal* and Hugh Thomas.

from the Asian mainland. With a land area one-fifth the size of the United States and the fifth-largest population in the world, Indonesia in 1988 presented a bewildering cultural diversity. Its dominant ethnic group, the Malays, had given Indonesia its identity and its official language, Bahasa Indonesia (Malay). But the Malay language was only one of the over 250 distinct native dialects spoken in Indonesia, a country populated by diverse ethnic groups including Chinese, Indians, Arabs, Micronesians, and Melanesians. The country with the largest Islamic population in the world, at a time when Islamic fundamentalism was sweeping Southwest Asia, Indonesia had shown itself to be relatively tolerant. A pluralistic society, it embraced Islam, Hinduism, animism, and Christianity.

In the 40 years following the declaration of independence in 1945 and the defeat of the Dutch colonialists in 1949, the overall trend of the Indonesian economy had been positive, but subject to vicissitudes. It was a roller coaster ride of development. The country's founder and first president, Sukarno, was a populist visionary, an international revolutionary, a gifted orator – and an economic disaster. He cemented peasant support for his regime by widespread land reform, yet by the mid-1960s he had dismantled liberal democracy, closed the economy to outside competition, ruined the plantations, embarked on an ineffective and costly military confrontation with Malaysia, introduced chronic budget deficits, nationalized the financial sector, and ushered in hyperinflation.

In September 1965, following an abortive coup allegedly backed by the Chinese Communists, General Suharto seized power and suppressed the coup in a campaign which sporadically degenerated into a pogrom against the Indonesian Chinese, who dominated private commerce. Suharto brought the economy under control. He mandated that the annual government budgets should be balanced. And he declared that his "new order government" was based on Sukarno's ideology of "Pancasila" – five principles on which the nation was founded:

1. Belief in one supreme God
2. Just and civilized humanity
3. The unity of Indonesia
4. Democracy led by the wisdom of deliberations among representatives
5. Social justice for the whole of the people of Indonesia

Meanwhile, Sukarno, stripped of authority and under house arrest, slid into obscurity. Sukarno died in 1970.

The Roaring Seventies

The 1970s saw a stable Indonesia under effective military control exercised through a consensus "party," the loosely organized Golkar (Golongan Karya, or "Functional Group"), made up of the civil service, the armed forces, women, students, and other groups. The Communist Party was banned; other parties were prevented from organizing, and Golkar dominated the political scene. Economically, Indonesia followed a path of development of state-dominated domestic industries to service the protected domestic economy. In agriculture, Indonesia moved from being a grain importer to self-sufficiency.

The government introduced a transmigration program, by which poor farmers from overcrowded Java (with 2000 people per square mile) were given government subsidies to resettle the sparsely populated regions of East Kalimantan on the island of Borneo (with a population of 38 people per square mile) and Irian Jaya on the island of New Guinea (with 8.5 people per square mile). The program not only proved expensive, but also ran afoul of environmentalists who saw it increasing the deforestation of Indonesia's tropical forests and contributing to the breakdown of tribal cultures. The government saw it as an economic and cultural expedient, relieving population pressure, homogenizing national culture, and simultaneously reducing the largest source of tropical forest depletion – the slash-and-burn cultivation techniques practiced by indigenous tribes.

The Indonesian currency, the rupiah, was made freely convertible and pegged to the U.S. dollar. The domestic banking sector was revitalized with the reintroduction of privately owned commercial banks, and, under the close supervision of the Central Bank, a thriving money market and a secondary market in promissory notes and trade bills emerged. Like India during the same period, Indonesia became a major recipient of World Bank loans, primarily for agricultural development. Foreign private capital also began returning to Indonesia, and domestic savings became increasingly available to finance development.

An additional boost to the economy in the 1970s came from oil. The Indonesian economy had traditionally been an exporter of commodities – rubber, tropical wood, coffee, and spices – but in 1967 oil exports became number one, a position they would continue to hold through the 1980s. By 1975, oil and petroleum shipments accounted for 75 percent of all exports. Unwilling to run budget surpluses to soak up liquidity, Indonesia was saved from serious inflation largely by government expenditures on regional development programs. Indonesia chose to pursue economic self-sufficiency by fostering infant industries – steel, cement, petrochemicals, consumer products – behind high import barriers. Autarchy brought with it a complex system of government licensing of monopolies in production and trade. The system provided a perfect vehicle for patronage.

Corruption, the bane of the Indonesian economy, thrived in the 1970s. Widely considered at that time to be a cultural imperative and an integral part of doing business in the country, it took on its most grotesque proportions in the Pertamina scandal. The state-owned oil company, Pertamina, the largest monopoly in the country, was directed by Suharto's friend and comrade-in-arms, General Ibnu Sutowo. In March 1975, Pertamina defaulted on some short-term debt. Subsequent government investigation revealed that Pertamina had piled up debts to external leaders of over US$10 billion. The government covered Pertamina's debts, but thereafter ruled that no state-owned corporation could borrow without the specific approval of the MOF.

The Eighties and the Berkeley Mafia

The boom of the 1970s turned into the bust of the 1980s as the price of oil steeply declined. As shown in Exhibit 1, Indonesia's oil exports fell from US$15 billion in 1982 to US$5.5 billion by 1986. As the trade balance deteriorated, it was offset by aid financing of projects and raising debt in international financial markets, which brought with it higher debt service obligations.

Faced with the deterioration of its terms of trade, Indonesia demonstrated uncommonly good economic sense. It adhered strictly to its balanced budget dictum, reformed its fiscal system

EXHIBIT 1   Indonesian Trade Accounts Reported by the Central Bureau of Statistics (Millions of U.S. Dollars)

| | Exports | | | | | |
	1982	1983	1984	1985	1986	1987
Crude petroleum and products	$15,493	$13,553	$12,477	$ 9,083	$ 5,501	$ 6,157
Natural gas	2,906	2,583	3,541	3,635	2,776	2,399
Plywood	270	509	668	825	1,002	1,759
Rubber	602	849	954	718	726	987
Ready-made garments	116	157	296	340	519	598
Coffee	342	427	565	556	818	535
Sawn wood	234	257	282	307	360	442
Textiles	36	112	188	220	279	418
Shrimp	181	194	196	202	285	352
Aluminum and bauxite	22	141	219	255	204	254
Spices	79	94	112	126	209	240
Tin and products	379	315	275	247	153	161
Palm oil	96	112	63	166	113	144
Tea	90	120	226	149	99	119
Fertilizer	10	47	37	80	127	86
Logs	332	291	172	9	2	2
Others	1,140	1,370	1,611	1,669	1,632	2,483
Total	$22,328	$21,131	$21,882	$18,587	$14,805	$17,136

| | Imports | | | | | |
	1982	1983	1984	1985	1986	1987
Machinery and equipment	4,406	4,164	3,393	2,699	2,866	3,720
Chemicals	1,419	1,467	1,646	1,514	1,500	1,803
Mineral products	3,684	4,285	2,864	1,451	1,283	1,301
Transport equipment	1,815	1,484	1,622	889	1,214	1,073
Base metals	2,130	1,833	1,459	1,331	1,186	1,317
Resins and plastics	539	616	648	571	659	738
Textiles, yarns, etc.	505	409	437	405	436	573
Paper and paper products	307	338	375	267	302	368
Vegetable products	471	878	609	469	471	467
Prepared food and drinks	579	267	159	134	211	228
Others	1,004	611	670	532	590	1,303
Total	$16,859	$16,352	$13,882	$10,262	$10,718	$12,891

to increase its tax base, replaced the corrupt customs service with a Swiss audit service, opened some previously protected sectors of the Indonesian economy to the rigors of competition, successively devalued the rupiah while maintaining its convertibility, and oversaw the reduction of government expenditures (excluding debt service) by over 25 percent in dollar terms from 1985 to 1987.

These programs were implemented by a group of technocrats in key government ministries, enough of whom had been educated on the U.S. West Coast that they came to be called "the Berkeley Mafia." They faced no domestic opposition to their draconian methods and were applauded for their efforts by the World Bank and the IMF. More significantly, inflows of private capital continued and exports of nontraditional manufactures increased. Exhibit 2 chronicles some of these macroeconomic developments.

Project Background

The Kalimantan Paper Project had been discussed among planners, both inside Indonesia and out, for the better part of two decades. It was born of the idea, tested successfully in Brazil,

EXHIBIT 2   **Indonesian National Economic Statistics Reported by the IMF (Millions of U.S. Dollars)**

	1982	1983	1984	1985	1986	1987
Balance of payments						
Merchandise exports*	$-19,747	$-18,689	$-20,754	$-18,527	$-14,396	$-17,206
Merchandise imports	-17,854	-17,726	-15,047	-12,705	-11,938	-12,710
Trade balance	1,893	963	5,707	5,822	2,458	4,496
Exports of services	1,527	1,177	1,398	1,612	1,576	1,610
Imports of services	-8,878	-8,592	-9,128	-9,445	-8,204	-8,484
Net private transfers	0	10	53	61	71	86
Net official transfers	134	104	114	27	188	142
Current account balance	-5,324	-6,338	-1,856	-1,923	-3,911	-2,150
Direct investment	225	292	222	310	258	307
Portfolio investment	315	368	-10	-35	268	-37
Other long-term capital	4,556	4,663	2,769	1,605	2,356	2,302
Basic balance	-228	-1,015	1,125	-43	-1,029	422
Short-term capital	526	731	476	-98	1,295	642
Errors and omissions	-2,151	467	-620	651	-1,269	-435
Counterpart items	-26	-12	-10	58	75	248
Change in reserves†	1,879	-171	-971	-568	928	-877
Petroleum output (1980=100)	86	85	88	83	87	70
Average exchange rate‡	661	909	1026	1110	1282	1643
Wholesale prices (1980=100)	119	142	161	168	182	215
Consumer prices (1980=100)	122	137	151	158	168	183
Fiscal policy (trillions of rupiahs)						
Expenditures	13.0	15.6	17.5	20.9	20.7	26.6
Revenues	14.4	16.6	17.9	21.2	23.3	28.5
Surplus (+)						
Deficit (−)	1.4	1.0	0.4	0.3	2.6	1.9

*Import and export data are reported to the IMF by Bank Indonesia and differ from those compiled by the Central Bureau of Statistics (reported in Exhibit 1) as to scope, method, and timing of coverage.
†A negative number denotes an increase in reserves.
‡In Indonesian rupiahs per U.S. dollar.

that forest plantations of fast-growing tropical pine and eucalyptus, which mature in 8 to 14 years, can provide a cheaper source of high-quality pulpwood for paper than can the temperate forests of North America and Europe, which require 25 to 50 years to reach maturity but which have traditionally accounted for the lion's share of the world's supply of paper.

The Original Investors

In the late 1970s, a group of Indonesian Chinese businessmen active in the timber trade (the Investors) formed a venture to turn the dream into reality. They calculated that, with proceeds from log sales of clear-cutting, and with the commitment of the government to protect the domestic market for the printing and writing paper which they would produce, they could operate a profitable integrated timber, pulp, and paper facility. Through their contacts within the army, the Investors secured the right to use for the Project a sparsely populated, suitable region on the Celebes Sea coast north of Samarinda in East Kalimantan.

The site offered not only suitable terrain for clear-cutting and subsequent planting of the forest plantations, but also exploitable growing timber. The existing stands of trees included three types of usable wood – pulpwood, lumber, and hardwood logs. The pulpwood could be used by a pulp mill and, when mixed with high-grade imported pulp, could produce paper of reasonable quality. For the economics of the Project, this meant that paper could be produced during the first decade, while the seedlings were maturing. The lumber-grade trees could be turned into sawn lumber for the local building market. The hardwood logs could be exported to Japan, South Korea, and Taiwan for the production of plywood and veneer.

Moreover, the site included a deep-water bay, where a pier to facilitate transportation of raw materials and finished goods could be built. Nearby settlements of Javanese migrants promised a reliable source of production and forestry labor.

In 1981, the Investors hired a technical consultant and, based on its positive recommendation and according to its specifications, they tendered for bids on the required equipment. They hired Metropolitan Bank as their financial consultant, on the basis of out-of-pocket costs, plus a per diem, plus a flat success fee of 1/2 percent on the foreign component of the financing arranged in the event that the project was successfully financed. Of the five bids received, a consortium led by KND of Germany presented a proposal considered jointly by the Investors, Metropolitan, and the technical consultant to be the most advantageous. Metropolitan worked with the Investors and KND to negotiate the most advantageous terms from the export credit agencies concerned.

By mid-1983, however, the Project had lost its initial momentum. Three similar projects in Indonesia and two in neighboring Malaysia had also gone out to tender. The Indonesian government had refused to become involved with guarantees on the necessary export credit loans. The Investors, while clearly having the means to contribute substantial equity, were reluctant to do so except on a highly leveraged nonrecourse basis – where loans to the Project not guaranteed by the Investors would be far in excess of paid-in capital. Since, in Metropolitan's judgment, the market was in no mood to entertain nonrecourse financings in Indonesia, the bank billed the Investors for fees and expenses incurred and closed its files on the Project. It thus came as a surprise to Metropolitan when, on April 1, 1988, Kalimantan Paper showed itself to be very much alive.

The Project Revised

The Project as it was resurrected in 1988 was almost identical to the original. Its components were:

> *Hardwood log sales.* During the first 10 years of project operation, while the plantations were being established, there were to be hardwood log sales from the clear-cutting of up to 185,000 cubic meters per year, a 12 percent upward revision from the original project's estimated maximum hardwood log sales volume.
>
> *Plywood production.* A state-of-the-art finished and prefinished plywood plant with output capacity of 50,000 cubic meters per annum would be set up with output to be exported or sold domestically. Hardwood logs for veneer production would be sourced from the project's own lands during the first 10 years of project operations, and thereafter would be purchased from other Indonesian producers.
>
> *Pulp and paper production.* As previously, an integrated manufacturing facility would be purchased on a turnkey basis from an overseas equipment supplier, producing sulfate pulp for in-house production of 108,000 tons per annum of fine coated and uncoated printing and writing paper.

The KND consortium was still the favored equipment supplier: Its updated bid, which formed the Investors' costing basis of the project, involved obtaining one-third of the equipment from West Germany, one-third from Canada, and one-third from various other countries, including the United States, Austria, and Japan. Technically, the new project differed from the original project only in that the medium density fiberboard plant had been dropped and the sawmill (whose equipment requirements could be sourced domestically) had been spun off by the Investors as a separate venture. Project management had yet to be determined. Although the Investors had considerable expertise in the timber business, they were newcomers to both forest plantations and pulp and paper production.

From a marketing perspective, the emphasis had changed. In the intervening years, the Indonesian government had shifted its policies from import substitution to export growth and had implemented a ban on export of hardwood logs. Thus the paper, originally to be sold domestically, was now being emphasized as a world-class competitive product that could be sold either domestically or internationally. The logs, originally destined for export, were to be sold for processing in Indonesia. Demand for paper in the region was growing. Moreover, only one of the five similar projects that in 1983 had gone out to tender had actually been completed, although the others sporadically showed signs of life.

Politically, the inclusion of a new partner was crucial. Mr. Tham Ohnhow, also known as Mr. Ibraihm Hanaffi, a businessman with diverse interests including sugar, textiles, timber, property development, and finance, had joined the Investors. As a friend of the Suharto family, he managed to bring the MOF to the negotiating table.

The Investors considered that the Project's $745 million cost could be funded as summarized in the schedule drawn up jointly by the Bank of Surabaya and KND and given in Exhibit 3. The Project's main sources of financing were to be export credit loans (US$360 million), equity (US$150 million), and a syndicated Eurodollar loan (US$100 million), with a revolving rupiah debt and internal cash generation making up the balance of required funds. The Bank of Surabaya,

EXHIBIT 3   **Cash Flow Summary for Construction Period (Millions of U.S. Dollars)**

	Outflows				
	1989	1990	1991	1992	Total
Equipment[1]	$150.0	$240.0	$180.0	$ 30.0	$600.0
Working capital	8.0	4.0	2.0	38.0	52.0
Resource/Plantation	22.0	0.0	3.0	3.0	28.0
Preproduction	5.0	13.0	7.0	1.0	26.0
IDC[2]	2.7	9.7	·13.9	12.8	39.1
Total[3]	$187.7	$266.7	$205.9	$ 84.8	$745.1
	Inflows				
Equity	50.0	50.0	50.0	0.0	150.0
Export credits[4]	82.0	111.0	140.0	27.0	360.0
Eurodollar loan[5]	20.0	80.0	0.0	0.0	100.0
Rupiah loan[6]	29.9	11.2	−0.4	−17.4	23.3
Cash generation[7]	5.8	14.5	16.3	75.2	111.7
Total[3]	$187.7	$266.7	$205.9	$ 84.8	$745.0

[1]Includes imported plant and locally obtained equipment.

[2]Interest during construction on rupiah and Eurodollar loans at 12% and 9% interest. Loan drawdowns and repayments are assumed to occur on June 30.

[3]Columns and rows may not add exactly due to rounding errors.

[4]Under negotiation. Covers 85% of imported costs plus 100% of IDC on export credit loans at 8% interest.

[5]Under negotiation; at 9% interest.

[6]Under negotiation; revolving loan at 12% interest.

[7]From precommissioning operations, largely log sales.

under the advice of the Investors, had projected cash flows for the completed Project based on a detailed set of assumptions (see Exhibits 4 and 4a). Given the realization of those assumptions, it was anticipated that the offshore loans could be serviced with an overall 8-year tenor available as of January 1, 1989, with 4 1/2 years grace and repayments to principal being made in eight semiannual installments starting in June 1993 with the last payment on December 31, 1996. Various interest and exchange rates valid as of the end of April 1988 are given in Exhibits 5 and 6.

Export Credits

In order to stimulate the export of capital equipment to purchasers whose ability to finance the equipment was limited, the governments of each of the industrial countries had developed its own system to extend fixed-rate loans to foreign equipment purchasers. These export credit loans were called *buyer credits* (to be distinguished from supplier credits extended to an exporting firm to be reloaned to the exporter's customer at the exporter's risk). Originally intended simply to be credit conduits, the various export credit agencies, under pressure of export competition, gradually changed the nature of buyer credits into a form of export subsidy providing, in effect, submarket concessionary financing to importers of capital equipment.

EXHIBIT 4   **Cash Flow Summary for Loan Amortization Period (Millions of U.S. Dollars)**

	1989	1990	1991	Sales[1] 1992	1993	1994	1995	1996	1997	1998
Logs:										
Volume (000s cm³)	$50.0	$100.0	$105.0	$185.0	$185.0	$150.0	$102.0	$ 80.0	$ 50.0	$ 30.0
Revenue	10.6	22.5	25.0	46.7	49.5	42.6	30.7	25.5	16.9	10.7
Plywood:										
Volume (000s cm²)	0.0	0.0	0.0	25.0	50.0	50.0	50.0	50.0	50.0	50.0
Revenue	0.0	0.0	0.0	26.8	56.9	60.3	63.9	67.7	71.8	76.1
Paper:										
Volume (000s tonne)	0.0	0.0	0.0	40.0	97.0	108.0	108.0	108.0	108.0	108.0
Revenue	0.0	0.0	0.0	65.6	168.8	199.2	211.1	223.8	237.2	251.4
Total sales	10.6	22.5	25.0	139.2	275.1	302.0	305.7	317.0	325.9	338.3
				Costs (see Exhibit 4a)						
Timber costs	4.8	8.0	8.8	14.4	15.3	13.7	10.8	9.7	7.7	6.3
Plywood materials	0.0	0.0	0.0	2.4	5.1	5.4	5.7	6.0	6.4	6.8
Paper materials	0.0	0.0	0.0	13.1	33.7	39.7	42.1	44.6	47.3	50.2
Labor	0.0	0.0	0.0	12.6	13.4	14.2	15.0	15.9	16.9	17.9
Maintenance and repairs	0.0	0.0	0.0	12.6	13.4	14.2	15.0	15.9	16.9	17.9
Administration	0.0	0.0	0.0	3.8	4.0	4.3	4.5	4.8	5.1	5.4
Insurance	0.0	0.0	0.0	5.0	5.4	5.7	6.0	6.4	6.8	7.2
Total costs	4.8	8.0	8.8	64.0	90.2	97.1	99.2	103.4	107.0	111.6
Cash flow before capital expenditures and debt service	5.8	14.5	16.3	75.2	185.0	204.9	206.5	213.6	218.9	226.7
Term loan principal Repayments:[2]										
Export credits	0.0	0.0	0.0	0.0	90.0	90.0	90.0	90.0	0.0	0.0
Eurodollar loan	0.0	0.0	0.0	0.0	25.0	25.0	25.0	25.0	0.0	0.0
Interest expense:[3]										
Export credits	0.0	0.0	0.0	0.0	28.8	21.6	14.4	7.2	0.0	0.0
Eurodollar loan	0.0	0.0	0.0	0.0	8.9	6.6	4.4	2.1	0.0	0.0
Rupiah loan	0.0	0.0	0.0	0.0	2.8	2.8	2.8	2.8	2.8	2.8
Total debt service	0.0	0.0	0.0	0.0	155.5	146.0	136.5	127.2	2.8	2.8
Debt service cover	na.	na.	na.	na.	1.19	1.40	1.51	1.68	78.28	81.07
Inflation index[4]	106	112	119	126	134	142	150	159	169	179

[1]Volume figures are thousands of cubic meters for logs and plywood and thousands of tonnes for paper. Output price assumptions, based on 1988 prices, are

logs per cubic meter US$200

plywood per cubic meter US$850

paper per tonne US$1300

[2]Term loans are repaid in eight semiannual repayments starting in June 1993 and ending in December 1996. Rupiah principal outstanding at the end of construction period is left as working capital facility through life of project.

[3]Interest is capitalized during construction. Interest rates are assumed to be 8% on export credits, 9% on Eurodollar loan, and 12% on rupiah loan.

[4]The inflation rate applicable to costs and revenues is 6%.

EXHIBIT 4A **Annual Costs of Supplies for Plywood and Production of Pulp and Paper (Thousands of U.S. Dollars)**

Plywood

Item	Costs*
Urea formaldehyde resin	$ 1,768
Catalyst	95
Wheat flour	510
Knives and saws	23
Fuel and lubricants	110
Sander belts	13
Miscellaneous	30
Shipping	
Lumber dunnage	165
Plywood dunnage	73
Steel strapping	19
Fuel	
Fuel oil	686
Diesel	288
Total	3,780

Pulp and paper

Item	Costs
Salt cake	1,443
Purchased pulp	10.725[†]
Filler clay	2,725
Fuel oil	1,890
Salt	475
Sulfur	24
Sulfuric acid	43
Limestone	305
Alum	633
Resin	1,234
Starch-size press	1,588
Coating clay	2,608
Coating starch	318
Coating latex	880
Others	3,025
Total	28,011

*All costs are capitalized during first 3 years of construction except timber costs for log production.
[†]Required only before the first plantation crop matures in 2001.

Wishing neither to put their exporters at a disadvantage, nor to pay out increasing subsidies, the developed countries concluded the Berne Union as an international agreement to regulate the extent of these export subsidies. The Berne Union stipulated, for example, that credit could not be extended for more than 85 percent of the exported equipment value, and specified the

EXHIBIT 5   **Interest Rates**

Interest Rate Description	Rate, %
Euromarkets	
April 2, 1988, 6-month LIBOR	
U.S. dollars	7 1/8
Japanese yen	4 3/8
German deutschemarks	3 5/8
Eurobonds (7-year fixed rates)	
U.S. dollars	9.23
Japanese yen	5.06
German deutschemarks	5.98
April 2, 1988, US$ fixed swap to LIBOR	
7-year (bid – ask)	9.30–9.38
10-year (bid – ask)	9.51–9.59
Japanese long-term (fixed) prime	5 5/8
Export credit consensus rate	8
U.S. domestic credit market (week ending April 1, 1988)	
Aaa seasoned bonds	9.53
Baa seasoned bonds	10.75
High-yield bond premium over Baa bonds	+2.5–+3.5

EXHIBIT 6   **Exchange Rates**

Currency	Rupiahs per Unit
U.S. dollars	1653.28
German deutschemarks	998.85
Japanese yen	13.3251

minimum fixed rates of interest which could be charged – so-called *consensus rates*. To achieve another objective of export credits, that of providing aid to less developed countries, the consensus rates were divided into three categories, with the lowest interest rates being applicable to category 3, or underdeveloped, countries, which included Indonesia. The consensus rates were adjusted on a semiannual basis, in January and July. In spring 1988, the category 3 consensus rate was 8.0 percent.

Export credit agencies used one of two methods to structure loans. The first method involved the agency extending credit directly to the importer. This usually involved the agency funding its long-term assets with generally shorter-term liabilities. This structure was used by the Export Import Bank of the United States, the Export Development Corporation of Canada (EDC), the Export Import Bank of Japan, the Export Import Bank of Korea, and others.

The second method involved the agency acting merely as guarantor to the participating commercial banks with respect to both the principal risk and the interest spread over the lending bank's cost of funds. On each interest payment date throughout the course of a given loan, the borrower would remit interest to the lending bank at the fixed consensus rate which had been prevailing at the time of the signing of the commitment to lend. And on each interest payment date, the lending bank would then remit to the export credit agency the difference, if positive, between (1) the applicable consensus rate and (2) LIBOR plus the spread (agreed at the time of loan signing between the bank and the export credit agency), or receive from the export agency that difference, if negative. In the event of a default on the principal, the lending bank would receive full payment of principal from the export credit agency. Although export credit agencies usually worked only with the exporting country's domestic banks in arranging buyer credits, it was common in large transactions for those domestic banks to syndicate to foreign banks parts of the arranged credit facilities. This second method was in widespread use in Europe by such agencies as the Export Credit Guarantee Department of the U.K., Hermes Kreditversicherungs AG of West Germany (Hermes), Compagnie Francaise d'Assurance pour le Commerce Exterieur of France, and Mediocredito Centrale of Italy.

Export credit agencies in general were prepared to assume either the sovereign obligation/guarantee of the country of the importer or the obligation/guarantee of a commercial bank of first-class international standing. Thus, if Kalimantan Paper were to be eligible for export credits, those export credit loans would have to be guaranteed either by the Indonesian MOF or by a well-known commercial bank in a developed country. The guaranteeing commercial bank could extend its guarantee in return for appropriate guarantee fees and credit support. The form of that credit support was a matter of negotiation, but might take the form of counterguarantees (from other international banks, local banks, business entities, wealthy individuals, etc.), mortgages or liens over property, assignments of proceeds of contracts and commercial guarantees, assignment of take or pay contracts, government undertakings with regard to preferential treatment of the project, or letters of comfort.

Official application to export credit agencies for funding could only be made by the exporter. However, because of banks' involvement with lending, especially in the second structure described above, the help of a bank in securing advantageous export credit terms for any large export of capital equipment was often useful. Thus KND had secured for the Kalimantan Paper Project, initially with the help of Metropolitan and later with the support of Deutsche Handelsbank, the export credit agencies' letters of intent.

With KND as the Project's principal contractor, approximately one-third of the equipment to be obtained from outside of Indonesia would be from Germany, one-third from Canada, and one-third from the rest of the world. KND and Deutsche Handelsbank had been in contact with Hermes, the German export credit agency, and with the EDC of Canada.

Hermes had indicated that it would be prepared to be the guarantor and interest support provider to the funding banks in a $120 million loan with a fixed annual rate of interest of 8 percent. For the prospective principal funding bank, Deutsche Handelsbank, this would be highly lucrative business: it would earn a 5/8 percent spread over LIBOR for booking the risk of its own government. Hermes in turn would require – in addition to various fees to be paid by KND – the guarantee of the MOF or a prime international bank.

The EDC of Canada had committed in a letter of intent to provide up to $115 million in term financing at a fixed annual rate of interest of 8 percent directly to the importer in return for receipt of a guarantee from a prime international bank or the MOF and various undisclosed fees to be received from the exporter.

Since the subcontractors for the remaining imported equipment had not yet been selected, export credit financing terms for loans covering the final third had yet to be negotiated. However, on most projects minor suppliers' export credit agencies tended to match the terms of major suppliers' export credit agencies, and it was anticipated that the remaining $125 million of export credit equipment financing could be secured on terms not significantly different from those indicated by Hermes and the EDC.

Positions of the Decision Makers

The Investors

As members of an often mistrusted Chinese minority, the Investors saw the Project as a means to make a long-term, high-visibility contribution to the development of the Indonesian economy. In the short run, the Project would cost a significant investment, but, in the long run, it should prove to be highly profitable. The Investors had determined that they could afford an equity contribution of US$150 million cash to be paid in over the first 3 years. Most of that amount would be for various preproduction expenses, in addition to covering part of the 15 percent equipment down payment and the price to the Indonesian government for the timber rights. The Investors were anxious to limit their exposure, and categorically ruled out the possibility of serving as unconditional guarantors of the whole Project.

The Investors argued that they were taking a high risk in investing in a facility using plantation technology untested in Indonesia. Only after 2001 (i.e., after the first plantation trees on the clear-cut land had matured and had been harvested) would the feasibility of that technology be established. Hence, the Investors had negotiated with the government considerable discounts on the timber tax, which constituted the largest part of the annual timber costs. More important, they still had the right to use the Kalimantan forest site from which they were permitted to harvest hardwood logs for up to 10 years, provided the Project was implemented. The Investors planned to concentrate log harvesting in the early years, which would both meet the clear-cutting needs of the plantation and maximize early cash flow for debt service. The logs would be sold to the Investors' own mills elsewhere in Indonesia, and were expected to bring profits to those mills of roughly 75 percent of their purchase price from Kalimantan Paper. In addition, contracts for the preproduction site preparation, civil works not part of the turnkey contract, and marine insurance on equipment shipments were expected to be awarded to interests under the control of the Investors.

The Investors were eligible for a 5-year corporate tax holiday following commissioning. With full loss carryforward of the initial years of operation, they anticipated that no corporate income taxes would be payable on their venture before the year 2000.

Although they were confident that the Bank of Surabaya and other local bankers would provide short-term rupiah funds for working capital of up to $60 million, the Investors did not wish to use these for term financing because of the volatility of rupiah interest rates. In the early eighties, rupiah interest rates had touched 100 percent on several occasions, and in recent years had frequently exceeded 20 percent, although their current level was 12 percent. The bank they were closest to among the three foreign banks invited was the Kamakura Bank of Japan. KBJ had flexibly provided low-cost facilities to Mr. Hanaffi on many occasions, and other members of the Investors had worked with its leasing subsidiary in Jakarta. The Investors had originally engaged Metropolitan as its financial adviser because of the bank's project-financing experience and contacts with export credit agencies. They viewed Metropolitan as entitled to its success fee if it earned it by lead-managing the final financing package. Their acquaintance with Deutsche Handelsbank was recent but positive. They were keen to use the export credit loans which Deutsche Handelsbank was helping to arrange and to take advantage of the 8 percent concessionary U.S. dollar financing.

Notwithstanding the cash-flow projections and negotiations carried on to date, however, the Investors remained highly flexible with regard to the capital structure of the Project. They would consider any serious financing alternative.

The Ministry of Finance

Coming to the negotiation table at the express request of the Minister, the MOF negotiating team wanted to be seen as promoting the fundamental interests of the Indonesian economy while dealing flexibly and positively with the favored, high-profile Project. The MOF wished to support the Project, both because of the laudable aims of Mr. Hanaffi and his colleagues, especially in bringing new technologies to Indonesia, and because that support would be seen as a signal to the international business community of the favorable Indonesian investment climate. However, the MOF was equally concerned that it be seen as even-handed, especially in the light of the fact that the Project involved one of the country's depletable natural resources – hardwood timber stands.

The MOF was reluctant to give its unqualified guarantee for any nonconcessionary financing. It was common practice on nationally important forestry and agricultural projects involving export credits for the MOF to take counterguarantees from Bank Bumi Daya, the government-owned bank for estate agriculture and forestry. Bank Bumi Daya, in turn, would normally require a mortgage over the imported plant and equipment as security for its guarantees. At the conference table the MOF was able to speak on behalf of Bank Bumi Daya in negotiating security and guarantee fees.

The MOF wanted to continue to demonstrate that the Republic of Indonesia's credit was excellent, in spite of the country's problems, and that it could command funds from a well-rounded syndicate of international lenders. It was well aware of the pricing and terms of credits arranged in the Euromarkets (see the accompanying box) and, notwithstanding its reduced need for funds, over the past 3 years it had annually entered the Euromarkets to raise from US\$300 to US\$350 million. That annual exercise had just been completed in late 1987. Led by the Bank of Tokyo and Morgan Guaranty, the loan offered 8-year funds at LIBOR plus 0.625 percent for the first 6 years, rising to 0.75 percent for the final 2. Yet with Indonesian loans trading on the secondary market at prices equivalent to spreads of LIBOR plus 1 percent, the subscribers to the BOT-Morgan loan were overwhelmingly Japanese banks. Hence the MOF was concerned that the Project not be seen as yet another Japanese deal.

The Bank of Surabaya

The Bank of Surabaya, with assets of about US\$2 billion equivalent, was one of the largest of the sixty-five private banks in Indonesia, and one of the few allowed to deal in foreign exchange.

Euromarket
Transactions
from
*International
Financial
Review*

The following items were reported in International Financial Review *in the months immediately prior to April 1988. Each item is followed by a short explanatory note.*

Turkiye Electric Kumura (Turkey) signed in late December 1987 a DM485 million project-related financing for the Ambarli Natural Gas Combined Cycle Power Plant. The financing includes a DM140 million 13-year tranche guaranteed by OKB (the Austrian export credit agency) priced at LIBOR + 3/4%, a DM59 million tranche guaranteed by CESCE (the Spanish export credit agency) priced at LIBOR + 7/8%, and a DM118 million 7-year Euroloan guaranteed by the government of Turkey priced at LIBOR + 1 1/4%. Front end fees to participating banks were 1/2% on the OKB tranche, 5/8% on the CESCE tranche, and 1% on the Euroloan.

> *Note:* Participating banks invited to participate in the financing must take pro-rata portions of each of the three tranches. The OKB- and CESCE-guaranteed tranches are generously priced through interest rate support agreements with the lending banks which give the borrower a concessionary fixed rate of interest. Because of the high yield on the export credit tranches, the under-writing banks have been able to reduce slightly their interest rate spreads on the Eurodollar tranche – where banks take less desirable Turkish sovereign risk.

The Republic of Indonesia's drawdown period on its existing US$750 million 8-year loan signed in February 1984 priced at (1) LIBOR + 3/4% and (2) US prime + 20 b.p. with a cap of 215 b.p. over the 90-day CD rate was due to expire in February 1988 with only $50 million drawn. The borrower gave notice that it would draw the entire remaining US$700 million. Funds are to be used for paying down other existing facilities. Agent banks are Bank of Tokyo and Morgan Guaranty and the lending banks are a syndicate of widely distributed, international commercial banks.

> *Note:* The strategy of the Indonesian MOF is to use the most inexpensive funds available for its general needs while maintaining flexibility with regard to availability of funds. This facility had been considered relatively expensive (otherwise it would have been used previously) but it remains cheaper than the current price of new sovereign Indonesian debt (otherwise the MOF would have let the facility lapse undrawn). By drawing down the loan, Indonesia will receive 4-year money at LIBOR plus 3/4%.

Pertamina (Indonesia) signed a US$316 million nonrecourse project loan with a maturity of the lesser of 12 years and 5 months or 10 years after project completion to finance the construction of an oil refinery. Tranche A (US$189.6 million) is to be provided by a finance company owned jointly by Mitsubishi Corp., Mitsui & Co., Sumitomo Corp., C. Itoh & Co., Nissho Iwai Corp., and Indonesia Petroleum. Tranche B (US$126.4 million) is to be provided by LTCB, BOT, IBJ, and Indosuez. Proceeds for loan repayment are paid by the purchaser (under a take or pay contract) of the refinery's offtake, China Petroleum Corp. of Taiwan, into a New York escrow account for the banks.

> *Note:* Although Pertamina (the project sponsor) is state-owned, the debt service obligations of the oil refinery will explicitly not be backed by the government. There are few details of the transaction because, unlike syndicated facilities which are advertised to large numbers of banks worldwide, this is a club loan with few lenders. The tranche A lender is a single-purpose finance company (set up only to finance the oil refinery) owned mainly by the Japanese engineering and equipment companies who will build the refinery. The tranche B lenders are four banks. Once the refinery is producing product, whether or not the contracting purchaser (China Petroleum Corp. of Taiwan) actually picks up the product, it must pay according to a specific schedule and specified dollar amounts for specified amounts of output. These funds – which are sufficient to amortize tranche B – will be paid not to the oil refinery but into an escrow account for the banks.

Republic of Indonesia in March 1988 signed a ¥100 billion 15-year facility with the Japanese Export Import Bank. The loan is divided into two parts: Tranche A is a ¥70 billion concessionary tranche priced at 5% and tranche B is a ¥30 billion commercially priced facility. It is led managed by BOT, DKB, Fuji, IBJ, Mitsui, and Sanwa. The funds will be lent to specific projects approved by the Indonesian government.

> *Note:* This general facility is available for equipment imports of many projects, each of which will be much smaller than the Kalimantan Paper Project (and the largest of which would probably not exceed ¥5 billion). Financed equipment will necessarily be from Japan. The Japanese Export Import Bank actually will provide loan funding and will receive as security the guarantee of the Indonesian MOF. In each case the MOF will be counterguaranteed by an appropriate state-owned domestic bank which will take the imported equipment as security for its guarantee and will

receive an annual guarantee fee appropriate to the risk of the project. As the commercial rate of interest on yen is exceeded by the Berne Union consensus rate, the consensus rate rule does not apply.

Thyssem Rheinstahl Technik, Indonesia, is arranging financing for its US$916 million petrochemical plant in Avun, Sumatra. The plant was canceled in 1983 and was reactivated following the addition of US$60 million in equity from the Suharto family to the existing US$140 million equity. US$716 million is to be financed through export credits and commercially.

Note: The item demonstrates that the Kalimantan Paper Project is not the only one which was previously canceled and has now been revived. This project enjoys the support of Indonesia's first family and is being financed partly on a commercial basis and partly on a sovereign basis (i.e., through export credit guarantees).

Although the Bank of Surabaya was overshadowed by all of the five state-owned banks, which together accounted for 80 to 90 percent of outstanding credits in Indonesia, it was one of the few which had international experience – in part developed through servicing the financial needs of clients such as Mr. Hanaffi. It had active interbank lines with Metropolitan Bank, Deutsche Handelsbank, Kamakura Bank, and many other global commercial banks, and had recently established a merchant banking subsidiary. By law, the Bank of Surabaya's assets could be financed by interbank borrowings only to the extent that such borrowings did not exceed 15 percent of liabilities. Recent deposit base growth, however, had depressed the Bank of Surabaya's interbank borrowings to less than 10 percent of liabilities, giving it additional room for asset expansion.

With foreign exchange assets in excess of US$500 million equivalent (largely interbank deposits), the Bank of Surabaya tended to maintain a net asset position in foreign exchange, having a natural foreign exchange deposit base of less than one-quarter of its foreign exchange assets.

The Bank of Surabaya, which had dealings with each of the Investors in the Project, saw its role as the local banker to the Project. It was keen to serve as the local financial advisor to the Investors and to collect fees for that service. Unofficially in that role, it had already produced updated cash flows in cooperation with KND. Having worked with those projections, it was keenly aware of the degree to which the sales volume, cost, price, and timing assumptions implied in the projections affected project viability. It was confident that the projections affected project viability. It was confident that the projections constituted a "best guess" as to project outcome, but that the actual realization would be subject to considerable variation.

The Bank of Surabaya considered that, with the participation of other domestic banks, it could arrange for as much working capital and short-term rupiah financing as the Project needed – provided the credit was appropriately structured. It could serve as domestic loan agent for

Project monitoring and would be happy to take the role as collateral agent for loan security. Because its valued customer, Mr. Hanaffi, was leading the Project, the bank's staff members had a strong incentive to do whatever they could within the strictures of prudent banking to see the Project successfully financed.

Metropolitan Bank

Metropolitan's team was more than a little miffed that the Investors, without having formally terminated Metropolitan's advisory role, were no longer using Metropolitan in an advisory capacity yet were working from Metropolitan's original feasibility studies and were using the arrangements which Metropolitan had earlier negotiated with the export credit agencies. Metropolitan's legal department advised that, notwithstanding the lapse of time, the advisory agreement (which either party could terminate at any time without penalty on 90 days' notice) was still clearly in force. Thus, it concluded Metropolitan would have a case against the Investors for failing to meet their obligations under the advisory agreement in the event that binding commitments to finance were signed while the advisory agreement remained in force. In that event, a U.S. court of law would award Metropolitan the 1/2 percent fee regardless of who made the final deal. Bad feelings apart, however, Metropolitan was most anxious to further its long-term relationships in Indonesia. Metropolitan's credit committee, fully aware of the status of the Indonesian economy and in agreement with the credit risk rating given to Indonesia by the international financial press (see Exhibit 7), was comfortable in principle with Indonesian risk. Any loan of the size contemplated by the Project, however, would have to go before Metropolitan's credit committee, which would thoroughly assess the acceptability of the risks involved. In particular, the effect of output price variability on project viability was of concern (see Figure 1).

Management, which would have to approve any loan, was concerned with the risk-return trade-off. With considerable project finance experience, Metropolitan was keen to consider complex arrangements which could justify higher spreads and fees from the borrowers and could entice providers of capital – either debt or external equity – with sufficient expected return to justify project risk. Metropolitan's legal department would have to sign off on any documentation and had been particularly concerned that offer letters reflect the kinds of detailed specifications of availability, security, representations, warranties, covenants, and events of default which would be required in the final loan documentation, in order to minimize complications in finalizing the eventual loan agreement negotiations. A checklist for those specifications (see Exhibit 8) had been circulated to the appropriate departments in the bank.

Deutsche Handelsbank

Deutsche Handelsbank was coming to the table to continue serving its good client, KND, and to be first in line to receive the LIBOR plus 5/8 percent spread which it would earn for West German government risk on the Hermes-guaranteed export credit loans. Deutsche Handelsbank considered Indonesia to be a bit risky, but it had relatively little Indonesian exposure on its

EXHIBIT 7   The Top 50 Countries in Institutional Investor's Country Risk Ratings, 1988

Country	Rank		Rating (out of 100)	6-Month Change	1-Year Change
	1988	1987			
Japan	1	1	94.6	−0.8	−1.4
Switzerland	2	3	94.1	1.0	−0.1
West Germany	3	2	93.1	−1.0	−1.1
United States	4	4	91.0	−1.5	−3.1
Netherlands	5	5	87.0	0.5	0.0
United Kingdom	6	6	86.7	0.3	0.0
Canada	7	7	85.9	−0.1	−0.6
France	8	8	84.9	0.1	0.9
Austria	9	9	84.1	0.7	0.9
Sweden	10	11	80.8	0.4	1.0
Norway	11	10	80.3	−1.1	−1.9
Finland	12	12	78.5	0.3	0.6
Italy	13	13	77.6	0.6	0.6
Belgium	14	14	77.4	0.9	0.7
Taiwan	15	15	76.3	1.5	1.8
Singapore	16	16	75.4	1.6	0.6
Spain	17	19	73.5	1.3	1.8
Denmark	18	18	73.0	0.4	0.1
Australia	19	17	70.7	−2.2	−5.7
Hong Kong	20	20	69.2	0.6	−0.1
U.S.S.R.	21	22	65.4	0.1	−0.1
New Zealand	22	21	65.2	−0.2	−1.9
China	23	23	64.8	0.2	−2.0
South Korea	24	25	62.5	1.9	2.7
Ireland	25	24	62.4	0.0	−0.8
Saudi Arabia	26	26	60.3	−0.3	−0.4
Kuwait	27	27	58.5	0.3	−0.4
East Germany	28	28	58.4	0.9	2.1
Portugal	29	31	56.5	2.2	2.3
United Arab Emirate	30	29	56.3	0.9	0.9
Thailand	31	32	55.9	2.2	2.3
Malaysia	32	30	54.4	−0.2	−2.6
Qatar	33	33	54.3	0.7	0.5
Czechoslovakia	34	35	54.3	1.2	1.3
Bahrain	35	34	53.7	0.6	0.3
Iceland	36	36	52.8	1.3	1.1
Oman	37	37	50.2	−0.1	−0.3
India	38	38	49.9	0.2	−0.7
Bulgaria	39	39	47.7	−0.4	−1.1
Greece	40	41	46.5	0.8	−0.5
Hungary	41	40	46.4	−1.5	−3.3
Indonesia	42	42	43.2	−0.7	−2.4
Algeria	43	43	42.6	−1.2	−3.3
Cyprus	44	44	42.2	1.9	2.1
Turkey	45	45	40.5	0.5	0.8
Colombia	46	47	39.1	−0.1	−0.7
Trinidad and Tobago	47	46	38.4	−1.7	−2.1
Papua New Guinea	48	48	37.4	−0.9	−1.3
Cameroon	49	49	36.0	−0.7	−1.9
Jordan	50	51	36.0	−0.4	−1.3

FIGURE I   **Log and Pulp Price Trends Reported in International Finance Statistics**

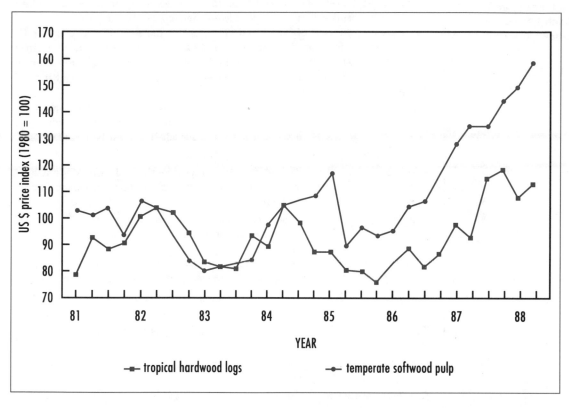

books, was under the gun from management to increase lending spreads on international business, and was, in general, asset-hungry. To date, the bank had been uncomfortable with project risk in developing countries unless it was very well secured and richly priced; however, the bank's role as KND's banker led it to take the initiative on this particular transaction. The negotiating team felt that, depending on the attractiveness of the Project, bank management might be willing to consider participating in Indonesian sovereign risk and even in Project risk. As a universal bank which had considerable equity holdings in some of its domestic German clients, moreover, Deutsche Handelsbank was familiar with the attractiveness of taking equity stakes to increase the expected returns from lending. It would be the job of the negotiating team to seriously reevaluate Project feasibility and, based on that, to negotiate a financing package which met the bank's risk-return criteria.

With regard to legal standards in any financing offers and subsequent documentation, Deutsche Handelsbank's requirements were similar to Metropolitan's.

The Kamakura Bank of Japan

Notwithstanding its role as an outsider in the Kalimantan project, KBJ enjoyed several advantages over its rivals. It was comfortable with the credit risk of the Investors, having dealt with many

EXHIBIT 8
Metropolitan Bank's Euroloan Offer Checklist

This checklist is a reference only with regard to *minimal* requirements for a Euroloan offer. Requirements will vary considerably – depending on the country and status of the borrower, the type of facility, and the nature of the security. No offer can be made before credit committee approval. Credit applications must contain indicative terms of offer. *All* offers are subject to documentation. All documentation must be referred to internal bank counsel for comment and approval *prior* to negotiation of documentation with client.

Borrower.	Exact identity of the borrower must be stated. The extent to which the loan obligations ae shared by its group (i.e., parents, owners, and subsidiaries) must be clear.
Lead managers.	Banks arranging the facility.
Agent for lenders.	Bank which will act as agent for the lenders, making disbursement, accepting payments, setting interest rates, and disbursing information.
Security.	Guarantees, mortgages, liens, assignments of proceeds, receivables, inventories, completion guarantees, take-or-pay contracts, etc.
Security agent.	The bank designated to administer the security on behalf of lenders.
Amount.	Total principal amount of facility and currency (or currencies).
Tenor.	Time from initial availability date to final payment of principal and interest.
Drawdown period.	Period during which loan principal may be drawn by borrower.
Conditions precedent.	Conditions to be fulfilled before the loan agreement becomes effective. These always include proof of corporate identity and integrity, directors' resolutions regarding lending, directors' certificate authorizing disbursing signatory, appropriate registrations and government authorizations, appointment of agents for service of process, and receipt of favorable opinions of local and New York (or U.K.) counsel. They may also include receipt of guarantee, surveyors reports, budgets, contracts, offtake agreements, contracts, completion guarantee, management agreements, letters of comfort, registration of collateral, etc.
Conditions of disbursement.	Conditions on which each drawdown is made, including amount and required notice. These conditions always involve a certificate of borrower requesting the drawdown amount and payment method and a restatement that the loan's representations and warranties are in force and that no event of default is occurring. They may include certificates of authorization from the project manager, the company parent or owners, guarantors, government agencies and/or other third parties.
Amortization.	Principal repayment timing and amounts.
Prepayment option.	Time at which the borrower can repay loan in whole or in part and fees (if any) payable on early repayment.

Interest.	Interest periods are defined. The U.S. dollar rate is usually expressed as a spread above LIBOR, an average of offer rates quoted by three named reference banks for lending dollar funds to first-class banks in the London interbank market. Other pricing standards are the U.S. CD rate, prime and treasuries.
Commitment fee.	A periodic fee on the undrawn but available balance of loan during the availability period. If drawdown is over several years, there may be lower fees negotiated on undrawn but unavailable funds in early years of drawdown.
Front end fee.	The flat fee awarded to the arrangers of the loan (and distributed at their discretion to other participating banks).
Agency fees.	Annual fees payable to the agent(s).
Expenses.	Legal, printing, telex, telephone, travel, and advertising fees incurred in arranging and monitoring the loan.
Withholding gross-up.	All payments to be made free and clear of taxes or withholdings and, in the event of such withholdings, to be grossed-up so that the amounts received after taxes and withholdings are the amounts agreed in the offer.
Representations and warranties.	The borrower warrants that it has power to enter into the loan, that the loan will not cause any other credit agreement of its parents or subsidiaries to go into default, that it is under no material litigation and that no event of defaults have occurred. It must agree to submit periodic financial statements (and possibly other documentation) and to deliver any other information relating to its business, assets, and condition as the banks may require. Other representations and warranties may be required.
Covenants.	The borrower pledges that it will not without the prior written consent of the banks allow to exist or permit to be created any mortgage, charge, pledge, lien, or other encumbrance over all or any of its present or future revenues or assets. Covenants typically also include the borrower's pledge to keep certain specified debt equity and debt service ratios and dividend payout restrictions, and to maintain existing management, ownership, lines of business, etc.
Events of default.	If the borrower fails to pay any sum due under the loan, if any statement in the loan agreement (or guarantee or collateral documents) is found to be false, if the borrower breaks a covenant, if an event of default occurs under any other indebtedness of the borrower, if any parent or subsidiary of the borrower is unable to pay its debts as they fall due or declares bankruptcy, if the security guarantee becomes invalid, or if it becomes unlawful for the borrower to perform any of its obligations under the loan agreement, then the banks can declare all amounts outstanding to be immediately due and payable, and a higher rate of default interest, to be stipulated in the loan agreement (usually an additional 1%), will be charged thereafter on outstanding amounts.
Applicable law and jurisdiction.	Laws of the State of New York or Laws of England.

of them individually on other transactions – invariably relying on their personal guarantees. Moreover, it was prepared to book more Indonesian sovereign risk, having been a major purchaser of Indonesian debt in the secondary market, and it felt that it could easily place with other Japanese banks any underwriting which met its own high credit standards. KBJ's leasing subsidiary in Jakarta had done several innovative financings, and although KBJ did not have the project finance expertise of Metropolitan or Deutsche Handelsbank, it was widely considered to be the Japanese bank most comfortable with reasonable developing-country project risk. As was the case for the other banks considering the Project, KBJ's commitment to the Project would have to be predicated on solid credit analysis of Project viability.

KBJ officers assigned to the negotiating team were sensitive to what they perceived as Indonesian borrowers' anti-Japanese biases. Recently they had been told by one of KBJ's domestic clients that the Project's original tender for bids had given Japanese equipment suppliers insufficient time to allow them a fair chance to submit the winning bid. Moreover, the client contended that, even if the initial bid of KND was the best in 1981, the lapse of time since then called into question whether the Project was being awarded to the currently lowest priced contractor.

Conclusion

As each decision maker prepared for the meeting to begin in Jakarta during the second week of April, each reconsidered the Project. Each participant had something to gain from the Project, as long as it was structured to allow those gains, but each could achieve the desired Project structure only with the cooperation of other decision makers. Thus every decision maker had not only to accurately evaluate its own Project risk-return trade-offs, but also those of all project stakeholders. Only in this way could an optimal financing scheme be achieved.

Glossary

absolute advantage   The production cost advantage enjoyed by one country over another when one (or both) of two products can be produced more cheaply in the first country.

ad valorem duty (tariff)   A customs duty or tariff assessed as a percentage of the value of the item.

affiliate   A unit, either partially or wholly owned, of an MNC; includes subsidiaries, branches, joint ventures, and any other legal form implying at least partial control over the entity.

air waybill   An air transport document that performs the same function as a bill of lading.

appropriate technology   Technology suited to the factors of production in the country where it is used. For example, appropriate technology would be relatively labor intensive in countries where labor is relatively abundant.

arbitrage   The simultaneous purchase and sale of something in several markets to profit from a difference in price in the various markets.

Association of South East Asia Nations (ASEAN)   A regional economic integration agreement among Brunei, Indonesia, Malaysia, the Philippines, Singapore, and Thailand.

back-to-back letter of credit   A form of financing in which the exporter uses the importer's letter of credit as a basis for seeking credit from a bank. The exporter can then use the back-to-back letter of credit to pay its supplier (such as a manufacturer).

balance of payments   A statement summarizing the economic transactions between a country and the rest of the world during a specified period of time.

balance of trade deficit   A situation in which the value of a country's imports exceeds the value of its exports for a specific period of time.

banker's acceptance   A form of posttrade credit in which an exporter sells to a bank, at a discount, an account receivable in exchange for immediate payment.

basic balance	A portion of a country's balance of payments that measures all the current account items plus the long-term capital account items.
bill of lading	A document used in shipping as evidence of a contract for shipping merchandise and as a document of title to be used in claiming the goods from the carrier. It is issued by the shipping company or its agent and is used as evidence of a contract to ship the goods. The bill of lading shows that the exporter delivered the goods to the shipping company. Shipments by air use air waybills and shipments involving several types of transportation (e.g., rail to air to truck) may use a combined transport document.
branch	An office or extension of the parent company that is away from the parent company headquarters but is not a separate legal entity.
Bretton Woods	An agreement made near the end of World War II to promote exchange rate stability and facilitate the international flow of currencies.
buffer stock	A commodity system utilizing the stocks of commodities to regulate prices.
Caribbean Common Market (CARICOM)	An eastern Caribbean regional integration group that includes former British colonies.
cartel	An organization of suppliers that attempts to monopolize the supply of a product and fix its prices.
centrally planned economy	An economy in which the government, rather than free-market activity, controls the allocation of resources.
certificate of product origin	A document issued by regulatory agencies in the country of origin that provides evidence that the goods were made in a particular country; it is needed so that various tariffs and regulations imposed by the importing country can be assessed.
commercial invoice	Invoices written by the exporter that describe the details of the merchandise and the terms of payment.
comparative advantage	The advantage gained through trade by two (or more) countries when each produces those products that are relatively cheaper to make and imports the other products.
confirmed letter of credit	A letter of credit that is confirmed by a bank other than the one that opened it.
consolidation	The process of preparing a consolidated statement by combining the financial statements of related entities (such as a parent and its subsidiaries) to show their combined operations.
convertible currency	A currency that can be exchanged for another currency without restriction.

corporate culture	The common values, behavior patterns, institutions, and so on among employees of a corporation that are distinctive to the corporation.
Council for Mutual Economic Assistance (COMECON)	A regional association for economic integration composed essentially of those countries that were within the Soviet bloc of influence.
countertrade	A sales transaction requiring the seller to generate foreign exchange for the purchasing country.
culture	The specific learned behavior patterns, values, norms, and institutions that are distinctive to a society.
customs union	A form of regional economic integration group that eliminates tariffs among member nations and establishes common external tariffs.
devaluation	A formal reduction (by government action) in the value of a currency in relation to another currency.
direct foreign investment	Sufficient investment in an operation in a foreign country to obtain significant management control.
direct quote	A method of quoting exchange rates that reports the number of units of the home currency given for one unit of a foreign currency.
divestment/ disinvestment	The reduction in amount of an investment, or selling, or otherwise disposing of an investment.
dumping	Underpricing a product (usually below cost or below the home country price) in a foreign market.
duty (tariff)	A tax levied on imported goods.
economic integration	The expansion of commercial and financial ties among countries through the abolishment of economic discrimination.
economic union	A type of economic integration group that combines the characteristics of a common market with some degree of harmonization of monetary and fiscal policies.
economies of scale	Lower costs achieved because of efficiencies associated with large scale production.
embargo	A type of quota that totally disallows the import of a specific product (or all products from a specific country).
ethnocentricity	The belief that one's own group is superior to others and that what works for the firm in its home country should also work in other countries.

Eurobond	A bond that is denominated in a currency other than that of the country of issue.
European Currency Unit (ECU)	A currency unit whose value is determined by reference to the value of a weighted average of the currencies of the European Community.
European Monetary System	A system involving most of the members of the European Community designed to promote exchange stability within it.
exchange rate	The price of one currency in terms of another currency.
exchange risk	The risk that losses can occur as a result of changes in the relative values of two currencies.
expatriates	Employees who are not nationals of the countries in which they are working.
Export-Import Bank (EXIM Bank)	An agency of the U.S. government specializing in lending to support U.S. exports.
export license	A license issued by the regulatory agency in the country of origin giving the exporter the legal right to export the goods being shipped.
export management company	A company that acts as an export department for other companies or acts as an agent for manufacturers.
export trading company	A company specifically established by law to export and import goods.
expropriation	The seizure of a company's assets by a government without (or with inadequate) compensation.
extraterritoriality	Government extension of the application of its laws outside its territorial boundaries.
Foreign Corrupt Practices Act (1977)	A U.S. law that prohibits certain kinds of questionable payments, such as bribes, by U.S. companies doing business abroad.
foreign exchange	Currency of another country, or a financial instrument that facilitates payment from one currency to another.
Foreign Sales Corporation (FSC)	A special form of corporation created by U.S. tax law that U.S. companies can use to shelter some export income from taxation.
Foreign Trade Organization (FTO)	A government agency, usually organized along product lines, that handles foreign sales and purchases. These are found primarily in communist countries.
foreign trade zone	A physical area in which the government allows firms to delay or avoid paying tariffs on imports. Payments of tariffs are not made, if made at all, until the goods are removed from the zone into the country where the zone is located.

forward rate	The exchange rate between two currencies quoted for future delivery.
global corporation	A company that integrates its international business activities.
hierarchical relationship	A vertically defined structure that has several layers between the highest and lowest levels.
home country	The country in which a multinational corporation's headquarters are located.
host country	Any country outside the home country in which a multinational corporation does business.
import substitution	An industrialization policy that focuses on creating domestic industries that will offer products and services currently imported.
indirect quote	A foreign exchange quote that uses units of foreign currency per unit of domestic currency as its basis.
industrial espionage	Illegally obtaining protected technology (such as processes, customer lists, or pricing policies) from a business.
inspection certificate	A document issued by regulatory agencies in either the exporting country or the importing country providing evidence that the goods have been inspected and meet the prescribed standards for goods of that type.
insurance certificate	A document issued by the insuring company specifying that the goods are insured and spelling out the terms of the insurance contract.
international Fisher effect	The relationship that implies that interest rate differentials on similar instruments between two countries will be offset by exchange rate differentials between their currencies.
International Monetary Fund (IMF)	An association of national governments organized to promote exchange rate stability and to facilitate the international flow of currencies.
international monetary system	The system for financial transactions between the governments of countries.
irrevocable letter of credit	A letter of credit that the issuing bank agrees not to revoke prior to the payment date without the consent of all parties named in the letter.
joint venture	An organization whose ownership is shared by two or more firms.
letter of credit	A document through which the importer's bank agrees to pay the exporter under specified circumstances. Most letters of credit are designated as confirmed and irrevocable, which means that once accepted, they cannot be changed.

licensing	An agreement whereby one firm gives the right to another firm to use assets such as trademarks, patents, copyrights, or other technology in exchange for a fee or royalty.
market economy	An economy in which the free market is used primarily to determine resource allocations, prices, and investments.
mercantilism	An economic philosophy equating the possession of gold or other forms of monetary assets with wealth. Trade activities, aimed at increasing wealth, are directed or controlled by the government.
most favored nation (MFN)	A policy of international trade among GATT members that requires extending to all other GATT members any trade barrier reduction granted to another country.
multinational corporation (MNC)	Another term for *multinational enterprise*.
multinational enterprise (MNE)	An organization that operates subsidiaries, branches, or other controlled affiliates in countries other than its home country.
nationalization	The forced sale of companies to the government.
Organization of Petroleum Exporting Countries (OPEC)	A cartel of major oil-exporting countries.
par value	The benchmark value that a government sets on its currency in terms of other currencies.
payment document	A document that ensures that the exporter receives payment for the goods. The most common form of payment is a letter of credit.
pegged exchange rate	An exchange rate system that fixes one country's currency in terms of another country's currency.
political risk	The risk to a business and its employees that stems from possible unexpected changes in the political environment. Risks can include disrupting supplies and markets, nationalizing the industry, or kidnapping employees.
portfolio investment	The purchase of debt or equity instruments (stocks, bonds, etc.) as an investment rather than to obtain management control.
Protestant work ethic	The view that hard, physical work is a valued personal and social behavior and a means to salvation.
purchasing power parity	An explanation of exchange rate changes based on keeping prices of goods in different countries fairly similar by offsetting inflation differentials with changes in the currency exchange rates.
quota	A restriction on the quantity of imports of a particular product that a country allows.

repatriation	The transfer of an expatriate back to a home country assignment or the transfer of foreign subsidiary profits to the home country.
revaluation (of currency)	A formal increase (by government action) in a currency's value in terms of another currency.
Second World countries	Communist countries.
sight draft	A bill of exchange that is payable immediately when presented to the party obligated to pay.
sogo sosha	The Japanese term for trading companies that import and export merchandise.
sovereignty	The power of a national government to control the land, people, and organizations within its borders.
special drawing right (SDR)	A composite currency that serves as the official currency of the IMF and is used for transactions within it. Its value is based on a weighted average of the U.S. dollar, Japanese yen, German mark, French franc, and British pound.
specific duty	A duty or tariff assessed on the basis of a specified amount per unit or weight rather than as a percentage of value.
spillover effects	Benefits that accrue when an activity has positive impacts on parts of a firm's (or country's) business other than those intended.
spot rate	The exchange rate between two currencies quoted for immediate delivery.
subsidiary	A company that is owned by another company.
subsidy – export	A financial advantage, such as the direct payment or tax advantage, offered by a government to domestic firms to enable them to compete more effectively in foreign markets.
tariff	A tax levied on imported goods.
tax haven	A country with low or no taxes on foreign source income.
terms of trade	The amount of imports that can be purchased by a specified amount of a country's exports.
Third World countries	Generally used to refer to the less developed countries, primarily in Africa, Asia, and Latin America.
time draft	A bill of exchange that is payable at a given future date or a given period after sight.
transfer price	The price for goods sold to units of the same company.

translation risk
The possibility that a firm's financial statements will be changed in domestic currency terms due to the restatement of values from one currency to another.

turnkey project
A project involving constructing an operating facility and training personnel and then transferring that facility to the buyer when it is ready.

value-added tax (VAT)
A tax levied on a firm based on the value added to the product by that firm.

vertical integration
Controlling different stages of production or distribution of a product.

Zaibatsu
The form of Japanese holding company that controlled major industrial empires prior to World War II.

Name Index

Company Index

Subject Index